Mimi Johnson
Dept. of Sociology

MATRILINEAL KINSHIP

MATRILINEAL KINSHIP

EDITED BY

David M. Schneider
and Kathleen Gough

UNIVERSITY OF CALIFORNIA PRESS
Berkeley, Los Angeles, London

University of California Press
Berkeley and Los Angeles, California

University of California Press, Ltd.
London, England

First Paperback Edition, 1973
California Library Reprint Series Edition, 1974
ISBN: 0-520-02529-6 (paper-bound)
0-520-02587-3 (cloth-bound)

Library of Congress Catalogue Card Number: 61-7523

Printed in the United States of America

To Audrey I. Richards

PREFACE

This book has grown out of a Social Science Research Council Summer Seminar which met at Harvard University in 1954. It appears just one hundred years after the publication of J. J. Bachofen's *Das Mutterrecht* (1861), which first posed matrilineal descent as a problem. That the two publications are not quite of the same order goes without saying, but the period between them has certain continuities.

Bachofen argued that human society began in a state of "primitive promiscuity," in which there was really no social organization and no regulation of behavior, sexual or otherwise. Matriliny, the second stage of cultural evolution, Bachofen argued, was associated with the invention of agriculture by women. In this stage women ruled the household and the state, and passed their names and property to their children. Essential to the matrilineal stage was a set of religious beliefs which centered, naturally enough, on an Earth Goddess. Indeed, the political structure and descent rule, according to Bachofen, merely reflected the cult of a female deity and depended directly on the religious mentality of women. Only late in the evolution of culture was this system thought to have given way to a patrilineal and patriarchal one.

Other nineteenth-century writers, notably McLennan, Tylor, and Morgan, agreed on the priority of matriliny over patriliny. They disagreed, however, as to the nature of matriliny, how it arose and how it finally yielded to patrilineal descent.

The nineteenth-century theorists wanted, on the whole, to establish general laws of cultural development, not merely particular historical sequences. In attempting to formulate such general laws they looked to the systematic interconnections among institutions within a particular culture and tried to explain them on a variety of grounds: in terms of other institutions, historically antecedent conditions, psychological states, or the biological nature of man. Yet despite their great intellectual gifts their theories were at best open to serious doubt.

Quite apart from the question of the legitimacy of their problem or the general nature of their explanatory framework, one shoal on which there was much foundering was that of the empirical referents for the concepts and categories of comparative analysis. Was "matriarchy" a single, indivisible entity and if so had it ever existed? Was "matriliny" the same as "tracing relationship through the mother"? Was "residence with the family of the bride" the "natural concomitant" of matriliny? Was the avunculate an integral part of "the matrilineal complex" and hence invariably a survival of a prior matrilineal state wherever it occurred? What was "matriarchy" and how did it work? What was "the avunculate" and how did it work?

Whatever the merits of the early theorists, and they were many and cannot be overlooked, they posed a succession of problems of this sort which the era of modern intensive field work has done much to unravel. Thus Bachofen's contention that matriliny (descent through women) and matriarchy (rule by women) were but two aspects of the same institution was accepted only briefly. For as evidence was sought in terms of which his contention could be evaluated it became clear that the generalized authority of women over men, imagined by Bachofen, was never observed in known matrilineal societies, but only recorded in legends and myths. Thus the whole notion of matriarchy fell rapidly into disuse in anthropological work.

Similarly, descent groups formed in terms of the matrilineal principle were confused at first by a kind of semantically inevitable error, with "tracing relationship through the mother"; ink pots spilled over in the heated effort to disentangle these two notions and their correlates. Morgan (1877) was particularly important in clarifying this problem. It was first suggested that matrilineal descent groups were an inevitable concomitant of this mode of tracing relationship and, indeed, matrilineal descent was defined in those terms. But it soon became evident that most societies were observed to relate members to both the kinsmen of the father and the kinsmen of the mother but that only some of these had organized descent groups as distinct from categories of kin. Hence descent had to be treated separately from the manner of tracing relationship and came to refer only to the form of social grouping, while the mode of tracing relationship was no longer expected necessarily to yield descent groups.

A closely related difficulty was the early suggestion that the true matriarchal or matrilineal complex did not include the husband or father and therefore could not include a discernible nuclear family as a social group. This followed from the idea that in true matriliny "kinship was traced only through the mother" and therefore there could be no social father. This view was consistent with the prevalent assumption of a stage of primitive promiscuity as the state prior to matriliny, for if promiscuity did settle down to orderly relationship it must first have settled in terms of mother-child relationships; only later, when paternity could be demonstrated, could the father-husband be brought into this unit. A further source of confusion which not only exacerbated this problem but created confusions of its own was the identification of kinship relationships with biological relationships. Kinship was held to be essentially the social recognition of biological facts: that is, that the social relationship of mother and child was essentially the social aspect of their biological relationship; that the social relationship of father and child was the social aspect of their biological relationship. So, the argument ran, until biological paternity could be established—at least on probabilistic grounds—there was no basis for the idea of social paternity. A mother had to be able to locate the biological father of her child before he could become the social father of her child. It followed therefore that descent groups were biological as well as social groups.

It took the clear statement of such assumptions, and the heated controversies of the time often forced their clear statement, to generate the kind of empirical research which alone could cast light on them. By now we know that though descent groups may be established in terms of matrilineal principles this does not mean that relationships cannot be or are not traced through the father as well as the mother, for the establishment of a descent group is something quite different from the principle in terms of which relationships among its members are traced. Social paternity need not be and often is not identical with biological paternity, nor is a descent group necessarily composed of biologically related members. The essential clarification which has occurred consists in the recognition that real biological relationships are distinct from and need not necessarily correlate with the social designation of a kinship relationship; in the distinction between a mode of tracing a kinship relationship and the formation of social groups of kinsmen.

Yet another difficulty which required clarification was the notion of residence, but this problem is even now far from clear. When matriliny and matriarchy were identified with each other as an indivisible unit it was difficult to see residence as anything but matrilocal. If women indeed had the power over men that was postulated, how could a man take a woman away from her group? For a time "matrilocal marriage" was used almost interchangeably with matriliny. In separating the variables of descent and residence, however, the precise referent for the notion of residence was left very uncertain. Tylor (1889), for instance, spoke of residence with the "family" or at the "home" of. N. W. Thomas (1906), who introduced the terms "matrilocal" and "patrilocal," did so specifically in terms of their parallel to the terms "matrilineal" and "patrilineal" but, except for acknowledging that they were not entirely satisfactory, left the matter as it was. Rivers in 1914 still used the bride and groom as the points of reference and continued, as had Tylor, to refer only vaguely to "the wife's people" as the place where the groom lived in matrilocal residence. In 1936 Firth first used the term uxorilocal, and in 1947 Adam suggested the paired terms virilocal and uxorilocal on the ground that "matri-" and "patri-" referred to "mother" and "father" respectively, while the concern was not with them but with the husband and wife, for whom the roots "viri-" and "uxori-" were more appropriate. But in 1949 Murdock specifically stipulated the parents of the couple as the defining criterion, matrilocal residence being defined as residence with the bride's mother, patrilocal as residence with the groom's father. In 1957, however, he altered these definitions so that matrilocal residence meant that the couple lived with the bride's matrilineal kinsmen; patrilocal residence meant that the couple lived with the groom's patrilineal kinsmen. In 1953 Hogbin and Wedgwood added community to the referents of residence and proposed a whole new set of terms.

With these uncertainties in the definitions of what appear to be crucial terms the possibility of the husband and wife living with the husband's matrilineal relatives was only appreciated slowly. Despite the fact that excellent accounts of this form of residence were available for some time it was not until 1938 that Kroeber coined the term "avunculocal," using the groom's mother's brother as the point of reference for the residence of the couple. Nor did this form of residence appear as a feature of historical reconstruction or evolutionary theory in any significant role before then. Perhaps the major difficulty in seeing avunculocal residence as anything but anomalous was in part a consequence of the semantic confusion generated by the term "patrilocal," since in both cases the couple did indeed live with the "groom's family" or "people." At the same time the urgent insistence on the association of matrilineality and matrilocality as the only "natural concomitants" simply left no room for avunculocality. As late as 1914 Rivers maintained this position, saying, "Mother-right in its typical form is associated with a mode of marriage most suitably called 'matrilocal' in which the husband lives with his wife's people" (Rivers, 1914b: 851).

Equally important was the almost unalterable conviction in the face of readily available evidence to the contrary that residence meant co-residence, and the possibility of a married couple living apart was not dignified as a form of residence at all. Murdock in 1949 did not recognize it formally, though in 1957 he used the term "duolocal" for it. The evidence that this form of residence occurred among the Nayar, Ashanti, and the Ga of West Africa was available in the literature for many years.

One direct consequence of the seminar's concern with this problem was Goodenough's paper "Residence Rules," published in 1956. In attempting to organize the material on Truk, Schneider raised the question of the apparent discrepancy between Fischer's and Goodenough's residence data, and this particular problem was settled in Goodenough's paper by what appears to be a considerable advance in clarifying some of the problems of residence.

The early twentieth century saw a widespread revolt not only against the particular theories of the nineteenth, but against cultural evolution in general. In America, Boas and his students turned to highly specific historical reconstructions. They eschewed all theories of general development on principle. In Britain, by the 1920's, Malinowski and Radcliffe-Brown, though holding very different assumptions from each other, condemned wholesale as "conjectural history" both the general evolutionary theories and the specific historical reconstructions of previous anthropologists. Both turned instead to analysis of the functional connections between contemporaneous institutions of a society. They emphasized that even if one could discover the historical origins of any particular institution, such knowledge would not explain why it persisted in its current setting today. Radcliffe-Brown, in particular, showed that many of the customs which the evolutionists had seen as survivals (such as certain patterns of kinship terms), when carefully investigated, made better sense in their present, real context than in any hypothetical previous one. Where customs were found whose existence could not be readily "explained" in terms of their relations with other institutions of the contemporary society—such as, for example, rules of descent themselves—these tended to be brushed aside as fundamentally inexplicable "historical accidents."

In modern social anthropology, therefore, matrilineal kinship systems came to be studied merely as particular examples of functionally integrated social structures, or else within the context of wider theoretical interests, rather than as the foci of special problems. Malinowski's monumental study of the Trobriand Islands in 1914–1918 concerned a matrilineal people, but he directed his attention to a general understanding of the interrelatedness of institutions, and used the matrilineal character of Trobriand society only incidentally to counter some general theories of psychoanalysis. Similarly Radcliffe-Brown, in 1924, used the specific theme of avuncular relations among the patrilineal Tonga and in various matrilineal societies in the general cause of his war on survivals and conjectural history. And although he contrasted patrilineal and matrilineal systems in his 1935 paper, his focus seemed to be on unilineal systems in general and he did not devote detailed attention to matrilineal systems as such.

Nevertheless, it is the work of these writers and their students which today offers the most fruitful insights into the special characteristics and problems of matrilineal descent. Malinowski's ethnography provided the first full-dress description of a matrilineal system in operation. Even today his are some of the clearest statements on the general position of the male in matrilineal societies, his equivocal relationship to his wife and children, the special importance of his relationship with his sister and sister's husband, and the conflict between a man's loyalties to his natal and his conjugal kin. Radcliffe-Brown, with a different theoretical orientation and a clearly structural view, also influenced most of the succeeding work on the structure of unilineal systems. The concepts of these two writers concerning matriliny have since been especially valuably documented and extended in the field studies of Fortune, Richards, Eggan, Fortes, and, more recently, Mitchell, Colson, and Turner.

British social anthropology has so far tended to be distinguished by depth of analysis of particular societies and by discussions of general concepts, rather than by extensive cross-cultural research into problems of co-variation. This makes the more remarkable Audrey Richards' paper of 1950 on the comparative study of Central Bantu matrilineal societies. This paper reintroduced, in a framework of modern anthropological theory, problems peculiar to matrilineal societies, and systematically compared and contrasted household composition, domestic authority, residence, inheritance, and succession patterns, in relation to subsistence base and to political structure, for six closely related matrilineal groups. In our view Richards' paper marked a major advance in the analysis of matrilineal descent groups. It provided the immediate stimulus for the present research, and for this reason the book is dedicated to Richards.

In this book three types of approach appear, now separately, now blended. One interest, shared by all the authors, is in the structural analysis of particular matrilineal societies, in their mode of operation and in the generalizations that can be made about all of them. Another interest is in cultural ecology: it is concerned with the significance for the form of a kinship system of the technico-environmental features of the culture in which it is found. A third interest is evolutionary: it is concerned with a typology of general levels of cultural development and, within this framework, with the implications of the evolution of the technical, political, and economic spheres of culture for the evolution of kinship systems. The second and third interests, shared especially by Gough and Aberle, derive much from American Culturology as represented by Leslie A. White and his students.

In this third interest especially the book takes up again the problem which the nineteenth-century theorists left in mid air. There is no question but that much of the confusion and entangling underbrush which tripped the nineteenth century theorists has been cleared away by the advances in both structural analysis and in analysis of the relationship between technico-environmental conditions and the institutions of kinship. But it is equally clear that much remains yet to be done in this area before we can say that even most of the underbrush is gone. It is precisely this problem which remains an open question: is adequate control over structural analysis, including technico-environmental relations, a prerequisite to the development of general laws of cultural development, as some people feel, or must the efforts to solve these go hand-in-hand, distinct but interrelated problems?

In general the authors have different degrees of commitment to these three interests. Not all the authors agree with all the conclusions drawn in the book, and each takes responsibility only for his or her own contribution. It is important to note that the different approaches and conclusions are indeed compatible.

The original seminar out of which this volume grew was convened by Schneider, because he felt that—except for Audrey Richards' work —insufficiently systematic attention had been paid to matrilineal systems and, particularly, that knowledge of their structure lagged behind that attained for patrilineal systems. The present volume is not a record of the seminar itself, but rather embodies thinking which originated there and developed beyond the point at which the seminar left off.

In the Introduction Schneider attempts to state, in theoretical terms rather than as empirical generalizations, the constant features of the structure of matrilineal descent groups. Such constant features occur within a variety of cultural frames and in a variety of ecological settings.

The actual organization of any particular group must therefore be seen not only in terms of its structural constants but as a product of those features in interaction with cultural and ecological conditions peculiar to the group. In selecting organization of matrilineal descent groups as the focus of the problem, it is not implied that the descent rule is in any sense causal or determinate, or even that it is the most important aspect of a particular kinship group, such as the Nayar *taravād* or the Ashanti lineage. On the contrary, the particular determinants of each particular case, both in its present condition and in its historical background, remain to be established. All that the delineation of the constant structural features of matrilineal descent groups can do is to state certain limiting conditions inherent in that mode of organization.

Part One of the book provides expositions of nine matrilineal systems. Each chapter includes material on what the author believes to be the crucial variables in dealing with matrilineal descent. The chapters in this part are not, however, intended as a random, stratified, or typical sample of matrilineal societies. The decision to use certain data for the seminar, to be worked up for presentation later in book form, stemmed from the original selection of members for the seminar. The aim, of course, was to find as many members as possible who had had firsthand experience, particularly recent field experience, with matrilineal peoples. This was not entirely possible for a variety of reasons. Gough, Aberle, Colson, and Basehart had all worked with matrilineal groups, but Basehart's Oneida materials did not prove suitable because of certain gaps in the data on the traditional system, which could not be filled from historical records. Fathauer knew the Trobriand and Northwest Coast literature and had worked with it for some time. Schneider had worked in Micronesia among a people who had been supposed to be matrilineal but who proved instead to have a system of double descent. He was, however, familiar with the Micronesian literature in general and had available to him excellent material on Truk. He was also able to discuss this material with Ward H. Goodenough and with John and Ann Fischer, who had recently worked there. It was hoped that this would make up for his failure to find matriliny where it was said to be.

The selection of societies did provide a wide diversity of types of matrilineal system. Drawing them from four continents minimized the possibility that any constant features discovered might result from diffusion rather than from matrilineal descent. The traditional Navaho and Plateau Tonga societies were examples of loosely structured, acephalous tribes; similarities between them proved particularly interesting in view of their great diversity of cultural origin. Both rely not only on cultivation but also on herding—unusual for matrilineal peoples. Truk and Trobriand are examples of more tightly structured matrilineal systems with relatively settled cultivation, organized into chiefdoms. The Ashanti were a large, matrilineally organized state, while the Kerala castes were differentiated occupational and social strata within still larger states. The six regions offered, also, a wide variety of residence patterns: irregular among the Plateau Tonga, dominantly matrilocal among Navaho, Trukese, and North Kerala Mappillas, dominantly avunculocal among Trobriand Islanders and North Kerala Nayars, and with a custom of "visiting spouses" among Central Kerala Nayars and a high proportion of Ashanti.

The chapter on the Navaho consists of new, unpublished information and a synthesis of the enormous literature on this well-studied group. Aberle has worked among the Navaho intermittently since 1940. He was fortunate in having access to some census data not widely available.

When she first presented it to the seminar, Colson's paper on the Plateau Tonga contained a large amount of material not published at that time. She later included much of this information in her book (Colson, 1958). The editors are especially grateful to her for redrafting her original paper to minimize overlap with her other published work, yet at the same time to highlight those aspects of the society which had special interest for the group.

The materials on Ashanti, Trobriand, and Truk are drawn from published literature. Each chapter is specially organized with reference to the ecological and social structural variables which, as the seminar progressed, came to seem most significant for the comparative study of matriliny. Anyone who has attempted to wade through Malinowski's voluminous writings will appreciate the magnitude of Fathauer's task and the skill with which he condensed the information into a straightforward account of social structure. Basehart, too, faced knotty problems in reconciling accounts of the political structure and of kinship among the Ashanti, and the editors feel he has solved many of them. The chapter on Truk contains some information not published elsewhere, kindly supplied by Ward H. Goodenough and John L. Fischer in response to enquiries which arose out of the seminar discussions.

The chapters on the Nayars and other Kerala castes contain a synthesis of historical literature, together with much hitherto unpublished material collected in the field. It is hoped that the information on the

Central Kerala Nayars may be of especial use to theorists of kinship, who have long been interested in this group because of the former absence among them of any organized nuclear family.

In Part Two Gough treats problems of variation in matrilineal systems, paying particular attention to the determinants of variation in descent-group structure, residence, patterns of interpersonal kinship relationships, and marriage preferences. She derives her hypotheses from investigation of the nine cases presented in Part One and from six other matrilineal systems for which literature is available.

Part Three is also comparative, but where Gough used a small number of cases, each treated as a whole system and in detail, Aberle selects more limited variables and treats statistically a large number of cases which were readily available through Murdock's *World Ethnographic Sample*. While concentrating on ecological determinants of social structure, Aberle also returns to some of the problems posed by the nineteenth-century writers who tried to stipulate general evolutionary sequences of culture. There are, of course, many differences in Aberle's approach. Perhaps the chief one is that he does not regard matrilineal descent as a primary characteristic of one general stage of cultural evolution. Rather, he sees it as one of several modes of descent possible in at least three general stages: namely, the acephalous, egalitarian tribe; the ranked, but not politically centralized, chiefdom; and the small-scale state. The problem of the incidence of matrilineal descent thus becomes, for Aberle, a problem not of general but of specific evolution.

The editors thank the other four participants for their patience and good will in corresponding over long distances, and in redrafting their chapters to suit changing plans for the book.

United thanks go to the Social Science Research Council for its excellent program of summer seminars, of which this book is but one product. The council's financial support made the six-week seminar possible, provided a Navaho informant for part of the period, and provided for a reporter who kept a valuable daily record of the discussion.

Harvard University and the Department of Social Relations gave generous hospitality, a meeting place, and such facilities as were available.

Professor Fred Eggan of the University of Chicago offered wise counsel in assembling the membership of the seminar and in first stating the problems for discussion. He joined the seminar for a short period. His advice proved excellent, his participation was enlightening, and his encouragement, particularly in the preparation of this volume, has been unflagging.

Dr. Titiev, Dr. Fortes, and Dr. Turner were of much help to Gough in her work on Part Two, in reading and commenting on preliminary versions of the various chapters.

Marshall Sahlins came to the seminar as its reporter, immediately following the completion of his doctorate. His official task was to keep a record of the discussions, which he did with immense diligence and consummate skill. Fortunately he also participated fully in the seminar and contributed many of its most fruitful ideas. He was invited to write a part of the book, but declined. He is, however, clearly represented in the thinking that went into Parts Two and Three of this book. Added warm thanks are due Barbara Sahlins for the long hours she put into typing the original manuscripts.

D.M.S.

CONTENTS

Part Two

Variation in Matrilineal Systems

Part Three

Cross-cultural Comparisons

The Distinctive Features of
Matrilineal Descent Groups

The aim of this introduction is to develop an initial theoretical rationale for certain features of matrilineal descent groups which distinguish them from their patrilineal counterparts. The patrilineal descent group is used as a point of contrast throughout.[1]

The problem is to put forward theoretical statements, not empirical generalizations. That is, I am concerned with some of the logical implications of a set of definitions, and the task is to show how the implications follow from the definitions so that they may have both predictive and analytic utility. For if certain conditions indeed follow logically from the way in which matrilineal descent groups are defined, then they should in real life (when they do match these definitions) be concretely constituted as predicted, and such conditions would be constant for such groups.

By concerning myself with the descent system it might seem that I somehow assume that descent is "causal" or "primary" or "important." I would explicitly disavow such assumptions. In order to say what is "important" or "causal" one must first specify "in respect to what." Descent may be "important" with respect to the patterning of certain relationships, such as marriage, or it may be but one of a series of relevant conditions. Descent may be unimportant to the techniques by which certain pottery designs are executed. I am therefore exploring

[1] Most of the central ideas in this chapter were developed during the course of the SSRC Summer Seminar so that D. F. Aberle, H. Basehart, E. Colson, G. Fathauer, K. Gough, M. Sahlins, and F. Eggan were particularly important to it. Each of them then contributed specific comments on earlier drafts which materially advanced both the thinking and its presentation. In addition, Raymond T. Smith, Erving Goffman, Robert F. Murphy, Richard N. Henderson, Clifford Geertz, and Melford Spiro offered helpful comments and suggestions. The reader will immediately note how much is owed to the pioneering work of Dr. Audrey I. Richards, and particularly to her very important paper (1951), "Some Types of Family Structure Amongst the Central Bantu" (*in* Radcliffe-Brown and Forde (eds.), *African Systems of Kinship and Marriage*).

the nature of matrilineal descent groups, not evaluating their importance for culture, for evolution, or for anything of that sort. I only assume that descent is a limiting condition in every kinship system; that there is a "coherence" or "logic" to a particular type of descent system such that it is not compatible with some forms of social organization but may be more or less so with others. My aim is, in a sense, to try to lay bare the structure of one particular type of descent group and the implications of this structure and so illuminate its internal "logic." My aim is definitely not to argue for the priority of descent in any sense—functional, causal, or historical.

Kinship must be distinguished from descent. Kinship defines a number of statuses and their interrelationships according to a variety of rules or principles and distinguishes kinsmen from non-kin. Descent, as the term will be used here, forms a unit of consanguineally related kinsmen. It is the existence of a unit which is crucial here, and the unit must be culturally distinguished as such. Such a unit cannot include all kinsmen, nor can it include kinsmen who are related in any way other than consanguineally. Descent as such thus refers to the socially stipulated rule by which the unit is constituted. Since the unit is a consanguineal one, each member is affiliated with the unit through his parents [2] and in no other way.

There may be, for instance, a patrilineal or matrilineal line which an observer can trace, or which a member of the society can trace, but unless this line is culturally distinguished in some way it does not constitute a descent unit.

A descent unit has members affiliated according to a particular rule, systematically applied. *Unilineal* rules or principles for the affiliation of descent unit members are those in which sex is systematically used as the distinguishing criterion, so that those kinsmen related through one sex are included and those related through the opposite sex are excluded. When male sex is the distinguishing criterion the descent

---

[2] See text below for definitions of the terms "parents," "mother," and "father." The usual definitions of "kinship" and aspects of kinship like "descent" tend to rest on assumptions of biological relatedness used either as an element in the definition of analytic categories or as a formal assumption implicit or explicit in some concrete system. There is no doubt whatever that many concrete systems, such as the American kinship system, use notions of "blood" and biological relationship in defining certain kinship relations. But my conviction is that biological relatedness, *used as an analytic category in terms of which kinship systems may be compared and analyzed,* has been as much of an impediment as a useful tool in understanding kinship in general. This is obviously not the place for an essay on this subject, but it is necessary to point out that I avoid biologically based definitions so far as possible.

principle or rule is called *patrilineal.* Ego is thus patrilineally related *to* females, but *not through* females for the purpose of constituting a particular descent unit. His initial relationship is of course through his father. From the point of view of the observer, either within the society or outside it, a patrilineal descent unit consists in consanguineal kinsmen related through males. When female sex is the distinguishing criterion the principle is called *matrilineal.* In the latter case the individual's initial relationship is to his mother and through her to other kinsmen, both male and female, but continuing only through females.

In unilineal descent, by definition here, an individual's affiliation is only rarely maintained for less than his lifetime.[3] His affiliation is ascribed automatically according to the rule of descent and follows from his association with his mother (or, in patrilineal descent, through her to his father). Choice is open to the affiliating individual only under rare and unusual circumstances.[4]

A particular society may use one or more different principles of descent. The descent *system* of a society is defined by the inventory of the different principles of descent which are employed in that society. If a society uses only one of the two unilineal principles, regardless of what other principles occur, the system is designated by the name for the particular unilineal principle which is used. Thus a system which includes the matrilineal principle but does not include the patrilineal principle will be called a *matrilineal system,* regardless of what other principles may also be used. If both matrilineal and patrilineal principles occur, the system is called *double descent* and is

[3] The particular problem to which this provision is addressed is that of the stability of group membership and the stability of an individual's commitment to a particular descent group. Two likely sources of instability are those which arise through adoption or similar circumstances, and those which arise through voluntary or involuntary shifts of group membership.

Adoption, given the definition of "mother" used here, is simply that situation where the formal responsibility for the child's care is relinquished by one woman and taken over by another. It is necessary that the capacity for placement and affiliation are transmitted at the same time. This is not, of course, the case in some concrete systems. But the specific provision against such a contingency is introduced here since, if there were a high rate of adoption and if each adopted person could retain his ties through his first mother as well as his ties by adoption, a large number of persons might gain membership in two or more unilineal descent groups.

[4] Firth (1957) and Goodenough (1955) have drawn attention to certain systems in which the individual elects to join one or another descent group, that of his mother or that of his father. As they have clearly shown, the membership of such groups is quite different from what are here defined as unilineal descent groups, and so must be ruled out of consideration here. The crucial definitional element appears to me to be the element of choice between mother's or father's group.

thus clearly separated from a matrilineal system. My assumption is that the presence or absence of principles of descent other than the unilineal principle does not seriously affect the theory being developed here. Even under conditions of double descent what follows concerning matrilineal descent groups is not seriously altered.

A particular principle of descent affiliates a number of kinsmen, but these kinsmen may or may not be socially defined as a kinship *unit*. That is, unilineal lines may be traced or unilineal affiliation between two kinsmen may be traced, but all unilineally affiliated kinsmen may still not be accorded the status of a unit. When kinsmen, affiliated according to one or the other of the unilineal principles, are treated as a unit for some purpose I will speak of a *descent unit*.

The descent units of a unilineal descent system may have different forms of organization. This theory applies only to one such form of organization, that is, to *that descent unit or portion thereof which engages as a whole in activities with respect to which decisions must be made from time to time and in which all adult male members do not have equal authority*. I will call this a *descent group* to distinguish it from descent units otherwise organized, as well as from aggregates or categories or other collectivities. The term "descent group" is thus similar to what has elsewhere been called a "corporate descent group."

A descent group is a decision-making group. In order to reach decisions and to carry them out effectively the group must have the power to mobilize its resources and capacities. To do this it must somehow structure authority so that the necessary decisions can be reached and enforced and so that sanctions can be applied in cases of failure to conform. The minimal condition for such a structure is that authority be differentially distributed among the members of the group.

Thus a lineage or clan which owns property, which assembles for legal, administrative, ceremonial, or other purposes, and which has a head, is an example, though not the only example, of a descent group as here defined. The Nayar *taravād*, described later in this volume, fits this definition. The *taravād* holds property jointly, acts as a unit with respect to ceremonial as well as property matters, assembles on certain ceremonial occasions, and has at its head the *kāranavan*. On the other hand, a named clan whose members are dispersed over hundreds of miles, which never meets or acts as a whole, which has no leader (such as the Navaho clan), though it may be a significant kinship unit in terms of which exogamic rules are phrased and reciprocal hospitality granted, is not a descent group by this definition. However, descent groups may be found within such dispersed unilineal units, as is the case with the Trukese lineage (chapter 3). Further, there may be more than one kind of unilineal descent unit present, or more than one level of unit organization in any given society.

There are, finally, three conditions which are, by definition here, constant features of unilineal descent groups regardless of the principle in terms of which the descent group is formed. They are "constants," of course, strictly in the sense that the theory requires them as characteristics of descent groups. These three constants, in combination with matrilineal descent, give matrilineal descent groups their distinctive characteristics. These are: first, women are responsible for the care of children, with every child being the primary responsibility of one woman; second, adult men have authority over women and children; and third, descent-group exogamy is required. I will discuss each of these briefly.

It is necessary in defining descent, descent principles, and hence the descent group, to define the terms "mother" and "father," since descent principles depend on the affiliation of each person through one or the other or both of these statuses.

The woman who has primary responsibility for the early care of the infant and child is its *mother*. The *father* of the child, for present purposes, is that person who is married to the child's mother at that time during the child's early life when the child is formally affiliated according to some descent principle.[5]

In the definition of "mother" the words "primary responsibility" are critical. I do not mean by this that the woman who has "primary responsibility" for the early care of the child must bear the child, or nurse it at her own breast or wash it with her own hands or, later on, actually prepare its food herself. Nannies, mammies, or servants of all sorts may very well be engaged to do the actual work, but they must be distinguished from that woman who has "primary responsibility" for the child. Indeed, the mother may have no actual say in the selection of the nurse or servant, and the mother may not even see the child for long periods of time, but she is "primarily responsible" for it in that these tasks are done for her; when such tasks are undertaken by others it is not "their" child but the "mother's" child.

From these definitions the role of the mother entails three analytically separable elements which may, in any concrete system, be fused into one. *Responsibility* for early care, the *actual care* itself, and *social*

[5] I am well aware of the difficulties of defining "married to" and so leave the term undefined here except to indicate that as a minimal definition, the person through whom the child is affiliated, if it is not the child's mother, is, therefore, its "father."

placement or *affiliation*. The woman who is primarily responsible for the care of the child is by definition here the woman through whom the child is affiliated with other kinsmen, either through his mother (matrilineal descent) or through his mother's husband—the father (patrilineal descent).

The role of mother has been defined as that of the woman primarily responsible for the care of a particular child. I add now that this is one aspect of the role of women in general. This means that by and large all women, or almost all women, are expected to be responsible for the care of children. This does not mean that in fact each and every female member of any particular society must care for at least one child. It only means that this is part of the definition of the role of a woman, and that so far as it is possible women will play this allotted role. Whatever other roles are allotted to women (that they hoe corn, make beer or beds, or become possessed by spirits), at least child care is required by this theory.

A second aspect of sex-role differentiation has to do with authority. It has already been stated that a necessary condition of this theory is that adult members of the descent group do not all have equal authority; this is required by the definition of the descent group as a decision-making group. Quite apart from the roles of men and women in the descent group itself is the general question of the roles of men as men and women as women. The role of women as women has been defined as that of responsibility for the care of children. I now add that the role of men as men is defined as that of having authority over women and children (except perhaps for specially qualifying conditions applicable to a very few women of the society). Positions of highest authority within the matrilineal descent group will, therefore, ordinarily be vested in statuses occupied by men.

The responsibility for the care of children is quite different from the distribution of authority. The responsibility for the care of children is one aspect of the role of adult women regardless of what other statuses they occupy. A woman may be a sister as well as a wife, a daughter as well as a mother, but none of these need alter her responsibility for the care of children. But the authority allocated to one status may very well be directly affected by the other statuses which the person occupies. Hence status stipulations may be of the utmost significance. Statuses in turn become relevant within a particular context or sphere of action. The status of wife has relevance to the domestic sphere; the status of mother's brother in matrilineal systems, to the descent-group sphere. The allocation of authority within the domestic sphere must be distinguished from the allocation of authority within the descent-group sphere and these in turn distinguished from the religious sphere, the political sphere, and so forth. Within a particular sphere of activity the authority of men and women, occupying the statuses appropriate to that sphere, may be differentially distributed. And if all spheres are compared to see how authority is distributed between men and women, there may be a systematic correlation such that male-held statuses have authority over those statuses occupied by women or children. For our purposes only two spheres are immediately important: the domestic sphere and the descent-group sphere. It is sufficient, then, to define the male sex role as having authority over the statuses occupied by women within the context of each of these spheres. This means that men of the descent group have authority over the women and children of that descent group, that adult males of the domestic group have authority over the women and children of that domestic group.

The matrilineal descent group—for this theory to hold—must be exogamous. Note however that it is the matrilineal descent group as such which must be exogamous, not the larger unit within which it may be imbedded. Thus the clan of which any particular matrilineal descent group may be a segment may be without a rule of exogamy in the sense that marriage may be permitted within it, but the matrilineal descent group itself must be exogamous.

From these definitions it might seem that matrilineal and patrilineal descent groups are precise mirror images of each other, identical in their structure except for the superficial point that in one group membership is obtained through the father, in the other through the mother. Otherwise, every element is identical. The groups are both defined as decision-making units which hold some activity in common. The roles of men and women are identically defined in both groups, men having authoritative roles and women having responsibility for child care. Both groups, by definition, are exogamous.

Despite the fact that the elements are the same, there are certain very obvious differences between matrilineal and patrilineal descent groups. Perhaps the first and most profound is that in patrilineal descent groups the line of authority and the line of descent both run through men. That is, both authority and group placement are male functions. In matrilineal descent groups, on the other hand, although the line of authority also runs through men, group placement runs through the line of women. The lines of authority and group placement are thus coördinate in males in patrilineal descent groups, but separated between males and females in matrilineal descent groups.

This is, I believe, the fundamental structural difference between matrilineal and patrilineal descent groups. From this difference all others follow.

The two differences which are consequences of this structural difference and which are in turn fundamental to all others are, first, that matrilineal descent groups depend for their continuity and operation on retaining control over both male and female members. Second, that the sex role of the "in-marrying affine" is different in matrilineal and patrilineal descent groups.

By "in-marrying affine" I mean simply the spouse of the person whose children belong to his or her own descent group. That is, the husband is an in-marrying affine with respect to his wife and her children in a matrilineal descent group; the wife is an in-marrying affine with respect to her husband and his children in a patrilineal descent group. However, once the term "in-marrying affine" is so defined, one can go on to ask about the role of the in-marrying affine with respect to his own group, the descent group into which he is married, the nuclear family into which he is married, and the kind of linkage he constitutes between his own and affinally related descent groups.

(1) *Matrilineal descent groups depend for their continuity and operation on retaining control over both male and female members.* Women are required to care for the new members of the descent group and to give these new members their membership in the group (since a child belongs to the group of its mother). The control which the matrilineal descent group exercises over its female members must ensure that the children will achieve primary orientation to the matrilineal descent group and develop primary ties of loyalty to it. If males are required for authority roles then they, too, cannot be relinquished by or alienated from the group.

Male members of a matrilineal descent group might be of three kinds: those who now play authority roles and hence are required for the current operation of the group; those who are likely to succeed to those roles and who cannot be lost to the group if it is to continue when the present incumbents become incapacitated or die; and those unlikely to succeed to authoritative roles.

It is conceivable that the matrilineal descent group might exercise either no control whatever, or very little control, over this last category of males, for they are not directly required for the maintenance and perpetuation of the group. Thus it might be possible for men of this category to break all ties with their own groups. That this would then constitute a serious source of strain which would tend toward the weakening or disruption of the system of matrilineal descent groups is, however, clear on analysis.

If a portion of the men of the matrilineal descent group broke all ties with their group, but still recognized the rule of exogamy, they would marry women who were members of other matrilineal descent groups. Having neither authoritative roles in their own group, nor the prospect of gaining any, such men would be put in a position where three alternate courses of action were open to them.

First, they might attempt to become assimilated into the matrilineal descent groups of their wives, competing for authoritative roles via avenues of influence with members of those groups—an inherently unstable situation.

Second, they might attempt to gain control over their wives and children and remove them from the control of their matrilineal descent group. Such a situation would seriously weaken the matrilineal descent group, though it might not destroy it.

Third, they might remain unassimilated and yet not attempt to gain control over their wives and children, but just "live in peace" with their affines. Men in such a position, without ties to, or the backing and support of their own group, would find themselves in a difficult position against their organized affines. They would become dependents, and at the mercy of their affines. A group of "second-class citizens" might thus emerge and, if they could not be drained from the society, might constitute a serious threat to its continuation as a system of matrilineal descent groups. In short, this last alternative would result in an unstable situation which would tend to shift toward either of the first two.

I have argued here exclusively in terms of authority roles and succession to such roles and without reference to one of the important "givens" of the situation: namely, that the matrilineal descent group is being treated here, by definition, as a unit which has decision-making functions with respect to some activity. Such an activity and such corporate organization directly entail an "interest" on the part of each member which in turn implies "rights." Perhaps the matrilineal descent group holds an estate in common from which its members derive their sustenance. Even though a man has no prospect of succeeding to an authority role, he has a right in that estate as a member and has an interest in maintaining that right, and though he may never succeed to headship, he need not, for that reason alone, become alienated from the group. He remains bound to that group by the commonalty of its members' interests.

If we consider those men who have no prospect of succeeding to positions of authority, the crucial consideration—which requires that even these men cannot be completely released from their matrilineal descent groups—cannot be such rights alone. For it would seem perfectly possible for a man to exchange his rights in his matrilineal descent group for equivalent rights in the matrilineal descent group of his wife. It is precisely the fact that such an exchange constitutes a threat to the integrity of his own group as well as to his affinal group that makes this the crucial consideration. For it follows directly that if an in-marrying affine obtains the same rights as a member, he becomes in effect a member, and the organization and membership of the group cannot long remain that of a matrilineal descent group. The only condition under which men of this sort do not constitute a direct threat is when they can be kept in the position of in-marrying affines and not permitted to share rights equally with members.

But the question of rights is not an all-or-none matter, though the question of membership is, by definition. There may, thus, be degrees of *alienation* of a man from his own matrilineal descent group, and degrees of *assimilation* into his wife's group, just as there are obviously degrees to which he is *depended* on by either his own or his affinal group.

The *dependence* of a member on his matrilineal descent group and of his group on him thus varies inversely with his *alienation* from his group. His alienation from his own group would vary inversely with his *assimilation* into his affinal group. One extreme of this relationship would be the case where a member was completely independent of his own group and alienated from it, and completely assimilated into his affinal group. In such a situation it would not seem possible for matrilineal descent groups, as defined here, to continue. The opposite extreme would define the strongest kind of matrilineal descent group; namely, where members were (except for the requirement of exogamy) completely dependent on their own group, not alienated from it in any way, and in no way (beyond the minimum conditions for marriage) assimilated into their affinal groups. The weakest groups would be those in which some proportion of members were alienated from their descent groups, independent of them, and greatly assimilated into their affinal groups.[6]

    [6] The idea of variable descent-group "strength" requires more specialized treatment than can be given here. Suffice it to say that certain simple distinctions can profitably be made in dealing with this matter. First, consistency of descent principle as a factor should be kept apart from the question of descent-group "strength" until its role in whatever is defined as "strength" is determined. The not uncommon device of continuing a patrilineal line by the fiction that the daughter's husband is really the son is an example of inconsistency of descent principle. Similarly, the patrilineal principle is clearly transgressed when parts of a patrilineal unit are related through a woman. Second, the notion of "strength" has at

What I have said thus far contrasts with the situation in patrilineal descent groups. Patrilineal units cannot afford to relinquish control over male members, who fill authoritative roles as in matrilineal descent groups, but they can afford to lose a considerable degree of control over their female members, provided that they gain proportionate control over the women marrying into their group. Thus the patrilineal descent group can lose complete control over its female members in exchange for complete control over its wives. This follows from the stated conditions that female members of a patrilineal descent group cannot add new members to their group, and are *not* required for authoritative roles in their group, though females of other groups are required for the perpetuation of the group. Further, the women of patrilineal descent groups can exchange rights in their own group for rights in their affinal groups without becoming a source of strain or a threat to the system of patrilineal descent groups.

This dependence of a matrilineal descent group on both its male and female members might be phrased as an interdependence of brother and sister. A brief review of the difficulties inherent in this phrasing raises certain points worth noting.

Such a view of the problem might argue that a sister depends on her brother for protection, care, and managerial and authority functions, while the brother depends on his sister for the perpetuation of his descent line and the provision of an heir.

The interdependence is not, and indeed structurally cannot be of *one* brother on *one* sister or even of brothers on sisters. All too often there may be no brother, or the ratio between brothers and sisters may be far out of balance, so that there may be many brothers and one sister or many sisters and but one brother. What *may* happen is that all women of a descent group may depend *for a time* on a single man, the head of the group, who may be a brother or the eldest male of

---

least two distinct references which might well be kept apart. On the one hand it may be used as a statement concerning the mode of internal organization of a unit, as is done here, where the focus is on the strength of the bonds among members. On the other hand it may be used to refer to the position of the unit vis-à-vis other units in the society. Thus, for example, "strength" in the first sense refers to the degree of loyalty which can be expected from members of a descent group. In the second sense "strength" refers to the position of the descent group in the total social structure as crucial or not, as playing a "vital" role or not, as "strategic" or not. Although there is some reason to believe that any group which commands extraordinary degrees of loyalty from its members is likely to play a strategic role in the social structure, it is possible that a single, crucial function can be performed by a social unit which commands little loyalty from its members, but just enough to maintain that group.

the group, while other males are away for longer or shorter periods.

It is true, however, that the symbolic statement of the interdependence of male and female members of a matrilineal descent group is often *phrased* by the people themselves as an interdependence of brother and sister and this may be particularly so where the descent group itself is organized as if it were composed of siblings. Or, the problem of binding the allegiance of out-marrying females of a matrilineal descent group may be solved by providing them with food; in order to make a definite assessment of the responsibility for the one who provides the food which is sent, particular brothers may be paired with particular sisters when this is possible. But because a woman's husband receives his wife's food from a particular brother of his wife does not mean that her children perpetuate only that brother's descent line, nor does it mean that the woman depends on that particular brother alone for providing her children with guidance, with a village, and with plots in a village to which they may go when grown. Thus in these cases too, despite the symbolic phrasing of the relationship in terms of brother-sister interdependence, the basic interdependence is between members of a group, not between particular persons or statuses.

The interdependence of male and female members in matrilineal descent groups is thus primarily a phenomenon of descent *groups,* not of pairs of persons or pairs of statuses.

Further, the real or symbolic interdependence of brother and sister is by no means distinctive to matrilineal descent groups but occurs among patrilineal descent groups as well. Where patrilineal descent groups practice marriage by sister exchange the interdependence of brother and sister is clearly evident. Among such people a woman's marriage may be directly dependent on her brother's marriage, and where one fails for any reason the other must necessarily fail too. Similarly, among those patrilineal people where bridewealth is a significant element of marriage, the marriage of a man may depend on the bridewealth which his sister first brings in, so that in some groups brother and sister may be paired off and the brother cannot marry until his sister's marriage brings in the bridewealth necessary for his marriage. Also, the partial dependence of a woman on her brother's protection is quite clear in many patrilineal groups.

The interdependence between men and women in matrilineal descent groups does have one important implication for brother-sister relationships where the kinship system defines group membership in terms of birth and the group views birth as a consequence of sexual relations. Let us take as a given feature of the descent groups with which we are concerned the prohibition of sexual relations between brother and sister. Patrilineal descent is consistent with the demands of this incest taboo in a way that matrilineal descent is not. In the patrilineal case a woman's sexual and reproductive activities are the primary concern of her husband and her husband's group, and not of her brother. In this sense there is a consistency between the prohibition against sexual interest between brother and sister and the locus of concern with a woman's sexual and reproductive activities. On the other hand, in matrilineal descent groups a woman bears children who perpetuate her own and her brother's group, and her sexual and reproductive activities are a matter of direct concern for her brother— although she is a tabooed sexual object for him. (2) *In màtrilineal descent groups there is an element of potential strain in the fact that the sister is a tabooed sexual object for her brother, while at the same time her sexual and reproductive activities are a matter of interest to him.*

There is no reason to believe that this potential strain is always recognized and adapted to, implicitly or explicitly. Nevertheless, the fact that this strain is implicit in matrilineal descent groups but absent in patrilineal descent groups means that it may, under certain conditions, generate modes of adaptation to it which will be distinctive to matrilineal and not patrilineal descent groups.

It is possible that the occasionally reported "ignorance of paternity" may have such adaptive functions, among others. Where, along with matrilineal descent the belief exists that the sexual act bears *no* relation whatever to conception and reproduction, this belief might be interpreted as a condition which separates sexual from reproductive activity. By thus separating these two activities and denying the relationship between them, it is possible that both brother and sister gain firmer control over their incestuous impulses. The brother's unqualified interest in his sister's reproductive activity may thus be uncontaminated by any implications of interest in her as a sexual object. Similarly, his renunciation of her as an object of sexual interest need not impair his concern for her reproductivity or her offspring nor need it infuse these relationships with more or less disguised sexual overtones.

A second possible adaptation to this potential strain is that of brother-sister respect [7] or avoidance. Respect and avoidance, which almost always prohibit elements of a sexual nature, might be seen in this

[7] I do not include those relations between brother and sister which are primarily limited to deference in this conception of "respect." By respect I mean those types of relationships which tend to minimize contact and narrowly channel interaction between the two.

context as special devices over and above those usually associated with the maintenance of the incest taboo. They are especially appropriate in minimizing the strain imposed by the brother's and sister's prohibited sexual interest in each other and yet maintaining their common concern for the continuity of their matrilineal group through the reproductive activity of the sister.

Here again, however, we must be explicit in noting that this strain need not necessarily generate specific institutionalized modes of adaptation, nor need brother-sister avoidance or respect be the only possible adaptation to it. Nor does it follow that brother-sister avoidance or respect has this and *only* this function. It may very well occur in patrilineal descent groups with quite different functions than this.

I turn now to those distinctive features of matrilineal descent groups which follow from the sex role of the in-marrying affine alone, or from the combination of this factor with that of the interdependence between men and women of matrilineal descent groups. These center on the in-marrying male in matrilineal descent groups, first as husband-father, second as husband, then as father. From there I proceed to the situation of the children as a sibling group.

(3) *Matrilineal descent groups do not require the statuses of father and husband.* The statuses of mother and wife, on the other hand, are indispensable to patrilineal systems.

The bond between mother and child has a certain base in the nursing and care situation which is not paralleled by the genitor-child relationship. It is the psychobiological quality of the mother-child relationship which makes the status of mother indispensable to the maintenance of patrilineal descent groups. It is precisely the psychobiological quality of the genitor-child relationship which makes no such requirement of matrilineal descent groups. All that is required is that the genitor belong to a descent group which is different from that of the mother.

In matrilineal descent groups it is the fact of responsibility for care by a particular woman that validates membership in a particular matrilineal descent group, and the psychobiological bond between a child and the mother who cares for it will be overlaid by these social elements. Every mother will be a member of a descent group and every descent group will look to the authority of its males. Though every woman must depend on one or more males for authority functions, these males are by definition members of her group. Genitors, therefore, may come and go with only the weakest links to the mothers of their children and with no more formal ties than those required by the fact that sexual activity must be ordered and regulated. Where the father-husband status is present in matrilineal societies, it must be accounted for on grounds other than that of matrilineal descent.[8]

In patrilineal descent groups the relations between mother and child are of an irreducible minimum and are necessarily present, while in matrilineal groups the relations between father and child have to be built from the ground up, from the little which is inherent in the situation. Therefore, (3a) *the status of father-husband can vary within fairly wide limits in matrilineal descent groups.* The status of mother-wife, on the other hand, can vary within much narrower limits in patrilineal systems.

In patrilineal descent groups recruitment of new members is through the males of the group. In those concrete societies where sexual reproduction and birth are conceived as crucial criteria there is an important sense in which men, in such patrilineal descent groups, have child-bearing functions which are symbolized in what Richards has called "the ideology of descent" (Richards, 1950: 213). Women may be regarded as mere receptacles, or they may be believed to contribute nothing more than a favorable medium for the development of the foetus. But there are distinct limits to how far women may be regarded as irrelevant to the recruitment process, for by definition here women do care for the children and men do not.[9]

[8] This is perhaps an important point at which to reiterate the fact that this attempts to be a theoretical statement and that this is a deduction from the theory. It does *not* say that since matrilineal descent groups do not require husband-fathers, it follows that a statistical survey of concrete cases will show them to be consistently absent in matrilineal descent groups and invariably present in patrilineal descent groups. No such contention is expressed or implied in this chapter. All that is argued is that matrilineal descent groups do not require the status of husband-father. That social conditions other than matrilineal descent *do* require such a status seems self-evident from its prevalence in concrete systems.

[9] There is a line of thought which I cannot follow up here but which merits some attention. By the definitions used here, it is only required that some woman be primarily responsible for the care of the child from its very early years, and that this role is expected of women generally. It is not stipulated that the woman who bears the child must be the woman who cares for *that* child. Given these definitions, the question arises as to whether it is necessary to this theory that women actually bear children. All that would be required is that some woman be primarily responsible for its care after birth, and that the child become a member of the matrilineal descent group of the woman who cares for it. There is the added stipulation that the ascription of descent-group membership cannot be arbitrarily repeated with great frequency and that it cannot be multiple. That is, the definitions insist on the stability of group membership and the stability of membership of the vast majority of individuals, ruling out multiple or sequential memberships.

There must be some provision for obtaining new members for a group if old members die. Otherwise the group would become extinct. Such provision might be met by women bearing children, or it might be met equally well by test tubes bearing children. The only argument which I can imagine at this time which might

(3b) *In matrilineal descent groups the position of the in-marrying male is such that even his biological contribution can be socially ignored to some advantage to the matrilineal descent group, and an ideology of descent developed which ignores the male role in conception.*[10]

The basic limit on the variability of father-husband roles in matrilineal descent groups is that of the degree to which he can be incorporated into the descent group of his wife, or the degree that his wife can be incorporated into his group. These limits are simply that, on the one hand, if women's children are assigned to their father's descent group the system ceases to be matrilineal. Therefore the tie between women and their own groups must be such as to permit the allocation of the child to the mother's group and to no other. On the other hand, so long as the woman's descent group locates authority functions over that group in the hands of its male members, the authority of a husband over his wife and her children is thereby limited.

(4) *The institutionalization of very strong, lasting, or intense solidarities between husband and wife is not compatible with the maintenance of matrilineal descent groups.* This is not true for patrilineal descent groups (cf. Gluckman, 1950; Fallers, 1957; Schneider, 1953).

By institutionalization I do not mean the relatively random occurrence of such solidarities in a very small portion of the population. This would constitute a source of strain, but not a systematic source of

---

challenge this view is that there is some inherent connection between birth and child care such that the woman who bears the child is, in some statistical long run, even if not in each particular case, the only woman who could properly assure that child of survival and proper socialization. Implicit here is the notion that childbirth somehow motivates women to care for children, a task that no one would want to undertake otherwise. This argument does not seem tenable.

Here again I am interested in showing the practical *analytic* irrelevance of biological links to kinship relations and descent systems. The social recognition of biological facts obviously occurs in some concrete kinship systems and obviously has certain functions, but I have difficulty in seeing that these are in any sense *required* by kinship systems or crucial to their analysis.

[10] Here again is a theoretical statement. It does not follow that in the real world the biological role of the genitor is only ignored in matrilineal descent groups and is invariably present in patrilineal descent groups. There are well-known cases where the role of the genitor is ignored in both matrilineal and patrilineal descent groups. All that is argued here is that, other things being equal, matrilineal descent groups can ignore the biological role of the male in conception without in the least disturbing the system and it is implied that from the point of view of the matrilineal descent group alone there might be certain advantages to this. Where, in concrete matrilineal descent groups, the social recognition of the male's biological role in conception is evident, this cannot arise from the fact that this recognition is *required* by, or even a likely consequence of, matrilineal descent-group organization.

strain. What I mean essentially is that where stable marriage is a normative element such that there is strong and consistent pressure on *all* husbands and wives to be firmly bound to each other, this will constitute a source of strain on the matrilineal descent group.

There is always potential conflict between the bonds of marriage and the bonds of descent; given exogamy, they are bonds which cannot coincide but pull each party to a marriage in different directions. If the bonds of marriage are maximized as against the bonds of descent this means that in any situation of conflicting loyalties the bonds of marriage are more likely to be sustained than those of descent. Conversely, where the bonds of descent are maximized, narrow limits are set on the degree to which the bonds of marriage may develop. In such a situation there are a variety of modes of adaptation to such potential conflict. Interests may be sharply segregated, various rights clearly delineated and allocated, or situations distinguished so that when one set of loyalties applies another is held apart and so on. But every such adaptive device is in one sense merely an impairment and a limitation on the maximization of one or the other set of ties which stabilizes the conflict.

If matrilineal descent groups are to be maintained, therefore, and if women are necessary to those groups for continuity, women's ties to their husbands must not be such that the priority they assign their marital ties supersedes that which they give to their matrilineal descent group. Similarly, if a man is needed to fill authoritative roles in his matrilineal descent group, he cannot accord such priority to his marital relationship that he fails to play this critical role in his own group.

Strong bonds of solidarity between husband and wife, and stable marriage, are possible with patrilineal descent groups in proportion to the degree to which the tie of the wife to her own unit is relaxed. Precisely because a woman can be practically entirely freed from obligations to her patrilineal descent group, her ties to her husband can be maximized to the point where they take first priority, and a system in which stable marriage is institutionalized can ensue. In the extreme case, therefore, there need be no conflict between the bonds of marriage and descent for a woman in a patrilineal descent group when her bonds of descent become practically nonexistent for her. Where a woman's tie to her own unit is greatly weakened or nearly severed she may become largely if not wholly dependent on her husband and his patrilineal descent group and the stability of the marriage may in such a case be a direct function of the degree of her dependency. Her severed or weakened tie to her own unit means, in such a case, that she is not free to return to her unit in divorce. Where a woman's tie to her own unit is so severed, her husband and his patrilineal descent group may gain a considerable degree of control over her, thus enforcing her bond to her husband and her dependence on him and his patrilineal descent group, regardless of her own inclinations. In short, the *independence* of men and women in patrilineal descent groups permits a degree of *alienation* of women from those groups, which in turn permits a high degree of *assimilation* of wives into their affinal groups.

Dependence and control are not, however, the only directions which the relationship between husband and wife may take in patrilineal descent groups. Strong, emotionally intense solidarity may develop between a woman and her children, and these may further reinforce her ties with her husband. I will return to this point shortly.

Thus far I have spoken of the bonds of marriage versus the bonds of descent and suggested that there is a necessarily inverse relationship between them: the greater the priority accorded to the bonds of marriage, the weaker the bonds of descent and the lower their priority. This is, of course, not only true for matrilineal and patrilineal descent groups, but for certain other descent systems as well. The only significant difference between matrilineal and patrilineal descent groups that I have pointed out thus far is that the bonds of marriage can be fully stressed in patrilineal descent groups because the bonds between a woman and her own unit can be practically severed. It should be quite clear, however, that this statement only holds true from the point of view of the woman as in-marrying affine. It cannot hold true for her husband, since his membership in and obligations to his patrilineal descent group require that from his point of view, no matter what the bonds of marriage may be, his own descent bonds must take priority; otherwise he will tend to be pulled out of and away from his descent group in situations of conflict of interest between his marriage bond and his descent-group bond.

I have been concerned only with the very general point that the development of strong bonds of any kind between husband and wife tend in the long run to be incompatible with the maintenance of matrilineal descent groups. It is appropriate now to consider a particular kind of bond likely to be significant, namely, that of authority.

The sex role of men makes them more difficult to manage as in-marrying affines than women, and hence in-marrying men are a special source of potential strain for matrilineal descent groups. In patrilineal descent groups the allocation of authority by sex is such that men as men have authority both within their descent group and over its in-marrying affines. The lines of descent and authority are thus coördinate. In matrilineal descent groups, on the other hand, such lines are not coördinate. Men have authoritative roles within their descent group, but their authority over their wives must be sharply limited. Conversely, the authority of a woman as in-marrying affine is no threat to her husband's patrilineal descent group because, by definition here, her husband has authority over her.

Males as in-marrying affines in matrilineal descent groups thus pose a problem in that they are in the position where they have a firm base upon which to develop the kind of authority over their wives that can lead to the disruption of the system of matrilineal descent groups. *(4a) Matrilineal descent groups require the institutionalization of special limits on the authority of husbands over wives.* Although every social system will necessarily set limits on authoritative roles, patrilineal descent groups do not, by their nature, require any other limits than those inherent in the problem of maintaining any system of social relations. Matrilineal descent groups, as I have suggested, do require special limits over and above those minimally necessary to systems of social relations in general.

The essence of the limitation of the husband's authority over his wife is, of course, the clear allocation of spheres of male authority so that males as descent-group members have kinds of authority which males as in-marrying affines do not have. On the other hand, men by definition here have authority over women and children. It follows, therefore, that husbands will have some authority as men over their wives and children, and the problem then becomes one of the specification of spheres of husbands' authority as against the spheres of male descent-group members. It is thus to be expected that a domestic sphere over which the husband has some authority will be clearly distinguished in concrete cases from the descent-group sphere. Since the woman must act both as a descent-group member and as a wife-mother she will tend to find herself in a position where her loyalties are in some degree split between her descent group and her husband. In part this is a problem of the integration and balancing of opposing loyalties, minimized to a great degree by the clarity with which her role toward her husband and her role toward her descent group are defined. Nevertheless, the husband's tendency to maximize his sphere of authority will be balanced by the male descent-group members' tendency to maximize and maintain their sphere of authority.

Relations between male in-marrying affines and male descent-group members will thus necessarily reflect this state of affairs. On the one hand, and perhaps as an extreme situation, it would seem very unlikely that wife's brother and sister's husband would have a warm, intimate, supportive relationship in matrilineal descent groups. A joking relationship similarly seems unlikely. However the relationship is specifically structured, one central element in it is the problem of maintaining the limitation over the husband's authority and its confinement to a domestic sphere and correspondingly maintaining and limiting the authority of the male members of the descent group to the descent-group sphere.

In this connection there is another problem entailed in matrilineal descent groups which is different in patrilineal descent groups. (5) *Matrilineal descent groups have special problems in the organization of in-marrying affines with respect to each other.*

In patrilineal descent groups it is possible for the woman, as in-marrying affine, to be so alienated from her own group and so assimilated to her husband's group that she can, in effect, be fully identified with her husband's position with respect to their son's wife. A woman may thus become her husband's executive and judicial arm with respect to her son's wife, and the son's wife, alienated from her own group, may be clearly subordinated to her mother-in-law. From the point of view of the son's wife, of course, her alienation from her own group is proportional to the degree to which she can be so subordinated. The stronger her tie to her own group, the weaker the control which can be exercised over her. However, because men cannot be alienated from their matrilineal descent group they present problems with respect to their organization as in-marrying affines.

Two problems are particularly evident. The first is that the daughter's husband represents a position more difficult to control than does the son's wife. Second, the father-in-law cannot be in a strong position to exert authority over daughter's husband or any other in-marrying affine.

The crucial condition for each of these problems lies in the attachment of males to their own matrilineal descent group. Where each daughter's husband retains a tie with his own unit, and where the bond of marriage is not strongly binding and he may leave it easily, the clear subordination of the daughter's husband would not seem easy, though it may be possible under certain limited conditions. Correspondingly, the father-in-law cannot be so closely assimilated to his wife's matrilineal descent group as to become his wife's executive and judicial arm with respect to their daughter's husband. The executive and judicial arm of the woman of a matrilineal descent group lies elsewhere than with her husband. Though a man may indeed have an interest in his daughter and thereby in his daughter's husband, he is not in a position to exercise a great degree of authority lest he usurp this descent-group function. The generational difference between father-in-law and son-in-law may provide a base on which their relations can be structured, but the degree of authority which one can wield over the other cannot be expected to approximate that of mother-in-law over daughter-in-law in patrilineal descent groups.

One situation in which relations among male in-marrying affines are clearly organized is that of prescribed cross-cousin marriages (matrilateral, patrilateral, or bilateral). Here relations among the in-marrying men are structured prior to marriage and continue after marriage.

(6) *Where bridewealth or bride service occurs with matrilineal descent this transfer of goods or services cannot establish such rights in children as allocate them to any group other than that of their mother.*

This is perhaps so self-evident as to require almost no comment. Matrilineal descent groups are replenished by the children cared for by its female members. Where rights over children are formally vested in the father and his descent group, the claims of the matrilineal descent group are vacated. Such transfer of goods and/or services are more likely to establish rights in the wife, particularly to labor or sexual activity.

(7) *The bonds which may develop between a child and his father tend to be in direct competition with the authority of the child's matrilineal descent group.* The bonds between mother and child in patrilineal descent groups do not necessarily constitute such a source of competition.

Father-child bonds are of two kinds: those of authority and those of positive affect. The father, when present, is likely to participate in some degree, however small, in the process of socialization. As a male, and as an adult male, he is thus—by definition of his age-sex role and quite apart from his kinship role—in a position of some authority over his children. For matrilineal descent groups, therefore, there is the problem of segregating and limiting the father's authority over his child so that it does not, and is not likely to, supersede the authority of the child's descent group. The situation with respect to husband and wife is, thus far, precisely paralleled by that between father and child. Nor are these two problems independent of one another, for the statuses of husband and father are occupied by the same person. This tension between a man and the matrilineal descent group over the control of the wife and children has been called "the matrilineal puzzle" by Audrey Richards, who went on to analyze the varieties of family form which reflect various balances of this tension in Central Africa (Richards, 1950: 207–251).[11]

The second type of bond between father and child which may develop in matrilineal descent groups is that of strong, positive affect. The relationship between potestality and bonds of positive affect is such that when, as in patrilineal descent groups, the father has authority over his children, there are likely to be compensatory affective ties through the mother to the child's mother's brother. Conversely, in matrilineal descent groups, where the father's authority is necessarily limited and weak and where authority is located in the office of matrilineal descent-group head, it is precisely with the father that compensatory affective bonds are most likely to occur (cf. Radcliffe-Brown, 1924; Homans and Schneider, 1955).

(7a) *In matrilineal descent groups the emotional interest of the father in his own children constitutes a source of strain, which is not precisely replicated in patrilineal descent groups by the emotional tie between the mother and her children.*

As was indicated in the discussion of marriage in patrilineal descent groups, emotionally intense solidarity may develop between a woman and her children and this affective bond may further reinforce her ties with her husband. Her alienation from her own unit may leave her free to develop such bonds with her children without affecting her own unit since she is not required to play a role in it. Thus the stability of her marriage may contribute to the unity and integrity of her husband's patrilineal descent group—partly by the loyalty she brings to it, partly by reinforcing the bonds between her children and their father and, through him, to their own descent group. Again, this need not necessarily be the case, but is a direction which it is possible for such relationships to take in patrilineal descent groups.

---

[11] Richards phrases this conflict as one between father and mother's brother. I suggest that the structural conflict is essentially between the father and the children's matrilineal descent group. It is certainly true that often the mother's brother is the head of the descent group and is its spokesman. It is equally true that the mother's brother is often perceived by the father as the locus of his difficulties. In fact, it is the descent-group head as such (who may or may not be the particular wife's brother) who must actively counter the father's efforts to control wife and children, but the locus of the strain is in the maintenance of the authority structure of the descent group against threats from outside it.

In patrilineal descent groups, the stronger the authority of the husband over his wife and the father over his children, the stronger the compensatory affective bond is likely to be between the mother and her children. But the strength of this bond is unlikely to become a base upon which the mother can build that kind of authority relationship which subverts the authority of the patrilineal descent group over those children. This is unlikely because the mother does not have, at the same time, an important political or authoritative role in her own patrilineal descent group, and because her authority as a woman is limited by the authority of her husband over her. That this bond may become an avenue for political alliance between two distinct patrilineal descent groups is obvious and too familiar to dwell upon here. But the analytically crucial question is whether or not this bond has significant potentialities for disrupting or subverting the authority of the patrilineal descent group over its members.

In matrilineal descent groups, on the other hand, the strong affective bond between father and child is one which can more easily become the basis for the kind of authority relationship which, as Richards' analysis shows so clearly, can easily run counter to the authority of the matrilineal descent group. That the father has some authority over both his wife and children, that he is independent of his wife's matrilineal descent group through the weakness of his marital tie, that he has a firm base in his own group, and that as a man his role tends generally to have significant political aspects, all put him in a strong position to subvert the authority of the children's group over them by inviting them to yield rights in their own group in exchange for rights in his group. This is especially so for the son, less acute for the daughter.

Economic coöperation between father and child, especially son, and the advantages of politically important rank in a father, where these occur, are two common kinds of especially serious threats to the integrity of matrilineal descent groups. Where a father and child can collaborate in economic relations and where such collaboration is in part based on a bond of strong positive affect, the alignment of the father and child against the child's descent group poses a particularly serious threat. Similarly, where the father can confer the privileges and advantages of a superior prestige position on his child, as against the position which he obtains through his own matrilineal descent-group membership, his child becomes particularly vulnerable to the temptation to exchange his rights in his natal group for such gains as can be had through his father.

There is, however, one very significant difference between the development of strong ties of positive affect between father and child and mother and child which is constant for both matrilineal and patrilineal descent groups, but which nevertheless functions differently in each. The psychobiological relationship between mother and child, by its nature, is such that strong positive affect is most likely to be developed, and since it is the first such bond in the child's life it becomes an element of more than superficial value. It is not necessary to detail the very profound psychological meaning of the mother for the child. It is only necessary to reiterate that by definition, in this theory, mothers are necessary to children as fathers are not, and to assume that the bond between the child and its mother is particularly likely to be a firm and enduring one. The bond between the child and its father, in matrilineal descent groups as in all others, tends to become established somewhat later than that of the child with its mother, and tends too to be ambivalent in affect.

It would follow, then, that children of one woman by different fathers are still more strongly tied to their mother than children by different mothers are tied to their one father.

If this is so we might expect that the children of different mothers by one father in patrilineal descent groups would on this basis alone be more likely to constitute a consistent line of cleavage than children of different fathers by one mother in matrilineal descent groups. In other words, there will be, on the basis of affective ties alone, a tendency toward fission along the lines of half-siblings in patrilineal descent groups, while that tendency should be markedly less in matrilineal descent groups.

On the basis of the different structural relevance of affective ties alone, then, (8) *the processes of fission and segmentation in matrilineal descent groups do not precisely replicate those of patrilineal descent groups.*

But affective ties are by no means the only elements involved. Men as in-marrying affines in matrilineal descent groups are bound to their own groups and tend to develop only weak marital bonds. Men constitute a source of potential strain in matrilineal descent groups because of their authority over their wives and children. Hence special limits must be imposed on the authority of men with respect to their wives and children. One important way to limit the authority of men over their wives and children, and thereby their influence on the organization and continuity of matrilineal descent groups into which they marry, is to minimize the importance of differences in paternal origin for the children by different fathers and one mother of a matrilineal descent group. Or, (8a) *differences of paternal origin are less likely to be used as criteria for creating structural divisions within a matrilineal descent group than differences of maternal origin are in the process of segmentation in patrilineal descent groups.*

Perhaps the crucial element here is the strength of the wedge which can be driven between a child (particularly a son) and his matrilineal descent group by economic coöperation and the transfer of property between father and child. This does not mean that the different fathers of children by one woman in matrilineal descent groups cannot undertake such economic coöperation or such transfer of property. It only means that this constitutes a potential threat of considerable significance which, if matrilineal descent groups are to survive as such, must be carefully countered by some mechanisms which offset or diminish that threat. Thus for instance the children of one mother may constitute a sibling group which holds property in common, and the property which the father of one sibling gives him must be pooled with the property which another father gives another sibling. For when siblings hold different property through different fathers, the first and most important division among them has taken place. This first and firmest link with their fathers constitutes the first break with their matrilineal descent group. This alone may not break up matrilineal descent groups. But it does constitute a focus of great importance for the realignment of bonds which may very well bring about the termination of the matrilineal descent group.

I have spoken here of children of different fathers by one mother and children of different mothers by one father. I have used this very general construction to cover certain situations. In either form of descent group these situations could occur as a result of polygamy or serial monogamy, that is, the children of one father by different mothers might, in patrilineal descent groups, be the children of polygynous wives, while the children of one mother by different fathers might, in matrilineal descent groups, be the children of a polyandrously married woman. Similarly, the children of one father by different wives in a patrilineal descent group might be the children of one father's successive wives, while the children of one mother by different fathers might, in a matrilineal descent group, be the children of one mother by a series of successive husbands.

There are other considerations which make the processes of fission and segmentation different in patrilineal and matrilineal descent groups.

In a patrilineal descent group any man who can acquire a wife is a potential head of a new segment. In any concrete case there may be insuperable obstacles to his founding a new segment, but in one respect he is self-sufficient: the new unit has its authoritative member (the male) and its "socially reproductive" member (the male) and a wife to care for children, the new members. In a matrilineal descent group no male can found a new segment unless he is able to pair off with one or more sisters or other matrilineal kinswomen (and their husbands), through whom social placement will occur, and no female can found a new segment without a male from her own group to fulfill the authoritative roles.

It is clearly more probable that any male can find a wife to care for his children than that he can find a sister or other female kinswoman to perpetuate a matrilineal descent group. The same situation holds in reverse: it is clearly more probable that any female can find a husband than that she can locate a brother or other matrilineal kinsman to act in the necessary authoritative roles. If we examine this proposition in the context of a single generation, then (8b) *brothers can more easily be the foci for the process of segmentation in patrilineal descent groups than can either brothers or sisters in matrilineal descent groups.*

In a patrilineal system, succession to authority may occur through unigeniture (e.g., succession by a son). The precise analogue for matrilineal systems would be from mother to selected daughter. This analogue does not apply, however, since authority is vested in male-held statuses. The nearest available analogue is that from a man to his eldest sister's eldest son, and so on. This system is possible, but unlikely in matrilineal systems. (8c) *Precise pairing of a male and a female member of a matrilineal descent group is relatively more difficult to achieve and, other things being equal, lateral succession (elder brother to younger brother, etc.) would be more likely than unigeniture in matrilineal descent groups.*

Further, (8d) *in dividing property, lateral processes would be more likely.* If property is divided among sons in a patrilineal system, it can be managed by each of those sons. If it is divided among daughters, the problem of allocating managers (brothers of those daughters) still remains. If it is divided among sons for the benefit of the daughters and their children, we still have the same problem.

Given these problems in the area of segmentation, succession, and inheritance, there would be a marked tendency to keep female siblings together in matrilineal descent groups under the leadership of one or more elder males. Succession would go from one male to another; even when it went from eldest sister's son to eldest sister's son, younger sisters and their children would be expected to remain with the group. Hence, (8e) *two or three generations of matrilineal kinsmen are more likely to stay together than to split up.* Where splitting occurred, it would likely be with reference to relatively remote matrilineal kinswomen. This bears on the possibilities of ranking lineage segments. Such ranking depends on perceptible splitting and, although it is not precluded in matrilineal descent groups, large descent groups with internally ranked segments can occur more easily in patrilineal than matrilineal descent groups.

Finally, the difficulties in separating collateral lines as social groups should be reflected in kinship terminology. (8f) *Matrilineal descent groups would be more likely to merge lineal and collateral relatives terminologically than would patrilineal descent groups.*[12]

(9) *Isolated communities (or smaller groups) consisting of matrilineal core and in-marrying spouses are extremely difficult to maintain.* The monolineage community implies the special segregation of the descent-group members of one sex from the other. Patrilineal descent groups, which can sever or radically reduce its bonds with its female members, face no difficulty here. The women are not needed to reproduce for the group nor are they required for the exercise of authority; the group can survive quite well without them. Where a woman's bonds to her own group are so minimized, spatial separation does not matter. For matrilineal descent groups, on the other hand, the greater the spatial separation, the less the degree to which either sex can fulfill its obligations to its group. Where communities are spatially distinct yet near each other, these difficulties are minimized, so that distinct matrilineal monolineage communities might only be expected under such circumstances (cf. Murdock, 1949).

In conclusion, I would raise a problem concerning one of the definitions used at the outset, namely, that authority over the joint activity of the descent group is held by male descent-group members. If authority is not specified as allocated to male members, a wider number of possible arrangements is conceivable than can be dealt with here. For this reason I have felt it necessary to retain the definition in this form. But one possibility is also thereby excluded which merits some attention and that is the possibility that male descent-group members

---

[12] This proposition must be checked after eliminating non-sororal polygynous groups from account. Non-sororal polygyny, which is associated with patriliny, is also associated with collateralizing terminology; hence a spurious relationship might be found.

have no authority within their own descent group, but that that authority is held by in-marrying male affines. That is, that husbands have authority over or manage the joint activity of the descent group of their wives. What, then, would happen to such a descent group?

The crucial question is that of descent-group maintenance; that is, the problem is one of balancing those conditions which would tend to disrupt the group as a group against those conditions which would favor maintaining the group as a group. In-marrying male affines, unrelated to each other and alienated from their own group (since they exchange authority over their wives for authority over the women of their own descent group), would gain authority over their wives, but the problem would arise of their relations with each other and of their relations to the other women of the descent group into which they marry. Each man, having authority over his own wife, would be in a position to disrupt the bonds between women and require his wife to focus her primary loyalties on him. The jointly held activity of the descent group would thus become fragmented into domestic pieces, bits shared by each woman and managed by her husband independently. The descent group would thus be disrupted primarily as a consequence of the lack of some form of organization among male in-marrying affines, comparable to that which obtained among male descent-group members. In any concrete situation the particular form which descent-group joint activities took would, of course, be an important consideration in determining the specific outcome. If the descent group held land in common the matter might be rather different than if it held rights in some ceremonial activity. But the pressure of the husband to gain control over his wife and children would not be balanced by the capacity of the women to hold their group together, since husbands have authority over their own wives and children. Such a situation would therefore tend toward the disruption of the matrilineal descent group.

But what of the situation where the in-marrying male affines are already organized prior to marriage, as would be true with matrilateral cross-cousin marriage. Would the same tendency for each husband to single out his own wife and gain complete control over her prevail, or could there be, in such circumstances, a coalition of in-marrying managers acting on behalf of the descent group or their wives?

The problem in this case would center on the problem of the control over children, particularly male successors. If the husbands control the descent-group activity of their wives, and if the husbands must bring in sisters' sons as successors, then the husbands must retain such bonds with the women of their matrilineal descent group as will enable them to hold their sisters' sons to their obligations as successors. This in turn means that the husbands as husbands must relinquish enough control over their own sons to permit the sons to become the successors of their mother's brothers. This would mean that the joint activity of the descent group is the management of the joint activity of another descent group. But this simply maintains matrilineal descent groups centered on joint activities requiring decision making, and entails all the distinctive features of matrilineal descent groups thus far considered; that is, it maintains the descent group's control over its recruitment, over its male and female members, and maintains this control as against the in-marrying male affines.

Where unorganized in-marrying male affines gain authority over their wives and children, then, it is unlikely that matrilineal descent groups as defined here can persist. Where matrilineally organized in-marrying male affines undertake to manage the joint activities of their wives' descent group, this merely becomes the joint activity of the matrilineal descent group of the in-marrying male affines and all the conditions distinctive to matrilineal descent groups continue to prevail.

The necessity for defining authority over the joint activity of the descent group as allocated to male members therefore arises only because failure to specify who holds this authority leaves more possibilities open than can be fully considered in this treatment, not because it is conceivable that male members can exchange authority in their own descent group for authority in the descent group into which they marry.

PART ONE

Nine Matrilineal
Kinship Systems

Introduction to Part One

We have tried in Part One to offer the reader analytic accounts of as wide a variety as possible of matrilineal societies, within the limits placed upon the writers by time, available literature, and their own knowledge.

First, the "example" societies are drawn from geographically remote regions—North America, Africa, Oceania, and India. This fact has historical and thus methodological implications. Granting obvious connections between the four Kerala groups, granting possible linkages between Truk and Trobriand, and even granting possible links between Ashanti and Tonga, the six societies nonetheless include end products of at least four historically independent developments of matrilineal descent. This being so, we may reasonably conclude that any common features occurring in all of them do not stem from common historical origins but from the essential nature of matrilineal descent.

Second, the examples embrace extremes with regard to type of natural environment, degree of technological complexity, and extent of political centralization; or rather, they embrace such extremes as seem likely to occur within the total world spectrum of matrilineal societies. The Navaho's semidesert country contrasts sharply with the tropical rain forests of Ashanti and Kerala, the Tongan savanna, the volcanic Trobriand Islands, and the coral-fringed islands of Truk. Traditional Trukese or Trobriand stone and shell tools are a far cry from the plough agriculture and irrigation works of Kerala. The total absence of hereditary, ranked political offices among Tonga and Navaho contrasts with the feudalistic kingdoms and politically administered trade of Ashanti and Kerala.

Such obvious cultural and social structural differences between the example societies render the more striking those common social structural features which issue from the central fact of matrilineal descent. What are these common features?

Notice first that in spite of the great variety of residential rules and of specific rights and obligations, the matrilineal descent group, in all these societies, tends to maintain a relatively high—and even—control

33

of both its male and its female members. This contrasts with the great majority of patrilineal descent groups, which in large measure surrender their female members to the control of the latter's husbands' groups. Connected with this general feature of matrilineal descent groups is the pivotal, strongly binding, yet highly ambivalent character of the brother-sister relationship. Always it combines recognition of the brother's interest in his sister's procreativity with the strict prohibition of sexual interest in her. Next, in the relations between proximal generations of the descent group, the mother's brother's role, more or less authoritative, is conspicuous. Correlatively, one finds in all these matrilineal societies a conscious counterpoising of the role of the woman's husband to that of her brother, and of the role of father to that of mother's brother. The exact content and relative weighting of these relationships varies greatly—as, for example, between Navaho and Central Kerala Nayar. But in all cases what is noticeable is that the rights and obligations of the husband and father are carefully limited and precisely defined—in contrast to the more "omnibus" character of these roles in patrilineal societies. There is, further, in all cases a marked and customarily recognized tension and opposition of interests in general between conjugal and paternal relationships, on the one hand, and those of each individual to his or her matrilineal descent group, on the other.

These common features of matrilineal systems are posited by Schneider in his general theoretical essay. Further, Schneider is able to show the logical connections between these features and the way in which they issue from three fundamental circumstances: namely, the existence of organized matrilineal descent groups, the exogamy of these groups, and the sexual division of functions involving female care of children and male assumption of authoritative roles. The ethnographic accounts in Part One thus provide strong empirical support for some of Schneider's logical deductions concerning the necessary correlates of matrilineal descent.

In addition, Schneider's theoretical statement contains certain negative hypotheses concerning institutions which are unlikely to occur with matrilineal descent. These hypotheses include, first, the unlikelihood of a clearly defined organization and authority structure among the spouses of members of a matrilineal descent group, even though the spouses might in some cases be recognized as a category having similar interests. A second negative characteristic concerns the difficulty of maintaining a strict rule of unigeniture in matrilineal societies. A third negative hypothesis is that the husbands of ancestresses of a matrilineal descent group (in contrast to the wives of ancestors in patriliny) are unlikely to be made the focal points of segmentation within the descent group.

The ethnographic accounts in Part One lend tentative support to these negative hypotheses, in that none of these features occurs with regularity in the societies which were examined. Satisfactory validation of these hypotheses would, of course, require examination of a much larger proportion of the world's matrilineal systems.

Plateau Tonga

The Plateau Tonga [1] are a matrilineal people who contrast in almost every conceivable way with the Ashanti or the Nayars described later. In pre-European days among the Tonga, political organization as we know it, with an orderly relationship between groups or statuses intermediated through a set of official positions, did not exist. Economic organization was of the simplest, with only an embryonic development of specialized occupations over and above the primary division of labor between the sexes. Unused land was a free good, and the ownership of cultivated land was unimportant. Tonga religion had neither a priesthood nor any hereditary religious officials to give a focus to the general alignment of people in groups. Shrines and their attendant cults were independent of one another.

In the absence of definite crystallized social groupings, the Tonga probably rival the Navaho as the simplest of the societies which have been chosen to illuminate the problems of matrilineal organization. Yet, despite this, once one abandons any attempt to force a more orderly arrangement upon a people who apparently had no affinity for it, it is possible to find a comprehensible organized set of relationships permeating Tonga life which can be defined as social structure. Matrilineal affiliation is only one of the organizing principles of Tonga social structure, but it dominates the structure and it is the only one which operates through time to maintain the adherence of the Tonga to distinctive groupings within the society.

[1] Much of the substance of this account has been incorporated into my book, *Marriage and the Family among the Plateau Tonga.* The material was collected during the years 1946–1947 and 1948–1950, when I served as research officer and director of the Rhodes-Livingstone Institute. The field research was financed by the Colonial Development and Welfare Grant. The original manuscript prepared for the Social Science Research Council Seminar for the Study of Matrilineal Kinship has been slightly revised for inclusion here. Most of the revisions have been for the purpose of shortening the manuscript, though at a few points I have sought to clarify the presentation.

Population and History

The Plateau Tonga inhabit the Mazabuka District of the southern province of Northern Rhodesia. Their territory runs about 60 miles from east to west, and 70 miles from north to south, though attempting to draw a firm line between them and their neighbors is impossible. They are surrounded in all directions save one by peoples who speak variants of the same language. To this language Doke has given the name "Tonga." He classifies it in his Central Bantu Zone (Doke, 1945: 31). A number of the other groups which speak "Tonga" also bear this name. Very possibly "Tonga" was originally a foreign word. I doubt that originally the Mazabuka or Plateau Tonga had any common name for themselves or saw themselves as a unit set off from their neighbors.

In 1950 there was still no adequate census of the African population of Northern Rhodesia. Estimates placed the total Tonga population of Mazabuka District as between 85,000 and 120,000. The population is certainly increasing; the fertility ratio, computed from my census of 22 villages located in four different neighorhoods, is roughly 805. Mortality is high, but there is reason to think that it is not great enough to offset the high birth rate. Population densities are again sheer estimates, but they are not impressive in comparison with densities found in many other areas of the world: in 1946 it was estimated that the Tonga reserves supported a density of 58.2 persons per square mile (Allan et al., 1948: chap. II; and Colson, 1951a: 99–100). It should be remembered, however, that this is a purely agricultural region with no towns and no industries.

The Tonga have no recorded history prior to 1853, when Livingstone first encountered them on his trek from the upper Zambezi eastward to the Indian Ocean. Nor do they have any traditional history of their own which would allow us some time perspective on the development of their society. The most that can be said about their antecedents is that probably Tonga-speaking people have been settled in this area for some centuries. Possibly prior to the nineteenth century they had some more developed form of economic and political organization which disappeared in the turmoil of the nineteenth century, but there is no clue to this either in the accounts of early travelers or in their own present organization. For at least some seventy years, from about 1820 to 1893, their area formed a buffer zone and common raiding ground for two expanding states, the Kololo-Lozi and the Ndebele. The Tonga made no organized resistance to these raids, although they lost their cattle and many of their people vanished into slavery or died of hunger in the famines which followed the destruction of their granaries (Colson, 1950). Commonly they took refuge in flight. Raiding ended in 1893 with the defeat of the Ndebele nation by the settlers of Southern Rhodesia; the Lozi had already ceased their raids—though not their claims to dominate the Tonga, from whom they periodically collected tribute. When the Lozi made their treaty with the British South Africa Company in 1890, they ceded these chimerical rights to the Tonga country to the company, and much later the company in turn ceded these to the British Crown when Northern Rhodesia passed directly under the British Colonial Office in 1923.

In 1899 the company established a police post in the Tonga area, and in 1903 civil administration was begun from a district headquarters built within the region. The administrator and his police force assumed the political function of maintaining law and order. Self-help and vengeance were banned; slavery was abolished. At approximately the same time a direct tax was levied on every able-bodied man, and from that date it has been essential for the Tonga to have some source of cash income.

In 1906 the Rhodesian railway was extended through Tonga country. In its wake came a number of mission stations and the first European settlers. Because the soil was fertile, the area free of tsetse fly, and the climate tempered by the high altitude and relatively healthy, the region was attractive to European settlement. About 1913 a block of land adjacent to the railway was set aside for European occupation. Those Tonga who lived within the scheduled area were ordered to move and had to find land for themselves within what were to become the Tonga reserves. Meantime the Tonga were drawn to work as labor migrants in the developing economy of Southern Rhodesia. There they could earn money for tax and for such luxuries as cloth, iron, and other goods available in the trading stores. Some stayed for only short periods and then returned home; others remained and were lost to their kinsmen in the reserves. Their absence was offset to some extent by the return of former captives now freed from servitude among the Lozi and Ndebele, many of whom wandered back to the region with only vague memories to guide them in their search for the villages and kinsmen from whom they had been stolen many years before.

Tonga residence patterns are extremely fluid, but in attempting to understand them it must be remembered that factors external to their society have been operating for many years to favor mobility. In addition to the dispersion brought about by the raids, there followed the displacement of blocks of population because of the creation of the European zone. The early labor migration and the return of former slaves have also played a part, albeit a minor one, in shifting people about. More recently two new influences have been at work. With the development of the Northern Rhodesian Copper Belt in the 1920's, the Tonga began to abandon labor migration and to turn to the production of cash crops for the market provided by the concentration of labor at the mines. There was a tendency for men to move as close as possible to the borders of the European belt as this also brought them nearer to the buying stations on the railway line where they could dispose of their crops. Beginning with the late 1930's, the Northern Rhodesian government began the building of dams and the digging of wells to open up areas where lack of surface water had hitherto discouraged settlement. Population pressure has increased to the point where it is necessary to hunt for new fields, and many people have moved from the overcrowded regions to the new areas in the west.

There have thus been good reasons for the Tonga to move from one area to another; and since 1903 the administration—by guaranteeing the safety of individual life and property—has also made it unnecessary for the Tonga to protect themselves by remaining in close contact with bodies of kinsmen who could come to their defense. Later on, I shall emphasize mobility as being inherent in the Tonga social system, but I am aware that the system may be an adaptation to what in many cases has been forced mobility (cf. Colson, 1951c).

New political institutions have also been developed during the last fifty years. From the beginning the administration has had to rely upon the building up of some sort of local authority to maintain order and provide for the peaceful settlement of disputes. In the early days such leaders as could be located were given an informal recognition which tended to institutionalize their status. Later, under the Native Authorities Act of 1927, the government instituted a hierarchy of authority. The district was divided into a number of chieftaincies, each under a man who received the official title of chief. To each chief was attached a Native Authority Court, with jurisdiction to hear civil disputes arising under native custom and with a limited jurisdiction to try minor criminal offenses. The assemblage of chiefs with their counselors then formed the Native Authority of the Plateau Tonga, with the right to pass ordinances and rules binding upon all the Tonga of the area. Tax funds are used to provide the authority with a limited budget, from which salaries are paid to the chiefs, court assessors, and the messengers attached to each chief. Boundaries between chieftaincies are delimited, and the authority of the chief is upheld by that of the administration. Since the end of World War II, under general colonial policy, stress has been laid on the development of what is now known as local self-government. The central government thus impinges more and more on the life in the reserves and is creating a local bureaucracy as an agent of its purposes (cf. Colson, 1948b).

It is necessary to mention these external forces and the new developments resulting from them, but henceforth I shall largely ignore them and attempt to built up a model of the Tonga social system, in relation to kinship, without much regard for the external forces which have been operating upon it. There is one exception to this statement. The development of a cash-crop economy has profoundly affected the Tonga family and the whole area of kinship relationships. Its influence will be related to some of the present stresses in the kinship organization.

Kinship and Local Groups

THE CLAN

The most enduring units in Tonga society are the clans. These are named, dispersed, exogamous units in which membership is derived through matrilineal descent. Representatives of all the clans are found dispersed throughout the Tonga area and the same clans appear everywhere with the exception of the northwestern portion of the country, where the clan system resembles that of the Ila and Sala. Clans are not corporate bodies. They own no property, have no ritual centers or leaders, and never on any occasion assemble as a group. At first glance they appear to be functionless, though fellow clansmen recognize claims to one another's hospitality. Each clan is linked or paired with several others in a relationship of which joking is only one aspect of a wider range of duties and rights. The clan joking partnership has an important role to play in the field of social control, and here probably lies the answer to the problem of why clans continue to exist despite the absence of organized activities in relation to their members. It is only with reference to the clan joking partnerships that any body of Tonga folklore exists to explain the origin of a particular institution or set of relationships (cf. Colson, 1953b).

THE MATRILINEAL GROUP

The corporate unilineal groups are much smaller bodies of kinsmen which I term "matrilineal groups." The Tonga word for such a group is *mukowa,* but this is also used for clan and has the general meaning of species, kind, sort, type. Matrilineal groups are dispersed, though not to the same degree as clans. They are unnamed. Theoretically membership rests on actual descent, through females, but exact genealogical ties are usually irrelevant either for ensuring membership or for assignment of position within the group. In Tonga ideology matrilineal groups have no internal differentiation based on descent, i.e., the descendants of one woman are not set off as a unit from the descendants of her sisters. A matrilineal group is a corporate body since it has a common legal personality vis-à-vis all other similarly organized bodies. Inheritance, succession, provision and sharing of bridewealth, vengeance, and a common ritual responsibility are functions of the group. A group does not hold a common estate in land or in movable property. The members of a group hold a joint right to inherit one another's estates, but on a death the estate is divided among the heirs. During his own lifetime a man has full control over his own property, whether this has been acquired by inheritance, from bridewealth, or by his own efforts. Matrilineal groups range in size from those composed of only a few adults to some which have around a hundred adult members. They may have a recognized head, but this is a matter of personal domination rather than of institutionalized authority (Colson, 1951*b*: 12–17; Colson, 1951*c*).

Matrilineal groups of the same clan are not linked together in any fashion save by their common clan membership. The Tonga have no vestige of a segmentary lineage system nor have they evolved any system of perpetual kinship between either kinship or local units to give a rigid structure to their society.

Links between matrilineal groups cut across clan boundaries and are tied to the life span of particular individuals. Every person is "an honorary member" of his father's matrilineal group. In all matters which concern him, his matrilineal kinsmen (*basimukowa*) are brought into contact with his father's matrilineal kinsmen (his *basyanausi*). The two groups continue their coöperation throughout his life, but on his death the tie which joins them vanishes. Each matrilineal group is thus associated with a large number of similar groups of other clans as it coöperates with the groups of the fathers of its members and with the groups of the children of its male members. But these ties change with each death and with each marriage and do not form permanent linkages between groups (Colson, 1951*a*: 143–151).

Clans, matrilineal groups, and the secondary linkages between matrilineal groups produced by the tie with the people of the father are based on kinship, or at least on descent. Of equal importance in Tonga society are groups based on residence, where descent is largely irrelevant.

RESIDENCE

Residence is usually virilocal but it is not otherwise determined by any rule which associates the husband residentially with a given body of kin. Every fully adult man—and every fully adult unmarried woman—may live where he chooses. A man usually prefers to live near those to whom he or his wife can trace some relationship, but in some cases he uses merely the ties of clanship, or, indeed, he may settle among strangers. Any village or neighborhood is therefore composed of people related to each other by a diverse assortment of kinship ties, with a sprinkling of strangers who have yet to develop any ties, even affinal, with the local people. For sixteen villages of my census, I analyzed the kinship links determining the village residence of adult males. Thirty-four and one-half per cent were living with matrilineal kin; 39.5 per cent, with patrilineal kin; 9.2 per cent, with the wife's kin; 8.1 per cent, with the husband of some female relative; 8.5 per cent had no kinship ties with others in the village at the time of settling there (Colson, 1951c: 48–51). If one took adult women as the point of departure for analyzing residence patterns, the number whose only tie to the village was traced through a spouse would be significantly increased.

Most people do not remain permanently attached to a single village throughout their lives. In the same sixteen villages only 36 per cent of the adult men and 20 per cent of the adult women were living in the villages of their birth (Colson, 1951c: 42). This mobility is not a product of a system of avunculocal residence; for although there is a tendency for men to move to join matrilineal kinsmen in later life, these moves are not necessarily to a mother's brother, and the tendency is not very great. The Tonga ideal is free choice of residence, which they say is characteristic of the free man in contrast to the slave, who had to live where his owner wished.

NEIGHBORHOODS

The largest local group which can be considered a unit with some enduring focus is the neighborhood, which today may consist of from four to eight villages and usually therefore has a population of around 400 to 600 individuals (Colson, 1951a: 151–161). This area is today commonly referred to as a *katongo*. In the past apparently the word *cisi*, today reserved for chieftaincy, was equally applied to the neighborhood.

Headmen of the villages in a neighborhood may or may not be able to trace kinship ties to one another. Or rather, though they can usually trace some relationship if the villages have been in the same neighborhood for any length of time, the relations frequently are through a network of affinal ties.

Figure 1-1 shows the spatial layout of villages in two neighborhoods and the kinship links between the headmen.

In the ordinary round of daily life, membership within a neighborhood may be of more significance than membership within a matrilineal group. All land which is not immediately under crops or occupied by dwelling places, and which has no claim against it on the grounds of such former use, is common to the neighborhood and may be taken at will by any individual living there. The fields of those living in different villages may be scattered among each other; the cattle intermingle at the common pastures. Wild produce, firewood, potting clay, basketry materials, and the like may be collected without let or hindrance by all members of the neighborhood. Strangers might also collect them but have little incentive to do so since they would then have the labor of transporting their spoils to their homes. Hunting and fishing are neighborhood matters, rather than the concern of a single village or a single homestead. Work patterns also emphasize neighborhood obligations: in clearing fields, weeding, harvesting, building a hut—whenever large numbers are required for a sudden spurt of activity—neighbors are summoned. Kinsmen resident in the same neighborhood are also expected to help, but by virtue of their local affiliation.

All residents of a neighborhood have an obligation to attend the funeral of any one who dies within the neighborhood. Kinsmen, wherever they may live, must also come, for they too are concerned in the death. But the importance of a person as a member of a neighborhood finds its expression in the common obligation to mourn for one another. Moreover, each person is expected to die in his own neighborhood, which is the area where he has his hut and where he cultivates. If he dies elsewhere this is an offense against that land, which he pollutes by his death; his kinsmen must pay with an animal from their herds, which is ritually slain and eaten by all members of the offended neighborhood. This sends the dead man's spirit back to the neighborhood in which he lived, where alone he has the right to die. The neighborhood may also be polluted by the spilling of blood upon its soil. Those responsible for a homicide will have to pay damages to the neighborhood, which then proceeds with the purification of its soil. In either case, general neighborhood misfortune or personal misfortune

NEIGHBORHOOD I

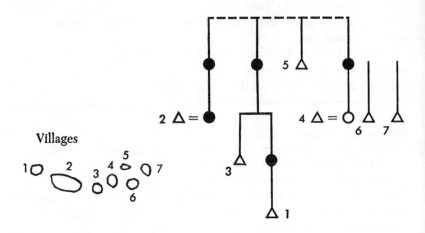

Villages

NEIGHBORHOOD II

Villages

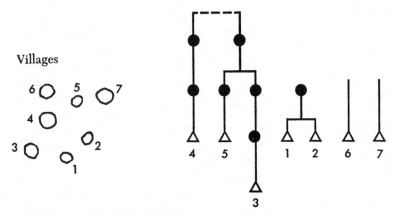

Broken lines indicate genealogical relationship unknown.
Continuous lines indicate known genealogical relationship.
Shaded symbols indicate person shown is dead.
Unshaded symbols indicate person shown is living.

Fig. 1-1. Kinship links between village headmen.

to any resident of the neighborhood may be attributed to failure to carry out the purification.

All members of a neighborhood are subject to the ritual authority of the local rain shrines and must take part in the general harvest festival in which thanks are given for a good crop. As soon as a person moves into a neighborhood he falls under the authority of the local cult and no longer observes that of the neighborhood from which he comes. For the cult is concerned with matters in which members of a neighborhood fare alike, and in which their fortunes may be very different from the fortunes of persons resident in other localities. All members of a neighborhood may be subject to localized disasters such as drought, plague, or epidemic. Through the local shrines and the attendant ritual, the group seeks to obtain rain and a bountiful harvest and to avert disaster in the form of epidemics and drought.

Neighborhoods may have a recognized leader, whose counsel and advice is sought by those within the neighborhood, and who from time to time may even organize the neighborhood for some particular activity. Such a leader may be called *sikatongo* ("owner of the neighborhood") or *ulanyika* ("owner of the land"). These, of course, are simply convenient translations. "Owner" here has no connotation of actual ownership. The leader has no right to allocate land, nor indeed can he exclude strangers from the area. He may derive his position and title from the fact that he, or his predecessor, was the first to settle in the area. His authority is dependent largely upon his personal qualities. It does not become institutionalized so that it can pass on to his successor, who will be a member of his matrilineal group. If the successor is not a strong man, he is disregarded. Usually the position of sikatongo is linked to the custodianship of the local shrines. Shrines, however, are not necessarily permanent cult centers, and as the influence of those who have instituted them wanes they are likely to be replaced by new shrines instituted by new leaders, frequently from another matrilineal group, who in turn have their brief moment of authority (cf. Colson, 1948a).

At any one moment a person is primarily associated with a particular neighborhood, but he is free to move from one to another. As soon as he has built his hut and cultivated a field in the new neighborhood, he becomes as truly a member of it as one who has lived there for many years.

INTER-NEIGHBORHOOD TIES

In many of their activities men are drawn outside their neighborhoods to come in contact with those resident in other localities.

During the dry season, the failure of surface water in many areas once made it essential that cattle be moved to dry-season camps in localities with permanent water. Such movements involved a radical rearrangement of cattle and herdsmen but did not affect the majority of the residents of a neighborhood. Most people remained behind in the permanent villages, and only herdsmen accompanied the cattle to the camps. All cattle from a neighborhood did not go to a camp or camps in a single locality. Each cattle owner might establish his own camp, wherever he would, without regard to the plans of the other men of his neighborhood or of his kinsmen. Cattle might have to be driven through a number of intervening neighborhoods before they reached the site of the camp. In the area about the camps, herdsmen found themselves associated with herders from various neighborhoods as well as in close contact with permanent residents of the locality.

It was a potentially explosive situation, but I could learn nothing about what happened when quarrels broke out between herders from different camps or between herders and local residents. In the western areas the dry-season camps still persist, but though the Tonga—and the western Tonga especially—enjoy a good fight, violent quarrels seem to be in abeyance for the period that the camps are occupied. The owner may safeguard his individual camp through an arrangement with a near-by resident of the area where the camp is situated. This man takes upon himself the obligation of warning others that the site has a prior claim upon it. He may also give some protection to the cattle and their herders while they are at the camp. But for safety on the route to and from the camp, the owner once had to trust to the general pacific intentions of those whom he encountered.

Other occasions also call for people to leave their own neighborhoods to visit other localities. Kinship obligations include the duty of visiting kinsmen who are ill or subject to some misfortune, and of attending funerals and other ritual occasions, such as the puberty ceremonies of girls. Kinsmen are usually scattered over a number of different neighborhoods, and in fulfilling his obligations to them a man must range fairly far from home.

In addition to these individual movements, there are occasions when a number of neighborhoods coöperate in some activity, though these times are fewer today than in the past. In former days, when hunting was more important than it is today—when the game has been killed over much of the area and fields and villages occupy former hunting grounds—yearly game drives assembled the men of four or five or more neighborhoods. The neighborhood claiming the right to the hunting ground summoned the others, and each neighborhood was assigned a section of the line of hunt. When a dispute arose over an animal claimed by men from different neighborhoods, the resulting fight mobilized neighborhood against neighborhood. If a man were killed or injured in the brawl it was left to his kinsmen to demand compensation and the claim lay against the one who had inflicted the injury, and his kinsmen, rather than against the neighborhood. When the floods subsided at the end of the rainy season, those living adjacent to the fishing grounds summoned other neighborhoods to take part in fish drives in the rivers and pans of their area. Here again there was direct coöperation for a common purpose involving men from different neighborhoods.

In their individual movements from one neighborhood to another, people were safeguarded to some extent by their personal ties of kinship, or by certain other ties which will be treated later. But since each neighborhood could not live completely unto itself, especially in those areas where the needs of the herds brought about annual shifts, there must have been some measure of acknowledgement of a field of wider local interests than the neighborhood itself. Equally, on occasion, their common suffering underlined their common dependence on natural forces and, therefore, their common interest in maintaining the correct ritual relationships which were thought to influence these forces. Strictly localized droughts afflicted small areas every year, but every few years a general drought reduced wide areas to famine conditions. Widespread epidemics affecting both cattle and people also occurred from time to time in the past.

Occasionally some man or woman who played upon the wider territorial interests or the feeling of common interdependence before a general misfortune was able to swing a number of neighborhoods into allegiance to a common shrine, or induce them to acknowledge in some slight fashion his personal authority. Such a figure was Monze, referred to by early travelers in Tonga country as a chief of a large area. His general authority was certainly nebulous, and neither he nor any of the other similar claimants for recognition ever built up any group of officials for the maintenance of control. These larger territorial units, without any firm underpinning of constant daily interaction to sustain them or any body of officials who have an interest in the maintenance of a common unity, quickly disappear again. These wider units leave as evidence that they once existed only the unsubstantiated boasts about the general importance of some shrine or statements about the respect once shown to some half-remembered leader.

Neighborhoods therefore are not part of a larger territorial organization, and with this there is an absence of terms to denote those who might have authority over a wide area. The term *mwami*, which today is commonly translated as "chief," seems to have meant simply "important person," "rich person." It did not refer to an official position.

VILLAGE AND HAMLET

Within the neighborhood there is a further subdivision into two smaller units, though the original nature of one of these is a matter for speculation. The larger, and the more speculative, is the village or *munzi*. Today the village has a very real existence because the administration has used it for the last fifty years as the basis for its administrative system. Even so, it is still necessary to define a village as that unit which is under a headman recognized by government (Allan *et al.*, 1948: 34–53; Colson, 1951*a*: 110–121). Some villages are compact units, set apart from other villages. Others consist of a number of small hamlets which are spatially separated, but still have some territorial separation from the hamlets incorporated in other villages. In other instances the huts or homesteads of a number of villages are so intermingled that it is possible to delimit each village only by asking to which village each hut is attached. The administration has attempted to limit the minimum size of villages by the rule that each village must contain at least ten taxpayers, i.e., ten adult able-bodied men. It has also sought to limit the physical dispersal of the village huts by a rule that villagers must live within a certain distance from their headman. It has also insisted that every man be registered within a recognized village. All three rules are now being dropped, and only the last has been fully enforced over the years.

The village is known by the official name of its headman, which is inscribed in the village registers at the district office. The successor of the headman, who is chosen by the villagers with a veto power resting in the hands of the administration, assumes the same name. Usually the successor belongs to the same matrilineal group as the previous headman, but the villagers may choose someone from another group if they wish. The village is fixed neither in membership, for its members may move to be replaced by newcomers, nor geographically, for the village may move in space about a neighborhood or from neighborhood to neighborhood. But so long as the village name remains on the books, it remains an official unit despite changes in location and composition.

Some villages are fairly strong units with forceful headmen who make their wishes felt. Others are purely administrative devices. The general lack of cohesion in the village is shown by the fact that it has no common property in land or in other goods, no common set of activities differentiating it from neighborhood or hamlet save those allocated to it by the administration, and no general ritual which unites its members.

There is a strong probability that the local units smaller than the neighborhoods were formerly the hamlets. Livingstone and other early travelers commented on the small size of Tonga villages. Livingstone was told that formerly the Tonga had lived in large villages but that they had scattered out into hamlets and homesteads as a defensive device in the face of the raids of the early nineteenth century. In the northwest, where ecological conditions limit the number of sites available for year-round residence, villages may always have been fairly large and compact. Elsewhere the hamlet has been the important residence group for at least the last century. In terminology, the Tonga do not distinguish between village and hamlet even today. The same word, munzi, is applied to both. Today it is possible to distinguish verbally between a village headman and a hamlet head, for the first is commonly known as sibuku, "he of the book" or "owner of the book," referring to the fact that his name appears in the district register of villages. The old term simunzi, "he of the village," applies equally to both.

Hamlets vary in size from single homesteads up to groupings which may provide housing for nine adult males with their families. If they grow larger and can thus meet the administration rule governing the size of villages, they usually hive off from the parent village under a headman of their own choosing and then become recognized as an independent village. This, however, simply gives official recognition to the de facto independence of the hamlet. In former days, when there was no higher political authority which had the power to grant or refuse recognition of independence, village and hamlet were probably one and the same thing.

A hamlet usually has its head, who speaks for the members and is concerned in all their affairs. The hamlet is usually known by his name, which may even survive his death if his successor comes to live within it and obtains the adherence of the other residents. Formerly each hamlet may have had its own cattle kraal under the authority of the hamlet head. The head also had some ritual authority over his people: when the new grain ripened, his people ate of the new crop only after they had gathered to be treated by him with medicine; at this time they also shared a common meal made from the new grain. Before planting, the hamlet head and his chief wife had ritual intercourse to give fertility to the seed, and the treated seed was distributed to the others in the hamlet to be mixed with their own seed for planting. After the harvest each household made beer for the harvest festival, held at the homestead of the hamlet head. Finally, the hamlet head contributed a pot of beer on behalf of his hamlet to the neighborhood festival held in conjunction with the rain ceremony.

The hamlet is thus a more integrated unit than the village, but it is also more easily broken at the present time. Since it is not officially recognized by the administration, no formalities are involved in a shift from one hamlet to another within a village or in breaking out to form a new hamlet. Hamlets are easily disrupted, especially where they are composed of an alliance between two or more adult men each with his own group of followers. Old members move out, new ones move in, splits may occur in which a large proportion of the hamlet follows a malcontent to form a new unit or to join with some other established hamlet. Again, there is no hamlet ownership of land to tie its members to the hamlet or to one another. A man may continue to cultivate his old fields even though he has withdrawn from the hamlet, and new-comers can take up land within the neighborhood without an appeal to hamlet heads.

Usually those resident within a hamlet have some fairly close tie of kinship between them, but these ties are of very different types, subject to many kinds of disruptive pressures. In the last analysis, probably the hamlet exists simply because men must live somewhere and it is usually pleasant to have at least a few close neighbors to help in the daily round. So long as they remain together, they must live in some kind of harmony. If this becomes impossible, they move apart and either find new associates or for the moment try the blessings of a more solitary existence.

Today the headman of a village usually has his own hamlet, unless the village is a compact unit, and within it his position is very much that of any hamlet head. His position is not clearly differentiated from that of the other hamlet heads. Recognition by the administration tips the balance in his favor, and if he is a strong man he can use this to subordinate the others to him. If he is not, they follow their own inclinations with little regard for his position over them. If they quarrel, they may still remain associated as a village since this is a formal measure to please the administration and neither needs to impinge upon the activities of the other.

Figure 1-2 shows the kinship links between adult people living together in the various hamlets of one village and also the links between the hamlet heads. To simplify the presentation, I have chosen the village in my census which has the greatest number of intra-village kinship links.

HOMESTEADS

The smallest residential group is the homestead, occupied by an immediate family and its adherents. It consists of a hut or a series of huts, depending on a number of circumstances: whether the head is monogamous or polygynous; whether or not the boys are of an age to have their separate hut or huts; whether or not there are unmarried adult men or women attached to the family because they are for the moment without a spouse and therefore incapable of establishing a separate household of their own; whether or not a young couple is attached to it for the first years of marriage before being given permission to have an independent household. A homestead may be the equivalent of a hamlet, or a hamlet may be composed of a number of homesteads set in close proximity to one another. My impression is that the small isolated homestead is becoming an increasingly common feature of the Tonga landscape as many of the pressures which held people together are relaxed. But the hamlet as an alliance of a number of homesteads probably has a long life ahead of it, for only a large homestead can maintain itself over any long period of time without outside assistance.

The homestead is the basic subsistence unit. Its members share the work of the fields, the care of cattle and other livestock, and the domestic work. The homestead is also a ritual unit under the charge of the married man who heads it, and the ancestral spirits (*mizimu*) which are concerned with him are thought to extend their interest over those under his protection (Colson, 1954: 55–62).

Relationships Based on Other Than Kinship and Residence

The groupings already described are those of primary importance in Tonga life. They fall into two categories. One is phrased in terms of kinship: clan, matrilineal group, and the cross-linkages between matrilineal groups. The other has a territorial basis: neighborhood, village, hamlet, and homestead. Each person is involved in the whole gamut of groups belonging in each category. But in one, his allegiance is settled at birth. In the other, since residence is voluntary, he has a choice with respect to the units with which he will associate himself.

Of less importance are a number of other relationships. One is a matter of ascription since it is based on age. The other two involve

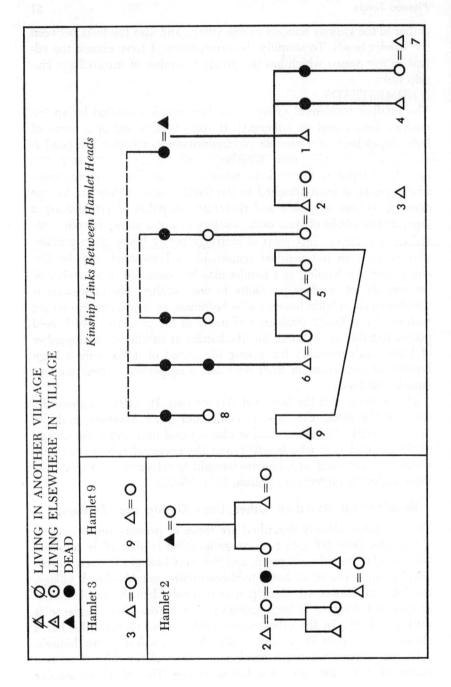

Kinship Links Between Hamlet Heads

△ LIVING IN ANOTHER VILLAGE
⊘ △ LIVING ELSEWHERE IN VILLAGE
▲ ⊙ ● DEAD

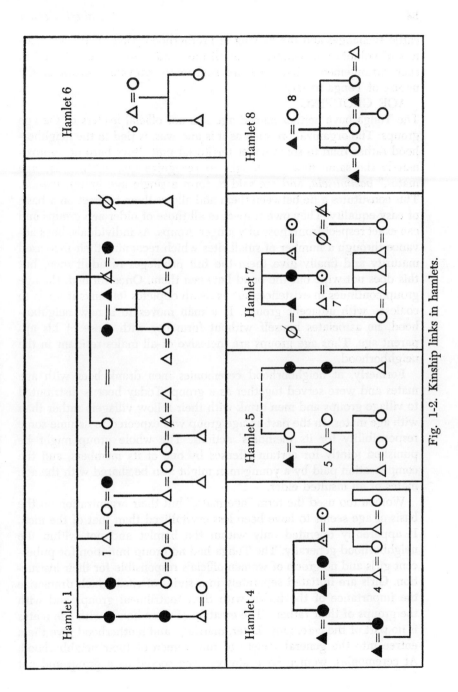

Fig. 1-2. Kinship links in hamlets.

cattle exchanges and the making of brotherhood pacts. These are matters of voluntary association. Not all men and women are involved in such arrangements, but they are sufficiently prevalent to affect the nature of Tonga society.

AGE GROUPING

The Tonga have neither named age sets nor official leaders of the age groups. The organization, such as it is and was, is tied to the neighborhood rather than to some wider territorial unit. Boys born at approximately the same time are taught to recognize one another as "age mates," *basimusela*, and are said to form a single age group, *musela*. This constitutes a tie between them and allows them to meet on a basis of easy equality. They owe respect to all those of older age groups and can exact respect from those of younger groups. As individuals, boys advance through a number of small rites which recognize their increased maturity and finally give them the full privileges of adult men, but this does not wipe out the bond between them. Once formed, the age group continues in existence, but as death depletes its ranks it tends to coalesce with adjacent groups. If a man moves to a new neighborhood, he associates himself without formality with those of his apparent age. Thus age groups are inclusive of all males resident in the neighborhood.

Formerly, at neighborhood ceremonies men drank beer with age mates and were served together as a group. Today beer is distributed to village groups and men drink with their fellow villagers rather than with age mates. In the past an age group was expected to assume some responsibility for its members' actions. The whole group might be punished jointly for certain offenses by one of its members, and the compensation paid by a young man might also be shared with the age mates of an insulted elder.

Women too used the term "age mate," but their organization on the basis of age seems to have been less crystallized than that of the men. It apparently operated only within the hamlet and not within the neighborhood generally. The Tonga had no group initiation for pubescent girls and no group of women officials responsible for their instruction. Girls are initiated separately in a series of rites which dramatize the importance of the bonds with their matrilineal groups and with the groups of their fathers. The creation of close bonds with age mates is no part of the ceremony. Later, marriage and motherhood give them entree into the general society of the women of their neighborhood. At ceremonies, women have always been served as a group and not according to age or village associations. Fines and damages were never assessed against women's age groups.

CATTLE LINKS

Age grouping strengthens ties within a neighborhood and provides a simple differentiation for the male residents. Cattle loans create a wider network of ties relating people who may live in widely separated areas. Cattle owners send many of their animals to other men for herding and, in turn, in their own kraals they hold cattle belonging to others. This system has its obvious utility. A man does not have the whole of his herd in a single spot where it might be wiped out by an epidemic or, as in the past, by a single raid. His creditors and others who might have a claim upon him cannot judge his assets from an inspection of his kraal, and one who contemplates settling a claim by absconding with an animal has his enthusiasm dampened by the knowledge that he may well be involving himself in a new set of complications if by chance he makes off with a beast belonging to someone other than his creditor (Colson, 1951b: 17–24).

The system of loans has other effects. Each man who owns cattle has the possibility of building up a series of claims against others who, by accepting the loan of one or two animals, become in a sense his clients and tied to his interests. The owner retains his ultimate rights to the animals and their increase, but the herder has the right to use them while they remain in his possession. The owner may resume his property whenever he wishes, but so long as he has no pressing need and the herding arrangement remains satisfactory to him, he is at some pains to maintain it. In some instances herding arrangements have continued for several generations, the heir of each man confirming the original loan. As the cattle increase, the herder may transfer part of the increase on to other men, who then become his clients while he remains responsible to the owner for the well-being of the animals. Thus ultimately an owner may have an indirect tie with men who are not personally known to him and with whom he has no firsthand contact.

Each wealthy man is likely to be the center of a far-flung network of cattle links, and wealthy men also attempt to build up alliances with one another by exchanging cattle. Cattle links may be established with kinsmen, with affines, with age mates, with friends. Frequently the links bind together men of different neighborhoods.

Just as the dispersal of kinsmen through the hamlets of a number of different neighborhoods once made it difficult for men to unite in an attack against any local group, so did the dispersal of cattle diminish the likelihood of direct action against the property of others. The threat of attack forced others in the vicinity who were not directly involved to intervene with informal pressures to force the settlement of a dispute before either side had taken drastic action. Thus even before the administration imposed its peace, it was possible for men to move through wider areas than the neighborhood; disputes had to be settled peaceably or too many people besides the disputants were affected by the resulting disruption of kinship ties and cattle ties. Only those living far apart could afford to attack one another (cf. Colson, 1953a).

BROTHERHOOD PACTS

Beyond the range of the close network of relationships which bound the people of one neighborhood to those within their general vicinity, brotherhood pacts gave a certain safeguard to the wanderer and provided for a limited exchange of goods between areas. Pacts were most commonly created between men living in widely separated areas where ordinarily no generalized pressure could be brought to bear to ensure life and property. A man who wished to trade in a distant area created a pact with a local resident, who then guaranteed his person and the safety of his property.

Brotherhood pacts gave a greater assurance of safety than could be found in the general claim to hospitality from a fellow clansman or a clan joking partner. Such claims did not set up any real expectation of protection against the attacks of others although it presumably prevented the host from taking action against his guest. Those of the same clan or those who were clan joking partners ought not to enslave one another, but they could ignore encroachments upon the life or freedom of one who could only cite his membership in a clan as claim against them.

That neither brotherhood pacts nor clanship was effective protection for the individual is pointed up by the constant emphasis of older people upon the necessity of staying within the area within which general amity prevailed. They stressed that marriages ought to take place with people belonging to kinship groups with which previous marriages had been contracted; this offered protection to the spouse, who otherwise settled among strangers.

Men and women who in their gradual shift from neighborhood to neighborhood drifted beyond the effective range of their kinship ties were lost to their matrilineal groups, whose other members were not prepared to venture into strange territory to avenge the misfortune of those who would have been wiser to remain near at hand. Distance was an effective solvent of kinship ties, for the obligation of mutual protection disappeared when intervening miles made it unlikely that the principle of mutual responsibility would be applied. Those who settled in remote areas had the task of building up around them a new network of ties to secure their position within the set of neighborhoods with which they were now associated. They might at first place themselves under the protection of some local leader as semidependents, then develop a set of affinal ties through marriages with local people, and in the next generation find themselves again in the possession of an effective matrilineal group related to others in the community through claims upon paternal groups. Once this was done they were again secure and could offer protection and hospitality to kinsmen who might follow them. If all contact ceased, then within a generation or two, as the memory of their common origin was forgotten, kinship faded into clanship and the area from which they originally sprang became alien territory into which they ventured at their own risk— though a brotherhood pact might give them some security.

Ecological Influences

The geographical features of Tonga country are probably related to the small size of the neighborhoods, the dispersed nature of the matrilineal groups, and the general mobility of the Tonga population.

Much of the area consists of the fairly flat plateau country stretching mile after mile, with little relief or obvious difference to give a focus to local sentiment. Along the northwestern border runs the Kafue River in its wide grassy flood plain, which is covered with water for a part of the year. Elsewhere open river bottoms sometimes break the monotony of the bush. To the east the plateau breaks fairly abruptly into the valleys running down through the Zambezi Escarpment in a belt of rugged country scantily inhabited by a closely related Tonga group.

The topography of the escarpment influences the rainfall on the plateau. As the clouds rise through the escarpment hills, they are deflected by the narrow valleys and ridges so that rainfall upon the plateau is often extremely localized. If there is to be a crop, rains must fall at the right times, and whether or not particular showers fall may be critical. Over a period of years adjoining areas may receive the same amount of rainfall and have an equal number of good and bad harvests, but in any one year they may have quite different luck. One may have almost a total crop failure; the other may have a sufficiency. The localized variation in rainfall seems to be at least one factor involved in the small size of the neighborhoods which are united about a common rain shrine.

Variable rainfall is also a factor in making the dispersed nature of the matrilineal group into an asset rather than a liability. On occasion it is essential for everyone to have some claim on food produced in other neighborhoods. Those with valuables—cattle and hoes (and slaves, in former days)—can buy food if they can find people with a surplus. Those who have exhausted their wealth, or who have none, could once depend only upon their personal claims against others. They could beg food from kinsmen with the expectation that they would be fed so long as there was food to be divided. They could approach fellow clansmen or clan joking partners or "pact brothers," though with less assurance of support. Failing these, their only resource was to sell themselves or some child into slavery in return for grain. Old people are still alive who were sold as tiny children in return for the food which allowed their elders to survive. Although today the administration arranges for the importation and sale of grain in times of general famine, in a hunger year people walk miles across the country to beg from kinsmen living in neighborhoods where there is some hope of finding food. The kinsmen may grumble, but so long as anything remains in their granaries or they have funds with which to purchase grain, they are likely to divide with their indigent relatives, knowing that another year may reduce them to the same straits.

Prior to the 1920's, when the Tonga began to produce for a cash market, they did not plant to obtain large surpluses beyond the need for subsistence. In a normal year a neighborhood produced enough to be self-sufficient and had some slight excess above its needs. This was not enough to serve all from a near-by area who might be reduced to seeking food, but if the indigent scattered widely throughout the surrounding country, they could be maintained. It was also impossible to predict which localities would have a surplus and which would be short of food. For sheer survival, therefore, it was an advantage to have those against whom you had a claim scattered in as many different neighborhoods as possible; it was also an advantage that all residents in the neighborhood should not have their claims concentrated in the same areas.

Under the circumstances, a dispersed kindred was less vulnerable than a highly concentrated one and in a better position to weather local periods of scarcity, though the advantage was gained at the cost of the general efficiency of kinship groups as effective units for concerted action. When real famine struck, many died. Only those tough enough to survive on what could be grubbed from the bush were left and they might have wandered far from their original homes in the frantic search for food. The history of a matrilineal group often begins, "So-and-so came here to escape the famine in such-and-such a place. He liked it here and decided to stay. Then others followed him, and now it looks as though we are different from those who stayed in the old area."

Famines, together with raids, did their share in checking the growth of population and holding it below the point of critical density. During the nineteenth century, land pressure may have existed in a few refuge areas. Over the rest of the country there was land and to spare. Quarrels and counterclaims about land simply did not occur until the developing land shortage of recent years. If a man wished to move he could always find fields in the area in which he wished to settle.

There were few obvious differences in natural resources to make people prefer one area over another. Soil fertility did vary but under the traditional system of shifting cultivation, with its slash-and-burn technique, the differences were not sufficiently important to play much of a role in determining residence. Fields were cultivated for a few years and then allowed to go back to bush while the cultivator found new fields. Cleared land was a wasting asset and not a carefully maintained piece of property whose value increased with the labor spent on it. The staple crops were annual ones—millets, sorghums, maize, groundnuts and ground beans, and cucurbits—and there were no holdings in orchard or root crops.

Water for household purposes was sufficiently common for there to be no need to hold fast to sites adjacent to springs or perennial seepages. Cattle might have to be driven to dry-season camps, but the best dry-season pastures were in regions likely to be flooded and unsuitable for agriculture or pasture during the rains. Potting clay, wood, thatching grass, and the food products of the bush were generally available.

The material possessions of men did not tie them permanently to one spot. Houses, granaries, and cattle kraals were temporary structures, as they usually are today, and within five to ten years of their building were in ruins. They were abandoned without regret by their owners, who shifted to new sites free of the debris and vermin which quickly overtake a homestead. The abandoned homestead site had some value because its soil was fertile, but the fertility was quickly exhausted under a crop of rank tobacco and it reverted again to bush. Soon only an occasional potsherd or an abandoned grindstone remained unscathed by the attacks of the termites to give evidence that the site was once inhabited. The unmarked graves of its inhabitants were forgotten, for the ancestral ritual is centered in the houses of the living, not in the graves of the dead.

All wealth consisted in movable property: livestock (cattle, goats, chickens, and pigeons), hoes, spears, guns, and slaves. Household possessions were few in number: pots, baskets, wooden mortars and stamping poles, grindstones, small wooden stools, and perhaps a drum or two. Most people had a few personal ornaments and a store of medicine. All of these were transportable and could be distributed on the death of their owner. They served neither to prevent people from moving freely nor gave them a reason to stay together with the hope of obtaining something through inheritance.

Today the wealthier men are investing in improvements which have a permanent value. Land shortage is also apparent, and men are reluctant to abandon fields when there is little hope of bettering their lot elsewhere. Stumped land is not lightly abandoned nor is land whose fertility has been increased by careful handling. Land is now regarded as a form of property, and has already entered into the inheritance system. Men are building brick houses, digging wells, and planting fruit trees on their holdings. But these are recent developments which began to affect the majority of Tonga only after the end of World War II.

Family Structure

The household, which is a residence unit, can be seen as a structural device which locks together various matrilineal groups since it includes, in the husband and wife, representatives of at least two such groups. It can also be analyzed as a unit in which individual men, women, and children adjust to one another in terms of certain kinship roles. It is with this field of kinship relationships that I propose to deal in this section.

THE HOUSEHOLD

The household is the group which combines about a common fire and consists of those people most intimately associated as a domestic unit. Each adult woman—after her marriage has become firmly established —is entitled to have her own fire and to cook independently. This establishes a new household. Households therefore are usually small, with a single adult male and female as their nucleus. I have analyzed 245 households drawn from two neighborhoods. Of these, 32 contained no adult males (households of widows and divorcees); 179 contained 1 adult male; 26 contained 2 adult males; 7 contained 3 adult males; 1

contained 4 adult males. No household had more than 4 adult men. Of the same 245 households, 2 contained no adult women (instances where an older man had managed to provide for his food without depending upon another household); 220 contained 1 adult woman; 20 contained 2 adult women; 3 contained 3 adult women. No household had more than 3 women.

A few households have no adolescent or child members. Most have a varying number, the greater proportion of which are the offspring of the married couple in whom the household centers. But the household is not identical with the immediate family. During its lifetime it requires the labor of a number of children of both sexes and of various ages to perform various tasks if it is to be independent. From time to time, therefore, it will have to borrow children from the kin of either husband or wife to meet its needs. It may also assume responsibility for orphaned or otherwise homeless children related to either spouse. Some of the children produced by the couple will in turn be sent to live with relatives to help them with their work or because temporarily they are a burden to their parents. The children themselves have a voice in the matter and may prefer to live with other relatives. The children resident in a household therefore vary considerably over the course of several years.

POLYGYNOUS HOUSEHOLDS

When a man is married polygynously, two or more households share a single male head. In my census of 22 villages in four neighborhoods, I found that 24 per cent of the married men (73 out of 307) had 2 or more wives. The greatest number of wives recorded for any man in the census was 6. The great majority of polygynists have only 2.

Usually the wives of a polygynist have adjacent huts within a single homestead. If their quarrels make this inadvisable, the husband may build their huts in different sections of the hamlet. He rarely has to resort to such measures; if life becomes completely unbearable one of the women is likely to solve his dilemma by divorcing him. I encountered two cases in which a polygynist had his two wives living in different villages. Most men would not consider such an arrangement. It would involve them in cultivating fields in different areas and make it necessary to move ploughs and oxen back and forth or to borrow this equipment, which today is considered essential for cultivation. The double location also runs counter to one of the important motives for polygyny, which is to be the head of a large homestead and to have the labor of a number of wives and their children to work the man's own field. As far as the women are concerned, such separateness removes the mitigating advantage of polygyny—the presence of another woman who helps provide the food for the husband and his visitors, and to whom one can turn for assistance in times of illness.

Each woman, and her household, is considered an independent unit, and the various households centering in a polygynist should have no close kinship ties to each other save through his. A man may not be married simultaneously to two women of the same matrilineal group, paternal half-siblings, paternal parallel cousins, a woman and her father's sister, or a woman and her mother's paternal half-sister. He may marry two women of the same clan, or women whose fathers were of the same clan. I found no instance of a man married to women who called each other cross cousin, though such a marriage might be admissible. Occasionally a man marries one woman and another whom she has previously addressed as "mother"—the former wife of someone whom she called "father." This happens even in arranged marriages but it is still considered undesirable. The rules of marriage go even further in maintaining the independence of the households founded by women. Two men who are uterine siblings or maternal parallel cousins should not marry women who are uterine siblings or maternal parallel cousins or closely related through paternal links. Thus each wife is secure in the knowledge that her own matrilineal group and the matrilineal group of her father—the two kindreds which should maintain her rights—have no overlapping interests in the households of her co-wives nor are they likely to be involved in the households revolving about her husband's brothers. Equally, she cannot be placed in a position of rivalry over a husband's attentions with a woman with whom she is otherwise identified. When the wife dies, her husband may marry one of her relatives. Occasionally, her matrilineal group will even provide him with a substitute for his dead wife, but it is not obligated to do so. In any event her successor may never be her uterine sister.

In polygynous families, as in all others, each wife is entitled from the time of marriage to her own hut. When her separate household is established, she becomes entitled to her own kitchen, her own field, and her own granary. She can be required to work only in her own field and in the separate field of her husband. Neither she nor her children need work in the field of her co-wife. The produce from her field is reserved for the use of her own household; if she shares it with a co-wife in distress this is on her own initiative. If her crop fails, her husband must provide for her household from his own field or he must purchase grain. Each wife has equal rights of maintenance and should fare the same in items of food provided by the husband and in clothing for themselves and their children. Each wife is entitled to an equal share of the husband's attentions; he should spend an equal number of nights in the hut of each.

The first wife to be married has the status of chief wife. Her house is placed on the right hand and is known as the house of "the father." A subsequent wife is known as a "small" wife, and her house is placed to the left and is known as the house of the mukowa, the matrilineal group. Any further wives have the same status and their houses too are identified with the mukowa. The chief wife has for certain purposes a higher ritual status. The husband should sleep in her house before departing on a journey and immediately after his return. The chief wife should be consulted in advance of the other wives. But any attempt on her part to subordinate the other wives after they have established their own households is an attack upon their positions which would be countered by the claim that they too are free women and not slaves to do her bidding. In this their relatives will support them. The children of the chief wife have no advantage over their half-siblings, for in relation to their father and his kin they are all of the same status.

So long as the man who forms their common bond lives and the marriages are maintained, polygynous households are closely united in many of their activities. The wives may form a common work team. If they are on friendly terms they assist in common household duties, look after one another's children, and give assistance and comfort in times of illness. Their children play and eat together. The boys may share a common sleeping hut. All the children address one another as siblings and are counted as such, while they address their mother's co-wives as "mother." The women themselves address one another as "my co-wife." They may refer to the child of a co-wife by the same term they use for their own child.

Polygyny, despite the rules which seek to regulate it, is considered a delicate affair, difficult for a man to manage comfortably. It is made the more difficult because Tonga women have an ideal of companionship within marriage which is incompatible with polygyny; if one wife succeeds in her aim it is only at the expense of the others. Men expect their wives to be jealous of one another and to quarrel over the husband's favors. It is believed that co-wives often resort to various love medicines in an attempt to gain first place with the husband and that they may use sorcery to kill a hated co-wife or her children. Sometimes the tension between the wives explodes into open accusations of dealings in sorcery. Sometimes, however, the wives form a common front against their husband, abetting one another in love affairs, going off in companionable couples to beer parties and funerals (leaving him at home to shift for himself), and siding together in any quarrels that may arise with the husband.

Whether the wives' alliance is bitter or happy, it lasts only as long as their marriages to the common husband endure. On divorce each wife departs, and usually those who have formed her household go with her. If the husband dies there is a disruption of all the households centered in him, and his matrilineal group appoints a representative to purify the wives, thus releasing them for remarriage. His matrilineal group, the wives, and their relatives then discuss the inheritance of the widows. They should be inherited by men of the dead husband's group, but they have a choice both with regard to whether they will be inherited and to the selection of the new husband. Co-wives may be inherited by different men, which means that henceforth they live in separate homesteads. One or all may refuse to be inherited, which again usually involves their separation and an end to any tie between them. A woman who refuses to be inherited goes off to live with her own relatives until she remarries and her new husband pays bridewealth to the relatives of her dead husband. A woman who is past childbearing may settle in the homestead of one of her adult children. In any event, the end of her marriage severs any legal relationship with her dead husband's group.

It is unlikely that the children of co-wives will remain closely associated after the death of their father, especially if the widows have separated. If they continue to live in the same village they will have little interest in one another once they are grown. They are not members of the same matrilineal group, they have no interest in one another's households, they have no particular obligations to one another. If they live apart they are likely to forget each other. The Tonga adult is frequently uncertain as to the number of his father's wives and their affiliations and to the number, the names, and the present whereabouts of paternal half-siblings. This contrasts with the ability to remember the wives and children of male members of the matrilineal group, who continue to stand in a close relationship to the kindred of their dead father. Paternal half-siblings are the common responsibility of members of their father's matrilineal group, but this does not create a community of interests which hold them together.

THE INITIATION OF A HOUSEHOLD

Households most commonly come into being as the result of a marriage which is recognized as having some probability of permanency. A test period of several years, during which one or more children may be born, therefore intervenes between marriage and the setting up of the household.

Men formerly married rather later than they do today; most men now seem to marry about the age of twenty-five. Informants claim that girls once married immediately after their puberty ceremony. Case material indicates that most commonly there was a delay of two or more years. Today women marry about the age of sixteen to eighteen. Approximately 40 per cent have born a "bush" child before marriage, though it is usually begotten by the man whom the woman expects to marry. But once her pregnancy is discovered, all marriage negotiations must cease until the child is some months old. Whether the lover marries her or not, he is entitled—and today is forced by legal action—to make a payment which establishes him as the legal father of the child, and his paternity is not altered by the mother's subsequent marriage to another man.

Informants say that formerly marriages were arranged by older relatives without much regard to the personal wishes of the couple. Today, under a rule introduced by the administration, the woman's consent is necessary. Since men have been in a position to earn their own bride-wealth, they have had the acknowledged right to choose their own wives, but they still consult older relatives whose coöperation is essential if the marriage is to be fully recognized by the community.

The suitor then sends a deputation to the guardian of the woman, who may be either her father or her mother's brother. The guardian consults with other relatives of her parental generation. If they agree to accept him the suitor is informed, and from that moment an avoidance relationship is initiated between him and the woman's parents and all persons of their generation. There remains to be negotiated the amount of bridewealth to be paid and the selection of the household to which the couple will be attached during the first period of the marriage. In former days, when personal safety was a factor to be considered, the woman's relatives might agree to her marriage to a man of another neighborhood only if he came to live among them for a probationary period. If they found him trustworthy he was then entitled to remove his wife wherever he wished to live, especially if he had kinsmen where he planned to settle. Today the couple may still settle initially with relatives of the wife, but most commonly they are attached to some relative of the husband.

The man builds a hut for his bride in the homestead of some established couple: his parents, his grandparents on either side, his mother's brother, his brother, his married sister, or the man for whom he has been working. If this is a polygynous marriage, the couple will be attached to the household of the first wife. The man then sends the preliminary marriage payments to his bride's guardian and his bride is sent to him. Wherever she has been living, the marriage ritual is phrased as though she comes from her father's house and from his guardianship. It is the rights in her and her children which vest in her father and his line which are transferred to the husband. The matrilineal group never relinquishes any of its rights in her, though it shares equally in the marriage payments.

At this stage the husband obtains rights over his wife's labor, rights to control her movements, and rights over her sexuality. He is the father of any children born to her, whether or not he begets them. If she dies in childbirth, he cannot be sued for damages. But if he delays in making his final marriage payments and his wife's relatives become impatient, they may claim that these rights have now lapsed. The relatives may impound the wife until he agrees to complete the payments. If he is recalcitrant or unable to pay, they formerly claimed the right to marry the woman elsewhere, saying that with her labor she had already offset the value of the preliminary payments. Today this is no longer permitted.

In any event, until a man has made his final payments he is not entitled to the full privileges which inhere in the status of a husband. He has not been given the right to initiate a new household through his wife. They may not have a cooking fire at their house; the wife may not brew beer there; she may not cook separately to provide for his food; and he may not dedicate the house to his ancestors, who have not yet been apprised of the fact that the marriage has taken place. Both he and his wife must rely upon the ritual offices of other members of their matrilineal groups to approach the ancestors in their behalf and in behalf of their children. Furthermore, if the husband tries to collect damages for his wife's adultery, her relatives will claim that the damages are rightfully theirs since the husband is still only a lover. If the wife dies, her matrilineal relatives will refuse to purify him unless he pays for the privilege. If the husband dies, his matrilineal relatives may not inherit the wife unless they pay the bridewealth. Again, the argument is that the husband is still only a lover.

To obtain the full complement of marital rights and to establish a household, the final marriage payments must be made. This is the *ciko*, which today consists of approximately four head of cattle. Like the preliminary payments, this is divided equally between the wife's matrilineal relatives and her father. They then arrange the ceremony of "greeting," which relaxes the avoidance between them and the husband and makes him free to visit their homesteads. Shortly thereafter, each sends a representative who together install the fireplace and ritually introduce the wife to cooking. Soon thereafter, their representatives come to set grain to soak within the house in preparation for brewing beer. When the beer is ready, the husband pours an offering at the door and installs his ancestral spirits as guardians of the household. Henceforth he and his wife are recognized as fully mature members of the community, and when they die they become ancestral spirits in their own right (Colson, 1954: 62–65).

A man therefore establishes a household only with the consent and coöperation of his wife's relatives. His chances of obtaining a position of importance in the community—the headship of a homestead, a hamlet, or a village—are dependent upon his maintenance of a household. This he can do only so long as he maintains control over his wife. Once he has made his final payment he can demand that his wife's relatives uphold his prerogatives and he expects them to return her to him if she runs away without cause. If he abuses his power she may still seek refuge with her relatives. If his fault is serious, they may demand damages from the husband before returning his wife; if they refuse to return her, they should return the bridewealth. Until it is returned, the husband's rights to his wife's sexuality are still intact. He may sue her lovers for adultery; he is the legal father of any of her children. These rights lapse only when the bridewealth is returned by the wife's relatives or when a new suitor pays bridewealth to the first husband and thus obtains full marital rights in the woman. The first husband retains his rights to any children born up to this point; the new husband is the legal father of subsequent children.

Despite the important role of the conjugal family and the household, divorce is fairly frequent, though certainly less common than in many matrilineal societies. In the twenty-two census villages, there were 330 men who were married at the time of the census or who had been married at some previous period; of these, 31 per cent had been divorced at least once. In the same villages, 486 women were either married at the time or had been married previously; 26 per cent of them had been divorced at least once. I suspect that the majority of divorces occurred during the probationary period, but I cannot document this. Still, long-established unions sometimes end in divorce, and if a woman is fully determined to leave her husband she usually accomplishes her purpose.

If a divorcee or widow refuses to contract another marriage, the rights which formerly vested in her husband largely accrue to her, rather than reverting to her male relatives. She can maintain a household of her own in which she is the undisputed mistress, as she is now mistress over her own actions. In the past she could become the head of a hamlet or village. Today, since village headmanship is an administrative position, the official headman is always a man, but a few women act as hamlet heads. Informants recall noted amazons who rid themselves of unwanted husbands and succeeded in inducing their daughters to follow the same path. The women then lived together in a separate homestead or hamlet, accepting as lovers men who did not become permanent members of their establishment. They acquired cattle which were herded by their sons. Most women who become *nabutema* (widows or divorcees) live within the homestead of a male relative who is careful not to intervene too closely in their affairs. Their position contrasts strongly with that of the single male. Once he has lost his wife he becomes dependent upon others and can never have a household or approach his ancestors unless he can acquire a wife. Old women chuckle happily at their independence; old men try desperately to find wives through whom they can once more establish a household unit catering to their wishes and giving them prestige and ritual potency.

So long as the household contains a married couple, it is theoretically under the authority of the husband. He represents it in the community composed of the other households of the neighborhood. It is known by his name. Individual members of the household remain identified with their matrilineal groups, but so long as they live within his household they must accept his leadership. The rights accruing to his position are part of his estate and are inherited by his matrilineal kinsmen, though during his lifetime he alone has the right to exercise them.

The actual authority of the husband, of course, is affected by many circumstances. In the past it was at a maximum where a man married his slave; he then had absolute rights over both her and their children, who belonged to the matrilineal group of their father as well as to his household. Conversely, it was minimal where the husband was a slave married to the sister or the sister's daughter of his owner, or where he was married to another slave. Today it is somewhat diminished if the husband is a poor man living as a semidependent in the homestead of his wife's relative. The husband's authority is also affected by the relative ages of husband and wife; in most households, it is buttressed by the fact that he is the oldest person within it. In 77 per cent of extant marriages (drawn from eighteen of the census villages), the husband is at least five years older than his wife; in 44 per cent of these marriages he is at least ten years older; and in 20 per cent he is at least fifteen years older. Years and experience then enable the husband to fill his role effectively. Where a young man is married to a much older inherited wife, or where the couple are of approximately the same age, the husband is likely to find his nominal rights set at naught, while the wife runs the household.

This does not affect the fact that the husband is formally in charge of the household. This comes out clearly in instances where a man marries a mature woman who already has her own house and granary. In addition to the payments which he makes to her relatives to establish the marriage, he makes a further payment directly to her to give him rights of ownership in the house and the crop she has grown. The house has previously been under the guardianship of the woman's ancestral spirits, to whom she made offerings at the door. These are now removed as guardians and the husband installs ancestral spirits of his own line who henceforth protect the house and its inmates. If the wife wishes to make offerings to her ancestors she must now pour the offerings at the bed posts or at the center post of the house, leaving the doorway to her husband. Thus the husband becomes ritual head of the household at the same time that he assumes the control of its affairs.

HUSBAND AND WIFE

Certain aspects of the husband-wife relationship have already been covered and need not be repeated here. In some respects it is an easy, informal relationship of partnership and friendliness, though formal etiquette stresses the superior position of the husband.

The husband has considerable authority over his wife, and her relatives transfer to him the right to exercise physical punishment. After her marriage, neither her father nor her mother's brother may lay a hand upon her, though they may chastise her verbally. A brother is always forbidden to use any form of physical violence against his sister and he should be wary even of verbal criticism. Thus only the husband is in a position to chastise a woman, for his own relatives may not exert any physical force over her. The husband has the right to discipline his wife if he suspects her of adultery, for neglecting his comfort, or for failure in deference. One of the arguments used to dissuade men from building on their own is the risk they run of beating a wife to death if no one is near to hear her cries and intervene. In a number of instances men have actually done this and have then committed suicide when they saw what they had done.

The husband exercises discipline, however, only when his wife fails in her duties to him. In the rest of her activities she acts as a free agent or as a member of a matrilineal group. A husband therefore is held to have no responsibility for actions of his wife which involve her with others. If she is sued for damages, he may refuse to help her. She must settle the matter with the assistance of her relatives, though the husband should be present when the affair is discussed. If she wishes to sue for damages, she does so on her own behalf or through the agency of her own relatives, and her husband has no right to the compensation which may be paid to her. Equally, her property may not be taken to settle claims which arise against the husband.

The wife has certain rights against her husband. He must sleep with her and beget children. If he fails, he should arrange with a cross-cousin or a friend to perform the service for him while he acknowledges the resulting children as his own. But he may make such an arrangement only after consultation with his wife's matrilineal kinsmen; otherwise they will sue him for prostituting her. If the wife is ill, the husband must join with her relatives in finding a diviner and he must bear a portion of the cost of treatment. He must provide her with a hut, a field, a hoe, and a certain number of household utensils. He must clothe her and her children. If he fails in any of these respects, his wife has grounds for divorce.

Until the last few years the husband was expected to clear land to provide fields for himself and his wife. The seed for their first crop was provided by their relatives and it was mixed together before planting. They worked their fields together and the resulting crop was their property. They produced only for their own subsistence; the disposal of any surplus was not in question. In the event of the death of husband or wife, any food remaining in the granary was used to feed those who attended the funeral. In the event of divorce, there might be a division of the crop, but more commonly the in-marrying spouse simply abandoned his or her claim.

Today, when land is in short supply, a couple may have to beg a field from any near-by relative or acquaintance who can spare one. The field is still assumed to vest primarily in the husband. If he later assigns a portion to his wife, she will refer to him as the donor even though it was originally given them by one of her relatives. But if he dies or they are divorced, the field will remain in her possession if it originally came from her relative.

In working their fields, husband and wife and the children attached to their household form a single work team with duties apportioned according to the traditional division of labor between the sexes. The husband and boys clear the land. Today they are responsible for the transport and spreading of manure, for ploughing, and for cultivation, since these tasks depend upon the use of oxen, whose handling is reserved to men. The wife, with the assistance of the girls, plants the seed, does most of the hoeing, and is largely responsible for the harvest. The wife uses the crop from her field for feeding her household, for brewing beer, and for making gifts. Once stored in her granary it comes under her supervision. Her husband has no right to take grain from her granary, nor may he arrogate to himself the right of doling out the daily provisions. If she has a surplus, however, she may sell it only with her husband's consent. He may then insist upon a division of the proceeds and even take a major portion of the money realized. The money which he leaves to her becomes her property, with which she may deal as she pleases. She may buy clothing for herself and her children or she may invest in livestock or goods to form her personal estate. The crop from the field allocated to the husband belongs to him. He is expected to reserve a portion of the crop to provide for emergencies. The remainder he sells to cover the cash needs of his household. But he has exclusive rights to any money he realizes and may spend it as he pleases. He need not even inform his wife of the amount which he obtained.

The introduction of ploughing has reinforced the husband's rights over fields and crops. Because the plough and oxen used in the fields are usually his, he claims that he is entitled to all the proceeds over and above that needed for food without regard to whose field produced the crop. If he has also provided the seed, his certainty that he is absolute master of the crop is increased. Today some husbands even claim a share in the wife's groundnuts, a crop in which the wife's privileges have always been greatest. The result is that many wives today feel that they are being exploited as laborers. This gives rise to considerable bitterness which sometimes breaks out into furious quarrels between husband and wife about the ownership of crops.

On the other hand a woman is free to earn, through other channels, money over which the husband has no claim. She may contract to brew beer from maize supplied to her, and the money she receives belongs to her. She may sell baskets or pots, or receive fees as a diviner. She may acquire livestock or chickens either through purchase or through gift, from her own relatives or even from her husband. She can refuse her husband's request that she kill a chicken from her flock to feed him and the household and tell him that they will eat chicken when he produces one of his own. If she has oxen, she may refuse to let her husband use them even to work their joint field, and her husband is without redress. Usually she sends such property to her own relatives for safekeeping to avoid any risk that her husband's matrilineal relatives may claim them as part of his estate in the event of his death.

Such questions of ownership highlight a major strain in the Tonga household at the present time. Members of the household who work together belong to different inheritance groups. The strain probably has always been present, but new conditions have made it evident to all concerned. Once the household was a unit which produced for its own subsistence; by and large its members consumed all that was produced. There was no question of the use of the surplus for supporting a standard of living higher than the general level or of its investment in capital goods and savings with permanent value. This is no longer true, and the ultimate disposition or use of wealth produced by a household is a matter of concern to many people, who have different claims upon it.

Members of the husband's matrilineal group see the wealth produced as a potential part of his estate over which they have rights of inheritance to the exclusion of the wife and her children. They resent his use of his wealth to raise the standard of living of his household since this means that the wife and children are "eating" the wealth. They are also resentful if he uses it to endow his wife and children, through outright gifts. The wife and children on the other hand see the wealth as largely the product of their labor. Its conversion into capital goods or savings—though this for the moment may give them security or a better living—means that eventually their work goes to endow the husband's relatives. The situation is particularly difficult for the wife of one of the new class of farmers who becomes accustomed to some slight luxury and the importance of being the chief woman in a large homestead. Her husband's death inevitably means a drastic change in her position, for even though she agrees to be inherited her husband's wealth will not pass intact to the successor. Much of it will be divided among the numerous heirs, and she will henceforth hold a minor position in a poorer homestead. She therefore tries, while she can, to divert as much as possible of her husband's wealth into the hands of her children, or she encourages them to break away from their father so that their labor does not go into his estate. To some extent her efforts here bring her into conflict with her husband, who wishes to keep his sons as members of his homestead and as workers in his fields. Meantime both she and her children, as well as the husband, fear the sorcery of the husband's matrilineal relatives, who would find advantage in his death and meantime see good reason to dislike the wife and her children.

The position of the husband as the leader and controller of the household's activities clashes with the matrilineal organization of Tonga society and leads to tensions affecting various relationships: husband and wife, a father and his children, a man and his matrilineal heirs, the wife (and her children) and the husband's matrilineal relatives.

I suggest that tensions within a matrilineal system vary with the amount of disposable wealth, the way in which this is accumulated, and the way in which it vests in persons. Potentially the most unstable type of matrilineal system may well be found in neolocal or avunculocal peasant societies with a surplus to be converted either into permanent wealth or differential living standards.

PARENTS AND CHILDREN

Children grow up in a household in which almost invariably there is a male head who exercises authority over them and their mother, or over them and the woman who is responsible for their care. If they are in their father's household, he has the right to their work and to their respect. If they are living with a maternal relative, the authority and the right to discipline them vests in this man. Only if they are living with a stepfather will they have considerable immunity from discipline, for the man will be afraid to punish them lest this antagonize their mother. By and large, the freedom of children lies in the fact that once old enough to move about they have a choice in the matter of their residence and thus of their guardian. The Tonga say that a child must be permitted to decide where it will live; otherwise it will cry that it is being treated like a slave, whereas it is a free person. Children may therefore live with their father, even though their mother is dead or divorced. They may leave him to live with a mother's brother, a grandfather, an older brother, a married sister, or, if living and remarried, their mother and stepfather. Since the labor of children is essential for the ordinary work of a household, they are always welcome. Some children grow up mainly with their parents; others live almost entirely in the households of other relatives and know their parents and siblings only casually. This may affect their adult residence and their choice of the kinsmen with whom they identify themselves most closely.

Legally, however, paternal rights and duties are not abrogated by distance or a lack of personal contact. These rights inhere in the man who gave the child the first of his two "ancestral" names (Colson, 1954: 27–31). This will be the man who acknowledged paternity in the case of the "bush" child born to an unmarried girl; it will be the husband in the case of any child born to a married woman. With the name goes a guardian spirit of the paternal line, which is thereafter identified with the child. In a sense, a child is an affiliated member of his father's matrilineal group. He is commonly addressed by his father's clan name. His father's group assumes certain responsibilities for him and contributes to a son's bridewealth. Though he is not a member of their vengeance group, they share with his matrilineal kin the obligation of paying compensation for his offenses. If he is killed, they join with his matrilineal kin in exacting vengeance or compensation, and they have a full share in any compensation paid. When he is in difficulties with his matrilineal group, they are expected to urge his claims. If his matrilineal kin accuse him of witchcraft and the accusation is proved false, they may demand compensation for the insult shown to them through their child. On the other hand, they are expected to show moderation in urging their own claims against him. If he kills his father—as has happened in several instances in the past—they may not proceed against him, for he is their child. Under no circumstances does the father or the paternal kin have the right—nor did they in times past—to sell a child into slavery. Thus a child can grow up securely in its father's household.

In turn, children must respect their father and those of his generation. If a son curses or strikes his father, this is *malweza,* a matter which involves a mystical retribution affecting the offender or the one offended or any member of the group with which either one is identified. The subsequent death of either man may be attributed to malweza, but there should be a ritual reconciliation in which the son acknowledges his fault.

Many of the rights and duties devolve upon the father himself even though his children may not be living with him. He should send them gifts of clothing. He should be informed if they are ill and consulted about the choice of a diviner and the type of treatment to be used. If the diviner attributes the illness to an ancestral spirit of his line, he or his representative must come to pour the offering.

A man may not have seen his daughter since her childhood, but he must still be summoned for her puberty ceremony. He may claim the right to have her secluded in the house of one of his relatives. When the daughter marries, he must be informed and his share of her bridewealth be given to him. When the bride is sent to her husband, his representative must pour the offering which informs the ancestors of his line that she has departed from her guardian's house to be married.

If she is married without his consent, he may sue her maternal relatives for damages and also refuse to recognize the existence of the marriage. A girl's stepfather, even though he has reared her from childhood, has no say in her marriage nor any share in her bridewealth, unless he be the heir of her dead father.

A man's rights over his son are also emphasized, though perhaps less emphatically than they used to be. Formerly a boy presented his first game either to his father or to his father's representative. Thereafter, whenever he killed a large animal a portion was due his father's people. When a labor migrant returned home with goods or money, he was expected to call his father or his father's representative, present the man with the key to his locked box, and stand aside while the man made his choice of its contents. Later he had to share some of his wealth with his matrilineal kinsmen, but he had the right to decide what and when he would give.

Today, when a man obtains a new plough or some other agricultural tool, he must use it first in the field of his father or his father's representative. Only then is he free to use it in his own field. If a man is chosen to succeed to the name of a member of his matrilineal group, a beast from the dead man's herd must be paid to the young man's father as an acknowledgement of the latter's rights in his son. When a man's household is established, his father or his father's representative is expected to take part in the dedication of the house to the ancestral spirits. If the father is dead, it is his spirit which is installed as the particular guardian of his son's first household. The most frequent offerings are made to spirits of the father's line, and these must be made through some matrilineal kinsman of the father (Colson, 1954: 60).

When a man or woman dies, a portion of the estate is inherited by the father and his kin. They must take part in the funeral rites, and when they depart they are said to take with them the guardian spirit which they gave at the naming. When a divination is sought to find the cause of death, representatives of the father must join with representatives of the matrilineal line, for it is among all these relatives that the source of the deadly sorcery is most likely to be found since they are all heirs and profit from the death.

Father and children are thus conceived as closely associated. Moreover, the relationship to the father is primarily a personal one to the father himself. Only secondarily does it devolve upon other members of his matrilineal group, either because of his death or because he appoints someone as his representative.

So far I have dealt with the standards of father-child relationship without regard to how it works in actuality, when it must adjust to the widely different experiences of various people. If children live with their father there is usually a warm affectionate relation between them while the children are still small. As they grow older, this relation alters. The daughters are drawn into the activities of their mother and older sisters almost as soon as they can walk. They eat with the women and begin to be trained for their future work. Discipline is usually left to the mother, who is in direct charge of their work, but despite this she becomes their confidant and mentor and a more formal relationship develops with the father. By the time they near puberty, the father will disavow any knowledge of their affairs. A man does not inquire directly into the sexual life of his daughter. If he suspects that she is pregnant, he must ask her mother or her mother's brother or some other relative to question her. He himself does not handle the resulting negotiations to collect damages. When his daughters marry, they go off to join their husbands, and the husbands then have first call upon their services.

Small boys remain longer in close association with their father, since by the age of four or five they are drawn into the eating group of the men. But the affection between father and son is soon subject to a severe test which begins when the boy starts work as a herdsboy; when he tires of the task, his father still drives him to the cattle kraal. There are quarrels about his derelictions from duty, which grow heated if the cattle have been left free to invade the fields or if they have suffered from his neglect. As a boy grows older, he realizes more and more clearly that he is herding cattle in which he has no ultimate interest, save for the payments which will be made to help him with his marriage. As he learns the difference between matrilineal and other kin, his attitude toward his father changes and there is a loosening of the tie between them. Meantime, the authority which his father exerts over him as the head of the working team of the household results in a more formal relationship which replaces the old familiarity. If the son acquires property, it is in his own control. Usually he sends it to a matrilineal relative for safekeeping to prevent its seizure by his father's heirs in the event of the latter's death. If he settles near his father, he gradually diverts more and more attention to the affairs of his own household. Eventually he will probably move out to form his own homestead. The father may rail that his son ate at his fire for many years and he now wants his son to remain nearby so that he may eat at his son's fire whenever he so desires. But he has no power to prevent the move.

The more generous a father is to his children, the more he resents their independence or their being drawn to matrilineal kin. Much that he does for his children is an act of grace rather than a legal responsibility. A mother's brother does not expect undue gratitude from a sister's son who claims his rights; a father who assists his child feels that he is not under obligation to act in this fashion and he therefore expects his child to show his gratitude by an unfailing allegiance. If his son or daughter offends him, he is likely to threaten them with the withdrawal of assistance and stress that their real tie is with their maternal relatives.

Father and children may quarrel, but children are never accused of using sorcery against their father, in whose death they find no advantage. Men say, "How can we trust our sons? They trust only their own matrilineal group." At the same time they feel secure in their relations with their children as they do not with matrilineal kinsmen. For this reason some men have opposed the introduction of a legal will or a shift to familial inheritance because this might give their children a motive to wish their death.

The mother's rights and duties in her children are assimilated to those of the matrilineal kin. An old Tonga proverb states, "A woman is only a sack." It was believed that the formative element in conception was blood which came from the father, and that the woman only molded it into a child. Some now argue that both father and mother contribute blood to the child. Yet today many are questioning a system of descent which affiliates a child with its mother's line, whereas formerly they accepted it without question. The old formulation was that the head and right arm belonged to the father; the body and left arm to the matrilineal group. This association is a common ritual motif. Nowadays men snort and argue that the whole of the child belongs to the father since he has paid bridewealth for the mother. Their carping, however, has not succeeded as yet in altering the descent system.

From their mother, children derive their clan affiliation and their set of clan joking partners. From her they also take their membership in the group which regulates inheritance and which was formerly the vengeance unit. Through her and her kin they receive the second of the "ancestral names" given in infancy, with which is associated a guardian spirit of the matrilineal line. Through the mother they gain their affiliation to the ancestral spirits which they may approach directly.

Most of the incidents of the children's lives show a balancing between the claims of the father's line and that of the mother. But whereas the paternal claims are largely focused in the father himself, the rights and obligations of the maternal line are diffused very widely and lie not against a specific person but against the group as a whole, or against a general kinship category within it.

The status of the mother is therefore much more personal than is that of the father. The tie between mother and child is also of a different nature since it is unlikely to be subject to the same pressure of property interests and direct authority. At the same time it is profoundly affected by the residence of the child and whether or not it grows up in its mother's household.

During its infancy a child has first call upon its mother's attention, though after the first few months it spends most of its time in the care of a child nurse, thus freeing the mother for her other work. But the mother should not become pregnant again until her child is able to walk freely. The birth of the next sibling ends the first child's domination, and the mother's attention will shift back to him only if he becomes ill and thus dependent upon her care. Only the last-born child has a longer period of domination, and is therefore expected to be "spoiled." The mother is the first disciplinarian, though she leaves to the play group much of the task of training her child in the adjustments needed for living with other people. Her later role depends upon the child's sex.

Daughters come directly under her supervision as they learn the skills required of women. They must respect her, but on the whole they have a familiar relationship with the mother as their confidant. A girl continues to live in her mother's house until her marriage, and she may confide to her mother's keeping tokens received from a lover. After her marriage she usually makes frequent visits to her mother's house; if possible, she returns there for the birth of her first child. Her mother has an important voice in her marriage; and if the daughter sues for divorce, the court will usually consult the wishes of her mother before settling the case. If the mother says that she refuses to agree to the continuation of the marriage, this is generally the end of the matter. Widowed or divorced women frequently return to settle near their mothers, or an old woman may move to join a daughter and a son-in-law. Formerly women gave only a single shrill at the birth of a boy but shrilled mightily when a girl was born; for it was in daughters that a woman found security for her old age. Today she is more likely to turn to her son, for a son-in-law is usually unwilling to spend his money upon her.

After his childhood a woman is not in direct charge of her son's activities. His work is herding, which places him immediately under the supervision of the older herdboys and ultimately under the authority of the father. He eats with the men. At about the age of ten, he moves from the family house to one of the boys' houses. Here he lives until he goes off to work or marries. His mother will see to it that he is fed, but he cannot demand services from her. He owes her respect, but this is no barrier to a close affectionate relationship; he may even caress his mother. He frequently consults her; even as an adult he is likely to listen to her advice. Perhaps the clearest indication of how the Tonga feel about the mother-son relationship is found in the words sometimes addressed to a man who is being urged to give his wife the respect which is her due: "You must respect her, for your wife is your mother. Like your mother she feeds you and cares for you. She is your mother indeed." A woman may use her influence to tie her sons to their father or she may urge them to go off to live with matrilineal relatives; but so long as she is alive and with their father, the sons are likely to live nearby in established homesteads of their own, where they may remain even though she subsequently leaves her husband to go elsewhere. If she is old, they may urge her to leave her husband to live in their homesteads, and they then assume the obligation of her support.

It is malweza for a man or woman to curse or strike the mother. Indeed it is more heinous than a similar offense against the father. Quarrels do occur; people speak bitterly. But I heard of no instance where an adult struck his or her mother. Informants could remember no instances of matricide, but they agreed that if a woman were killed by her child no action could be taken against the offender. Finally, I know of no instance where a child was believed to have used sorcery against its mother.

Women get a certain grim satisfaction from the thought that their children are more firmly attached to them and their matrilineal group than they are to their father. A wife ended an argument over the ownership of crops by saying, "All right, you men can take the groundnuts, but the children belong to us!" Her husband growled, "To you! You mean they belong to your relatives." She replied, "It is the same thing. They belong to us." Women do not found new segments of the matrilineal group through their children; they pass on the right of membership in the undifferentiated whole. Thus, even if a woman accumulates property of her own, it is not inherited by her children to the exclusion of the other members of her matrilineal group.

THE INDEPENDENCE OF HOUSEHOLDS

The independence of a household is assured by the dominant position of the husband and the control he has over his wife and children. Various restrictions affecting relationships within the nuclear family operate to secure the autonomy of the individual households in which its members function and dramatize the severance between them.

These restrictions are of greatest force between a man or woman and his or her oldest child. A father may never handle the negotiations for the marriage of his oldest child; he must appoint someone else to represent his interests. If the oldest child is a daughter, neither father nor mother should receive any portion of her bridewealth. They may hold bridewealth for subsequent daughters, but it is more graceful for them to turn it over to other kinsmen. When a daughter is sent to her husband, the father's representative pours an offering at the door and announces, "I now throw away my daughter, so-and-so. She has gone to be married to such-and-such." But the father himself may not make the offering nor should he be present when she leaves. Neither parent may follow the bridal party to take part in the further ceremonies. Parents are honored guests, but they must never sleep inside the house of a married son or daughter; other accommodations must be found for them. A child may never sleep with his or her spouse (or a lover) within the parental house, though a married daughter may stay there if she comes to visit by herself. A mature son always finds other sleeping accommodations. The oldest child may never be attached to the parental household for the probationary period of marriage.

Children equally have no right to intervene in the sexual life of their parents. A son may not hold his mother's bridewealth. If she is a widow or divorcee, he may not sue her lover or act as his mother's representative in claiming damages. A son should not have an affair with his father's wives, whom he should treat as mothers. If a son breaks this taboo, it is a greater offense than if a sister's son were involved. Sons do not inherit these women after their father's death, and they should never marry one who has been their father's wife or mistress. The father should not marry the ex-wife or mistress of his son. Either action is disreputable and borders on incest. It is definitely regarded as incest if a daughter has an affair with her mother's husband.

Parents are discouraged from interfering in the households of their children. In the courts today interfering parents are told: "You must not meddle in your child's household. Your child now belongs to another house. If you meddle, you will ruin the marriage. You have no right there." Such strictures are usually directed against parents, though the meddling of other kin may be equally damaging. Some parents conscientiously refrain from meddling, and old widows may remain in hamlets where they have no close relatives in preference to moving into the vicinity of their children. Nonetheless, parents are suspect, especially the parents of the wife. Men resent a woman's visit to her parents, fearing that she will there find encouragement to love affairs or plans for a new marriage. They also resent the refuge against ill-treatment that a wife finds with her parents or her mother's brother. In a number of instances men were accused of attempting to poison their parents-in-law or the wife's mother's brother with the hope that their wives, deprived of a refuge, would become more subject to them. Informants say that this is not uncommon. The husband's relatives seem to impinge less upon the sphere of the wife, or women are more long-suffering. At least I know of no instances where a wife was accused of sorcery against them, and informants thought it an unlikely proceeding.

SIBLING RELATIONSHIPS

Uterine siblings are recognized as having a close bond which must be countered lest it wreck the dogma that the matrilineal group is undifferentiated. Despite this, proximate siblings are thought to have an underlying hostility towards one another because of "milk." A child is expected to dislike its next younger sibling who robbed it of its mother's milk, and this dislike is reciprocated. It is expected to have a very close relationship with the second following sibling, for whose care it is generally responsible. But the expectation of antagonism and affection is not formalized into any institution of linked siblings.

"Milk" may lie only between uterine siblings. Their identity also appears in other ways. It was once the custom for children to have their upper front teeth removed at about puberty. Uterine brothers had their front teeth removed in strict order of seniority; in the same fashion, uterine sisters also followed the rule of seniority. Marriage should occur by seniority; brother following brother, and sister following sister.

Sexual taboos are strong between uterine siblings and only secondarily enforced against classificatory siblings. No uterine sibling may receive a share in the trifling gifts distributed to classificatory siblings of a bride. A man should have no contact with cattle of his uterine sister's bridewealth. If he drinks the milk or eats the meat, he may become sterile. Careful fathers avoid the danger by sending bridewealth from their daughters to other relatives. No man may be consulted about his sister's marriage, hold bridewealth for her, or intervene in her quarrels with her husband. A man may not sit upon his sister's bridal stool, which in some situations is a symbol of the marriage. Brother and sister should never sit or lie on the bed where the other has slept with his or her spouse. These last rules apply between classificatory as well as uterine siblings.

Sisters may share neither the same lover nor the same husband; brothers may not have the same mistress. For a man to have an affair with the wife of his uterine brother is incest. It is reprehensible to have an affair with the wife of a classificatory brother. A brother and sister might marry a sister and brother, but the marriage is disliked on the grounds that it closely associates brother and sister in their sexual lives. When a man or woman dies, the surviving spouse is purified by ritual intercourse with a member of the matrilineal group of the dead, but a uterine sibling should never be chosen for this purpose. If the matrilineal group wishes to continue the alliance with the husband, they may not offer a uterine sister of the dead woman as a substitute wife; they must find a woman from another womb. A man should never inherit his uterine brother's widow, though this is happening more frequently today.

In other respects the relationships between siblings are not hedged with great formality. Sisters have great freedom with one another. They rarely quarrel openly, but if they do it is patched up with no great harm done. An older sister frequently rears a younger one sent to her as a nursemaid for her first baby and then stays on to grow up in the household. As for male siblings, it is openly acknowledged that brothers often fight. If they come to blows, they come to blows, but it is not malweza and there is no ritual reconciliation. For a man to strike a sister *is* malweza, and it is regarded more seriously than physical violence offered to a father, a mother, or a mother's brother. (The last is hardly malweza at all.) The Tonga can give no reason why quarrels between brother and sister are considered more serious than quarrels between other relatives. I think it relates to the fact that a man's eventual security in a body of matrilineal kinsmen lies through his sister. He may quarrel with his brother and lose contact with him; that is simply the loss of a man. If he quarrels with his sister and loses contact with her, he has lost the source of the matrilineal group. If sisters quarrel and move apart, each is capable of initiating a new matrilineal group.

Sisters therefore may quarrel; brothers may be at violent odds; but brother and sister must never quarrel nor should a man use harsh words to his sister. Brother and sister should always deal in tones of friendly concern.

In later life the relationship between siblings is affected by the development of their interest in their own households. This may strain their friendship. Brothers may live in the same village but they rarely inhabit contiguous huts. Usually they move apart when each feels strong enough to have his own homestead; frequently they live in different neighborhoods, sometimes miles apart. They usually summon one another to consult on matters of general concern and expect to help each other in an emergency. They may arrange to hold the bridewealth for one another's daughters and are very likely to provide the animal killed by the father's side for a girl's puberty ceremony. But each brother has absolute claims over his own household and over any property that he acquires. When a man dies, his uterine brother will probably be declared *musololi,* the leader of his funeral and the administrator of his estate until the inheritance is arranged. He will receive a portion of the estate, but probably no larger or only slightly larger a portion than that which is inherited by any other male of the matrilineal group. Despite this, each is likely to suspect the other of sorcery against him.

Brother and sister may live in close proximity for many years. It is fairly common for a man to settle either with his sister and her husband or with his wife's brother. The two households then may coalesce in many activities and form a single unit for the preparation and consumption of food. A widow or a divorcee may live with her brother, but he must build her a separate hut. In any event, if a man grows wealthy he is likely to begin to view his sister and her children with only slightly veiled hostility. Their presence is a constant reminder of the ultimate rights of his matrilineal group to his estate. He may admit that he ought to help his sister and her children: that he should provide food if they are hungry; that he should help with clothing and school fees; that he should help pay claims against his nephews as they grow older, and assist them with bridewealth; that he should help them find fields and begin the accumulation of farming equipment. At the same time he may claim the boys to herd his cattle or help in his fields, and in any emergency he calls upon his sister's daughters to help in his own household. He expects eventually to lose his sister's daughters to their husbands, but the attempts of his sister's sons to establish autonomy are met with resistance. They are his potential heirs and they ought to remain attached to his household to contribute their work to the building up of the estate. If they stay, he then begins to suspect them of anticipating their inheritance by becoming the lovers of his wife, and he also suspects them of sorcery. He, on the other hand, may be suspected of bewitching them. The tension that then lies between a man and his sister's sons reflects back into the brother-sister relationship. She may accuse him of sorcery and blame him for the death of her children. In one instance a frightened and suspicious woman induced her son to dispose of her brother with a hatchet after a number of deaths had been laid at his door.

The Matrilineal Group and the Wider Field of Kinship Relationships

THE UNDIFFERENTIATED MATRILINEAL GROUP

In Tonga dogma, the matrilineal group is not internally differentiated into segments based on common descent. The Tonga admit that uterine siblings may feel themselves a unit in contrast to other members of the group; that the own mother is usually more important than a classificatory mother; and that a man is likely to take a greater interest in his own sister's children than in classificatory sisters' children. But these are unpleasant facts rather than values enshrined in the social structure.

Rights and obligations vest in the matrilineal group as such and not in particular segments. I have suggested elsewhere that this may be due to the dispersed nature of the group:

Members of a matrilineal group who do live close together are also in constant associations with people who belong to other groups—indeed, the majority of their associates will be outsiders. Since people are surrounded by outsiders, amongst whom they live and with whom they cooperate in ordinary activities, membership within the matrilineal group as a whole is the overwhelming fact that they stress. The relationships which they have with outsiders are different in kind from those which they have with each other, and the differences in degree that may mark their own relationship sink into unimportance and are barely recognized in the dogma of the group. This is the more true since members of a matrilineal group act alone on very few occasions. Their corporate activity takes place within situations where outsiders are also present. At a funeral, and in subsequent mourning ceremonies, all those living in one neighborhood should participate. All attend, but the members of the matrilineal group concerned have special roles in the ceremony. Girls' puberty ceremonies are occasions for general neighborhood gatherings, but again the matrilineal group involved has a special role to play. Formerly when they gathered to protect a member, or to seek vengeance for some offense against him, they were posed as a united group against a similarly mobilized unit. People see themselves therefore in general as members of an undifferentiated body of matrilineal kinsmen, in contrast to the outsiders who are also present (Colson, 1954: 37).

To ignore for the moment the matter of generation, it can be said that the customary rules governing inheritance and the rights to seek asylum and protection are in conformity with the dogma of unity. Uterine siblings and their descendants have no greater right than other members of the group to share in an estate. Indeed, uterine brothers, though they may inherit property from one another, may not inherit one another's households. A woman's bridewealth is not necessarily taken by her own mother's brothers to the exclusion of her classificatory mother's brothers, though today there is a tendency for this to happen. Men accumulate property for their bridewealth by approaching any matrilineal relative whom they think likely to be able to help them.

The dogma is also reflected in ritual, for each matrilineal group is thought to have a single body of ancestral spirits, any one of whom may affect any member of the group, and to whom all members of the line have an equal right to appeal. Any fully adult person may approach these ancestors on his own behalf. Ancestral shrines and localized foci for the ancestral cult do not exist.

Matrilineal groups are thus structurally undifferentiated. They are also usually small, which is probably a reflection of the first condition. An undifferentiated body grows unwieldy as it increases in size. The fact that the group is supposed to coöperate as a body with various other matrilineal groups which have either begotten its members or which contain the children of its male members is also relevant here. Small groups can coöperate in this manner without undue strain. Large ones would find it either difficult or impossible to maintain such relationships unless a rigid system of preferential mating kept the number of coöperating groups at a minimum. This, however, would defeat the effective role of the interplay of a diffuse network of kinship ties in maintaining peace throughout a region.

To maintain the system, matrilineal groups must lose members. Geographical mobility provides for this, since those who wander too far away to be able to maintain close ties are automatically eliminated.

GENERATION

The differentiation within a matrilineal group which is stressed is based on generation. Alternate generations are classed together and aligned against proximate generations. Among the men of a matrilineal group there are only three kinship categories: brother, mother's brother, sister's son. Men of alternate generations call each other "brother"; men of proximate generations call each other "mother's brother" and "sister's son." This distinction is of some importance as between the men themselves, but it is most emphasized as it outlines their rights and obligations to the women of the group.

Thus, no brother may be involved in the marriage of a woman whom he calls sister, nor may he hold her bridewealth. Instead, he has responsibility for the marriages of his sisters' daughters and in this his sisters' sons may not interfere. He may not intervene in the marriages of his sisters' daughters' daughters, who are again his sisters; the marriages of these women are in the hands of his sisters' sons. Brothers are roughly equated as equals, though they differentiate among themselves according to seniority of birth. No brother has authority over another brother, including a sister's daughter's son. Brothers are all "fathers" to each other's children and share a common responsibility for them. Once a man is dead, his paternal role is taken over by his brothers, and for this reason his ideal successor is found in a brother who comes from a different womb.

"Mother's brother" and "sister's son" have a different type of relationship. Mother's brother has authority and should be treated with respect. To a certain extent he is equated with "mother" and in him vest the rights that a mother has over her children. Mothers' brothers arrange the marriages of their sisters' daughters and hold their bridewealth. They share with the fathers of these women the responsibility for the maintenance of the marriage. Formerly the mother's brothers had the right to sell their sister's child into slavery, though I could not learn if the right was vested in a single individual or if it could be exercised only with the consent of all the mother's brothers. It is the mother's brother who should represent the matrilineal group in any incident in which a person is concerned. It is also the mother's brother who has the greatest obligation to provide support and assistance. A man claims bridewealth from his mother's brothers with a greater assurance than he asks his brothers for assistance. The claim for assistance, however, is not based on a claim against the man who holds the mother's bridewealth, for this is not held by any man of the mother's brother's generation.

Women are less clearly placed in respect to one another. Usually their relationships are phrased in terms of sisters, mother-daughter, and grandmother-granddaughter. But grandmother and granddaughter may be classed together as sisters, and even address one another as such on occasion.

KINSHIP TERMINOLOGY

Within the matrilineal group, there are the following sets of relationships:

> brother-brother
> sister-sister
> sister-brother
> mother-child
> mother's brother-sister's child
> grandmother-grandchild.

The last pair may be equated with the brother-sister or the sister-
sister relationship, but otherwise there is no uncertainty about the
usuage. All members of the group are collectively referred to as
basimukowa.

Each person is also related to another matrilineal group, his
basyanausi, the people of the father. Here the principle of equating
alternate generations and the custom of cross-cousin marriage are at
odds and make for some confusion in terminology. All those whom the
father calls "brother" are "fathers" and their children (who are not
basyanausi) are siblings. All women whom the father calls "sister" are
today called "mother," and they in turn call the child of any brother by
the term for child. Formerly there was a special term for "father's
sister," but informants are uncertain if a woman also had a special
term for her brother's child. Children of father's sister and children of
mother's brother are cross-cousins, a relationship of licensed familiarity.
Bilateral cross-cousin marriage was formerly a preferred marriage and
even today it is fairly common, though coming into disrepute. This
introduces some ambiguity into the relationship with the children of
father's sister's daughter. Since you may marry their mother, they may
be children. Since they are equated with your father, they are "mother"
and "father." Father's sister's son does not produce members of the
basyanausi. Usually people do not use kinship terms for his children
unless some actual marriage has renewed the tie. But female ego,
since she may marry their father, may refer to them as "child"; her
brother can therefore refer to them as "sister's child." Mother's brother's
children's children may be similarly treated, or they become simply
grandchildren since they tend to treat all members of their grandfather's group as one.

Father's mother is "grandmother." Her brother is usually called "grandfather," though within his own matrilineal group he is equated with the paternal cross-cousin. Father's father and mother's father are "grandfather." They all respond with the term "grandchild." But there is a difference in attitude toward some persons classified as grandparents and grandchildren which contrasts them with others also placed in this category. Mother's mother who is usually "grandmother," is treated as a sibling and joking (especially with any sexual overtones) is forbidden. Joking is permitted with father's mother and father's mother's brother who are assimilated to cross-cousins. Joking is also characteristic of the relationship with father's father and mother's father, and here it is extended to include all those of the matrilineal groups of these men. All the males are grandfathers, all the females grandmothers.

The matrilineal groups of father's father and mother's father have no real role to play in relation to their "grandchildren." Real authority has passed from them to the basyanausi and basimukowa. The grandparental groups receive only a small token from the bridewealth of their granddaughters and are not expected to assist with the bridewealth of their grandsons. Marriage back into the matrilineal groups of either father's father or mother's father is considered an excellent thing, though marriage with the real grandfather is not permitted.

Great-grandfathers are so remote that they are no longer classified as kin, and there is no cultural norm for dealing with the matrilineal groups to which they belonged. For that matter, few people can remember the names or group affiliations of great grandparents who have been dead for any length of time.

Affinal ties are of considerable importance. All men married to women of a matrilineal group have special obligations to it. When the matrilineal group is involved in a ceremony where many people attend, it is to these affines that it looks for assistance. The men act as brothers, get the firewood, cook the food, and perform the other work about the homestead. Most of the labor falls to the more recently married men, while those who have been long married can relax and perform only token labor. Any affine married to a woman of the matrilineal group is considered an ideal person to act as an intermediary if the group has to negotiate a contentious matter. The affine has its interests at heart, since his children are members of it, but he is not so closely identified as to be considered a party to the dispute.

Nevertheless, one does not distinguish in terminology between affines married to members of one's matrilineal group and all other affines. Instead, affines are divided into two categories, according to the generation of the spouse. Sister's husband and brother's wife (either sex speaking), husband's sister, husband's brother, wife's brother, and wife's sister are equated and with them are included spouse's grandparents and grandchild's spouse. All are *mukwaasi*. This is a joking relationship comparable to that existing between cross cousins. Indeed the term mukwaasi and the term for spouse can be extended to the cross cousin. Cross cousin's spouse is rarely called by a kinship term, but some people say that mukwaasi might be used.

All other affines, i.e., those of proximate generations, are *mukwe* and avoidance is the rule. Mukwe include all of spouse's parents' generation and the spouses of all those in the generation called "child" or "sister's child." The rigid avoidance goes into abeyance some years after marriage, though some vestige always remains. The avoidance is always least between a man or woman and the real parents of the spouse, and between a man and the person who poured the offering when the wife was first sent to him. Ego is likely to address spouse's own parents with the terms "father" and "mother," and over the years the relationship with them may develop into something resembling the parent-child relationship.

Other affinal relatives are likely to be addressed in terms drawn from consanguineal relationships. Thus all "fathers'" wives are addressed as "mother," and so is mother's brother's wife. The husbands of all "mothers," including father's sister's husband, may be addressed as "fathers." The husbands of all "grandmothers" are "grandfathers"; the wives of all "grandfathers" are "grandmothers." Behavior should be in accordance with the term used though it is recognized that this is only a courtesy extension of the term.

Affinal terms are applied only between the person who contracts a marriage and the relatives of his or her spouse. The respective relatives of the two spouses are not thought to be in a direct relationship and they do not adopt kinship terms for one another. Thus husband's mother and wife's mother do not use kinship terms. The paternal and maternal relatives of both spouses are brought into close contact with each other through the creation of the marriage, but they see their common interests as vesting first in the particular household created by the couple and then in the offspring of that household. They do not thereby become kinsmen to one another.

So far I have outlined the kinship terminology as though it were regularly applied. The use of terms in reference is fairly regular, but in address the Tonga use terms in a haphazard fashion without much regard to actual behavior but rather as courtesy forms of address to those whom they encounter. They may also dispense with kinship terms of address even when dealing with close relatives and use instead clan names, teknonymous names, or nicknames.

The term *mukwesu*, which is said to mean sibling—though it is rarely used for anyone regarded as a real sibling—may be used as a form of address to any member of one's own clan or to any child of one's father's clan. The term for "father" may be used to any older man who is not one's mother's brother; for that matter I have heard it used to younger men and even to women. The term "mother" may likewise be extended to any older woman or to any female. Grandfather and grand-mother are less widely used, probably because people prefer to be addressed as "father" or "mother," but the terms may be applied to all members of the grandfathers' clans; these people then reply with "grandchild." Cross-cousin terms and the terms for mother's brother and sister's child are more strictly applied. The latter terms tend to be held within the matrilineal group, but it is perfectly regular for a man to use the term for "sister's child" for the children of his female paternal parallel cousin; they reply with "mother's brother."

Kinship terms as such, at least in their wider usage, are of slight importance to the Tonga, who think systematic usage is important only with respect to those belonging to the basimukowa and the basyanausi. I amused them by attempts to work out what they should call remote relatives. After careful consideration they usually agreed that the term could be used, but would add that nobody would be fool enough to bother.

PREFERENTIAL AND PROHIBITED MARRIAGES

In this section I shall draw together material scattered throughout previous sections on preferential and proscribed marriages. The Tonga would sum up the rules by saying: it is a good thing to marry where you already have relatives, either consanguineal or affinal; it is wrong for two closely related siblings of the same sex to marry those who are also closely related siblings; if between relatives, marriages must be within the appropriate generation; no marriage may occur within the clan, or between siblings.

Clans are exogamous save with respect to those brought into the clan through slavery. Slaves were always affiliated to the clan and the matri-lineal group of their owner, but this did not create a barrier to mar-riage for the first and second generation. Once the slave link was for-gotten, the rule of clan exogamy was applied. Clan exogamy is still accepted. In twenty-two villages I recorded only two instances of intra-clan marriage where a slave link was not involved. In one instance the couple also belonged to the same matrilineal group, which made the matter still more disgusting for the Tonga. When I asked how such a marriage could occur, informants said simply, "They must know in their own hearts why they did such a thing. They must be fierce people." Sexual relations between clan members, and thus between members of the same matrilineal group, are also regarded as incest but occur more often. I recorded two instances of incest between a man and his sister's daughter, three instances involving classificatory brothers and sisters, and one involving a woman and her classificatory son.

All marriage and sexual intercourse is prohibited between brothers and sisters whether or not they are of the same clan and matrilineal group. Paternal half-siblings, paternal parallel cousins, and the children of any two men of a matrilineal group who call one another brother are thus prohibited. One may marry a child of one's father's clan. The children of paternal half-brothers would probably be forbidden to marry. Maternal half-siblings and maternal parallel cousins are forbidden to marry, but the majority of these marriages are also banned by clan exogamy. I have recorded no instances of such marriages. Occasionally people so related, as the children of two classificatory "brothers," have become lovers, but the affair is treated as incestuous when discovered.

Marriage or sexual relations between father and daughter, or mother and son, are considered incestuous. This applies equally to classificatory relationships, but I am not sure how far the barrier to marriage is extended. In one instance a man's heir was the paternal half-sister's son of the widow. He wished to inherit her and found some support for the scheme among his matrilineal kin. The widow refused, arguing that it was unthinkable that she should marry her "son." In other instances, those who have stood in a father-daughter or mother-son relationship because of the classification together of alternate generations have pressed a marriage against the wishes of their kinsmen and finally succeeded in carrying their point. Two instances of such irregular marriages occur in figure 1–2. The marriages are definitely irregular, but I do not think that they are classified as incestuous. Marriage between a real grandparent and grandchild is prohibited and is probably incestuous. Marriage between classificatory relatives of this type is desirable.

Marriage of a man to two closely related women is almost equivalent to incest. Two women of the same matrilineal group may not be married simultaneously to the same man, nor should paternal half-siblings, paternal parallel cousins, a woman and her brother's daughter, a

woman and her paternal half-sister's daughter. Two closely related
men of the same matrilineal group should not marry closely related
women of another matrilineal group. Headstrong men and women may
set at naught the wishes of their relatives and enter into these forbidden marriages. In one instance a man married two women who
were daughters of full brothers; in another instance two men who
were maternal parallel cousins married women who were full sisters.
Neither set of marriages was liked, and the first was considered a rank
scandal.

The Tonga are likely to cite such marriages as the result of the breakdown of the controls exercised by the kinship groups. But there has
always been a possibility of acquiring a semilegality for unions which
are looked upon with disfavor, for each matrilineal group is concerned
only with upholding its own kinship rules. The offended matrilineal
group may refuse its consent and give no recognition to the marriage.
The other group may given its consent and recognize the marriage. The
man who married the paternal parallel cousin of his wife was unable to
obtain the consent of the woman's father's matrilineal group. They
refused to recognize the marriage and would not visit his homestead
except at times of mourning. The woman's own matrilineal group,
which was not related to the first wife, gave its consent, accepted
bridewealth, and proceeded to treat the marriage as an established
fact. A man who married his mother's mother's brother's daughter—a
woman who ranked as his father's sister and therefore terminologically
was his "mother"—had no support from his own matrilineal group who
were the "fathers" of the woman. They refused to take bridewealth,
chortled each time his wife left him, and in general made it clear that
they did not recognize this as a real marriage. The woman's matrilineal
group accepted the marriage. In neither case would the older people
of either group have arranged a marriage of this type. Faced with an
accomplished fact, the group which is not directly concerned is inclined to accept it.

The reaction of the offended group is a characteristic Tonga sanction.
If a person is not consulted when he should be or if his advice is
flouted, he refuses to concern himself with the results of any action
taken. When a woman complained about the brutality of her husband
to a member of her matrilineal group, the man replied, "I agree with
you. I never wanted you to marry him. But your father arranged the
marriage without consulting me, so I can do nothing in this affair. It
concerns only your father." The guardian of another woman arranged
her marriage without consulting her other "mother's brothers" or her

"fathers." These people then refused to avoid the husband as an affine, claiming that they had no knowledge of the marriage since they had not been consulted. They told the husband to avoid only the guardian, the only one who "knew" about the marriage. The guardian later impounded the wife when the husband failed to pay increased demands for bridewealth. The husband approached the woman's closest relatives to ask for their intervention. They said that they would like to help him but that they could do nothing, never having been consulted about the marriage.

Approved marriages were either with those classified as cross cousins or with classificatory grandparents or grandchildren, or with those to whom there was some previous affinal link. Marriage with a clan joking partner was also considered desirable because such a marriage gave some protection to a spouse in association with affinal relatives, since the single marriage was then not the only link between them. It was also argued that people ought to marry within the same neighborhood, as this was the most effective protection of all. Today there is no longer this emphasis upon protection, since a wider organization has assumed responsibility for maintaining peace and order. The Tonga are moving away from preferential marriage arrangements based on kinship, and certain types of preferred marriages are beginning to be considered undesirable. Some people now say that cross-cousin marriages are wrong, but too many of the extant marriages fall into this category for there to be any feeling that they are incestuous.

In sixteen villages, 23 per cent of the extant marriages were between cross cousins. Marriage with mother's brother's daughter accounted for 13 per cent, marriage with father's sister's daughter for 10 per cent. Both personal cross-cousin and classificatory cross-cousin marriages are included in the figures. The trend away from cross-cousin marriage, however, is shown in the material relating to the marriages of the males of seven villages which occurred between September, 1946, and August, 1950. These men married as follows:

Mother's brother's daughter	3
Father's sister's daughter	1
Inherited wives	4
Woman related by some consanguineal tie other than cross-cousin	3
Woman related by affinal tie	11
Unrelated women	34

If this material is representative, the great majority of Tonga marriages today are between nonrelated men and women. I have also classified these marriages by locality as intra-village, intra-neighborhood but not intra-village, and between neighborhoods. The results are as follows:

Intra-village 10
Intra-neighborhood 15
Between neighborhoods 31

The numbers involved are small, but if these villages are typical, then marriages between consanguineal kin are becoming rare, but there is still a strong tendency for people to marry within their neighborhood.

In any event, cross-cousin marriages must always have been a minor proportion of all marriages, since it ran counter to the rule that closely related men should not marry wives who were closely related to one another. The Tonga have tended to invest their marriages in building up a diffuse network of relationships with many different matrilineal groups represented within a series of neighborhoods, in preference to channeling them in a single direction which would reinforce but a single set of ties.

Summary

Tonga society is composed of several types of units organized on different principles; of these, groups based on residence and kinship are the most important. In the kinship groups the rule of matrilineal descent is emphasized. In residence, personal choice is the rule. Yet the basic building blocks of the local units consist of independent households under the direction of the husband and father. Each household head is also a member of his matrilineal group, which has an interest in the maintenance of his household. This forms part of his estate which the group has the right to inherit. Men rise to positions of prominence within a local community through their control of households, which are based on their wives and children who are members of other matrilineal groups. Within the household therefore you find a focus for the intersecting interests of a number of different matrilineal groups.

This interdependence of kinship groups is doubled because each person is affiliated too with his father's matrilineal group, which also has an interest in the household of its child. Each household is a nexus for the coöperation of four matrilineal groups, but the same groups should not have similar interests relating to a series of households. This is prevented by the rule that a man may not be married simultaneously to two women who bear a close relationship to one another and that two closely related men may not have wives who are closely related. Marriages therefore involve each matrilineal group with many others of its kind, and their coöperation is necessary if the household units are to function without disruption.

The high degree of geographical mobility is probably related to the relative independence of the household, which sets it free to shift its residence without regard to the residence of the kinsmen of its members. At the same time the incorporation of its members into a number of matrilineal groups gives it protection if it does not move outside the range of effective kinship relationships.

With the scattering of kinsmen and neolocal residence, there is a lack of internal organization within matrilineal groups and also a lack of institutionalized leadership. Clashes between generations are played down by the rules which prevent those of proximate generations from quarreling over rights in the women of the group and the children of these women. Each generation of men is assigned rights over a particular generation of women, but this very rule makes it difficult for one man to dominate the whole of his kinship group. Nevertheless the emphasis upon the generational principle is a factor in preventing the internal differentiation of the group into segments based on descent.

Today the development of cash-crop farming, with the possibility of accumulating wealth, is intensifying the tensions in a system based on a male-centered household combined with matrilineal inheritance. Moreover, as the old functions of vengeance and protection have dropped away from the matrilineal group while inheritance and rights to economic assistance are coming to the fore as unifying principles, there is a tendency for groups to break down into small bodies of uterine siblings and their immediate descendants through females. Many Tonga, especially those who are most involved in the new economic systems, desire a shift to familial inheritance, and this will probably occur in the not too distant future.

Meanwhile most Tonga are still sufficiently close to the subsistence level and still sufficiently imbued with the old values that there has been neither a shift to familial inheritance nor a complete repudiation of the old dogma that the matrilineal group is basic to society and that within it all members are equally related.

Navaho

An attempt to describe the kinship system of the Navaho on the basis of the available data must be considered foolhardy or valiant. There is so much published material on the Navaho that this essay cannot pretend to cover it thoroughly (cf. Kluckhohn and Spencer, 1940). Sources on kinship span at least a hundred years, and differences in reporting must partly reflect historical changes. In addition, there are significant regional variations. Authorities agree that Navaho kinship relationships are exceedingly flexible and have been for some time. There are numerous acceptable alternatives in some situations and competing norms in others. Where there has been much research, there is something less than complete agreement. No less than twelve field workers have tried to pin down the Navaho clan group system, and have provided us with twelve somewhat different solutions (Packard, 1882; Matthews, 1890; Franciscan Fathers, 1910; Curtis, 1907–1930; Reichard, 1928; Sapir, MS; Hill, n.d.; Carr, Spencer, and Woolley, 1939; Government Survey, MS; and Haile, 1941). There are important disagreements about some norms. Three reports on kinship terminology vary slightly (Reichard, 1928; Haile, 1941; Hill as reported in Bellah, 1952).

When this chapter was first drafted, in the summer of 1954, I was tempted to believe that ethnological work on the Navaho had been of poor quality. More and more immersion in the data has convinced me that the ethnographers are not vague, but are reporting a situation of genuine flexibility and are reflecting the broad range of past and present variability among the Navahos. This essay will attempt, among other things, to account for this flexibility and variability. There is, furthermore, a consistency among reporters on major details. Had my own field work among the Navaho been primarily in the area of kinship, it might not have taken so long for me to accept flexibility and variation. As it is, I do not have very much field data of my own to fall back on. There are, however, some critical gaps in the published

record, and at such points I have sometimes supplied my own con-
structions, for later testing.

This chapter is based on the major authorities, on unpublished
manuscript sources kindly lent me by a number of people, on published
life histories, and on a few interviews with informants.[1] My use of unpublished materials and the existence of conflicting views on important
points have faced me with a special editorial problem. To report the
results of the analysis of unpublished data is simply to add another
opinion to the many now available, and to report only my own views
where there are others is misleading. For the benefit of the general
reader I have presented broad conclusions or omitted detail at certain points in the chapter, assembling the substantiation or further
information in a section entitled "Supporting Evidence."

The Navaho Country

The present Navajo Reservation [2] occupies a territory of about 23,500
square miles, mainly in northeastern Arizona but reaching into Utah
and New Mexico (*The Navajo Yearbook*, 1957: 131; hereafter des-

[1] Through the kindness of Clyde Kluckhohn, I have had access to the field notes
of the Ramah project, and to manuscript field notes of W. W. Hill, Edward Sapir,
and Robert L. Packard. Robert W. Young, of the Navaho Agency, has made Government Survey materials available to me, and these have been of particular assistance. The Soil Conservation Corps Economic Survey (here called Government Survey) consisted of the following professional staff: Frederick H. Blair,
Jr., J. Nixon Hadley, Gordon B. Page, Solon T. Kimball, John H. Provinse, and,
for part of the time, Lloyd Fisher and Truman Peebles; the Navaho staff included:
Thomas Attson, Dannie Bia, Alfred Bowman, Phillip Emerson, Nelson Gorman,
and Hoske Naswood. Several of the professional staff—in particular, John H.
Provinse and J. Nixon Hadley—have provided helpful comments. The data of
the survey include: a concordance of several authorities' clan groupings and a final
grouping which is more satisfactory than any other known to me; a reasonably
complete census of clan membership in sixteen out of eighteen administrative units
of the Navajo Reservation; a census of inter-clan marriages for the same areas;
a list of types and frequencies of Navaho households. The Social Science Research
Council provided informant fees which made it possible to work intensively for
four days with Jimmie Dapah, a Navaho formerly of Coolidge and Pinedale. I have
benefited from criticisms supplied by Clyde Kluckhohn, Evon Z. Vogt, and the late
Gladys Reichard, and from new data supplied by Clyde Kluckhohn. David Goldberg has advised me in the analysis of some of the Government Survey data. I have
had statistical and clerical assistance from Hope Leichter, Robert L. Carroll, and
David P. Street. Funds for this assistance were supplied by the Social Science
Research Council and by a Ford Foundation Behavioral Studies Grant. A Faculty
Released Time Grant from the Horace H. Rackham School of Graduate Studies of
the University of Michigan provided time for the final revision of this chapter.

[2] The official designation for the reservation is "Navajo"; the standard ethnological designation for the tribe is "Navaho." This accounts for the apparent vacilla-
tion in spelling which characterizes this essay.

ignated TNY). In addition, however, there is a large area in north-western New Mexico adjoining the reservation where Navahos live on trust-patent lands, intermingled with the holdings of white ranchers and farmers. The extent of these holdings is not known to me. There are also two separate Navaho enclaves in New Mexico, at Puertocito and Canyoncito. The Ramah Navaho, although administratively detached from the Navajo Agency, and only weakly affiliated with the reservation Navaho, are not so completely cut off as these other groups. The tribe, which is said to be increasing at about 2 per cent yearly, now numbers around 78,000 (TNY, 1957: 310).[3] Density figures for 1950 were: Arizona, 1.9 per square mile; New Mexico (reservation only), 3.7 per square mile (*ibid.:* 277–278). The land is definitely overpopulated for the present mode of subsistence.

In altitude the country ranges from 2,800 to 10,000 feet above sea level, almost all of it at elevations between 4,000 and 7,000. Fifty-five per cent of the area is classified as desert, 37 per cent as steppe, and 8 per cent as humid (*ibid.:* 132). Mean annual rainfall varies in different areas from 5 to nearly 13 inches per annum, with a rough association between altitude and amount of rain. Killing frosts vary considerably, so that the growing season may be as long as 200 days, or as short as 90. Summer rains may be torrential and destructive or there may be serious drought. Agriculture is always a precarious business. Minor irrigation, using floodwaters, is common, but intensive irrigation with works of any size is feasible in only a few places. In recent years there have been government irrigation projects at such sites. Finally, the country has been on the downgrade of an erosion cycle since 1880. Erosion seems to have been rapidly accelerated by overgrazing, which has been observable since at least 1915. Erosion has reduced available farm and pasture land, while overgrazing has caused a retrogression in the quality of forage for stock. (Foregoing section except as noted from Hill, 1938.) The country is rugged and beautiful, but difficult for farming and herding.

Navaho History

Navaho is an Apachean language, and the Apachean group belongs to the Athabaskan linguistic stock. On the basis of lexicon, distribution data, and glottochronology, it can be regarded as a certainty that the Apacheans originated in Canada and migrated to the Southwest,

[3] This essay was drafted in 1954 and revised in 1959. I have attempted to bring it up to date at only a few points, since there has been very rapid change on the Navaho reservation in the past few years.

probably as a group (Sapir, in Mandelbaum, 1949: 213–224, 456–457; Hoijer, 1938 and 1956; for the theoretical basis see Sapir, *op. cit.*: 455–458; Dyen, 1956). This implies that the proto-Apacheans were hunters and gatherers, with small local groups and a low level of political integration. The Apacheans are thought to have arrived in the Southwest 900 years ago or less. Possible proto-Navaho ruins date from A.D. 1106, identifiable Navaho sites from A.D. 1541—the year of Coronado's arrival in the Southwest (Underhill 1956: 16, 24; the dates are based on dendrochronology).

The archeological record indicates that, before the Navaho arrived, the Pueblos had certain cultural items which are now shared with the Navahos. Hence it can be inferred that the Navahos acquired from the Pueblos: agriculture, sand paintings, masks, altars, prayer sticks, etc. Through Pueblo contact the role of the "inspired" shaman, important in several other Apachean groups, must have been reduced to the diviner role, with concomitant development of the role of the learned singer. The Navaho, however, did not develop a Puebloan priesthood. At whatever time this absorption of Pueblo items began, it must have been facilitated by Pueblo-Navaho alliances against the Spanish in the early seventeenth century (Forbes, 1959: 199) and by the collapse of the Pueblo revolt of 1680. When the Spanish returned to the area, many Pueblo Indians fled and lived with the Navaho (Underhill, 1956: 41–51).

Having turned from hunting to a combination of agriculture and hunting through Pueblo contacts, the Navaho acquired livestock and techniques of animal husbandry based on Spanish patterns. These patterns were acquired through various chains of communication stretching ultimately to Mexico, as well as by direct contact with the Spanish and contact through the Pueblos. Horses were probably acquired as early as 1606. "From 1606 until the late 1620's the Navaho and the Indians of Jemez were the principal opponents of the Spanish and therefore the principal raiders for livestock" (Forbes, 1959: 202). Nevertheless, in 1630 Benavides speaks of the Navahos as "very great farmers," estimates their number at 30,000, which is impossibly high, and fails to mention any use of livestock (Underhill, 1956: 36). By the first half of the eighteenth century, Navaho possession of modest numbers of horses, sheep, goats, and cattle is amply attested. Depositions of Spanish witnesses recorded in 1745, covering the period 1706–1743, report Navaho herds of sheep and goats, and of small numbers of horses; they also record cattle tracks, although witnesses saw no cattle. Population estimates range from 2,000 to 4,000. Weaving of wool is mentioned. Most witnesses refer to "some small herds of sheep"; the largest number mentioned is 700 (Hill, 1940*a*).

Extensive weaving is reported by the second half of the eighteenth century, and a report of 1795 refers to their sheep as "innumerable" (Underhill, 1956: 68–69). Thus the transition from agriculture, hunting, and no livestock to agriculture, hunting, and extensive livestock, took something less than two hundred years. By the mid-nineteenth century, Navaho society was differentiated by wealth and by "slave" and free status. The rich seem primarily to have been interested in maintaining holdings and keeping the peace, the poor in raiding. "Slaves" were presumably captive non-Navahos; their descendants were free (based on Roessel, 1951; Underhill, 1956).[4]

Certain inferences about the Navaho period of agriculture and hunting may perhaps be drawn from a comparison with the Western Apache, who are, after the Navaho, the most agricultural of the Apaches, and who had not acquired any considerable amount of stock until recently. The comparison would suggest that during the period of agriculture and hunting, Navaho matrilineal clans, and sub-groups within clans, had some degree of localization based on the monopoly of adequate agricultural land—land, that is, which had some water resources. This same period would have seen the development or the intensification of the leadership of chiefs of local groups. Thus the installation of a headman described by Hill involves agricultural, not herding, hunting, or warfare ritual (Hill, 1940*b*). With the development of a livestock base, I assume, came an expansion of population (since more territory became exploitable), a greater flexibility of residence patterns (since agriculture was no longer so important for survival and hence agricultural lands with good water resources were less valuable), and probably an increase in the size of local groups.

In 1863 Kit Carson proceeded against the Navaho, whose relations with the surrounding Mexicans and Americans had become increasingly hostile. By destroying their crops and rounding up their livestock, he forced them to submit to internment at Fort Sumner, New Mexico, where they remained from 1864 to 1868. Over 8,000 entered Fort

---

[4] Roessel's work, although issued in mimeographed form, is not easily available. I have not personally consulted all the sources he has cited and quoted, but I list them here to make evaluation of my generalizations easier.

Thomas, Alfred B. *Forgotten Frontiers.* Norman, Okla., 1932.

Gregg, Josiah. *Commerce of the Prairies.* 1844.

Calhoun, James S. *The Official Correspondence of James S. Calhoun.* 1915.

Letherman, J. A sketch of the Navajo tribe of Indian Territory of New Mexico. *Tenth Annual Report of the Smithsonian Institution.* Washington, D.C., 1856.

Sumner and over 7,000 returned. Some Navahos hid out in the back country during this period—perhaps a few hundred, perhaps as many as 5,000. Thereafter the Navaho were effectively pacified. Ultimate legal control passed into the hands of the United States government. Beginning with a small amount of livestock issued by the government, the Navahos soon redeveloped large holdings. The period 1868 to 1933 was one of population and territorial expansion, and probably of relative well-being. Thus the Navaho almost completely rejected the Ghost Dance of 1890 (Mooney, 1896: 809–811; Hill, 1944) and had no major nativistic reactions until the late 1930's, during and following livestock reduction. At that time there were a few visions of the destruction of the whites and the peyote cult entered the area, spreading rapidly after 1936 (Aberle and Stewart, 1957).

Whether or not my reconstructions regarding social change among the Navaho are accepted, it is evident that in a period of 400 to 1,000 years the Navaho have gone from a simple hunting and gathering economy to one based on agriculture, hunting, and gathering, and from there to add livestock to their subsistence base. The last transition required less than 200 years. In the past 100 years came still other changes: increasing dependency on wages and marketing of herding surplus. Each of these major steps, it must be assumed, required significant modifications in kinship structure.

Navaho Economy

Navaho livelihood has four bases: farming, herding, crafts, and employment. A few parts of the country are primarily agricultural (Shiprock, Fruitland, Dinnehotso, Many Farms, and Canyon de Chelley). All except Canyon de Chelley are sites of government irrigation projects. Other areas depend heavily on herding, with very limited agriculture (principally the northwest and southwest parts of the reservation and the Black Mountain country). Here the growing season is too short or the rainfall too scanty for farming of any scope. The remainder is classified as mixed farming and herding. In all except the intensive agricultural areas farming provides subsistence crops, with little or no sale of produce. Corn, beans, squash, and sometimes potatoes are the principal crops.

Livestock was formerly the basis of wealth, prestige, and conspicuous consumption. It provides meat, one of the most important articles of gift exchange. Sheep are the main livestock base, used for meat, wool, and hides; goats are also important in the same ways. Horses are used for transportation and draft and are occasionally eaten. Formerly the owner of a large herd of horses had great prestige. There are burros and mules and a few cattle.

Many women card, spin, and weave the wool into blankets, for use or sale, and some men are skilled silversmiths. But craft activities do not seem to be a major source of income today.

At least as far back as 1881, when the railroad was being built near the reservation, Navaho men have been willing to do wage labor (Matthews, 1897: 22). This suggests that there was always a fair-sized group whose livestock and farm holdings were small enough to make other forms of income desirable and to make absence from home possible. In 1915, for example, 24 per cent of families on the southern Navajo Reservation had no sheep (TNY, 1957: 331). The government began livestock reduction in 1933 and systematic reduction in 1937, with serious effects for the economy.

The details of the grazing program are important for understanding the Navaho situation. The aim of the program was to reduce livestock to the carrying capacity of the reservation, and to do so by cutting the holdings of larger owners while maintaining smaller owners at their current levels. The reservation was divided into eighteen Land Management Units or districts. Range specialists calculated the carrying capacity of each district. A livestock census was made and livestock permits were then issued. A maximum permit was determined for each district. Every owner with more stock than the maximum permit was asked to sell off his stock until he no longer exceeded it. Owners with less than the maximum were frozen at their current level. Thereafter each owner was to sell stock each autumn to stay at or below his permit. No new permits were issued to new family heads after that date, although permits could be subdivided for inheritance.

The maximum permit varied by district, from 275 sheep units to 61. (One sheep or goat is one sheep unit, a cow is equivalent to four sheep units, a horse or a burro to five. These equivalencies are based on the amount of range required for each type of animal. A permit of 61 would allow, for example, 51 sheep and 2 horses, which is not sufficient to support a family.) In areas with very low regular permits, some individuals, often those who had not in fact reduced their stock, were given supplementary special permits. Even the largest regular permits, however, afforded only a fair livestock subsistence base. Permits were issued to Navahos who appeared on government rosters as "owners"— often the senior man of the household so appeared—and many actual owners were passed over in the process.

During the reduction period, livestock were improved by government programs so that more meat and wool were produced by the reduced herds than by the previous, more numerous ones. This increase, however, was only modest, and the frozen level of Navaho livestock did not in any way keep pace with a rising population. The Navaho reaction to the program was bitter.

No one can hold a permit larger than 350 sheep units (as of 1954). People purchase permits within these limits, but the cost is high and sellers are few. Even people with unfilled permits do not want to sell, since they might later want to use them.

The permit system was introduced to combat a serious overgrazing problem. With a rapidly increasing population the control of livestock holdings by the government also has the effect of forcing Navaho men and Navaho families into seasonal wage labor at an accelerating rate.[5] The main sources of jobs are the railroad section gang, towns near the reservation, and (especially for family labor) the bean, beet, and carrot fields.[6]

Most jobs either require a man to leave his family for part of a year or remove a family from the reservation for part of the year. Relatively few Navahos have settled permanently in towns, although the number is increasing. There is an active government resettlement program, but some Navahos have relocated without this assistance (for figures on recent resettlement, see TNY, 1957: 317).

As befits a sheepherding people, the Navaho settlement pattern is one of scattered nuclear or extended households, rather than the compact villages found among the Pueblo Indians.[7] There are denser settle-

[5] In 1953 interviews with random samples of individuals from Mexican Springs and Aneth showed that male respondents and the husbands of female respondents had been employed at some time during the past fifteen years in nineteen out of twenty-four cases in Aneth and twenty-nine out of thirty-two in Mexican Springs. In each community the question was inapplicable to one informant, an unmarried or long divorced or widowed woman. Full job histories were secured from men only. Of eight men in Aneth, four had been employed from seven to fifteen years of this period; in Mexican Springs, eight out of thirteen men had been employed for a similar period. In Aneth, remote from the employment scene, seven out of eight men had been employed for an average of three months or less during the years they worked; in Mexican Springs six out of thirteen had been employed a similar average length of time, but there were five men who had been employed an average of nine months or more per year of employment. Mexican Springs is near the job market, and some men can work in town and live at home.

[6] The recent discoveries of oil, natural gas, and uranium on and near the reservation have supplemented employment opportunities near home. This development has occurred largely since this paper was first drafted.

[7] It is sometimes argued that sheepherding does not account for the difference between Pueblo and Navaho settlement patterns, particularly since many Pueblos have large numbers of sheep. It is my argument that when the Navahos acquired

ments in areas of more intensive cultivation, but each cluster of hogans, or traditional-style dwellings, is still surrounded by its own fields and corral, so that even there, there is no compact village.

Typically, then, a hogan or a cluster of hogans is separated from the next cluster by a space of a quarter of a mile up to several miles. Sheep crop close. If a village pattern were to be used, either the flocks would quickly denude available range, or they would have to be taken great distances, or they would have to remain very small.

Navahos shift seasonally from one hogan to another, or from a hogan to a tent or shelter, but a hogan is often used for many years. Hence it seems unwarranted to consider the Navahos nomadic, although they are often transhumant (see also Hill, 1938: 18).

Stored wealth consists of livestock, jewelry (which can be pawned with a trader for cash), and money, although bank accounts and accumulations of cash in the home are rare. Many a Navaho family is almost continually in debt to a trader, who allows credit for futures in the Navaho's meat, wool, and hides, and nowadays for futures in wages, Railroad Retirement Act checks, and the like.

The Units of Navaho Social Organization

This section will briefly outline the nature of Navaho social units. Later the operation of kinship units will be described in detail. I shall begin with the United States' government's relationship to the Navahos, touching on pre-Conquest political organization in this connection.

GOVERNMENTAL STRUCTURE

The U.S. Bureau of Indian Affairs is a branch of the U.S. Department of Interior. The bureau is headed by a commissioner, whose office is in Washington, D.C. There are a number of area directors under the commissioner, each of whom ordinarily controls several agencies. The area office which includes the Navajo Agency is at Gallup, New Mexico. The general superintendent of the Navajo Agency is located at Window Rock, Arizona, on the Navajo Reservation, near Gallup. Below the agency level are staff officers (education, forestry, roads, etc.), and

---

sheep, they were living in more marginal agricultural environments than were the Pueblos, that consequently they had not tended to develop compact villages before they obtained sheep, and that they subsequently accommodated their agricultural activities to the requirements of herding. The Pueblos, already settled on the major nuclei of good farm land and living in compact villages, did not tend to build up large herds when they first acquired sheep because they could not protect them from marauding groups like the Navaho. Even later they tended to accommodate their herding practices to their agricultural requirements. Recently the expansion of Pueblo herds was curtailed by government programs.

line officers—the supervisors of the nineteen Land Management Units or districts. Four of these districts are almost entirely or entirely off reservation; in these cases agency control over the areas is minimal. The supervisors have few independent powers, operating with mandates from the Window Rock Office. The average Navaho finds himself far from the locus of the power that affects him. In addition there is room for misunderstanding and conflict over policy between the several administrative echelons above the district.[8]

The agency controls law and order enforcement, although this function is being transferred increasingly to the tribal organization. It also manages schools [9] (except for those which have been transferred to the control of the states of Arizona and New Mexico), agricultural extension training, forestry, livestock programs, and a host of other services. Health facilities are now administered by the U.S. Public Health Service. Like other citizens, Navahos are eligible for Old Age and Survivors' Benefits and Aid to Dependent Children.

TRIBAL COUNCIL

A Tribal Council of 74 elected members administers many tribal affairs under government supervision. Its powers have been increased over the years and it has more and more important decisions to make. For working purposes it has developed seven committees (as of 1957), which prepare recommendations for the total body. The budget administered by the council was nearly $2,250,000 in 1954 and rose to more than $6,600,000 in 1957 (TNY, 1954: 129; 1957: 123). A considerable amount of this budgetary increase results from mineral leases and royalties. Although members of the tribe do not always understand or agree with the actions of the council, it is a unit of major significance. The Tribal Council in its present and previous forms, however, is a creation of the agency. There was no central governing body of the Navaho tribe in pre-Conquest times.

[8] The selection of an appropriate "ethnographic present" for this description is difficult. In general, this description applies to the period from 1935 on. But during much of this time there were only eighteen districts, an additional off-reservation district having been recently created. After 1954 the reservation was divided into large sub-agencies, with more power allocated to sub-agents than had accrued to supervisors. This was, in a way, a return to a division of the area into units like the several independent agencies which preceded the consolidated agency of 1935. It also put administrators with power into more direct contact with local communities than had been the case after 1935.

[9] Between 1928 and 1945, little more than a third of Navaho children between six and eighteen were in school. In 1950, 55 per cent were in attendance, and since 1953 the figure has been 85 per cent or more (TNY, 1957: 310). During 1935–1936 there were 8 Navahos in college; in 1956–1957 there were 294 (ibid.: 311).

Nevertheless, some authorities describe an assemblage of the entire tribe during the winter. It is not clear whether the assemblage was largely for ceremonial purposes and especially connected with a particular war ceremonial (cf. Sapir and Hoijer, 1942: 274–279), or whether it involved planning of organized warfare and exhortations on the general welfare of the tribe (Reichard, 1928: 108–111). These and some other accounts suggest that the group assembled for a few days, dispersed for a longer period, and then reassembled, continuing thus all winter. But it is not clear whether they dispersed to their usual homes, or whether they built shelters or hogans near the central gathering place for the winter. Sometimes it is implied that they remained together all winter (cf. sources cited and Matthews, 1890: 94; Van Valkenburgh, 1936: 18–19). Reichard suggests that these assemblies occurred every two to four years (*loc. cit.*); there seems to have been none since around 1800, although perhaps one was planned just before the Navahos were taken to Fort Sumner. The simple problem of feeding a gathering of this size for any length of time would require some sort of pattern of dispersal and reassembling to conduct a winter-long ceremonial. Whatever the functions of this assembly, it could not have been a Navaho governing body, but only a coördinating session, and one which has been in abeyance for a century and a half.

LOCAL COMMUNITY

Some authorities have said that the Navaho did not have communities, but only families and loose political units. Whatever may have been the case in the past, communities exist today. A Navaho not only identifies himself as a member of a particular locality, but is able to state who else belongs to the local group and who does not. Even in cases of ambiguity, the reasons for the ambiguity are clear. Thus a man may say, "Joe lives at Tohatchi but he sends his children to Mexican Springs School. He attends chapter meetings at both places." A community usually has as its center one or more trading posts, a school, and sometimes other government offices.

Some years ago agency personnel developed a chapter system to replace the traditional local headman. The aim seems to have been a more structured local group with more organized participation in decisions and local action. The chapter has three officers: chairman, vice-chairman, and secretary, elected annually by popular vote of a community. Sometimes there is a chapter house. Chapter meetings are called at the desire of officers, of members of the community, or of government agents, to discuss and plan action on matters of community or agency interest. Sometimes this is merely a matter of announcements and discussions. During the stock-reduction program, however, chapters became foci of organized opposition to reduction and the government stopped encouraging them. Nevertheless, in 1949 these units survived in many places (Kimball, 1950). Elections were held, meetings continued, and the local Tribal Delegate used the chapter and its officers to communicate with the people, through meetings and informally. In a few places the old local leadership pattern may survive, and there are some areas where there is neither organized traditional leadership nor modern chapter. In recent years the government has again supported chapter organizations.

Community boundaries are clearer in some areas than in others. In an area like Black Mountain, where until recently there was only one school and trading post for a widely dispersed group of 4,000 people, subdivisions of the region are particularly unclear. In Mexican Springs, by contrast, the school district, trading area, and chapter are almost exactly coextensive, and there is a definite feeling of community membership.

It may be assumed that prior to Fort Sumner the Navaho fell into local groups, each headed by a leader. The size of these groups is not clear; Hill suggests a range of 60 to 200 people. The leader was selected by consensus and ritually installed for life. There was some statistical tendency for the position to pass from father to son, although other kinsmen and non-relatives also succeeded. The theoretical norm was, however, selection by consensus (data on tendencies from Kluckhohn, personal communication). The leader was expected to know the Blessing Way ritual (Hill, 1940b). According to Hill, his powers were mainly those of exhortation, although Goldfrank (1945, 1946) suggests that in communities with irrigation the leader was stronger than elsewhere. This, however, is denied by Collier (1946). Such leaders did not lead war expeditions. War leaders seem to have been self-selected and ritually trained, and to have commanded volunteers (Hill, 1936: 6–8). It is probable that a group of local leaders was likely to acknowledge one among them as preëminent and to be guided by him in matters which transcended the community. The events leading up to Fort Sumner make it amply clear that there were important respects in which neither local nor preëminent leaders could control the tribe. Thus treaties made by major leaders were abrogated by individuals who were interested in raiding and who could mobilize followers (Underhill, 1956: 77, 81–82, 96).

THE CLAN GROUP

The clan group consists of a set of two to six or more matrilineal clans which consider themselves to be affiliated. In most cases such a group is exogamic, but sometimes it is said that a clan is "distantly related" to another, and marriage is permitted. These groups are unnamed.

THE CLAN

The clan consists of a group of people who consider themselves matrilineally related, the relationship being stipulated rather than reckoned. It is a named, exogamic unit, dispersed, and not organized. Clans vary in population from about 3,600 to 1.

THE LOCAL CLAN ELEMENT

This unit consists of the members of a given clan residing in a given area, plus some of the close relatives of these members living in nearby areas. It is loosely organized and constitutes the unilineal unit of collective responsibility and joint action. It is, of course, exogamic. In the literature we read of one "clan" proceeding against another, or of the members of a "clan" coöperating to give a ceremony. The dispersion and size of most clans make it impossible to believe that the clan in fact organized in any such way. It is necessary to assume that some local section of a clan took action, and this section I have termed a local clan element (hereafter LCE). Interviews with Jimmie Dapah have provided supporting evidence for this inference.

EXTENDED FAMILY, COÖPERATING UNIT, AND OUTFIT

An extended family consists of a set of fairly closely clustered, nuclear families and/or individuals or married couples, living in separate hogans but coöperating closely, and united by consanguine ties. The majority of extended family units are matrilocal, but bilocal and patrilocal instances are found.

In some areas a larger unit of families forms a network of coöperation. This is dubbed the coöperating unit by Collier (1951) and is somewhat smaller than the mutual-aid unit which Kluckhohn and Leighton (1946) call the outfit. In such networks the links between nuclear families can be either consanguineal or affinal.

SINGLE HOGAN UNIT

The most frequent residential unit occupying a single hogan is that of husband and wife or wives, with or without unmarried children. There are, however, a variety of other types: widowed or divorced men or women, with or without unmarried children, grandparent and married or unmarried grandchild, and so on. Many hogan units exist apart from a residential extended family, and of course many more are included in such extended families.

The Navaho Kinship System

In the previous section, Navaho kinship units were presented briefly and schematically, with no hint of the empirical and theoretical problems involved. It is now necessary to deal with these problems, to elaborate on the definitions presented earlier, and to describe the operation of important units. The previous outline began with the most inclusive unit, the tribe, and dealt with progressively smaller units. This section will depart from that order, dealing with the clan first, as a necessary prelude to the understanding of other units based on lineality.

THE CLAN

A Navaho matrilineal clan consists of a category of persons who regard themselves as members of a named, matrilineal, exogamic unit, membership being ascribed by birth. Adoption is extremely rare. Navaho mythology accounts for the origins of many of these clans, but does not concern itself with genealogies of clans or their sub-groups. In a few instances the origin story states that all the members of a particular clan are descended from a particular woman, but in others the origin story deals simply with the beginnings of a group. Clan membership, correspondingly, is stipulated, not reckoned. The clan has no head, is not organized, does not congregate, and does not hold property. Exceptions to this statement would be localized clans of small size, which would thus approximate the LCE, discussed below. The functions of the clan include prohibition of marriage or sexual relations between members, and the provision of hospitality and assistance. A traveler attempts to locate members of his own clan, who can be expected to feed him, give him shelter, and otherwise assist him. Exogamic and hospitality functions are also located in one's father's clan and one's clan group, in more attenuated form.

Breaches of the incest taboo, although they disturb the LCE and the community, bring supernatural disaster only to the incestuous partners. Their relationship should be discontinued, and formerly Moth Way was performed over them. This ceremony is now obsolescent, and Moth Medicine is sometimes used. The selection of the chant is based on the theory that incestuous people are liable to go crazy and fall into the fire like moths, or to have their vitals consumed by moths. Alternatively, they might sicken and die, become insane, or produce deformed or insane offspring. Navahos joke about incest: a person who gets cramps in his hand or feet is jokingly told that this must be the result of sexual relations with a member of his own or his father's clan (Hill, 1943: 16).

Some Navahos believe that rituals belonged to particular clans in the past, but no such clear structuring exists today. In the case of hunting ritual, now obsolescent, it was considered desirable, but not essential, to have a woman of the Deer Spring Clan present for a portion of the ceremony (Ramah files). Some clans seem to have had insignia, and in the mythology a few had "pets," although these animals cannot be shown to have had totemic characteristics. Today some informants speak of members of one or another clan as having common psychological characteristics—generosity, slow speech, or a tendency to joke.

Except for hospitality and support, all activities which previous writers have attributed to the Navaho clan are, in my view, functions of the LCE and are discussed in that connection.

Changes of clan affiliation through adoption are not known today, although double affiliations and adoptions may once have occurred (Franciscan Fathers, 1910: 432). Clans became extinct, and Reichard states that there is no evidence that adoption was used to avoid extinction, without, however, explicitly denying that adoption from one clan to another ever occurred (Reichard, 1928: 29). Since neither land, livestock, ceremonial prerogative, nor political position were clan-controlled, there would be little reason for such adoption (cf. Reichard, *loc. cit.*). Nor would property considerations be of great importance for adoption within a smaller unit, a portion of the clan, as will be seen when inheritance and ownership are discussed. A child was sometimes transferred from one family to another through some consanguine link, in the interests of caring for the child or of securing labor for his parent's sibling or his grandparent, but this did not affect clan affiliation. Such adoption into a clan as is recorded was of non-Navaho slaves or the children of non-Navaho female slaves, and served the purpose of providing non-Navahos, or the children of non-Navaho women, with a clan affiliation. Thus the children of a Hopi woman slave became members of their Navaho father's clan (*ibid.:* 17). Again, a Walapai brother and sister became affiliated with the clan of their owner, Many Beads, whose mother reared them. Each married a Navaho; they became free as adults. (Based on Kluckhohn, 1956: 364 and personal communication clarifying clan affiliation, ownership, and subsequent status. The attribution of a different clan affiliation—in Kluckhohn, *op. cit.:* 373—is an error.) Probably the children of a slave woman and a Navaho man acquired membership in their father's clan. I do not know what happened in the case of the children of two slaves. Some slaves must not have been assimilated to extant clans, for there were so-called "slave" clans, that were said to be the descendants of captives.

Much of the remaining discussion of the clan is based on a survey carried on in the 1930's by the Soil Conservation Corps Economic Survey (hereafter called the Government Survey), some of the results of which have been made available to me by the Navajo Agency. Details are supplied under "Supporting Evidence, A." In the 1930's there were around 50 Navaho clans. They ranged in size from about 3,600 to a single individual. There were a small number of very large clans, and a large number of smaller ones. Thus four large clans made up nearly 40 per cent of the population, whereas some twenty-six small clans accounted for only 13 per cent of it. These figures indicate that at the clan level there is no process of orderly segmentation or opposition and balance of units of like order or size.

The clans are not ranked in terms of authority or economic perquisites, and only weakly in terms of prestige. There is some slight prestige associated with the four "original" clans of the origin myth, but different versions of the myth disagree as to which are the first four clans. Among those usually included are both large and small clans. Membership in the "Mexican" clan is not highly valued, because it originated from captives. The origin myth does not seem to glorify large clans; some of the largest clans are said to be of Pueblo origin (cf. Matthews, 1897; Young and Morgan, 1954: 20–27; Reichard, 1928: 24).

In sum, the clan is a matrilineal exogamic category, membership in which is stipulated. It is egalitarian in character, lacks authoritative functions, and holds no property; it is unorganized. Clans are not ranked with respect to each other. They are variable in size and in degree of localization. Undoubtedly clans have arisen by the division of old clans, by sizable increments of population resulting from the flight of Pueblos after the collapse of the Pueblo Revolt, and by the capture of slaves (cf. Reichard, 1928: 11–50; Underhill, 1956: 41–57).

THE CLAN GROUP

A clan group is a set of clans considered to be affiliated. The groups are not named. Ordinarily clans within a group cannot intermarry, but sometimes a clan is said to be "distantly related" to another and marriage is permitted (Reichard, 1928: esp. 44–56; Young and Morgan, 1954: 20 et passim). The nature of the affiliation is variously described in myth. Sometimes it is said that a woman of one clan gave rise to another clan. Perhaps a man of one clan is said to have acted in a particular way—and so "his" group has since been known by a new name, the process of descent being left unspecified. Or two clans are said to have met and traveled together and therefore are connected. Hence it seems better to speak of the clans of a group as "affiliated" rather than "related."

In some cases a clan group connection can apparently be used or disregarded. One may either claim members of another clan as kinsmen, or marry a mate in that clan and treat its members as affines (Young and Morgan, 1954: 24). Or one clan may claim affiliation with another, but the second may reject this claim (*ibid.:* 21).

The clan grouping problem is vexing not only because of such ambiguities as these, but because different ethnographers, and different informants consulted by the same ethnographer, provide different groupings. (For further details, see "Supporting Evidence, A.") I have followed the practice of the Government Survey. Although we have seen that in the 1930's clans ranged from 3,600 to 1 in membership, clan groups were more nearly of the same size, ranging from just under 2,000 to nearly 5,600. Some clans were assigned to no group, but these constituted only about 900 individuals, less than 3 per cent of the population. There were nine clan groups and eight unassigned clans.

The functions of the clan group are evident. They permit the extension of claims for hospitality and support beyond the clan itself. The importance of this will become clear when the LCE is discussed. Yet with great differences in size among clans, a system of extending exogamic prohibitions beyond clan borders could create problems. Thus, if the three largest clans belonged to the same clan group, nearly a third of the Navaho population would form an exogamic unit. In fact, however, the ten largest clans are distributed among eight exogamic units. Clan groups tend to include one large clan and some small ones, or two to four clans of intermediate size and some small ones, etc.

Since no legislative act imposed this grouping on the Navahos, it is probable that two processes are at work to prevent the agglutination of very large clans. The first is a tendency for any clan of very large size to separate from other very large clans, when the maintenance of so large an exogamic unit becomes cumbersome. Large clans, whose members can find assistance everywhere, have nothing to gain from maintaining affiliations. The second is a tendency for smaller clans to seek affiliations, or to seek to maintain affiliations with larger ones. Thereby they can gain or retain assistance from many people in many places.

HOSPITALITY AND EXOGAMY

Navahos today travel extensively, and must have done so for many years. Migration of families has occurred in the recent past, and must have occurred long before Fort Sumner days. True clan localization does not exist. Extension of kinship ties over a wide range is important, both for migration and for visiting. Roughly speaking, the kin from whom one expects help are the kin with whom one may not marry. Thus, traditionally, a Navaho should not marry into his own clan, his clan group, his father's clan, and (weaker prohibitions) he should not marry into his father's clan group, nor marry anyone whose father is a member of the clan to which his own father belongs. Data on observance of these prohibitions are supplied elsewhere in this paper.

A Navaho can expect help from members of his own clan, his father's clan, and his own clan group—especially his own and his father's clan. Extended affinal connections and non-kin may also provide assistance, but this is an act of supererogation. In his home community a man may use traceable kinship through all lines to secure help. Hospitality will be based on friendship as well as kinship, and particular individuals are well known to be generous or niggardly hosts. But away from home extended kinship dominates in attempts to secure help and hospitality. Thus when I have traveled with interpreters, hospitality has often depended on my interpreter's locating a classificatory relative, basing his claim to aid from a stranger on clan connections of one sort or another.

THE LOCAL CLAN ELEMENT

The LCE is a far more important unit in day-to-day life in the community than the total clan. The same rules of grouping, exogamy, hospitality, and aid, which apply to clans as wholes, have enhanced significance in relationships within and between LCE's of a community.

My basis for postulating the existence of the LCE is the impossibility of the whole clan's acting as a unit or carrying out the functions commonly attributed to it. More than half the Navaho clans are distributed over ten or more districts—that is to say, over more than half the reservation. Only ten small clans are limited to two districts or less, and even in some of these instances the districts do not adjoin. By reason of size and distribution, the clan is not generally suitable for organized action. It may well have been organized when the Navaho were a small tribe; in the case of small, localized clans it may still be. But the informant, speaking from the perspective of his own and neighboring communities, can perfectly well say, "If I am ill, *my clan* will help with the ceremony," and mean *the clan members he knows*.

Lack of ethnographic attention to the LCE as a distinct group makes it difficult to delineate the exact structure and functioning of this unit. Although it may be centered in a particular community, it is not rigidly confined to one community: members of a clan in one community may well call on some members of their group ten to fifty miles away and, with improved communications, perhaps further. (Men and women away at work are a special case. Today they may return several hundred, or even a thousand miles for a ceremony or other crisis.)

According to Jimmie Dapah, formerly of Coolidge and Pinedale, the LCE had a head. In the case of his own LCE it was his mother's oldest brother, who was later followed by her second brother. (The pattern of succession was discussed no further.) The term he applied to this head, *sahastói,* he regarded as a respectful term for mother's brother as well, and recognized that it has a more general application. In fact it is used generically to refer to an elder, elders, or elder maternal clansmen, and cannot be regarded as a kinship term (Haile, 1950–1951, 1: 166; Kluckhohn, personal communication). The sahastói acted in the following contexts: to demand damages from another LCE, to collect damages from his own kinsmen for another group, to mobilize the group to contribute to a ceremonial, and to send out messages to collect more distant kinsmen. I can find no specific mention of such a figure elsewhere. The Franciscan Fathers refer to settlements "reached privately and by representative members of the disputing clans" (1910: 439). It is at least possible that the LCE had several leaders, each representing a group of immediate matrilineal kinsmen. One of these leaders may have been paramount. Leadership of the LCE must not be confused with leadership of the community, although Navaho statements occasionally lend themselves to such confusion. Thus Matthews states that Navaho local chiefs were spoken of as leaders of particular clans, although in fact they were heads of local units (Matthews, 1890: 104–105). Today community leaders are not spoken of as clan heads.[10]

It would appear that the LCE as such did not hold land, although it may have monopolized it. The Franciscans' views are of particular interest because they are relatively early ethnologists in the area: "In many districts land is held *in severalty* by members of one or affiliated clans to the exclusion of all others" (Franciscan Fathers, 1910: 265, italics supplied). Yet, they say, "The farm is, as a rule, property of the husband who disposes of it before death" (*idem*). Fr. Berard Haile stresses the separate ownership of plots and denies that concentration of clan members in an area implies LCE ownership of the land (Haile,

[10] In the Western Apache case, the chief of a large local group holds an hereditary position, transmitted by clan and lineage, the clan normally being "the dominant nuclear clan of its local group" (Goodwin, 1942: 169). The same may originally have been the case among the Navaho.

1954: 6). He says that a large group of clan members would never "exclude others, *if* sufficient grazing or arable lands were available in that locality" (*ibid.:* 5, italics supplied). His "if" seems fairly important to me. He concludes, "No territory, springs, grazing or other lands are set aside and claimed as exclusive clan or clan group property" (*ibid.:* 6). Nevertheless, it appears probable to me that at one time, prior to the emergence of large herds, land was owned or monopolized by the LCE or by the small clan. First, many clan names are simply place names. Second, when the Navaho lacked sheep, permanently watered farm land must have had far greater value to them. Finally, such control by the LCE is reported for the Western Apache (Goodwin, 1942: 152–155).

Perhaps the most critical economic aspects of the LCE is its members' mutual aid. If a Navaho falls ill, he most commonly requires a ceremony to cure him. Lasting from two to nine nights, these ceremonies can require anything from a small fee to the ceremonial practitioner and hospitality for a small group of kin and neighbors, to a much larger fee and a cost of several thousands of dollars to feed hundreds of people for nine nights. The primary burden of these expenses falls to the patient's LCE, with almost as heavy demands on his father's. Affines may contribute, out of kindness rather than out of formal obligation, as may friends. In the case of a very large ceremony, LCE's of other clans in the patient's clan group may also be involved. Theoretically every ceremony should be repeated four times—at rather widely spaced intervals of up to several years—over the same patient. After the first performance the local representatives of the clan group are particularly likely to be called on for assistance.

Formerly the LCE must have had great importance in disputes. "All clansmen were responsible for the crimes and debts of other members of their clan, hence it was in their own interest to prevent murder, rape, and theft on the part of any and all clan relatives" (Kluckhohn and Leighton, 1946: 65). The exact mechanisms for settling various kinds of disputes are not entirely clear, but it would seem that even in cases of murder the preference was for settlement by individuals, the LCE entering the picture when individual efforts failed. Arbitration by a third party or by a headman was also possible, although the arbitrator could only attempt to adjust the payment or put pressure on the offender to pay or on the parties to a quarrel to desist.

The Franciscans state that inter-clan (LCE) quarrels were common, with settlement "reached privately and by representative members of the disputing clans. In some instances a case may be submitted to a

neutral party . . . though an unofficial settlement is much preferred"
(Franciscan Fathers, 1910: 439). The Franciscans say that in cases of
murder a life would be taken for a life, with the murdered man's clan
(LCE) members exacting the penalty. Most of their discussion of
murder, and much of Fr. Berard's, however, centers on weregild.
"Formerly" the compensation consisted of "almost the entire wealth
. . . of the offending clan. Later [there was] . . . a penalty to the
value of five and more horses for a woman, and three or four for a
murdered man . . ." (*loc. cit.*). Note the greater value placed upon
a woman. Slaves could be used as payment for a killing.

Several of Hill's informants describe the meeting of two LCE's in
connection with a murder: the offending party's clan piled up goods
until the injured clan element was satisfied. Apparently the mother and
father of the murdered man took their pick of the goods, and the rest
of the clan thereafter scrambled for the remainder (Hill, n.d.). This
lack of precise patterning resembles the inheritance settlements following a person's death (see below). In both cases there is a lack of
attention to the economic status or prestige of the individuals affected
by the settlement, and a corresponding tendency toward leveling economic fates rather than building up the wealth of selected senior individuals.

Inability to pay resulted in the death of the murderer at the hands
of the offended group—but this was compensation, not punishment.
Often the murderer seems to have been quick to offer compensation in
goods or slaves. Sometimes, however, the result of a quarrel or of a
murder was to bring LCE's into threatening opposition. If one LCE
was particularly important, the other might have to call in related
LCE's or even friendly ones (Haile, 1954: 7–8; for an account of a
dispute see Dyk, 1938: 160–163). Fr. Berard speaks of arbitration by
the headman "of the tribe," but this must be a lapse, since there was
no such figure—unless he means the head of a large local group. The
"clan" (LCE) also stood ready to protect a woman at the hands of her
husband. Formerly it protected the sexual rights of its men. It backed
a widower's claim to marry again into his wife's clan, and it held the
privilege of releasing the widow of a clansman from the claim of the
deceased's clan mates to remarry her (Franciscan Fathers, 1910: 434,
432). These last privileges appear to have lapsed completely at present.

Today the functions of the LCE in disputes have been much reduced. The agency controls law enforcement through tribal police and
Navaho courts. Nevertheless, many cases are still settled between individuals or LCE's, by compounding, without court intervention. In the

past the strength of a man's support clearly determined the outcome of many disputes. The Franciscans state that there is no traditional Navaho word for law (*ibid.*: 440).

Theoretically quarrels between clan members must be settled within the clan without external intervention (Hill, n.d.), but Dyk records a case in which a headman and a policeman play a role in such a dispute. He considers that intervention by non-clansmen may not be a recent phenomenon (Dyk, 1947: 87–93, 192–193).

It is clear that the LCE is not a highly organized group, nor one in which strong authority is exercised. It is therefore of interest to note that witchcraft accusations involving blood kin and "clansmen" (here undoubtedly members of the LCE) are fairly common. Of 164 "victims" of witchcraft in Kluckhohn's cases, 89 were said to be blood or clan relatives of the witch; and of these, 59 were siblings of the supposed witch. Thirty-nine were affinal relatives of the witch (Kluckhohn, 1944: 34). These data summarize community discussions of witchcraft, and differ in nature from Kluckhohn's tabulation of 103 cases where informants "accused (or repeated accusations against) their own relatives." In this group of 103, 14 involved accusations of a mother's brother and 81 involved affines. Apparently Navahos believe in general that consanguine kinsmen are likely to bewitch other kinsmen, but within their own specific networks of kin they fear affines more than consanguines.

G. E. Swanson has recently advanced the hypothesis that witchcraft or witchcraft fear is prevalent in those societies where important "unlegitimated" relationships are prominent—relationships not subject to adjustment by authoritative figures, yet important enough that avoidance of forceful conflict or final breach is critical (Swanson, MS). Carrying this one step further, one might infer that *within* a given society, witchcraft or apprehensions of witchcraft will occur in relationships which are important but not strictly regulated by organized authorities, and that the witchcraft complex secures conformity where other means are weakly developed. The LCE has a weak authority structure and, as will be shown later, authoritative relationships among affines who have married into the same family unit are not firmly structured. Yet coöperation is required in both instances. And indeed witchcraft fears and accusations center about consanguines and affines.

To summarize, I suggest that the LCE, although not highly organized, operated as the major unit of aid outside the extended family, bore the major responsibility for a person's derelictions, and served as the major agent for an individual in disputes which could not be handled on an interpersonal basis. In all these respects, it can be assumed that the first resource was a person's own LCE, the second his father's, and the third the LCE's of his clan group. Ethnographic accounts of "clan" functions must perforce involve a smaller unit than the clan, and it is this unit I have called the LCE.

Each Navaho community consists of a core group of large LCE's and smaller branches of various clans. In some instances these smaller groups may be small LCE's; in some cases they are probably closely affiliated with a larger LCE of their own clan in a nearby community; in some cases they may have no such backing and are probably dependent on various affinal or consanguineal kinsmen for support. (Data on localization and size are presented in "Supporting Evidence, B.") It is even possible that in some cases the numerically dominant clans in a community may be divided into two or more LCE's. The larger the community, the more clans are to be found in it; but the pattern of a few large clans is found in all cases. Two to four clans make up at least 50 per cent of the population of almost all communities for which data are available. The remainder of the population is to be found in some seven to eighteen smaller clans, the number of clans increasing with community size. The numerically predominant clans are exceedingly likely to belong to different clan groups.

The larger LCE's are thus not likely to be bound together by a common clan group membership. The tendency for one group of siblings to marry another, or for a group of siblings of Clan A to marry members of Clan B, creates many affinal connections between large LCE's in any given generation. The children of such "bunches" of marriages, however, are excluded from marrying into their father's clans, so that consanguine ties exist in that generation, and different affinal connections must be sought. In each generation many potential mates can be found within the larger LCE's, but sometimes there must be marriages into other units. With a flexible residential rule, in time this gives rise to the existence of representatives of other clans, in smaller numbers, within the community.

The largest clans on the reservation tend to be among the largest LCE's many communities, but the localization of some of the smaller clans also brings about their numerical dominance in some communities.

The Navaho tribe has been expanding in terms of territory, population, and number of communities for some time. One might suppose that the natural unit for the development of a new community would be two intermarried sibling sets. Such a unit would provide a new, isolated community both with an effective unilineal unit and with family units. In fact, however, it appears that the first families to enter an area do so as nuclear units, and are joined by other families linked to them by any of a variety of consanguineal ties. Interpersonal ties of kinship, rather than the ties of clan membership, bring families together in a new community (see "Supporting Evidence, B").

THE FAMILY

Residence pattern and composition The expressed Navaho preference is for matrilocal residence (husband and wife live with or near wife's mother). Patrilocal residence (husband and wife live with or near husband's father) is acceptable but far less common. Independent nuclear families are found in large numbers. Forms of residence which bring together a man and his sister's son are extremely rare and in most cases cannot be regarded as avunculocal in intent. They are likely to involve cases where a young man resides with his sister and her husband and children, or where an older man and his children (or his wife and children) reside with his sister and her husband and their children (sororilocal residence), or where a woman and her children (or husband and children) live with her brother and his wife (fratrilocal residence). Death of the senior generation of an extended family results in the breakup of the unit, the middle generation then forming neolocal or new extended families, depending on whether children of this middle generation are married and residing with their parents at the time of the breakup. Hence Navaho families can properly be described as falling into two types, independent monogamous or polygynous units, and lineal units (Murdock, 1957: 669–670). Nevertheless, I have followed the terminology of Navaho specialists in referring to the lineal units as "extended families." In the 1930's the rate of polygyny was probably between 5 and 10 per cent of all marriages, equally distributed in independent and extended units (see "Supporting Evidence, C").

Regional variation in family composition is evident, but not marked, in the Government Survey. This is not surprising. There are differences between Land Management Units, with respect to herding-agriculture balance and density of population, but there are also fairly marked variations within districts, which tend to attenuate interdistrict differences. The percentage of extended family units varies from 36 to 64. (In Dinnehotso, then a new agricultural community centering on a government irrigation project, extended family units drop to 11 per cent, but this is a result of recent resettlement.)

Roughly speaking, a high percentage of extended family units is found in the western half of the reservation, in more thinly populated and less agricultural units. Agriculture and density tend to coincide, so that the effects of these two variables cannot be easily disentangled.

Percentage of polygynous marriages has a somewhat similar distribution. It ranges from none to 12 per cent. The western, stock-raising, thinly populated area contains the majority of districts above the median; and the eastern, agricultural, densely populated, the majority below the median. Kluckhohn and Leighton (1946: 55) consider that the large, polygynous family is helpful for livestock operations.

With respect to matrilocal tendencies, the percentage of all *extended* families that are purely matrilocal ranges from 54 per cent to 92 per cent among districts, but all except two districts fall in a narrow range of 60 to 79 per cent. The matrilocal bias seems not to fit density, agricultural bent, or geography; it makes no obvious pattern. Kluckhohn and Leighton estimate that 85 per cent of families on the western reservation live matrilocally, a higher figure than that supplied by the Government Survey. They used a different basis of computation, however: percentage of all *nuclear* families living with wife's matrilineal kinswomen (*loc. cit.* and personal communication).

The interpretation of data on Navaho residence is by no means easy. I have concluded that it would be fair to assume that in the 1930's nearly two-thirds of all Navahos lived in extended family units, the remainder residing in separate nuclear families. Two-thirds of extended family units were matrilocal; about one-ninth of extended family units were patrilocal; and the remaining two-ninths were mixed. (For documentation of these statements, see "Supporting Evidence, C.")

Rules Relating to Marriage

Incest, exogamy, preferential mating. Incest prohibitions and exogamic rules coincide. A Navaho should not marry: members of his own clan; members of his clan group; members of his father's clan (according to most authorities); by the same token, members of his father's clan group, although this is probably the weakest prohibition; individuals whose fathers are members of his own father's clan. In this last case, the two are "born for" (children of) the same clan and are classified as siblings. Thus an individual may not marry any real or classificatory cross or parallel cousin of his generation. Some authorities report a preference for marriage into the father's father's or mother's father's clan.

Available data show that infractions of clan exogamy are extremely rare, and marriage into the father's clan only slightly less so. Marriage into the mother's father's and father's father's clan are much more common, but apparently make up only a small number of all marriages. As late as the 1930's, breaches of clan group exogamy were also exceedingly rare (see "Supporting Evidence, D").

It is possible that in the past the Navaho practiced classificatory cross-cousin marriage, but there is no ethnographic data to support the view that such a pattern has been acceptable within historic memory (see "Supporting Evidence, D").

There is a strong tendency for any marriage to initiate a set of similar marriages on the part of the kin of the two spouses. This tendency, of course, can be expressed only if two groups of some size are represented. Thus, in the case of two large LCE's, a man's marriage to a woman may result in his brothers' and sisters' seeking marriages with her brothers and sisters, and vice versa. Extensions of this principle are also found: a man and his sister's son may marry two sisters; or a set of siblings may all marry individuals from a particular clan. (Cf. Reichard, 1928: 67–69; Carr, Spencer, and Woolley, 1939: 254–255; Spuhler and Kluckhohn, 1953; Zeldith, 1959.) There are also mild preferences for remarriage into the same family or LCE on the death of the initial mate. The levirate and the sororate seem at one time to have been quite strongly developed. The Franciscans report, "Upon the death of her husband general good custom required the widow to marry his brother, or some close relative of her late husband" (1910: 432). The parallel requirement existed for men. If the clan of the deceased spouse had some reason to abrogate this commitment, it could do so, but only if it supplied the living spouse with a release before the spouse made his (or her) claim for a new mate from the clan of the deceased. The claim of the deceased spouse's clan was valid for two years. "The clans also assert their traditional rights, holding the widow until she obtains her release either by marriage (and divorce) or by their consent. In the event of a refusal other clans avoid her, though such a release is at present often purchased by sexual intercourse with one or other clan relative of the deceased, after which all obligations are considered fulfilled" (*ibid.*: 432–433). No such degree of formalization has been observed by other, later workers. Reichard (1928) specifically denies the levirate. What remains, however, is certainly an attitude of preferential opportunity for further marriages between the surviving spouse and the deceased spouse's clan members.

Each of these preferential patterns tends to build up relatively high frequencies of marriage between two LCE's at any given point of time. Both statistical and normative preferences within circumscribed areas are demonstrated by Navaho community and kinship studies (e.g., Carr, Spencer, and Woolley, 1939; Spuhler and Kluckhohn, 1953; Reichard, 1928: 68–69; Collier, 1951). But beyond this there does not seem to be any true pattern of specific preferences for marriages between two clans which operates on a reservation-wide basis.

Polygyny is forbidden today by tribal law, although many Navahos still regard it as morally acceptable, and the law is weakly enforced. As has been said, a reasonable estimate of the rate in the 1930's is 5 to 10 per cent. According to Stephen, polygyny was once very common, more than 50 per cent of married men having two or more wives (Stephen, 1890a). The first three men to enter the Ramah community (1869–1874) all contracted polygynous unions (Kluckhohn, 1956). Marriage to a wife's sister or classificatory sister was preferred. An extension of this pattern was stepdaughter marriage, often used by an older woman to hold a younger husband. Non-sororal polygyny was practiced, but presented problems: if both wives practiced matrilocal residence, a man would have to live alternately with, and work for, two separate families. Sisters, or mother and daughter married to the same man, belonged to the same consumption unit and indeed most commonly resided in the same house.

These marital preference patterns seem to be reasonable accommodation to various features of Navaho social organization. They tend to alleviate certain strains in family relationships which are discussed below. Thus marriage of two brothers to two sisters provides companionship to a man in his outsider status in his wife's family. (It also creates certain strains, since men married to two sisters tend to be sexually jealous of one another, and this is at least as true of brothers as of non-kin.) Marriages of a brother and a sister to a sister and a brother unite to some degree the interests of the two families: a man whose mother asks him to work for her is then contributing to the support of his wife's brother's family, so that his own mother-in-law is presumably less concerned at the temporary loss of his services. To a lesser degree, the marriage of a set of siblings to a set of clan mates has somewhat similar effects.

From the point of view of inter- and intra-familial solidarity, however, cross-cousin marriage would have similar effects. Notably, the Tonga, who practice cross-cousin marriage, forbid sororal polygyny and brother-sister exchange and the marriage of two brothers to two sisters. Colson suggests that the combination of *all* these forms of preferential marriage interrelates a small set of local unilineal units very closely, and that this is incompatible with a range of social relationships like that of the Tonga; the same argument would apply to the Navaho. Western Apache society employs all these devices, and there we do find more localized and smaller-scale networks of social relationships.

The Navaho patterns permit a fair degree of intra-community marriage and closely unite larger LCE's. The results are the usual network of cross-cutting ties at the community level. Thus the two largest outfits of the Ramah community have been repeatedly tied together by marriages (Kluckhohn, 1956).

It is clear that the wide range of Navaho relationships is itself the result of an expanding population: a population which has not only moved into new territories but which has filled in the interstices in already settled areas. This has occurred in the context of an economy based not on important, fixed agricultural estates, but on movable herds, so that extensive travel to find a new locale was possible. A strong preference for cross-cousin or classificatory cross-cousin marriage would presumably create relatively permanent ties within communities, or between adjoining communities, and would thus be disadvantageous during this expansion. The Navaho preferences, on the other hand, unite growing communities without inhibiting further expansion. This may possibly account for the choice of these mechanisms rather than cross-cousin marriage. The explanation is tentative, however, in view of the unsettled character of Tonga social life for the past hundred years, and the presence there of cross-cousin marriage. In any event, it cannot account for the prohibition of real or classificatory cross-cousin marriage, but only for a lack of preference for this form. It is my unsubstantiated belief that this prohibition grew up in an earlier period—either during the population expansion which resulted from Pueblo immigration or during the early years of stock raising—as a response to an increase in the number and size of exogamic groups, and the consequent need to expand the connections of affinity.

Establishing a marriage. Marriages may be primary or secondary. Primary marriages are those which are not conditional on the nature of a prior marriage of either partner, and secondary marriages are those which are conditional, as in sororal or stepdaughter polygyny, sororate or levirate. Primary marriages may involve two previously unmarried individuals, a previously unmarried male and a previously married (divorced or widowed) female, the reverse of this, or two previously married individuals. By definition, secondary marriages always involve at least one partner who has been previously married, or is now married and whose prior marriage affects the choice of his spouse.

Among the Navaho, marriages may occur with or without ceremony, with or without prior arrangement through the parents, and with or without bride price. Arranged marriages are on the decline. Traditionally, arrangement, bride price, and ceremony were most likely in the case of a primary marriage involving two previously unmarried individuals. Ceremony is less likely to occur in primary marriages if either partner, especially the girl, has been previously married, and is very unlikely if both have been married. A bride price should be given wherever there is a ceremony, but may also be given when there is none (Dyk, 1947: 172). Bride price is not unknown for a woman's second marriage, but is not required. Primary marriages in which either partner (but especially the woman) has been previously married, are not likely to be arranged: the parties are no longer in the control of their natal families in this respect. Secondary marriages are arranged in a somewhat different sense than primary ones: although the first wife may press a sister or daughter on her husband, and although consultation among kin is involved for the old custom of sororate or levirate, a family council followed by formal representations to the family of the bride by the family of the groom is not required. (Cf. Franciscan Fathers, 1910: 446–453; Reichard, 1928: 139–141; Dyk, 1947: 171–172, 174, 179–181, 191–192, 198–200, 213, and the passages in the autobiography to which these notes refer; Sapir and Hoijer, 1942: 307–317 and footnotes; also, Kluckhohn, personal communications.) Ceremonies do not occur when a previously unmarried girl enters a polygynous marriage with her sister's or mother's husband (Kluckhohn, personal communication).

It is convenient to consider first the most elaborated form of marriage, involving two previously unmarried individuals, in its most traditional form. Minor contradictions among sources are extensive enough to make detailed annotation difficult; the basic sources have been supplied above. There is general agreement that the groom's kin initiate action, going to the bride's kin. According to some views, the groom himself may ask for a particular marriage to be arranged, and the bride will then be consulted. According to others, marriages are arranged by the parents but the children are consulted. Sapir and Hoijer state that formerly neither child had any say (1942: 532). A representative of the groom's family approaches the bride's family, to see if the marriage is acceptable and to negotiate the bride price. The representatives variously mentioned are the mother's brother, father, mother, father's father, and a friend. Sapir and Hoijer assert that the mother's brother is most commonly the negotiator, the father next (*loc. cit.*). Other writers are less definite. The bride price should theoretically be contributed by the groom's clansmen (Dyk, 1947: 172) or by the groom's own and father's clansmen (Jimmie Dapah). It is distributed to the bride's clansmen (Dyk, *loc. cit.*) or to the bride's clansmen and father's clansmen (Jimmie Dapah). Dapah also says that affines may contribute.

The traditional bride price ranged from one or two up to ten to fifteen horses, although twelve horses (Franciscan Fathers, 1910: 446–453) or more (Sapir and Hoijer, 1942: 532) were considered bad luck. Cows, bulls, and perhaps sheep and other wealth were sometimes given, more often for a previously married woman than for a first marriage (Dyk, 1947: 172). The bride price was larger if the bride's family was wealthy (Haile, 1954: 14). I have no information more recent than the 1920's on amount and kind of bridewealth. The bride price should be distributed on the day of the marriage, but sometimes there are delays (Dyk, *loc. cit.*). In the event of divorce, even after a very short interval, the bride price resides with those who had received it. The bride price is, among other things, payment for the groom's sexual rights in his wife (Kluckhohn, personal communication). There is no evidence to suggest that the man is paying for any paternal rights. A man who takes a second polygynous wife from a different clan than the first wife's should pay his first wife's family (Reichard, 1928: 503).

The Franciscans assert that virginity is not valued, but Dyk states that the bride price is returned if the girl is not a virgin (Dyk, 1938: 150).

After negotiations for bride price are completed, a date is set. On that day, the groom's party appears with the bride price at the bride's home. The bride's mother is not present in the house, since she is now to be avoided by the groom. The girl's father or her mother's brother carries out the "basket ceremony," presenting a basket of mush and pollen to bride and groom. Both eat out of it. Advice to the young people from the relatives on both sides follows this. The bride's family provides a considerable feast to the groom's party, and are assisted by contributions from their own kin. Thereafter the young people normally reside with the bride's mother's family, but not in her house. Residence arrangements are usually made as part of the negotiations (Dyk, 1947: 213).

I have indicated that various kinsmen may play a primary role in the arrangement of a marriage. This may strike the reader as ambiguous. It is therefore worth noting that the Navahos themselves do not seem to have firmly established rules in this, as in many other connections. An example is Old Mexican's account of his daughter's marriage. It was arranged with the halfhearted acquiescence of Old Mexican and his wife, Old Mexican often saying that it was up to his wife but finally taking the steps that led to the marriage. At the time of the marriage, his wife's younger son by a previous marriage objected vigorously because he had not been consulted and because he did not approve. Yet others present seemed to think that the young man had nothing to say—or at least nothing to say once the arrangements had occurred (*ibid.*: 150–154).

The bride price is not in any sense the property of the bride. It is, in the main, redistributed among her kin. She enjoys the use of it only in matrilocal residence, and then only by virtue of its being available. The marriage ceremony makes husband and wife each "property" of the other. Both Dyk (1947: 185) and Haile (1954: 14–15) use this word, indicating their awareness that they are "property" in a different sense from ordinary goods. Traditionally, it also made each partner the potential sexual property of the rest of the clan, a point already discussed in connection with the levirate and sororate. This, perhaps, accounts for the tendency even today for individuals to seek subsequent mates in the same clan, in the event of divorce. The tendency of a group of siblings to marry another group has already been discussed and partly accounted for on other grounds; the levirate and sororate can be regarded both as a form of social insurance for the widowed and as a perpetuation of LCE ties. But remarriage into the same clan after divorce is somewhat more difficult to account for, except by reference to a "lien" established by a first marriage. The critical question would be whether marriages with bride price are more likely to lead to such events than those without, and whether a man's second marriage into the same LCE, after divorce, is less likely to require bride price than marriage into a new LCE.

In spite of the inter-group relations established by a marriage, there is also an important sense in which a marriage frees both partners for all subsequent marriages, in the event of divorce. Such marriages do not require the mediation of kin, nor do they require bride price or ceremony. (Ceremony is unlikely, but second bride price is possible.)

It would be a mistake to think of the bride price as a tremendously important economic consideration; in some cases it is small. In cases where the girl is wealthy it may possibly serve as a barrier for poor families, although the literature does not indicate whether this is the case. Even a poor family might be able to call on the assistance of others to make up the bride price. It is counterbalanced by the bride's family's feast, which requires a fair expenditure of sheep. It clearly does not cement the relationship, prevent divorce, or give the groom or his kin extensive rights, except for sexual rights. It would appear to be primarily a gift of prestige goods, expressing approval of the union by both families, and more important, expressing a more or less permanent connection between two LCE's. The goods themselves symbolize especially male wealth, since it is males who are primarily concerned with the care of horses and who use them as a sign of status.

Some first marriages are contracted by the couple's coming to live together, or more commonly by the man's coming to live with his wife. These seem to be as binding, and no more so, than the basket ceremonies. Reichard says, "If gifts are not given a marriage is not considered legitimate but practically no discrimination would be made against it. A woman might marry after bearing a child or two and her husband would care for her child as his own. If two people go off and live with each other they are not considered to be married but if a child is born the man may give the woman's family horses and they would sanction the union" (Reichard, 1928: 140–141). Dyk's views are somewhat similar: "Young and old often take up a common residence with no very serious intent, or, as we might say, with their fingers crossed. Under such conditions the payment of a bride-price would be folly, since it is not returned upon separation, except in cases where a 'virgin' proves to be otherwise" (Dyk, 1947: 172). He also says that the bride price "is to cement bonds between kith and kin and to give some assurance of permanency to the wedding" (*loc. cit.*); yet biographical materials scarcely suggest that basket-ceremony marriages are stable (cf. Dyk, 1947, *passim;* Dyk, 1938, *passim;* Leighton and Leighton, 1949, *passim;* Vogt, 1949, *passim*). "In the old days cross-cousins married without social sanction. They married in secret, no gift was given and no ceremony was held; hence the union was not legitimate" (Reichard, 1928: 60).

Dyk seems to suggest that only tentative unions lack bride price; Reichard, that if the parents disapprove, no bride price is given and no "legitimate" marriage occurs, and similarly, that if the couple initiate marriage without the bride price it is not "legitimate." Haile, on the other hand, indicates that after divorce a woman may arrange her own subsequent marriages without bride price and does not indicate that these marriages are "illegitimate" (Haile, 1954: 14; Kluckhohn has data supporting Haile—personal communication).

The question of the status of various types of Navaho marriages is thus not entirely clear. It would appear that first marriages are more likely to involve ceremony and bride price, and that this is particularly true for the children of people of status and substance. On the other hand, a considerable number of second unions—and even of first unions—seem to be far more casual. We do not know whether, under the more casual conditions, the claims of either party on the other's kin group are diminished.

Legitimacy. We now turn to the question of the status of children conceived or born under irregular conditions. Unmarried mothers sometimes practice abortion and infanticide; so do some women whose pregnancy has resulted from adultery. When the woman is unmarried, others sometimes believe that she terminated the pregnancy in these ways because of incest or even sexual relations with animals. (Navahos believe that children may result from intercourse between a woman and an animal—generally the coyote, in folklore.) Premarital births are regarded unfavorably, and there are a number of pejorative terms for such children.[11] On the other hand, abortion and infanticide are regarded even less favorably than illegitimacy. Navahos say of a bastard that its kin "like it as well as any other baby" and "the mother takes care of it and the girl's family all bring it up" (Bailey, 1950: 99).

Premarital pregnancy leads to marriage in some instances, ordinarily with payment to the girl's family. In other cases there is no marriage but damages are collected. In earlier days these could be quite large (*ibid.*: 100). "Where the fatherhood is disputed (as it so often is) the father's clan is most often stated as unknown. On the other hand, when the father or his family happen to have high prestige, the chil-

---

[11] A common term is *yótashkii* (*wótashkii*), which, it can be inferred, is derogatory from the translation given: "bastard." On the other hand, the precise denotation and the connotations of this term are not known to me. Another is *jóhonaa'ái ba'álchíní*, literally "children of the sun"—or nobody's children. The reference here is to the myth of the birth of Changing Woman's children, after she had been magically impregnated by the sun. In the myth, these children are told that they are *yótashkii* when they first ask who their father may be (Matthews, 1897: 107). A third derogatory term is *k'a bizhii*. "It means 'braided arrow' and they laugh at [a child] that way" (Bailey, 1950: 99). The reference is again mythological. A child may be called *bizhé'é doo bééhózinii*—roughly translated as "his father is unknown" (*loc. cit.*). Robert W. Young questions the term "k'a bizhii" for an illegitimate child and states that it refers to the barrel cactus (personal communication).

dren and their maternal relatives will boldly state the father's clan as accepted fact, and this is often resented by the 'father' and his immediate relatives" (Kluckhohn, personal communication).

According to Dapah, a child born of an adulterous union would be "born for" its genitor's clan. Kluckhohn says (personal communication) that in some cases the legal and adulterous half-siblings would sometimes recognize their different parentage by the use of cross-cousin or other terms which stressed their anomalous situation. It may be assumed that if such a birth resulted in divorce and the mother's remarriage, the child's status would be no different from that of any child of a casual union.

What is badly needed is information on the degree to which children born under such irregular circumstances as described above suffered an attenuation of particular claims on their father's kin. It is clear that they were not seriously handicapped socially, and I am reasonably sure that, where the father was known, affiliation to the father's clan would follow, with normal extensions of exogamy and hospitality.

It should also be mentioned that exceedingly casual arrangements are often referred to as marriages: a man who has sleeping partners in, say, four communities, is said to have "four wives."

Divorce. Navaho marriages increase in stability with age, but divorce is quite common. "Only about one woman out of three and one man out of four reaches old age with the same spouse. . . . Some of these changes are the result of deaths, but the majority are consequent upon desertion" (Leighton and Kluckhohn, 1947: 83). The wife may go to her mother's hogan and stay there, not coming to the husband's hogan; the husband may leave, returning only rarely to get more and more of his belongings. Traditional custom did not hold the husband responsible for the welfare of the wife or of the children once he had left the wife, but American law is now enforcing support in some cases. If a woman's family were willing, some of the children might accompany him, but this is rare (Kluckhohn, personal communication). Divorce seems frequently to result from the adulterous behavior of one of the partners, but personal incompatibility, failure to work adequately, and refusal of sexual relations are all bases. The Navaho recognize that either a man or a woman may be the cause of a sterile union; sterility sometimes leads to divorce (Bailey, 1950: 20). Divorce has no ceremonial forms. Even in the symbolic levirate described earlier, the "marriage" rather than the divorce is ritually expressed through intercourse—the divorce occurs by the woman's leaving her partner.

Marriage and legitimacy: interpretation. The materials on marriage are evidently not entirely clear or consistent. Three reasons can be assigned for this. First, the forms have changed in recent years. Arranged marriages are less common. Casual and non-ceremonial unions occur more often. Second, Navaho social life seems to have a considerable degree of flexibility in areas like the arrangement of marriages, where African materials, for example, have led us to expect a considerable rigidity. In the section on ownership and inheritance I shall indicate some of the bases for various sorts of flexibility. Finally, what is needed is a tabulation of marriages as primary, secondary, first, second, etc., with a parallel charting of bride price, ceremony, and the like, and a careful investigation of the status of so-called "illegitimate" children and "illegitimate" unions.

Even so, several conclusions can be drawn. Arranged marriages had their principal importance as signs of family status and as bases for inter-LCE relationships. The first of such marriages tended to result in others, both through polygny, the sororate and the levirate, and through second marriages after divorce. They provided preferential claims for men and women for future marriages—claims which have very much diminished in importance since the days of which the Franciscans wrote. Marriages after divorce were far less likely to involve such arrangements. Children born out of wedlock entitled their mother's LCE to a claim against the father's LCE. But the status of the illegitimate child was not strikingly inferior to others. So far as I know, illegitimacy could not deprive a child of its claim to connection with the father's clan, if the father were known. And its membership in its mother's clan was established by birth.

Current conditions. Today the law permits claims on the father for support, if the child is illegitimate. Marriages should theoretically be registered with the tribe, whether they occur by tribal custom (both arranged and casual form), in churches on the reservation, or in churches or registries off the reservation. Tribal law, however, accepts unregistered marriages so long as there is no barrier in the form of a previous marriage under state law. Such marriages are legally binding and divorce must occur in state courts, whereas the "tribal custom" marriage is easily dissolved.

Property and Inheritance.[12] The norms of Navaho economic relationships, including those of ownership and inheritance, are extremely

[12] I am particularly indebted to Marshall D. Sahlins for discussions on this subject.

flexible, and indeed in some respects ill-defined. My initial reaction was to blame this state of affairs on the ethnographers, but reading case materials and reflection have led me to another view. Although I introduce it with reference to economic matters, its applicability is clearly broader than that.

Fundamentally, the explanation of this situation is rapid and long-continued culture change. Contemporary Pueblo Indian groups represent perhaps 3,000 years of adaptation to an agricultural economy, more than 800 years of which involves an adaptation to the type of relatively well-watered, concentrated agricultural bases which they occupy today. Even in the period since they were conquered, until very recently in the Rio Grande area, they were not heavily involved in a wage economy, nor did they have considerable amounts of surplus produce to sell. Only since the conquest of the Navahos in 1868 have Pueblo flocks become sizable, and even then the Pueblos have tended more to adapt herding to an agricultural base than to adapt the reverse. On this agricultural base they have developed firmly institutionalized corporate kin groups or communities and a degree of regularity of institutional forms not found among the Navahos.

When the Apachean hunters entered the Southwest some 600 to 900 years ago, their conceptions of property must have been very simple. Personalty—clothes, hunting gear, etc.—must have been privately held and, to judge from contemporary customs, destroyed at death. This probably included the habitation. Hunting territories must have been controlled by bands. Game and gathered produce must have been allocated either commensally in the family, or by reciprocity or very low-level redistributive processes in the local community. Although kinship must have been the dominant mode of social relationships, organized authoritative, firmly structured kinship units must have been lacking above the family level.

The period of mixed agriculture and hunting was presumably one in which personalty continued to have more or less the same content. Extended family, lineage, or small-clan monopoly of agricultural territory perhaps developed. Judging by the Western Apache, it never became so elaborated as in the Pueblo case. At least three reasons must be assigned for this. First, this period of adaptation to agriculture was far shorter than the Basket-Maker and Pueblo development: 600 years at most, and perhaps only 2 to 300. Second, the lands occupied were marginal and scattered, so that the communities must have remained smaller than with the Pueblo. Third, some of the more marginal lands

must have gone out of production from time to time—as they still do
—leaving a family dependent on hunting and on reciprocity with kin.
This would still further weaken a corporate landholding unit.

Hard on agriculture and hunting followed herding, agriculture, and
hunting, a development which occurred within a maximum span of
200 years. In essence, the rules of personalty were extended to stock—
even to the tendency to destroy much stock at a man's death. But herds
and the fortunes of herding made it possible for some individuals to
amass large quantities of goods and left others leading a marginal
existence. Tendencies toward corporate units based on land were
weakened—if, as I infer, they existed—and finally destroyed, as livestock became more important.

Two opposing patterns of economic relationships developed. One
was that of a precapitalist non-cash economy based on kinship. The
relationships appropriate to this form demanded the constant equalization of economic differences. The patterns conducive to equalization
are found primarily with respect to the role of the "rich" and the
"leader," the significance of ceremonial, and the forms of inheritance.
A rich man should be generous; a headman should be especially
generous. Ceremonies involve feeding those who attend, and literally
thousands of dollars worth of livestock and other goods could be consumed in the course of one of the larger ceremonies. The larger ceremonies were given by wealthy families (Kluckhohn, 1937: 73, 76, 81).
This tended again and again to reduce the size of large stock holdings.
The inheritance forms tended to fragment holdings and prevent a line
from building up wealth. All these forms, then, tended toward equalization (cf. Kluckhohn, 1944: 63). It would help if we knew that large-
scale consumption during ceremonies began in the herding period.

On the other hand, beginning in the Spanish period, there were trade
goods to be bought, and wealth became an advantage. By the mid-
nineteenth century we find the rich, the poor, and the thieves, with
differences of interest between rich and poor—the rich desiring peace
and the poor, war. But real involvement in a market system and the
breakdown of a kinship society commenced in the late nineteenth
century, after the American conquest. In the late nineteenth and early
twentieth century one man amassed a fortune unknown to earlier
generations of Navahos, although he still operated in part in a kinship
idiom—"farming out" portions of his herds to kinsmen, exchanging a
portion of the yield for their labor. Today a Navaho can be seriously
concerned about transmitting his estate.

Between 1706, when the Navahos were modest herdsmen, and 1958, livestock has changed from personalty to real wealth; farming, from basic subsistence to an ancillary but important pursuit; wage and other market relationships, from trivial to overwhelming significance. This combination of economic forces, in so short a time, can scarcely yield perfectly consistent or clear forms. At times we can expect the modes of relationship of hunters and gatherers, and at other times, the modes of small entrepreneurs. With this background we are ready to inspect Navaho ownership and inheritance.

There are some conflicts between various sources on land inheritance, not all of which can be referred to changes in practices over time. It is important to remember that the quality of a field depends primarily on the availability of water and not on soil differences. Where there is adequate run-off water, the land seems to be permanently reusable under native cultivation, probably because of the repeated deposition of alluvium. "Fields were distributed along the courses of perennial and intermittent streams, on the gentle slopes below escarpments, on the flood plains of ephemeral streams, and on the alluvial fans at the mouths of streams" (Hill, 1938: 20). Natural flooding and irrigation were used to water fields. There was some dry farming. Although well-watered sites must have been treasured, erosion might make them worthless; there has been an erosion cycle in the area since 1880 (*ibid.*). Dry farms might be abandoned because of poor rainfall. Population expansion resulted in continual exploitation of new areas, and "there has always been sufficient land to satisfy the demand" until recent years, at least (*ibid.: 22*). Under these circumstances, failure to inherit land did not reduce a man to poverty or starvation, and in some areas there was little farming.

Hill's information comes from informants who were old in the 1930's; few of them are alive today. I assume that they were aged 50 to 90 when he worked, and that the period described is 1840–1900, in the main. The fundamental pattern he describes is that of "inherited use ownership." The first person to work a field set up a permanent claim on the land, transmitted to his heirs in perpetuity. Yet if he were clearly not using the land, another person might do so. The permanent right nevertheless resided with the first person and his heirs. If some one planted on a field and the "owner" came back to claim its use, he might dig up the unsprouted seeds or receive a share of the harvest —either by agreement with the planter or through arbitration by a third party (*ibid.: 21–22*).

There is no disagreement among authorities about inherited use ownership, but there is as to the lines of transmission. According to

Hill, "In the case of a man, his sister's son normally inherited the right. . . . In the absence of the nephew the heirship went to a brother or sister. In recent years, however, this system of inheritance has broken down and there has been a tendency for the land to pass directly to a man's children. In the case of real property held by a woman, the normal inheritance is still from mother to children" (*ibid.:* 22). The Franciscans say that "The farm is, as a rule, property of the husband, who disposes of it before his death" in cases where farms are more or less permanent (Franciscan Fathers, 1910: 265). In the 1920's and before, says Haile in a comment on the Franciscans, women also owned fields and parents might give fields to both sons and daughters (Haile, 1954: 16). Collier, who did her field work in 1938, reports that as a couple grows older, farm land is ordinarily divided among the daughters, but that sons may receive land if there are few or no daughters. If sons inherit, there is subsequent conflict as to whether their land should revert to their matrilineal kin or go to their children. She reports a dispute: a man from Navaho Mountain married to a woman from Shonto maintained fields in both communities. At his death his brother took the field at Navaho Mountain and claimed the one at Shonto, because the dead brother had worked it. The widow, however, kept the Shonto field, which was at her family's place.

Verbal wills were traditionally made (Hill, 1938: 22). Improvements, such as fences, are individual property, as are small irrigation ditches, but more extensive irrigation works are "the common property of the tenants" (Franciscan Fathers, 1910: 265). Where the water supply for irrigation is steady through the summer, "clashes over water rights are not uncommon" (Haile, 1954: 17). Major irrigation works are recent, and norms for smaller ones do not seem to have become clearly established. Inheritance of improvements is not further clarified.

It can be assumed that patrilineal inheritance is becoming more common, but it may well be that there has been conflict over inheritance of land for some generations. It must be remembered that land inheritance is not so critical as in some societies.

Hill reports that trees are owned by those who plant them. Fr. Berard, however, records an instance in which the owners of the fields, not the planters of the trees, claim control of some peach trees in Canyon de Chelley. They permit other people to gather there but control the amounts picked and apparently ask for some goods in return. In this instance the trees were planted at some time before Fort Sumner, and there was a subsequent dislocation of population during the Fort Sumner captivity (Hill, 1938: 23; Haile, 1954: 18).

Authorities disagree about ownership and control of pasture land. According to Kluckhohn, extended families have the use right to range land, as in the case of farm land (Kluckhohn and Leighton, 1946: 59). Howard Gorman gave the same information to J. Nixon Hadley (Hadley, personal communication). Van Valkenburgh mentions ownership of springs and pasture lands (1936). On the other hand, Haile says that in theory pasture land is not owned (1954: 18). Perhaps the issue at stake is ownership in our sense: exclusive right to a piece of land, including the right to dispose of it as the owner sees fit. This certainly is not the Navaho pattern. There is general agreement that individuals and groups succeed in controlling areas of pasture; Haile says that in some areas owners of large flocks manage to keep others off. Furthermore, if a man can afford to develop his own water resources, for example by installing a pump, he controls the surrounding range by controlling the water for stock. Kluckhohn says that wealthy owners with large outfits monopolize tracts of pasture (Kluckhohn and Leighton, 1946: 59). It is probable that recent crowding has resulted in conflicts over grazing lands; Mexican Springs informants say that clashes began only in the 1930's. Collier mentions conflict over springs and pastures at Klagetoh, a relatively densely populated area, but says there is none at Navaho Mountain, where population is thinner. She is speaking of 1938 (Collier, 1951).

It seems probable that in the past there was some *de facto* control of portions of pasture land by families and larger groups living nearby or habitually using them, and that this control was recognized as their right. Other areas were probably not "staked out." Herders were obligated to keep herds away from unfenced cultivated fields and standing crops, but compensation for damages by stock was sought only when the damage was considered malicious (Haile, 1954: 18).

Fluctuations in rainfall and in the supply of water for stock would make pasture areas vary from year to year in their utility, so that control could not be very tight. There was also the opportunity for families to move to new land. With a rising population and a stable reservation, competition must have increased. Pumping stations and wells would also increase the value of some pasture areas. Hence both conflict and efforts to define use patterns more sharply would be enhanced. It must be stressed, however, that even today there is no rigid definition of ownership of pasture lands. But fenced lands cannot be used for pasture without permission.

Navaho houses fall into two general classes, the traditional *hogan*, which is, roughly speaking, round, and the *kin*, or square house. Hogans are one-room houses with dirt floor and smoke hole. They are built to face the sunrise (not the true east)—so that the direction varies with the season in which they were built (Van Valkenburgh, personal communication). Today some hogans have stoves, windows, doors, and composition roofing; they are never divided into rooms, and the dirt floor is a constant feature. A ceremony must be held in a hogan, not in a square house. The "square" houses are square, rectangular, or even L-shaped. They may have two rooms; they ordinarily have a floor, windows, door, stove, and no smoke hole. They may be made of stone or wood, ordinarily of logs but sometimes of siding. A few more elaborate cement-block houses with several rooms are beginning to appear. An extended family unit ordinarily consists of two or more hogans, reasonably close together. (An "extended family" consisting of an old woman and two unmarried grandchildren would require only one hogan.) Each reproducing family unit ordinarily occupies one hogan, although the possibility exists that other odd kin may be co-resident.

Traditionally, if a death occurred in a hogan, a hole was broken in the north side (the north being the direction in which spirits travel), and the house was abandoned. This usage I would regard as a survival of the treatment of a house as personalty, something so closely identified with the dead—and of such relatively little importance—that it cannot be used after the death of a person closely associated with it. As more work is involved in the building of more elaborate houses this usage becomes uncomfortable, and a deliberate effort is made to remove a dying person from the house before he can "contaminate" it with his death. Even so, Navahos may not want to remain in that particular place after the death. In any event, if an older person dies and his mate remains in the hogan, no problem of inheritance exists. If a young woman dies, her husband is likely to leave—again, no problem. If both parents are dead, the extended family breaks up and all parties may well relocate—if only by a short distance—and again there is no problem. For this reason the inheritance of houses was not traditionally a problem, although with better housing and less observance of traditional mortuary custom it will become an issue.

For the living, the rule is that "ownership is vested in the builder" (Haile, 1954: 11), the person supplying or paying for the materials and labor. This apparently might mean ownership by husband, by wife, or by both (*ibid.*). Haile does not say what would happen to a jointly owned house in case of divorce. Kluckhohn (personal communication) says that behavior is variable: if the wife leaves, the husband keeps the house, and vice versa; if the house is located in an area where many kinsmen of one spouse reside, this is also likely to influence the decision. It can be assumed that in an extended family unit the kin of one spouse would have had far more to do with the construction of the house than the kin of the other, and hence would have a greater claim. In most instances it would be the wife's kin who would have such a claim.

Livestock, rather than fields or houses, forms the most important Navaho property.

Sheep and goats are given a particular earmark to identify ownership by man, woman and child. Cattle, horses, mules and burros are branded in modern fashion, and brands are frequently registered in the counties of the states. There are possibly more women owners of sheep, while men may specialize in cattle and horses, but all are desirous of owning both sheep and cattle. Many parents therefore assign ewes and cows to their infant children, a nucleus the natural increase of which is often considerable when the children graduate from school. . . . If needed in an emergency the consent of the children is asked. . . . The wool and lamb crop is entirely at the disposal of the individual owner who also disposes of the hides and pelts . . . where the size of the herds requires additional herders the owner pays the expenses of herding, lambing and shearing (Haile, 1954: 19).

This admirably concise statement sums up the best available information on control of livestock. Fr. Berard, however, says (*ibid.*) that the custom of allocation of sheep to children "is perhaps more frequent in families of the monogamous type," a remark not further elucidated. Jimmie Dapah reports a slight variant on the pattern of allocation to children: when a boy marries, his family allots stock to him. Dapah also says that the flocks of a husband and wife belong jointly to both, so that a divorce should result in a split, share and share alike. But, like other authorities, he notes that a young man does not usually bring his sheep to his wife's camp at once—which seems to imply at least an initial holding in severalty.

Matrilineality, matrilocality, and individual holdings do give rise to complications. Thus a young man is reluctant to bring his sheep to his wife's house, lest he lose some in the event of a divorce—either through arguments about allocation of the yield of the flocks or through pressure from her kin. Yet if he leaves them with his sister, he may find that his flocks do not prosper, though hers do—it is always his sheep that get killed by coyotes (Kluckhohn, personal communication).

Traditionally, "Property, especially inherited property, . . . belongs to the clan, though the bulk of it presumably will go to the closest relatives, real brothers and sisters, parents, uncles and aunts, and children if the deceased is a woman. The remainder will be distributed among the deceased's friends, spouse, and children if the deceased is a man. These latter bequests are made as a matter of courtesy. There are no legal obligations involved. The distribution is usually supervised . . . by the most influential male kin" (Dyk, 1947: 185). This generalization is amply supported by case materials in Dyk's two Navaho life histories (1938; 1947). He points out that various personal and immediate factors may influence the division, adding, "Wills are technically binding, and a man's will leaving nominal sums to friends, children, wives, would normally be executed. But one which were to leave all to a man's wife, children and friends might very well be set aside" (Dyk, 1947: 185). Formerly, slaves and horses might be killed immediately after a man's death, and Dyk records one case in which two slaves requested to be killed (*ibid.*: 60–61).

It is important to note that traditionally the matrilineal kin who appeared at or shortly after the funeral were those among whom the dead man's property was divided (cf. Dyk, 1947: 168; 1938: 279). This practice makes it clear that inheritance patterns do not maintain an estate and are not primarily oriented to precise definition of kinship bonds, but rather operate to disperse the estate.

In a fictional work which was written to illustrate contemporary Navaho usage, Reichard provides two interesting cases. In one of these, a man left the bulk of his property to his sister's daughter's son, who had been the only one of his kin who had taken the trouble to learn ceremonial lore from the old man. This was against custom, since the man's sister's sons would have the right to expect the bulk of the property. He had also left ten sheep to his wife and each of his children, and a cow to each child. This was also against custom, in terms of the size of these bequests (small though they are), and yet the wife and children could have sued in court for a larger share, following American law. A remote relative (type unspecified) persuaded all the kin to acquiesce in the will: first, because the sister's daughter's son had given the old man so much attention; second, to avoid litigation in American courts. This case illustrates both the older norms and current partial shifts. In the second case a woman of another tribe had married a Navaho. On being widowed, she could have been dispossessed from ten acres of irrigated land used by her husband. A community meeting resulted in the decision to maintain the widow on the ten acres and to assist her with her herding (Reichard, 1939: 114–119).

These materials indicate fairly clearly the pressures of several levels of Navaho development. The destruction of a portion of a man's property is a survival of the treatment of sheep as personalty. The division of herds after death is a reflection of a kinship-oriented society (and specifically a matrilineal one), in which the maintenance of the living is important but in which wealth lacks capitalistic significance. In Reichard's case materials this phase is still dominant, with somewhat more recognition of the substantive justice of the claims of a man's wife and children, but court procedures and the maintenance of estates for children are beginning to intrude. We can assume that this feature will become increasingly prominent, and that there will be corresponding stress on children's inheritance of father's property.

Jewelry was individually owned, represented stored wealth, could be pawned with the trader for credit used to buy consumer goods, and was probably traditionally buried with the owner—again a reflection of primitive personalty (cf. Sapir and Hoijer, 1942: 431–433). Adair, however, says that some—indeed, much—of a man's jewelry is preserved. He may distribute it before he dies, or it may be ritually purified and used after his death (Adair, 1944: 99–100).

Ceremonial lore is thought of as owned. I refer here to the Navaho "sings," ceremonies in the main having curative functions. Although they can be taught free of charge, ordinarily there is a fee, which may be less for a kinsman than for a non-kinsman. To know a "sing" is to have a lifelong means of earning, since the patient must pay for a sing; if he is impoverished, the payment may be a mere token, but the sing is not valid without payment. Kluckhohn reports one sample of singers. Of thirty individuals, sixteen learned from consanguine kinsmen: six from fathers, three from fathers' brothers, three from various blood relatives in father's clan, three from mother's brother, and one from other blood relatives in own clan. Two learned from members of their clan group, but otherwise none learned from clansmen or father's clansmen beyond the bounds of immediate, traceable kinship. One learned from a stepfather, and five from affines. Six learned from individuals where there was no tie of kinship or clanship. In the latter instances considerable amounts were paid for the teaching. In all cases taught by kinsmen, only the fees for the first sing held by the learner were paid to the teacher. The predominance of father's kin is notable in this sample. A sing may be taught to several persons without weakening in power, but the singer will often hold back a portion of the sing, failing to teach it to his pupil. This is considered important for his own health, but it is believed that kinsmen hold back less. (All statements

except the last are from Kluckhohn, 1939, but with figures revised by
personal communication from Kluckhohn.)

The ceremonial kit necessary to hold the sing is another, separate
matter. Not all singers own the appropiate pouch and kit (*jish*);
some borrow them. A man who has learned a sing must try to assemble
his own. If a man owns a kit and teaches his son the ceremony, the
son inherits the pouch after his father's death. If no son knows the
ceremony, the pouch reverts to the father's matrilineal kinsmen,
whether or not one of them knows the sing. It can, indeed, be sold by
such an heir. Once a man has inherited such a pouch, the same rules
would apply at his death—it would pass to his son or revert to his own
matrilineal kinsmen. Fr. Berard does not believe that clan inheritance
of ceremonies is involved here—that it is rather a matter of immediate
matrilineal kin (Haile, 1954: 31–32). A number of Kluckhohn's informants comment that there was once an association of clan and
chant, and one said that transmission from father to son has destroyed
this (Kluckhohn, 1939: 64–65).

There was a great deal of private—or perhaps better, exoteric—
lore, songs, and prayers performed by man to benefit the herds and
farming activities which sustained his family. Farming songs were
taught freely to any one who wanted to learn: as "essentials" to life,
they could not be guarded; they were not paid for (Hill, 1938: 61). On
the other hand, when Old Man Hat taught his son songs for livestock, the old man seems to have been concerned that he might die
soon and that the boy would not be given these songs by other paternal
clansmen. The boy was then living far from his mother's kinsmen
(Dyk, 1938: 258). It is conceivable that farming songs pertained to
subsistence and were freely transmitted, whereas livestock songs were
conducted with wealth and were not. Yet one of Hill's informants says,
"I have always been a poor man. I do not know a single song (i.e.,
ritual)" (Hill, 1938: 52).

Learning the skill of silversmithing follows a pattern very similar to
that of learning a sing. One does not pay a relative, but does pay a non-
relative. Of fifty cases listed by Adair, eighteen learned from fathers,
fourteen from matrilineal kinsmen, including eight brothers, and thirteen from affines, including five women who learned from their husbands (Adair, 1944: 89–92).

In sum, I suggest that variation and casual practices with respect to
property are real features of the traditional Navaho scene, and not reflections of poor ethnographic research, and that they can be interpreted as the product of the recency and speed of Navaho technological

and economic change. There are survivals of a hunting and gathering ideology, which now serve equalizing functions. There are other, newer practices aimed at equalizing, essential to a kinship-based society in which it became possible to create large differences in livestock holding, without corporate kinship units to redistribute the gains on a year-to-year basis. Finally, there are practices which arise out of the incursion of wages, cash, and Western legal norms. It may well be possible to gather more specific materials on some of these issues, and to demonstrate in more detail which norms apply under what circumstances, but the picture here presented is in general outline accurate and reasonably full. I stress this because an earlier reading of these materials led me to a different conclusion.

The Family Unit in Operation Most of the discussion that follows refers to the extended family unit, and specifically to the matrilocal extended family unit. Omission of the patterns relating to patrilocal cases overlooks only 15 per cent of all extended family units. The independent nuclear family unit, which must account for some 36 per cent of all individuals, will be slighted, and this is more serious.

Spatial distribution. It has already been said that the ordinary extended family includes a minimum of two hogan units, one for the couple of senior generation, and one for the reproducing family unit. Mother-in-law and son-in-law traditionally could not occupy the same hogan because of the mother-in-law avoidance taboo. Even today, when this taboo is largely disregarded, separate residence is usual. There may, of course, be three, four, or half a dozen hogans, neighboring or up to a half-mile apart. Sometimes there are more houses than families, since a hogan may be maintained for ceremonial purposes and a square house built as well, the family occupying either one. Except in primarily agricultural areas, one such hogan cluster may be quite far from the next. There are sheep corrals, and storage huts in some instances. Fields may adjoin houses or be several miles away. The water supply, whether by stream, pond, or windmill, is ordinarily from a few hundred yards to several miles away, and water must be hauled— ordinarily in large metal drums. Some locations are distant from generous supplies of firewood, which may also have to be hauled.

Division of labor. Discussion of this topic requires some reference to different historical periods. Traditionally, warfare and hunting were male occupations; gathering, primarily female. Men seem to have been the principal owners of horses and cattle and to have cared for these animals—a process much less time-consuming than herding sheep, since horses and cattle could be turned loose to forage for themselves.

Herding the sheep was primarily the concern of women and children, and women tended to own most of the sheep (Franciscan Fathers, 1910: 257–258; Stephen, 1890*b*).[13] Hill's account of Navaho agriculture indicates that both men and women did agricultural work, but that the bulk of cultivating fell to the men. Often the women were gathering or processing gathered seeds when the men were hoeing (Hill, 1938: 15–18). The Franciscans, writing somewhat earlier than Hill, remark that traditionally agricultural labor "was shunned and usually assigned to captive slaves, so that the hastqin, or lord, might be enabled to devote his time in some noble raid or in complete inactivity," a statement which implies that agriculture was principally a male activity (*ibid.:* 259; Stephen, 1890*a*, supports this inference). Weaving, the making of pottery and baskets, cooking and child care were women's activities, and the vast majority of ceremonial practitioners were males. The heavy work of building houses was presumably a male activity.

Today's situation is different. Presumably the shift results from the cessation of warfare. Men continue to be in charge of caring for horses and cattle; they also take care of saddles, harness, and wagons, and now repair automobiles. Men drivers far outnumber women. The care of horses remained a major activity for many years after Fort Sumner, and ownership of many horses endowed a man with high prestige. More men than women owned horses, and men were larger owners. Beginning with livestock reduction in the 1930's, the management of horses became less and less important. Thus in 1928 there were nearly 70,000 horses, with a Navaho population of about 40,000, whereas in 1957 there were less than 26,000 horses and the population was about 83,000—although some off-reservation horses have been omitted from the count (TNY, 1957: 310, 382). In most areas cattle have never been an important item in the economy.

[13] It is at least possible that the Navahos acquired an important number of horses before they became much involved in sheepherding. Forbes, whose interest is in the transmission of horses in the Southwest, does not make the earliest date of acquisition of sheep explicit (Forbes, 1959). Under these circumstances the horse would have greatly magnified the importance of the man's role as a warrior. Not too many years after, sheep would have entered the economy, first as an unimportant supplement, later becoming a significant item. This postulated sequence would help to account for the tendency for men to own and care for horses, and women, sheep. It would imply that the Navaho did not so much acquire a pastoral complex (horses, sheep, and cattle—cattle being of minor importance in all except a few areas), as a horse-and-raiding complex, allocated to men, followed by a sheep-pastoralism complex, allocated to women. Functional reasons for maintaining this division continued until Navaho pacification in 1868.

Today both men and women herd sheep, although where possible children are put in charge of the herds. Sometimes even very young children may herd, but each year there are more children in school and less available for herding.[14] The loss of child labor is undoubtedly affecting family organization. Shearing, dipping, and lambing, now and in the past, call for the nuclear or extended family, the outfit, or even the community to organize the activities.

Today sheep are owned by both men and women. In the 1930's permits were issued to Navaho owners during the livestock reduction program. These permits tended to favor males as livestock owners, since the permit was most often issued to the "head of the family" for the sheep he brought in for dipping. These might include the sheep of other family members.

Men still do the bulk of farm work, although both men and women hoe. Male predominance in farming is particularly evident where horse-drawn ploughs, cultivators, and so on are in use. Men do the major work in building houses, corrals, and fences, although women assist. Men haul water and wood. Silversmithing is primarily a male activity, of less importance as wagework becomes more prominent, and women continue to weave. Pottery and basket making are still women's work but are done by very few women. Wage work, available since at least 1881, is of major importance since World War II and is largely either a male activity or a family enterprise. Care of the house and children and cooking are women's sphere, although men will assist in all of these or even take them over from time to time as the situation may dictate. (Foregoing from Kluckhohn and Leighton, 1946: 50; from personal observation; and from sources indicated.)

A comparison of earlier ethnographic descriptions with those of the 1940's suggests that as the warrior role was eliminated and hunting became minor, male participation in farming and herding and male ownership of sheep increased, although male control and care of horses continued. Livestock reduction in the 1930's caused another shift. Today sheep and, especially, horses are becoming less significant, and wage work is rising greatly in importance.

The reasons why the Navaho could remain matrilineal in spite of a heavy pastoral dependency can be partly understood in terms of some

[14] Until the turn of the century, the proportion of children in school was negligible; by 1908 it was only 10 per cent; by 1918, 19 per cent; by 1928, it had risen to 37 per cent, remaining in the neighborhood of one-third until after World War II. By 1957, 91 per cent of children were attending school at least part of the year (TNY, 1957: 310).

of these facts. Let us assume, as seems reasonable, that after they became agricultural and before they acquired herds, the Navaho had a
matrilineal, matrilocal bias, and that men did a fair amount of raiding.
Spanish herds of horses and sheep would have provided a further
impetus for male raiding activities, and raiding would give men a
primary interest in horses. Women would necessarily be left in primary
charge of the sheep, which demand daily care. A matrilocal bias would
be supported, rather than undermined by any increase in male raiding
and warfare, and the consequent absence of men from their homes. If
the system had not been matrilineal to start with, women might not
have become owners of sheep, but given the division of labor and prior
matrilineality, this was possible. The cessation of warfare enhanced
men's interest in herds of sheep, and there was nothing to prevent them
from ownership. Within a little more than sixty years, however (1868–
1933), livestock reduction forced men into the wage market, under
conditions which demanded frequent absence from home but did not
permit the accumulation of much cash. These circumstances tended to
support matrilocality and did relatively little to undermine matrilineality.

Families in flux. The residential unit, either as a day-to-day affair
or viewed over a longer span of time, appears to the outsider to be in a
state of considerable flux. On any given day a man might be absent
from his wife's family unit for any of several reasons: a half-day or
full-day trip to the trading post; visiting matrilineal kin or father's kin;
several hours chasing the horses, which are not ordinarily corralled or
hobbled at night; taking out the sheep if need be; farming on a plot of
his wife's family a half-mile or a mile away; working for his mother and
her family on a plot near her place; looking after his own sheep, left
with his sister; dipping sheep; attending or conducting a ceremonial
(any of the last might require several days' absence). He might also be
absent for one to three months on a job. A man might be in the army.
Several men in the family might be absent from some combination of
the above causes.

A woman might go to the trading post, to visit kin, to assist kinswomen in a ceremony, etc., but she is more likely to be at home. If a
non-kinsman visits her in her husband's absence and spends much time,
especially if he goes into the hogan, adultery is suspected.

Children might be at school, out herding, or visiting a neighbor.
One entire nuclear family might be absent visiting, attending a ceremonial, going to the trading post, or be gone for several weeks to the

bean or beet fields, off-reservation, employed as seasonal agricultural laborers.

There might well be increments, as well as decrements: a visit from the wife's brother or her brother and his family; a visit from the husband's parents, and so on.

The entire family might move from a summer to a winter hogan, or back; a portion of the family, one entire nuclear family, or a single adult might be away at a sheep camp in summer. Indeed, summer and winter family groupings are not necessarily identical. Hill says that only one or two members of the family went with the herds, in times past, leaving in June or July and returning for the harvest in August (1938: 18). Navaho management of flocks is transhumant: in most areas they move from lower to higher pastures in the summer. The higher pastures may be near or far; in Mexican Springs, a few miles up the mountain produces a complete change of climate. In areas where such a marked change of altitude is available, the mountains provide the summer pasture and the flats the winter. The mountain pastures cannot be reached in winter and are well-watered in summer, whereas the flats receive less rain and are poorer pasture in summer. The dead, dried summer grass and browse, however, provide flatland fodder for the flocks in winter. In areas where there is little or no altitude contrast, it is nevertheless desirable to move the sheep to some summer pasture, reserving another area for the winter.

The demands of farming, however, do not necessarily fit with those of herding. The mountains afford a shorter growing season, and the flatlands more potentiality for runoff water and minor irrigation. Hence it may be necessary to divide the family unit to manage the herds in the mountains and the farms below. Even where there are no mountains, as at Greasewood near Ganado, farms are concentrated in a large, shallow valley and sheep must be moved out in the summer. To move them out in the winter would be to live in scattered, exposed sites, far from school and trading post, during the snows. As transportation and roads improve, as farming and herding decrease in importance by comparison with wagework, and as population becomes denser, however, Navaho families tend to occupy the same site throughout the year, and even to live in the mountains in the winter—at least in the Mexican Springs area. Where farm land and herding area are widely separated, the family may move with the herds, and one or more members may ride down to the farm and work as needed.

Over a longer period there are the normal increments and decrements of the marriage of daughters, bringing in sons-in-law, the departure of sons, in most cases, and the death of various members, particularly infants and the aged. But in addition, husbands, even in their fifties, may leave their wives, and new husbands appear. "Figures on 1,000 cases from the Ramah region show that only four children out of ten lived from birth to marriage with their own parents" (Leighton and Kluckhohn, 1947: 46). Adoption of children in and out of the residential unit by sisters, grandparents, and so on, adds to the turnover. Adoption may result from needs of the grandparents, inability of the parents to care for the children, the children's being orphaned, and, in some instances, illegitimacy. The lot of the adopted child is variable. There is no clear-cut differentiation between adoption and caring for a child. Orphans cared for by grandparents and more remote kin may lead rather miserable existences.

These facts make it difficult to make a structural analysis which is not misleadingly static. Family biographies would be required to complete the picture, and only life with the Navaho can give a sense of the daily movement of personnel.

The extended family. Our "typical" unit, which is actually only one of dozens of concrete types, will consist of a husband, wife, two daughters and their husbands, the young children of these couples, and a younger unmarried brother of the two married women. An older brother of the two married women may be imagined as residing about a mile away with his wife's family.

Production and consumption. Sexual and age division of labor has already been discussed. The entire family may hold one common field, worked by the men or by the men and women, depending on the activity, or a common field and separate fields, or only separate fields. Separate fields are worked predominantly by one man or by a married couple and their children. Many factors affect the choice of one versus another of these alternatives. Thus at Navaho Mountain the early settlers selected the best lands, in the canyon. These are often used as extended family plots. As families expanded, they began also to work fields further upland, and later arrivals might have only upland fields. The upland fields are smaller and tend to be worked as separate nuclear family plots, whether or not they supplement extended family plots. At Klagetoh there is a slight difference in organization. Camps are smaller on the average than at Navaho Mountain, but in many instances sets of camps are united in larger groups, called coöperating units; these larger linkages are lacking at Navaho Mountain. All single-hogan units have one field each. Most coöperating units have more than one field, but there is an average of more than seven hogans per unit and only two to three fields per unit. Single-hogan and multiple-hogan camps tend to have but one field per camp, and some fields are shared by more than one camp. Farm land here is of better quality and more widely distributed. Thus a Navaho extended family might coöperate in working one field, or coöperate on one field and work others as single-hogan units, or have only single-hogan unit fields, depending on locale, settlement history, and many other factors.

Herding arrangements are equally flexible, depending largely on size of herd, stage in the family cycle, etc. At Navaho Mountain most families which herd their sheep in one flock have small herds, or consist of units where a young husband has not yet brought his sheep to his wife's residence, or both. Those families which split their herds include camps with many sheep and camps where the parental generation owns many sheep and wishes to keep them separate from the smaller herds of married children.

At Klagetoh the situation is roughly comparable for camps, but coöperating units, which are geographically dispersed, split their herds correspondingly. In addition there is some use of paid herders.

Larger-scale farming and herding operations utilize larger units: the camp supplies the larger needs of the nuclear family for labor, and the coöperating group, sometimes friends or neighbors or even the community, supplies the larger needs of the camp. The hauling of wood and water is more likely to be a camp than a nuclear family affair.

It is the hogan which is the unit for the preparation and consumption of food, but cooked food may be sent from one hogan to another in the same camp, so that there is considerable sharing.

Data on more recent handling of wages among kin are not available to me. It is my decided impression that for many years each hogan has maintained separate credit accounts with the trader, but I am not certain on this point.

Although, as has already been said, sheep are "owned" by individual members of the family, this is an ownership which involves far less than full rights of disposition. Meat consumed by the extended family is drawn from the herds of each of its members, and is shared among the constituent nuclear families. Wool is similarly taken from the animals of the total family herds for use. (Data on fields, herds, work groups, and consumption units are drawn from Collier, 1951.)

The production units of the extended family, then, at times consist of each nuclear family working separately, on fields or with herds; at other times one such nuclear family assists another, as in shearing, or the entire group may work together on a field. In addition, every in-marrying male retains obligations and rights in his mother's group and may be working the stock and the farm, providing labor or goods for ceremonials, etc., at her residence. He may receive fair-sized gifts of food from her fields or herds, and in the event of illness it is his natal kin—his own family, his mother's and his father's LCE—who bear the cost of a ceremonial for him. The same is true for the unit into which he has married: his wife's brother has parallel rights and duties.

Authority. A portion of the patterning of authority is implicit in the previous analysis of productive activities; some of the more delicate relationships will be discussed in connection with patterns of communication. How much authority is exercised in daily life by various members of the family is partly a function of such variable features of Navaho life as the use of common versus separate fields, or common versus separate herding of livestock. The sharing of a field or joint herding of livestock calls for more coördination than do separate enterprises. It is my impression that a good deal of the coördination is handled by the senior male, but that he has few sanctions to impose and operates with some delicacy. Kimball and Provinse, however, indicate that he does a great deal of authoritative direction of the activities of his sons-in-law. They also remark:

After the son-in-law has established himself as a responsible person in the eyes of his wife's father, he is then permitted and encouraged to establish separate residence and assume the nearly complete care of his family. This separation is frequently marked by the division of the flock with his taking over those which belong to himself and his wife, the construction of a hogan some distance away, and a greater freedom and latitude in movement and decision. Those ties which bind family to family, by reason of either blood or marriage, are seldom completely severed (Kimball and Provinse, 1942: 22).

These writers tend to see the relationship of a man with his son-in-law as more authoritative than do my informants, and tend to describe a process of segmentation different from the one I have set forth. It may well be that final dispersal of siblings takes place after the parents' death, but that some siblings move away earlier, a view suggested by Kluckhohn and Leighton (1946: 57).

In matters of socialization, according to Jimmie Dapah, it is the parents who have primary responsibility. They may scold, scare, shame, threaten, or beat the children. The father's disciplinary role is not limited by the fact that he is of a different clan than are his children. Rather, if both father and mother are concerned that their children are misbehaving, they may request either the children's mother's father or the children's mother's brother to speak seriously to the children. A beating may be threatened but a serious lecture is more usual. The children hang their heads and are likely to listen and try to obey. In addition to intervening by request, a child's mother's brother or mother's father may deliver a moral lecture on his own initiative. In both respects, according to Dapah, the mother's father is more likely to act than the mother's brother, since the former is co-resident in the family unit and sees what is going on.

It would appear that this type of disciplining is particularly effective because it puts the child in a serious relationship with a kinsman other than those who supervise him daily. It is difficult to see this as the "clan's" claim to discipline the child, since the mother's father is also a common choice for serious discipline. And for the same reason, it is difficult to see the father's disciplinary role as being *replaced* by that of the clan—rather it is *supplemented* by formal, external discipline.

The disciplinary position of a stepfather or stepgrandfather is, however, considerably weaker than that of a real father or grandfather—unless the stepkinsman is of the same clan as the real one; in that case, his rights are equivalent. So clan considerations are not irrelevant. The relatively strong disciplinary role assigned to co-resident kinsmen—father and mother's father—would appear to result from the lack of any highly organized matrilineal unit and from the lack of definite patterns of localization.

I have drawn principally from Dapah, but it can be said that in general Navaho biographical materials do not display frequent cases of disciplining at the hands of the mother's brother. Against the picture that I have drawn, however, must be set Kluckhohn's generalizations, based on detailed work at Ramah and extensive experience elsewhere. "The mother's brother was, and to an appreciable degree still is, a severe disciplinarian" (Leighton and Kluckhohn, 1947: 101). Mothers' brothers "assumed many of the disciplinary and instructional functions which fall to the lot of the father in white society" (Kluckhohn and Leighton, 1946: 58).

The mother's brother, we have already said, was traditionally important in marriage arrangements; he was a source of inheritance after death; and a matrilineal kinsman was ordinarily in charge of the redistribution of an estate after a death.

Avoidance and joking relationships. This section will deal not only with familial patterns but with other avoidant and joking relationships. There was only one absolute avoidance in the Navaho kinship system: that between mother-in-law and son-in-law. They were not to see each other. The obligation to avoid was mutual, and the penalty was supernaturally caused blindness. The justification was mythological. The Navahos themselves considered this marked avoidance to be respectful. There was, I believe, one element of asymmetry. I have often heard of Navaho men's leaving their own hogan so that their mother-in-law could enter, but I have not heard of a woman's leaving her own hogan so that her son-in-law could enter. Nevertheless, in most contexts the party who arrived to find the other already there would retreat. One term for mother-in-law or son-in-law was "the one I don't see." Today, mother-in-law avoidance is observed by a decreasing number of individuals, the pattern tending to survive in less acculturated areas.[15] Although there was once far more avoidance, even traditional practice permitted a mother-in-law and son-in-law to agree from the beginning not to avoid one another. There were also special circumstances that abrogated avoidance. If a man married a woman and then her daughter by a prior marriage, no avoidance was instituted toward the older woman—who was now, in fact, mother-in-law for the new marriage. If a man had had sexual contact with a woman and later married her daughter, he was not required to avoid the woman. If both parties were very old, avoidance might be abandoned by agreement. In a crisis which required coöperation, as in the case of a sudden severe illness in the family, the taboo might be abandoned (Dyk, 1947: 173). Lastly, if a man performed a sing (ceremony) over his mother-in-law, something done only in a serious emergency, the avoidance relationship was thenceforth broken, and they called one another mother and son (Ramah Files). In this connection it should be mentioned that if a man performs a sing for his wife—again something that occurs only in serious emergencies—she becomes as his sister, and there can be no more sexual relations between them (Kluckhohn, 1947: 57–58). Thus it would seem that a mother-in-law who has been sung over is sexually taboo, and avoidance can therefore be done away with. There is unquestionably an undercurrent of sexual avoidance in the relationship, even though a mother-in-law is, in any event, normally a

---

[15] In 1953, in a random sample of twenty-five Navahos from Aneth and thirty-two from Mexican Springs, two people in Aneth and four in Mexican Springs now avoid their mothers-in-law or sons-in-law (or did while both lived). In Aneth three people who once practiced avoidance have stopped doing so. In Aneth fourteen individuals, and in Mexican Springs, seventeen, have never practiced avoidance. The remainder of the cases have never had a mother-in-law or a son-in-law. My impression is that in the more traditional Black Mountain area avoidance is commoner.

proscribed sexual contact, as are the wife's married sisters. (The latter norm, however, is sometimes broken.) One Navaho in his fifties informed me that when he married he told his father that it did not seem to him logical to "respect" his mother-in-law by avoiding her. Rather, he said, he would respect her by helping her. I asked him what he called her. "Mother," he said. "Otherwise people would have thought there was something peculiar [sexual] going on."

A relationship of mild avoidance exists between brother and sister. Men should not look at women's genitalia, or they may go blind. So girls are trained from early childhood to keep their skirts down. The first males from whom they guard themselves are, of course, brother and father. Once a brother and sister have passed puberty, they may not use the dual form of the verb to one another, or refer to joint activities they may have carried out. The Navaho language has a singular, dual, duoplural (two or more), plural (more than two), and distributive plural (several independent things). Use of the dual implies that the brother and sister as an exclusive pair are doing something together, and hence carries a connotation of incest. A brother and sister do not ordinarily travel together without other companions except by permission of their parents. At least traditionally a brother and sister were not to hand objects to one another. This prohibition was stringent when both were married, weaker if only one was married, and inoperative if both were single. It came into operation with marriage, not puberty. Thus brother-sister avoidance becomes more marked with age, whereas mother-in-law avoidance tends to weaken with age.

A number of partial avoidances among affines are dealt with in a later section on communication. Only one requires mention here. A man should not visit his wife's sister's hogan, lest her husband become suspicious. He usually is, in any case, even if—and perhaps especially if—the two husbands are brothers or clan brothers.

Although there are avoidant aspects of the brother-sister relationship, there is also patterned joking between brother and sister, as well as between brother and brother, and sister and sister. Such joking must not have sexual content. A woman might say to her brother, "I heard you got rich, taking care of your livestock every day." A man might joke with his sister: "I heard you were the best one at making blankets (or at cooking)." Or a brother might say to a brother, "Why are you so dirty? Get your wife to bathe you and wash your clothes." The foregoing comes from Jimmie Dapah. Hill notes derogatory jokes about "personal appearance and behavior" and mild practical jokes. He says that the same patterns are extended to parallel cousins (Hill, 1943:

21–22). These jokes, then, can be either outlandish exaggerations of a person's good fortune or skill, or derogatory.

Joking is permitted with both parents. According to Jimmie Dapah, a man might say to his father, "Hello, shaadaaní," a kinship term which, in this context means, "man [of proximate generation] who married a woman of my clan." Thus he removes his father from a paternal to a purely affinal relationship. There is a parallel form for the mother, "Hello, shizhá'áád," which term in this context means, "woman [of proximate generation] married to a man of my father's clan." In this way the son underscores his connection with his father's clan and treats his mother as an in-law. I failed to ask whether these jokes were permitted to daughters. Other joking with parents occurs, but the content was not investigated. Presumably sexual joking is not permitted.

With the maternal grandfather "good" jokes (not further specified by Dapah) are in order. Only the mildest sexual referent can be involved; thus one could say, "Grandfather, there's a young lady that wants to see you." Joking challenges to race or wrestle are acceptable. "Good" jokes with father's parents are said to be permissible, but I have no further information on content from Dapah, except that jokes about wrestling and racing are again permitted.

According to Hill, joking with paternal grandparents was more extensive and less restrained than with maternal grandparents. Between paternal grandparents and grandchildren there is much joking about wrestling and running, apparently centering about the actual incapacity of the grandparents for these activities, about supposed physical or personal deficits of grandchildren, joking about the grandrelative as a sexual partner, and joking about the sexual deficits or excesses of grandrelatives. Joking with maternal grandrelatives is similar, save that it was milder and sexual references were muted or absent (Hill, 1943: 22). Reichard, however, denies the possibility of joking with paternal grandparents (1928: 88). Hill's account is too circumstantial to take Reichard's denial very seriously.

With mother's brother, the sister's son has a symmetrical and complicated joking pattern—at least complicated for a non-Navaho. Either might say to the other, "Hello, báshíschíín bakạ'," which might be rendered, "Hello, male married to the women of the clan for which I am born." Fundamentally, this joke is similar to that with the parents —it emphasizes affinal rather than blood connection. A woman cannot marry a man of her father's clan. She and her brother are "born for" their father's clan—descendants of that clan. Her son is "born for" her husband's clan. Thus by necessity mother's brother and sister's son, al-

though members of the same clan, must be "born for" different clans
—their respective fathers' clans. The mother's brother cannot marry
into his own father's clan, but the sister's son can marry into that clan
—his own mother's father's clan. Indeed that is nominally a preferred
marriage. The sister's son, on the other hand, cannot marry into his own
father's clan, but the mother's brother can marry into that clan. So, in
theory, the taboos of one are the opportunities of the other. Furthermore, either may accuse the other of keeping women from him—presumably the women of the other's father's clan. The two may joke
roughly about sexual matters—comparative size of genitals is a permissible topic. Finally, the word "baką'," translated as "male," is itself
vulgar. It is a word used to distinguish the sex of animals, not of hu-
mans (although used with perfect propriety for animals or for chant
names—Male Shooting Way, etc.). A woman may refer to her husband as her "male," but this is crass usage. Hence the word has marked
sexual overtones. According to Dapah joking with grandparents and
parents should be "nice," or "good"; this joking is considered "rough."

There is another stereotyped joke between mother's brother and
sister's son which plays on the same theme. One might call the other
"shaadaaní," and the other might reply with the reciprocal kinship
term "baadaaní nishłį." In this context, the first speaker is claiming the
second as an in-law, specifically, as some one of proximate generation
who has married a woman of his father's clan. The second replies, in
effect, "I *am* your in-law," thus accepting this role in jest. Then the first
speaker takes some article or articles of clothing from the second, as a
symbolic brideprice. The clothing is later returned.

Still another play on sexual themes is found between mother's
brother and sister's son. One might assert that a particular girl was the
other's wife or lover, selecting an unmarried and undesirable girl—a
cripple or a crazy woman. In one such case, the subject of the joke
died, and the mother's brother and sister's son who had been jesting
about her each accused the other jokingly of having killed her by rape.
This indeed is rough joking. Other derogatory joking occurs, according
to Hill (1943: 22).

There are parallel jokes between mother's brother and sister's
daughter, but the deliberate coarseness found in the joking between
mother's brother and sister's son is lacking. Mother's brother says to
sister's daughter, "Hello, báshíschíín be'esdzáán" ("Hello, wife of the
men of my father's clan"). The reply is, "Hello, báshíschíín bahastiin"
("Hello, husband of the women of my father's clan"). In both instances
proper terms for husband and wife are used, instead of the coarse

"male" which appears between mother's brother and sister's son. The explanation is as before: the two are "born for" different clans, and each may marry a partner from the other's father's clan, whereas each is blocked from marrying into his own father's clan. The use of in-law terms also occurs, but without the brideprice element. A man might say to his sister's daughter, "Hello, shizhá'áád," (in context, "Hello, in-law, woman married into my father's clan"). Or she may say, "Hello, shaadaaní" ("Hello, in-law, man married into my father's clan"). With appropriate shifts of terminology these jokes can be made with a mother's sister. I did not inquire about joking relationships with father's brother and sister. Reichard says that joking is permitted (1928: 87).

Hill's data essentially corroborate Dapah and supply information about paternal kin. According to Hill there was a reciprocal joking pattern between children and parents, and between nephews and nieces and paternal and maternal uncles and aunts. "In the case of children and their mother or maternal aunt each accused the other of cohabiting with members of the father's clan. In the case of the paternal aunt the child substitutes his or her clan and vice versa" (Hill, 1943: 22). As for father and paternal uncle, "Each group accused the other of cohabiting with members of the other's clan . . ." (*ibid.*). Forfeits or gifts were requested in jest. Maternal uncle and nephew and niece requested mates from each other, as did father and child and paternal uncle and child. Maternal uncle and nephew joked about the size of each other's genitals (*ibid.*).

Male cross cousins may make rivalrous jokes about wrestling and racing. A man may also joke with either a male or a female cross cousin about the cousin's having a "second spouse." This joking occurs in the presence of the cousin's actual mate and has its hazards, since the mate may not consider it funny at all and may start an argument over the supposed rival. Dapah's views are corroborated by Hill, who says that the most strenuous joking occurs between cross cousins of opposite sex, that the "second spouse" jokes and similar jests can occur between any cross cousins, and that derogatory and obscene joking is common (Hill, 1943: 21).

Where joking about racing, rolling in the snow, or wrestling occurs, these activities may ensue—the two may race, or wrestle, or one may throw the other in the snow. This is a part of the joking relationship.

Jimmie Dapah denies that one may joke with any affine, but Reichard states that rough joking with father-in-law is permitted (Reichard, 1928: 88, reaffirmed in personal communication).

In addition to these jokes among close kin, there are a group of pat-

terned joking situations in the wider context of relationships which
center about loyalty to one's own clan, one's father's clan, or one's
spouse.

Navaho clan names are analyzable and meaningful—"salt people,"
"red running into the water people," "many goats people," etc. Correspondingly, it is easy to make joking references to a clan. If a person
makes a joke about a clan name, and he is not a member of that clan,
nor "born for it," any individual who *is* born for that clan might grab
a forfeit from the jester—perhaps his hat. A man would only claim
such a forfeit for a joke directed at his father's clan name, but a woman
might make the claim for her own clan as well, although she is not
very likely to do so.

If a woman is clumsy or does something stupid, some one might say,
"You don't think well, as your father's clan does" ("Báshóólchínígí
dó'óhólyą́ą́da"). This remark might be made to a group of women
working together. The women may then take a bracelet from the joker
or rip his clothes. There is no recovery for this. A man would not make
this joke with another man, but with women. Hill reports a slight
variant: derogating a man by saying that he is just like the members
of his father's clan (1943: 16).

Another type of joke centers about personal names. Traditionally
Navahos had personal names which were not used for address or reference, except under unusual circumstances, such as in certain ceremonials. They were therefore known by nicknames, which were used
for reference; it was impolite to use a person's nickname in his presence.
(Etiquette in these matters is changing rapidly.) A man's public name,
then, might be "Salt's Son-in-Law" (the son-in-law of a prominent Salt
Clan man), "Yellow Man" (in reference to coloring), "Slim Man,"
"Beautiful Singer," etc. A man from Ramah might be called "Onion,"
since this area is known to the Navahos as Onion Springs. If Fred's
sister is married to a man named Onion, and another man, Joe, makes
an obvious joke about the name—by saying, perhaps, "I would sure like
to bite into an onion"—then Fred will try to take an article of clothing
from Joe. Onion himself might or might not be present; he would not do
or say anything. This joking and forfeit pattern applies to any one who
makes a jest about the name of another person's sibling's spouse.

The outlines of the patterns of joking relationships were developed
by interviews with Jimmie Dapah, but many of his statements are corroborated by Reichard and Hill, as well as by scattered interviews of
mine and by the Ramah files, which have good material on sibling
jokes. Further exploration is required, since there are some contradic-

tions among these sources. I turn now to a partial interpretation of the joking patterns.

Essentially, these jokes seem to be plays on the ambiguities of group loyalty established by descent and marriage. Every Navaho is affiliated with two clans, his own and his father's. His relationships to his own clan mates are complicated by their marital relationships—and of course by his own marriage. Very close kin thus differ in their affiliations and loyalties, and every one has a special stake in kinship groups of which he is not a member. (This approach is essentially that of Radcliffe-Brown, 1952: 90–116.)

Thus, jokes with a father stress ego's membership in his own clan and his father's affinal connection with that clan. Jokes with ego's mother bring out ego's birth connection with his father's clan, and his mother's affinal tie with that group. Jokes with the mother's brother emphasize differences in paternal affiliation. On the other hand, jokes with cross cousins do not play on differences of clan affiliation.

A second set of jokes is concerned with the marital relationship, but without the play on affinal versus consanguine ties. This set includes joking about a lover, between mother's brother and sister's son or between cross cousins. In the case of cross cousins it is a play on the delicacy of the marriage tie and may go astray.

A third set of jokes involves infringement of others' rights or sensitivities. A man claims to have married a woman of his mother's brother's (or sister's son's) father's clan; he jokes about some one's father's clan; he jokes about some one's sibling's spouse. All of these jokes require major or minor forfeits. It is striking that, for the most part, these do *not* involve ties to one's own clan, but the more remote affiliations to affines and father's clan.

Siblings do not jest about divided affiliations by descent—since they share the same paternal clan affiliation—but rather stress rivalry and separation.

It would be easy to argue for an explanation of some of these joking patterns in terms of incestuous strivings. Whatever the merits of such an argument, it would seem that a more general explanation, covering the entire range of jokes about affinity and clan affiliation, is possible: an explanation which focuses on group membership and inter-group relationships as the underlying source of the humor.

Members of a clan joke about the things that divide them: different paternal affiliations. Parents and children joke about their different affiliations. Brothers and sisters joke about their different fortunes and their marital ties, if in a rather cautious fashion. Cross cousins, whose affiliations are clearly different, joke about the delicacy of the marriage bond. Outsiders press home jokes centering about a person's paternal affiliations or his siblings'—not his own—in-laws. In-laws do not joke, according to Dapah, although Reichard says that father-in-law and son-in-law do. In general, the non-joking and avoidant relationships create the ties about which the jesting revolves.

One jokes with others about their father's clan and their more remote in-laws, but must repay these jokes with a forfeit. Every delicate relationship is a joke for some one else; every joke is about some one else's delicate relationships. The joking system largely reflects the tensions of multiple allegiance to own clan, father's clan, and affines. Immediate incestuous tensions are only one feature of the total pattern.

In addition, the roughest joking is permitted with the mother's brother, the man with whom relationships may at times grow very strained.

The wrestling and rivalrous jokes are not clear. They seem to involve individuals who use self-reciprocal kinship terms, or who can do so. The cross-cousin and father's parent terms are self-reciprocals; the mother's father term can be so treated. They involve both cases where physical competition is between the decrepit and the young, as between grandrelatives, and where it is between people of equal vigor.

Patterns of communication. In various discussions with Navahos, I have been impressed by their vagueness about matters of authority, and their common unwillingness to admit that any one is "in charge" of anything, except that an individual is in control of himself. By the same token, the literature of the Navaho is not particularly clear on this general topic. This reluctance goes very far indeed. In many instances, when I asked Navahos how many years their children should attend school, they replied, "It's up to them." The apparent vagueness of the literature regarding authority reflects in large part certain important features of Navaho social relationships. First, there are quite a number of areas of activity in which an individual can make his own decision, or in which a husband and wife can arrive at a joint decision—especially where there are separate fields and herds for each nuclear family. Second, and far more important, there are a number of crucial relationships in which a certain ambiguity about "who is in charge" has more positive functions than any sharp definition of the situation could have.

This is by way of prologue to the present materials. When I began to interview Dapah in the summer of 1954, I anticipated a leisurely exploration of authority with an articulate informant already thoroughly accustomed to discuss the details of his culture, and a man who welcomed the opportunity to do so. In many areas Dapah was full of information, but I was blocked in my discussions of authority by a series of bland replies—that it depended on the situation, that no one was in charge, that the example I employed had never come up in his experience, and so on. By trial and error I hit upon the device of asking a series of questions about requests for assistance: Whom can one ask directly for assistance or favors? and what intermediaries must be used where direct communication is considered awkward? The results, set forth below, are not available elsewhere. Based, as they are, on a single informant, only partially corroborated by a more casual conversation with Paul Jones, they may be in need of correction. Nevertheless, they supplement the materials on authority previously provided, develop the patterns of partial avoidance in Navaho kinship in great detail, and complement the discussion of joking relationships.

To begin with, Navahos see two types of relationships with kin— relatives with whom one is "bashful" (*yá hasin,* bashfulness), and relatives with whom one is not. Among the free relationships are those of parent and child, mother's brother and sister's child, and father's sister and brother's child. (I did not secure information about father's brother or mother's sister, but these are almost certainly not bashful.) Between brother and sister, between a man and his parents-in-law, between a man and his wife's siblings and siblings' spouses, there is bashfulness, although this is not an exhaustive list. Bashfulness makes a person hesitant to ask favors or assistance directly. In addition, however, he may be reluctant to seek assistance from people who are his seniors in age or generation, whereas they may feel free to seek his. This is not a matter of bashfulness. In general, Dapah considers that men tend to be bashful with each other and with some women, whereas women tend not to be bashful with each other. The materials are presented in detail.

Nuclear family:
(1) Mo-Ch. Each asks the other directly.
(2) Fa-Da. Fa asks Da directly; Da usually asks Fa directly, or may go with Mo to Fa.
(3) Fa-So. Fa asks So directly; So may go directly but will usually ask Si or Mo to speak to Fa.
(4) Parent-married Da. Same as before marriage.
(5) Parent-married So. Mo now asks SoWi; Fa asks So directly. Reciprocals as before marriage. (In spite of what Dapah says, I doubt

that Mo goes to SoWi unless they happen to be in the same place. Otherwise, I think Mo communicates directly with So when they are together or sends a message to him, and that he then discusses the request with his Wi.)

(6) ElSi-YoSi. ElSi asks YoSi directly. YoSi may ask directly or use a parent as an intermediary. Marriage does not alter this pattern.

(7) ElBr-YoBr. Same as 6 above except that YoBr may also use Si as an intermediary.

(8) ElSi-YoBr. (Marriage alters this relationship and many that follow. Henceforth these abbreviations will be used: "sg," single, "ma," married.)

ElSi sg-YoBr sg. Direct requests are made by both.

ElSi ma-YoBr sg. Direct requests by both.

ElSi sg-YoBr ma. Failed to check.

ElSi ma-YoBr ma. ElSi goes to YoBrWi, or sends her children to ask YoBr. YoBr will use his Wi to reach his ElSi or send his children.

(9) ElBr-YoSi.

ElBr sg-YoSi sg. ElBr asks YoSi direct; she uses Mo as intermediary.

ElBr ma-YoSi sg. ElBr asks YoSi directly. She may use his Wi as an intermediary or go directly to him.

ElBr sg-YoSi ma. ElBr may approach YoSi directly or approach her through their Mo; he will be reluctant to approach her directly when her Hu is there. (The pattern Dapah indicates would require that the YoSiHu absent himself, so that her Mo may talk to her—provided that avoidance was being maintained. I failed to discuss this explicitly.) YoSi goes direct to ElBr, or sends her children.

ElBr ma-YoSi ma. ElBr uses his Wi or Ch as intermediary; YoSi uses ElBrWi or her own Ch as intermediary. (Marriage does not alter the relationships of siblings of same sex. When a man marries, his Si must turn to his Wi to reach him, so that now it is female affines who communicate directly.)

Other cognatic relationships:

(1) FaSi-BrSo. FaSi asks BrSo directly, but BrSo will ask his own Fa's permission before acting. BrSo asks FaSi directly.

(2) FaSi-BrDa. Not checked. Almost certainly same as 1.

(3) MoBr-SiCh. Each asks the other directly.

(4) MoFa-DaSo. MoFa goes to his Da, who consults with her Hu. If they agree, DaSo is sent to MoFa.

(I did not check other grandparental relations, or parents' siblings of same sex. I assume they parallel the relationships with parents.)

Affinal relatives:

The first group are the affines of a "typical" matrilocal household.

(1) WiMo-DaHu. If avoidance is observed, messages pass from WiMo through her Da, and from DaHu through his Wi. I do not have information as to whether this persists when avoidance breaks down, but I am reasonably certain that many messages are so transmitted. Should a woman ask her Da to communicate something to DaHu and be refused—for example, if the girl considers the request unwarranted or embarrassing, the WiMo might stand outside the Da's hogan at some time when DaHu was inside, and shout her request (or other comment) at her Da. This, however, is an extreme step.

(2) WiFa-DaHu. WiFa uses his Da to communicate with his DaHu. As in the case of WiMo and DaHu, this is easily managed. The Da usually goes to her parents' hogan early in the morning, and there the plans for the coming day are made. According to Paul Jones, if the WiFa had to make a request of his DaHu before the Da had made her visit, he would come to the Da's hogan, and there discuss the matter with the Da, never addressing the DaHu directly. She would then communicate with her Hu and transmit the result to her Fa.

The relationship is very sensitive. If WiFa were to ask that his DaHu round up the horses and water them on the way back, he would not ask the DaHu if he had watered them when the horses arrived. To do so would imply that he had given an order and was supervising its execution. Rather, he looks to see if the horses' hooves are muddy—a sign that they were watered—or asks tactfully, "Did they drink a lot?" In this and the instances that follow, after the initial awkwardness of the request is over, the two men work and talk together perfectly directly. If, however, WiFa wishes to scold DaHu, he should be most circumspect: "There are people who behave in such and such a fashion; it would be better if they did not . . ." and so on. DaHu also uses his Wi as intermediary in making requests of his WiFa.

(3) WiSi-SiHu. A woman uses her Si as an intermediary to her SiHu. This is reciprocal for the SiHu. Relative age is not a consideration.

(4) WiSiHu-WiSiHu. A man goes to his Wi, who goes to her Si, who goes to her Hu. In a Navaho extended family, these affinally connected men must in fact work together in many situations. Nevertheless, in initiating coöperation, they can communicate only indirectly—or at least this is preferred. Sometimes a group task is initiated when one of these men begins a job which clearly requires assistance. The others

may simply come to help without being asked, or they may be urged to help by their wives.

(Thus within the matrilocal household, a young man seeks help only through his Wi and is solicited for assistance only through her. She communicates freely with all members of the group except her SiHu, and uses her Si as intermediary there. Of course this is etiquette at its most proper. Men who co-reside for a long time eventually develop more direct communication, if the relationship is smooth. And if such men are kinsmen prior to marrying into the same household, the communication patterns appropriate to the consanguine relationship continue to obtain.)

The next group includes relatives who might reside in the household, but who more commonly are in separate households.

(5) HuMo-SoWi. Each ordinarily makes requests directly of the other. Sometimes, however, a woman's Hu is used as an intermediary to the HuMo.

(6) HuFa-SoWi. No adequate data.

(7) HuSi-BrWi. Reciprocally direct.

(8) YoBrWi-HuElBr. A woman makes requests of her HuElBr through HuElBrWi if he is married; otherwise through HuMo. He uses the reciprocal channels.

(9) HuBrWi-HuBrWi. They may communicate directly or through HuMo. This may be a bashful relationship.

(10) WiBrWi-HuSiHu. The woman communicates through her HuSi, the man through his Wi.

(11) WiBr-SiHu. A man often uses his Si to make requests of his SiHu, and vice versa. If the WiYoBr is single and resident in the household, a man might consult his Wi first and then approach her Br directly. He should be particularly generous to such a resident WiYoBr, buying him presents such as shoes and pants, perhaps giving him a horse, suggesting—but not arranging—a possible marriage, contributing to the brideprice. This gift giving is asymmetrical, since the WiYoBr is in no position to reciprocate fully. Such a pattern would not be followed for a married WiBr.

(12) MoBr-SiDaHu. MoBr uses SiDa as an intermediary.

(13) MoBr-SiSoWi. MoBr goes directly.

There are a few additional comments on request patterns both within and outside kinship bonds, and on kinship etiquette. Although a man should give presents to his wife's younger unmarried brother, and may give them to his wife's younger unmarried sister, gifts to a wife's married sister would imply an adulterous relationship. A man uses the same polite forms of the verb with his wife's sister, single or married, as he does with his own sister.

There are situations other than those described above—where children are used as intermediaries—although these have not been checked systematically. Thus, if the neighbors are butchering, a family may send its children over to stand around. Although they would request nothing, they would ordinarily be given meat to take home.

A man who encounters a friend alone and wants his help, asks him directly. The friend would ordinarily, but not invariably, consult his wife before making a definite commitment. If a man who wants help finds his friend with the friend's wife, he speaks in a general way about his needs, without making a direct request. "We are rounding up the horses, and we are having a hard time without enough men around to do the work." The husband and wife would consult, and the friend might then help out.

Interpretation. The interpretation which follows must be regarded as tentative, since it is based almost entirely on the information provided by a single Navaho, with some corroboration from a second.

In general, the communications of consanguine kin and of husband and wife are direct and unimpeded. Age and generation differences sometimes produce asymmetrical patterns. Thus the mother is sometimes used as an intermediary when a junior consanguine needs leverage in asking the assistance of senior kin. No intermediary is used for the mother herself. Mother's brother-sister's son relations are handled directly. The direct communication of brother and sister is disrupted by marriage, and particularly by the brother's marriage. Then his wife or his sister's children serve as intermediaries.

A man's communications with both male and female affines are largely indirect, whereas a woman's with female affines are often direct. This asymmetry is not reflected in kinship terminology, it will later be seen.

These facts can largely be accounted for by reference to two things. First, within the Navaho extended family, each nuclear family operates partly in a fairly self-contained fashion and partly in coöperation with the other nuclear families in the unit. Isolated nuclear families retain somewhat similar coöperative ties with other nuclear or extended families and do not constitute a special case for the argument which follows. Second, of course, the position of the Navaho male and female differs in the nuclear and extended family and in the network that connects such families to each other.

Each nuclear household requires a close working partnership of husband and wife. Once the husband has moved his flocks to his wife's hogan, the couple must attempt jointly to build up their flocks, even if these flocks are separately owned. To some degree they work the farm jointly and are bound to the trading post by a joint credit account. A woman has an interest in her husband's herd, since her children's herds will be partly established through gifts from him. (Today, of course, they may even inherit more than token amounts from him—but today there are fewer sheep.) In all these ways they find their interests partly segregated both from the wife's extended family and from the husband's natal family. Yet each nuclear family needs the services of others for many enterprises: rounding up the horses, trips to the trading post, shearing, and so on. The sheep may be herded jointly for the larger unit, or a field worked in common. In the past the senior generation normally owned more of the stock than the juniors, so that daughters and their husbands had a real interest in helping to care for the livestock, from which they received at least part of their food. The senior male of such an extended family was the natural coördinator of such economic activities as required joint action or assistance, and his sons-in-law were his most readily accessible adult labor force.

But each in-marrying male is also seriously involved with his natal family. He has a lasting commitment to work for his mother, father, brothers, and sisters, and to contribute to them. He has the expectation of receiving gifts of produce and meat from them. He contributes to ceremonials held for them, and ceremonials for his benefit are managed at his mother's or sister's house and contributed to by his kinsmen. Formerly, at least, he often arranged the marriages of his sister's children, inherited from his senior matrilineal kinsmen and expected his estate to be distributed to his junior kinsmen. Formerly, he was bound to them in feuds and efforts to get compensation for injuries.

Thus he is neither simply subservient to his wife, nor absolutely under the control of her kinsmen, nor a complete outsider with unimportant functions in the nuclear and extended family. But neither is he a person fully integrated in the extended family whose outside interests are severed. As father-in-law, and coördinator of activities important to all members of each nuclear family in the extended family group, he can expect that his sons-in-law will carry out his wishes, however indirectly he may express them. But as an outsider, whose sons-in-law all have outside attachments, he is in no position to command. And he must recognize that nuclear family interests also require protection, so that husband and wife must consult before his plans are accepted. As son-in-law, he is on sufferance but is necessary, too. As brother-in-law, with no support from age and generation seniority, he is dependent on his wife's tie with her sister, and the sister's leverage with her husband—or dependent on establishing an informal relationship of good will with his wife's sister's husband. His relationship to his mother-in-law is the most delicate of all. Her position as senior member of the matrilineal core of the household is impregnable, but his position as partner of his wife in a joint undertaking is a significant one, even if not a stable one. The avoidaace relationship seems to reflect this.

A woman is less dependent on her affines. She seldom needs to seek help from her husband's kin or her brothers' wives. When she does, she goes to another securely rooted person—her husband's sister, her brother's wife, and so on. The link may be tenuous between them, but neither is in a "delicate" position in her own household. It is particularly interesting to note that when she is deprived of this security through residence with her husband's family, relationships with his kin may grow quite tense (cf. Kluckhohn, 1944: 57).

It would appear that Navaho channels of communication illuminate authoritative, solidary, and coöperative relationships, and that questioning of informants in the area of communication provides details on these relationships which are difficult to secure in other ways.

Interpersonal Kinship Relationships

The previous section dealt with Navaho kinship units. Analysis of the structure of the extended family, however, demanded systematic presentation of joking, avoidance, and communication. Hence these subjects will be discussed as briefly as possible in this section.

RELATIONSHIPS IN THE NUCLEAR FAMILY

Husband-wife The conjugal relationship is complicated both by the matrilineal ties of the partners and by the fact that the nuclear family is so frequently embedded in an extended family unit.

Authority. The wife clearly has the right to make many demands on her husband, acting often as the agent for her mother, father, and sisters, to secure his services for extended family needs. In many major decisions, however, either mutuality or male authority over female is found. Kluckhohn and Leighton consider that the husband is formally head of the family (1946: 55). Nevertheless it is notable that in a standardized situation Navaho women were observed to win argu-

ments with their husbands in a majority of cases, whereas the reverse
was true for Mormon couples (Strodtbeck, 1951). The husband's
authoritative situation presumably increases with neolocality or as he
becomes the senior male of an extended family.

Economic allocation. In daily life each spouse produces for the other,
the husband providing wages and farm produce, caring for the horses
and doing some herding, the wife often doing the herding and always
the weaving. Neither has real freedom to dispose of his own produce
or of the other's property without due consultation. A husband is not
likely to move his flocks to his wife's hogan until after the marriage
has stabilized somewhat. This would imply that, although their holdings
are theoretically separate and are separated at death, it may not be too
easy to distinguish them. Formerly a wife inherited little from her
husband, and vice versa. Today a wife seems often to inherit sheep
and farmland from her husband. The reverse is probably less common, although some Navahos consider it normal. Each fulfills demands
of his own consanguine kin for aid and hospitality.

Solidarity. It is customary and correct to speak of the marital bond as
weak. It is not buttressed by barriers to divorce, and each partner retains natal ties of the greatest importance which may conflict with the
marriage bond. These have been discussed at some length. It would be
easy to overstress this fragility. The effect of membership and non-
membership in the peyote cult casts some light on the issue. I know of
many cases where siblings or parents and children are divided on
the peyote issue, one kinsman being a member and another holding
strong views against the cult. But divisions within the extended family,
whether between consanguine or affinal kin, are relatively rare. Where
parents and children or siblings do disagree, they are likely to be living
in separate family units. There are a few cases where husband and wife
are divided by the fact that one is a cult member and the other is not.
I know of no case where the wife threatened to leave or left her husband because he was a cult member and she would not join. I know
of several where the wife entered the cult and the husband refused to.
If the husband took the stand that he would leave his wife if she did
not quit the cult, the usual result was that she did relinquish her membership. Thus the crucial units of extended family and husband-wife
tie are not so subject to the divisive forces of factionalism as are the
intense and ordinarily affectionate ties of siblinghood and the parent-
child relationship.

There are also some pressures toward the reconciliation of marital
differences. The extended families (especially consanguine members)

of the two partners, or the two LCE's of the partners, or the local headman, or a singer (formerly), or the chapter meeting (today) may arbitrate the quarrels of husband and wife and attempt to reconcile them.
These same agents would act where reconciliations did not occur but
where damages were to be collected. Theoretically, damages may be
collected from a husband who beats his wife. Also, in theory, a wronged
mate collects from an estranged spouse's "seducer," although this is
probably rare in practice.

MOTHER-CHILD

Authority. A mother may discipline her immature children, has authority over a resident married daughter, and expects her non-
resident, as well as her resident sons, to respond to requests for
their services. Jimmie Dapah says, however, that a man who finds
his mother-in-law's requests in conflict with those of his mother would
do well to obey his mother-in-law. One cannot argue with her, whereas
a mother can be told that "they held me" to work for the wife's household. Arguments can occur without serious breaches in the bond, and
the relationship is clearly not one of implicit and invariant obedience
(cf. Dyk, 1938: *passim*). Serious misbehavior in childhood may result
in the use of a child's mother's father or mother's brother as a last disciplinary resort.

Economic allocation. The mother has a good deal to say about her
daughters' day-to-day work. I have no information about her control
over her sons' work. They are probably under their father's direction.
Mothers transmit sheep and land (in inherited use ownership) to their
children. They expect support from their children in old age.

Solidarity. The relationship is conceived of, and seems to be both
strong and intense for, sons and daughters. Respect seems to be taken
for granted rather than enforced, and mild joking is permitted. The
mother is the focal point for the children when they want the aid of
consanguine kin and hesitate to ask for it. Little negative feeling is
manifest. According to Kluckhohn there may be some latent hostility
toward the mother, engendered very early in connection with weaning.
This finds only the most indirect outlet, as in dreams (Kluckhohn, personal communication). Projective tests show no "systematic hostility
to either parent" (Henry, 1947: 105–106).

FATHER-CHILD

Authority. There is no conception that the father cannot discipline
his children because they belong to another matrilineal unit. He may
use wife's father or wife's brother for supplementary serious discipline, and both of these kin have independent rights to instruct

and verbally chastise a child on their own initiative. The father is commonly mentioned by sons as the primary source of their instruction in technology and values; mother's brother is almost never mentioned in these connections. Probably a father's authority over his son is more weakened by his son's marriage than is the case for the mother. If the father and mother remain married, the mother's requests for assistance from her married son also serve the father. The married daughter is more directly under her mother's control than her father's.

Economic allocation. A father's labor is the major source of economic support for his immature children if the marriage remains intact. Unmarried sons help their fathers with farm work and the care of livestock —and indeed children may do the bulk of the family's herding. The father has a claim to his children's support in old age, but if his wife is dead he also has a claim on his own kin, who may well fill the breach. There are conflicting patterns of inheritance: formerly the bulk of property went to matrilineal kin, but it is likely that own children will be more and more favored as time goes on.

Solidarity. There is a high rate of divorce. There are a fair number of cases in which a woman dies young, her children remain with her kin, and their father remarries elsewhere. Hence ties between father and children are often weakened. There is no traditional claim of children on their father for property or support after a divorce, and a divorced man may maintain little interest in his children. In cases where the marriage is stable, the relationship can be described as intense (affectionate and intimate) but not strong; it does not compete successfully with the mother's claims in case of divorce, or with the bonds to a man's natal family. Projective test results have been mentioned above. My own observation and at least two life histories show that the relationship can be very positive and affectionate (Dyk, 1938; Kluckhohn, 1945). Kluckhohn's short life history of Bidaga and some of my own field observations indicate that a strong and effective father can be a son's major role model, whereas I can call to mind no case in which the mother's brother appears in this light (Kluckhohn, 1945).

BROTHER-BROTHER

Authority. The older brother has some authority over his younger brother. My informants consider this to be weak, but Reichard states that it can be very strong (personal communication). It can be assumed that the head of an LCE would have more authority over his younger brothers than would otherwise be the case.

Economic allocation. In childhood, brothers work together; in later life they coöperate in assisting their natal family. Unless two brothers marry into the same extended unit, however, their mutual economic interests may be slight as they grow older. In matters of inheritance, presumably a brother, as a close kinsman, often receives a fair amount of stock from a dead man's estate, but matters of personal relationships and the presence or absence of the living brother at the division of the dead man's herds modify this.

Solidarity. Overtly the relationship is positively toned. It is structurally weak, since each man has obligations to his family of procreation which override his ties to his brothers. Joking is permitted and often centers on comparative economic well-being, thus expressing the disjunction of commitment to different economic units. Sexual jealousy is not uncommon. Although brothers should not seduce one another's wives, this occurs. The jealousy is maximized when the two live in the same extended family unit, according to my informants. Reichard has not found this to be the case (personal communication).

SISTER-SISTER

Authority. The elder sister has authority over the younger. The scope of the authority is not known to me. In an extended family, presumably the mother's authority over all daughters would limit the scope of a sister's authority. Reichard states that in those cases where a widowed or divorced elder sister and a younger married sister co-reside, the older has authority (personal communication). The same would be true in the case of two married sisters. Joint households consisting of two sisters in the senior generation are extremely rare.

Economic allocation. Mutual assistance in household tasks is common. One may inherit a portion of the other's estate, with all the qualifications discussed in the earlier section on inheritance.

Solidarity. This bond is fairly strong; how intense it may be I do not know. Clearly the husband-wife bond is strong enough to separate sister from sister when their parents are dead.

BROTHER-SISTER

Authority. The older of the two has authority over the younger. The areas of authority differ for older brother and older sister. An older brother, for example, might be involved in the approval of his sister's marriage.

Economic allocation. Each has claims on the other, but a sister's claims for service are more extensive: for work, gifts of meat and produce, and ultimately for a portion of her brother's estate for her children, in the traditional system. She may be "trustee" of his sheep during the early years of his marriage. This is a source of trouble between them.

Solidarity. The tension between commitment to the unilineal group and to the family of procreation is most marked in the brother-sister relationship. It can be highly ambivalent or even negative. A man does not especially want to leave his sheep in his sister's charge, although he often does, *faute de mieux.* In many cases he is very much interested in establishing his own children with their herds, and rather less involved in the fate of his sister's children, although they traditionally become major heirs after his death. The fact that avoidance patterns increase in intensity after marriage suggests that each feels a conflict between conjugal and consanguine claims.

OTHER RELATIONSHIPS

Mother's Brother-Sister's Child   At this point I shall depart from the previous system of categories, in order to discuss some of the problems of the avuncular relationship among the Navaho. There has been sufficient analysis of disciplinary authority, authority in marital arrangements, inheritance, etc., to cover the general topics dealt with for other relationships. The fundamental problem is the empirical difficulty which arises in discussions of "the" mother's brother. In many societies it is reasonable to speak of "the" father, since many children will have but one, or at any rate one at a time. But in no society can there be a guarantee that a woman will have one mother's brother. She may have several, or none. Hence the question arises as to whether one particular brother plays "the" mother's brother role, or whether all do—and if only one plays this role, the question arises as to how one brother is selected, and what the child's relationship is with the remainder. If there is no mother's brother, what principle of substitution of more remote kin is utilized—if any? In the Navaho case, these questions are not fully answered. What does emerge, however, is a strong impression that there are at least three modes of relationship between mother's brother and sister's child: the avuncular role, the clan-mate role, and the LCE head role.

The avuncular role. Mother's brother disciplines, arranges marriages, and, traditionally at least, is a source of inheritance for sister's child. On the other hand, especially today, he may be in conflict over the claims of his sister's children and his own. As has been said, he seems less likely to be a major source of identification than does the father. In Navaho life histories, the mother's brother does not frequently emerge as a central figure in childhood and adolescence. Father's teachings and father's discipline are mentioned far more often than mother's brother's. Indeed, among the fifteen short life histories of young veterans provided by Vogt, the mother's brother is prominent in the recollections of but two. Vogt himself, using data which supplement the informant's own comments, considers the mother's brother to be important as a source of influence in six of these fifteen cases. He mentions that in two cases the informant had little contact with his mother's brother; in two additional cases, the relationship is described as that of peers. In three cases Vogt does not mention the mother's brother's importance, and I assume it is slight (Vogt, 1949). Rapoport mentions a case in which a mother's brother demanded that his sister's young son live with and work for him, treating him very harshly, but Reichard considers this atypical (Rapoport, 1954: 110–111; Reichard, personal communication). It seems fair to conclude that the mother's brother has more importance in life crises (marriage, for example), in affairs of the LCE, and in matters of grave discipline and major decisions, than in daily relationships. (Cf. Vogt, 1949; Rapoport, 1954; Dyk, 1938 and 1947; Leighton and Leighton, 1949; Kluckhohn, 1945.) Leighton and Kluckhohn regard this relationship and that of brother and sister as the most "bipolarized" in the Navaho kinship system, and it is clear from what has been said that the brunt of conflict between co-residential and matrilineal ties is borne by these connections. They observe that since mother's brother and sister's son are each resident in a matrilocal household other than their natal unit, whereas a sister's daughter is resident in the unit to which the mother's brother himself retains an allegiance, trouble between mother's brother and sister's son is more common than between mother's brother and sister's daughter (Leighton and Kluckhohn, 1947: 101–102).

Witchcraft accusations also indicate the tensions in this relationship, although the available data do not show the distinction between sister's son and sister's daughter. Of 103 witchcraft accusations aimed at kin tabulated by Kluckhohn, 14 were directed against mother's brother. Eighty-one were directed at affines, "with son-in-law accusing father-in-law being much the most prominent of these" (Kluckhohn, 1944: 34). The remaining 8 accusations were aimed at miscellaneous consanguine kin. Thus, although affinal targets are nearly four times as frequent as consanguine, nearly two-thirds of consanguine cases involve mother's brother. Evidence of tension also comes from Kluckhohn's tabulation of 324 cases of physical fights associated with drinking. More than 90 per cent of these fights concerned the following pairs: husband-wife; son-in-law-father-in-law; brothers-in-law; brothers, real or classificatory; and maternal uncle-sister's child, real only, and presumably mostly between males, since women are far less often involved in physical brawls (Kluckhohn, 1944: 54). The source does not provide a more detailed breakdown.

The clan-mate role. The joking between mother's brother and sister's son is symmetrical and egalitarian. Its overt tone is rough but intimate. Among the various terminological alternatives for this pair is a self-reciprocal term; another possibility is a reversal of terminology by generation in favor of relative age. In addition, a woman may call her mother's brother "my son," and he may reply "my little mother." These usages suggest to me that in some contexts a mother's brother is viewed more as a fellow clansman than as a generationally differentiated, authoritative figure. Leighton and Kluckhohn consider the joking as an outlet for the tensions of the authoritative relationship (Leighton and Kluckhohn, 1947: 101–102).

Head of LCE. The senior male of the LCE seems to have played an important part in mobilizing the kin group for large ceremonies and in treating with other, similar figures in cases of disputes. Presumably in this capacity a man had some authority over the junior members of the LCE and may have had more authority over his own sisters' sons than would ordinarily have been the case. His LCE authority, however, may have been different in kind from the usual avuncular authority. At any rate, classificatory mothers' brothers do not seem to appear as prominent targets of hostility in the cited materials from Kluckhohn.

Probably there were some mother's brothers with whom both an "avuncular" and a "clan mate" relationship were maintained, and others where the relationship was far more that of clan mate. Rough joking may be directed at any mother's brother, so that there is no reason to suppose that the authoritative role outlawed it. On the other hand, the slim data available suggest that a particular mother's brother was likely to have the most authoritative role, and that this stemmed from the relationship of that man to his sister. Thus the Ramah field files state that a woman tries to select a particularly sagacious brother for what is here termed the avuncular role, but the files do not provide case data. One case suggests that a woman tends to rely on an older brother for advice (Leighton and Kluckhohn, 1947: 100–101).

Father's Sister-Brother's Child A father's sister is said sometimes to have asked her brother for one of his sons, to raise. The nephew was expected to help her, and eventually she expected to pay the brideprice for him (Ramah files).

Maternal Grandparents Mother's father is instructor and at times disciplinarian, by request or on his own initiative. If the mother-in-law taboo is observed, the mother's mother sees her grandchildren mostly in her own hogan, and can discipline them immediately. Children of unmarried mothers, or orphans, may be reared by grandparents, who may expect especial support in old age from such children. Sometimes a woman will request and receive one of her daughters' children for this purpose. In recent years there have been cases of refusal by grandparents to send such wards to school, on the theory that if the children are kept at home they are more likely to continue to aid the grandparents as the old people become helpless.

Paternal Grandparents   They are not likely to be in the immediate vicinity of the child's natal household. They have far less authority than maternal grandparents. The relationship is in theory intimate, in spite of the reduced contact.

Affinal Relationships   These have been discussed elsewhere, as have the ramifications of relationships to own and father's clansmen.

Kinship Terminology

The terms for consanguine kin used in the kinship charts are drawn from a manuscript by W. W. Hill, which provides the most complete set of terms available. Terms for affines are based on my interviews with Jimmie Dapah. They are in accord with published affinal terms, but make up a more extensive list than is to be found elsewhere. There are variations among published sources (e.g., Reichard, 1928; Haile, esp. 1941 and 1950–1951). It is probable that there are variations in terminology by region, depending on the farming-herding-wagework balance, and by generation. The terms presented are reference terms, but all may be used in address except affinal terms.

The minor variations do not obscure the general outlines of Navaho kinship terminology. It is a classificatory system, since at many points it merges lineal and collateral relatives. It provides both bifurcate merging and bifurcate collateral terms in the first ascending generation. Cousin terms are Iroquois. At certain points the unity of the unilineal group is expressed in overriding of generations, but not at those points which would provide Crow terminology. There is some use of self-reciprocal terminology, but far less than in the other Western Apachean systems (San Carlos or Western Apache, Chiricahua, and Mescalero).

The major variations in the published materials occur in terms assigned to descendants of grandparents' siblings and children of cross cousins. These variations do not affect the classification provided above. Interviews with Dapah and with Charlie DeJolie of Kaibitoh suggest that a shift toward Hawaiian cousin terms and generation terms in the

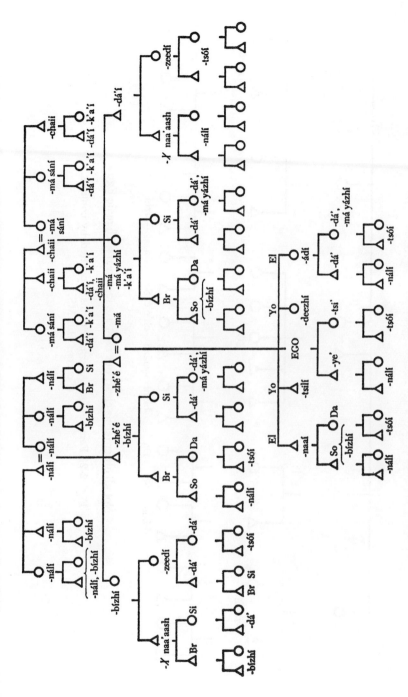

Fig. 2-1. Male ego. Alternate terms separated by commas. (Source: Hill MS.)

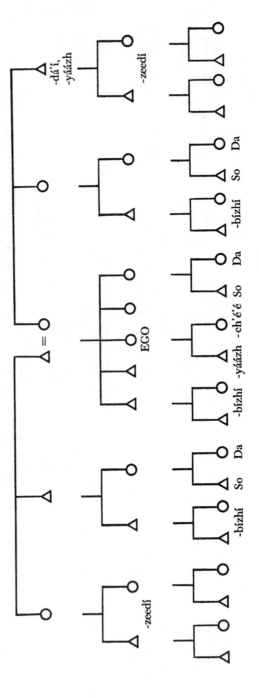

Not all other terms clear, but most are identical with male Ego's.

Fig. 2-2. Female ego. Alternate terms separated by commas.
(Source: Hill MS.)

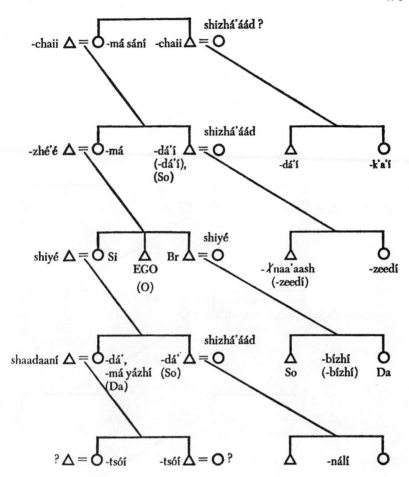

Fig. 2-3. Ego's matrilineage—male or female. Alternate terms separated by commas. Terms in parentheses are for female ego only; terms for the same positions not in parentheses are for male ego only. (Source: Hill MS; Informants.)

first ascending generation may be under way, but there are not enough data to develop this point further. Hill and Edgerton, of the Summer Institute of Linguistics, state that in the area near Farmington, New Mexico, cross-cousin terms are sometimes used for father's brother's child (personal communication, 1959).

Extensions of kinship terms within own or father's clan and to the clan group are as follows. Locally, the individual may know the genealogical relationship and apply terms accordingly. This, of course, ap-

plies to own and father's clan. Traceable relationships to members of
the clan group are unlikely. Where relationships are not known, and
toward members of the clan group, terms are cued to those employed

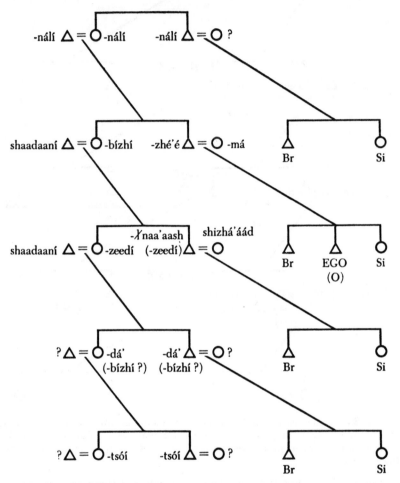

Fig. 2-4. Ego's father's matrilineage—male or female. Alternate terms
separated by commas. Terms in parentheses are for female ego only; terms
for the same positions not in parentheses are for male ego only.

by one's parents. Older people are more likely to know genealogical
connections than are younger ones. In visits to other communities, a
Navaho may try to trace actual genealogical bonds: "My mother said
she had a sister who went to such and such a place—that, I guess, is

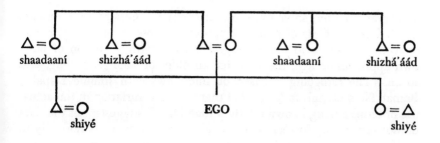

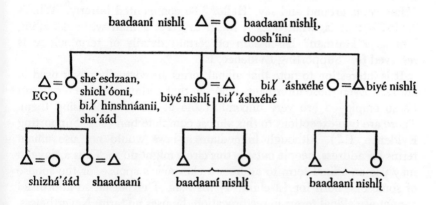

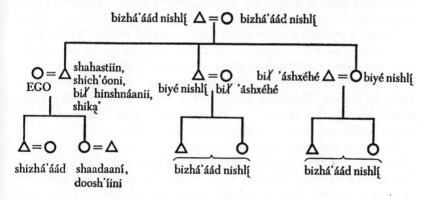

Fig. 2-5. Affinals only. Alternate terms separated by commas.
(Source: Informants.)

your grandmother; so you are my 'sister's son.'" Otherwise, terms are applied on the basis of apparent appropriateness. A much older man or woman is likely to receive a grandparent term, a person of one's own approximate age, the term for an older or younger sibling, and so on. (The foregoing is based on interviews with Jimmie Dapah.) Ramah file materials indicate that there is more variation in the actual use of terms among known relatives than Dapah suggests, but the data do not permit any further conclusions. It is good manners normally to use kinship terms in addressing non-relatives and strangers. One old man in the Sweetwater area complained—correctly or not—of the manners of some of his neighbors since they had joined the peyote cult. "They come around and say, 'Hello,'" he commented bitterly. "What's 'hello'?"—that is, what does it mean to greet a man without hailing him as a kinsman? Discussion of certain details of terminology is reserved for "Supporting Evidence, E."

It is interesting to note that affinal terms are virtually never used in address. Even those informants who say that certain of these terms can be so employed are very uncomfortable at the idea of using them. There are two exceptions to this almost complete ban (see "Supporting Evidence, E."). Although immediate in-laws would not use affinal terms for address, people outside this circle might do so. Thus a Navaho may use an affinal term to address a clansman's spouse, or the spouse of some one born for (a child of) his clan. The person so addressed cannot use affinal terms in reciprocation; he uses no term. Nevertheless, provided that these kin are remote connections of his spouse (through the paths mentioned), the use of these terms is not offensive. Indeed, a man might receive hospitality while traveling from a member of his wife's clan.

The other exception is the use of these terms for joking. But the jokes occur where no relationship of affinity actually exists. In the trading post, one friend might call another "shaadaaní," and this is considered hilarious. The friend might reply, "No, I'm not!" or might accept the claim by saying, "Baadaaní nishłį́" ("His in-law I am"). Either reply would be regarded as comical. The use of this joke, with forfeit, between MoBr and SiSo has already been described.

Affines use consanguineal terms toward each other wherever possible. The criteria for selecting these terms are not known. Dapah's father-in-law asked Dapah to call him "older brother," and in turn called him "younger brother." Dapah and his wife's sister's husband called each other "cross cousin," although they were unrelated. One might surmise that his father-in-law wished to retain seniority and minimize authority, whereas he and his brother-in-law wished to stress equality and separation.

The barrier to the use of affinal terms in address fits the delicacy already noted in these relationships. The nature of these ties is not to be stressed. The use of consanguine terms seems to be an effort to surmount the tensions of the relationship. The use of the terms for rough joking where there is no affinity fits with the general tendency to joke about the disjunctions of descent and affinity.

In-law terms are extended as far as consanguinity goes. A person's father's clan are his kin; their spouses are his affines. Spouses of fellow clansmen are affines. Spouses of children of men of the clan are affines. There is a radical segregation of all affines from all consanguines. This is not surprising for ego's own generation, but many kinship systems extend consanguine terms to some or all of ego's parents' siblings' spouses. Perhaps the Navaho failure to do so rests on the partial segregation of each nuclear family: a mother's sister's husband does not, in fact, act as a proxy father in daily life.

Conclusion

This section will review and interpret some general features of Navaho kinship and discuss further research needs.

INTERPRETATION

The question as to why the Navaho kinship system is matrilineal is answerable only in part by reference to present conditions. But these conditions largely account for the *kind* of matrilineal system found here. Matrilineality has its roots in earlier Navaho history, whether or not the specific explanations supplied in this chapter are accepted. The contemporary situation is one where men are the major agricultural workers, where both men and women own stock, where children, women, and men tend stock in approximately that order of importance, and where men are primarily responsible for wage work, which is growing in importance. It would be difficult to argue that these conditions promote matrilineality. On the other hand, it is self-evident that the present conditions permit matrilineality. They may to a degree support the matrilocal pattern, since a core of consanguineally related women who coreside and coöperate is adaptive when men spend much time away from home in wage work. This, in turn, probably provides support for the matrilineal ideology. The women's ownership of stock, the continuing importance of farming and herding, and the fact that kinship, not market, still regulates so much of community life, all make possible the temporary survival of the matrilineal principle.

Leaving aside the most recent effects of modern wage work, Navaho ecology and economy seem to me to combine and create the following effects on Navaho kinship. First, a variety of factors requires a loosely organized local descent group. Families must locate and relocate with due regard for the demands both of farming and herding, and these demands often do not coincide. The resources base for agriculture and pastoralism is unstable: fields useful at one time may disappear through erosion; decline in rainfall may eliminate the utility of some fields for several years at a time; pasture good in one year may be poor another; fixed dependency on rigidly allocated resources would be unsatisfactory. Second, there were factors promoting widespread kinship ties. The introduction of livestock permitted expansion and migration. This probably further reduced the possibility of tight local organization, and made the extension of clan and clan group affiliations over great distances very important. Third, equalization devices are required. The Navahos lack a clear-cut, hierarchically ordered descent group to manage wealth in livestock. On the other hand, they entered the world of market relationships and entrepreneurial livestock management only recently. The economic demands of ceremonials tend to disperse the flocks of the wealthy in old age, when ill health takes its toll, and the inheritance pattern tends to prevent marked concentration of wealth in family lines.

Fourth, given a relatively weak unilineal unit and matrilocality, the extended family unit has special features. The interests of each nuclear unit are partly separate from the extended unit and partly tied to the operations of that unit—or the operations of a more dispersed group of kin. In addition, each man retains obligations to his natal kin.

Hence the husband's *de facto* authority is relatively extensive for a matrilineal system, as is that of the senior male of the extended family. The role of the mother's brother represents an additional demand on the sister's son, different from that of the father. It is more likely to be supportive of parental authority in childhood than in competition with it. The relationships of affines are delicate. They are neither strangers, each of whom makes an independent contribution to the unit into which they marry, nor in any sense fully integrated. They are interdependent yet separated by group membership, if they are males. For women, the interdependence with female affines and with affines outside the extended family is ordinarily far less, and the relationships correspondingly are more direct and less delicate.

PROBLEMS

Further work is required on many topics: changes in current Navaho kinship usages of all sorts; variations by generation and economic base; clan groups, including clan legends and clan histories; content of joking relationships; barriers to communication among kin (the description here is based largely on the word of a single informant); actual address practices prevalent among affines; case histories on inheritance and settlement of disputes; the existence of the postulated LCE and its structure; the avunculate—which mother's brother does what with which sister's child; and details on farming and herding locations by family. Whatever the difficulties, it would still be possible today to get full information on these topics, using generationally stratified informants, to cover the period from at least 1890 to the present.

Supporting Evidence

A. CLAN NAMES, CLAN SIZE, AND THE CLAN GROUP PROBLEM

The Government Survey omitted all of district 13, 75 per cent of district 9, and smaller percentages (28 per cent or less) of districts 12, 14, and 16. It is virtually complete for the remaining districts. Field workers began with a list of 74 clan names culled from ethnographies and from several informants. The final census located living members of only 45 of the clans, but turned up one new clan name. Since several small clans have only ten members or less, it is probable that a few additional extant clans might have been discovered in a 100 per cent survey. Thus, Carr, Spencer, and Woolley (1939) found a previously unknown clan with 111 members in the Chaco Canyon area. It is not listed in the Government Survey. Fifty seems a reasonable estimate for the total number of extant clans. Reichard's estimate is identical (personal communication).

The large number of names for clans with no living members is intriguing. Some are undoubtedly names for clans now extinct. Since many clan names appear in the origin myth, Navahos are likely to name these clans, even if they do not personally know members of them. The Navaho are aware of the extinction of some clans (cf. Young and Morgan, 1954: 21). Other names may be alternative terms for extant clans, or even names of clans which have been absorbed by larger clans, although this process has not been documented.

In dealing with the question of clan size, certain adjustments of the survey figures have been made to simplify statistical operations. The Government Survey estimates a population of 35,500 Navahos, but for

4,700 the clan affiliation was not determined. All of district 13 was omitted from the survey, an estimated group of 950 persons. Figures were readjusted as follows. First, the population of district 13 was omitted from the calculations, leaving a total population to work with of about 34,500. Second, within each district persons whose affiliations were unknown were allocated to the clans for that district in the same proportion in which persons of known affiliation were found. Thus, if Clan A made up 10 per cent of the population of those whose clan affiliation was known, and there were 700 persons of unknown affiliation, then 10 per cent of 700 was added to the known population of Clan A in that district, for a new estimated figure; and so for the remaining clans. In this way the unknowns were absorbed. The readjustment was based on the dubious assumption that the unknowns in the district were a random sample of the district's population. This step was necessary, however, for an analysis of clan distributions over the entire reservation. The adjusted figures are used throughout this chapter. Use of the original figures, however, would not alter any of the conclusions.

The mean clan size is 749, the median 377.5. The largest 4 clans make up 39 per cent of the population; the largest 10, 64 per cent; and the first 20, 87 per cent. Twenty-six clans make up the remaining 13 per cent. In absolute figures, there are 3 clans of more than 3,500; 2 clans of 2,000 to 2,800; 8 clans of 1,000 to 1,500; 22 clans of 100 to 999; and 11 clans of less than 100. There are no clans in the size interval 1,501 to 2,000. The Government Survey rank order corresponds closely with Reichard's rank order for a smaller sample (Reichard, 1928: 24).

Clan groups range from just under 2,000 to nearly 5,600, the smallest clan group containing 5.7 per cent of the population and the largest, 16.2. By contrast, the largest clan contains more than 10 per cent of the population, and the smallest, a negligible fraction.

The Government Survey's system of clan grouping is based on consensus among previously published sources and informants used for the survey: Matthews (1890), Bourke (1890), Franciscan Fathers (1910), Reichard (1928), and a small group of knowledgeable informants. Clans were assigned to groups on the basis of a majority "vote" of published authorities and informants. The result was 9 clan groups and 8 unassigned clans. Clans were listed as "unassigned" where there was no consensus at all, or where there was agreement that they belonged to no group. Some of these could probably be assigned.

It is clear that there is no reservation-wide, universally valid clan-group system. Nevertheless, the "majority rule" Government system has a general validity. Subsequent to the development of this grouping, the Government Survey tabulated inter-clan marriages over a very large part of the reservation. The clan groups that had been set up proved to be overwhelmingly exogamic, so that the Government system is heuristic, even if it is not definitive.

The composition of clan groups is as follows. Four clan groups contain 1 large clan each (2,800 or above) and no other clan of more than 500 members. Three clan groups have 2, 3, or 4 clans of 900 to 2,000, the other members being smaller than 900. Two clan groups have 1 clan of 1,100 to 1,300 and other smaller clans. Of the 4 clan groups with·very large clans, one is a clan group only by courtesy, since it contains only 1 clan; nevertheless, it is always described by informants as belonging to a group which contains other, extinct clans.

It remains to discuss the disagreement both between Navahos and between anthropologists as regards clan groups. To begin with, it is worth stressing that there was enough consensus among informants and anthropologists for the Government Survey to set forth 9 clan groups. When the size, distribution, and lack of formal organization of the clans are considered, it seems probable that such agreement as is found represents in part a survival from an earlier period, with a smaller population. It is hard to conceive how members of two clans which are today spread over the length and breadth of the reservation could agree that they are affiliated, if this affiliation were the immediate product of current conditions. (This is less true if one of the clans is found in a narrowly circumscribed area, but few clans are so circumscribed.)

What kind of a system this may have been can only be conjectured, but the Western Apache afford an interesting comparison. This tribe has clans not unlike those of the Navaho, and indeed with some overlapping names. The Western Apache system is a rather complicated one, in which Clan A and Clan B may maintain an exogamic relationship, but each may have other exogamic affiliations not shared by the other—a linked clan system. The system is associated with clan localization, clan control of land, and with processes of community growth and segmentation not found today among the Navaho (Goodwin, 1942; Kaut, 1957). Kaut, indeed, has suggested that the apparent vagaries of the Navaho system might be understood by using the Western Apache as a model for further investigation of the Navaho case. There are some faint traces of linkage among the Navaho. There are inform-

ants who insist that certain clans are affiliated with two groups. Some
such cases are to be explained by the fact that what is now seen as a
clan with a dual affiliation itself had multiple origins. Thus women
from one Pueblo might each become affiliated with a different clan.
Their children might be the start of new clans, each of which would
maintain a clan-group connection with the father's clan. Thus there
might be a "Jemez Pueblo" clan affiliated with Clan A, and another
with Clan B. In time, the two "Jemez" clans might be regarded as one,
but the two affiliations might survive. At any rate, some so-called
"Pueblo" clans have such double affiliations. In other cases, however,
we may have the remnants of a linked-clan system like that of the
Apache.

We cannot, however, be sure whether the Navahos once had such a
system, or once had a phratry system. There are, however, circumstances which lead to ambiguous clan affiliations, in addition to the
possible breakdown of a linked-clan system. One of these, attested for
Navaho Mountain (Collier, 1951), is the filling of a community with
two large LCE's of the same clan group. Although this may not happen
too often, certainly the most likely outcome is a failure to recognize
the existence of the clan group, and the establishing of marriages between the two LCE's. Under these circumstances, informants from this
area will have an interpretation of clan groups at variance with members of another area. Another possibility, ambiguously suggested by
the Franciscan Fathers, is that a "slave" clan will be claimed by that
clan in a group which enslaved the progenitor, but not by other clans
in the same group, and that furthermore as the "slave" clan itself
became large and important it might reject the affiliation as a relic
of previous low status. Two sources of ambiguity could thereby arise:
affiliation of the slave clan with but one clan in a group, so that clear
phratry patterns would fail to be evident, and unilateral claims of
affiliation (cf. Franciscan Fathers, 1910: 431–432).

The lack of consensus on clan groups would not, however, seem to
be a mere result of the fact that the clan-group system is breaking down.
In the 1930's, as pointed out above, there were few marriages within
the clan groups postulated by the Government Survey, and we would
rather expect the exogamy to break down before memories of the system
disappeared, than that any clear picture of the system should disappear
while exogamy survived.

In sum, the clan group is probably fluid, extends the range of exogamy
and thereby widens the circle of people treated like matrilineal kinsmen, and merits further study.

B. LCE AND COMMUNITY

Data on the clan composition of communities can be found in the Government Survey, in Collier (1951), and in Spuhler and Kluckhohn (1953). The Government Survey divided Land Management Units into "sub-units" and provided a tabulation of clan membership for 52 of these sub-units. In the case of 4 units in district 14, the "sub-units" are chapters and can be regarded as equivalent to what I have called communities. In the remaining 48 instances, I have assumed that they are communities, although they might possibly be arbitrary divisions of a district. In terms of size they resemble communities. These sub-units range in size from less than 50 to more than 1,200. The number of clans runs from 3 per unit to 28. The median sub-unit is about 350 in population, and the median number of clans, 16. There is a close correlation between number of clans and community size. Units tend to be small in the west and larger in the east, where the center of Navaho population is found.

For purposes of analysis, communities were grouped into three categories: those with 3 to 12 clans, those with 13 to 19, and those with 20 to 28 clans. Clans were rank ordered in terms of size, and each community was then examined to see how many of the largest clans were required to make up at least 50 per cent of the population, and how many of the smaller clans made up the remainder. In communities with 3 to 12 clans, the median number of larger clans required to compose 50 per cent or more of the population was 2; the median number of clans composing the remainder was 7. In communities with 13 to 19 clans, the median number of larger clans was 3; the median remainder was 14. In communities with 20 to 28 clans, the median number of larger clans was 4; the median remainder was 18. Although the range of clans was from 3 to 28 per community, and of population from less than 50 to more than 1,200, in no case did it require more than 6 of the largest clans to make up at least 50 per cent of the local community. In almost all cases, the remaining population consisted of a considerably larger number of clans. Thus the range of large LCE's making up at least 50 per cent of the community is narrow—from 2 to 6, and in most instances from 2 to 4, in spite of great variation in community size. Larger communities, however, contain many more relatively small clans than do small ones. Furthermore, in almost every case the numerically preponderant clans are drawn from different clan groups (using the Government Survey clan grouping). Indeed, in only two cases are even two of the largest clans members of the same group.

The same situation is found in the communities described by Collier and by Spuhler and Kluckhohn. In their descriptions are found instances where smaller clans are represented by only one or two adults. In the Government Survey, the range of size of the largest clan contingent in the 52 communities is from 16 to 216.

Hence it seems probable that each community has as its core a few large clans. In some cases these clans may be large enough so that they contain two or more LCE's. Smaller clans may comprise LCE's in some cases, but may be attached to neighboring LCE's in others. In still others, individuals may have almost no members of their own clan in their community of residence or neighboring communities.

Naturally, the largest among the Navaho clans tend to be among the dominant clan contingents of a number of communities. This tendency, however, is offset by the localization of some smaller clans. The largest of all the Navaho clans is among the four largest clan contingents in 26 of the 52 communities surveyed by the government. The second largest clan is found in this position in 22; the third in size, in 21; and the fourth, in 17. On the other hand, 29 other clans are found among the largest 4 clan contingents in at least one community each, so that 72 per cent of all clans occupy such a position in one or more communities. Indeed, 1 clan with a total membership of only 76 is represented among the 4 leading clan contingents in one community.

These figures have implications for the fact that the largest clan contingents in a community are commonly members of different clan groups. Since the largest Navaho clans are distributed among several clan groups, and since these same clans tend to be among the largest clan contingents in a number of communities, simply by virtue of being large and widely distributed, the result is a situation in which the largest clans in a community are often of different groups. Nevertheless, smaller clans do appear as the largest contingents in some communities, and this is probably not the only factor at work to account for the non-exogamic relationship among large clan contingents.

Probably marriage is one device by which additional clans appear in a community, which in turn would tend to provide access for clans not of the same group as those already present, and to provide less access for others. By the same token, since marriage into the father's clan is forbidden, communities are likely to have more than two large clan contingents, given any tendency toward marriage within the community.

It has been pointed out that a nucleus of two sets of intermarried siblings would be theoretically ideal for beginning a new community, since it would provide both families and the core of two LCE's. Data on the history of settlement of three communities indicate a different pattern of settlement. In the case of Ramah, a full chronology of settlement is provided by Kluckhohn (1956). In the case of Navaho Mountain and Klagetoh, chronology is less detailed and the reconstruction is correspondingly somewhat less certain (Collier, 1951). At Navaho Mountain and at Ramah there is no evidence that a group of brothers and sisters moved together. At Klagetoh there are more brother-sister links, but no special sign of effort to preserve them: at one point families resided with husband's kin, at another with wife's, and at still another with neither. It would seem safe to conclude that particular ties with kinsmen, rather than any "architectural" principle which would maintain an LCE nucleus, were active in bringing new families to an area after the first settlers entered. This is not too surprising, considering the absence of corporate landholdings and the flexibility and weakness of the LCE.

C. FAMILY RESIDENCE PATTERN AND COMPOSITION

Support for generalizations on this topic is provided by the Government Survey made in the 1930's, which covered nearly 3,700 family units in all but two areas of the reservation—virtually a complete survey of the Navaho population. The survey shows that 53 per cent of Navaho family units consist of the "biological" family (these and other terms used by the survey are discussed below); 32 per cent are matrilocal, 5 per cent are patrilocal, and 10 per cent are mixed. These figures, which would seem to suggest that matrilocality is relatively rare, require interpretation. "Biological" families include all independent consumption units consisting of husband, wife, and children; of a man and his children; of a woman and her children; of a husband and wife or wives with no children in residence; or of husband, plural wives, and children. There are 1,958 "biological" units, of which 81 per cent consist of husband, wife, and children. This 81 per cent of "biological" units might contain as few as 3 persons (husband, wife, and 1 child), and as many as 12 or so (husband, wife, 10 or more children). On the other hand an extended family ordinarily consists of at least two adult generations. It does not in all cases: a widow and her grandchildren are tabulated as a "matrilocal" rather than a "biological" family, for example. Thus at a minimum an extended family might include only 2 persons, e.g., a woman and her granddaughter, but at a maximum it might include a woman and her husband, several immature children of this couple, several adult daughters of the couple, husbands of these daughters, and children of the daughters. It could conceivably range as high as 50 individuals, although this size is unlikely.

In this census of family units, then, every "biological" family is one unit, and every "matrilocal," "patrilocal," or "mixed" consumption group is one unit. Yet it is exceedingly likely that the extended family units are larger, on the average, than the nuclear families. The government figures, however, do not permit any deduction as to how much larger the extended units may be. For this I have used Collier's figures for Navaho Mountain and Klagetoh (Collier, 1951). At Navaho Mountain the median size of a nuclear family which is not a part of an extended family is 7; the median for extended families is 15. At Klagetoh the median size for nuclear families is 5, and for extended, 10. It would seem fair, then to assume that on the average extended families contain twice as many individuals as nuclear ones.

The ratio of "biological," matrilocal, patrilocal and mixed *units*, we have seen, is 53:32:5:10. If we make the assumption that there are approximately twice as many *individuals* in an extended unit (matrilocal, patrilocal, or mixed), as there are in a "biological" unit, the ratio *of individuals* living in the various types of units would be 53:64:10:20. If these ratios are reduced to percentages, they provide figures as follows: 36 per cent of *individuals* reside in nuclear families; 44 per cent, in matrilocal; 7 per cent, in patrilocal; and 13 per cent, in mixed units. Thus it is reasonable to assume that about 64 per cent of Navahos in the 1930's resided in extended family units, and that the majority of them lived in matrilocal units. The number of nuclear ("biological") families is large, and the percentage of individuals who live in such units is also considerable. It must be remembered, however, that some of the nuclear units result from the breakup of extended units after the death of the parents, and may become extended units in their turn.

At approximately the same time as the Government Survey, Collier made detailed studies of the Navaho Mountain community and a portion of the Klagetoh area. It is important to note that her data indicate a substantially lower figure for percentage of all families that are nuclear families. In analyzing her materials, I have treated her "camps" as family units, since they consist of coresident, closely coöperating sets of nuclear families. Of 9 such camps at Navaho Mountain, only 2 are solitary nuclear families, or only a little over 20 per cent. Of 31 such camps at Klagetoh, 15, or slightly under 50 per cent, are solitary nuclear families. The Government Survey also indicates a lower percentage of "biological" families in District 2, which includes Navaho Mountain, than in District 17, which includes Klagetoh, but the percentages are 49 per cent and 55 per cent respectively. Thus Collier's figure for Klagetoh is reasonably close to the Government Survey, but that for Navaho

Mountain is at marked variance. It is possible that Navaho Mountain, as a recently settled area, is atypical, but no final judgment can be made.

Of all cases in the Government Survey where the senior "family" of a unit, nuclear or extended, consists of a husband and wife, or wives rather than a widowed or divorced man or woman, only 5 per cent are polygynous (150 cases). Polygyny in the second generation is even rarer, being found in only 14 units. (Some of these cases might involve two polygynous marriages in the second generation of the same family, but this is unlikely.) In only one case do we find a plural marriage in both the senior and the second generation.

These figures are very low. Gladys Reichard suggested to me that many cases were concealed, an assumption which seems reasonable in view of increasing Navaho sensitivity to Western reactions to polygyny. On the other hand the basic data were compiled by anthropologists aware of Navaho attitudes. There are various ways of estimating the possible error. One is to make the extreme assumption that *every* case in which the senior generation includes a man and his wife's sister, but not his wife's sister's husband, is a case of concealed polygyny. This would add less than 2 per cent to the total percentage of polygynous marriages, a negligible amount. If we assumed the same ratio of concealment for the second generation, the increment is infinitesimal. This leaves out of account stepdaughter marriages and cases in which a man is married to women in two different consumption units. Such forms of polygyny are rarer than the sororal forms, so that the concealed group would again be small. It seems fair to assume that of all Navaho marriages in the 1930's not less than 5 per cent nor more than 10 per cent were polygynous. Polygynous unions are equally represented in independent and extended units.

Again Collier's data may be inspected for more detailed but less broadly gathered information. At Navaho Mountain her data indicate 20 conjugal sets (husband and wife or wives), of which 2 are polygynous—10 per cent. Of these 2 sets, 1 involves a man and 3 wives, the wives being distributed among 3 consumption units, and all 3 women being of the senior generation of their camps. The other involves a man married to 2 sisters, the second generation of their camp. At Klagetoh, of 33 conjugal sets, 4 (or 12 per cent) are polygynous. One of these involves women in 2 camps, both of senior generation; 2 involve senior-generation polygyny; 1 involves second-generation polygyny. The detailed investigation here conforms closely to the higher figure estimated from government figures. Kluckhohn and Leighton provide a similar figure, 7 per cent, for an unnamed community (1946: 55).

The vast majority of independent units are headed by husband and wife, as are the majority of extended units. The survey does not make it possible to distinguish the widowed from the divorced. It shows "husband" alone or "wife" alone as heads of some "biological" families, and "widow" or "widower" as heads of extended families; no mention is made of divorce or separation, although all sources agree that divorce is common. Hence it is fair to assume that some proportion of solitary husbands and wives, or "widows" and "widowers," are divorced. In using these data, however, I shall follow the compilers' nomenclature. Of 1,958 nuclear families, 84 per cent are headed by a husband and wife or wives, with children; 5 per cent consist of a husband and wife with no children. A woman and children make up 6 per cent; a man and children, 4 per cent; and solitary individuals, 1 per cent. These figures are susceptible of two interpretations. One is that the incomplete nuclear family is not a viable unit in Navaho culture, so that such units tend to become attached to other units as part of extended families. It is, however, equally plausible to assume that these units are relatively young families, so that widowed status is rare, and that either divorce or widowhood is followed by remarriage for this younger group.

In the 1,712 extended families, husband and wife or wives head the unit in 62 per cent of the cases; widow, in 31 per cent of the cases; and widower, in 7 per cent of cases. In these latter cases it is exceedingly unlikely that more than a fraction involve divorced men, since such men are unlikely to retain their children. They might, however, head extended units which include a brother and/or sister and their children. A negligible percentage is made up of sibling groups which coreside but have no children with them. Percentages of widows and widowers for matrilocal, patrilocal, and mixed households do not differ to any important degree.

Presumably the units headed by widow and widower have older heads on the average than those headed by husband and wife or wives. This is suggested by household composition. In the case of households headed by husband and wife or wives, 24 per cent of resident sons-in-law have no children; in the case of households headed by a widow, 8 per cent have no children. In the case of husband-and-wife-headed households, 27 per cent of resident daughters-in-law have no children; in the case of widower-headed households, 9 per cent; and in the case of widows, 13 per cent.

The very large discrepancy between the number of extended family units headed by widows (31 per cent) and widowers (7 per cent) is somewhat difficult to interpret. Part of the difference must be accounted for by higher death rates for older men than for older women, combined with a general tendency for men to be older than their wives at marriage. Another portion may represent a greater tendency for older men to remarry than for older women to do so, although it must be remembered that older Navaho women do sometimes marry younger men.

It is tempting to assume that the Navaho extended family remains together while the senior woman is still alive but tends to break up if she dies, even if her husband is still alive. Under these circumstances, the number of extended families headed by a widower would be considerably smaller than the number headed by a widow. In that case, however, we should find a fair number of men living attached to sisters' families, sister's daughter's families, etc., and a small number of women living alone or thus attached. No such marked preponderance of men is found. We might assume that a woman's children tend to remain with her when she is widowed, whereas a man's children tend to separate, the father remaining with one of his daughters. This state of affairs, however, would not account for the above percentage difference, since a unit of a woman and her daughter or daughters would be a single extended family, and a unit of a man and his daughter or daughters would also be a single extended family in the government census. In sum, the percentage difference is not satisfactorily accounted for, and there are no data satisfactory for drawing conclusions regarding the exact sequence of events in the breakup of the extended family in each generation.

It is clear, however, that it does break up. Extended family units involving two or more siblings and their spouses in the senior generation are exceedingly rare. Of 1,712 units, there are 68 such cases, or less than 5 per cent. Nearly half of these include two sisters and their husbands; two thirds of the remainder include a brother and a sister and their spouses; the rest involve two brothers and their wives. Even rarer are cases in which the senior generation consists of a married couple plus a sibling of one of them and the sibling's children, sibling's spouse being absent. There are only 30, or less than 2 per cent. I have tabulated these various categories in detail, since in each case we can assume the existence of an extended family with two mature siblings in the senior generation. It could be argued that a number of cases have been overlooked by omitting cases of a childless, mature, divorced or widowed individual (one without children or whose children have left the family of orientation), who is attached to a sibling in a sort of extended family unit. I assume that many cases of coresident solitary siblings involve younger, unmarried siblings, but in any case the percentage of all families with any coresident sibling of either the husband or the wife in the senior generation is very small. Hence the data conclusively show that Navaho extended family units almost invariably segment completely at the death of the parents. (In some cases, of course, several children may have moved away prior to this event.)

In spite of the enormous diversity of types of kin found attached in various instances to the Navaho extended family, 80 per cent of extended family units include one or more of the following types of kin, whatever else they include: son-in-law, daughter's children, daughter-in-law, son's children. The remainder are considered extended families by virtue of the addition of assorted kin: wife's or husband's sibling, wife's or husband's sibling and children, great-grandchildren, etc. Furthermore, 70 per cent of all extended units contain either son-in-law or daughter's children, with or without additional kin.

Of extended units headed by a husband and wife or wives, 29 per cent do not include a child's spouse or child's child. Widow-headed units contain only 5 per cent of such cases; and widower-headed, only 9 per cent. Perhaps this reflects a tendency for dependent, incomplete families and solitary individuals to attach themselves to fully functioning extended units, rather than to units handicapped by widowed heads, but this is uncertain.

The Government Survey provides two types of tables: a list which shows every combination of kin found in Navaho families, and how often that combination occurs (analyzed above), and a list which shows the number and percentage of cases in which each single type of kin is found. The second list contains overlapping categories: thus it states in how many cases daughter's children are present (or son's children), but one cannot determine from this list in how many cases both are present. Nevertheless, it provides a rough measure, in brief form, of some of the features of household composition presented above.

Table 2-1 shows what percentage of families have within them each of various types of kinsmen in addition to the senior family and its offspring. Married daughters are considered a part of the senior family for these purposes, but sons-in-law are considered additions to this family, and so for other kin types. Only the most frequent types have been included.

D. DATA ON INCEST, EXOGAMY, AND PREFERENTIAL MATING

Reichard states that Navahos prefer to marry into their fathers' clans,

but other authorities state either that these marriages are prohibited
or that they are rare (cf. Carr, Spencer, and Woolley, 1939: 255).
Reichard's own data provide perhaps the largest quantity of material
suitable for testing the tendency for marriage into the father's clan. To
make such a test, we selected the longest genealogy from each area
in which Reichard worked. This provided 7 genealogies and 580 mar-

TABLE 2-1

Common Co-residents

| Relative present | Number | Per cent | |
		Total	Extended Units
DaCh	1,064	29	62
So-in-l	806	22	48
SoCh	264	7	15
SoWi	247	7	14
WiSi	131	3.5	8
WiSiCh	121	3.5	7
WiBr	117	3	7
DaDaCh	81	2	5
HuSiCh	72	2	4
HuBr	52	1.5	3
DaDaHu	52	1.5	3
HuSi	35	1	2
HuBrCh	27	0.5	2
WiSiHu	24	0.5	1
WiBrCh	19	0.5	1
HuBrWi	16	0.5	1
WiBrWi	14	0.5	1
HuSiHu	12	0.5	1

riages, or 45.6 per cent of all marriages in all genealogies (1,273 total).
In these 580 cases, information was lacking with respect to the clan of
husband and/or wife in only 10 per cent of cases, but for the more
remote clan ancestry of husband and wife it ran 57 per cent or more;
thus information is lacking on either husband's father's clan or wife's
father's clan, or both, in 98 per cent of cases. Percentages of marriages
were calculated, then, on the basis of cases where information is avail-

able for the relevant clan affiliations—and sometimes this involves very small numbers of cases. On this basis, marriages of a man and woman of the same clan constitute .19 per cent of cases; marriages into father's clan, 3.2 per cent; marriages of people whose fathers were of the same clan, 4.3 per cent; and marriages into grandfather's clan, 9.1 per cent of cases, of which the majority are marriages into the father's father's clan.

Carr, Spencer, and Woolley provide a sample of 247 marriages from Peublo Alto, with rather more information on father's and father's father's clans, so that the percentage of unknowns rises only as high as 66 per cent. (The difference is not in the quality of field work, but in the nature of the data. Carr, Spencer, and Woolley were trying to ascertain parental affiliations of living individuals; Reichard's genealogies contain deceased individuals, whose father's father's clan might well be unknown to the living.) In their sample, using cases where information is available as a base, there were no infractions of clan exogamy. Marriage into father's clan occurred in .8 per cent of cases where information is available; marriage into mother's father's clan, in 12.4 per cent of cases; and marriage into father's father's clan, in 14.1 per cent of cases. Thus, although Pueblo Alto informants do not mention a prohibition for the father's clan, they almost never choose such marriages.

These two samples provide roughly comparable results. Marriages into father's clan are so infrequent as to support the views of those ethnologists who state that the relationship is prohibited. Marriages into the grandfather's clan, although an expressed Navaho preference, are also rare enough to be of relatively little significance, when it is considered that even in the absence of preference many such marriages are likely to occur. With a few large clan contingents in every community and with a prohibition against marriage into the own and father's clan, there is a reasonable possibility of random selection of a grandfather's clan (cf. Zelditch, 1959).

The data of the Government Survey of the 1930's provide further information on clan exogamy and its breaches, but cannot be used for the question of preferential marriages, since there are no data on partners' paternal or more remote clan connections. The survey tabulates extant marriages by clan affiliations of the partners for 14 districts out of 18, covering the vast majority of marriages at the time—a total of 4,385. Only 29 occurred between members of the same clan, or .66 per cent. Reichard shows .19 per cent, and Carr, Spencer, and Woolley record no breaches for 1 area. Hence it seems fair to say that there was almost no breakdown in the observation of clan exogamy as late as the mid-1930's. The frequency of breaches of exogamy in the government data is roughly proportional to clan size, so that the 3 largest clans have the largest numbers of transgressions. The frequency is also proportional to the number of marriages surveyed in each district. Thus there are 6 breaches in district 17, where 672 marriages were tallied, and only 1 in district 9, where but 68 marriages were tabulated. It might be claimed that acculturation is responsible for breaches of exogamy, but the eastern part of the reservation is both the more densely populated and the more acculturated. Given the rarity of all breaches, and the narrow range—from 0 to 6 cases per district—it seems simplest to assume that size of population is the critical variable for the period under consideration.

I turn now to observation of clan-group exogamy. On this subject Reichard's data provide no information, since she used exogamy itself as one criterion for establishing the clan groups. The government list of clan groups, however, was based largely on informants' "votes." Hence this grouping may be used in connection with the tabulation of 4,385 marriages as a partial check on clan-group exogamy. There are only 70 breaches, or 1.6 per cent. Undoubtedly some of these marriages were not regarded as incestuous by the participants, since clan groupings do vary by area. Hence this figure is probably too high. When it is considered that little other than informal pressure penalizes breaches of exogamy, these figures reflect a strong tendency to maintain clan-group taboos as late as the 1930's, in the face of considerable acculturation.

As for cross-cousin marriages, there is an Enemy Way song which implies sexual contact between cross cousins. Dapah explains this as a device for keeping secret the identity of the person for whom the song is being sung. McAllester indicates that the song is used to tease cousins who are dancing together (McAllester 1954: 40, 41; song 42 and musical text).

The Western Apache, who permit and prefer this marriage, sing songs in which the term for cross cousin is used to refer to a sweetheart (Goodwin, 1942: 302). Both the existence of the songs and the Western Apache preference for such marriages suggest that they may once have been a Navaho pattern.

To investigate the problem of possible preferences for marriage between certain clans, the Government Survey data on marriages between clans in fourteen districts have been combined into one master table. This table has not yet been subjected to careful statistical analysis; inspection indicates, however, a strong tendency for marriages between clans to be proportional to the size of the clans in question, except for the exogamic patterns previously discussed. It is possible that there are departures from this tendency marked enough to be called "preferences." A detailed analysis of inter-clan marriage in three districts indicates that within each district there are some departures from the frequency predictable on the basis of clan size and exogamy. Nevertheless such higher than normal pairings between two clans in one district are not paralleled by similar high frequencies between the same two clans in the next. Hence there are no data to support a hypothesis of reservation-wide clan marriage preferences. It is quite possible, however, that in any given area some informants will say, "We of Clan A prefer to marry into Clan B." Fundamentally, all such preferences are probably reflections of the size of the clans in the area, and the preferential familial patterns listed above.

E. KINSHIP TERMS AND USAGES

Consanguine terms are here listed as stems. They are never so employed, either in reference or address. They occur only with prefixes, "my, our, your, their, one's," etc. A trivial exception is a tendency of young children to address their mothers as *má* instead of *shimá* (my mother). Readers who wish to consult lexicons are advised that kinship terms sometimes appear as stems, or with the *shi-* (my) prefix, or with the *ha-* (one's) prefix. The orthography used here is that of Robert W. Young and William Morgan, who also supply a fairly complete set of terms (Young and Morgan, 1951: 255–259).

I shall begin by discussing variants and special usages with reference to consanguine kin, passing then to affines and finally to group terms. All consanguine terms may be used for reference and address.

The *-náli* term is self-reciprocal, applied to FaFa or FaMo or SoCh. It seems to be extended to FaFa lineage, but some informants are inclined to say that more remote connections of FaFa are not really kin. It may be pluralized when a senior refers to his juniors (my grandchildren), but not when a junior refers to his seniors.

The term for MoMo and certain other kin in her generation is *-má sáni* (literally, old mother). Some sources provide *-chó* for MoMo, but some informants insist that it can be used only for MoMoMo. Some informants permit *-má sáni* for MoElSi, but others restrict it to the grandparental generation.

The reciprocal for *-chaii* (MoFa) is *-tsói* (DaCh). But often *-chaii* is used as a self-reciprocal between two men of equivalent age—even two young men—who are clan relatives or unrelated. Neither will call the other "grandchild" under these circumstances.

There is an alternative term for Fa, -taa', which is generally agreed to be obsolescent for kinship reference or address. Some informants say that it may be used for Fa; others deny this. It appears in addressing deities in prayers.

FaBr may be called by the term for Fa (-zhé'é), or "little" Fa (yázhí, little). The reciprocals are the terms for So and Da ms. FaBr may also be called by the term -bízhí, which is used for FaSi as well. The reciprocal is also -bízhí. The FaBr or FaSi may refer to BrCh collectively using a pluralizing suffix, but the BrCh may not use this collective form for the FaBr as a group, or for the FaBr and FaSi taken together. MoSi may be called by the term for Mo, may be called "little" Mo, or may receive a separate term, -k'a'í. This last is rare and seems to be obsolescent. Some informants do not know the referent of the term.

The charts provide the reciprocal pair shidá'í-shidá' for MoBr-SiSo. There are several variants. The two may address each other self-reciprocally as shidá'í-shidá'í or as shidá'-shidá', or even reverse the terms, so that MoBr calls SiSo shidá'í and he replies, shidá'. In the last case, the MoBr is usually younger than the SiSo. An alternative sometimes mentioned for MoBr is shahastói, but this is in fact not strictly a kinship term, being translated "my elder," and not necessarily to an elder kinsman. Dapah suggests that this is used for the head of the LCE. According to Haile (1941), a man may address his SiSo as "my young man," and his SiDa as "my young woman," a usage which would appear complementary to the use of "my elder." Young and Morgan provide the following: "hatséłke'é, plural of tsiłké, youth; used in referring to one's grandsons and nephews as a group. Hach'eeke'é, plural of ch'iké, maiden, is used in referring to one's granddaughters and nieces as a group." The terms may be used by a man or a woman (Young and Morgan, 1951: 258). They seem to suggest bilateral extension of these terms, as seniority usages, whereas Haile implies unilateral use. Young, however, says that these terms are broadly applied, since they mean "my young man (young woman)" (personal communication).

MoBr may call SiDa "little mother"; she may similarly call him "my son." The same variant pairs of reciprocals are also found as in the case of MoBr-SiSo.

Two sibling terms not charted are -k'is, sibling of same sex, and -lah, sibling of opposite sex. These words are losing their value as kinship terms, or even as extensions of kinship. Between males, the -k'is term means little more than "friend," and there are terms for "friend" which have a stronger connotation of intimacy. Although Haile insists that these terms can be used only for true Br and Si (1941: 58), some informants assert that they should be used only *outside* the family—they are too remote to apply to close kin. This is a fairly recent development. Half-siblings use the same terms as full siblings for address and for reference, unless the context requires further specification. This is true whether the link is through Fa or through Mo.

ElSi may also call a considerably younger Br "my son," and he will reply, "my (little) mother" (Reichard, personal communication).

There are two cross-cousin terms, *-í naa'aash,* used only between males, and *-zeedí,* used between females, between male and female, and (uncommonly) between males. The first of these terms is analyzable as meaning, "he who goes about with me" (Young and Morgan, n.d.: 103).

Matrilateral cross-cousins may be further distinguished descriptively as "my cross cousins born for me"—i.e., descended from my clan, and patrilateral cross cousins as "my cross cousins for whom I am born." If a Br and a Si marry a Si and a Br, the children of the two marriages are cross-cousins "born for each other." The Navahos enjoy various complicated "plays" with terminology which are based on this double linkage.

As indicated on the charts there are separate terms for So and Da, ms and ws. There is another difference in usage between the two. The term for children is *'álchíní.* When a woman speaks of *sha'álchíní,* my children, she refers to her own sons and daughters. A man uses the same term to refer to his family—to his wife and children. It would appear that clan affiliation may account for this difference. The term for parents is *shischíinii.* There are a number of terms for first-born, last-born, and the like, and routine ways of indicating whether two children are born of the same parents or merely of the same mother and different fathers, or vice versa. Two children born for the same clan (whose fathers, that is, are of the same clan) have a standard term for expressing this relationship. Most of these last usages do not involve terms of reference or of address, but are simply standard ways of describing relationships.

Affinal terminology cannot be discussed without the use of possessive prefixes, since, as will immediately become apparent, the application of the terms would otherwise be entirely unclear. Affinal terms are almost never used in address.

Basically, there are only three stems involved: *-aadaaní,* used for male affines in the first ascending and descending generations; *-zhá'áád,* used for females in the same generations; and *-yé* (to marry), for affines in own generation. (Note that this is not the same stem as *-ye',* So ms.)

These three stems are then treated in two different ways. Ego refers to individuals who have married his own consanguine kin, using the first-person possessive prefix, *shi-*, or *sh-*, and the appropriate stem. On the other hand, when he speaks of his wife's consanguine kin, he uses the same stems in the same generations, but with a different prefix and an additional word. He uses the third-person possessive prefix, *bi-*, his (her) and adds *nishłį*, I am. Thus, SiHu he refers to as *shiyé*, roughly, "my in-marrying one." But he refers to WiBr as *biyé nishłį*, "his in-marrying one am I"—as it were, taking the perspective of the other. And so for the other two stems. Thus a man who is asked to identify another might reply, "That is my son-in-law." But if the son-in-law is asked to identify his father-in-law, he replies, "I am his son-in-law."

In every case where *nishłį* can be used, *nishłíini* may be substituted, with only a trifling difference in sense: *baadaaní nishłį*, "I am his (her) son-in-law" (or other relative covered by this stem); *baadaaní nishłíini*, "the one whose son-in-law (etc.) I am."

There are also minor variants for all of the terms employing the *-yé* stem. Thus for *shiyé* may be substituted *shá'áyéhé* or *sha'áyééh*, the latter two being free variants. Young translates the latter two terms as "the one who marries for me." He says that Navahos are likely to use the term *shiyé* for their own siblings' spouses, although they may use the other terms. The variant terms are, however, more often applied to individuals married to members of one's clan than to immediate kinsmen. They convey more the conception of someone "married into my unit" than of someone "married to my kinsman" (Young, personal communication). The reciprocal term based on the variant stem is *bá'áshhéhé*, which may similarly be used to describe any one of the appropriate generation belonging to the unit into which ego has married. It may be translated, "for him (her, them) I married" (Young, personal communication).

Thus those who marry ego's consanguines are "his" in-laws—belonging to him. On the other hand, his wife's consanguine kin do not belong to him—he belongs to them. These usages are perfectly symmetrical for male and female speakers, in spite of the asymmetry of the relationship discussed in an earlier section.

The last class of affinal connections are those who have married ego's spouse's siblings. They are termed *bił 'áshxéhé*, and the term is self-reciprocal. Roughly speaking, the term carries the meaning, "one married into the same unit (into which I married)." The term *t'áálá'íigé* is an alternative for this, and contains the stem for "one" and the stem for "marry," conveying approximately the same meaning as the other term. Mother-in-law and son-in-law also refer to each other as *doosh'íinii*, "the one I don't see." The term for co-wife is *yił 'iyé*. There are no terms for child's spouse's parents, and some informants would claim that there are no terms for some of the affines described above.

Terms for stepparents vary, depending upon whether there is a prior relationship to ego. Thus if own FaBr or MoSi or a clansman of Fa or a clanswoman of Mo replaced the deceased parent, *-bízhí*, the term for FaSi and one of the terms for FaBr, would be used for a stepfather, and *-k'a'í*, one of the terms for MoSi, for a stepmother. Otherwise, the terms *shaadaaní*, for stepfather, and *shizhá'áád*, for stepmother, would be used, thus classifying them as affines (Reichard, 1928: 86).

The polite reference and address terms for a spouse are *shahastiin* and *she'esdzáán*. The word *hastiin* has almost the force of "Mr.," when used without the possessive, and *'esdzą́ą́* is a similarly respectable way to refer to a woman. There are two self-reciprocal terms, the first satisfactory for reference or address, *shich'óóni*, roughly "friend" or "companion," a word which can be applied by a man to a man or woman friend—not checked for a female ego; and *bił hinshnáanii*, "we two live together," used for reference. The terms *shiką'* and *sha'áád*, my male and my female, although often supplied gleefully by informants, are distinctly vulgar. I do not know if they are ever used in address. In reference they are jocular and coarse.

The foregoing treatment of affinal terms deals with terminological classification. I turn now to details of the uses of affinal terms. As has been said, most informants agree that one should never address the immediate affines to whom the terms apply as *shaadaaní*, *shizhá'áád*, or *shiyé*. None find the idea of using them for immediate affines agreeable. The reciprocals of these terms can never be used in address. The self-reciprocal *bił* . . .term is never used in address.

Exceptions to the almost total bar to the use of affinal terms in address have been discussed in broad outline above. More concretely, the clan mates of a man's wife's father will all call him *shaadaaní;* clan mates of a woman's husband's father will all call her *shizhá'áád*. Thus the spouse of a person born for one's clan is always regarded as of a different generation, and presumably of the first descending generation. A man's wife's own clan mates will call him *shaadaaní* or *shiyé* and its variants, depending on their perspective. Those who regard his wife as a generation above or below them will use the first term; those who regard her as of their generation will use the second. The same usage will apply toward a woman: her husband's clan mates will call her *shizhá'áád* if they equate him with the first ascending or descending generation;

and *shiyé*, etc., if they equate him with their own generation. Children
of male members of one's spouse's clan may address one as *shiyé*, thus
assuming generational equality.

I turn now to group and categorical terms. *Shik'éi* means "my relatives." It apparently applies to the entire group to which any consanguineal term is normally applied. There is a term for clan relatives,
shití'ízini (Haile, 1950–1951, 1: 104). A clan is *diné'é*, which also means
"people," or *dóone'é*. Clans in the same group as one's own are described
as "related." Jimmie Dapah says that a group of strangers may be addressed as *kwáasiní*, which he considers to signify "my relatives of some
sort or other"—i.e., of indefinite relationship. Haile translates it as
"acquaintances" (*ibid.* 210). There is a collective term for all those
married into a given clan: thus, *kiiya'áanii yáají' da'ayé*, all those married to members of the *kiiya'áanii* clan.

Truk

Ecology and History

Just east of the center of the Caroline Island group lies Truk, a complex atoll made up of a great ring of reefs and coral islets within which rise seventeen small, volcanic islands. Although the lagoon ranges from 30 to 40 miles in diameter and has an area of 822 square miles, and although just over 9,000 people live in this area (Goodenough, 1951: 19–25), we are here concerned with only one of the high islands, Romonum. The ethnographic work of Goodenough, Murdock, Gladwin, and the Fischers all converged on Romonum, although each worked on other islands in the Truk group as well. Since all the work was done within a period of about four years, it refers to the same island, the same people, and the same time period.[1] The work of the earlier German ethnographers, dating from the turn of the century and the work done for the U.S. Commercial Company just as World War II ended are not referred to here.

Romonum has an area of 0.288 square miles (Goodenough, 1951: 21), a population of 230 in 1946 (Gladwin and Sarason, 1953: 68), and a population density of nearly 800 per square mile.

Dogs, cats, rats, pigs, a few cattle, and fruit bats occur, but they play a very small part in the diet. Staple food is supplied by the breadfruit tree, which matures in about fifteen years and produces for about 150 years. Breadfruit is stored and fermented in pits for off-season consumption, during which time taro, sweet potatoes, and manioc supplement the diet. Yams are not grown, and coconuts and bananas play only a small part in providing food. Fish, although highly valued,

[1] I am indebted to Ward H. Goodenough and John L. Fischer for reading successive drafts of this chapter, offering corrections and suggestions, and providing information beyond that published in their monographs and papers. They are not, of course, responsible for the form I have used, or for my interpretations of their data. Work done since 1954 by Marc Swartz was not available when this was written.

are a supplement to the primary reliance on vegetables, especially bread-fruit (Goodenough, 1951: 23–24).

Truk came under effective foreign control just over sixty years ago, when Germany acquired it from the nominal rule of Spain. Prior to this, Western contacts were limited to brief, often violent visits by an occasional ship and later to the presence of a handful of traders and missionaries, who first appeared in the latter part of the nineteenth century (Goodenough, 1951: 25). Early contact was minimized by the widely held belief, fairly well founded on fact, that the Trukese were a hostile and unfriendly lot (Gladwin and Sarason, 1953: 39–40). The pacification of Truk was not accomplished until 1903 (Goodenough, 1951: 25). Since then changes have occurred, but we are informed that they have not been of major significance for social organization. Goodenough (1951: 26) notes, "Despite the discontinuance of warfare, an almost complete conversion to Christianity, a high proportion of literacy, and considerable modification in technology, Trukese society is still a vigorously going concern, its pattern of organization little changed by the events of the past 50 years." All sources seem to concur in this judgment.

Descent Groups and Property

There are at least 42 matrilineal clans on Truk, averaging about 250 members in each (Goodenough, 1951: 82), though some clans are on the point of extinction while others have far more than the stated average figure. The clan is an exogamous descent unit with relatively weak ties of kinship between members. Demands for hospitality may be made in the name of common clan membership, but such demands are made only when no other, firmer ground can be given. The clan has no chief, controls no land, and holds no ceremonies or meetings (*ibid.*: 82). Goodenough speaks of them as "name groups," which seems an appropriate designation.

The sub-clan on Truk consists of the members of a clan who share a traditional common ancestry, usually about events in the past which marked the splitting of a particular lineage. The sub-clan, thus, is described by Goodenough (1951: 86) as "a large lineage whose constituent descent lines have their corporate holdings in different districts and on different islands where they function locally as independent lineages while retaining membership in their parent lineage." Ties of hospitality exist, extending, in the old days, to wife lending, and sub-clan members may call on each other at times of food shortage.

The unit of next smallest size is the ramage, a group of sub-clan mates who are organized into more than one major property holding group but who are members of the same political district. The ramage has a recognized leader, the oldest among the leaders of its constituent property groups, and unity as a special task group.

Most often, however, there is but a single property-holding group, the lineage, and no larger unit like the ramage exists (Fischer, 1950: 6). The term ramage is thus confined to situations in which two or more property-holding groups have emerged through fission but are not yet fully separated.

The ramage has a chief, *sömwonum ejinag* (chief of the clan), who has authority only with respect to activities which the related property groups agree to undertake as a group. He has no control over the property of the constituent property groups except his own. Ramage tasks are usually restricted to large fish drives and preparations for feasts.

The ramage may arise either through the growth and splitting of a single property group into two, or through the immigration and establishment of persons as property groups in a district where they have clan mates who are already a property group and with whom they establish such coöperative connections (Goodenough, 1951: 87).

The central unit of Trukese social structure is the lineage, which consists of a group of persons who can usually trace actual genealogical connection with each other through the female line and who hold collective title to certain plots of land. The members of a lineage do not belong to any larger property-holding group, although some of its members may hold title to some other lands and thus constitute a smaller property-holding group within the larger unit. Such a sub-unit within a large unit is to be distinguished as a "descent line" (*ibid.:* 77).

There is no Trukese word which means lineage. A lineage may be referred to as a *tetten* (line) of a clan, sub-clan, or ramage. Before the missionaries came, *jetereges* or *cö* were used to designate this group, the latter term meaning "people"; now the word is *faameni*, the Trukese rendition of the English word "family," which is also applied to the sub-clan. Other ways of referring to a lineage are by the clan name of its members or by the name for its lands or estate, "the people of such-and-such a place." In Trukese thinking, each property group has a locality even though its holdings may be widely scattered (*ibid.:* 66–67).

Prior to the German occupation, in 1901, there used to be associated with each lineage a dwelling (*jimw*), occupied by the women of a lineage and the husbands of those who were married, and those young males who had not yet reached puberty. A large jimw was usually partitioned into sleeping compartments, one for each married woman and her husband with their small children, and a separate one for the unmarried girls past puberty. Where a lineage was small, however, a smaller house served. Today, the large jimw are little used. Instead, smaller houses, still occupied by the women of a lineage singly or in pairs (*ibid.:* 67), are clustered about a common hearth (*fanag*). Where the lineage is quite small there may be no common hearth with its associated earth ovens (*ibid.:* 69); there is, instead, a cook house associated with each dwelling.

A large and important lineage might have a meeting house (*wuut*), which usually stood by the shore, where it served as a canoe house as well. Here the unmarried young men of the lineage slept, as well as men of the lineage or husbands of the women when observing sexual taboos. The meeting house was the lounging place for men during the evening, where they visited and told stories; visitors were put up here, too. There are no such meeting houses today, a situation which imposes some strain on the sleeping habits of the young, unmarried men who, it is sometimes stated, should not sleep in the same house as their sister.

Each large dwelling used to have a menstrual hut associated with it where the women of the lineage were isolated during their first menses, where they prepared and ate their meals during subsequent menstruations, and where the women went for childbirth. Menstrual huts are no longer used (*ibid.:* 69).

Dwelling sites used to be shifted about once in a generation's time in order to keep them near breadfruit trees which were bearing well, so that the supply of this staple would always be near at hand. The Japanese administration required that houses be situated close to the shore, and such moving about was rare (*idem*).

On Romonum, lineages range in size from 3 persons in the smallest to 34 in the largest. Roughly 13 functioning lineages are distributed between two political districts. The nucleus of each lineage, often its entire membership, is composed of the matrilineal descendants of a group of real or classificatory siblings who founded it as a property-holding unit. Genealogies may be traced back four or five generations, seldom further, and are often traced to a man. This man may have been the husband of the ancestress of the lineage, and though his name will be remembered, hers may not, nor those of her siblings (*ibid.:* 70).

The inclusion of persons in the property group other than actually related martilineal kinsmen arises in two ways: first, through adoption, second, through the client relationship. Persons adopted when they are still infants become fully fledged members of the adopting parent's lineage, losing membership in their natal lineage. If, however, adoption occurs later in life the adopted person is likely to retain membership in both units, meeting obligations to both and deriving such rewards as he may from both. Such a situation is not usual. Client members are present when only one or two surviving members of a particular lineage affiliate themselves with the lineage of their father, or when a woman marries virilocally and, being without local lineage affiliation herself, is taken into her husband's lineage where her children will continue to occupy client status until they acquire property in their own right sufficient to set themselves up as an independent lineage.

The lineage as a property-holding unit can be distinguished from the lineage as a group of matrilineally affiliated kinsmen, and indeed is so distinguished to a certain extent in Trukese thinking.

The lineage as a property-holding unit is conceived of as a group of siblings, whatever the actual genealogical relations among its members may be. The bonds between true siblings are considered to be closer than those of any other relationship. Siblings are expected to support each other regardless of the situation or its possible consequences. Anything which their collective efforts produce in the way of property belongs to all of them as a group. Any property which they may inherit from their father belongs to all of them as a group. Such property is administered by the oldest brother in the interests of the group, whose members may not put it to personal use without his permission. The oldest brother is called *mwääniici*, "senior man," and he represents the group to outsiders. He allocates property as it is needed, may order the younger siblings of the group to work, and supervises such work. The division of labor by sex largely separates the activities of men from women, and the women thus tend to work as one team, the men as another. So the women have their *finiici*, "senior woman," who orders them to do various jobs, supervises their work, and represents them.

Younger siblings must obey and respect their older siblings of the same sex, and this is so both in theory and in practice, anyone failing in this being severely censured. Sisters must obey and respect their brothers regardless of their relative age in years, provided only the brothers are past the age of puberty.

Own siblings are defined as the children of one woman; children of one woman by different men are also own siblings, but children of one man by different women are not. Children are automatically members of their mother's lineage and, regardless of the particular genealogical tie, are conceived of simply as younger siblings from the point of view of the lineage as a property-holding group. Thus a child may be in the same lineage as his mother, mother's sisters, mother's sisters' children, and so forth, but as a member of a property-holding group he is related to them as sibling, older or younger depending on their relative ages. In contexts concerned with their collective property holding, members of the lineage refer to each other as "sibling" (*ibid.*: 31–33).

Women have equal rights with men in the ownership of property of all types, but their role is often less obvious owing to the dominance of brothers over sisters.

The Trukese are interested in property primarily for its productive or practical potentialities rather than for prestige or nonmaterial rewards. Nevertheless, the Trukese have a very strong, deeply emotional attitude of attachment to their land. The Trukese place a high value on having enough food, "perhaps," says Fischer (1950: 15), "even higher than do many peoples. They are chronically afraid they are not going to get enough food. Land they identify with food. A man speaking of his land will often simply use the words 'my food' instead of 'my land.' A threat to their land is a threat to their food." Each small piece of land, on the hills as well as on the shore, has a separate name. Many of the names are simply descriptive of the location but others are named to commemorate some important legendary event in the family history which occurred there.

Ownership may be of two sorts: *full* and *divided*. Where there is full ownership the individual or group has full title to the property. Where ownership is divided, one owner will have *provisional title* and the other *residual title* (Goodenough, 1951: 34).

Inheritance should be clearly distinguished from other forms of title transfer. Inheritance has to do with the succession to title occasioned by the death of its former holder. Goodenough states the Trukese rule of inheritance succinctly: "any property to which a man, woman or corporation (lineage) holds full title at the time of their death or extinction is inherited by their children" (*ibid.*: 145). In the case of a lineage, its "children" (*jëfëkyr*) are the offspring of its men. Thus, when a man dies, those holdings to which he alone has full title pass on to his children, but his lineage continues to hold title to such plots as the man had provisional title to, since on death provisional title is lost and full title reverts to the residual title holder. A lineage loses members by death and gains members by birth or adoption. So long as that lineage has members it has not died (or become extinct). Therefore the children of the men of that lineage cannot inherit from it. When, however, a lineage has no surviving women of childbearing age it usually permits its remaining men to make gifts of their holdings to their children. As provisional title holders, the children thus acquire full title to the gift when their father's lineage becomes extinct (*ibid.:* 45).

A person who makes improvements on property has full title to these improvements, provided he has the owner's consent to make such improvements. Thus a house or tree may be owned separately from the land on which it stands, while cleared and cultivated soil is separable and may be separately owned from the land or territory of which it is a part. The house, the cultivated soil, and the planted tree are all improvements to which their makers have full title regardless of the ownership of the land on which they stand (*ibid.:* 35).

Except for two restrictions, inheritance and lineage membership, a full title holder may destroy, lend, give, or (nowadays) sell his property as he sees fit. He may not present his property as a gift to someone other than his heirs, his own children, without the latter's consent. Likewise, a junior member of a lineage may not dispose of property to which he alone holds title without the approval of his mwääniici, for the lineage head has the right to call upon the junior member to employ that property in the lineage's interests where that may be necessary.

The situation of divided ownership may arise through the giving of a gift, *niffag*, which transfers provisional title to the recipient while the donor retains residual title. The most important situations of this sort are two: first, the allocation by the lineage of certain plots to certain members for their use; and second, a man's gift to his children of property to which he may hold full or provisional title. The allocation of plots of land held jointly by the lineage to certain of its members is such that the lineage retains residual title; the users, provisional title. When the lineage member who holds provisional title to certain plots dies, full title reverts to the lineage, which may then, through the mwääniici, reallocate these plots. Often the holder of provisional title will share the plots with a younger sibling or a sister's child, and as the provisional title holder becomes old and ceases to take an interest in these plots, the junior member is tacitly confirmed as the provisional title holder. This should not, as Goodenough points out, be confused with matrilineal inheritance, since the full title is not conveyed. The lineage retains its right to full title and its right to decline to allocate those plots to the particular junior. If the junior does obtain them, it is because he has generalized rights in those plots anyway, by virtue of his birth, and not because of the advanced age or death of the provisional title holder. That *this particular* junior gets provisional title to *these particular* plots is merely a matter of convenience for the lineage in dealing with the problem of allocation.

Since a husband works plots to which his wife and her lineage hold title, and since the husband is responsible for improvements in these plots, he gains title to those improvements. As his natural heirs, his children inherit the improvements which their father made (*ibid.*: 42). Plot and improvement thus revert fully to the lineage on the father's death, though the sibling group of children retain full title to their improvements.

On the other hand a lineage may permit a male member to make a niffag of plots to which he has provisional title to his children, who then become the provisional title holders but only when the lineage itself has enough for its own needs. The children's father becomes residual title holder of any improvements he has made on it (which his children will inherit full title to), and the father's lineage retains residual title to the holding minus the improvements. The children owe their father a portion of the produce of the trees he planted for them, and owe their father's lineage, in the person of its mwääniici, a portion of the produce from that to which it holds residual title (*ibid.*: 43–44).

The Trukese say that men prefer to give some of their land holdings to their own children and some to their sister's children. This is what in fact usually happens, according to Fischer (personal communication). At times the gift is made by the senior man of the lineage who can override objections from within his lineage and give considerable portions of the lineage holdings to his children. At other times it may be done by a junior (but not very young) member of a lineage in the face of lineage opposition and this may then become the basis for considerable tension, litigation, and ill will after the death of the older people; the lineage retains its sense of ownership while the children claim full ownership.

Regardless of the gifts of land, a father will plant trees and cultivate gardens for his children on land they hold as members of their lineage, and these are given as gifts to the children. So long as the man is alive, the children must give a portion of the products of gifts to their father. On the father's death, full title passes to the children. The question of whether both the pattern of transferring plots to own children by gift and the rate at which it occurs are of long standing and stable is of course difficult to answer. Goodenough indicates that the pattern at least is of pre-occupation status, and seems to imply that the rate at which it occurred has been relatively stable since aboriginal times. Fischer (personal communication) is less certain and is only willing to agree that this transmission from father to children is older than the German administration. It is his feeling that it occurs somewhat more frequently now than it used to.

An important element in the gift from father to child is the fact that this obligates the child to give a portion of the produce continually to the father. As the father gets older and can no longer work, his status as residual title holder obliges his children to give him a share of the produce. This is a form of old-age insurance, although, as will be seen, it does not always work well for the older person.

The division and subdivision of plots through successive gifts of fathers to their children keeps provisional holdings fairly equitably distributed (*ibid.*: 44). At the same time, however, it reduces individual holdings with each generation. Goodenough states that a man's holding on a given plot may consist of one tree. Further, this process tends to scatter holdings widely about the district. This in turn has bearing on the nature of the community, in that a given lineage has its holdings scattered throughout the holdings of other lineages, so that regardless of the compact nature of the residence group, its worked holdings are scattered.

Acquisition of property has thus far been dealt with as deriving from inheritance from father to children, from gifts from father to children, and, of course, through birth into a lineage. There are other ways in which property can be acquired, but none of them are as important as those already discussed. These include sale or exchange, which can occur but actually occur rarely; conquest and seizure, which transfers full title, and although relatively rare, is structurally important in that it involves reshuffling of political organization as well as the tendency to assemble many small holdings back into a larger block; and finally, a form of gift called *kiis*, which will be described later. Further, although the discussion has proceeded in terms of land and improvements on it (trees or gardens), these same regulations apply to various other kinds of property such as canoes, magic, dances, and so forth. We will not be concerned with these here.

Where the lineage acts with reference to the property it holds, all members are regarded as siblings. Where it happens that ego's mother's brother is the senior man of a lineage, he is called elder brother. When, however, the context is one which does not concern the joint holdings of the lineage, mother's brother is called "father." The eldest male of the lineage, its mwääniici, is its head and the next oldest male of the lineage, who will succeed him, is *mwääninyk* (*ibid.:* 74).

As head of his lineage, the mwääniici administers its property. He allocates use shares to the junior members, who hold them under provisional title from the lineage. A mwääniici must be consulted by his juniors before they take any action which might affect the welfare of their group, such as getting married or selling or giving away important personal property. It is the mwääniici who calls meetings of the lineage in the lineage wuut. He represents his lineage to the district chief. He has the right to veto proposed marriages of his junior lineage mates, although in the end the junior may force the withdrawal of the veto. He may order the lineage members to harvest from their own personal holdings and to put the harvest in the lineage pool, to bring this produce to the lineage cook house, to prepare and process it, and to bring the finished product as a presentation to the district chief. The lineage head initiates and leads the work of storing breadfruit for preservation in the pits used by individual members. If there is a big land-clearing project undertaken by the lineage, it is the mwääniici who organizes and supervises it (*ibid.:* 75).

The finiici, or senior woman, has a comparable role where the activities of women are concerned. She supervises the management of the household in which they live together and directs and organizes their coöperative work, such as reef fishing. She keeps track of the food supply and informs the mwääniici of the state of affairs in the household. She may also report to him any behavior of any woman's husband which she deems out of order. Like the mwääniici, she has veto powers over the marriage of junior members of either sex, although here too, the junior member may, by one stratagem or another, win out (*idem*).

Succession to the office of mwääniici is theoretically by birth order within a generation level: the oldest man of the oldest generation at any given time is head. In fact, however, if the oldest man in a younger generation is considerably older, actual age takes precedence over generation. Where two men are of roughly equal age, generation seniority will prevail (*ibid.:* 76). It is worth noting that where the lineage contains two or more collateral lines, headship does not reside in one line to the exclusion of the other; both lines are treated as indistinguishable elements in the lineage and headship passes to the oldest person regardless of line. Lines within a lineage are not ranked (*idem*).

It will be recalled that any group of own siblings may constitute a property-holding group with respect to certain properties, but it takes its place within the lineage in holding rights in lineage-held property. This situation may arise when a group of own siblings either creates property by its collective efforts or inherits property from the father. Like any individual member of the lineage, these siblings may not dispose of their property freely but must consult with the lineage head, and may be called on to contribute from their personal holdings in the lineage's interest (*idem*). It is not unusual for each set of siblings within a lineage to have such holdings of its own, as well as its common lineage holdings, since each set of siblings will have a different father and each set of siblings will regard itself as an especially close and effective work unit. This descent line, as Goodenough calls it, is thus one of the more important points at which fission can be expected. When the descent line, which need not include own siblings exclusively, holds large amounts of property and contains a relatively large number of persons, it tends to be in a better position to split off and also to have reason to do so. It acquires greater autonomy within the lineage by virtue of its holdings. The fact of its common holding, in which other lineage members do not share equally, tends to make the bonds between its members firmer (*ibid.*: 78).

Fission begins when the women of a descent line establish themselves in a household separate from that of the other women of the lineage. This is only possible when these women hold title to land which is not part of their lineage holdings. Such separation also requires that they have an elder sibling of each sex who can act in the roles of mwääniici and finiici. The actual split occurs when the whole lineage formally divides its holdings so that the new descent line takes out its share, gaining full title to it (*idem*).

Fission is inhibited by the relative stability of population; often a descent line may consist of two or three brothers, without a sister whose children can continue the group. Such a group of brothers may take in a female of a collateral descent line who can bear children to it, thus fusing two descent lines. Likewise, fathers do not often have sufficient land to pass on to their children to encourage the children to begin a distinct descent line (*ibid.*: 77–78).

It is important to note, moreover, that the process outlined above only tends to occur: where the lineage is very large; where the sibling group which splits off consists of uterine siblings; where the sibling group has elder members capable of acting as male and female head respectively; where ample land is available to the lineage; and where the particular sibling group which splits off has enough land to manage. Ordinarily, however, the gifts by a father to his particular children are gradually merged with the property of the lineage of which they are members, managed by a mwääniici. Having managerial rights with respect to all members of the lineage, the mwääniici manages whatever holdings a particular member or group of members of the lineage may have. If siblings have need of that property, the mwääniici is responsible for its allocation to them for their use. Further, it should be explicitly reiterated that (according to Goodenough) such splits, if and when they occur, occur between the children of different sisters, and never occur between the children of one mother. The number of different fathers involved is irrelevant. The closest, firmest bond is between uterine siblings. Second is the bond between the children of sisters. A woman may have married two different men and had two children by each. The gift by one father to his two children tends to be amalgamated with the gift of the second father to his two children, and the whole unit is managed by the eldest sibling as the mwääniici of that unit (Goodenough, personal communications).

Marriage

Marriage is forbidden between members of the same clan, sub-clan, ramage, lineage, or descent line. In addition, it is forbidden to marry anyone who is recognized as a consanguineal relative, which includes members of one's father's lineage, though not his ramage, sub-clan, or clan. Normally the young people themselves initiate the match, but marriages may be arranged by the parents of the couple.

Divorce is possible, and, to quote Goodenough (1951: 121), "if it [the marriage] doesn't work out, there is little hesitancy in getting a divorce." I have been unable to obtain divorce-rate figures, but all sources agree that it is both permitted and "not uncommon." Fathers continue to be responsible for the child's food and shelter after divorce.

Extramarital affairs are practically universal. Both sororate and levirate were practiced in former time but have become less common today. Formerly, it was held that a man should marry some woman of his deceased wife's lineage unless such a person could not be supplied, at which time he would be released. Similarly, a woman "should" marry a man of the deceased husband's lineage.

Formerly polygyny was permitted, but it was rarely practiced because the difficulties were so considerable. A man might be married to two sisters, in which case he would live in one place, but it was believed that the sisters would quarrel too much. Alternatively, a man might be married to unrelated women, in which case he would have to alternate his residence between the houses of the two wives. The demands of two separate brothers-in-law tended to impose severe strain on a husband. In fact, polygyny seems always to have been rare, and mainly a function of the levirate (*ibid.:* 122–123).

Residence

The choice of residence on Truk has recently been clarified by Goodenough (1956: 30–34). It is worth quoting him directly and at length in view of the precision with which he deals with the relevant considerations.

. . . the cornerstone of [Trukese] social structure is the property-owning corporation, which, because it perpetuates its membership by a principle of matrilineal descent and is a segment of the community rather than being widely extended across community lines, I chose to call a lineage. No individual can exist independent of some lineage affiliation. If he goes to another community he must either affiliate with one of its lineages or remain outside the community pale without food, shelter or protection. If it has enough adult members and access to a suitable site, a lineage has its own dwelling house (or cluster of houses) which is regarded as the place where it is physically located. A large lineage may contain two or even three separately localized sublineages. Lineages may move from one site to another as they gain right of access to different plots of land; house sites are not regarded as permanent. There are several ways in which a lineage may have right of access. It may itself own the ground under full or provisional title; one of its members may hold personal title to the ground; or a sublineage may be the owners. A lineage may also be localized on land which belongs to a man who has married into it. When this happens, the understanding is invariably that the man's children, who are members of the lineage, have received the land in gift from their father, so that in localizing here the lineage has moved, in effect, to the land belonging to one of its members. With the tendency nowadays for the lineage to be localized in a cluster of smaller houses instead of a single large one as in former times, the site may consist of several adjacent plots under separate ownership; but each case will conform to the pattern above—three adjacent plots, for example, being held by the lineage, one of its members, and one of its husbands respectively. The need for juggling of this kind has also been increased on Romonum Island with the movement of all house sites to the beach, during the decade before World War II. The point of importance to note, however, is that a man who is living on land which he got from his father is in all probability not living in the extended family associated with his father's lineage, but in that associated with his or his wife's. Let us now see what are the possible choices of residence open to a married couple within this setting.

The first thing to note is that the choice is always between extended family households. Couples do not go off and set up in isolation by themselves. The only exceptions to this are native pastors and catechists whose residence is determined by their occupation. (They find it necessary, however, to try to make some arrangements for domestic cooperation with a neighboring household.) The important question for a married couple, then, is: to what extended families does it have access? It has access by right to the extended family associated with the lineage of either the bride or the groom. A member of a lineage which is not localized becomes a dependent of his or her father's lineage for purposes of shelter. The extended families associated with the wife's father's lineage and the husband's father's lineage form, therefore, a pair of secondary possibilities for choice of residence. At any one time, however, a couple has but two alternatives: on the one hand the wife's lineage, or, if it is not localized, then her father's lineage, and on the other hand the husband's lineage or, if it is not localized, then his father's. Other things being equal, as long as one party to the marriage belongs to a lineage which is localized, this lineage will be chosen before joining the other's father's lineage. Resort to a father's lineage of either spouse is, therefore, a fairly rare occurrence. Other things being equal, moreover, a couple will regularly choose to live with the extended family associated with the wife's lineage rather than that associated with the husband's. It is regarded as proper for one's children to grow up in the bosom of their own lineage in close association with their lineage "brothers" and "sisters," with whom they are expected to maintain absolute solidarity, no matter what the circumstances, for the rest of their lives. Given matrilineal descent as the principle of lineage membership, regular residence with the extended family associated with the husband's lineage would keep lineage brothers separated from one another until adulthood and lineage sisters would not normally live and work together either as children or as adults. Choosing to reside with the wife's localized lineage, therefore, is consistent with the high value placed on lineage solidarity.

But what are the considerations which make other things unequal? Under what circumstances do people regularly choose in favor of the husband's localized lineage even though the wife's lineage is localized? And under what circumstances do couples prefer to reside with a wife's father's lineage household rather than the household associated directly with the husband's lineage? What are the factors, in short, which favor a husband instead of his wife and a secondary instead of a primary affiliation?

Most instances of residence with the husband's lineage household occur in cases where the wife's lineage is not localized because it does not have enough adult women to run a separate household or lacks access to suitable land. But there are other circumstances favoring such residence. Ultimate responsibility and authority in a lineage is vested in its adult men. If residence with the wife's kin would take the husband too far away from where his own lineage house is located, it may appear advisable for him to bring his wife to live at the latter place. As the physical distance between the husband's and wife's lineage households increases and as the importance of the husband in his lineage affairs increases, the greater the liklihood that residence will be with the husband's kin. Where the husband or his lineage is in a position to provide the children with far more land than the wife's lineage, and at the same time the husband and wife come from communities too widely separated to make it possible to reside in one and maintain the land in the other, residence will be with the husband's kin. If the husband's lineage will soon die out, so that his children will take over its lands, these children may organize as a new lineage temporarily operating jointly with the survivors of their father's lineage. Such of these children as are women may bring their husbands into what may be regarded either as the wife's or wife's father's localized lineage (the former as one looks to the future, the latter as one looks to the past).

Finally, it may happen that a young couple may be requested to reside with elder relatives in a household in which they do not have any *right* to live. In Fischer's census, for example, I note the case of an elderly man residing with his wife's localized kin group. He and his wife have no children. Nor are there junior kin in his wife's lineage who do not have greater responsibilities to others in the household (judging from my genealogical data). Living with them are this old man's sister's daughter and her newly acquired husband. As head of her lineage, the old man has obviously pulled her into his household with the consent of his wife and her kin (who are thus relieved of undue responsibility). She has no other reason for being there, and the arrangement will terminate when either the old man or his wife dies. Temporary arrangements like this one, made for mutual convenience and with the consent of those concerned, may be on the increase today. I suspect, however, that one hundred years ago they would also have accounted for the residence of up to five per cent of the married couples.

The foregoing, then, are the considerations which I believe the Trukese have in mind when they decide where they are going to live.

. . . It should be clear that while land-ownership in Truk is a factor which limits the number of sites where a lineage can be localized as an extended family, individual couples are concerned with what extended family they will join, not with whose land they will live on (except in the case of inter-community or inter-island marriages already noted). To use land ownership as a basis for differentiating types of residence choice, therefore, seems to me to be artificial. . . .

Since it is extended families between which the Trukese choose, we may list the types of residence which are descriptive of the possibilities inherent in their social structure as follows:

1. Residence with the extended family associated with the wife's lineage.
2. Residence with the extended family associated with the husband's lineage.

3. Residence with the extended family associated with the wife's father's lineage.
4. Residence with the extended family associated with the husband's father's lineage.
5. Residence by arrangement with a specific kinsman in an extended family in which one is otherwise without residential right.
6. Residence independent of any extended family—one a hypothetical possibility until recent times, now involving church officials and a few persons seeking to break with traditional ways.

Residence of type 1, above, is conceived as ideal and is at the same time structurally integral. The role of the division of labor between the sexes in this arrangement is succinctly stated by Goodenough (1951: 127):

. . . the organization of the lineage as a tight cooperative group is strengthened by its being localized in a particular place in a house occupied by its women, who operate as a cooperative team. For such a team to be effective, there have to be enough women to satisfy certain minimum working requirements. Fishing, for example, is an important feminine activity. The techniques involved require a minimum of about four women in order to get a reasonable catch. For an extended family to function adequately, therefore, there must be enough young women to do the necessary work and at least one woman of sufficient age and experience to direct it intelligently. There have to be men in the form of husbands or brothers to prepare those foods (such as breadfruit) which it is a male responsibility to provide. If there are not men in a lineage, its women are dependent on their husbands, whose primary responsibilities are with their own lineage. If the men of a lineage are few, their share of responsibility toward their lineage sisters is proportionately greater. All these factors are of importance in determining whether or not the women of a lineage can afford to live in matrilocal residence when responsibilities to their sisters are heavy.

The six types of residence which Goodenough lists are given in terms of the primary consideration entering into the residential decision, namely, affiliation with an effective extended family unit. But residence has traditionally been treated for comparative purposes in terms of the spatial alignment of primary and secondary relatives. What spatial alignments of kin emerge from the six residential types Goodenough lists for the Trukese?

Goodenough's type 1, if followed consistently, would yield an alignment of matrilineally related *women* with their husbands. Type 2 would yield an alignment of matrilineally related *men* with their wives. Type 3—residence with the extended family associated with the wife's father's lineage—would yield an alignment of women whose fathers belonged to the same matrilineage. "The Trukese have standard expressions for this kind of relationship; the women would all be *pwiipwi winisam,* 'siblings through fathers,' or *jëfëkyren eew sööpw,* 'heirs (as distinct from members) of the same lineage'" Goodenough, 1956: 35). Type 4, residence with the extended family associated with the husband's father's lineage, would yield "an alignment of men who were *pwiipwi winisam,* whose fathers belonged to the same matrilineage" (*idem*). Type 5 would not yield any systematic alignment since it would depend on the specific kinsman chosen. Type 6 is, of course, neolocal residence.

The frequencies of actual residential arrangements on Romonum in 1947, according to Goodenough's typology, follow. The frequencies appear to be consistent with his conclusions.

Type of Residence	Number	Per cent
1	46	71
2	10	15
3	0	0
4	1	1.5
5	3	5
6	4	6
undetermined	1	1.5

The problem of the distance between the localized natal groups of bride and groom has already been alluded to. Goodenough (1951: 145) makes the point clearly that "Since matrilocal [i.e., type 1 above] residence takes the men away from their home lineages, most of them marry women whose lineage houses are within a few minutes walk of their own." People are not restricted to their district for their spouses. Since Romonum is 0.288 square miles in area, marriages within Romonum itself do not impose distance as a problem. It is only marriages between residents of Romonum and other islands in the Truk group which might make such a problem significant, and the evidence suggests that although such marriages occur and are not prohibited by any specific rule, they are infrequent.

Fischer (personal communication) provides some precise figures on this point. He writes that the following ratios of on- to off-island marriages (either husband or wife from another island) obtain for the following islands in the Truk lagoon: Pata, a peninsula of Tol island,

38:5; Uman (one district), 27:3; Parem, 26:14; Fefan (Ununno district), 19:3.

The clustering of houses on the island of Romonum is today distorted by the administration requirement that houses be located on or near the beach so that overwater privies may be used and thus conform to hygienic standards set forth by the administration. Goodenough, however, gives a map of aboriginal dwelling units (1951: 133). From this it can be seen that houses were located well back from the beach "as a defence against a surprise night attack from the sea" (*ibid.*: 132) and occurred with some light density toward the center of the island; lineages with more than one house often had these houses separated from each other at some distance, with other lineage dwellings intervening; there was no marked clustering which could be described as a village, hamlet, or ward unless the entire island as a unit be regarded as the community, village, or hamlet. It is in no sense possible to regard this as a monolineage community.

Production and Distribution

The productive roles of men and women, husbands and brothers, wives and sisters, split mainly along the male-female axis. The major food is breadfruit, and men climb the trees, harvest and collect it, peel and steam it, pound and prepare it. A woman depends on a man for this task, and primarily a women depends on her husband, only secondarily on her brother, although he may well help. Actually a man will work both for his sister and his wife, and although he must see that his sister's breadfruit supply is taken care of, he is concerned that his sister's husband take care of it. Similarly, cooking in bulk for later use is a man's task; the day-to-day, small preparation of each meal falls to the women. When cooking is done on any scale, however, it tends to be the husbands of one household who will cook enough for the whole of their wives' lineage and themselves. Women in small groups do much of the shallow-water fishing with hand nets, while spear fishing, trolling, or setting are done by teams of men. Husband and wife's brother will often coöperate as a fishing team, while a group of sisters, women of a lineage, do the inshore fishing together.

The breadfruit, prepared in bulk for storage and later use, is obtained from those sources to which either the wife or the husband has access. The wife is allotted trees by the mwääniici of her lineage. If those trees are bearing and ready for picking when the food is needed, they are used. Her husband is responsible for feeding his children, and food from such trees as have been allocated for his use by the senior man of his lineage, and which may be bearing and ready for harvesting, may be used. If food is needed and neither husband nor wife has access to trees ready to be picked, one or the other will appeal to their respective lineage heads, and food will be found.

The symbolic value of food throughout Micronesia is difficult to overestimate. It enters into every relationship, every crisis, almost every ritual, and it is the center of a complex of psychological concerns and anxieties that have not yet been clearly unraveled for any Micronesian culture, though its existence is clearly perceived and remarked on by almost every ethnographer. Truk is no exception. As has already been mentioned, the lineage's estate is often called "food" (Fischer, 1950: 15). Gladwin and Sarason (1953: 52–53) report:

> . . . it is in matters related to food that the solidarity between kinsmen finds its most explicit expression in everyday life. Food is normally shared with the other members of one's lineage whether there is a lot or only a little available, and a man will usually give some also to his wife's relatives. This sharing is no small gesture, as the quantity of food given away will usually exceed that kept for one's own household and always represents a large outlay of work involved in both production and preparation. But as a man makes the rounds of his relatives, distributing the packages of food he has prepared or the fish he or his wife have caught, he knows that these same relatives will be preparing food themselves in a day or two and will soon make a return gift. As food spoils quickly in the warm, damp atmosphere of Truk, this system actually makes it possible for a person to prepare food less frequently than would otherwise be the case. In a closely knit lineage the various households in effect take turns in providing for the whole group. That the sharing of food is not entirely motivated by unselfish ideals is also shown by the observed fact that older people beyond the productive age often do not get their full share in the lineage distribution and, not being able to provide for themselves, may suffer real privation.

Food exchanges, in one form or another and developed to one or another degree, are also a general Micronesian characteristic. On Truk one lineage will challenge another to a food fight, and the members of each lineage will work desperately for days and weeks to produce more food than the other. This culminates in a great feast in which each lineage tries to consume the output of the other, although only after each item has been carefully counted and the victor determined. Usually, despite everyone's effort to stuff himself well beyond capacity, there is food left over. It may in part be distributed to persons of other lineages, but this is a weak effort and the surplus usually spoils (*ibid.:* 58).

The gift of food also plays a role in the relations between the district chief and the lineages constituent in his district, in that this gift symbolizes their relations.

Interpersonal Kinship Relations

An important aspect of the organization of the lineage lies in its internal differentiation. It is helpful to proceed to describe the internal differentiation of the lineage by first considering kinship terminology.

On Truk, kinship terms are used "(1) when the question of kinship is relevant to the context of a conversation, (2) when one wishes to avoid using a personal name, and (3) in order to coerce behavior under exceptional circumstances" (Goodenough, 1951: 93). Ordinarily, personal names are employed. Under extraordinary circumstances the use of a kinship term may in effect be a conditional curse and is strongly disapproved of as such by the Trukese. Goodenough (*idem*) says, "if a woman is reluctant to give me something I want I may say: *mwäänumw, mwäänumw,* by your brother, by your brother, give it to me. She would then bring sickness or death on her brother if she failed to grant the request."

Six consanguineal and two affinal terms characterize the system (all from Goodenough, 1951: 94–100):

jinej. Applied to any woman of a higher generation: Mo, MoSi, FaSi, MoMo, FaMo, etc. and extended to all females of ego's father's lineage, ramage, and sub-clan (but not clan), such as FaSiDa, FaSiDaDa, etc., and are also extended affinally to any woman whom ego's wife (or husband) calls by that term, or the wife of any man ego calls *semej.*

semej. Applied to any man of higher generation: Fa, FaBr, MoBr, FaFa, MoFa, etc. and extended to all males of ego's father's lineage, ramage, and sub-clan (but not clan) such as FaSiSo, FaSiDaSo, etc., and also extended affinally to any man whom ego's wife (or husband) calls by that term, or the husband of any woman ego calls *jinej.*

pwiij. Applied to any sibling of same sex: a man to his brothers, a woman to her sisters, and extended to MoSiCh of same sex as ego, the child of anyone called *semej* or *jinej* if they are of ego's sex, and spouse's siblings if of same sex as ego.

feefinej. Female sibling, man speaking. Extended as *pwiij* except that for "sibling of same sex" read "female sibling M.S." throughout.

mwääni. Male sibling, female speaking. Extended as *pwiij* except that for "sibling of same sex" read "male sibling F.S." throughout.

neji. Applied to anyone of a lower generation: So, Da, SiCh, BrCh, GrCh, etc. and extended to the children of men of ego's descent line, lineage, ramage, and sub-clan (but not clan) such as MoMoBrCh, MoBrCh, BrCh, SiSoCh, and extended to the children of those called by sibling terms.

pwynyej. Applied to own spouse, anyone whom my spouse calls *pwiij*, and to the spouse of anyone ego calls *pwiij*, e.g., Hu, Wi, WiSi, HuBr, BrWi (M.S.), SiHu (F.S.).

jeesej. Applied to sibling-in-law of same sex as speaker, spouse's sibling of opposite sex, and to anyone whom my spouse calls *mwääni* or *feefinej*, and to the spouse of anyone whom ego calls *mwääni* or *feefinej*; e.g., WiBr, HuSi, BrWi (F.S.), SiHu (M.S.).

I follow Goodenough's analysis (1951: 94–96) of the terms in detail here. He points out that

It is apparent that the Trukese kinship system is fundamentally . . . of the so-called Hawaiian or generation type, in which parental terms are extended to all relatives of one's parents' generation, sibling terms to all relatives of one's own generation, and child terms to all relatives of one's children's generation, regardless of how they are actually related. The Trukese notion that the people of a lineage stand in a parental relationship to the children of its men, its *jëfëkyr*, has redefined what constitutes a higher and lower generation, thereby altering the framework of the Hawaiian type of kinship system. This redefinition is a logical outgrowth of the organization of lineages and descent lines as corporations [property-holding groups] whose members are regarded as siblings. It is possible that at one time a person stood in a dual relationship to his mother's brother's son just as he now does to his mother's brother, calling his cousin a sibling when they interacted simply as kinsmen but calling him a child when behaving as a member of a corporation [property-holding group] toward one of its *jëfëkyr*.

On my father's side the *jëfëkyr* relationship redefines what are higher and lower generations. Since I am an *jëfëkyr* of my father's descent line, I am a child of his descent line as a whole. All the members of his descent line therefore stand in a parental and thus higher generation to me. Hence all the men of my father's descent line (e.g., FaMoBr, FaBr, FaSiSo) are my fathers: *semej*. All the women (e.g., FaMo, FaSi, FaSiDa) are my mothers: *jinej*. The parent terms are extended to members of other matrilineal kin groups to which my father belongs, including his lineage, ramage, and subsib [sub-clan], but not including his sib [clan].

The same considerations apply optionally to the lineage and subsib of my mother's father, since I am the child of their *jëfëkyr*. Even more remotely one can extend this to the members of one's father's father's lineage, but in practice this is not done.

Since all the children of all the men of my descent line (e.g., MoMoBrCh, MoBrCh, BrCh, SiSoCh) are in turn my *jëfëkyr* including of course my own children if I am a man, they are regarded as of a lower generation and

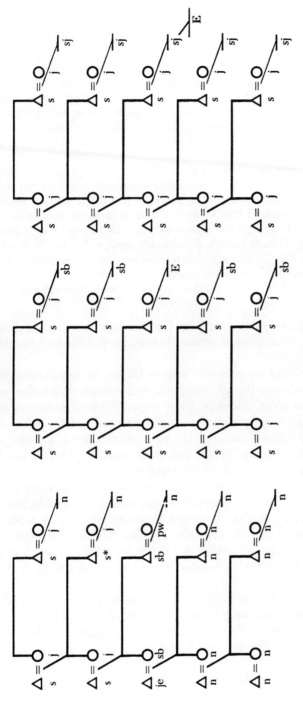

E = ego; s = *semej*, Fa; j = *jinej*, Mo; sb = sibling; n = *neji*, Ch; je = *jeesej*, sibling-in-law same sex speaker; pw = *pwynyej*, spouse.

*MoBr may be called *semej*, Fa, or older brother (*jääj mwään*).

Fig. 3-1. Trukese kinship terms. (After Goodenough.)

are hence my children: *neji*. This usage is extended to include the *jëfëkyr* of my lineage, ramage, and subsib, but does not include the *jëfëkyr* of my sib. The children of my *jëfëkyr* are in turn of an even lower generation and hence are also *neji*.° [°A person is in a position to recognize this relationship with the children of his *jëfëkyr* much more readily than they are to reciprocate. While a man lives, his lineage mates recognize kinship with his grandchildren, but he usually dies before his grandchildren have reached puberty or adulthood and are fully aware of the connection and prepared to act accordingly.—Goodenough's note]

Since all the *jëfëkyr* of my father's descent line (e.g., FaMoBrCh, FaBrCh, FaSiSoCh, and FaCh by another marriage) stand in the same genealogical relationship to my father's descent line that I do and are, like me, "heirs" of that descent line, I consider them to be in my generation and hence call them siblings: *pwiij, feefinej, mwääni*. This usage is extended to the *jëfëkyr* of my father's lineage, possibly his ramage, but not to those of his subsib or sib. The Trukese say: "He is *pwiij* because we are *jëfëkyr* of the same *sööpw* (lineage)." Since the *jëfëkyr* of my father's descent line and lineage are my siblings, their children are of a lower generation and are hence my children: *neji*.

Lineage diagrams constructed from Goodenough's analysis are shown in figure 3-1. Relationships, described below, are summarized in tables 3-1 and 3-2.

Father and mother are primarily responsible for the socialization and care of their children, though other relatives classed with father and mother share to some extent in these responsibilities. Authority and the right to discipline lie in the hands of father and mother primarily, and only rarely will anyone else take such action for a child who has not yet reached puberty. When the child reaches puberty, the father's authority ceases, as does his right to discipline the child. Although the mother retains the right to exercise some authority she is usually not capable of doing much. No one outside the child's lineage except the father ever has the right to discipline him. A woman's brother may interfere with his sister and her husband in the matter of discipline. The right of a child as a dependent of his father, and the child's right to the father's provision for his food and shelter is clear, and this continues even after divorce.

Conversely, children are supposed to take care of their parents when the latter are old and incapacitated. In fact, old people tend to be neglected except when there is plenty and to spare for the young people; then the surplus goes to the old.

The relation between father and daughter becomes constrained when the daughter reaches puberty, so that the father is, as the Trukese put

TABLE 3-1

Status Scale of "Setting Oneself Above Another"

Ego in Relation to Other	Must Not Use Fight Talk	Must Not Speak Harshly	Must Not Refuse Request	Must Avoid	Must Crawl
Man to semej	No	No	No	No	No
Man to jinej	No	No	No	No	No
Man to feefinej	No	No	No	No	No
Man to Hu of feefinej	No	No	No	No	No
Man to Wi	No	No	No	No	No
Man to Wi's ygr pwiij	No	No	No	No	No
Woman to semej	No	No	No	No	No
Woman to jinej	No	No	No	No	No
Woman to own Da	No	No	No	No	No
Woman to Da of pwiij	No	No	No	No	No
Woman to Hu	No	No	No	No	No
Woman to Hu of ygr pwiij	No	No	No	No	No
Woman to Hu's feefinej	No	No	No	No	No
Man to Wi of ygr pwiij	Yes	No	No	No	No
Woman to own So	Yes	No	No	No	No
Woman to Hu's ygr pwiij	Yes	No	No	No	No
Man to ygr pwiij	Yes	Yes	No	No	No
Man to Wi's older pwiij	Yes	Yes	No	No	No
Woman to ygr pwiij	Yes	Yes	No	No	No
Woman to So of pwiij	Yes	Yes	No	No	No
Woman to Hu's older pwiij	Yes	Yes	No	No	No
Man to male neji	Yes	Yes	Yes	No	No
Man to Wi of older pwiij	Yes	Yes	Yes	No	No
Woman to Da of mwääni	Yes	Yes	Yes	No	No
Woman to Da of Hu's pwiij	Yes	Yes	Yes	No	No
Woman to So of Hu's ygr pwiij	Yes	Yes	Yes	No	No
Woman to Da of Hu's feefinej	Yes	Yes	Yes	No	No
Woman to So of Hu's feefinej	Yes	Yes	Yes	No	No
Woman to Hu of older pwiij	Yes	Yes	Yes	No	No
Woman to Da's Hu	Yes	Yes	Yes	No	No
Woman to So's Wi	Yes	Yes	Yes	No	No

TABLE 3-1 (continued)

Ego in Relation to Other	Must Not Use Fight Talk	Must Not Speak Harshly	Must Not Refuse Request	Must Avoid	Must Crawl
Man to older pwiij	Yes	Yes	Yes	Yes	No
Woman to older pwiij	Yes	Yes	Yes	Yes	No
Man to female neji	Yes	Yes	Yes	Yes	Yes
Man to Wi's mwääni	Yes	Yes	Yes	Yes	Yes
Woman to so of mwääni	Yes	Yes	Yes	No(?)	Yes
Woman to mwääni	Yes	Yes	Yes	Yes	Yes
Woman to So of Hu's older pwiij	Yes	Yes	Yes	Yes	Yes
Woman to Wi of mwääni	Yes	Yes	Yes	Yes	Yes

SOURCE: Goodenough, 1951: 113, table 7.

it, "taboo from setting himself above" his daughter. He must not use "fight talk" in her presence, i.e., belligerent or threatening language and certain insulting expressions or gestures (Goodenough, 1951: 112), must not speak harshly to her, may not refuse a request she makes, and should avoid her presence. He also must not stand in her presence, or, more precisely, he must not be physically higher than she, so that if she is seated, he must crawl or crouch in passing. Crawling behavior is no longer practiced, but the other forms of avoidance are. A man must not see his mature sister's breasts exposed or joke sexually in public in her presence.

Although a man must not "fight talk," speak harshly with his son, or consistently refuse his request, there is no avoidance nor are any of the more extreme forms of respect behavior required. Relations between mother and son are marked by none of these restraints except that she must not use fight talk with him. A woman is under no restraint with her own daughter.

Any brother may concern himself with his sister's child, and she may request his intervention if she wishes, although on the whole this seems to be rare. It is only until puberty that the mother's brother may act thus; after puberty his role assimilates to that of "father" and an elder member of the child's lineage.

As has been indicated, it is the sibling relationship which is the keystone of the whole Trukese system, and the relationship which is

TABLE 3-2

Status Scale of Sexual Distance

Ego in Relation to Other	Joke Sexually in Public	Have Inter- course	See Breasts Exposed	Be Seen in Company	Sleep in Same House
Man with pwynywej (other than Wi)	A	A	A	A	A
Man with Wi	D	A	A	A	A.
Man with affinal jinej	D	D	A	A	A
Man with consanguineal jinej	F	F	A	A	A
Man with Da of Wi's mwääni	F	F	D	A	A
Man with female neji (except first above)	F	F	F	A	A
Man with feefinej	F	F	F	F	F

A = approved   D = disapproved   F = forbidden

SOURCE; Goodenough, 1951: 117, table 8.

stressed most is that of brothers. A man's own brothers as well as lineage brothers always provide unqualified support in his conflicts with outsiders. During adolescence parents cease exerting discipline; they may scold, but more usually will call on the boy's older brother to speak with him or beat him. Gladwin and Sarason (1953: 97) state: "Often this is more appropriate, for the misdeeds of an adolescent are quite likely to involve his brothers rather deeply. . . . [If he] gets himself into trouble he may well find himself in a fight and his brothers will have to come to his aid, often at their own peril . . . a man will thus often take the initiative in curbing his younger brother without the intervention of their parents."

An elder brother must be respected and obeyed, and has, as indicated, the right to discipline and give orders to a younger brother. A man must not use fight talk with his older brother, nor may he speak harshly to him or ever deny a request made him. The respect demanded of the younger brother requires a degree of avoidance. An older brother, however, may refuse a request of a younger brother and need not avoid the latter, though he should not speak harshly to nor use fight talk with his younger brother.

A man is permitted to sleep with his brother's wife, either older or younger (or with a wife's sister). He must, however, show his older brother's wife more respect than his younger brother's wife, in that, although they may sleep together or joke sexually in public, a man may not speak harshly to an older brother's wife nor refuse her request, as he may do in the case of a younger brother's wife.

Brotherhood is extended formally under certain circumstances to persons who have no blood relationship, and thereupon entails the rights and obligations of true brotherhood.

Sisters are not as close as brothers, nor as interdependent. Gladwin and Sarason (1953: 56–57) report: "To some degree this may be a function of the fact that to a man, his brother means support in time of crisis as well as a companion, while for a woman, it is her brothers, rather than her sisters who rally to champion her cause when need arises." To this might be added the fact that it is only in fishing that there need be any marked coöperation between sisters; the main productive roles are in the hands of husbands and brothers. Further, the sister's subordination to her elder sister, who may order her about and demand obedience, is not balanced by obligations for mutual support; in trouble, a woman depends on her brothers, not her sisters.

At puberty a brother must not sleep in the same house as his sister. He may not joke sexually with her in public or private, nor may he see her breasts exposed or be seen alone in her company. On the other hand, he may use fight talk, speak harshly, may refuse her requests, and need not avoid or crawl in the presence of his sister. A man's cherished possessions are held in his sister's house, not in his own, and so long as sex is avoided his relations with his sister may be very close and interdependent. As has been indicated, a sister is subordinate to her brother's authority and she depends on him, not on her sister, to help her out of difficulties and to come to her assistance in times of crisis.

A married man contributes labor and food to his wife's extended family and his own lineage, and divides his time between the two (Murdock and Goodenough, 1947: 341). The husband builds his wife's house, which is eventually inherited by the children, to be used by the daughters and their husbands. The husband is the prime economic support of his wife and contributes to the wife's lineage those products of his labor which consist of food. Men do the heavy preparation of food in bulk, and although they may both work for and cook for their own lineages, their primary effort is expended for their wives and wives' extended families. A man's wife's relatives may use his property much as if it were their own, borrowing his canoe or even appropriating a large share of his earnings if he is employed. In the event of a fight he is expected to side with his wife's lineage and help them, unless the interests of his own lineage are opposed.

On the other hand a man has exclusive sexual rights in his wife and has the support of her lineage in punishing any infractions which may be discovered. He expects his wife to treat him with deference, to take care of his clothes, and to fish and cook snacks for him. If she fails in any of these respects he may beat her, and—unless he is entirely unjustified or carries the beatings to extremes—her lineage will not interfere.

Although a man finds it easy to leave in divorce, merely using the pretext of adultery, the wife finds it considerably more difficult to terminate a marriage unless her husband consistently fails in his obligations, when her brother may tell him to leave. Further, if there are children, the husband continues to provide them with food and is responsible for providing them with a place to sleep.

Although Murdock and Goodenough, in an early paper written after a short initial period in the field, state that the husband exercises authority over his wife (1947: 341), Goodenough qualifies this statement later. With respect to the statement of Gladwin (1953: 306), "Men beat their wives with impunity and in general extend to them little consideration and few courtesies," Goodenough comments, in a personal communication:

I find little moral-legal basis for husband's authority over his wife. His wife may beat him physically, too, if she is strong enough. She is under no moral obligation to obey him any more than he her. [The statement that men have authority over wives] is based on limited field work and the visual observation of physical assertion and free scolding of wife by husband. Perhaps it should be stated this way: Men generally take precedence over women in public situations. A man may therefore publicly scold his wife more readily than she him. I see this as more a function of sex roles than marital ones. When married pairs are the units of consideration, one may say that the husband is normally spokesman for them both; his is the public face. Perhaps it would be best to say that the husband is regarded as the "leader" in the relationship where the public is concerned, but he does not have "authority" over her in the relationship itself, which is quite egalitarian.

His leadership is an expression of the principle that men are more "responsi-ble" than women in public matters. For a husband to snap at his wife about something reflects his assumption of responsibility; but for a wife to snap at him indicates his failure to play the male role adequately. Questions of face and sex roles rather than authority seem to me to be primarily involved.

Husbands married to women of a lineage are organized into gen-erations, each with its age-graded hierarchy. They derive their posi-tions in the age hierarchy of husbands from the positions their wives occupy in the age hierarchy of women of the lineage. The senior hus-band, therefore, is the man who is married to the finiici, the senior woman. Thus a younger man who is married to a senior woman has seniority over an older man who has married a junior woman. The age grading of husbands is important, says Goodenough, in the organiza-tion of activities which they undertake as a group and is also important in etiquette; it is always the senior husband present who opens pack-ages of mashed breadfruit at meal times and who starts the eating (Goodenough, 1951: 125–126).

Goodenough adds, however: "Now that the extended family is broken up into smaller households there appears to be less cooperation be-tween husbands than there was in former times. The husbands of the two or three women in a house continue to cooperate, however, fre-quently fishing together and jointly providing the food for their wives and children" (*ibid.*: 126).

Men who are married to women of a lineage have access to each others' wives as sexual partners, for a man may sleep with his wife's sister. The men who are married to sisters have a joking relationship which centers on rude references to the other's cleanliness habits or on statements that the other eats feces, and which is expressed in part also by sleeping with the other man's wife (ego's wife's sister). Cor-respondingly, a woman may sleep with and joke with her sister's hus-band, as a man may sleep with, and joke with, his brother's wife.

Although the house belongs to the lineage of the wives the husbands have the immediate responsibility for its maintenance and for building a new one should this become necessary. Ultimately this is the re-sponsibility of the men of the wife's lineage rather than of the husband's. The latter, however, are charged with the actual job as a kiis which they render to their wives' brothers (*idem*).

A wife's brother may make almost any demands on the sister's hus-band and these must be fulfilled. This is the only context in which reciprocity is not required in Truk. Such gifts of service or property, which may but does not often include pieces of land, are called kiis and are, according to Fischer (1950: 13), "marriage gifts." They not only may be made any time, but are in fact an on-going process of "payment for the woman," according to one of Fischer's informants (*idem*). Failure to meet the demands of a wife's brother are grounds for terminating the marriage, and the brother will tell his sister to request the husband to leave.

In conclusion, Gladwin (1953: 306 ff.) remarks on the fact that men in Trukese society seem to be dominant and secure, women subservient, insecure, and afraid to express themselves in the presence of men. Men are heads of households and lineages, hold political power and esoteric knowledge, take the initiative in the ever present adulterous liaisons while the women wait at home for a visitor or letter of assignation. Men have the important productive roles, women do not. Men beat their wives and women seldom can do much about it. Actually, according to the analysis of Rorschach and TAT materials, it turns out that it is the women who are secure and capable of responding adequately to situations of conflict or doubt, while the men are anxious and inadequate. Gladwin argues that this situation derives from the far more difficult adjustment problem the man faces: leaving home at puberty, having no real home till he is married, and then only being able to remain there on his good behavior. A woman stays home after her puberty, her husband comes to live with her, and must conform to her brother's demands. Where the man is responsible for the food supply, the woman has no such demands to meet and for two years after the birth of a child has few responsibilities except to the child.

Political Structure

Before the German occupation of Truk, around the turn of the century, each district was politically independent, the district chieftainship being the highest political office available (Goodenough, 1951: 129). (Fischer, in a personal communication, agrees on the whole, but suspects that Romonum, two districts now but formerly one, was before this time subordinate to another district and that there may have been alliances of districts under the leadership of one of them.)

The Trukese view is that the district starts as virgin territory to which a man stakes a claim. His children inherit it and form a matrilineal property group. Men of this group then bring in their wives, there being plenty of land, and provide for their children handsomely with large tracts of cleared land. Their children then duly inherit full title to these plots of soil and trees and found new lineages affiliated with clans different from their fathers'. "While the new lineages have full title to plots of soil which they acquire in this way in the new territory, they hold only provisional title to the territory from the founding lineage. In other words, by creating property in the form of soil and trees for their children, the men of founding lineages make a *niffag* of certain portions of the territory. Residual title to the territory is held by the original lineage. In this way the various lineages in a district owe the founding lineage the permanent obligations of a provisional title holder to a residual title holder. The newer lineages are also directly or indirectly started as the *jëfëkyr* of the founding lineage" (Goodenough, 1951: 136).

Within a particular district the clans are ranked, and this ranking has to do with the supposed seniority of the clan in the district. "The ranking of clans has no particular function other than to express the order of their immigration into a district, the clan first there being that of its chief. However, chieftainship can be wrested from one lineage by another and often has been in the history of Truk and Romonum" (*idem*). (Goodenough gives a full and intensely dramatic account of one such political struggle.) The victors then simply take the victims' place and say that they were the founding lineage (*idem*).

The district is thus a group of lineages which are in theory the patrilineal descendants of the chiefly lineage, which is in the position of the founding father. As titular father of his district a chief is regularly referred to as "my father-chief." He is considered responsible for the welfare of his dependent children. Goodenough makes the nice point that "We are presented with the interesting phenomenon of a society whose individuals are organized into matrilineal lineages, which groups are in their turn further affiliated matrilineally into ramages, and subsibs, and patrilineally into districts. . . . Truk presents the only instance known to the writer wherein one rule of descent is used to affiliate individuals while the opposite rule of descent is used to affiliate the resulting kin groups into a larger kin group" (*ibid.*: 138).

Succession to the district chieftainship is ordinarily from the oldest man of the chiefly lineage to the next oldest man. When, however, there are no adult men to succeed, succession goes to the oldest man of the lineage which is jëfëkyr (heir) to the chiefly lineage, which continues to hold it even though the women of the chiefly lineage may bear sons who grow to maturity.

Ideally, four feasts a year are given in the chief's honor. The men of the various lineages prepare breadfruit and the women fish. On the day of the feast each lineage brings its food in a procession, the men carrying giant bowls of breadfruit on frames and chanting as they walk.

The chief selects the largest for himself and his lineage and then re-distributes the rest to the assembled population. The distribution is made according to lineage and is roughly proportional to the size of each lineage.

The chief might call out his entire district for large fish drives and he receives the first fish caught. Otherwise he was a man of influence and prominence to whom dues and respect were owed but who held little formal authority. No regular ritual duties attached to the chief's office; these were instead performed by various ritual specialists. The chief was, in aboriginal times, the war leader and mediator in intra-district disputes.

The children of a chief were accorded special privileges in aboriginal times. Together with the next younger brother of the chief they had special seats of honor in the meeting house and were privileged to harangue the people. These privileges were held by the chief's own children, and when one chief was succeeded by another the former children retained these rights but could not transmit them.

Trobriand

All data on which this analysis is based are from the following works of Bronislaw Malinowski: *Sex and Repression in Savage Society; Crime and Custom in Savage Society; The Sexual Life of Savages; Argonauts of the Western Pacific;* and *Coral Gardens and Their Magic,* volume 1. The last-mentioned work has the most detailed description of Trobriand social organization. The most concentrated treatment of kinship is found in *The Sexual Life of the Savages.*

My job has been one of trying to pull together from the various sources information bearing on kinship and social structure. In spite of the fact that Malinowski did not make such a systematic analysis himself, it was gratifying to find that he presented enough of the facts in different contexts to allow for the construction of a comprehensible model of Trobriand social structure.

If detailed references were to be provided, the reader would be overburdened; there would be a reference for almost every sentence in the chapter. With a few exceptions, which have been noted, all the facts are attributable to Malinowski. The location of direct quotations has been indicated, but no attempt has been made to provide a reference for each factual statement.

Ecology

The Trobriand Islands are located north of the eastern tip of New Guinea. The main island, Boyowa, was the center of Malinowski's inquiries. It is an irregular piece of land 27 miles at its greatest length, 2 miles wide at its narrowest point, and 10 miles across at its greatest width. Population figures are not available but Malinowski says, "For a south sea tribe they have a very dense population" (1935: 8).

Subsistence is based primarily on agriculture. The natives grow yams of several varieties, sweet potatoes, taro, bananas, and coconuts, and in an average year they produce twice as much as they can eat. Famines seldom occur; several consecutive years of drought are required to produce serious starvation. Fishing is next to agriculture in importance.

In some coastal villages, more time is spent in fishing than agriculture. There is a regular pattern of bartering fish and vegetables between the coastal and inland villages. Hunting is of no importance and collecting plays a very minor part in Trobriand subsistence.

Social Units

The people are distributed throughout the island in villages of varying size. Malinowski does not give accurate figures, but my impression is that a small village might consist of from 7 to 10 adult males and their families. The largest village, Omarakana, probably contains 40 to 50 adult males and their families. (According to Malinowski the population was considerably larger a generation or two before his arrival in the area.) Each village is surrounded by its fields (some of which are allowed to lie fallow each year), its water hole, its fruit trees, and palm groves. Each village is under the control of a headman, who is the leader of the sub-clan of highest rank which is resident there.

The villages are combined into districts, each one under the control of a chief. The largest of the five or six districts on the island has from 18 to 20 villages. The size of the districts varies; a rough estimate of the largest is about 9 miles long and 6 miles wide. Almost every village in this district is within a mile of another village, and some are much closer than that. Marriage ordinarily should take place within a district.

The political and economic unity of a district derives from the status of chief. This official has the privilege of polygyny, which is denied to all but the highest-ranking members of Trobriand society. He welds his district together by taking a wife from each village, usually a sister or other close relative of the headman. It is incumbent upon a man to make large gifts of food, called *urigubu*, to his sister's husband. Thus a chief receives an extremely large income as urigubu from the headmen of all the villages in his district. This he distributes throughout the district in great feasts which strengthen the obligations of all his subordinates to him. He can feed large work parties or war parties as the occasion arises, and can translate some of the food into canoes and "valuables"—objects such as shell necklaces, shell armlets, and highly polished axe blades.

The chief of a district is the head of the highest-ranking sub-clan in the district. The Tabalu sub-clan has the highest rank in the Trobriand Islands, and its head is chief of the richest district, Kiriwina. To some degree, the chief of Kiriwina is the paramount chief of the whole island chain. He possesses rain and weather magic which can bring drought or good weather to all of the islands. His high prestige is recognized and deference is paid him outside of his district. In general, all districts recognize him as the person of highest rank in the entire area, but his political and economic authority is largely confined to his own district.

There is a certain amount of economic specialization among the districts. Some, such as Kiriwina, are largely agricultural but some fishing is done; others are exclusively agricultural. One small subdistrict, composed of three villages, specializes in crafts. These people do the woodworking, carving, and certain forms of basketry for the entire island system, and some of their work is bartered throughout New Guinea. These craft workers are considered of low rank and have become endogamous because of the unwillingness of any other sub-clans to marry with them. Another cluster of craftsmen is found in another district which is primarily agricultural. They make finely polished axe blades and other highly prized stone objects. These people, as well as the craftsmen previously mentioned, are supported by the chiefs and other men of high rank who give them presents of food and receive their products in return. In addition, they barter some of their products with commoners in various villages throughout the island. Sinaketa, a southern Boyowan district, and the island of Vakuta produce the highly prized, red shell discs used in the *kula* exchanges.

The Sinaketans, who specialize in spondylus-shell fishing and the manufacture of red shell discs, sometimes marry women from Kiriwina. This is mutually advantageous for reasons of agriculture, because of the differences in soil of the two areas. In Sinaketa taro is a major crop, and the urigubu consists of a plot set aside for the sister's husband. The taro cannot be ceremonially harvested and offered in bulk since it must be taken out of the garden as it ripens and eaten within a short time. Hence the sister's husband must dig his own taro as it ripens from the plot assigned to him by his wife's brother. When a woman from Kiriwina marries a man from Sinaketa, the latter receives his urigubu in the form of yams transported from the wife's brothers' fields in Kiriwina. This provides him with an ample supply of yams—not as plentiful in Sinaketa as in Kiriwina. In return, he can give red shell discs to his wife's brother in Kiriwina. The latter has plenty of yams but always desires more valuables.

The most comprehensive Trobriand social unit is the *kumila,* or clan. All humanity is divided into four matrilineal, totemic clans, each of which has a number of plants, animals, and fish associated with it. The Malasi clan ranks above the other three on the basis of a myth which describes the emergence of the animal ancestors of the four clans from the underworld. The people of a clan feel that they are "one body," and they are said to have certain personality and character traits in common. Clan members have a rather vague obligation to help each other when necessary.

The clans are exogamous units. Kinship terms are extended on a classificatory basis to clan members. Incest regulations apply within the clan, but it is not unusual for them to be violated by people who cannot trace a genealogical relationship. Clan incest lends a touch of spice to a love affair. Marriage within a clan, however, is a serious violation of moral conduct. A few such marriages are known, primarily in the highest clan, the Malasi, whose members also have the reputation of being the most frequent committers of incest.

There is no office of clan headman, nor is there anything like a clan council. The clan never acts as a unit. When the head of a sub-clan is sponsoring a great festival, the headmen of sub-clans belonging to his clan assist him in providing food. On such occasions, when the clan comes closest to concerted action, the contributions of each sub-clan is carefully noted and repayment is expected. The clan does not act as a unit in feuds, although all clansmen are supposed to feel a sense of loss at the death of a member. In general, the clan seems to be concerned chiefly with certain vague ties extending beyond the confines of the local district.

Clans are divided into *dala,* which Malinowski translates as subclan. Malinowski states that there are some thirty to fifty of these units but he does not say how many are to be found in each clan. Each subclan was originated by an ancestress, frequently accompanied by her brother, who emerged from the underworld in a particular spot. All descendants of the ancestress in the female line are members of the sub-clan. The membership is perpetual because dead souls are reincarnated, after a period in the underworld, as members of their own sub-clan. The members of a sub-clan regard themselves as "real kinsmen" as distinguished from clan members, who are designated as "pseudo-kinsmen." They believe that they can trace descent to the female founder, although in fact the counting of kinship genealogically does not go beyond the grandparent or great-grandparent.

Each mythological brother-sister pair took possession of the territory around the hole from which it emerged. This included a village site, the adjoining agricultural land, a water hole, and the magic associated with the land. In theory, and to a very considerable extent in practice, the sub-clans are localized. There is an association between one sub-clan, one portion of gardening land, one system of gardening magic, one ancestress and her brother, one genealogy, and one rank.

Each sub-clan is ranked with reference to all others, both within and without the clan. There are high-ranking and low-ranking sub-clans within each clan. In the Malasi clan, for example, there is the Tabalu sub-clan, of the highest rank in the Trobriand Islands, as well as two sub-clans considered to be the very lowest in rank. The Tabalu sub-clan is recognized as having the highest rank by all the sub-clans of all the clans throughout the Trobriand Islands. An individual's rank, therefore, is basically dependent upon sub-clan membership. All members, both male and female, have their rank determined at birth by entrance into a particular sub-clan. There is, however, one connection between sub-clan and clan rank in the supreme position of the Tabalu sub-clan. It is recognized as superior to the top sub-clans of the other three clans because, according to mythology, the Malasi clan outranks the other clans.

The eldest male of the eldest lineage is regarded as head of the sub-clan. If it is a high-ranking sub-clan he is regarded as a chief. The property and privileges of the sub-clan are vested in the headman, who, in most cases, is also head of the village belonging to the sub-clan. The sub-clan is an exogamous unit. Incest within the sub-clan is regarded as a serious violation of the moral code, and marriage is strictly forbidden. The sub-clan is characterized by collective responsibility. It is the effective unit in feuds and will take action to gain satisfaction for a member's murder by blood vengeance or damages. It will insist that a member's surviving spouse and children mourn properly for his death. The members of a sub-clan form a coöperative unit in most economic activities and all important ceremonial activities.

The sub-clans are apparently divided into lineages, but Malinowski does not provide much information on this subject; if this unit has a name, Malinowski does not give it. He does refer, however, to the fact that there is recognition of "senior" and "junior" lineages within the sub-clan (1935: 345–349). One of the lineages, in which descent is traceable, is regarded as the eldest and most important. This is important with reference to the headship of the sub-clan and its village. The office passes from a man to his own younger brothers in order of age, and then to a son of one of their sisters. There is no statement that the headship passes to the eldest sister's eldest son, but that is probably what happens in many cases. Factors of age, sex, and number of siblings and children must be taken into consideration in any actual case, and they may operate to modify the pattern. Ordinarily the heir apparent is either a younger brother or a sister's son of the incumbent, but if there are no men in these positions, or if they are too young or too old, a classificatory brother or nephew may succeed to the headship. In high-ranking sub-clans, lineages may split off and take over control of another village by a process to be described below. This is probably the basis for the formation of new sub-clans. Apparently lineages are not very formalized. They are composed of genealogical kin who coöperate economically and in many other ways.

There are two possible types of composite families in Trobriand social structure. The first is the extended family, which appears to be quite unimportant as a social unit. The reasons for this statement must be discussed since they have bearing upon the residence patterns followed by the Trobrianders. A man grows up in his father's household and village. After he is married he ordinarily moves to the village owned by his mother's sub-clan. The result is that a group of matrilineally related males inhabit a village or section of a village. This is generally termed "avunculocal residence," since a man goes to live in the village in which his mother's brother resides. However, it should be noted that this does not refer to the creation of a significant extended family.

The nuclear families of a man and his mother's brother are not combined in any way. They do not live together or eat together. They do not work together as a special unit, although both may be working under the direction of the headman of the village. The mother's brother does not direct the economic activities of his sister's son unless he happens to be the headman, in which case people standing in relationships other than sister's son are also subject to his direction. A man, since he has a claim based on his membership in the owning sub-clan, is not dependent upon his mother's brother for grants of land. Thus evidence seems to indicate that an avunculocal extended family is not a significant social unit. In the Trobriands "avunculocal" refers to the fact that a man leaves his father's house and village to live with his wife and children in a village or section of a village owned by his male matrilineal kin.

Occasionally a man will continue to live with his father, a situation which will be discussed below in greater detail. In this case a patrilocal extended family is formed, which has some significance. The son is dependent upon his father for land, privileges, and in general for his place in the community.

The other form of composite family that occurs is the polygynous household of chiefs or other men of high rank. The paramount chief of Omarakana, the capital of Kiriwina, used to have forty to fifty wives, each representing an alliance with some headman in his district. When Malinowski was there the number had been reduced to eighteen. Lesser chiefs have smaller numbers of wives. Each wife has a house in which she and her young children live. The chief has his own house, but he usually eats at the house of one of his wives. The houses belonging to the chief's wives are located contiguously along one side of the dance place. Only a small number of Trobriand men have polygynous households, the basic rule being monogamy. Each of the chief's wives cultivates plots of land with the assistance of her children. The chief helps each of his wives to some degree, but he also assigns men who are under obligation to him to assist each wife with the heavy tasks demanding male help.

The nuclear family is one of the important units in Trobriand social structure. A man, his wife, and their children ordinarily occupy one house. It is unusual for any remote relatives to stay with them. This household is an important unit in the gardening cycle: husband and wife work together in planting, harvesting, and caring for their plots of land. The husband has the heavier duties in connection with planting and harvesting, while the wife is responsible for the weeding. They work together, however, at most stages of the agricultural cycle.

The household's food supply comes from two sources: the plots cultivated by the husband and wife and the urigubu gift from the wife's brother. Husband and wife each own their tools and utensils. The wife cooks food for the family, is responsible for carrying water, and keeps the house clean. The father is very important in taking care of the children. Malinowski does not give accurate figures concerning divorce, but he says (1929: 142) that it is "not infrequent," and that the husband rarely takes the initiative. On the whole there is a fair degree of stability in the marriage relationship. Malinowski also feels that the affectional bonds within the unit are strong, as indicated by the following quotation (1929: 21): "Watching a native family at home or meeting them on the road, one receives a strong impression of close union and intimacy between its members."

The Social Units in the Village

The best way to understand the interrelationship of the previously described units is to study the composition of a village. A small village of medium to low rank will first be described; then the more complex organization of Kiriwina, the largest village in the Trobriands and the residence of the paramount chief, will be analyzed.

A small village of low rank may be composed almost exclusively of matrilineally related men and their families. These are the men of a sub-clan which has the mythological right to reside in the village and to use its lands and its magic. This is a close approximation of the "avuncu-clan," as the term is used by Murdock (1949: 68–74). It is hard to tell from Malinowski's account to what degree the wives of the men are integrated into the unit, but there appears to be some degree of integration. The sub-clan's ownership of the village and its lands is vested in the headman. An important part of his property is the garden magic associated with the soil. Sometimes the headman may delegate the duty of garden magician to a relative—usually a brother, sister's son, or son—but in a small village he would probably keep the magic himself.

The headman initiates the gardening cycle with a ceremony in which the plots to be cultivated are agreed upon. Each village has fields which are owned by the headman. Each field is divided into plots which are owned by the headman or individual men of the sub-clan. The headman announces which field is to be used and then asks which man will cultivate each plot. Each man will claim the plots which he has inherited. Sometimes a man has more plots than he can cultivate, and they are assigned to men who have few plots or are new arrivals in the village. Each man receives some plots to cultivate, whether or not he owns them; this applies even if he does not belong to the matrilineal unit which owns the village. The headman or garden magician then directs the collective activities which are demanded by various phases of the agricultural cycle.

In addition to the collective activity, each nuclear family does a great deal of independent work in cultivating its plots. Each man plants a garden for the use of his nuclear family, and another one for his sister's family. This will be the urigubu or harvest gift, which will be carried to his sister's household in another village. In a small community of low rank more than half of what is produced will be sent outside of the village. In addition to giving urigubu to his sister, each man is responsible for a contribution to the headman, which will become part of the latter's urigubu gift to the chief of the district who is married to the headman's sister or other close relative. Urigubu represents the right which a woman has in the product of the land of her sub-clan. Her brothers have the use of the land, but she is entitled to their economic support.

In addition to the matrilineally related males, there may be an adult son of the headman who has remained in the village. Such a man is

entitled to till plots by virtue of residence in the village. The members
of the sub-clan, however, have the right to terminate his residence
privilege at any time. During the gardening cycle such a man will
work under the direction of the garden magician, just like anyone else.
All residents, regardless of their affiliation, have a duty to coöperate in
communal garden labor, to obey the directions of the headman, and to
contribute to his urigubu as long as they reside in the village.

A large village of high rank, such as Omarakana, the home of the
paramount chief, has a more complicated structure. The village is in
the form of a circle around an open area which is used for dancing
and ceremonies. The chief's house is in the center area. Starting from
the entrance to the village and moving in a clockwise direction around
the circle, there are (1) a number of houses inhabited by the chief's
wives and some of his grown sons. Beyond this there are (2) a number of contiguous houses inhabited by members of a fairly high-ranking
sub-clan, the Burayama, who have a mythological right to be in the
village, and a number of houses occupied by commoners. The latter
are composed of (3) those having a mythological right to be in the village, and (4) those who are there solely because they are vassals or
servants of the chief. Continuing around the circle are (5) a number
of contiguous houses inhabited by members of the chief's sub-clan, the
Tabalu. These are the brothers, sister's sons, and other male maternal
kin of the chief, together with their families. Each of these groups will
be examined in detail.

The fact that the paramount chief resides in the village has an
important bearing on its composition. He has a large number of wives,
each of whom has her own house and plots of garden land to cultivate.
In addition, the chief will usually keep a number of his sons with him
even after they are mature. A man will ordinarily go to the village
of his sub-clan after marriage, where he has a claim to land. His
mother's brother will bring pressure to bear upon him if he delays too
long in coming, because the matrilineally related group of males is
strengthened by each addition, which may be useful in feuds or other
inter-village disputes. However, because of the high rank of a chief,
and particularly the chief of the Tabalu, the uncle will not object if the
chief wishes to keep his son in the village with him. The chief grants
his son the right to reside in the village, and may also give him privileges and magic which belong to the sub-clan. The son's right to reside in the community is usually terminated upon the death of the
father. His residence right is strengthened if he was married in infancy to his father's sister's daughter. This makes his right to remain

in the village even after his father's death almost, but not quite, inalienable. It must be remembered that the members of the chief's sub-clan have the right to drive out the chief's son if they choose to use it, since he is an outsider. This will rarely happen unless the son does some grave wrong to a member of the sub-clan. The fact that this is no idle threat is indicated by the fact that the favorite son of the paramount chief was forced to leave the village after having a member of the Tabalu sub-clan jailed by the colonial authorities.

No further comment is needed with reference to point 5, the matrilineal kinsmen of the chief. Their rights and duties are the same as those of the owner sub-clan in the small village previously described.

The members of the fairly high-ranking Burayama sub-clan of the Lukwasisiga clan (2), and the Kaluva'u (3), a commoner sub-clan of the Malasi clan, can be dealt with together. Both of these sub-clans had mythological rights to different parts of the territory near the village. Why should the Tabalu have a controlling position in a village where they did not originate? An understanding of how they gained control of Omarakana will provide considerable insight into the working of Trobriand social organization.

When a woman marries the headman of a sub-clan which is below hers in rank, she maintains her superior position and transmits it to her children. In this case the headman, who is desirous of keeping his son with him, is backed up by the superior rank of his wife and his son. Persons of higher rank possess immunity to the attempts of those of lower rank to regulate their residence. Thus the high rank of the son cancels the power of the owning sub-clan to evict him. The headman-father grants some land and other privileges to his son, and these privileges do not revert back to the father's sub-clan at his death, as normally would be the case, because of the high rank of the son. Furthermore, the son can live in his father's village as long as he wants to. Then if the headman's son's maternal nephews, who are of his subclan, come to reside with him after the pattern of avunculocal residence, they will inherit his lands and privileges, and the higher-ranking subclan will have taken firm root in the village. Gradually, over several generations, the ownership of almost all the lands will be relinquished by the inferior sub-clan and the sub-clan of higher rank will be in full control of the village.

This appears to have been the pattern by which the Tabalu took over control of the capital village of Omarakana. First the Burayama gained control from the commoner sub-clan, the Kaluva'u, and then were superseded by the Tabalu. The previous owners are not completely evicted; their mythological rights to residence and use of land are vestigially maintained. Both Burayama and Kaluva'u have a right to be in the village, but they are under the authority of the Tabalu chief; they must work under his direction, contribute to his yam house, and support him in all of his activities. The headman of each of the sub-clans which previously owned the village is permitted to keep title to a small amount of land. When the paramount chief decides to use some of this land he goes through the formality of consulting with the owners, who never oppose the chief's plans. This movement, which is documented for the village of Omarakana, is still going on. The Tabalu have taken control of several other villages in the district, and some outside of it, through the power mechanism of their rank.

Malinowski points out that mobility is correlated with high rank, while low-ranking sub-clans are characterized by territorial stability. Only one high-ranking sub-clan is still located in the area of its mythological emergence. The movement of the high-ranking sub-clans is toward the better agricultural lands. In time perspective, this may also be the mechanism by which new sub-clans are formed: a woman marries into a lower-ranking village; her son remains in that village; his sister's sons come to live with him. Since there is no immunity to rank power, the higher-ranking sub-clan gradually takes control. After a time they may forget or ignore their relationship to their original village, thus becoming a new sub-clan.

Since high-ranking women are frequently marrying into lower-ranking villages, the question may be raised as to why this process does not take place more rapidly. Accidental factors are part of the answer: a line may die out before it is securely established because of a lack of sisters or sisters' sons.

There is also a structural mechanism, patrilateral cross-cousin marriage, which promotes stability. Marriage to a father's sister's daughter in a matrilineal descent system, as Fortune (1933: 1–8) and Leach (1951: 28) have pointed out, means that grandfather and grandson will be members of the same sub-clan. Figure 4-1 may help to clarify the situation. The village belonging to sub-clan X is indicated by a rectangle. Since patrilateral cross-cousin marriage is accompanied by patrilocal residence, a man belonging to X sub-clan will keep his son of Y sub-clan with him. He will marry the son to his sister's daughter, who is a member of his own sub-clan. The son's son will be a member of X sub-clan and will reside in the village by right of ownership as well as the fact that his father will desire to keep him at home. Thus the privileges and land transferred outside of the sub-clan will be returned to it in the following generation. Since it requires several generations for the higher-ranking sub-clan to gain control, patrilateral cross-cousin marriage helps to maintain control of the village in the hands of the lower-ranking sub-clan.

It will be noted that the conservative aspects of this form of marriage depend upon a strong affectional bond between father and son, which leads the father consistently to transfer privileges to the son although he is not the legal heir, and to keep the son with him in patrilocal residence. On the other hand, a man has no desire to see his lineage perma-

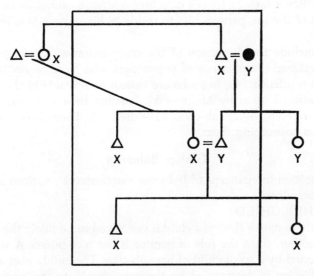

Fig. 4-1. Patrilateral cross-cousin marriage as a mechanism for maintaining control over land.

nently lose control of its village. Hence, if he can marry his son to his sister's daughter he will be able to keep his son with him and also be fairly sure that the property and privileges which he gives the son will return to the sub-clan in the next generation.

The customs associated with father's sister's daughter marriage are in accordance with this reasoning. Such a marriage is the result of an infant betrothal, contrary to the usual marriage pattern. A man has the right to ask his sister for her daughter as a wife for his son provided the children are not more than two or three years apart in age. Since the marriage is made in infancy, the members of the father's sub-clan are not worried about the advantages he gives his son since they know that they will get back these privileges in the next generation. Consequently, the rule that a man who is married to his father's sister's daughter may remain in the village after the father's death, while a man who has not made such a marriage must leave when his father dies, seems reasonable.

The marriage preference applies, however, only to infant betrothal with a real sister's daughter or her daughter, of approximately the same age as the son. Accidental factors of birth and death, therefore, prevent such a marriage from being made with regularity. Thus it is still possible for a higher-ranking sub-clan to gain control of a new village when a father's sister's daughter marriage cannot be made, but the rank of the son permits him to reside in his father's village permanently.

To conclude the discussion of the composition of the large village of Omarakana, the presence of commoners who have no mythological rights to residence (4), but who are vassals or servants of the chief, is not elaborated upon by Malinowski. Possibly they were captured in war, or are men whose sub-clans have died out. There is very little information concerning them.

Kinship Behavior

In this section the patterns of behavior manifested by various kin pairs will be described.

MOTHER-CHILD

According to native theory, a child is conceived to be solely the product of the mother, since the role of genitor is not recognized. A woman is impregnated by a spirit child of her sub-clan. The child's clan and sub-clan affiliation is determined by the relationship to the mother. The mother nurses her child for a year or two, also giving it soft food early in infancy. There is close contact between mother and child and a warm, affectionate relationship seems to be established. Discipline is very moderate; according to Malinowski, the mother does not deliberately punish the child in order to improve its character.

MOTHER-DAUGHTER

A daughter will inherit any titles or positions which her mother may hold; witchcraft is inherited by the daughter. While the daughter is living at home she helps her mother in the various duties of the household. A mother is interested in her daughter's marriage and exerts some control over her choice of a husband. The mother does this by consultation with her husband, who formally handles the marriage negotiations involving the daughter. At marriage the daughter leaves her parents' home and village. A mother has an obligation to help her daughter during pregnancy and at the delivery. A daughter may always return to her mother's house if she leaves her husband.

MOTHER-SON

A son is cared for in the same way as a daughter in infancy and childhood. There is a warm and affectionate relation between the two. A structural bond also unites mother and son, since he becomes a member of her sub-clan by matrilineal descent. The son leaves his parents' household when he reaches the age of twelve to fourteen years, to spend his nights in bachelor's houses with his sweethearts. He continues to take his meals at the parents' home. The son has a rather free-and-easy relationship with the mother. He does not have to keep his sexual affairs secret from her; if there is no sister living at home, a son may bring his sweetheart to spend the night in the parents' house. While he is young a son works with his parents on their plots of land. The fiction is that he is contributing to the urigubu of his mother, which is due her from her brother.

At maturity a son usually leaves his parents to take up residence in the village belonging to his sub-clan. While his mother is alive, however, her house is always open to him; if he is divorced before he is firmly settled in his own village he may return to his mother's household. The son has a duty to look after his mother; if she has no one else to provide her with urigubu he will assume this responsibility. Mother-son incest is regarded as impossible by the Trobrianders. There are no cases in memory or mythology.

FATHER-CHILD

Since the Trobrianders do not recognize the function of a genitor, native theory states that the father has no physiological connection with his children. He is regarded as an "outsider" since the children belong to the lineage and sub-clan of his wife, their mother. There is no mention of a father in Trobriand mythology. The father does play an important role with reference to his children, however. He shares fully in their care—feeding them, playing with them, washing them, and looking after them around the house. Children of an unmarried woman are considered unfortunate because "there is no one to nurse and hug them" (Malinowski, 1929: 21). A child's duties to the father later in life are phrased as being a repayment for the care the father has given him: it is "because of the nursing, because his hands have been soiled with the child's excrement and urine" (idem). A father shows deep and genuine affection for his children, and he appears to them as a loving and protecting figure. The father has some disciplinary functions toward the children, but his exercise of discipline is kept to a minimum. In spite of the fact that native theory recognizes no physical connection between father and child, they are said to resemble him. The feeding and fondling by the father are said to "mould the face of the child" (*ibid.: 257*). While it is recognized that the father has great love and affection for his children, his gifts to them and the services he renders in their care are phrased as if they were in payment of his sexual rights in their mother. As long as a father lives, his children have personal duties toward him in illness, economic distress, or when he is in danger from an enemy.

FATHER-DAUGHTER

Intercourse between a father and daughter is viewed with repugnance and strictly forbidden in spite of the theory that they are not really kin. This applies equally well to a stepdaughter. Violations of this taboo are known to occur. The taboo is not supported by supernatural sanctions since it is not a violation of the rule of exogamy. Reasons given for the existence of the rule forbidding sexual intercourse or marriage with a daughter are based on a man's relationship to the daughter's mother and on his relationship to the daughter in her childhood. There is the feeling that his marriage entitles him to sexual rights over only one woman of the mother's lineage. He should not sleep with his daughter because he took care of her as a child. Since he has control over his daughter's marriage, he has a duty to his wife to try to arrange a suitable marriage for her daughter.

The father acts as a representative of the mother—but with considerable independence of judgment—in deliberations about his daughter's marriage. He grants approval or rejects the daughter's suitor. The father may take the initiative by asking a boy to marry his daughter. He cannot object, however, if his wife's brother asks for the daughter on behalf of his son. A man relinquishes responsibility as guardian of his daughter's sexual processes to her husband in return for a present of valuables. A daughter may ask her father for assistance in becoming pregnant. He will perform a ceremony asking one of his ancestral spirits to transport a spirit child belonging to the daughter's sub-clan to his daughter so that she may bear a child. A man asks his sister to arrange for the making of a pregnancy cloak for his daughter. The father also has the duty of making protective gifts of food on behalf of his daughter to women who possess black magic which is effective during pregnancy.

FATHER-SON

The father-son relationship is characterized by strong affective bonds. A father tries to give his son as many advantages as he can: he gives him gifts, magical formulas, and land in the father's village. These rights must be relinquished at the death of the father unless the son has married his father's sister's daughter, which solidifies his right to remain in the village after his father's death, or unless the son is of higher rank than the father, in which case he usually can keep the privileges granted by the father and remain in the village if he so desires. Almost all fathers will do as much as they can for their sons and will desire to keep them in their villages, but it is men of rank—chiefs and headmen —who are usually most successful in this respect. In most cases the son will leave his father's village after marriage to live in the village belonging to his own sub-clan. The father has little or nothing to do with arranging his son's marriage unless he contracts an infant betrothal with his sister's daughter on behalf of his son. When the son gets married, the father, aided by his relatives, makes gifts of valuables to the bride's father. A son has a number of personal duties to his father: if his mother is dead the son will continue to give urigubu to his father if the latter has not remarried. A son has an important part to play in the funeral ceremonies attendant upon his father's death.

BROTHER-SISTER

The relationship between brother and sister is one of fundamental importance in the eyes of the Trobrianders. In mythology a brother and sister emerge together from the underworld, the sister to establish a sub-clan and the brother to act as her guardian. The relationship is one characterized by respect from the early years of life. There should be no intimacy between them. A sister should always respect her brother, bending down when he approaches, and obeying his commands in all matters. A woman should regard her brother as her guardian and the legal head of her family of procreation. Even as very young children, siblings of opposite sex should not play together. At puberty they must be residentially separated. A boy who has a sister living at home sleeps in bachelor's houses or the family yam house, and carries on his affairs with his sweethearts away from any possible contact with his sister. The sister sometimes leaves home also, going to live at the house of an elderly widowed aunt. Brother and sister may not share the same dwelling nor work together. They must have no knowledge of and take no interest in each other's sexual affairs.

As a general rule, of course, brother and sister do not live in the same village after they are married. The incest taboo between them is regarded by the natives as the one which must be enforced with the greatest stringency. Incestuous dreams of relations between brother and sister apparently occur with some frequency, and such dreams are very disturbing to those who experience them. Incest between brother and sister is apparently very rare, but in mythology there is one story in which the origin of love magic is based upon brother-sister incest.

Although a man is expected to function as the guardian of his sister throughout her life, he cannot interest himself in her marriage in any way. Only after her marriage is arranged by her father, after consultation with her mother, does the brother enter the picture: he is now obligated to provide urigubu for her new household. A man always plants a garden for his sister, which becomes the basis of his urigubu gift to her husband. The urigubu gift usually amounts to about half of a household's food supply. Although her husband receives the gift, it is conceived to be for the support of a woman and her children, and thus it represents her claim to a share of the products of the land owned by the sub-clan of which she is a member. It also represents a demand by the sister on her brother, since in some cases, although the brother is not cultivating land belonging to his sub-clan, he still owes an urigubu gift to his sister's household.

This is primarily a relationship between one brother and one sister. Where there are several siblings of each sex in a family, one brother is paired off with one sister for purposes of urigubu. If there is one sister and several brothers, the eldest brother will be responsible, but he will be helped by his younger brothers. If the only brother in a family has several sisters, some older and some younger than himself, he will be responsible for the urigubu of all. However, the sons of his elder sisters will help him not only with their mothers' urigubu but with that of his younger sisters as well. If the only brother has several sisters, all younger, then he will have to work very hard so that each will have some urigubu.

This pairing off extends to other things besides urigubu. A sister may ask her brother to make magic designed to get her impregnated by one of the spirits of their sub-clan. The brother who is responsible for a sister's food is the one who plays the main role of disciplinarian and tutor of her children. The other brothers are secondary in this respect.

Maternal parallel-cousins are only rarely involved in the urigubu relationship. If there is no brother, a woman's mother's brother will be responsible for her urigubu, and later her son will undertake this task; only if none of these relatives is available will the mother's sister's son be called upon to provide for her household. A man is generous in giving urigubu because this increases his esteem as well as the prestige of his sister and their lineage. There is a custom called "untying the brother's yam-house" (Malinowski, 1935: 189) in which a sister requests additional urigubu from her brother. If she knows that his yam house is full, she will ask her husband for a valuable which she will give to her brother. This entitles her to the contents of one compartment of his yam house. This may be considered evidence of a demand of the sister on her brother, but it also has some aspects of a tribute to him, since he receives a valuable from his sister's husband.

BROTHER-BROTHER

Structurally, the link between brothers is expected to be very strong. The factor of relative age is important. An elder brother is supposed to look out for his younger brother, and the latter is expected to reciprocate by showing respect and obedience. An elder brother has the right to expect a younger brother to give him assistance in filling their only sister's urigubu gift. A younger brother is frequently the heir of his elder brother. In such cases the younger brother may gain some of his heritage in advance of his brother's death by giving him several substantial presents. The elder brother then turns over the right to some land or some magic to the younger.

Affectively, the relationship between brothers may be warm and intimate, but sometimes it is characterized by considerable antagonism. The latter may be more common where the elder brother is a person of importance who has considerable property and magic which the younger brother covets. In myths, brothers are frequently at odds with one another, and the younger brother frequently receives more sympathetic treatment. A younger brother may resent the gifts given by his elder brother to the latter's son. When the younger brother pays his elder for some magic, as described above, he frequently feels that he has been cheated—the elder brother might not have given him the full spell. A son, who receives magic from his father as a free gift, never doubts that he has received the complete formula. In general there seems to be considerable tension in the relationship between brothers.

SISTER-SISTER

Not much information is available on this relationship, except that sisters are expected to be mutually helpful to each other. Authority based on age between sisters is not discussed by Malinowski, but the kinship terminology suggests that it may have existed. If sisters are living in the same village they will visit frequently and help look after each other's children. A sister will also come to help a woman in labor. A woman who has left her husband may take up temporary residence in her sister's household. In general, the sister relationship does not seem to be of significant structural importance.

MOTHER'S SISTER-SISTER'S CHILD

If the mother's sister is living in the same village, she frequently may care for her sister's children. In this case she shows much devotion to the children. The relationship is a warm one, paralleling that between mother and child but somewhat less intense. A sister's son has a duty to provide urigubu for his mother's sister if she does not have a closer male relative to undertake this responsibility.

MOTHER'S BROTHER-SISTER'S DAUGHTER

This is a restrained relationship, analogous in many ways to that between brother and sister. A woman is expected to respect her mother's brother, although they do not have very frequent contact with one another. The maternal uncle has nothing to do with arranging his sister's daughter's marriage except in the case of an infant betrothal to his son. The mother's brother may be instrumental in getting a child spirit to impregnate his sister's daughter. If her brother is not old enough, a maternal uncle will distribute food as payment to the women who have made a pregnancy cloak for his sister's daughter. A woman must give birth at the house of her father or her mother's brother; if she is of high rank it will usually be at the house of her uncle. In general there is a rather formal relationship between the two because they ordinarily do not live in the same village. The sister's daughter is expected to be respectful, while the mother's brother is concerned with the welfare of his sister's daughter.

MOTHER'S BROTHER-SISTER'S SON

The mother's brother is the person who has the greatest authority over his sister's son. The nephew may be his uncle's heir. In some cases the uncle from whom a man expects to inherit may be the man who instructed and disciplined him in his youth. However, as noted in the discussion of urigubu, this is largely a relationship between a particular mother's brother and a particular sister's son. Hence, the mother's brother responsible for a young man's socialization may die and be succeeded by his younger brother, in which case the young man now becomes the heir of a man with whom he had little contact in his youth. Such a man may be more inclined to favor his own son against his sister's son than would have been the case with the uncle who guided him into manhood.

A boy does not have much contact in childhood with his mother's brother since they usually live in different villages. As he grows older, his mother's brother begins to exert more influence on him. The uncle tutors his nephew in lineage and sub-clan traditions; he takes his nephew to work with him in the fields to which the youth has a claim.

At this period the relationship is friendlier than at any other time. The mother's brother introduces the youth to pride in his lineage, ambition, and promises of future wealth and prestige. As the boy grows older his mother's brother demands more work of him. The boy goes frequently to his mother's brother's house for ceremonies and feasts involving his own sub-clan.

A man lives with his parents until he is married, after which he ordinarily moves to his own village. As mentioned above, this does not mean that he forms an effective extended family with his mother's brother, but rather that they both now reside in the village where they belong. Unless the uncle is village headman they will be working together under the direction of an older kinsman. The mother's brother does have the right partially to determine the distribution of his sister's son's harvest. He may ask for a contribution to his payment to the chief, or ask the younger man to help with his mother's urigubu. A man may acquire some privileges prior to his uncle's death in the manner previously described. The nephew, as was seen for the younger brother, is likely to feel that he has been cheated. The relationship between mother's brother and sister's son is a structurally important, asymmetrical one, characterized by considerable tension. It resembles the elder brother-younger brother relationship in many ways.

FATHER'S SISTER-BROTHER'S SON

This is a relatively unrestrained joking relationship. The father's sister has a warm, permissive attitude toward her brother's child, in which sexual implications are prominent. Sexual joking is frequent, and intercourse with the father's real sister is considered right and proper although it does not occur too frequently because of the age difference. The father's sister's daughter is always available, however, and frequently utilized in this way. Ideally the father's sister's daughter should be the first person with whom a boy has sexual intercourse. Marriage with a father's sister seems not to occur, but her daughter is a desirable spouse. The father's sisters, real and classificatory, prepare a young man for certain ceremonial dances by dressing him and performing beauty magic over him. The sexual implications of the father's sister extend to all women of the father's sub-clan and clan. According to Malinowski, native theory extends these implications even further, to include all women not in a man's own clan.

FATHER'S SISTER-BROTHER'S DAUGHTER

The father's sisters have a number of duties, primarily ritual-ceremonial, toward their brother's daughter. When a woman is pregnant her father asks his sister to perform pregnancy rituals. She gets her kinswomen together and they make a pregnancy cloak and perform magic for their brother's daughter. After the child is born the father's sister cuts off the remaining piece of cord close to the baby's stomach in a ceremony three days after birth. A month after she has given birth, a woman is washed by her father's sister and other kinswomen of the father, after which time she is free to go outside of the house. On all these occasions the mother's brother or brother of the pregnant woman gives food gifts to the father's kinswomen in recognition of their services.

FATHER'S BROTHER-BROTHER'S CHILD

Malinowski has little to say concerning this relationship. Apparently it follows the pattern of the father-child relationship, but with less intensity. Since the residential pattern usually groups brothers together in the same village, a child will probably have considerable contact with the father's brother.

PARALLEL COUSINS

Maternal parallel cousins are regarded as siblings, but the obligations existing between them are not very significant. They observe the brother-sister taboo, but in an attenuated form. Maternal parallel cousins ordinarily do not grow up in the same village.

Malinowski does not describe the behavior of paternal parallel cousins. Ordinarily they will not belong to the same clan or sub-clan, so it is possible that they are not thought of as relatives. They may be in frequent contact in childhood since their fathers usually live in the same village. There is no information concerning sexual behavior or marriage between paternal parallel cousins of opposite sex. Malinowski reports that adolescents engage in numerous premarital sexual affairs within the village. The residence pattern means that a large number, possibly all, of the adolescents of opposite sex within the village will be paternal parallel cousins. It seems likely, then, that there is no prohibition on sexual relations between such cousins. Although not perfectly clear, the evidence seems to indicate that paternal parallel cousins should not marry.

CROSS COUSINS

As indicated above, father's sister's daughter and mother's brother's son are especially suited for marriage if they are about the same age. Such marriages are arranged when the cousins are infants, or at least before the age of ten. Malinowski does not say that they may not marry if they independently become interested in each other at a later age in the absence of an infant betrothal. Sexual joking is common between such cross cousins, and they are favorite sexual partners in their youth.

The relationship between father's sister's son and mother's brother's daughter is the opposite of that described above. These people should not marry or have intercourse. There are some violations of this prohibition, but they are strongly disapproved. The kinship terminology reflects this prohibition since father-child terms are used.

Male cross cousins are frequently placed in a competitive relationship because the father of one is the mother's brother of the other. The father's sister's son is called "father" and the mother's brother's son is "child." This usage fits with the fact that they are potential brothers-in-law if patrilateral cross-cousin marriage takes place. In this case the man called "father" will be expected to pay urigubu and give assistance to the one called "child."

There is no detailed statement as to the relationship between female cross cousins. They will ordinarily not be found in the same village. The father's sister's daughter will join with her kinswomen in performing rituals and making a pregnancy cloak for her mother's brother's daughter.

GRANDPARENT-GRANDCHILD

Malinowski says very little about this relationship, which probably reflects the fact that it is not very significant. The residential rules usually separate grandparents and grandchildren. The terminology for this relationship is self-reciprocal. The mother's mother and the daughter's son are sexually forbidden since they are members of the same lineage and sub-clan, but there is no horror connected with the idea of intercourse between grandmother and grandson—it appears to the natives only as a ridiculous possibility because of the discrepancy in age.

HUSBAND-WIFE

Something of the nature of this relationship has already been suggested in the description of the nuclear family. Husband and wife are a team in productive and domestic activities; they work together in most phases of the gardening cycle and share in the care of the children within the household. The husband owns the house and his tools. The wife owns the utensils which she needs for cooking and running the household. They do not inherit from each other.

The husband has an exclusive right to his wife's sexuality; he may beat her for adultery and claim damages from her lover. The husband will rarely initiate divorce proceedings because he will lose the urigubu which her brother gives him, and his children will leave with their mother. A wife may divorce her husband if he beats her badly or if she cannot get along with him. Apparently a marriage may sometimes be dissolved if the wife's brother engages in a serious quarrel with the husband and refuses to pay urigubu to the latter. This is rare, but one case was described by Malinowski.

The husband is considered to be master of the household because it is his house in his village. The wife, however, has considerable equality and influence because her brother has a great deal to do with the food supply of the household. A woman may outrank her husband, in which case he must obey her food taboos or she must have a separate set of dishes. In public they behave in a restrained manner, never overtly showing tenderness toward each other. According to Malinowski, the failure of a woman to bear children is a misfortune for her lineage, but is no reason for a husband to divorce her. Her prestige does not suffer in any way if she is barren. This is hard to reconcile with a man's great fondness for children, but he may be able to express this toward his brother's children.

The spouse is the chief mourner at the death of a man or woman, but the difficult mourning customs are more strictly enforced against the wife than the husband. A widow must wear her husband's jawbone around her neck and use his skull for a lime pot. She is secluded for a long period of time—up to two years if her husband was a man of high rank—in her husband's house. At the end of this time she is released ceremonially by the husband's kin. She then turns over the jawbone and skull to the husband's kin and leaves the village to live with some maternal kinswoman. A widower must observe mourning less rigorously and for a shorter period of time. In general, according to Malinowski, spouses seem to get along well together and feel considerable affection for each other.

RELATIVES-IN-LAW

Both a man and a woman call their parents-in-law by a special kinship term. Malinowski does not say what terms are used for son-in-law and daughter-in-law. It is possible that the parent-in-law term is used reciprocally, but Malinowski does not indicate this. Sexual relations between a man and his mother-in-law are forbidden. No other behavior patterns are mentioned by Malinowski. It seems clear that there are no patterns of formalized avoidance between parent-in-law and children-in-law. Contact with parents-in-law is not frequent since they are not normally in the same village as the husband and wife.

The relationship between brothers-in-law has already been indicated. The wife's brother is obligated to give urigubu to the sister's husband and to help him in house building, canoe building, or other activities. The wife's brothers also have an important part in carrying out a man's funeral and mourning rites. The relationship is an asymmetrical one, with most of the burden falling on the wife's brother. Brothers-in-law normally do not live in the same village.

There is no information on the relationship between sisters-in-law.

Sexual relations between brother-in-law and sister-in-law are strongly disapproved. The sororate and sororal polygyny are not approved although they occasionally occur. The levirate is disapproved except in the case of a younger brother who inherits the chieftainship. In this case he inherits the wives, who represent political alliances, of his elder brother. The contact between a brother's wife and her husband's brother is frequent since they usually live in the same village. The natives say that a wife's sister becomes something like a man's own sister, and hence sexual relations are forbidden.

Marriage

In most cases one of the premarital affairs engaged in by adolescents leads to marriage. A boy is largely a free agent in deciding upon a wife. A girl's relatives are concerned about her choice of a husband and her mother and father discuss the matter carefully. The choice of a spouse is limited by the fact that the rules of clan exogamy must be observed, and the married pair should be of roughly the same rank if possible. The girl's family is concerned with the industry and character of her suitor. A boy is interested in the size of the urigubu he may expect, in addition to the personal charms of his sweetheart. The number of brothers and sisters in her family is an important consideration in this respect. A girl's father plays a major role in the negotiations leading to her marriage. He consults with the mother as to the suitability of the daughter's lover, but has considerable independence of action. He can be trusted to act in the best interests of the daughter, in spite of the fact that she is not of his sub-clan, because he is fond of her and also because he does not want his son to be placed in the position of paying urigubu to a man of bad reputation. The girl's father may take the initiative by asking his daughter's lover to marry her, or the boy may bring matters to a head by doing favors for the girl's father.

After this the girl spends the night at the groom's house. In the morning her parents bring cooked food to the boy's household and the bride and groom eat together. This symbolizes the marriage. If an elopement takes place in the face of parental opposition, the couple may stay at the boy's house but they will refrain from eating together until the girl's parents demonstrate their consent by bringing the gift of cooked food. From the first moment of their married life, a couple eats food supplied by the girl's relatives, as will be the case all through their life together.

Following this, a series of gift exchanges occurs between the families of the bride and groom which may take a year to complete. These are summarized in table 4-1.

TABLE 4-1

Marriage Gift Exchanges

I	Girl's kin to boy's kin	(1) Cooked yams from girl's parents to boy's parents.
		(2) The girl's father, mother's brother, and brother each bring one basket of uncooked yams to the boy's parents.
		(3) The same relatives each bring one platter of cooked vegetables to the boy's house.
II	Boy's kin to girl's kin	(4) Repayment of gift 3 in same form by the boy's relatives to the girl's family.
		(5) Valuables given by the boy's father to the girl's father in repayment of gift 2.
III	Girl's kin to boy's kin	(6) A large quantity of yams at first harvest (urigubu) from the girl's brother to the boy.
IV	Boy's kin to girl's kin	(7) Gift of fish from the boy to the girl's father in repayment of 6.
		(8) Gift of valuables from boy's father to the girl's father in repayment of 6.

The last gift shown (8) is not always given. It will be made only if the young husband is very rich or if his father has not been able to make gift 5 prior to this time. Gifts 5 and 8 are binding on the husband, since they are not returned if a divorce takes place. These two gifts are equal in value to all of the other first-year gifts put together.

A marriage gives the husband exclusive sexual rights in his wife. In payment for this, he gives valuables to his wife's father, who has been the guardian of her sexual processes up to this time. In case of a divorce the valuables are not returned by the wife's father. If the wife remarries, however, her new husband must give a valuable to her former husband and another to the woman's father. In this way the first husband transfers his sexual rights to the second husband, and the wife's family is placed under urigubu obligations to the new husband by the second gift. The husband receives urigubu only for the duration of the marriage. In return, the husband gives occasional presents of valuables to the wife's brother or mother's brother. Thus a man gives food to his sister's husband and valuables to his wife's brother, and receives food from his wife's brother and valuables from his sister's husband. In this manner the entire district is welded together by a constant flow of food and valuables which move in opposite directions.

As the result of a marriage, the matrilineal kin of husband and wife have demands upon each other for services on certain ceremonial occasions, especially funerals and mourning ceremonies. The demands are primarily on the spouse and secondarily on the kin of the spouse.

After the marriage-gift exchanges are completed, the newly married couple is supposed to move to the village belonging to the husband's sub-clan. They have a claim on him, and he has a right to go there. However, a father may try to keep his son with him. High-ranking men are most successful in this because they have more advantages to offer the son and are better able to counteract the claims of the son's male kin. The mother is usually the father's ally in this attempt because otherwise all her children will leave the village. Certain regular mechanisms and rationalizations have developed to permit the parents occasionally to evade the demands of the system that their sons leave home.

The father of high rank will make it attractive for his son to remain with him by giving him special privileges, such as plots of garden land, fishing rights, and magic. These are subject to veto by the father's kin, and they terminate upon the father's death. If the father can arrange an infant betrothal of his son to his sister's daughter, the son's position in the village is strengthened. The fact that such a marriage will return alienated privileges to the sub-clan of the father in the next generation has already been discussed. In addition, certain personal considerations make it an attractive marriage from the point of view of the father and the son.

The son will be the brother-in-law of the father's heir. The latter will be obligated to provide urigubu for the son, and to assist him in other ways. Thus, the man who is most likely to resent the son's relationship to the father is placed in a position where he must coöperate with the son, and even regard it as his privilege. Another advantage recognized by the Trobrianders is that the father and his daughter-in-law will belong to the same lineage and sub-clan. A man may have to rely upon the attentions of his son and his son's wife in old age, and he will be better off if the latter is also his sister's daughter. He will feel safer from sorcery if the daughter-in-law is his own kinswoman. Patrilateral cross-cousin marriage permits the parents to keep their son with them, controls some of the tension between a man's heir on the one hand and his son on the other, and prevents privileges granted the son from being permanently lost to the lineage.

Kinship Terminology

The Trobriand kinship terms [1] are shown in figures 4-2 to 4-7. Those not specifically listed by Malinowski, but indirectly indicated in various contexts, are placed in parentheses.

Certain terms are extended widely in a classificatory manner. The term for father, *tama*, is extended to father's clansmen, and mother, *ina*, to mother's clanswomen. The term for sibling of opposite sex, *luta*, is extended throughout the clan in the same generation as ego. The terms for elder sibling of same sex and younger sibling of same sex, *tuwa* and *bwada*, are extended throughout the clan according to the relative age of the speaker and the person addressed in the same generation. The term for grandparent or father's sister, *tabu*, is applied to all women of the father's matrilineal lineage. The charts in figures 4-2 and 4-3 indicate that the system is of the bifurcate merging type, with Crow cousin terminology. One outstanding feature appears to be the usage of the term tabu, which is a reciprocal between grandparents and grandchildren, father's sister and brother's child and mother's brother's child and father's sister's daughter. The self-reciprocal term, *kada*, used between mother's brother and sister's children, also provides an interesting feature of the system.

The latter term may be crucial for an understanding of the system. At first glance it is strange to find men in an asymetrical relationship such as mother's brother and sister's child applying the same kinship term to each other. However, it must be remembered that this relationship tends to be activated in terms of authority by a particular mother's brother. Other men in the same relationship to ego do not behave toward him in a particularly authoritarian manner. The reciprocal term,

[1] E. R. Leach (1958) has published a stimulating and provocative analysis of Trobriand kinship which differs from the present treatment in some respects. Since Malinowski's published works do not seem to substantiate some of Leach's generalizations, detailed reference to his article has not been made here. The article is recommended, however, for those having a specialized interest in kinship and social structure.

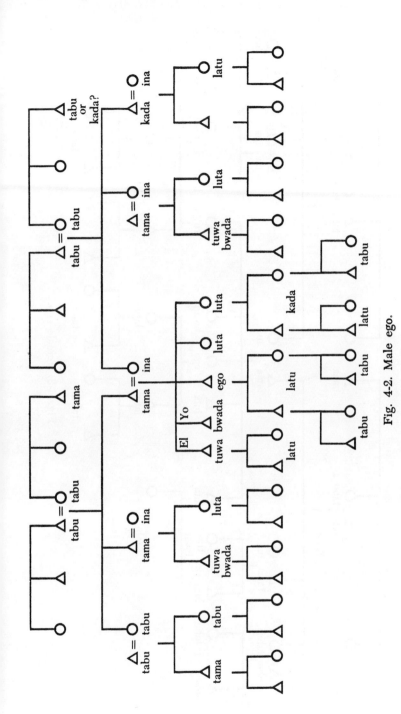

Fig. 4-2. Male ego.

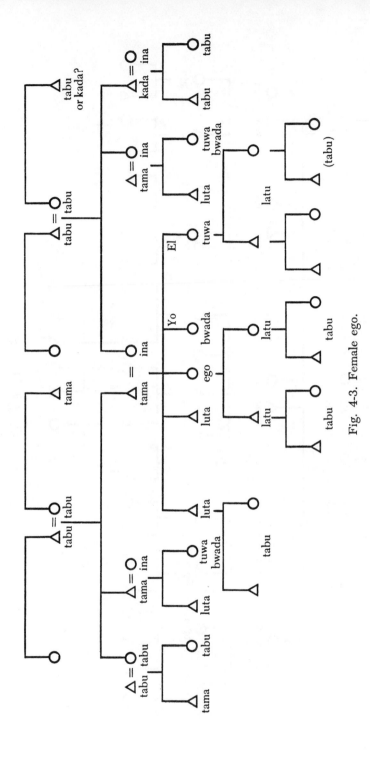

Fig. 4-3. Female ego.

kada, basically has the meaning of "male member of my lineage and sub-clan." From the standpoint of ownership of a village and its lands, it means "co-owner." People who use this term reciprocally are co-owners of a village and its lands, and the men form a residential unit. From the standpoint of an adult male in figure 4-4, the men of his village, who are co-owners as well as co-residents, are all either kada, if they are not of his own generation, or brothers if they belong to his generation.

Malinowski does not give a term for mother's mother's brother in his summary list, but in one analysis of urigubu contributions he does indicate the classificatory use of the term tabu for this relationship. If he is alive, the mother's mother's brother will also be co-resident with ego. As a matter of fact, he will probably be the headman of the village. In this case he will be referred to as "chief," if it is a high-ranking sub-clan, or *tokaraywaga*, which means "owner of the village." Malinowski indicates that only the close kinsmen of the chief use kinship terms in addressing him or referring to him. Thus it seems reasonable for the mother's mother's brother to be regarded primarily as "headman" by his sister's daughter's son. This is largely speculation, since Malinowski has not provided clear-cut terminological data, but that part of the analysis pertaining to the term kada seems well founded. It reflects the fact that the nucleus of a village is a two-generational group of matrilineally related males. The younger of the two generations is adult when it moves to the village. Together with the adjacent older generation, it forms the effective unit for coöperation in fighting or collective economic activity.

The term tabu, which is used reciprocally between grandparent and grandchild, father's sister and brother's child, and mother's brother's child and father's sister's daughter seems to have the meaning "consanguineal relative not of my sub-clan." The one definite exception to this is the mother's mother-daughter's child relationship. The available material does not permit a definitive analysis of the term. However, all the relatives who use this term are involved in an easygoing, permissive relationship with each other. The use of this term for father's sister and her daughter is extended to all women of the father's matrilineal lineage, as indicated in figure 4-6.

In summary, relating kinship terms to residential units seems to give a certain amount of insight into the system. A male child is born in his father's village where the older men are "fathers" and their wives are "mothers." People in his own generation are his own brothers and sisters, or the children of his father's brothers. The sisters of men in the

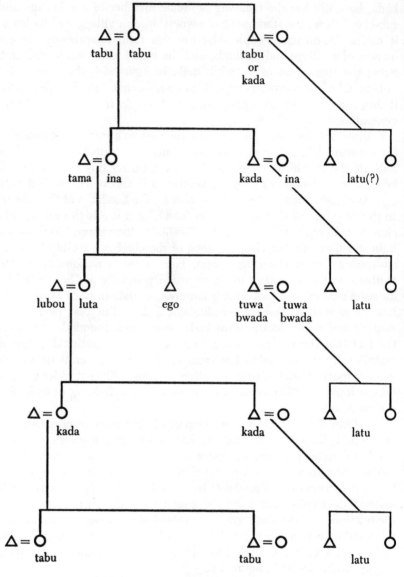

Fig. 4-4. Male's matrilineal lineage.

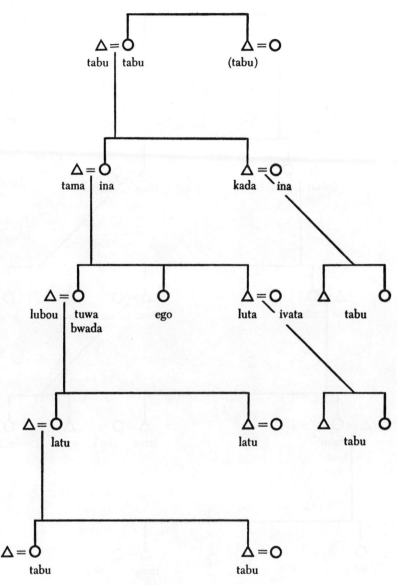

Fig. 4-5. Female's matrilineal lineage.

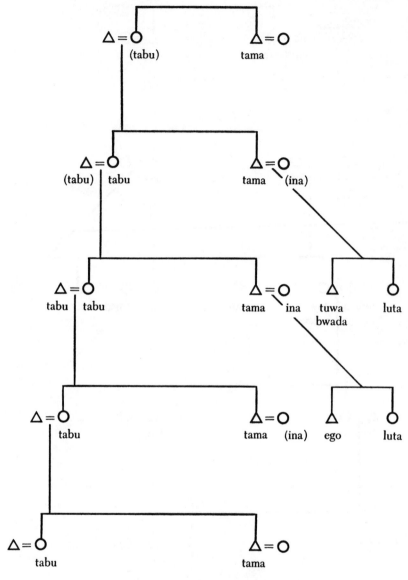

Fig. 4-6. Father's matrilineal lineage—male ego.

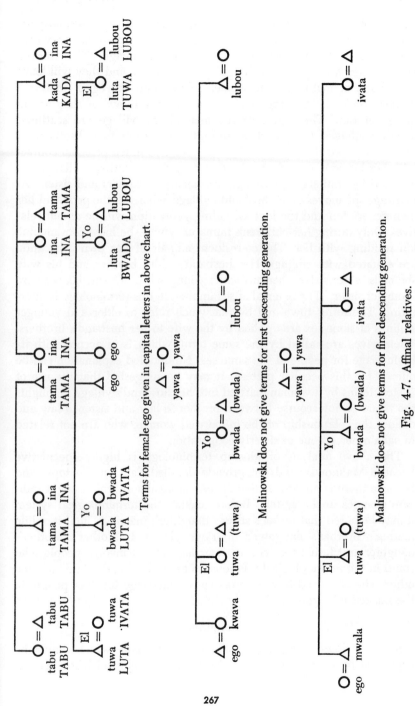

Fig. 4-7. Affinal relatives.

Terms for female ego given in capital letters in above chart.

Malinowski does not give terms for first descending generation.

Malinowski does not give terms for first descending generation.

267

village, who are scattered in other villages, are privileged sexual partners. When he reaches maturity a man moves to his own village, where
the men are either brothers or "members of the lineage." The children
of these men are equated with ego's own children, and they will leave
the village at maturity. The women in this unit are ego's "mothers"
if they are in the generation above, or "sisters-in-law" if they are in
his generation. The sisters of the men of the village are scattered
in other villages, supported by urigubu gifts from their brothers. It
should be noted that a woman does not have as much personal contact
with her kin as a man does. She grows up in her father's village, surrounded by "fathers," "mothers," and her own brothers and sisters. At
marriage she moves to her husband's village, where all the people of her
own generation and the first ascending generation will be affinal relatives. Only during her children's immaturity will she have consanguine
kin residing with her. The co-resident affinals of her own generation
are equated with siblings. Her husband's elder brother and his wife
she calls "elder sister"; her husband's younger brother and his wife are
"younger sister." The reversal of sex implied in this terminology is interesting. The terms tuwa and bwada which refer to elder and younger
siblings of same sex are applied by the wife to her husband's brothers.
Their wives are called by the same term, which is in accord with its
basic usage for people of the same sex. No detailed explanation can be
offered for this peculiar pattern. It may be suggested that the use of
"sister" terms by a woman married into her husband's village highlights
the taboo on intercourse between brother-in-law and sister-in-law and
defines the relationship of the in-married women, who are not related
to each other, as one of sisterly coöperation.

The above analysis of kinship terminology is highly speculative
because Malinowski did not provide detailed data on the topic and
because there is no information of an historical sort which might indicate changes in the system. Before leaving the terminological system
it may be noted that father's sister's daughter's marriage "fits" it, while
mother's brother's daughter's marriage does not. Mother's brother's
daughter and father's sister's son marriage would involve people who
stand in the terminological relationship of "father" and "child" to each
other. The approved form of cross-cousin marriage involves people in
the relaxed tabu relationship.

Summary

There is a limited supply of good agricultural land which cannot be
expanded by acquiring new territory. The agricultural labor of both

sexes is required. The sub-clan, the basic unit of Trobriand social structure, is founded upon the joint ownership of a village and its fields. The strength of the sub-clan is maximized by avunculocal residence, which groups matrilineally related males on their lands. Within the sub-clan there is a clear-cut authority structure with the headman performing important managerial, religious, and leadership functions. The effective nucleus of the sub-clan consists of the men of two generations, working and fighting under the direction of the headman.

The women of a sub-clan are supported by the food grown on its land by the men of the unit. This custom of urigubu, combined with the hereditary ranking of sub-clans, makes it possible for many villages to be welded into a more extensive, stable political unit under the control of a polygynous chief. The matrilineal clans regulate marriage and relate people over a still wider area, but they are weak units without leadership or significant political, economic, and religious functions.

A strong father-son tie develops within the nuclear family but this poses a threat to the matrilineal character of the system only in the case of artistocratic fathers. Their actions in behalf of their sons are counteracted by their matrilineal kin. Patrilateral cross-cousin marriage is a compromise solution which permits aristocratic fathers to favor their sons and at the same time prevents loss of rank, land, and privileges by the sub-clan.

Ordinarily parents are residentially separated from their adult children, and brothers from their sisters. This maximizes the strength of the sub-clan and permits economically significant marriage ties to be used as a politically integrative mechanism. It severs attachments of an intimate nature which might compete for an individual's loyalty to the larger units, sub-clan and chiefdom. A woman under avunculocal residence is isolated from her kin and children, which can lead her to seek affectional satisfaction from her husband. If she is economically independent by virtue of her tie to her sub-clan, her search may be rewarded. An intense affectional relationship between spouses does not seem to threaten the strong structural bond between brother and sister, which brings food to the sister and valuables to the brother.

Ashanti

Reports on Ashanti society and kinship organization present something of a paradox in that they suggest a combination of seemingly contradictory modes for the ordering of social structure, involving a hierarchical, differentiated, and stratified society, together with a segmentary lineage type of kinship system. The presence of matrilineal descent and succession contributes to the paradox, as it has sometimes been suggested that the matrilineal emphasis constitutes a limiting element for both of these developments.

The Ashanti paradox constitutes the focal problem of this chapter, which will attempt to answer two major questions: What is the nature of the relationship between the Ashanti kinship system and the structure of the larger social system? And to what extent does analysis of Ashanti kinship and domestic organization contribute to the understanding of problems of matrilineal kinship?

The Ashanti are one of the best known of the numerous Akan-speaking peoples, who live for the most part in the southern portion of Ghana. The Akan are divided into a large number of states of varied size, of which Ashanti has been the largest and politically most important since the eighteenth century. Although the Ashanti Confederacy centered in the forest country, the Akan are said to be relative newcomers to the region, which they occupied only about the end of the fifteenth century, when trade in gold and slaves with the Portuguese on the coast became important. The Bono state, an early center of Akan culture, was located about 100 miles north of Kumasi (the Ashanti capital), and is said to date from the fourteenth century (Manoukian, 1950: 9–13).

Primary source materials for this chapter are the works of Rattray, published during the 1920's, and those of Fortes and Busia, dating some twenty years later. The data are complementary to a degree, but differences in the theoretical frameworks guiding the investigations make the task of collation difficult. A further problem is presented by the increased tempo of change in modern Ashanti, as reflected in the materials of the contemporary investigators. I will not attempt to deal with problems of change, but will limit the paper explicitly to a consideration of traditional Ashanti society.

This chapter is divided into three major sections: an account of the traditional political structure of the Ashanti Union; discussion of political organization at the level of the individual Ashanti state and its relation to kinship structure; and an examination of traditional Ashanti kinship.

The Ashanti Union

THE SETTING

Under this heading I refer to ecological and certain non-ecological factors which are important in defining the setting in which Ashanti society operated.

Ecology The Mampong escarpment, a line of hills ranging in height from 1,000 to 2,000 feet, divides Ashanti into northern and southern portions of roughly similar area and markedly different character. Tropical rain forest of mixed deciduous type originally covered the southern plateau, while the north is savanna-orchard bush country. Although the two regions do not differ greatly in *average* rainfall and temperature, in the north the harmattan wind contributes to lower humidity and high evaporation. Where the south has an excess of water, the north faces a water shortage most of the year and extensive flooding of the lowlands for one or two months (Steel, 1948: 65).

Agricultural techniques and crops differ in north and south, reflecting the distinctive problems presented by the environment. Yams and guinea corn, staple crops of northern Ashanti, require greater farming skill than the large variety of crops (plantain, cocoyam, maize, cassava, yams, and minor vegetables) which can be grown in the south (Fortes, 1948: 12). Mineral resources appear to be confined to the south, where gold mining constituted an important element in the economy of traditional Ashanti.

Population concentration in the south, revealed by Gold Coast census materials, is probably not a recent phenomenon. Reliable statistics for traditional Ashanti are not available, but the 1921 census, which provides something more than an informed guess, may suggest the magnitude of population density differentials for the two zones. For northern districts the range of density was from 4.9 to 18.2 persons per square mile; for the south, from 26.9 to 54.6 (Steel, 1948: 69). The modern clustering of towns in the southeast has been facilitated by contact conditions, but the pattern is not new; this development is lacking in the north, where the few towns of any size are market centers of considerable antiquity (*ibid.:* 71). The first Ashanti census (1901) reported a total population of 346,000—possibly an overestimate, to judge by the 1911 figure of 287,000. By the 1948 census, the population had increased to 822,485.

There is no evidence of any serious pressure of population on land resources in traditional Ashanti; even with the large population increases of recent years, this has not yet become a major problem.

Subsistence The farming practice which provided the subsistence basis in traditional Ashanti is usually referred to as "shifting cultivation," but this phrasing requires considerable qualification when applied to southern Ashanti. In fact, the system of garden cultivation which even now produces the major portion of the food supply in the villages closely approximates settled agriculture. The older village settlements tend to be surrounded for a depth of one-half to one mile by permanent lineage food farms; when the fertility of one plot declines, it will be allowed to remain fallow and another plot will be utilized for next year's farm. For a given year one person's garden plot might range in size from a quarter to one-half an acre (Fortes, 1948: 14). The crops from these small plots are more than adequate for the needs of the domestic unit: staples like plantain, cocoyam, and palm nuts produce throughout the year and provide a natural larder, virtually eliminating both storage problems and the possibility of food shortage. Lineage lands were utilized for the food farms; as Fortes (1948: 14) points out, the necessity of shifting the farm site periodically favors lineage control, since individually owned plots would need to be much larger than the gardens actually cultivated for domestic use. Garden land in the ordinary village is sufficiently plentiful for non-lineage members to borrow plots without payment.

The environmental distinctiveness of northern Ashanti is reflected in the markedly different subsistence pattern of the region. Whereas food farming in the south is primarily in the hands of women, the staple crops of the north are cultivated by men. Yams and maize provide the major contributions to the food supply; their production is seasonal, as compared with the uniform produce of the southern staples. It is reasonable to expect that relatively large amounts of land would be required for effective farming. The small population density of the north as compared with the south is consistent with this view, as is Busia's statement (possibly with reference to North Ashanti) that farms sometimes were made jointly by lineage members (Busia, 1951: 47).

Unfortunately, I have been unable to discover detailed information on subsistence practices for this northern region.

Other Situational Elements   At this point I wish to introduce two considerations which will be treated in other contexts in the body of the paper. The first is that Ashanti society as we know it crystallized during a period of chronic warfare. The traditional history of the development of the Ashanti Union [1] attributes the consolidation of political ties among states of the Kumasi area to the need for united action in warfare to counter the exactions of a powerful southern neighbor.

The importance assigned to conflict and military action in this traditional account legitimizing the Union forecasts later history, as there were few years without external or internal warfare up to the final Ashanti defeat by the British. The significance of warfare is indicated further by the fact that in Kumasi, leading state of the Union, the traditional lineage-based military organization shifted toward military units of heterogeneous lineage composition. In other states, the lineage-derived titles of chief's councilors were replaced by titles referring to the official's army position.

The second factor I should emphasize is that *prior* to contact, Ashanti was a society with some degree of complexity in role differentiation. Social stratification reflected differentiated political and economic status and took the form of a division into chiefs, commoners, and slaves. Ashanti dogma, particularly the idiom of kinship, tended to minimize status distinctions and consequently they have sometimes been insufficiently emphasized. I do not suggest that traditional Ashanti had a class structure marked by rigid boundaries, but it was true that achievement in many areas was qualified by ascriptive criteria.

POLITICAL STRUCTURE

For the purpose of this chapter, I consider "political structure" as referring to the distribution of power, authority, and responsibility with respect to considerations of territory. In this section, therefore, I am concerned with significant territorial units in Ashanti, and will deal only incidentally with the structuring of political elements in kinship units.

Information is lacking as to size of territory and the population of states comprising the original Ashanti Union. Three of the nine states were said by Rattray to have been "comparatively unimportant" in the early period, but this exhausts the information in sources consulted (Rattray, 1929: 73).

---

[1] I follow Busia (1951) in referring to the confederation of states of traditional Ashanti as the "union."

Authority   Political relationships at the level of the Union and, partly, *within* member states, conformed to a type of authority allocation I will term "feudal." In paradigmatic form, an authority structure of feudal type has A exercising over B, who is responsible to A; B has authority over C, and C over D; responsibility is from the lower to the higher. However, A has no direct authority over either C or D; A can communicate to D only through B via C. A is D's superior, but the attempt to exert direct control over D would involve power rather than authority (cf. *ibid.:* 96–102).

The superordinate authority in this feudal structure was the head of the Kumasi State, who became the Asantehene. The legitimacy of the new political order was asserted through the traditionally approved mechanism of priestly supernatural inspiration. The priest Komfo Anotche, lawgiver and originator of the Golden Stool, the sacred symbol of the Union, is linked in Ashanti tradition with the first Asantehene, Osei Tutu, and regarded as cofounder of the nation. The successors of Osei Tutu, installed upon the sacred stool, performed ritual sacrifices to the royal ancestors which were asserted to be essential for the well-being of the entire political community.

I would argue that the stability of the feudal authority structure described is inversely proportional to the number of intermediate authority wielders. The problem of the maintenance of conformity to political order at the level of the Union may be expected to be acute; statements by Fortes (1950: 252) and Busia (1951: 87) support this assertion. The states making up the Union continued largely autonomous and central controls were precarious. Among the factors which countered the tendency to secede were: 1) Union warfare against external enemies, which required approval of all member states and their united support; 2) the fact that states subordinate to the Asantehene in theory had equal voice at Union councils regardless of state size. Since *some* states at any given time were likely to support Kumasi against insurgents, strong combinations among the disaffected were more difficult to achieve; 3) the practice of "de-stooling," which made it possible to remove an unsatisfactory ruler while retaining the traditional order; 4) kinship relations, both clan and affinal. The Asantehene had permanent kinship affiliations with the heads of subordinate states, couched in "uncle-nephew" or "brother" terms; he also maintained perpetual affinal relations with a number of lineages; 5) the symbolic importance of the Golden Stool, which, as Busia emphasizes, made secession an "offense against the gods" (1951: 57).

Formal statements of the Asantehene's prerogatives tend to overemphasize the degree of his control of subordinate chiefs. The contrast between Ashanti ideology and practice in these respects is well illustrated by the operation of the judicial system.

The Ashanti distinguish between "household" cases and those which involve "things hated by the tribe" (Busia, 1951: 65; Rattray, 1929: 294–339). Formal court process is associated with the latter type of offense; it is commonly instituted by the swearing of an "oath," which is an oblique reference to some misfortune of the ancestors and consequently a ritual offense. With the development of Kumasi as the superior Ashanti authority, the Asantehene's oath became a basis for judicial action in all states, though not the only basis. The Asantehene delegated authority to hear *his* oath cases to the heads of Union states, but reserved the right to impose sentence himself. Other prerogatives of the Asantehene which vest his office with autocratic trappings are similarly subject to compromise or flexible in practice. (Rights of the Asantehene are listed in Rattray, 1929: 104–105; cf. also Busia, 1951: 17). Further, the Asantehene was not immune to legal process; a national tribunal of the heads of states could be convened and the Asantehene arraigned before it. Like all Ashanti chiefs, he could be de-stooled.

Economic Elements The Asantehene had no control over the land of individual states of the Union, with the exception of his own state. Busia (1951: 60) has rightly emphasized the contrast here with European feudal land tenure. I would add the periodic chiefly control of external trade as a further contrast in the economic area. Together with lineage economic patterns, this limited the opportunity for the development of an *independent* merchant group.

The literature is not clear as to the role of the Asantehene in economic activity, as distinguished from that of other chiefs of states. I suggest that the following revenue sources were of greater importance for the Asantehene by virtue of his position: trading; spoils of war; court fines; special imposts, as for war (but only with the consent of chiefs of states, according to Rattray, 1929: 112); death duties. The Asantehene also possessed a very large number of slaves, and could increase their number by his periodic monopoly of trade to the north and by other means.

The special advantage of the Asantehene in trade included: a monopoly period when, for example, the trade paths to the kola market of the north were closed to all but the Asantehene's traders; the exaction of toll charges from other traders; the chief's weights, used for weighing gold dust, which were permitted to be heavier than those in ordinary use (Rattray, 1923: 304). Trade between Kumasi and the coast assumed considerable proportions by the nineteenth century and probably was important much earlier. The flow of trade was directed outside the Union, to the slave markets of the north and to the coast; Busia (1951: 89) indicates that there was little trade or other economic relations between the states.

Spoils of war might include the villages of defeated peoples. The Asantehene could allocate these to Kumasi favorites or to Union member states which had distinguished themselves in the military campaign. For the other revenue categories noted, the possible privileged position of the Asantehene does not require extended comment.

The Asantehene had ultimate control over the disposition of revenue, with the significant exception that it could not be turned into a private fortune. The profits of trading, death duties, and gold mining went to the "stool" treasury directly (Rattray, 1921: 116), whereas other revenues were distributed in accordance with custom to state officials, as "thank offering" to craftsmen, and to provide chiefly hospitality. The Asantehene and the head treasurer had joint charge of the chest in which large sums of gold dust were kept.

A de-stooled chief could take no property with him without explicit permission; generally he was allowed one wife, a small boy servant, and "a little" gold dust (Rattray, 1929: 116–117).

Military Organization   There was no permanent Union army; indeed, this appears incompatible with Ashanti feudal authority structure. Evidence that Kumasi state organization deëmphasized lineage elements in local organization suggests that a more efficient military structure was developed; Busia's remarks (1951: 97) support this notion, though he does not provide specific evidence of greater combat effectiveness.

Control of trade routes and the spoils of war, including captives, were dominant motivations for war. Data in support of this statement are skimpy, but major campaigns—against Denkyira and the Akim states to the south and Bono to the north—involve states wealthy from gold mining and control of trade (cf. Meyerowitz, 1952, *passim*).

For most states, army service was a lineage obligation, but Kumasi had military companies of heterogeneous clan composition and made extensive use of captives and slaves as soldiers (cf. Rattray, 1929: 120–121). Captives added greatly to Kumasi military strength; after a successful campaign the Asantehene created new military companies or enlarged existing ones to integrate captives into the army.

Soldiers were partly self-equipped and partly supplied with weapons and gunpowder by the state. As the striking power of the army became more dependent upon European firearms, the chief assumed primary responsibility for furnishing weapons and ammunition. The individual soldier carried his own provisions, but in extensive campaigns counted on living off the country.

In the field the army was divided into a number of task-oriented elements under their own commanders. The elements included scouts, the advance guard, main body, right and left flanks, and the rear guard. The Asantehene was commander-in-chief of the Union army if he took the field, while particular elements were commanded by various state chiefs with traditional rights to the positions. The dry season was the preferred period for campaigning. Rattray (1929: 125) reports of tactics that: "Strategy and deceit were of course legitimate weapons." (Cf. also the traditional account of the Ashanti conquest of Bono in Meyerowitz, 1952: 36–44). The rank and file might flee if the battle went against the army, but commanders were expected to fight to the last to defend the ancestral stools and to destroy themselves and their regalia by firing kegs of gunpowder when hope was lost. Major campaigns were planned carefully; several years might be spent accumulating the powder and shot deemed necessary for a distant campaign.

Succession   Rights to the office of Asantehene were vested in a lineage of the Oyoko clan. Busia states (1951: 98) that the royal lineage "had several branches," but he does not indicate whether or not all of the branches were eligible to succeed. A candidate for the vacant stool was nominated by the Queen Mother after consultation with the stool family. The nominee not only had to be formally approved by the Kumasi "elders" (i.e., the Asantehene's advisors, who were war captains or lineage heads) but also by the Union chiefs of states. The wide latitude of the succession rule permitted selection of a candidate on the basis of fitness for the position, while at the same time it would seem to have invited factional dispute. Records show that Union chiefs were embroiled in two succession wars in the late nineteenth century (*ibid.:* 98–99).

An Ashanti State

POLITICAL STRUCTURE

In this section my interest is in the examination of the political order based upon stratified segmentary lineages typical of the ordinary Ashanti state. The most detailed materials available refer to Wenchi, a rather small state in northern Ashanti at the edge of the forest zone, described by Busia.[2] The Wenchi location in Brong-speaking country does not augur well for typicality, but Ashanti influence in the region

[2] Wenchi, although a member of the Ashanti Confederacy, was not included in the original union.

has been evident for a lengthy period, and there does not appear to be a radical departure from the Ashanti pattern.[3]

Authority The formal political pattern of Wenchi conforms to the feudal authority type previously defined. The chief, selected from one lineage of two that were considered senior by virtue of having founded the town of Wenchi, ruled with the advice of councilors who were the heads of the six other lineages of the town.

Most (possibly all) of the "elders" in the capital were responsible to the chief for at least one village. The village was managed by a headman selected from the "founder" lineage of the village, assisted by other lineage heads as elders; the headman was directly responsible to his elder in Wenchi, rather than to the Wenchihene.

In practice the authority pattern of this system was subject to certain strains, which made it possible for the commoners ("youngmen") to play a critical role. The elders on the chief's council had to balance their responsibilities as representatives of their political subdivisions and lineages with their loyalty to the ruler. They could attempt to check a chief's departure from custom, but they could not oppose radical deviation too vigorously without suspicion of disloyalty. At this level, then, there could be no effective check on the decisions of a headstrong leader. Under these conditions, where the customary political organization was threatened, the informal organization of the commoners assumed a position of critical importance. The commoners appeared to be an aggregate of persons not holding office, and acting as citizens of the state without reference to lineage membership. Through their acknowledged spokesman, whose position was recognized by the elders, they could voice disapproval of the actions of the ruler. Thus, destooling of the chief was initiated by the commoners in the typical case. The commoners constituted a safety valve, redressing the lack of balance in the administrative system, and preserving the kingship at the expense of the king.

New villages in the chiefdom developed by immigration from elsewhere in Ashanti—primarily of persons displaced by warfare during the eighteenth and nineteenth centuries—and by normal segmentation processes.

The site of the town of Wenchi is said to have changed several times,

---

[3] The political organization of the Kumasi State differed from that of other states of the Union. The first Asantehene, Osei Tutu, is credited with the reorganization of the state through the use of the newly devised military machinery for administration. Busia presents a brief account of Kumasi state organization (1951: 91–96).

but whether this followed from the exhaustion of farm land or in consequence of warfare is not stated.

Stratification Materials with respect to lineage stratification for Ashanti generally, including Wenchi, are deficient. Neither Rattray nor recent writers seem to have examined this problem systematically and consequently there is a gap between the descriptions of the political order and the lineage order. I think this break can be bridged by taking account of lineage stratification, but I have little concrete evidence except for Rattray's largely implicit recognition of "class" differences in traditional Ashanti.

I have the impression that Ashanti dogma would deëmphasize the ranking of lineages. Discussions of genealogical position outside one's own lineage were discouraged by the maxim: " 'No one must disclose the origin of another' " (Rattray, 1929: 40).

At the clan level Fortes notes (1950: 260) that although the lineages of the Asantehene's Oyoko clan had superior prestige, every clan had a claim to importance in some area. "Hence all are considered to be of equal rank."

Wenchi materials are consistent with the following status discriminations among lineages: the chiefly lineage; Wenchi town lineages with stools—the "elders" held political titles as councilors to the chief and were village overlords; lineages of village headmen; "commoner" lineages.

Lineage and individual social mobility appear to have been possible. The founders of a village were its "owners" and were entitled to the office of headmen. I assume that a commoner lineage could found a village and thus rise in status, but I cannot demonstrate this view, other than to note that immigrant groups could establish villages in this way.

For the individual excluded from succession to political office by virtue of birth, status achievement was possible through success in war; manipulation of the supernatural—the "priesthood"; certain political offices, such as that of Okyeame (spokesman for the chief); the favor of royal fathers (for chiefs' sons).

Succession Succession to chiefship in Wenchi followed procedure similar to Ashanti. The Queen Mother consulted with senior men and women of all branches of the royal lineage and nominated a candidate. The candidate had to be approved by the hereditary officeholders of the state and by the commoners. The former, as lineage heads, retained their offices, providing for continuity in administration.

Property Political position at this level included rights with respect to land. Ashanti conceive of the earth as having inherent mystical powers and as belonging to the ancestors. As custodian of the land, the chief provided the link between the ancestors and their descendants. He had rights in the land which "co-existed" with rights of lineages and of individuals (Busia, 1951: 44). The chief was entitled to portions of animals killed and fish caught, to yearly first fruits, to treasure trove, and to mineral products. He had the right of *corvée* for his own farm, as well as for public works; at Wenchi this service was performed six times a year, and over one hundred men might participate on a given day. The chief's food requirements were heavy, not only for his own large establishment, but because he was expected to provide hospitality on a wide scale, and support artisans working for the stool. If the need was great, he could sell land after propitiating the ancestors and with approval of his councilors. Land which was not claimed by lineages could be allocated by the chief to strangers. I do not know whether this land could be alienated later, but I do not think it could.[4] Lineages had permanent usufruct rights in land. Problems of land allocation and usufruct rights will be examined in detail in the following section.

Taxing powers, court fines, and the other revenue sources were also available, in some degree, to state chiefs. The indirect techniques characteristic of Ashanti revenue collection made it possible for the chief to profit even when an impost was technically for the benefit of the Asantehene. The major element in the economic power of the chief consisted in control over services, rather than transferable wealth (*ibid.*: 50).

There are no indications that chiefly lineages, or other ranking lineages, had access to a greater amount of land, *as lineages,* by virtue of their status. A chief, after "enstoolment," was supposed to concern himself with problems of the state, not the lineage; his lineage had equivalent rights with other lineages, and was represented by an elder (the "clan" chief) on the chief's council. However, chiefly lineages were likely to be larger than commoner lineages and consequently more land would be required to provide for the larger number of economic units involved. I am not clear as to why higher-ranking lineages were larger, unless it is possible that they held a larger number of slaves whose female members could have been the starting point for attached segments of the lineage.

---

[4] However, Fortes maintains (1948: 13) that the state could take land required for public purposes "with or without the consent of the user and without compensation." Perhaps this is a modern development, since Rattray claims (1929: 355) that after land had been allocated by a "head stool" it was held "on a kind of perpetual tenure, terminable only by the wrongful act or negligence of the tenant . . ."

Military Service By virtue of lineage membership all able-bodied men were required to serve in the army of the chief. Lineage kin fought together under the leadership of the lineage head; even if a man did not live on lineage land, he was expected to meet this obligation unless he removed permanently to another chiefdom. I have no information as to the amount of time a man spent in military activity in any one year, nor do I know the age of initial conscription or of retirement from active duty. Aspects of military organization other than recruitment parallel the Ashanti organization discussed earlier.

Kinship Structure

The major questions addressed in this section are the nature of the linkages between Ashanti segmentary lineage structure and the differentiated political structure, and the organization of the Ashanti kinship system and the implications of the system for the study of matrilineal kinship.

In order to deal with the first problem it is necessary to determine the extent to which Ashanti lineage structure is accurately described as a segmentary type of lineage system. Here I follow Fortes (1950), in arguing that the evidence indicates that Ashanti lineages are segmentally differentiated, but that segmentation is not associated with political role allocation at differentiating points.

The central clue to the relationship between Ashanti lineage and political structure, as I see it, is to be found in the fact that each lineage is politically undifferentiated and comprises a single unit from this point of view. In terms of the superordinate political structure, the unitary lineage is represented by its elder, whose role is defined by the feudal authority system. Thus the lineage elder probably will be a councilor to the village headman or to the chief; the lineages cluster around some person with an office which interlocks with other offices in the political structure of the larger society.

Questions of particular interest with respect to Ashanti kinship center on what Richards has termed the "matrilineal puzzle" (1950: 246). The particular elements which appear significant for Ashanti deserve emphasis here, since they are presented only in descriptive fashion in the body of the section.

I interpret bilateral cross-cousin marriage in Ashanti as one solution to the matrilineal puzzle at the *domestic* level. Cross-cousin marriage here does not seem, even ideally, to structure relationships for the total society. The Ashanti themselves phrase marriage with cross cousins as a way of resolving the conflicting values of matrilineal kinship and paternity. This suggestion is, of course, neither novel nor original; I emphasize it in connection with Ashanti to point to the possibility that cross-cousin marriage in other matrilineal societies may have greater structural implications and require consideration of other than domestic elements for full understanding.

An acute problem for many matrilineal structures is that of residence. Where should husband and wife reside after marriage? Where should their children live? Schneider (SSRC Seminar) has suggested that access to strategic livelihood sources will be crucial here. Ashanti data, though not simple, seem to support this formulation. A boy will live with his parents, for example, until he reaches adult (non-dependent) status; then he is likely to move to his mother's brother's home where his legal claims to livelihood sources rest. If he remains with his father, it will ordinarily be found that he has secured special privileges, which he may enjoy for a time without full legal rights. After marriage he and his wife may live in duolocal residence initially, with each retaining their previous rights to resources. In terms of interpersonal relations, avunculocal residence may be thought of as a device for segregating the father-child and uncle-nephew conflict through a "time sequestration" of control and solidarity.

The kinship system will be described by reference to the following categories: kinship membership units; residential groupings; marriage; reciprocal relations among kinsmen; and terminological system.

Kinship role differentiation on the basis of generation, age, and sex will not be analyzed separately. Economic allocation in kinship structure is treated sketchily, not from choice but because this area is inadequately represented in available materials.

KINSHIP MEMBERSHIP UNITS

Clan   The widest and weakest expression of matrilineal unilineal relatedness is found in the clan. Clans are exogamous, named, nonlocalized units; all eight clans (seven clans, according to some authorities) are usually found in each Ashanti chiefdom. Clans are of roughly equivalent status, although a particular clan may be of greater importance in a given area.

Members of the same clan share diffuse hospitality obligations and in general behave toward one another as toward remote kin of the same maximal lineage (Fortes, 1950: 258).

Matrilineage   The localized lineage tracing descent from a known common ancestress for a period of ten to twelve generations is the basic unit for political, ritual, and legal purposes. Fortes has described the segmentary structure of the lineage: "each segment being defined in relation to other segments of a like order by reference to common and differentiating ancestresses" (*ibid.*: 255). Thus descendants of an alien slave woman become lineage members by attachment as a differentiated segment of the maximal lineage.

Formerly the maximal lineage may have been as important in the economic sphere as it now is with respect to political, legal, and ritual areas. Rattray's remarks (1929: 332–333) suggest that at one time this lineage held a joint estate, as anything "acquired by the joint labor or action of two or more members of the *abusua*" thereafter was controlled by the lineage head; the latter further had control over all *individual* possessions of a deceased member of the lineage. Fortes notes that "in theory any member of a maximal lineage is eligible for selection as heir of a deceased member if he or she belongs to the appropriate kinship category" (1950: 257).

Presumably with reference to North Ashanti, Busia states (1957: 47) that a "whole lineage" acquired usufruct rights over land and could exercise these rights in perpetuity. While it is possible that the economic solidarity of the maximal lineage in the north reflects the ecological distinctiveness of that region, it is noteworthy that Fortes' materials do not definitely exclude the possibility of a maximal lineage joint estate in the south, despite his emphasis on the lineage segment as the land holding unit (Fortes, 1950: 255–258). In an earlier publication he reported that "family land" could be held by a "lineage of any number of generation" (1948: 13).

Ashanti prefer to view the lineage as a unitary, undifferentiated grouping. They do not like to admit that membership may be a matter of degree, nor do they conceptualize the lineage as segmentary in character (Fortes, 1950: 255). This orientation, plus the moral prohibition against discussing another's origins, apparently makes precise discrimination of segments difficult. Fortes (1950: 257–258) describes a subdivision of considerable contemporary importance as including "the uterine descendants of an ancestress not more than four, or occasionally five, generations antecedent to its living adult members." This may be referred to as "the children of one womb" (*yafunu*). Land-ownership is vested in this segment; responsibility for assistance and aid to lineage members is greatest; it is the unit within which inheritance and the levirate operate in practice. This may be the segment which Rattray (1929: 333) distinguished as controlled by the "Fie-wura," or household head, who inherits and administers the "family" property for a group of unspecified depth.

The mother's brother who is an individual's legal guardian is the oldest living male in a more restricted segment than the estate-holding unit (Fortes, 1950: 270). This segment is of about three generations depth; the house of the leader is *de jure* a man's home, although Fortes indicates elsewhere that the legal home may be associated with a segment descended from a common grandmother (1948: 5).

Authority   The maximal lineage is headed by a male, who may also be a councilor of the chief. He is expected to consult the older men and women of the lineage and is assisted by a senior woman—the analogue of the Queen Mother in royal lineages. Duties of the lineage head include arbitration of disputes, direction of corporate lineage responsibilities, receipt of brideprice, consent for divorce, approval of the heir of a lineage member and of widow remarriage, and the performance of rituals in connection with male ancestral stools and the shrine of the lineage gods.

Leadership within the lineage segment of four to five generations depth was informal. An "experienced senior male" (Fortes, 1950: 258) was accepted as the authority figure by the consent of the senior members of the segment, male and female. Important administrative duties may fall to the leader, as Fortes notes: "If the segment owns land, or fishing rights, or other corporate property, he administers it, and his successor will be chosen by reference to his capacity to act as leader in the affairs of the segment" (*ibid.:* 258).

The lack of a formalized authority position for the segment head, when considered in relation to the possible heavy responsibilities of the post, suggests again that the maximal lineage formerly may have administered the estate. The segment head is recognized as an intermediate link in the chain of authority extending from a person's legal guardian to the maximal lineage head. The authority of the legal guardian of an individual, his "mother's brother," is discussed in a later section.

Rattray's analysis (1929) of the role of the household head provides no basis for precise determination of the nature of the unit over which this person exercised authority. Since he states that the "house father" performs rituals for the ancestors of the family, it might be assumed that reference is to the maximal lineage head (ancestral stools are limited to the maximal lineage); the head is also the arbitrator of household disputes. At the same time, the household head is reported to be the conservator and administrator of "family" property (Rattray, 1929: 4). Unfortunately, Rattray's materials are too vague to permit inference from the functions of the leader to the structure of the lineage unit.

The position of foreign slaves, over time, approximated that of free-born lineage members. Initially, however, a master had full legal and disciplinary authority over his slave, except that the latter could not be killed without the approval of the head of the state (*ibid.*: 33–46).

Land Allocation, Usufruct Rights, Inheritance Rights to allocate land rested with the leaders of the various sociopolitical units of the state. A chief could allot a sub-chief land "to eat upon" (*ibid.*: 351); in turn, the latter could provide land for a lineage, and the lineage elder, Busia states, "saw to it that every member of the lineage had a portion for his farm" (1951: 47). A lineage member had the right to farm on any unused lineage land (Fortes, 1948: 14), but formerly, at least, the head of the "family" had to be informed first (Rattray, 1929: 350).

Both men and women had the right to use land held by their own lineages. Marriage may have required some readjustments in land use, but I suggest that in most cases husband and wife continued to cultivate land which they had used previously. The majority of marriages involved persons from the same village, or from near-by villages (Fortes, 1950: 279); marriages of this type would raise no problems of accessibility to farm plots. However, if the parties to the marriage were from distant villages or had not farmed lineage land prior to marriage, other types of access to land were possible. Thus a wife could be permitted to farm on a part of her husband's lineage land; after her death, her daughters could continue to farm there, though the grantor lineage retained basic land-use rights (Fortes, 1948: 14; Rattray, 1923: 229–230). A man might be given land by his wife's lineage for the period of his life or the duration of the marriage, according to Rattray (1923: 229). Data are not available with respect to the particular conditions which gave rise to these types of usufruct grants, nor the frequency with which the grants were made. I have indicated two situations which might provide occasion for such grants; other possibilities include the displacement of a free-born Ashanti from his native state, and a specific lineage's shortage of land. It will be evident that this discussion is based on the assumption that the norm is for individuals to secure land through their own lineages, whereas the variations in access noted represent uncommon deviations from the norm. I do not know that this is so; it may be the usual thing for a wife to use the husband's lineage land. However, the context of Rattray's statement (1923: 229–230) on husband's access to wife's lineage land suggests that instances of this kind were rare.

Succession and inheritance rules stress sex, generation, and age. For an estate, whether that of the maximal lineage or any segment of the lineage, men have precedence over women, "brothers" over "sister's sons," and the senior over the junior. Potential successors to the position of trustee of a property-holding group of any scale were evaluated by the elders of the unit concerned in terms of personal qualities, as well as genealogical position. The heir was not only responsible for managing the property, but also for debts.

It was possible for an individual to acquire property through his own efforts, which he could then dispose of, in part at least, in accordance with his own desires. A man had exclusive usufruct rights to land which he cleared on his own (Rattray, 1929: 350), as he had to trees which he planted, and any other property obtained by his "unaided efforts" (*ibid.:* 335).[5] During his lifetime, a father could give a portion of his self-acquired property to a son or could will it to the latter after his death. It is probable that land could be transmitted in this manner in traditional Ashanti. Busia (1941: 43) indicated that a father could give his son a part of a farm if maternal kinsmen approved and customary obligations were observed (cf. also Matson, 1953: 224). On the other hand, Rattray reported (1929: 353–354) that the right of a son to continue to cultivate a deceased father's farm was contingent upon the levirate, although trees or crops given to the son belonged to him absolutely.

The emphasis on self-acquired property probably is not a recent phenomenon. Prior to the introduction of cocoa, the cultivation of kola provided a sort of cash crop which was a major item of trade in the markets of the north. The extent of kola farming in traditional Ashanti is unknown; it was formerly a "normal cash crop" in the forest zone village of Akokoaso, in Akim Kotoku, according to Beckett (1944: 75), but no great time depth may be involved here.

Rules with respect to the ownership and inheritance of immovable property, such as houses, are similar to those for lineage land (Fortes, 1948: 18). A father could provide a son land upon which to build a house; Rattray (1929: 354) suggests that the practice may be common: "Villages may grow up in this manner in which the houses and people are subjects of another chief, while the land on which the houses stand belongs to the Stool which possesses the land."

The above materials have been presented in some detail in order to emphasize the significance of self-acquired property in Ashanti,

---

[5] Women might also obtain property through their own efforts, although Rattray believed that if a woman's husband and children provided assistance, as in clearing the land, the crops would belong to the husband. On the other hand, help given by wife to husband "went to increase his personal wealth" (Rattray, 1929: 336–337).

particularly as a traditional means for dealing with one aspect of the matrilineal puzzle. The data also provide insight into the traditional view of the nature of land "ownership," whereby all land ultimately passed into trusteeship of a representative of a lineage or lineage segment. "The cycle seemed unending"; Rattray (1929: 334) wrote, "private property to-day was tomorrow again bound with fetters apparently unbreakable in the hands of the heir."

Patrilineal Linkages The classification of Ashanti kinship by some writers as a system of double unilineal descent derives from Rattray's reports (1923: 45–46) on the *ntoro,* which he regarded as an exogamous division based on transmission by and through males only. In a recent review of the character of the ntoro groups, Fortes emphasizes the minimal significance of this patrilineal element for the kinship system. Membership in "named quasi-ritual divisions" (Fortes, 1950: 266) is transmitted patrilineally, but ntoro are neither exogamus nor organized groups in any sense. The ntoro are included in a complex ritual ideology having to do with the notions of "soul" or "spirit" and with the moral value of paternity. Ntoro members are required to observe certain taboos and perform certain rituals; they are believed to have common personality characteristics.

The ntoro divisions do provide a basis for legitimizing the social importance of the male's paternal role in a society which otherwise places a dominant emphasis on matrilineal kinship. At the present time, the structural significance of these divisions is minimal; the traditional beliefs are esoterica known only to elders and those of chiefly lineages. It is possible that the ntoro were formerly of greater importance, but definite evidence is lacking.

RESIDENCE GROUPINGS

Village An Ashanti village was divided into wards or sections, in which the majority of the residents were members of a single lineage. At Wenchi, where the wards included several lineages, the houses of lineage members centered around the house of the lineage head. One ward had two lineages; a second, one; and the third, four lineages (Busia, 1951: 3). The lineages were stratified; there was a correlation between high status and a large population. While there was no rule of village endogamy, a strong preference for intra-village marriage existed.

Ashanti manifested a high degree of loyalty to their own village—that is, the village in which their lineage was located. They were called upon to help the village financially and in any necessary work of public service. In return, since a man was a citizen of the political

division to which the village belonged, he had the right to build a
house or cultivate a farm on any land in the division not already
allocated—after informing the chief, of course.

Household   The Ashanti household described by Rattray (1929: 3)
comprised a patrilocal extended family with the possible inclusion
of sister's children and unmarried uterine siblings of the male head.
It is true that for Ashanti men, the ideal was to head a household of
patrilocal type (Fortes, 1950: 262); this may have been the ideal for
men in traditional Ashanti. But Fortes (1948: 6) noted another
"preferred norm," where the preference was for a man's wife and
children to reside in their own matrilineal house—possibly a woman's
ideal, or that of her lineage. Statistical materials (Fortes: 1949)
document the practical significance of this second residence pattern
even in contemporary Ashanti; in the village of Agogo, the more
isolated of two communities studied, only one-third of the married
women lived with their husbands (Fortes, 1950: 262). Households of
patrilocal type probably were not statistically frequent in traditional
Ashanti except possibly among the chiefly class, where a son could be
induced to remain with his father in hope of political preferment.

In this section I depend upon Fortes' (1949) statistical material
for the analysis of the household, even though these data were secured
from contemporary communities and my concern is with traditional
kinship. However, no comparable figures for early Ashanti are known
to me; further, the wealth of information provided contributes to a
better grounded understanding of household problems in general
and, in this sense, has relevance for the traditional system.

Three major household types may be distinguished, based upon
the following residence patterns: duolocal, where each spouse remains with own matrilineal relatives; avunculocal; and patrilocal. In
the early years of marriage, residence was predominantly duolocal,
but with the passage of time could shift to avunculocal or patrilocal.
It is unlikely that the nuclear family of husband, wife, and children
was of structural importance in traditional Ashanti.

The traditional dwelling house comprised an oblong or square
compound, around which there were closed-in and open porchlike
rooms. In the center there was a courtyard, where women worked and
cooked and children played. The size of the compound varied; that
of a chief might cover a large territory (Rattray, 1929: 56–61).

Both men and women could be household heads; the critical
feature was ownership of a house, though age and generation were
factors. At Agogo 64 males were heads of household groups, as

compared with 57 female heads. The largest proportion of both male and female heads were aged 51 or over, reflecting the importance of the "time" factor in house ownership. There were a higher proportion of male than of female heads in the age categories from 31 to 50 (Fortes, 1949: 66); males have a somewhat better opportunity than females to secure their own houses during early adulthood.

For both townships, 45 per cent of households had a generation depth of two or less; 55 per cent included three generations, with a small number of the latter exceeding three generations.

Where women were heads, households tended to be segments of a matrilineage. When daughters married, they were likely to remain in their mother's household, so that duolocal residence was typical for the early years of marriage. The wife visited the husband in his home (Fortes, personal communication to K. Gough).

Ashanti ideology stressed that a man should have his own home, with wife and children living with him, but only about 26 per cent of Agogo married women lived with their husbands (Fortes, 1949: 77); among 41 of these women, almost half (17) were found married to cross-cousins. As Fortes remarked, "the norm at Agogo is so markedly against a wife's living with her husband that special circumstances must be looked for to explain the exceptions" (ibid.: 78).

Fortes' statistics support the Ashanti generalization that children live with their mothers or fathers while young and then move to their mother's brother's household. The frequency of avunculocal residence is not apparent from the data, but Fortes (1950: 262) stated that it is not "uncommon" for a man to have own children and sister's children living with him. A man would live in his wife's household only under highly exceptional circumstances.

Domestic Economy Formerly the household was probably the basic unit in the domestic economy, with joint production and consumption responsibilities. Busia referred to a "domestic unit" of large size, which engaged in joint cultivation. "The crops and fruits which were raised by the joint labour of the group were owned by the head of the family, but the members could collect food from it." (Busia, 1951: 47). Men of the lineage ate together in the house of the lineage head, the wives of married men bringing the evening meal to them there (ibid.: 6–7).

The decline in lineage solidarity in contemporary Ashanti is particularly marked in domestic matters (Fortes, 1950: 261). The household has little economic significance, neither engaging in productive activities as a unit nor maintaining a common food supply

(Fortes, 1949: 64). Every adult is expected to earn his or her own living (Fortes, Steel, and Ady, 1948: 168).

MARRIAGE

Marriage was forbidden between persons who fell within the broad range of the Ashanti conception of incest. The restrictions included a person's own matrilineage and its segments, if attached for more than four generations: any patrilineal descendant of father's father's father; the child and son's child of half-brothers by the same mother and different fathers; finally, any lineal ascendant and siblings to the fourth generation and any lineal descendant to the fourth generation, in both cases exclusive of ego's generation.

Legal marriage was determined by the payment of *tiri nsa* ("head wine") to representatives of the bride's lineage by the head of the husband's lineage. The payment ordinarily consisted of two bottles of gin, but was more elaborate for girls of high-ranking lineages. The bride's lineage could demand a further payment from the husband at any time after marriage. Parents might approve a period of cohabitation prior to formal marriage.

The payment of tiri nsa gave the husband exclusive sexual rights in the wife, made him legal father of the woman's children during the period of the marriage, and obligated the wife to perform economic and domestic services. In turn, the husband was responsible for providing food, clothing and, if necessary, housing for his wife and children, money for her debts, care in the event of illness, and sexual satisfaction; he had to obtain her consent before taking another wife.

Polygyny was permitted; probably it was unusual among commoners, except for marriage with slave women. Fortes (1950: 281) reported that 80 per cent of married men today have only one wife at a time; a "commoner" polygynist was unlikely to have more than three wives. There are no statistics with reference to traditional patterns.

Marriage with either cross cousin was a preferred form in traditional Ashanti. The incidence in the old days is unknown, but Fortes (1950: 282) found that 14 per cent of marriages for women aged 50 and over were of this type. Rattray (1927: 291) thought that there was a tendency to prefer marriage with mother's brother's daughter, but this is not well documented.

The divorce rate in modern Ashanti is high, over half of the men over 40 and women over 35 in Fortes' samples having been divorced at least once. It is probable, but not certain, that divorce was frequent in traditional Ashanti. Both sexes had the right to request divorce.

RECIPROCAL RELATIONS

Mother-Child   The crucial relationship in Ashanti kinship [6] was that between mother and child. The bond was one of great strength and intensity for both son and daughter. Moral rather than legal sanctions buttressed the mother's authority. She was seldom a punishing agent; rather, she stood for "unquestioning protection and support against the world at large" (Fortes, 1950: 264). Mother and daughter became closely identified through years of intimacy. There was not such constant contact with the son but she was his "trusted confidant." A son's first ambition was to build a house for his mother if she did not have one. Though always ready to succor her children, the mother expected obedience and respect from them. A mother was responsible for the moral behavior of her daughter.

Father-Child   A father had no legal authority over his children, but it was his "duty and pride" to care for them and provide them with a start in life. He was the primary disciplinary agent; the children's mother's brother could not punish except at the request of the father and mother. A father might make his children gifts of money or other property, including land to which he had right as an individual, while alive or on his deathbed. The relationship was thought of as one of mutual affection; a son or daughter "ought" to support an aged father, though there were no legal sanctions to compel this action. A father had charge of the moral education of his son; consequently he was responsible for paying damages if the son committed adultery. A son's labor or earnings went to the father as long as the former was a dependent.

A father's relationship with his son was more intimate than with his daughter. If the father was a craftsman, he would be likely to transmit this specialized knowledge to his son.

The father role was subject to some variation by virtue of the stratified nature of Ashanti society. Where the father held an important political office he was able to use his rank to retain control over the sons by providing them with special advantages. At Kumasi some "captaincies" were permanently allocated to the Asantehene's sons; filial sentiment and political advantage were united in these appointments, as they assured the rulers of servitors whose loyalty was undivided.

Mother's Brother-Sister's Child   The oldest living mother's brother (classificatory) of an individual's great-grandmother's lineage segment had sole legal authority over him. The relationship became par-

[6] The materials in this section have been drawn primarily from Fortes, 1950, but have been compared with other sources where possible.

ticularly important after an individual assumed adult status, when the legal norms embodied in the matrilineal lineage system were most effective. In traditional Ashanti the maternal uncle's area of control over sister's children was extensive—he could pawn his nephews and nieces, his approval was crucial for marriage, and he could demand that divorce be instituted. He could insist upon cross-cousin marriage and a nephew could not refuse, though a daughter might; likewise a niece could be forced to marry her uncle's son (Rattray, 1929: 20). Considerable ambivalence characterized this asymmetrical relationship, particularly with respect to inheritance and succession; this is evident in the Ashanti saying quoted by Rattray, "Nephews are your enemy" (*idem*).

Sibling-Sibling The relationship between siblings was considered to supersede all bonds except those between mother and children. This was not a completely symmetrical relationship, since age distinctions were observed and order of birth was important. Older siblings might punish younger brothers and sisters, while the mother's first-born was regarded as the head of the sibling group. Despite the Ashanti horror of incest, there was no avoidance between siblings of opposite sex. Sisters tended to become strongly identified with one another; they could not be wives of the same husband, either contemporaneously or by means of the sororate. A brother would entrust important matters to his sister rather than to his wife, while his sister was expected to support her brother against her husband. At the same time the relationship engendered considerable suppressed hostility, which became manifest in witchcraft accusations within the matrilineal lineage and devotion to "witch-finding" cults (Fortes, 1950: 275).

Husband-Wife The norms governing this relationship have been detailed in the section on marriage. The strong negative attitude toward childlessness was noteworthy—both men and women viewed the lack of children as "the greatest of all personal tragedies and humiliations" (*ibid.*: 262).

Paternal Half-Siblings There were no legally prescribed rules defining this relationship, which was structurally unimportant. Ties of sentiment between paternal half-siblings were usual and might form the basis of a lasting friendship.

Grandparents-Grandchildren Grandparents were the "most honored" among kinsfolk. The relation between grandparent and grandchild was one of warmth and affection. Grandparents might correct grandchildren, but called upon the parents to act if serious discipline was required. The grandmother might take over much of the care of a young daughter's children, especially during early years of marriage when the daughter was likely to continue to live in the maternal household. A woman should always return to her maternal home to bear her child.

Father's Sister—Brother's Child   A father's sister was entitled to respect but there was no deep attachment involved. She might scold brother's children, but could not actually punish them. Through cross-cousin marriage, she was a potential mother-in-law to her brother's children.

Parents-in-Law—Children-in-Law   Neither a son's wife nor a daughter's husband were required to use special forms of etiquette with reference to parents-in-law. The relationship was a diffuse one characterized under the heading of "special respect." Parents-in-law were to receive help and support from children-in-law, especially in the early years of marriage. Similar norms of respect and assistance held for sibling-in-law relations. The Ashanti recognized the potential strain in affinal relationships, and were likely to attribute marriage failures to in-law interference. The lack of formal patterning of avoidance and joking relationships here may be related to the possibility of limitation of contact between in-laws, which in turn would be related to Ashanti residence patterns.

TERMINOLOGICAL SYSTEM

Intensive analysis of the terminological system will not be attempted —indeed, the data are deficient for certain categories and can be supplied only through inference.

The extensive set of alternate terms is an outstanding terminological feature. This introduces varied possibilities in the concrete application of terms by a given ego, possibly in accordance with shifts in the social situation. The system lacks the neat precision of classic Crow-Hopi terminology, but its adjustability seems to fit with variable requirements of a large-scale, differentiated society.

The application of alternate terms makes it possible to stress any of the following: cross-cousin marriage; lineage elements in ego's generation, through the use of descriptive terms for FaBrCh, FaSiCh, and MoBrCh—own siblings and MoSiCh are then linked as siblings; the lineage principle, by the application of terms for Fa and FaSi to any member of Father's matrilineage, and of grandparent terms to any member of Father's Father's matrilineage; generation equivalence in ego's generation, by extension of sibling terms to all males of the generation—however, special terms are always applied to MoBrDa and FaSiDa.

Ashanti recognized seven generations in the kinship terminology.

TABLE 5-1

Ashanti Kinship Terms*
(After Rattray, 1923)

1. Nana (panyin)	Great-grandparent
2. Nana	$\begin{cases} \text{Grandparent} \\ \text{Grandchild} \end{cases}$
3. Agya	Father
4. Ena, 'eno	Mother
5. Sewa	Father's sister
6. Wofa	Mother's brother
7. 'Nua panyin	Elder sibling
8. 'Nua kuma	Younger sibling
9. Sewa 'ba	Father's sister's child
10. Wofa 'ba	Mother's brother's child
11. Agya 'ba	"Father's child"
12. Agya Wofase	"Father's sister's child"
13. 'Ba	Child
14. Wofase	Sister's child
15. Nana n'ka'so	Great-grandchild
16. Yere, ye'	Wife
17. 'Kunu Panyin	"Husband's older brother"
18. Ase	$\begin{cases} \text{Parent-in-law} \\ \text{Child-in-law} \end{cases}$
19. Akonta	Sibling-in-law
20. 'Yere kuma	"Younger sibling's wife"
21. Kora	$\begin{cases} \text{Wife's sister's husband} \\ \text{Co-wife (woman speaking)} \end{cases}$
22. Kuna, Ku'	Husband (woman speaking)

* Numbers are those used in the accompanying charts.
Terms are for a male speaker, unless otherwise indicated.

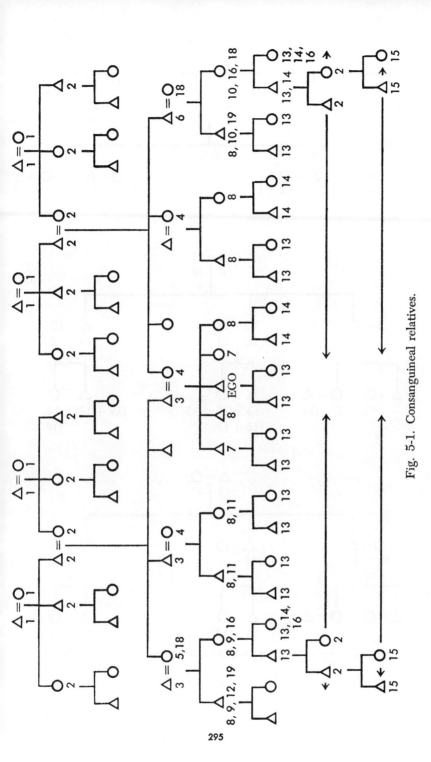

Fig. 5-1. Consanguineal relatives.

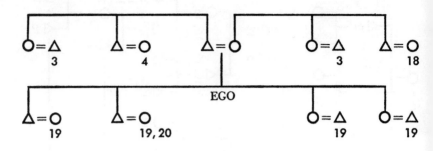

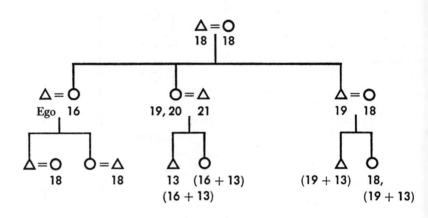

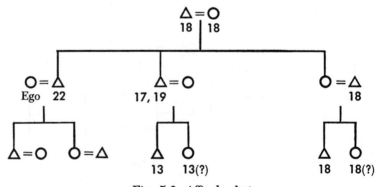

Fig. 5-2. Affinal relatives.

Rattray (1923: 31, 32) classed grandparents and grandchildren together under a single self-reciprocal term, but this may not be accurate (cf. Fortes, 1950: 276). Great-grandparents are referred to as
"old" grandparent, and great-grandchildren as "grandchild don't
touch my ear," since their touch is said to lead to the former's death
(Rattray, 1923: 34, 39).

In the first ascending generation applications conform to the bifurcate merging pattern. The pattern for the first descending generation grouped own Ch and BrCh together, with SiCh separate—presumably the pattern was reversed for female ego, though Rattray is
not clear (1923: 32). Similar differentiation between the offspring
of males and females is made for MoSiChCh and MoBrChCh. Data
for FaSiChCh are not complete, but alternative Ch and SiCh patterns
appear applicable here, as is the case for MoBrChCh. However, Fa-
BrChCh may also be classed as Ch, regardless of the sex through
which descent is traced.

Affinal relationships do not appear to be highly structured, but more
extensive information is required for analysis. Parents-in-law and children-in-law use a single self-reciprocal term. The use of consanguineal
terms for parents' siblings' spouses is interesting, but data for in-
terpreting this assimilation are lacking.

Nayar: Central Kerala

The Nayars, unlike the groups so far described, form only a part-society—a named category of castes within the social system of southwest India. An account of their kinship system therefore requires a sketch of the political and economic system in which they were embedded. It seems to have been the Nayars' role as a specialized occupational group within a complex society which accounted for the most unusual features of their kinship institutions.

The Nayars differ also from the other groups considered with regard to their relatively high level of technological development. At least from the first century A.D., Kerala's social structure was based upon plough agriculture with irrigation, specialized crafts, and overseas trade (K. M. Panikkar, 1945: 36). Productivity was sufficiently high so that more than one-quarter of the population could be exempted from manual labor and set apart as specialist, literate groups engaged in religion, government, warfare, and wholesale trade. The Nayars, as the ruling and military castes, formed the core of this aristocracy and probably comprised between one-quarter and one-fifth of the total population.[1]

Partly as a result of direct legal changes brought about since the British conquest of 1792, and, more deeply, as a result of the change to an industrial fuel technology, the Nayar system of matrilineal groups has been gradually disintegrating over the past hundred years. Some of the traditional functions of these matrilineal units are being taken over by the elementary family and by the wider, personal, bilateral kindred of each individual. Other former functions of matrilineal groups have passed to such modern bureaucratic institutions as government, army, law court, and school. Because this book is a comparative study of matrilineal systems, I shall concentrate on Nayar lineages and kinship in the "traditional" period before the British

---

[1] Buchanan estimated the population density of Central Kerala at 100 per square mile in 1800 (1807, II: 501). The density for Cochin State was 814 per square mile in 1931 (Census of India, Cochin State, 1931).

conquests; that is, from 1342, the date of the first useful Arabic account (Gibb, 1929) to the end of the eighteenth century. My sources include English translations of the writings of Arab, Italian, Portuguese, Dutch, and French visitors to Kerala, works by English travelers, government servants, historians, and anthropologists, and a few historical works by Indian scholars who make use of indigenous Malayalam and Sanskrit documents.

Modern changes in Nayar kinship are not evenly distributed throughout the population. Some of the traditional institutions and relationships persist, especially in villages most remote from the seats of government and from modern market centers. Many other traditional usages are remembered by older people. Because of this, my own field work in three villages of Kerala—between November, 1947 and July, 1949—was able to provide me with the organizational framework into which to fit the literary material, and supplied me with many details on the traditional system not hitherto published.[2] Some information was also gleaned from genealogies, manuscript histories of particular lineages, and translations of Malayalam documents relating to land tenure, property transactions, and religious rites.

Modern changes in Nayar kinship comprise a large subject, which I have already briefly treated elsewhere (Gough, 1952a; see also Rao, 1957: 74–142). A full account will appear in a forthcoming book.

Ecology

Kerala, or the Malabar Coast, lies in the extreme southwest of India beside the Arabian Sea. The coastline is some 360 miles long, the area about 14,908 square miles. It is divided from the rest of South India by the Western Ghats, a mountain wall broken only in the center by the Palghat Gap. From prehistoric to modern times, migrations took place from the eastern plateau of peninsular India into the coastal region, but until the coming of modern transport the mountains prevented continuous contacts between the people who became established there and their neighbors to the east. On the other hand, its position laid Kerala open to contacts by sea with many peoples, including Jews and Arabs (from perhaps 800 B.C.), Egyptians and Phoenicians (ca. fifth century B.C.), Romans (first century A.D.), Chi-

[2] My field work in three villages of Central and North Kerala was made possible by the grant of a William Wyse Studentship from Trinity College, Cambridge, and of an Anthony Wilkin Studentship from the Faculty of Archaeology and Anthropology, University of Cambridge. The preparation and writing of these chapters have been carried out with the aid of two grants from the Social Science Research Council, in 1954 and 1956.

nese (from at least the sixth century) and after 1498 the Portuguese, followed by the English, Dutch, and French (Logan, 1951, I: 251–254, 258, 294–399).

The coast falls roughly into three natural divisions: the coastal strip, the midlands, and the highlands rising into the Ghats (cf. Buchanan, 1807: 565–566). The coastal strip is flat and sandy. Its chief product is coconuts, with some rice and bananas. In the southern half it is broken by salt-water lagoons which for over a hundred miles form a continuous navigable chain parallel to the sea. Most of the chief towns are situated on the coast, divided by chains of little fishing villages. Many of the coast towns are ancient, and most of them lie at the mouths of navigable rivers which flow westward from the Ghats. From time immemorial raw materials, chiefly pepper, were brought by boat from the inland hillsides for shipment from these ports.

The midlands comprise low hills and fertile valleys. Broad strips of alluvial rice lands lie in the valleys, thinning out as the land rises into the foothills of the Ghats. On the hill slopes are gardens of coconut palms, bananas, pepper, ginger, and many fruit trees such as jack and mango. It was probably wild pepper which was exported in Roman times, but pepper and other spices have been deliberately cultivated at least since 1290 (Ricci, 1931: 326). Cashew nuts, introduced by the Portuguese, formed an additional export crop. Small merchant settlements, market-centers, and the military fortifications of petty chiefs existed at strategic points on river banks. Some of these centers grew into bazaar towns in the nineteenth century. But the mass of the population traditionally lived, as today, in scattered village communities on garden land surrounding or surrounded by fields of wet rice, the main subsistence crop. Wet-rice cultivation depended on plough agriculture with teams of oxen or water buffalo. Goats and chickens were the other significant domestic animals.

The highlands rising into the Ghats were covered mainly by deciduous forests. The foothills, interspersed with occasional rice flats, were sparsely populated by people of the same cultural groups as those in the plains. They eked out their wet-rice cultivation with garden crops of fruits, spices, and vegetables, with shifting hoe cultivation of dry grains on hillsides, and with forest hunting of elephant, deer, and pig. Higher in the mountains lived primitive tribes of hunters and shifting cultivators, having only occasional contacts with the kingdoms of the plains.

Throughout most of the area Kerala's rainfall varies between 75 and 170 inches, being heaviest in the north where the mountains are

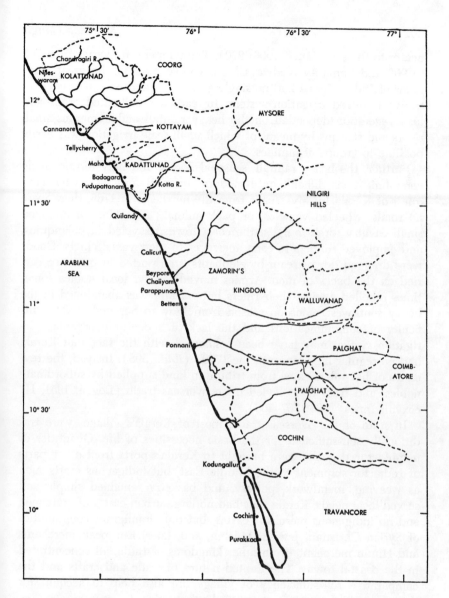

Fig. 6-1. Rough boundaries of the Kingdoms of Central and North Kerala in the mid-eighteenth century. (Adapted from C. A. Innes, 1908: 44–45.)

nearer to the sea (Innes, 1908: 270). The temperature varies from 70°
to 90° and humidity is always high. Unlike most of the great kingdoms of India, Kerala had no single great river and no extensive, centrally organized irrigation system. Instead, her cultivated crops and
lush vegetation depended on the heavy rainfall and numerous small
rivers and streams by means of which small-scale irrigation was easily
possible to groups of families.

Further, the heavy rainfall, seasonal floods, and hilly terrain made
communications difficult until modern times. Before the partial conquest of Kerala by Mysoreans from the northeast in 1766, there were
no roads, wheeled vehicles, or pack animals. The kings maintained
small cavalry forces only in the coast towns, traveled in palanquins,
and employed runners to carry messages to their vassal chiefs. Goods
were dragged downstream by elephants, transported in boats, or carried on the backs of men. Armies moved slowly; local nobles sometimes rebelled against their rulers but warfare was abandoned in the
heavy southwest monsoon season from May to September. The difficulty of communications and the lack of a centrally organized irrigation system may have been connected with the fact that Kerala
had no regular land tax until the 1730's (*ibid.*: 308). Instead, the revenues of her rulers came from tribute in kind supplied by subordinate
nobles, and from taxes levied upon overseas trade (Logan, 1951, II:
ccxviii; Innes, 1908: 307–308).

In spite of the overseas trade, most of Kerala's villages were traditionally self-sufficient for the basic necessities of life. Quantities of
manufactured goods were brought to Kerala's ports from other parts
of India for shipment to the Middle East, but indigenous crafts such
as weaving, metalwork, pottery, and basketry remained simple and
served local needs. Kerala thus had no large urban castes of craftsmen
and no indigenous merchant castes, but only immigrant communities
of Syrian Christian, Jewish, Muslim, and, later, European merchants
and Hindu merchants from other kingdoms of India, all concentrated
in the coastal towns. The limited nature of trade and crafts and the
comparative self-sufficiency of village life also help to account for
the relatively decentralized political structure.

History

Little is known of Kerala until the first century A.D. It then formed
part of the kingdom of Chera, whose capital was probably east of the
Ghats at Karur on the Kaveri River in the modern Trichinopoly district. Chera, like its companion South Indian kingdoms, Chola and

Pandya, appears to have grown powerful on the basis of trade with Rome. Like Chola and Pandya, it was a Tamil kingdom; Malayalam, the modern language of Kerala, did not diverge from Tamil until about the tenth century (Sastri, 1955: 400). It is clear from the Tamil literature of the Sangam period that the basic features of Kerala's division of labor, caste system and village organization, must have developed during or before the Chera period (*ibid.*: 110–140). The three South Indian kingdoms temporarily disintegrated in the late third century, probably as a result of a sharp decline in Roman trade.

There is no mention of any matrilineal caste like the Nayars in the Chera kingdom. When and whence they came is uncertain. The most plausible suggestion is that during the Chera period they were a matrilineal hill tribe occupying the Ghats under chiefs who owed a tenuous allegiance to the Chera kings. They may have descended to the Kerala plains as invading barbarians about the fourth century, when the Chera kingdom collapsed (Ayyar, 1938: 43). Little is known of Kerala between the Chera period and the thirteenth century. All or a part of it passed under the rule of a succession of viceroys (Perumals) from various South Indian kingdoms to the east of the Ghats. The date of the last Perumal is quite uncertain. Many writers concur in placing him in the early ninth century, but he may possibly have lived as late as the thirteenth. Nayar chiefs and Nayar soldiers are first mentioned in three copperplate inscriptions, tentatively dated late seventh, mid-eighth, and early ninth centuries. The inscriptions record grants of land and judicial privileges on the coast to settlements of Jewish and Syrian Christian traders (Logan, 1887, I: 265). The grants were made by rulers of Kerala, presumably Perumals, and were witnessed by Nayar chiefs of Venad, Ernad, Walluvanad, and Palghat. All these districts were famous Nayar chiefdoms in the later periods and persisted until the eighteenth century. The plates suggest that Nayar chiefs with private armies had emerged as vassals of the Perumals at least by the ninth century. By the mid-thirteenth century, at the latest, the greater Nayar chiefs had become independent small kings, and the Perumals had disappeared.

Chinese had resumed trade with Kerala sometime in the Perumal period, and in the thirteenth century this trade greatly expanded under the empire of Kubla Khan. Concomitantly, two coastal Nayar chiefdoms with strategic ports expanded into small kingdoms by conquering the surrounding inland chiefdoms and monopolizing their trade. In the north was the Kolattiri kingdom centered about Mount Eli, and in the south the kingdom of Travancore or Venad, centered about Quilon (Ricci, 1931: 326–330; Logan, 1951, I: 282–283). Chinese trade declined in the late fourteenth and early fifteenth centuries, but that of Muslim Arabs (who had visited the coast from the eighth century) greatly increased. In the fourteenth century a third Nayar kingdom around Calicut, in the center of the coast, had expanded with the help of Arab merchants (Major, 1857: 13–18). By the time the Portuguese arrived, in 1498, Calicut practically monopolized the Arab trade, and the Zamorin (king) of Calicut held overlordship from Pudupattanam south to Porakkad (Logan, 1951, I: 293–294; Ayyar, 1938: 273, 291). Trickles of trade continued in Kolattunad and Travancore, but the kings there had grown weak by comparison with the Zamorin. Kolattunad had become divided into three virtually independent little kingdoms, and the Travancore ruler had surrendered large powers to the subordinate local chiefs of his realm. Two other small kingdoms remained independent in the interior to the east of Calicut: Walluvanad and Palghat.

The period 1498 to 1792 was one of bitter struggle between European and Middle Eastern powers, who formed shifting alliances with native rulers for control of the pepper trade. By 1600 the Portuguese had practically abolished the Arab trade, but they were themselves driven from the coast by the Dutch in 1663. The English reached Kerala in 1615 and the French in 1725. Each European trading power allied itself with one or another Nayar ruler and took part in successive battles until, in 1766, the northern half of the coast was overrun by Muslim armies from Mysore to the northeast. The Mysorean occupation ended in 1792 with the settlement of the whole area by the English East India Company and the establishment of the British bureaucratic political system (Logan, 1951, I: 404–473).

Shortly before the Mysorean invasions Kerala was divided into nine small kingdoms and a number of border chiefdoms owing only tenuous allegiance to some king. The British after 1792 amalgamated the seven northern kingdoms (Kolattunad, Kottayam, Kurumbranad, Kadattunad, Calicut, Walluvanad, and Palghat) to form the Malabar District of Madras Province, pensioned their rulers, and brought them under a British district officer responsible to the government of Madras. Cochin, a small kingdom in the center of the coast, remained a native state under its own ruler subject to the advice of a British Resident. So also did the southernmost kingdom of Travancore, whose ruler had already in the 1730's established a standing army, dispossessed his Nayar nobles, and formed a bureaucratic government. Kerala remained divided in this way until after the independence of India in 1947. Cochin and Travancore were amalgamated in 1949 and, under popular pressure for the formation of linguistic states, the whole area was reunited as the State of Kerala in 1956. This state elected a Communist government in 1957.

After 1498 there were certain changes in Kerala's economy. Trade and towns expanded, gunpowder was introduced and wars became more devastating, and cash transactions became more prevalent among the aristocratic castes in villages (K. M. Panikkar, 1929: chap. XIV). But the basic form of the caste system and the pyramidal system of kingdoms, subordinate chiefdoms, and villages persisted with little change until after the Mysorean conquest. The Calicut kingdom gradually declined after 1498, for the Portuguese allied themselves with the small kingdom of Cochin to the south, freed it from Calicut's overlordship, and used it as a base from which to expel the Arabs and subdue the Zamorins. Nevertheless, with fluctuating boundaries Calicut remained the most powerful kingdom until the 1730's.

Although its internal political boundaries have shifted continually, Kerala is today still divisible into three major cultural areas. These are distinguished by differences in the names and numbers of the castes who occupy them, in dress, dietetic habits and ritual practices, and in the kinship systems of the several Hindu castes. The northern area, north of the Kora River, comprises the former kingdoms of Nileswaram, Kolattunad, Kottayam, and Kadattunad. This was the area dominated by the Kolattiri kings in the fourteenth century and at various periods thereafter. In British times it became the northern part of Malabar District and the southern part of South Canara District; I shall call it North Kerala. The central area comprises the former kingdoms of Calicut, Walluvanad, Palghat, and Cochin. It was overrun by the Zamorins of Calicut at various times between the fourteenth and eighteenth centuries. In British times it formed South Malabar District and Cochin State; I shall refer to it as Central Kerala. All the southern area (until recently, Travancore State) was at one time or another subordinate to the kings of Travancore. The political systems—and consequently the internal caste divisions of the Nayars and the forms of their kinship systems—differed in these three areas. Much confusion has arisen in the past because of failure to distinguish between the three regions. It has been assumed that the Nayars had one kinship system, whereas in fact they had three, with different terminological structures. In this paper I describe Nayar kinship in two kingdoms of Central Kerala: Calicut and Cochin.

Caste and Territorial Divisions

THE HIGH CASTES

The Nambudiri Brahmans   Throughout Kerala the Nambudiri Brahmans were the highest Hindu caste and the ritual and scholastic leaders. Today they form one hundredth of the population (Censuses of Madras, Cochin, and Travancore, 1931). Carriers of the Sanskrit language and of ancient Vedic culture, they are thought to have entered Malabar from the eastern plateau sometime after the fall of the Chera kingdom (Logan, 1951, I: 121, 243; Ayyar, 1938: 47). Most Nambudiris were landlords of substance, but they included a number of ranked occupational sub-castes of varying wealth. The greater landlords were managers of large temples, promulgators of religious law, legal advisers of the kings, priests of public sacrifices, or philosophers and Vedic scholars. The lower sub-castes, whose members owned smaller estates, included temple priests, physicians, and household priests and professional cooks who officiated at ceremonies in the Nayar castes.

The Nambudiris ranked ritually above the kings and were to some extent above and outside the political systems of the kingdoms. Alone of all the castes, they moved unmolested between enemy kingdoms. They held ceremonies attended by their caste fellows from all parts of Kerala and carried on their system of intra-caste administration independently of the administration of justice within the kingdoms. For the latter purpose they divided Kerala into *gramams* (caste areas) (Logan, 1951, I: 120). Over the whole region a dignitary called the Aravancheri Tamburakkal, who lived in the Calicut kingdom, was universally acknowledged as the ritual and administrative leader of the Nambudiris (Buchanan, 1807: 423–426; Ayyar, 1938: 23). He held the right to install the kings of both Calicut and Cochin, even though these rulers were traditionally at enmity. The field of social relations of the Nambudiris was thus the whole of Kerala and they played a role not dissimilar to that of the medieval Catholic church. Descent among the Nambudiris was patrilineal.

The High-Caste Nayars   Below the Nambudiri Brahmans in ritual rank came the royal *matrilineages* of the several kingdoms. Those in Central Kerala were Calicut, Walluvanad, Palghat, and Cochin. Although of Nayar origin, each of these lineages considered itself superior in ritual rank to the Nayar subjects within its kingdom. Between kingdoms, royal lineages disputed for rank and would not intermarry. Although exogamous, therefore, each royal lineage considered itself a separate caste. The Cochin lineage claimed descent from the Perumals and ranked as Kshattriyas, the second of the four divisions of all-India Hindu society. The Walluvanad, Palghat, and Calicut lineages, once vassals of the Perumals, were not strictly recognized as Kshattriyas in Brahmin theory and held the title of Samantans. Normally, the oldest man in each royal lineage held the kingship and administered customary law with assistance from Brahman advisers.

Each kingdom was divided into *nāds* (chiefdoms or districts). In the Zamorin's kingdom at the height of its power some of these chiefdoms had once been independent small kingdoms. They were conquered by Calicut in the late fourteenth and the fifteenth centuries. They continued to be ruled by their traditional monarchs, who paid tribute to Calicut. Among them were the chiefdoms of Beypore, Chaliyam, Parappanad, Bettem, and Punnattur. Each of these ruling lineages, although feudatory, retained a higher ritual rank than the Zamorin by virtue of its more ancient tradition of government. Similarly, some chiefdoms of the Cochin kingdom were governed by conquered feudatory rulers of higher ritual rank than the royal lineage. The small kingdoms of Walluvanad and Palghat, however, had no feudatories of higher rank than their royal lineages.

The other chiefdoms of a kingdom were ruled by hereditary Nayar chiefs (*nāduvaris*) originally appointed by the king, and these chiefs had more restricted powers than the feudatory monarchs. Most of them held the title of Samantan, but all were considered of lower ritual rank than their royal lineages. The Zamorin's kingdom (the largest) appears to have had twenty-eight such district chiefs in the fifteenth century. Each chiefly lineage, like each royal lineage, tended to regard itself as a separate caste acknowledging no peers.

Each chiefdom was divided into *dēsams* or villages. A village seems to have covered anything from one to four square miles, comprising both dry garden land and flats of alluvial rice land. Most of the land in each village was normally owned by one landlord family of higher ritual rank than the other occupants.

In some villages the land was owned by a Nambudiri patrilineal extended family, whose large house occupied a central position. In others it was owned by one or other branch of the royal lineage as part of the royal domain. There would then be a palace in the village and the senior prince of the household would act as village headman. In other villages the land was owned by the chiefly matrilineage of the district, whether this lineage were of feudatory royal rank or of vassal Samantan rank. Again in this case the chiefly family would live in a small palace and the head of it would fulfil the roles both of chief and of village headman. In other villages the land formed part of the estate of some large temple. These estates, called *sankētams,* were managed by assemblies of Nambudiris who held complete judicial rights over the lower-caste population. Finally, in yet other villages the land was owned by the matrilineage of a hereditary Nayar village headman (*dēsavari*) originally appointed by the king or by the chief of the district. The Nayar village headmen were drawn from castes ritually lower than those of their district chiefs. In Walluvaned and Calicut village headmen were usually drawn from the Kiriattil Nayar caste. The corresponding caste in Cochin was called Vellayma Nayars.

The landowning families in all of these villages were called *jenmis.* The eldest man of the extended family, whether patrilineal or matrilineal, had legal guardianship of his own family and, in another sense, of the village lands and inhabitants. He sanctioned marriages in all the castes, managed the land devoted to village temples, and paid the temple servants from its produce. A landlord family could not sell its land without the consent of the king and it usually remained on its site over many generations.

Villages were classifiable therefore as Brahman, temple, royal, chiefly, and Nayar headmen's villages. In some areas a group of villages of the same type might be adjacent to one another. In each village, subordinate to the landlord in ritual rank and administrative power, lived members of one or other caste of Nayar retainers or vassals. In modern times these castes have tended to combine as a single caste of "high-class Nayars," so that their former roles are difficult to determine. So far as I could discover they were as follows.

First, a caste called Kiriattil Nayars in Calicut and Vellayma Nayars in Cochin. Most village headmen's lineages were originally drawn from this caste, but after they had assumed office these lineages isolated themselves as a separate sub-caste of higher rank than ordinary Kiriattils. Ordinary Kiriattils appear to have been usually retainers in villages commanded by Nayar village headmen.

Second, a caste called Purattu Charna Nayars ("outdoor retainers") in Calicut. Its members usually lived in villages owned by a district chief or by the royal lineage. A special, higher-ranking subdivision of the caste called Pariccha Menons ("leaders of the shield") formed the Zamorin's private army and lived on royal land near Calicut.

Third, a caste called Agattu Charna Nayars ("indoor retainers") in Calicut. They also seem to have lived mainly in royal or chiefly villages. The men were often clerks in the palaces. In Cochin, castes two and three were amalgamated and were called Swarupattil Sudra Nayars or "palace servants."

Fourth, a caste called Pallichan Nayars, both in Calicut and Cochin. Its members also were vassals in the villages of royalty, chiefs, and of the greater Brahmans. The men were often palanquin bearers as well as soldiers.

Fifth, a caste called Sudra Nayars in Calicut and Illath ("Brahman house") Sudras in Cochin. The members lived in villages owned by Brahman families or on the estates of Brahmanical temples.

The mutual ritual ranking of these five castes seems to have varied in different districts. In some districts they ranked in the order given, and men of a higher caste might marry women of a lower caste; the reverse was in theory forbidden. In other districts the castes seem to have disputed for precedence and not to have regularly intermarried. In most areas the five castes occupied different villages or different sections of large villages, seem to have had little communication in peacetime, and did not normally interdine. In war, however, soldiers of these different castes interdined freely and spent the night in each others' homes. It is possible that sexual restrictions between these castes were also relaxed in war, but this point is uncertain.

In each village there were normally some four to seven matrilineages of the appropriate retainer caste. The separate households or property groups within each lineage had the hereditary right, granted by the king, to occupy stretches of garden land and to lease large plots of wet paddy land on long-term tenure from the village landlord. The tenure was called *kānam;* the tenant, *a kānakkaran.* In most villages the men of retainer lineages also owed military service to their landlord, ultimately on behalf of the king. (The military organization is discussed below.) Retainers were called *adiyar,* a word equivalent to "vassals," of their landlord. They participated in his household ceremonies and often waited upon him. Women of retainer lineages could be summoned as serving maids in the landlord's family; men, as bailiffs to collect the landlord's rents and organize the labor of his serfs.

The Temple-Servant Castes   In addition to the Nayars, other aristocratic castes often lived in a village. These were the temple servants, nowadays collectively called Ambalavasis. They are relevant to our discussion because they sometimes married Nayar women. The highest of these castes were the Chakkyars (or reciters of Puranic stories) and the Pushpagans (or flower gatherers for temples), which had patrilineal descent systems of the same type as the Nambudiris. They

ranked below Nambudiris but above retainer Nayars and certain matrilineal temple-servant castes. The latter included Nambyars, Puduvals,
and Marars, three castes of drummers, and Psharodis and Variyars,
castes of temple stewards.

The temple-servant castes were small and lived chiefly in villages
owned by Nambudiri Brahmans or in sankētams. Four types of temples
were distinguishable among the higher castes. First were the large temples of the sankētams, whose estates were managed by Nambudiris. They
were dedicated to all-India, Puranic deities, usually Siva or Vishnu.
Second, were the private temples of individual Nambudiri families in
villages owned by Nambudiris, which were small replicas of the first
type. Third were the private temples of royal and chiefly matrilineages, dedicated to Bhagavadi or Bhadrakali—the Nayar goddess of war, epidemic, land, and fertility. Fourth were the smaller
Bhagavadi temples of village Nayars, each collectively managed by
an assembly of Nayar retainers of one or more villages.

In the first two types of temple animal sacrifice was forbidden.
Offerings were of fruit, flowers, incense, and fire. The priests were
low-ranking Nambudiri Brahmans. Nayars might enter the outer
courtyards of such temples but might not perform rites there. In a
village which formed part of a sankētam there was sometimes no
Nayar population at all; a group of lineages of one or more temple-
servant castes replaced them as retainers of the Brahmans and as permanent tenants. In Nambudiri villages containing a temple of the
second type, one or two lineages of some temple-servant caste would
be attached to the temple, but there would invariably also be a group
of Sudra Nayar retainers with their own Bhagavadi temple.

In villages under a Nayar headman there might be only one Bhagavadi temple managed collectively by Nayars. One lineage of the Marar
caste might be present to drum in the temple, but the other temple-
servant castes did not work in Nayar village temples. Similarly, in a
royal or chiefly village containing a large Bhagavadi temple of the
ruling lineage, the temple-servant castes might be absent except for
one lineage of Marars. Persons of other temple-servant castes might
however come from nearby villages to assist at special ceremonies.

In Bhagavadi temples the regular priest was usually of a special low
subdivision of Nambudiris (Adigals). In addition a Nayar shaman,
attached to the temple, periodically became possessed by the goddess
and declared her will to the people. Daily rites in the Bhagavadi
temple were similar to those in a Brahman temple, but annual festi-

vals involved animal sacrifice by Nayars in which Brahmans and temple servants took no part.

Consistent with these differences in ritual practice, Nambudiris and temple servants were vegetarians and followed rules of non-violence. Royals, chiefs, and Nayar retainers were warriors and until modern times usually ate meat and drank liquor. The matrilineal castes of temple servants were otherwise culturally similar to Nayars, with whom they probably had a common origin.

Below the Chakkyars and the Pushpagans, the Nambyars, Psharodis, Variyars, and Puduvals disputed for ritual rank and would not interdine. These castes ranked roughly parallel to the district chiefs, with whom they had few social relations and did not interdine. They ranked above the retainer Nayars, who might receive food from them but might not give to them. Marars ranked below the other temple servants and parallel to retainer Nayars, with whom, however, they had few social relations outside the temple and did not interdine.

The Nayar Menials in Temples Below all these aristocratic castes came certain small matrilineal castes of menial, non-military Nayars whose work was largely connected with temples. Vattekad Nayars were oilmongers; Odatt Nayars, tile makers; Andura Nayars, temple potters. One Vattekad lineage was present in every village to supply oil for temple lamps. Often the headman of the Vattekad lineage was the shaman of the Nayar Bhagavadi temple. Vattekad Nayars also performed household tasks for Kiriattil Nayar village headmen, which ordinary Kiriattil Nayars were too proud to do. Odatt and Andura Nayars were very small castes,[3] and one lineage might serve six or eight villages.

The Nayar Servant Castes Below the temple menials came three matrilineal castes of servant Nayars with "degrading" occupations. Chidigans (called Attikurssis in the Calicut kingdom) were funeral priests of the higher matrilineal castes. Veluttedans were washermen of all the castes above them and Vilakkataravans were barbers of all the castes above them. One lineage of each was usually present in a village. Funeral priests ranked above barbers and washermen, who disputed for rank and would not interdine.

Social Relations among the Higher Castes The castes so far men-

[3] The kings permitted only Brahmans, royalty, and the greater chiefs to roof their houses and temples with tiles. Tile making was therefore a minor craft, and temple pottery was of superior quality to that used by commoners. The ordinary polluting caste of potters, Kumbarans, camped outside villages and exchanged their wares for grain.

tioned were called "high," "good," or "clean" castes. They lived in
a separate portion of the village around the temples and the landlord's establishment, with each house in its own fenced garden. Except for the servant Nayars all might enter either Brahman or Nayar
temples. Within this group, lower castes were forbidden to touch
higher castes because of rules of ritual pollution, but individuals of
different castes might approach each other within a few feet. Equal
interdining took place only between caste fellows, but members of
lower castes might *receive* food from higher-caste hosts. In ritual
terms these castes thus formed the upper ranks of society, although
only the Nayar retainers and those above them were economically
and socially aristocrats. Nambudiris and two small castes of their
temple servants were patrilineal; all the rest were matrilineal.

I have designated as "Nayars" all the castes which bear this title
today. They are not a unitary group but a named category of castes.
Traditionally, the title Nayar seems not to have been extended to
all these castes. Before 1498 the military Nayars or retainer Nayars
were called Lokar (Ayyar, 1938: 32). What the other matrilineal
castes were called is not known. "Nayar" was not then a caste name
but a title conferred by the king on lineages whose members had won
special military honor. The Portuguese called all the soldiers "Nayars"
and during the period of European trade it seems to have come into
use as a title held by all the military castes. Some Nayars say that
the temple menial castes and the matrilineal castes of washermen and
barbers usurped the title only during British rule, in order to raise
their status. The higher temple-servant castes, although matrilineal,
never adopted the title because they ranked above the military Nayars
and had honorable titles of their own. This paper primarily concerns
the Nayar military retainers, their village headmen, chiefs, and
royalty.

THE HIGHER POLLUTING CASTES

The high castes were the religious and secular aristocrats and their
personal servants. In many respects the polluting castes lived a separate social life, being located in a different part of the village. They
included, in order of rank, Tiyyars (called Iravas in Cochin), who
were palm-wine makers and tenant farmers, with twenty to forty
households per village; Kanisans or astrologers, with one to three
households per village; the artisan castes of blacksmiths, goldsmiths,
carpenters, bell-metal workers, and stonemasons (who ranked equally),
each with one to three houses per village; low-caste washermen and
barbers (who ranked equally), each with one to five houses per vil-

lage; and bow makers, each with about one to ten houses per village. Tiyyars, astrologers, washermen, and barbers had double unilineal descent: localized patrilineages with dispersed exogamous matrilineal clans. Artisans and bow makers had patrilineages only.

The polluting castes worked for each other and for the higher castes. Tiyyars held land on a sub-tenure from landlords and Nayar tenants. Astrologers and artisans gave services to the higher castes, to each other, and to the Tiyyars, who ranked above them. Barbers worked for all the higher polluting castes but not for the "good" castes, who employed the Nayar barber. Washermen laundered for all the higher polluting castes but not regularly for the "good" castes, who employed the Nayar washerman. However, the low-caste washerman's lineage owed services to the "good" castes at death, menstruation, and childbirth. Bow makers served Nayars and Tiyyars. Each of the polluting castes was endogamous and interdined only within the caste.

THE LOWER POLLUTING CASTES

On the outskirts of the village, in separate small hamlets, lived the very low castes of Parayas and Pulayas. Parayas were a small caste of basket and umbrella makers. Two or three households had a village right to serve all castes above them. Pulayas were until 1850 the agricultural serfs of Nayars, temple servants, and Brahmans (Buchanan, 1807: 370–372). As highly polluting castes, Pulayas and Parayas were theoretically forbidden to approach the high castes within a distance of sixty-four feet. They might not enter the "good" area of the village or walk on the main paths.

OTHER RELIGIOUS GROUPS

Muslims, called Mappillas, were concentrated in the Zamorin's kingdom, where they followed patrilineal descent. In 1931 they formed about 15 per cent of Kerala's population. Their presence dates from the ninth century, when Arab traders began to make converts, probably mainly from the Tiyyars and the coastal caste of fishermen. From the Arabs and from these converts there sprang a flourishing trading community which increased greatly in the fourteenth century (Logan, 1951, I: 192–197). The Zamorins derived a large measure of their power from the Muslims through taxes and naval support (Ayyar, 1938: 54). Muslims lived mainly in the ports and at inland trading posts on the banks of rivers. They were partly outside the village ranking system, which had its basis in differential land rights, and were theoretically outside the Hindu religious hierarchy. Nevertheless, Muslims were in some contexts accorded a rank ritually and socially between that of Nayars and Tiyyars.

The Christians of Kerala numbered about 20 per cent of the population in 1931. The Syrian Christians, the most ancient and numerous group, may be descended from Persian Nestorians; they were trading on the coast at least by 525 A.D. (McCrindle, 1897: 119). Christians were and are concentrated in Travancore and Cochin. They received land grants near the ports and enjoyed virtual self-government provided they paid taxes to the kings (Logan, 1951, I: 260–270; III: cxxi–cxxvi). As landlords, tenants, and administrators—as well as traders—they ranked socially parallel to the Nayars and were served in the same manner by Hindu polluting castes and serfs. Their trade declined after the Arabs became dominant on the coast, and some of them began to serve in the royal armies along with Nayars. The Portuguese converted some Syrians to Roman Catholicism, but the converts still retained the Syriac rite. All Syrians were readily distinguishable from the lower-ranking Latin Catholics, converts to Catholicism from Portuguese times who were drawn from various polluting castes.

The Economic System

The principles of reciprocity and redistribution,[4] rather than of market trade, dominated the village economy until toward the mid-nineteenth century. In villages, castes were characterized by hereditary occupations and correspondingly by hereditary, differential rights in the produce of village lands (Logan, 1951, I: 110–112, 269, 270, 599–600, 623). The village landlord and the Nayar tenants were the main redistributive agents, collecting in goods from the lower orders and redistributing them in customary shares. In all village economic transactions, *households*, and not whole caste groups or individuals, were the units of interaction.

The village landlord's household "owned" almost all the land in the village. "Ownership" meant both more and less than modern Western landownership (Logan, 1951, I: 602–603). The landlord might not sell his land without the consent of the king or of a chief, and sale was restricted to families of appropriate caste. He might not evict his tenants, village servants, or serfs without their consent unless they committed grave crime (*ibid.*, I:. 607). On the other hand, the landlord's ownership included judicial rights over the village population.

The landlord retained a portion of the land as his private domain for cultivation by his serfs. The rest was held by Nayar retainer households as non-cultivating tenants (*kānakkar*). The tenant's household

---

[4] For an analysis of the general operation of these principles in the Indian village economy, see Neale, 1957: 218–236.

originally rendered a portion of the produce to the landlord and additionally paid tribute in kind at New Year and at the succession of a new landlord or a new tenant on the death of the old (*ibid.*, I: 605–614). In return for their hereditary land rights tenants owed military and personal services to the landlord or to his military representative.

Each Nayar tenant household, like the landlord, retained a portion of land for cultivation by its serfs. Serfs were attached to the plots on which they lived, took the house name of their masters and were held as ancestral property. The master supplied the serf with daily rice, building materials, a house site, and special gifts at life crises and festivals.

Each tenant household also gave some lands to cultivating subtenant households (*verumpāttamdar*) of the Tiyyar caste. According to Logan, the latter traditionally retained one-third of the net produce and surrendered the rest to their masters (*ibid.*, I: 583).

The Nayar servant castes and most of the polluting castes of village servants (astrologers, artisans, bow makers, basket makers, etc.) owed their main services to the landlord, the Nayar tenants, or both. Each family held the hereditary service right of a village or occasionally of a small group of adjacent villages. Village servants gave their services to the appropriate higher-caste households when required. In return they received from each patron household customary biennial shares of rice and other goods after the two harvests of the year. Each servant family held a house site and garden from the landlord by hereditary right and was provided by its various patrons with the materials (metal, wood, etc.) of its craft.

Among the higher polluting castes, most of the village servants (astrologers, artisans, washermen, barbers, etc.) simply exchanged services reciprocally without making gifts of grain. Within this range of castes, however, Tiyyars, as cultivators, were subsidiary agents of redistribution, for they received the services of almost all the village servant castes and made biennial gifts to them of grain.

The village was thus almost self-sufficient for food and the daily necessities of life. In addition, part of its produce in rice and coconuts went out in the form of annual tribute given by the landlord to his district chief. The chief in turn gave tribute to the king and in addition rendered succession fees and gifts at life-crisis rites (Logan, 1951, II: ccxviii–ccxix; Ayyar, 1938: 270).

A large part of the king's revenue, however, came from taxes on overseas trade. Before 1500 the trade was in the hands of Arab merchants, who obtained pepper and other spices from inland landlords and tenants through indigenous Muslim middlemen. At that time the middlemen appear to have paid the villagers directly in cloth, metals, and luxury goods. Sumptuary laws confined the use of many imported goods to Brahmans, Nayars, and merchants. Other strategic goods such as metals and cloth filtered down from the landlords and tenants to the lower castes in the form of customary gifts at festivals.

During the period of European trade (1500 to 1792) markets and cash transactions encroached further upon the subsistence economy of villages. The kings prosecuted larger and larger wars and increasingly paid their Nayar soldiers in cash, even though they continued to muster them through the Nayars' "feudal lords." [5] As the pepper and coconut trade increased, new gardens came under cultivation and landlords and tenants often sold their spices for cash. The Nayar retainers seem to have received most of this cash from the towns, for as tenants they held the bulk of the village's garden lands as well as receiving their payments in war. From about 1550, therefore, landlords, who wished to maintain control of the economy, had to develop some means of extracting money from their tenants. Cash payments thus became a regular feature of the *kānam* tenure (Logan, 1951, I: cxxxi). The tenant periodically advanced a cash sum to the landlord as a kind of forced loan, the interest on which was then set off against the annual payment in kind. At the death of either landlord or tenant 13 per cent of the original sum was deducted from the loan as a succession fee. The tenant might then repay this amount in cash or revert to paying a larger share in kind. Later in the period cash renewal fees seem to have been exacted by landlords every twelve years. In some cases the tenant would prefer to surrender his land or to sell his right and move his family to another village. Sales of landlord rights, even (near the ports) to Europeans or Muslims, also increased. However, sale of either landlord or tenant rights remained disreputable, lengthy, and hedged about with legal restrictions until after the collapse of native rule (K. P. P. Menon, 1929: 309–310; Logan, 1951, I: 597 *et seq.*; II: cxxxv).

---

[5] I use the term "feudal" here without precise definition. In many respects the political structure of the Central kingdoms was comparable with that of the stronger Western European principalities such as Flanders and Normandy in the second half of the eleventh century. There was centralized control of the judiciary, of armies, trade, and coinage, but within each principality subordinate lords retained minor judicial powers and owned domains and private armies (Stephenson, 1942: 80–92).

European trade shook the foundations of the caste system in other ways. Ports grew larger, and within them European merchants employed Christian converts, artisans, and runaway serfs. Near the ports, serfs sometimes became slaves, being torn from their ancestral lands and sold or hired for cash.

Nevertheless, until the introduction of steam power in the second half of the nineteenth century, the technology and over-all economy of Kerala did not change very radically. Trade was still limited to surplus crops, luxury goods, and metals. Inland villages remained largely self-sufficient, with the lower castes excluded from cash transactions. Upward mobility was virtually confined to Muslims, Christians, and the Hindu aristocrats above the rank of Nayar retainers. It seems to have been this lack of basic change in the technology which allowed the persistence of a strict, hereditary rank order in villages and, within each homogeneous local caste group, of kinship as the main organizing principle.

War and Law

The traditional period was one of perpetual wars between adjacent kingdoms, interrupted only in the rainy seasons. A royal lineage's strength lay in its monopoly of gunpowder, coinage, and customs dues, its ability to use foreign and Muslim ships for naval warfare, and its control of the royal domains both as a source of produce and of Nayar retainers as soldiers. Through its superior wealth and military power a royal lineage could force feudatory princes and vassal nobles to muster soldiers throughout the kingdom in periods of large-scale war. Each district and each village was classified according to the number of Nayar soldiers it could customarily muster for war. In the Zamorin's kingdom the strength of royal feudatories varied between 18,000 and 1,000 Nayars; of Nayar chiefs, between 5,000 and 100; of village headmen, between about 100 and 25 (Ayyar, 1938: 278). Records of the muster of each feudatory were kept by the Nayar clerks of the palace. The primary duty of each chief was to assemble regularly the soldiers of his district for military exercises at the capital, and in time of war to lead them to battle, with the king himself at their head. Within the district military training was organized on a village basis. This might be done by a Nayar village headman, by the chief himself, or, in Brahman villages, by a Nayar military leader (Asan) who acted for the chief or the king. All Nayar boys of the retainer, village headmen, and chiefly and royal castes seem to have received a military training, although some, especially of the Agattu Charna caste, later became clerks (Dames, 1921: 18–19; A. Gray, 1887, I: 412–413).

The Nayars' traditional arms were the sword, shield, lance, and the bow and arrow, although gunpowder came into increasing use after the Portuguese arrived. Before 1500 battles were highly stylized (cf. C. A. Menon, 1911: 56; Ayyar, 1938: 118, 171). Not more than 10,000 were commonly brought into the field at one time. Severe loss of life was prevented by the employment of Brahman emissaries who, if fighting became intense, might enter the field and arbitrate between the leaders. If, however, the king or a chief were slain, his personal vassals had to fight to the death or until their honor was avenged by the slaughter of a corresponding leader on the enemy side (Logan, 1951, I: 138).

Later, with the introduction of cannon and fortresses by the Europeans, battles became more frequent and devastating. The Zamorin mustered a total force of between 50,000 and 60,000 at various times in the sixteenth and seventeenth centuries against the ruler of Cochin (Ayyar, 1938: 169, 182). The kings had to rely increasingly on paying their soldiers in cash rather than on sporadic feudal levies. Permanent conquest and the control of rich lands also became a more urgent aim of the kings as the overseas trade expanded. But the Nayar techniques of fighting and their code of honor persisted until British times.

Within each kingdom, law was administered at several levels. Each local caste group had its own periodic assembly of household heads to judge crimes (which were also sins) against the caste's religious laws. These included wrongful interdining and sexual relations with members of other castes. The chief punishments were fines for the upkeep of the caste shrine and temporary ostracism. Grave offenders were excommunicated with the consent of the chief. They then became the property of either king or chief and were sold as slaves to foreign traders. In the larger castes such as Tiyyars or Pulayas the local caste group was often contained within the village. The smaller castes of village servants each had their own assemblies extending over a group of adjacent villages.

Among retainer Nayars the local caste group might comprise the Nayars of one caste within one village, within a section of a large village, or within a group of two to four adjacent small villages. This area was called a *tara* in the Calicut kingdom and a *kara* in Cochin; we shall call it a neighborhood. Its assembly was called a *tara-kūttam* or *kara-yōgam* (Logan, 1951, I: 87–88, 132–133). The functions of intra-caste administration of the Nayar assembly are discussed later in connection with the lineage.

The village headman, assisted by representatives from the Nayar retainers, judged small civil cases concerning debt, petty theft, or trespass. He appropriated the fines in these cases (Munro, quoted in Ayyar, 1938: 288). Individual Nayars also arbitrated in small civil disputes carried voluntarily to them by disputants within their own or the lower castes. Serfs came directly under the jurisdiction of their Nayar or Brahman masters, who had the power of life and death over them.

In the castes above the serfs, larger civil disputes and grave crimes were judged in the court of either chief or king. Chiefs' (*nāduvaris'*) judicial powers varied with the size of their armies, but feudatory princes (*svarūpis*) retained complete judicial rights with power over life and death (Ayyar, 1938: 272). So also did the Brahman managers of temple estates, although they called upon some local chief to carry out their judgments. Murder, sacrilege, treason, the wounding of a cow or of a Brahman, indecent assault of a woman, and grave theft from a man of "good" caste were generally punishable by death (*ibid.:* 282). Brahmans and women, however, were never officially executed by order of the king. All offenses among Brahmans were tried by an assembly of the Brahman neighborhood, which, with the local ruler's approval, might excommunicate the offender. If a woman of any caste above serfs was convicted of a capital offense the king had the right to sell her into slavery.

The higher the cast, the wider the field of social relations. Among the serfs and the higher polluting castes this was confined to a group of adjacent villages. Among temple servants, village headmen, and retainer Nayars (apart from their excursions in war) the field of social relations was the chiefdom. Among chiefs and royalty it was the kingdom, and among Brahmans, Kerala.

Hypergamy in the Upper Castes

Each of the castes below Nayar temple menials was endogamous, as is usual in the caste system throughout India. But among the higher "clean" castes the integration of political offices and of the larger territorial units was strengthened by hypergamous marriages. By hypergamy I mean the marriage of a woman of lower caste to a man of higher caste.

In discussing hypergamy it is necessary to explain the descent system of Nambudiris. In the Nambudiri patrilineal extended family only the eldest son was permitted to marry (with Vedic rites) within his caste, and beget children for his family. Younger sons had recognized liaisons with women of the matrilineal castes, whose children belonged to their mother's caste and lineage by matrilineal descent. These hypergamous unions were regarded by Brahmans as socially acceptable concubinage, for the union was not initiated with Vedic rites, the children were not legitimized as Brahmans, and neither the woman nor her child was accorded the rights of kin. By the matrilineal castes, however, the same unions were regarded as marriage, for they fulfilled the conditions of ordinary Nayar marriage and served to legitimize the child as an acceptable member of his matrilineal lineage and caste.

If a Nambudiri eldest son remained childless the second son might marry a Nambudiri woman and beget children for his family. Unmarried Nambudiri women, of whom there were many, remained in their natal homes and were maintained by their fathers and brothers. The eldest son of a Nambudiri house might however have several Brahman wives (who lived patrilocally with him) and also several Nayar partners whom he visited in their homes. Nambudiri younger sons lived and ate in their natal households, headship of which passed from the eldest son down the line of brothers and then dropped to the next generation. In this way the Nambudiri family was prevented from splitting into segments and was enabled to maintain its ancestral estate intact over many generations. If in any generation a family had no son, succession was ensured by the adoption of a daughter's husband or of a man related through some cognatic tie.

The possible directions of hypergamous marriages in the Cochin kingdom are briefly as follows. In the royal lineages marriages were entirely hypergamous. In Cochin and Walluvanad royal women married only Nambudiris of the highest and wealthiest sub-castes within the kingdom. Royal men married women of chiefly lineages within the kingdom, of village headmen's lineages within their own domain, or of retainer Nayar lineages in the royal villages. In the Calicut kingdom royal women married either Nambudiris or the feudatory princes of higher rank and more ancient lineage than themselves. Royal men married women of the same lower matrilineal groups as in the Cochin and Walluvanad kingdoms. Women of the feudatory royal lineages married only Nambudiris; men married royal women or women of chiefly, village headmen's, or retainer Nayar lineages within their own area of rule.

Each Nayar chiefly lineage, like royalty, normally counted itself a separate caste and married only hypergamously. Women of chiefly lineages married the royals or feudatory royals to whom their lineages were immediately subordinate, or wealthy Nambudiris, usually of their own district. Men of chiefly lineages married women of village headmen's lineages within their district, or women of retainer Nayar lineages, usually in their own villages.

Village headmen's lineages occasionally contracted marriages reciprocally with other village headmen's lineages of the chiefdom which had originally sprung from the same retainer caste. They also provided wives for chiefs and Brahmans and husbands for retainer women, usually of their own villages.

Among temple servants, Nayar retainers, and Nayar temple menials the majority of marriages were between persons of the same caste. A few women in the Psharodi, Variyar, Poduval, and Nambyar castes married Nambudiris, especially those whose families managed the temples where they worked. A few such women also married men of the Chakkyar and Pushpagan castes, which had descent systems like that of the Nambudiris. A few men of these matrilineal temple-servant castes married women of Nayar retainer and Nayar temple-menial castes in the villages of their work. Nayar women were particularly convenient partners for temple servants and Nambudiri temple priests because of the latters' spatial distribution. Often a temple-servant lineage or a Brahman priestly family held the hereditary right of service in six or eight small temples in villages up to ten miles away. One man of the lineage might spend much of his life working away from home in one of the more distant temples. He would live on food previously offered to the deity, occupy a room attached to the temple kitchen, bathe in the temple bathing pool, and visit a local Nayar wife at nights, returning home for life crises and festivals.

Women of the retainer Nayar castes might receive husbands from all the castes above them. Sudra Nayar women living in Brahman-owned villages or on the estates of large temples were the most likely to form links with Brahmans and temple servants; Charna Nayars and Pallichans, with royalty or chiefs; and Kiriattil women, with village headmen. Thus hypergamous unions entered into by retainer Nayars in general followed the main lines of lord-vassal relationships. However, "odd" marriages with individuals of any higher rank in nearby villages were permitted.

Because the higher castes were much smaller than they were, the Nayar retainers probably gave less than 10 per cent of their women to men of higher caste. Men of the retainer castes made still fewer marriages in the castes of temple menials. The latter also received as husbands a few temple servants and a few Nambudiris of the lowest sub-castes of cooks and household priests. The temple-menial castes did not intermarry, and their men seem thus to have been confined to women of their own caste. Hypergamy stopped at this level and the Nayar servant castes were each endogamous.

The hypergamy of the Nayar office-bearing lineages fitted their gradual social mobility and lack of rank parity with each other. With time, because of the vicissitudes of war and conquest, a retainer lineage might be appointed as village headmen, and might later even aspire to chiefly rank. Several of the chiefly lineages of Kerala can be traced back to much humbler origins three to six centuries ago. Apart from the regular offices of rule over territorial units, commoner Nayar lineages might also attain special rank as ministers or military leaders. When a lineage received promotion in this way, its members in course of time declared themselves ritually higher than those of the caste from which they sprang and would no longer interdine or intermarry with that caste on equal terms. Hypergamy permitted these isolated office-bearing lineages to marry in unequivocally higher and unequivocally lower groups, but to side-step the awkward question of their precise rank in the hierarchy as a whole.

Hypergamous marriages, like all Nayar marriages, were tenuous and carried few obligations. Nevertheless, the dependence of aristocratic castes on each other for spouses and genitors must have strengthened relations between them. Hypergamy inextricably linked the secular and the religious hierarchies, whose interests in many contexts were opposed. Nambudiris waged a perpetual struggle to preserve their lands and judicial powers from encroachment by kings and chiefs. Their religious laws forbade bloodshed on the estates of their great temples. If a local ruler invaded such an estate or flouted its laws, the Brahmanical assembly exercised its religious authority to fine him in land, cash, or elephants and closed their gates till he repented. This does not mean that the kings were puppets of the Brahmans. When a king conquered a new district its Brahmans came over to his side. They gave him the right to protect their temples and to use their Nayar retainers in war, on receipt of a fine for any personal inconvenience they had suffered. They obviously needed the ruler's military protection of their religious and landed rights. The rulers in turn needed the Brahmans, for the whole social system was sanctioned by religious beliefs of which they were the chief exponents. Marriages at all levels between the religious and secular hierarchies pointed up this interdependence.

Among the Nayars hypergamy must also have cemented lord-vassal relationships. Older Nayars still take pride in the fact that their lineages have for centuries been fathered by chiefs, royals, and Brahmans. Traditionally, it was for the sake of this generalized filial bond that they were prepared to die in battle and, paradoxically, to deny themselves paternal rights in their own children.

Matrilineal Units of the Nayar Retainer Castes

THE CLAN

The clan was the largest matrilineal unit to which a Nayar commoner belonged. Its members believed themselves descended from a common ancestress, but her name was not normally remembered and the exact genealogical relationships between a clan's subordinate segments were often unknown. Occasionally, all of a clan's known members lived within a single Nayar neighborhood (*tara*). In this case the clan was co-terminous with the next lower order of matrilineal unit, which I call the lineage. More commonly, the clan had a nucleus of members within the neighborhood from which it originally sprang, together with outlying segments whose forebears had moved to other neighborhoods of the chiefdom. Clan affiliations among Nayar retainers do not seem to have extended beyond the chiefdom.

The clan was called a *taravād*, the word also used for the lineage and the matrilineal household unit. "Taravād" is derived from "tara," meaning "mound," [6] in this case the raised foundation on which a Nayar house was built. Its members derived a sense of unity from the belief that their matrilineal forebears sprang from the same ancestral house, and if the site of this house still existed they retained a sentimental attachment to it. The word "taravād" (befitting for a settled agricultural people) was in fact equivalent to the English "house" in its sense both of ancestry and of place. The clan was usually called by the name of its original ancestral house site.

The clan was exogamous and sex relations within it were forbidden. Those of its members who lived near and met often used kinship terms to address each other. If a death or birth occurred, clan members had to be informed by messenger. Upon receipt of the informa-

---

[6] Any kind of raised foundation of earth or laterite is called a tara. Tara (meaning "neighborhood") is derived from the large platform of earth round a sacred "milk" -exuding tree (*alstonia scholaris*) located near the Nayar neighborhood temple of Bhagavadi. The neighborhood assembly congregated on this mound.

tion they entered for fifteen days into a condition of ritual pollution. They might not eat with nor touch other Nayars, enter the temple or other houses, bathe in the public bathing pools of their caste, or eat meat or salt. Death pollution, and to a milder degree birth pollution, cut off the clan from participation in the social life of the caste. It isolated the members as a group set apart in a special and dangerous ritual condition, who had to observe taboos for their own and each others' safety. Its observance stressed the kinship connection of clansmen and marked their common concern on the occasion of an increase or decrease in their membership. Only those clansmen living within the neighborhood, however, were obliged to attend a funeral or visit a house of birth. Beyond these observances clansmen had only loosely defined rights of hospitality in each other's homes. As far as I am aware they never assembled as an organized group.

In time a clan might divide into two or more clans by the common consent of its members. The decision to separate depended both on geographical distance and on distance of relationship. If a segment of the core unit moved into an adjacent neighborhood its members might maintain clanship with the parent lineage for several hundred years thereafter. If they moved to a distant part of the district (say, fifteen miles away) their grandchildren might sever the connection. Severing clanship was called "cutting the pollution bond." Representatives of the branches met and decided not to inform each other of future deaths in their respective groups. Usually the outlying branch would soon afterward adopt the name of the oldest ancestral house site in its own vicinity as its clan name. Exogamy was theoretically preserved as long as matrilineal ties were remembered—usually, about three generations after the division.

Beyond the neighborhood, clan ties had no legal or economic concomitants and were relatively unimportant, their claims being subordinated to those of lineage, village, neighborhood, district, and kingdom.

THE LINEAGE

A lineage comprised those members of a clan living in one Nayar neighborhood, and it operated within the legal and social framework of this unit. As we have noted, the retainer Nayars of a neighborhood were of the same caste. They interdined and intermarried freely and the neighborhood was their unit of caste administration. A neighborhood might comprise the retainer Nayars of one village or of two or three adjacent villages, or occasionally Nayars of only part of a large village (e.g., a royal village) in which more than one caste of

Nayar retainers resided. A neighborhood normally contained some six to ten lineages and probably had a population of about three hundred Nayars.

The lineage was called a *taravād*. If it occupied the ancestral village of the clan its members used the ancestral house name as both clan and lineage names. If it lived elsewhere its members added a distinctive name, derived from their new locale, to the clan name. Each segment of a lineage occupying one house in turn had its own house name, and each Nayar had a personal name followed by the caste title. A typical Nayar name might therefore be "Thengiparambil Padikkil Kirakkutt-Velappil Govindan Nayar"—"Clan of the coconut garden, lineage of the gatehouse, household of the eastern garden, Govindan (personal name) Nayar." Usually one branch of a lineage continued to occupy and to rebuild the oldest ancestral home of the clan. The clan, lineage, and house names of these members would then be collapsed into one.

A lineage normally comprised some four to eight households, each a matrilineal segment of three to six generations' depth, including the youngest children and the common ancestress. Sometimes the households of a lineage might occupy adjacent gardens on a continuous stretch of dry land in the high-caste residential area of one village. Alternatively the houses of a lineage might become scattered throughout the high-caste residential areas of the several villages of the neighborhood. For it was possible for Nayar tenants, with the consent of the various overlords concerned, to buy or exchange the tenures of gardens. Further, a branch of a lineage which was expanding might be allotted the tenure of a newly developed garden at some distance from its former abode. Normally, however, the gardens in which their houses were built remained in the possession of one or other branch of a lineage over many generations.

Some writers would not apply the word lineage to the group which I am discussing. It was not always a lineage in the sense of a matrilineal group tracing descent from a common ancestress through a determinate number of generations (cf. *Notes and Queries in Anthropology*, 1952: 88–89). This definition applied to lineages which had occupied a neighborhood only for six or seven generations. It might also apply to an older lineage some of whose branches had died out, or to an older lineage whose membership had not happened to expand greatly over several generations. Often, however, there would be very old lineages whose most distantly related segments no longer remembered their exact genealogical relationship and whose members were no longer sure of the name of their founding ancestress. The reason for this was that over time, a lineage was formed from the successive divisions of matrilineal households springing from an original matrilineal household. As will be seen later, a matrilineal group occupying one house and jointly owning property divided into its component major segments to form two or more new households at a definite point in its development. Each woman was potentially the ancestress of a distinct segment. However, her segment would in fact become distinct only if she had two or more daughters who themselves lived to bear daughters. If she had only one daughter this woman replaced her in the lineage structure as the ancestress of her segment, and after three or four generations the existence of one or other of these women would be forgotten.

However, although exact genealogical relationships tended to be forgotten after some five to seven generations, the order of segmentation within a lineage was remembered because it was relevant to the reversion of property. If a household died out, its property was divided between those segments of the same order as itself which had sprung from the next larger segment. It is for this reason that I call the clan members of one neighborhood a lineage, for their order of segmentation *was* known and was relevant in this limited context. As far as I am aware, those branches of a clan which left their ancestral neighborhood lost their right to claim property in the village of their origin.

In other ways the order of segmentation was unimportant for the structuring of intra-lineage relationships. It is true that minimal segments of a minor segment which had jointly held property a generation previously, maintained a closer sense of kinship than did more distantly related segments. But segments intermediate between the household and the lineage had no special property, activities, or ceremonies, and their members never met to the exclusion of other lineage kin. Neither were whole intermediate segments mobilized in quarrels between individuals of a lineage. Quarrels were restricted to the households of the disputants and were normally settled through appeal to a popular, unrelated arbitrator. If they became serious they were forcibly settled by the intervention of the neighborhood assembly and of the village headman.

As a part of the clan, the lineage was exogamous, sex relations were prohibited within it, and ritual pollution was observed by its members at a birth or death. Outside the lineage and within the clan it is doubtful whether these rules could be enforced by law. Within the lineage they were legally mandatory. The local caste assembly, with the backing of royal or chiefly authority, could take action against offenders. Intra-lineage incest was indeed a crime punishable by death. As a matter of courtesy, lineage members extended appropriate kinship terms to one another.

Unless it was declining in numbers and had shrunk to the proportions of a single household, the lineage was not an economic unit. Its members did not jointly own an estate and did not coöperate in the production or distribution of goods. These functions accrued to the small segment of a lineage occupying a single homestead, which I call a property group. Lineage kin *were* the residual heirs of a property group which died out. However, such reversion of property was rare. A property group which had no childbearing women usually adopted one or more girls from some other branch of the lineage in order to perpetuate itself.

A "commoner" lineage had no headman. Its oldest man commanded special respect but he had no legal authority over the lineage as a whole. The office of headman of the lineage existed only in village headmen's, chiefly, and royal lineages. Here the political office was theoretically vested in the eldest man of the lineage, irrespective of branch. These lineages had a somewhat different structure, discussed below.

The members of a lineage engaged in coöperative activities at two major life crises: the pre-puberty marriage rite of girls, and the funeral of a member, followed by offerings to the departed spirit on the fifteenth and sixteenth days after the death.

Both of these occasions involved the caste assembly of the neighborhood and the institution of linked lineages or *enangar*. The caste assembly comprised the eldest men (*kāranavar*) of all the property groups. It met periodically on a mound (tara) near the Bhagavadi temple of the neighborhood to manage the temple's affairs. It also judged offenses against the religious laws of the caste.

Each lineage was linked by hereditary ties of ceremonial coöperation to two or three other lineages of the neighborhood. These linkages were reciprocal but not exclusive. For example, lineage A might have as enangar B, C, and D, whereas B might have A, E, and F, and so on. A chain of such relationships therefore linked all lineages of the neighborhood.

The enangar were partners who offered help in a ceremonial manner at all major life crises. They stood as formal links between the lineage and the total neighborhood group, which was called the *enangu*. In small neighborhoods, indeed, all the lineages were sometimes enangar to one another, although this seems to have been rare. At least one man and one woman of each of its enangar lineage had to visit a household for the life-crisis rites of its members, at which they gave ceremonial assistance and partook of a feast. These rites included the naming ceremony of a baby, the first rice feeding in the sixth month, the pre-puberty marriage rite of girls, the first menstruation ceremony of a girl, the first pregnancy ceremony of a woman, the offerings to a departed spirit which closed the period of death pollution, and the subsequent offerings each year to the spirits of recently dead members of a property group on the anniversaries of their deaths. Enangar also gave neighborly help on the day of a cremation and, during the fifteen days of death pollution, provided cooked food for the household of the bereaved.

Although whole lineages were linked as enangar to each other, a linked lineage acted as a collectivity only at the pre-puberty marriage rite, at cremations, and on the sixteenth day after a death. For the other life crises, each household of a lineage would invite as enangar partners only one household in each of their linked lineages with whom they had special customary ties. Similarly, the members of a household were not obliged to invite other branches of their own lineage to the minor life crises, although they might do so if they wished.

The enangar played their most important role at the pre-puberty marriage rite. Every ten to twelve years each lineage held a grand ceremony in its oldest ancestral house, at which time all immature girls of the lineage of one generation were ritually married by men of enangar groups. This ceremony, called *tālikettukalyānam* ("*tāli*-tying ceremony") had to be performed for each girl before puberty on pain of her excommunication from caste (Gough, 1955). Before it took place, elders of the assembly selected suitable youths of the enangar lineages as ritual bridegrooms for the girls. At the ceremony each bridegroom, in the company of representatives of every household in the neighborhood, tied a gold ornament (tāli) round the neck of his bride. Each couple was then secluded in a room of the ancestral house for three days and nights, during which, if the girl was old enough, sexual relations might take place. On the fourth day the bridegrooms departed. They had no further obligations to their brides and did not need to visit them again unless they wished. After the tāli rite, however, a girl was regarded as having attained the status of a mature woman, ready to bear children to perpetuate her lineage.

Shortly before or after puberty she might, following the ceremony, enter without religious rites into sexual liaisons with one or more men of her own or an appropriate higher caste. Similarly, a Nayar man (whether or not he had ever performed the tāli rite) might enter into relationships with any number of women of his own or an appropriate lower Nayar caste.

These marriage customs are further discussed below. Here it is relevant to point only to the role of the *enangan* bridegroom. Since the enangar stood to the lineage as formal representatives of the local caste group, it seems appropriate to interpret the tāli rite as a ceremony of group marriage, in which the caste group as a whole married the immature girls of the lineage as a whole.

The tāli rite was indeed both a religious and a legal transaction between the lineage and the enangu or neighborhood group. If a girl was discovered to have attained puberty before it had been performed, the assembly forced her property group to expel her and to perform her funeral rites, for she was thought to be ritually dangerous to her caste as a whole. For a woman, the tāli which she wore round her neck until death was therefore a sign that she had been ceremonially and legally accepted as a mature woman of her lineage and caste, "cleared" to bear children to perpetuate both groups.

The lineage similarly operated as a unit, and the enangar fulfilled similar roles as formal links with the caste on the occasion of a funeral. All adult males of the lineage who were junior to the deceased attended his cremation, which took place in the southwest corner of the garden of his house. Representative members of all enangar households also came to help with practical tasks and to provide ritual objects for the chief mourner's ceremonies, although they were forbidden to touch or to receive food from the mourners throughout their period of pollution. In the fifteen days after the death only the deceased's household, assisted by their special enangar households, took part in the collection of the bones and ashes and made offerings to the departed spirit. Other lineage members observed death pollution in their homes and were attended by enangar there. On the fifteenth day the lineage reassembled at the house of the dead. After many ceremonies its members were purified by the funeral priest from the pollution of death. On the sixteenth day final offerings were made to the spirit. The deceased's household then held a large feast, which was shared by lineage members and representatives from all houses of the linked lineages. This reception of food by the enangar from the hands of the deceased's matrilineal kinsmen marked a

formal recognition that the bereaved lineage, freed from its death
pollution, had been received back into the normal social life of the
caste.

Lineage members were also united in worship of their lineage
goddess or *dharma devi* ("goddess of moral law"). This goddess,
named differently in different lineages, was a species of the common
Nayar goddess Bhagavadi. Her idol was housed in a small shrine near
the oldest ancestral house or sometimes in the courtyard of the village
temple. She was believed capable of inflicting or withholding sickness and all types of misfortune. To ward them off, members
propitiated her with offerings of cooked food every year. The astrol-
oger might also advise an emergency propitiation. She had the power
to bless women of the lineage with fertility. On this account she was
worshipped before a tāli rite and also at the first menstruation ceremonies of a girl. In a somewhat vague sense, moreover, lineage members appear to have felt themselves collectively responsible to the
goddess for sins or ritual lapses on the part of one of them. It was believed that if any member failed to observe the religious laws of
caste, to perform household duties correctly, or to revere the goddess,
she might bring sickness or misfortune upon the lineage as a whole.

In spite of this sense of collective moral responsibility, the evidence
is unclear as to whether the lineage as a whole was held legally
responsible for any of its member's acts. It is true that the enangar
were the legal representatives of the local caste unit in its relations
with the lineage. This inter-lineage relationship was hereditary and
obligatory. It could not be entered into or permanently broken without the consent of the assembly and the chief of the district. If,
moreover, an individual infringed a religious law of the caste, it was
the duty of his lineage's enangar to summon a caste assembly to judge
and punish the offense. Crimes, which were also sins, against caste
law included incest within the lineage; dining or sex relations with
prohibited lower-caste persons; failure to perform the marriage rite
of a girl before she reached puberty; failure to observe pollution at
the birth or death of a lineage member or (on the part of an individual woman) during menstruation; failure to pay dues in kind
to the Nayar temple of the neighborhood. On being apprized of an
offense, the assembly's first recourse was temporarily to ostracize the
offender's household from the caste community. Ostracism meant
that the offenders might not enter the temple, bathe in public bathing
pools, enter the houses of other Nayars, employ the village servant

castes, or receive customary help from their enangar at life-crisis ceremonies. If the ostracism was not effected it was believed that the whole neighborhood would fall into disfavor with the caste goddess and might become prey to epidemic or crop failure.

The point on which I am uncertain is whether the lineage as a whole was ostracized, or whether other branches of the lineage normally retained their caste status by severing their own connections with the offender's property group. The latter actually occurred in a case in Cochin in 1924. A Sudra Nayar woman had sex relations with a man of the caste of Nayar funeral priests. Shortly after the assembly met, the other houses of her lineage repudiated all connection with the offender's household, which alone remained ostracized for a year. The woman and her lover then fled to Malaya. The household paid its fine and was reaccepted to caste. I do not know whether it was possible under native rule for a lineage to repudiate its responsibilities in this way.

Minor offenses, such as dining with low-caste people, were settled by the offender's property group paying a fine to the village temple. The offender and his household were purified from their pollution by certain ritual acts. They then gave a feast to their enanger at which they were publicly reaccepted to caste. Traditionally, graver offenses (such as the one above) met harsher penalties. The caste's judgment on such an offense traditionally had to be ratified by the district chief or by a royal officer. The offender was then either executed by his immediate matrilineal kin or surrendered to the king for sale into slavery. His household members performed his funeral rites and only then were they taken back into caste.

Whether or not the lineage as a whole was held collectively responsible for offenses against the religious law of the caste, it was not held responsible for civil wrongs judged by the village headman or for crimes judged by the chief or by officers of the royal court. The property group, headed by its kāranavan, and not the whole lineage, was responsible in cases of theft, debt, or other offenses concerning property which were judged by the village headman. With regard to a major crime, a Nayar who murdered another was tried in the court of the king or of a higher chief. If the murdered man was of the same or a higher caste than the murderer, the murderer was executed by a small group of Nayars selected by the judge. If the murdered man was of lower caste, the murderer's property group had to pay a fine to the district chief. Again, if a Nayar of any rank committed treason against the king, the king might order the execution of all members of his property group. Their land escheated to the royal lineage, but apparently no reprisals were made upon the lineage as a whole.

In spite of these laws of the kingdom a tradition did persist that the lineage of an offended Nayar had the moral obligation to avenge him (Logan, 1951, I: 169). Folk songs tell of blood feuds (*kudi-paga*) between lineages which apparently neither king nor chief could always quell, although the blood-feud tradition is not nearly so important as in North Malabar, where political centralization had advanced less far. In the central kingdoms feuds between commoner lineages and between village headmen's lineages could be most easily cut short by the higher authorities. Feuds between district chiefs' lineages were harder to quell and sometimes turned into small wars between districts, in which each chief amassed his feudal following behind him (K. M. Panikkar, 1929: 9). However, even in the twentieth century under the British legal system, protracted estrangements have sometimes existed between two retainer lineages of the same neighborhood, which would periodically break out in armed assaults between representative individuals or even, occasionally, in murder. In recent years inter-lineage conflicts concerning assault and libel have also often been waged in the urban law courts.

Three institutions existed through which kings and chiefs seem to have tried to handle and curtail inter-lineage aggression. During wartime the problem was presumably less acute because the soldiers were away from their villages fighting large battles under their feudal lords. But wars took place only in the dry season; in the monsoons extensive military operations were impossible. Instead, each wet season saw a period of intensive military training in village gymnasia. Intermittently in this season, champions of lineages, of villages, and of chiefdoms went to joust at chiefly and royal palaces for the entertainment of their lords. Thus, first, these occasions may have helped to canalize intersegmentary conflict in a manner conducive to the royal peace.

Second, if a Nayar assaulted another or insulted his lineage, the offended man might challenge him to a duel. On payment of a fee to the chief, each disputant brought one or several champions from his lineage to fight on his behalf. Each pair fought until one or both was wounded or killed. A duel might be postponed as long as twelve years until the two lineages had trained champions to their satisfaction (Logan, 1951, I: 170). Often it was not fought by the original disputants. Duels seem to have been fought mainly to avenge the honor of matrilineal kinswomen against accusations of incest with a lineage kinsman or of adultery with a low-caste man. Interestingly, these two forms of slander still occasion the bitterest inter-lineage disputes in modern villages.

Third, if a Nayar murdered another of the same rank, his lineage kin had the customary right to carry the corpse into the courtyard of the murderer's property group and burn corpse and house together. The royal and chiefly powers seem to have sanctioned this act as a form of private vengeance while reserving for themselves the right of trial and execution of the murderer.

In the law of the kingdom, therefore, the lineage was not recognized as a unit having legal responsibility for its members' acts. The state vested it with no property and no internal structure of authority. Its members were not required to accept responsibility for one another's crimes and civil offenses nor were they accorded the right of unrestricted vengeance. They were merely *permitted* (probably as a concession to more ancient custom) to support one another in certain restricted situations, provided they acknowledged the superior authority of the kingdom's judicial agents.

I have written of lineages as groups of true matrilineal kin, and so they often were. However, some procedure seems to have been found necessary to adjust the lineage system to the territorial organization. We saw that segments might hive off to other neighborhoods; this must have become more common as sales of landlord and tenant rights increased during the period of European trade. My informants in one Cochin village told me that traditionally, when a lineage segment moved to a new village, its members were adopted as retainers and tenants by the local landlord. They were accepted into the assembly of their new neighborhood and permitted to perform their first tāli rite jointly with some established lineage. Presumably they also took over the enangar of this lineage. In any case my informants thought it would be necessary to obtain the sanction of the chief or, in areas of temple management, of a Brahman legal authority called a Vaidigan, to obtain new enangar ties within a neighborhood. The joint performance of the tāli rite set up a bond of fictitious matrilineal kinship between the old lineage and the incoming segment so that their members had thenceforth to observe exogamy.

This procedure served to provide newcomers with ceremonial and marriage partners and to induct them into the microcosmic political life of the neighborhood. The new members, however, were apparently never completely accepted as "true" matrilineal kin. Thus death and birth pollutions were not extended to them by their host lineage. Instead, as we have seen, they continued to observe these rites for several generations along with their clansfolk elsewhere.

The information on this procedure is incomplete because it does not take place in modern times. It is not known whether a lineage segment ever became incorporated into a new retainer caste as well as a new neighborhood, although this seems unlikely. It is not known whether an indigenous lineage which shrank to the size of one small property group ever allied itself in putative matrilineal kinship with another established lineage. It is also uncertain whether major segments of a very large lineage might over time break the pollution bond and gradually cease to observe exogamy. Some evidence from a Cochin village suggests that this may have happened. Shortly before my stay a man and woman of two lineages which had the same enangar and had never been known to marry, entered into a traditional type of informal marriage relationship. Elders of the village then began to wonder whether the lineages had not once formed one lineage, either by true matrilineal kinship or by joint performance of the tāli rite. As they were unable to foist their doubts on to the junior generation the marriage persisted. Thus, what may once have been an ancient tie of lineage and clan exogamy was quietly broken. I do not know whether fission within a lineage was traditionally possible or whether it occurs only in modern times, when the neighborhood assembly and the lineage itself are both disintegrating.

THE PROPERTY GROUP

Structure The property group among Nayar retainers was a segment of the lineage having a time depth of some three to six generations, including the youngest members and the common ancestress. It therefore typically comprised a group of brothers and sisters (real or classificatory), together with the children and daughters' children of the sisters. This group was the joint-property-owning unit. Its members were from birth equal co-parceners in the buildings, land, movables, serfs, and all other property which had come to them from their matrilineal forebears, or had been conferred on them by their feudal lord, or had been acquired by the efforts of individual members. The group's oldest male member (kāranavan) was its legal guardian and represented it in the caste assembly.

When spoken of in its own right the property group, like the lineage, was called a taravād. When spoken of as a segment of the lineage it was called a *tāvari* (literally, "mother's line"). Tāvari could also be used of any intermediate segment of the lineage or of a minimal segment of one mother and her children within the property group. Each property group usually had a separate garden name in addition to its lineage name.

Residence   Among retainer Nayars of this area a property group usually owned only one homestead and was simultaneously a dwelling group. Occasionally among retainers, however, and more commonly among chiefs and village headmen, a property group which increased in size might build two or more homesteads on its lands. If the houses were adjacent they were usually occupied indiscriminately by members and cooking was done only in one. If the homesteads were some distance apart each might be occupied by a minimal segment of the group. The kāranavan would manage the resources of the whole group but would allocate provisions separately to each household. Separate cooking would be carried on.

Spouses lived separately in their natal units, with the husband visiting the wife. We shall call this type of residence *duolocal.*

A traditional homestead of retainer or village headman's rank centered about a large main building with two stories, separate staircases for men and women, and, in the middle of the building, a small courtyard open to the sky. The house faced east, and was fronted by a spacious veranda, used normally by men of the group and their male visitors. Within, a passage led to the central courtyard, round which rooms opened off on three sides. They included an ancestor shrine; several storerooms containing clothing in boxes, metal vessels, jewelry, weapons, and paddy (unhusked rice) in large wooden chests; one or more rooms for everyday use, each with sleeping mats, a bench, wooden stools and chests, and a rope to hang clothes; and a small room occupied by women during their delivery and menstrual seclusions. A roofed cloister with pillars ran between the open courtyard and the rooms. Beyond the courtyard to the west was a long, narrow dining hall with a large kitchen behind it. Behind this lay the back veranda, normally used only by women and children. Upstairs might be four or five bedrooms in which women received their husbands. Men born into the group seldom entered these upstairs rooms and were forbidden to use the women's staircase.

Outside the house in the outer courtyard a separate building served as a granary for paddy. The upstairs of this building was often set aside for the kāranavan's use. Here he slept, was served with food by women of the house, entertained co-villagers, and kept records of the group's economic transactions. If the group was large a second separate building was often reserved to junior men for reading, entertaining friends, or sleeping when they were not visiting their wives. A cowshed a few yards from the residential buildings completed the arrangements in a normal retainer homestead. In village headmen's and chiefly households whose women often had Brahman husbands a separate building with its own kitchen was set aside to entertain the men when they visited their wives.

The buildings and outer courtyard were surrounded by a shady garden of coconut, jack, cashew, and mango trees. Chiefs and village headmen had a private bathing pool with stone steps round it in their own gardens. Retainers more often bathed in the large public bathing pools attached to the temples and reserved for "clean" castes of the village. Men and women bathed and swam daily on opposite sides of the pool.

In the southwest corner of the garden an open space was set aside as the property group's cremation ground, entered only at funerals. In another corner was a dense shrubbery devoted to the snake gods of the group. Offerings were made there to small stone images of cobras, and if real cobras appeared they were regarded as manifestations of these deities.

A high bamboo fence surrounded the whole establishment. It was entered through a wooden gatehouse within which armed men might sit on guard in time of war.

Economic Activities The property group obtained almost all of its subsistence from garden and paddy lands held on tenure from the village landlord and cultivated by Tiyyar sub-tenants or by Pulaya serfs. The property group surrendered part of its produce in kind as dues to the landlord. It retained part for maintenance, stored part for repayment to its serfs as daily subsistence, and gave portions twice annually to the village servant households. Tiyyar tenants retained enough for their own needs, but gave the bulk of their produce to their Nayar masters. Increasingly during the period of European trade the property group also sold spices and coconuts to Muslim middlemen in exchange for cash or cloth. The cash was used to buy brass and silver vessels, gold ornaments and jewelry, and other luxury goods from the towns. The property group gave some cloth to its serfs and tenants at festivals once a year.

The kāranavan managed all these transactions and controlled the group's estate. He might allocate specific tasks of management to juniors, but no payment was made on behalf of the group, no crops were sold, and no goods were consumed without his consent. Junior men serving in the king's wars received small daily cash sums on an individual basis, but this money seems only to have sufficed for their food and other necessities while on the march or on service in towns. When they were at home in their villages their kāranavan assumed responsibility for each man's customary gifts to his wives in other households.

Within his own household the kāranavan personally allocated their subsistence to its members. Every few weeks he transferred quantities of unhusked rice, vegetables, and other stores from the granary to storerooms inside the house. They were then usually taken over by the eldest woman, who kept keys to the storerooms and chests and allocated daily supplies to the kitchen. In property groups with more than one homestead the kāranavan delivered quantities of paddy, salt, and coconut oil twice annually to each house according to the number of its members. Each house sent a person daily to the ancestral house to bring fresh vegetables, milk, buttermilk, and other perishable foods. In all taravāds the kāranavan controlled purchases from the town. Twice a year—at New Year and at the harvest festival—he distributed clothing to both male and female members.

Virtuous kāranavans were those who managed the daily affairs of the taravād with thrift, justice, and meticulous care, but who, through judicious planning, were able to lavish grand feasts upon caste members, tenants, village servants, and serfs at the major life-crisis rites. An aged kāranavan would enumerate with satisfaction the various feasts at funerals, tāli rites, and first-menstruation ceremonies which he had satisfactorily conducted. Each of the servant castes contributed appropriate goods or services in advance of these feasts, and each Nayar house reciprocated the hospitality when its own life-crisis rites came round. Besides reaffirming in a ceremonial manner the different types of ties between Nayars and between Nayars and the lower castes, the life-crisis ceremonies seem to have stimulated production and provided suitable foci for acts of economic redistribution and reciprocity.

The amounts of time spent by junior men of the taravād on different activities are no longer clearly known. We know however that at the age of seven a boy was inducted into military training in the village gymnasium; this training persists in a few villages, and includes fencing, wrestling, rigorous exercise, and very strenuous massage. Traditionally, Nayars also learned archery from a special caste of village servants (Vil Kurups). For a part of their time they attended a village school run by yet another caste of schoolteachers (Eruttacchans); almost all adult Nayar men and most women were literate

in Malayalam and some became famous poets during the sixteenth
and later centuries. A Nayar received his arms from his feudal lord
—a village headman, a district chief, or a prince—at the age of sixteen. From this time until, perhaps, late middle age, he seems to have
spent periods of each year away from his village attending military
exercises in the larger towns or fighting in the continual wars against
the North Malabar chiefdoms, Walluvanad, or Palghat, or between
Cochin and Calicut themselves. Evidently Nayars also spent long periods in their villages, at least in the monsoon seasons, for they policed
the villages, arranged village festivals, were bailiffs on the landlord's
domain, and paid regular visits to local wives. Nayar youths were also
obliged to attend with their seniors and fulfill ceremonial obligations
at the life-crisis rites of the landlord family. The rites were of course
conducted in a grand manner and served as a focus for the collection and redistribution of perishable goods throughout the village.

Nayar youths also did some cultivation of vegetables and spices in
the gardens of their taravāds. Every youth received a rigorous training in cultivation methods, land management, the keeping of accounts,
and the construction of houses, either directly from his kāranavan or,
more usually, from the brothers of his own mother. However, there
was no clear-cut allocation of differential authority and economic roles
among the junior men of a taravād in this area. This was evidently
not necessary because the bulk of the work was done by tenants and
serfs, whose management could be most easily controlled by a single
experienced man. It was enough that a young Nayar should learn *how*
to manage and to cultivate so that he might one day replace his kāranavan. Their military duties were obviously the important ones for junior
Nayars. It is unfortunate that we know next to nothing about how they
were organized in the army, or even if they fought in lineage groups
under the leadership of their mothers' brothers. All we know is that they
were for the most part recruited in lineages, with the members of one
lineage serving the same feudal lord.

The division of labor between the sexes was less rigid than in most
Hindu castes, but was well demarcated in daily life. Girls played with
boys, attended the village school, and even received training in the
gymnasium, until they underwent the tāli rite, usually at about the age
of eleven. After this they were segregated from the men of their lineage and concentrated their time on domestic tasks. For most purposes the group of matrilineally related women formed a single work
unit under the informal authority of the oldest (or oldest competent)
woman. She gave out produce for cooking and allotted to each woman

in her care particular daily tasks in connection with cooking, house-
work, the pounding of paddy, and the tending of small children. The
minimal unit of one woman and her own children, although having a
special solidarity emotionally, was given very little recognition in the
division of work. Women cooked communally in the kitchen, bathed
and washed their own and any children's clothes in company in the
bathing pool, and at the harvests moved in household groups to the
fields to help the serf women of their families in cutting paddy. Nayar
women's agricultural work, however, was subsidiary and they took no
part in the more arduous tasks of transplanting and weeding.

The women of a Nayar retainer lineage also owed services to women
of the landlord household to which their lineage was attached. Although their lower-caste rank prevented them from touching their mistress or entering her kitchen, they swept the house, accompanied its
womenfolk to their bathing pool, and did various household chores.
The landlord household normally chose three or four favorites from
among the lineages attached to them to perform these services, but
women of any retainer household might be summoned during the
special preparations for a feast.

Authority and Responsibility Property groups, rather than lineages,
were the main legal units within the local caste group. Their kāranā-
vans formed the neighborhood assembly. Within the assembly, a
kāranavan acted on behalf of his property group in managing the
Nayar temple, settling small civil disputes in his own and lower castes,
and adjudicating in cases of offense against Nayar religious law.

A kāranavan also represented his property group in its relations with
its feudal lord and with higher authorities of the kingdom. We have
seen that the property group and not the lineage held land on tenure
from its landlord, and that although a lineage was attached to a landlord by hereditary right, the landlord conducted all economic transactions separately with the head of each property group within it.
Similarly, each kāranavan was required to represent his own property
group in ceremonial attendance on his village landlord, the chief of
his district, or (if he were a direct vassal of the royal lineage) his
king, at religious festivals associated with the temples of these digni-
taries.

On behalf of his property group, a kāranavan was held legally responsible for his juniors in most types of legal offense. He paid their
fines from taravād funds if they were found guilty of petty theft or
debt before the village headman or the chief. If a member of the taravād was convicted in the royal court of treason, his kāranavan and

his whole property group might be put to death. Conversely, the property group as a whole was rewarded for extraordinary military valor on the part of one of its members. In a period of conquest of a new district, the king sometimes removed from office recalcitrant village headmen or even chiefs of the enemy side and replaced them with property groups from among his own following. Again, when a soldier died fighting with exceptional bravery, his chief sometimes rewarded his property group with a plot of land held on a special military tenure, under unusually favorable terms.

As we have seen, the property group had the prime responsibility for an individual convicted by the neighborhood assembly of offense against the religious laws of caste.

The kāranavan's day-to-day authority over his juniors was conferred upon him by his feudal lord, backed by the judicial authority of the king. He had the right to command and discipline all junior members. In cases of extreme disobedience he might inflict corporal punishment on the women or children, or cause a junior man of the taravād to do this. He seems to have had the right temporarily to expel from the household and to deny maintenance to junior men who insulted or disobeyed him. As manager of the estate he also had disciplinary rights over the taravād's tenants. In serious matters the tenants had recourse to the village headman, perhaps to the chief, but their own master settled minor disputes among them and fined them for small offenses. In law a kāranavan appears to have had complete rights of life and death over his property group's serfs. A very few cases are recorded of his exercising it to the full. More common are the stories of extraordinary loyalty between serf and master, especially of serfs who died fighting to defend their lords' homes. Their spirits were rewarded with a place in the taravād's ancestral shrine.

It is clear that whatever his *de jure* authority, the kāranavan's *de facto* authority was greater over women and children than over junior men, who were often absent on military service. It seems probable that at these times soldiers came under the direct legal control of officers of the kingdom and that in at least some contexts their property groups were not held responsible for them. We know for example that if a Nayar soldier murdered another he was tried in the court of the king or of a feudatory prince and, if convicted, was executed promptly by four or five of his peers, presumably without his property group being consulted or punished. Thieves caught within the boundaries of coastal towns seem to have been similarly dealt with (Barbosa, 1518, quoted in Ayyar, 1938: 284–286). It may be that their property groups were held legally responsible for Nayar men only when they committed high treason or when they became engaged in disputes and offenses within the neighborhood of their birth.

It seems probable that the kāranavan's powers over his juniors and over their property were limited by the codification of law which came about during British rule (Aiyar, 1922: 33–132). It is not clear whether he could traditionally alienate land without the consent of other adults of the taravād; during British rule he could not. British law also permitted appeal to the court by junior members for the removal of a kāranavan who could be shown guilty of gross mismanagement. He could then be set aside in favor of his immediate junior. An inefficient kāranavan could moreover be forced by the court to maintain accounts of his income and expenditure. Since 1933 in Malabar District and 1938 in Cochin, all kāranavans have been legally obliged to do this and to make available their accounts for inspection by junior members once a year, as provided in the Madras Marumakkattayam (Matriliny) Act, 1933, and the Cochin Nayar Act, 1938. However, few juniors avail themselves of this right, which is evidently repugnant to the traditional ideals of obedience and trust toward elders of the taravād.

Even traditionally, however, both junior men and women were often consulted in the management of the group's affairs. If a dispute arose between minimal segments of the taravād it was common for appeal to be made to an arbitrator of the caste from outside the lineage. The settlement agreed upon would be embodied in a document called a kārār, which legally bound all adult members. In large taravāds the allocation of separate houses and sometimes even of separate land to each segment was usually embodied in a kārār. All land continued to be managed by the kāranavan, but he paid a sum of paddy each year to the senior woman of each household from the land allotted to her segment.

Kārārs were, however, common only in village headmen's, chiefly, and royal property groups. Too little property was usually involved in the case of retainer Nayars, among whom effective daily management was divided between the kāranavan and the oldest woman. As we have seen, the former carried out all formal transactions outside the group, controlled the estate in toto, and disciplined men and boys. The latter organized feminine tasks and held more informal authority over women and small children. When the kāranavan was the son or younger brother of the eldest woman, management usually ran particularly smoothly. The oldest woman might indeed be de facto head of the group, maintaining its accounts in her own hands and counseling the kāranavan on his transactions with outsiders. When the oldest woman was the kāranavan's own or classificatory younger sister or sister's daughter her role was unequivocally subordinate and a formal division of duties was common.

Rites of the Property Group The property group jointly invited enangar households to the ceremonies of name giving, first rice feeding, first menstruátion, and death. The lineage as a whole held the tāli rite in its oldest house. However, expenses were divided between the property groups and food was cooked separately in their homes. Similarly, at a death the whole lineage observed pollution and attended the cremation, the gathering of bones on the seventh day, and the purification and feasting on the fifteenth and sixteenth days. But men and women of the deceased's own property group offered cooked rice to the spirit in their courtyard each day during the pollution period. The rites of chief mourner were performed by the junior man considered most closely related to the deceased—her eldest son in the case of a woman, and the man immediately junior to him in the property group in the case of a man.

The propitiation of cobra gods and of dead matrilineal forebears also united the group's members. The cobra deities (*nāgas*) could inflict or avert sickness in general but were especially believed responsible for the fertility or barrenness [7] of taravād women. If a woman failed to conceive, a performance was held at which men and women of a wandering caste called Pulluvar played instruments and sang songs to entice the cobras to appear. A group of women of the taravād, who had purified themselves by sex continence and fasting for several days, then became possessed by the snake gods. They performed a wild dance, bowing and swaying in a circle and sweeping their hair along the ground. In this condition they might speak with the voices of the gods and announce whatever propitiations were necessary to appease them. Sometimes one or more of the women fell into a trance.

It seems reasonable to suppose that the snake gods were worshipped as phallic symbols. They were definitely not regarded as the spirits of dead matrilineal forebears, yet were capable of withholding fertility or of causing women to conceive. Perhaps, therefore, they symbolized the procreative powers of past genitors of the property group, who

---

[7] Snake gods inflicted barrenness; the lineage goddess inflicted miscarriages and sickness in childbirth.

had been so essential to its perpetuation, yet so firmly excluded from its everyday affairs.

Within each Nayar house one room was devoted to the spirits of dead kāranavans. It contained a number of small wooden stools on which spirits were believed to come and sit. The ancestor shrine of the lineage's oldest house contained many stools placed there in turn for the kāranavans of past generations, reaching back to the foundation of the lineage. A newer house would contain only the stools of kāranavans of that house. Offerings of cooked food were made before each stool by the living kāranavan, in the presence of all members, twice a year. The kāranavans' spirits were vindictive rather than protective. They were prone to punish the taravād with sickness or financial loss if any of its members failed in details of ritual performance, in care of the property, or in piety toward matrilineal kin. I have suggested elsewhere (Gough, 1958) that the cult of dead matrilineal forebears served as a focus for aggressive impulses which had their origin in relationships with living matrilineal elders. At the same time it united the living in fear and reverence of the dead and reaffirmed the moral laws of the taravād. It also acted as a sanction against a kāranavan's own exploitation of his juniors, since the maintenance of right relations with junior kinsmen formed part of his pious duty to his forebears.

The Splitting of Property Groups Genealogies and property documents reveal that during the nineteenth century the property groups of retainer Nayars divided at a particular point in their development. This occurred when the property group comprised two or more discrete segments descended from sisters, each segment containing an adult male capable of becoming kāranavan of his branch. For a segment to be "discrete," its founding ancestress, whether herself living or dead, must not have a mother, brothers, or mother's brothers alive. Separation before this point was not possibly because the division of property was stirpital. Individual men, the managers of property, could not separate themselves from their own mothers or sisters. A man could therefore never be a member of a different property group from that of his own mother's mother's brother, mother's brother, or brother. Division could take place only between groups headed by men from different minimal segments (parallel cousins, a man and his classificatory mother's brother, etc.), who were no longer held together by submission to a common mother's brother, grandmother, or great-uncle.

It seems probable that the property groups of retainer Nayars divided somewhat earlier in their development during the nineteenth century than during the period of native rule. The reason for this is that during British rule Nayar men, having no other compulsory work, considered themselves old enough to become kāranavans by the age of thirty to forty, provided their appropriate elders were dead. In the traditional period, presumably, a man would be in arms until at least the age of fifty and would be unlikely to press for kāranavanship before that age.

Further differences in the patterns of division of property groups must have arisen from the marked increase in population during British rule. This is not documented until after the 1870's but from genealogies it appears to have begun between four and five generations ago. The increase would mean that more women, and a higher proportion of women, would have had enough living children to become the founders of discrete lineage segments during their lives or shortly after their deaths. Thus property groups in the nineteenth century would divide not only at an earlier point in their structural development but also more frequently than was the case during native rule.

The absolute size of traditional property groups was limited by the amount of land available to each. It can be roughly gauged by the size of the houses they left behind. It seems unlikely that a traditional retainer property group would contain more than twenty-five to thirty people, or fewer than six.

Interpersonal Kinship Relationships

I describe the relationships between kinsfolk as these have existed in the recent past in the most "traditional" households, making reference to earlier periods when this is possible.

WOMAN-SON

The relationship of mother and son was the strongest in the system in the sense of mutual obligation and the expectation of mutual love. A man should place the needs of his mother above those of all other kin. A woman should show equal concern for her children of both sexes, but it was expected that her primary attachment would be to her sons.

A woman's obligations to both daughters and sons in their early childhood included breast feeding to the age of two or three, care, especially in sickness, and instruction in cleanliness and in the man-

ners and morals of their caste. She might discipline them with slaps
and scolding but was usually indulgent. She taught her children to
look to her brother as their authority, and might either report their
conduct to him or (more commonly) try to shield them from his correction. A woman's duties to her adult son were to assist in cooking
for him, to serve him with food along with other men before she and
other women had eaten, and to assist in care of the house. She should
offer him counsel and comfort, respecting his wishes but attempting
to dissuade him from wrong. Her own moral conduct in the village
was a part of her duty to her children. If she infringed the religious
laws her shame fell also on them and they were the most likely persons to be visited with supernatural vengeance. A woman should accept the suggestions of her adult son with regard to her conduct. If
he became her kāranavan she theoretically owed him obedience in
law.

A child should respect his mother's teaching, although strict obedience to her was not demanded before the age of five or six. Throughout her life he should revere her, remembering that he owed to her
his membership of his taravād and all the birth-status rights of his
caste. For her sake he should maintain right relations with his matrilineal kinsfolk, submitting to his male elders and protecting his sisters and their children. A man should protect his mother from slander
or physical harm. When he entered the village after an absence he
must go first to greet her. While he stayed there he should live in his
natal house and make himself available to his mother's requests. He
should not incur her jealousy by visiting a wife for long periods in
the daytime, or by eating frequently in the house of a wife or of
friends. In all things he should place his mother's comfort and the
interests of the taravād above his private concerns. In her old age he
must offer comfort and companionship to his mother and after death
must perform funeral rites and make annual offerings on behalf of
her soul. Neglect of the mother by an adult son was the height of
impiety. The lineage goddess was believed to inflict sickness on an
impious son.

The etiquette of behavior between mother and adult son required
mutual respect and a certain restraint on both sides. Each stood when
the other entered the room, although they might later sit together and
converse informally. They discussed questions of property and the
affairs of the taravād in serious confidence, but undignified gossip
and talk touching on sexual matters were prohibited between them.

WOMAN-DAUGHTER

A woman was her daughter's immediate mentor and moral authority throughout her life. Whereas a son entered the company of men and boys after about the age of seven, a daughter returned to her mother's intimate care after the tāli rite. From her mother and from older women of the taravād a girl learned cookery, household and child care, manners, morals, and minor agricultural work. As her daughters came of age a woman took personal pride in their dress, jewelry, and physical attractions. It is said that formerly mothers and other matrilineally related women instructed girls in the arts of love. A woman should spend her life in her mother's household, and she should obey her, taking over from her more and more of the household responsibilities. She should defend her mother in disputes with other women, offer her companionship in old age, and perform funeral and anniversary rites for her soul after her death.

A daughter replaced her mother in the social structure and was expected to resemble her in character, as indeed she often did. A woman's constant care for her daughter's welfare became particularly prominent during the latter's pregnancy and parturition, when the mother must be at hand to offer counsel, good food, and medicines. So long as they respected her and did not encroach on her authority, she should welcome her daughters' husbands with cordiality. If, however, a husband's conduct gravely displeased his mother-in-law, she had the right to ask her daughter to reject him. A dutiful daughter would usually do so; if she refused, the mother might place her case before the kāranavan and request that the husband be dismissed.

Behavior between mother and daughter was usually informal, and they had few secrets from one another. In the privacy of their home and in the absence of men, matrilineally related women of today discuss their affairs and their neighbors freely, sometimes with hilarious mimicry. Mother and daughter were expected to have occasional quarrels. Indeed, there was often a deep undercurrent of rivalry between them which might break out into acrimonious mutual scolding. A daughter should bear patiently her mother's reprimands, but even though she struck her mother in anger her bad conduct would be forgiven more readily than the neglect of a son. A mother would also often try to shield her daughters from anger on the part of the kāranavan, of the mother's own brothers, or even of her sons. Mother and daughters usually maintained unity in disputes with other segments of the taravād, and it was axiomatic that mother and daughters stand united in disputes with other households.

WOMAN-SISTER'S CHILDREN

A woman and her sister's children should behave toward each other so far as possible in the same way as a woman and her own children. A motherless child was brought up collectively by his mother's sisters, usually attaching himself in particular to one of her younger sisters. As a member of their household who stood in a maternal relationship to them, a woman expected reverence, companionship, and practical help from her sisters' sons and a measure of obedience, companionship, and coöperation in domestic tasks from her sisters' daughters.

Terminologically and behaviorally, the mother's sisters were differentiated by age in relation to the mother. The mother's older sister received more respect than the mother, especially if she was the oldest woman in the household. Her role approximated that of the maternal grandmother after the latter's death. The mother's elder sister usually had children of her own by the time ego was born. She tended to advise ego's mother on how to care for him rather than tending him intimately herself. The mother's younger sister's role, by contrast, approximated that of a much older sister. Before she had children of her own, she often played the part of a long-suffering nursemaid and usually remained a favorite throughout her life. A mother's younger sister who was younger than ego was called by her personal name and treated as a younger sister.

Theoretically, attitudes proper toward the mother should be extended to all women of her generation within the lineage and clan. Actually, a rather sharp distinction was drawn between "mothers" of ego's own property group and those outside it. Behavior which was axiomatic within the property group became a matter of polite etiquette toward more distant kinswomen. Within the property group two or more sibling groups descended from sisters might oppose each other in adulthood. When the maternal grandmother and all males of senior generations were dead, their disputes might culminate in division of the property even while their mothers were living. Such inter-segmental disputes created strains in the relationship with the mother's sisters, but these ought not to become apparent in open quarreling.

WOMAN-DAUGHTER'S CHILDREN

A woman had strong control over her daughter's children. Her authority surpassed that of the mother and she retained the last word in matters of feeding or of care in sickness. At a time when her daughters were absorbed in childbearing and in relations with their husbands, she was deeply concerned for the future of her taravād as a group and took upon herself much of the moral training of her grandchildren. It was chiefly from the grandmother that children learned religious mythology and stories from their taravād's history. If she was the oldest woman of the house and if her son was kāranavan, a woman of strong personality might virtually direct the household, protecting the grandchildren both from their mother's indulgence and from their uncles' displeasure. She seldom inflicted corporal punishment but was obeyed by young children more readily than the mother. As they grew to maturity a woman tended to show indulgent pride in her grandsons as the pillars of her old age. By contrast she might show jealousy of her granddaughters and be a harsher judge of their manners and morals than was their mother.

MAN-SISTER'S SON

A kāranavan had special rights in and obligations to his sisters' children, some of which have been detailed. As their legal guardian he exercised the rights and obligations which normally accrue to the legal father in the higher patrilineal castes of India. He was responsible for his nephews' training in the laws and morality of their caste, in literacy, in agricultural work, and in military skills. Much of this training he often dispensed in person either before or after he became kāranavan. He was responsible for maintaining the junior men of his taravād and for guarding and, if possible, augmenting the ancestral property on their behalf. In turn they owed him obedience, loyalty, and submissive respect. A kāranavan might inflict a beating on a disobedient nephew under about the age of sixteen or might order a younger brother to do this on his behalf.

Relationships with all mother's brothers within the property group were modeled on that with the kāranavan. A man owed all of them respect and obedience within the framework of the kāranavan's jurisdiction. Often a boy's junior mother's brothers were absent from the taravād. When they were home the mother's own brothers took a special interest in him. They might play with him indulgently until he was about the age of three. After this he learned to respect them, to be quiet in their presence, and to fear his mother's report of his ill conduct to them. As he grew older it was usually from his mother's own brothers that a boy received detailed training in agricultural matters and it was they who most frequently chastised him. Throughout their lives a man owed obedience and loyalty to all men of senior generation in his taravād, and after their deaths, regular offerings in propitiation of their spirits.

The etiquette of behavior between a man and his mother's brothers was formalized to the point of avoidance. A boy or man might not touch his mother's brother. Before entering the uncle's presence he removed his upper clothing as a mark of respect. He might not speak first to the uncle but stood with arms folded and head bowed, attentively awaiting commands. He might not sit before his uncle except at mealtimes; he then sat down last and rose as soon as the uncle's meal was finished. When summoned for a lengthy interview he stood half hidden behind a pillar, holding his hand before his mouth lest his breath should reach the hearer. He might not chew betel leaves, smoke, spit, or use any but the most serious and respectful language in the presence of his senior. These rules of intercourse were most strict in the relationship with the kāranavan. For this reason a kāranavan absented himself as much as possible from family gatherings, living on the upper floor of the granary among his age mates of other lineages who came to visit him. With junior mother's brothers, who were more intimately responsible for his education, a youth's behavior was necessarily more relaxed. Even so, he observed the greatest possible formality, walked several feet behind them, and avoided them when he could.

A man should show loyalty to his mother's brothers in relations with outsiders, if necessary defending them with his life. He was expected to identify with them, receiving and perpetuating the noble traditions of his taravād. In fact Nayars did show great pride in the elders of their taravād as a group, exhibiting their virtues and hiding their weaknesses in the presence of strangers. There was regularly, however, deep hostility in their interpersonal relationships. The Nayars of today are well aware of this and expect acrimonious rivalry between the men of a taravād; hence, they say, the need for formal etiquette and strict ranking on the basis of age. A Nayar will speak of himself as bound to his taravād through natural love for his mother and sisters, and obliged for their sakes to maintain outward decorum in his relations with matrilineal kinsmen. In a modified form this suppressed hostility traditionally extended to all the men of the own, first ascending and second ascending generations. All male elders in the taravād might be collectively called kāranavar (singular, kāranavan). Within the property group they were numbered in order of age (irrespective of generation) as first, second, and third men. All owed loyalty and obedience to those above them and protection to those below them, but all envied their seniors and feared the rivalry of juniors. The mother's own brothers were, however, the prototypes for this generalized rivalry. Whether or not Nayars experienced Oedipal hostility to the mother's husband in their earliest years, there seems no doubt that a great part of their hostility to male elders became focused on the mother's brothers by about the age of five, and that much of it remained conscious. Thus occasional stories are told today of nephews who poisoned or stabbed their mothers' brothers and it is often remarked that kāranavans are "hated" and that "their position is not safe." Such tales of violence are regarded as shocking, but they do not arouse the horror with which a Hindu of the patrilineal castes would receive a story of patricide.

Relationships with the mother's mother's brothers were less intense and rivalrous than with the mother's brothers. Until the age of three or four a small boy might be a playful visitor to the room of the great-uncle who was his kāranavan. Often, this elder died while he was still small, so that the boy retained only affectionate memories of him. Otherwise he learned to behave with even greater formality to this elder than to his mother's brothers. He saw the great-uncle less often, however, and was seldom directly punished by him, so that the relationship tended to remain one of distant geniality.

MAN-SISTER'S DAUGHTER

As the head of her taravād a kāranavan owed his sister's daughter maintenance, shelter, and legal and physical protection. At her tāli rite and during her subsequent marriage relationships, only the sexual rights in a woman were lost to her taravād. All other rights, in her procreative powers and domestic services, remained vested in her taravād, represented by its kāranavan. He could command her obedience in the performance of household and minor agricultural work. He automatically became the full legal guardian of children born to her legitimately. If she seriously infringed the religious laws of her caste, for example, by having sex relations with a man of lower caste, it was his duty to expel her from the taravād and his right (very occasionally exercised) to put her to death by the sword.

In the nineteenth century, when monogamy gradually became customary, a kāranavan arranged the marriage of his sister's daughter. In earlier periods Nayar women seem to have exercised considerable freedom to select or reject their husbands. A woman might not, however, oppose her kāranavan's right to dismiss an unwelcome husband.

All the mother's brothers of a woman had the right to command her domestic services and to discipline her in minor ways. As in the case of a boy, they might play with her until she reached the age of three or four, after which they became somewhat feared authorities. A man might occasionally beat his sister's daughter, until the age of seven or eight, but he would not inflict heavy punishment unless he was sure of the child's grandmother's and her kāranavan's support. After she had undergone the tāli rite a man was forbidden to touch any junior woman of his taravād. His relationship with his sister's daughter thereafter became very distant. In accordance with rules associated with incest prohibitions, he might not be alone in a room with her and would scrupulously avoid suspicion of intimacy. He would absent himself when her husband entered the house, remaining on the outer veranda, in the separate men's building, or in the house of his wife. A woman must remain standing and remove her upper clothing when her mother's brother entered her presence. She must not speak first to him, must not laugh in his presence, and must respond with extreme submissiveness to his requests. When possible a man would communicate advice to his sister's daughter through some kinswoman senior to both of them. Thus, except to serve him with food, a woman had little direct intercourse with her mother's brothers.

Modern Nayars admit freely that the partial avoidance between men of the taravād, on the one hand, and that between men and women junior to them in the taravād, on the other, have quite different foundations. The former is a defense against aggression, the latter against desire. Nayars partially avoid their younger sisters and nieces, it is admitted, because otherwise they might be tempted to commit incest with them. As things are, in speaking with others, men often express a respectful tenderness toward their sisters' daughters and a pride in their qualities. Because of the difference of sex, and therefore of ambitions and interests, there is much less potential conflict here than in the relationship with the sister's son. By an orthodox kāranavan in particular, its young women are seen as the fine flower of his taravād. Whatever may be his more selfish inner feelings, he expresses gladness when there are many of them to perpetuate his matrilineal group. For their sakes and for the sake of the heirs they may bring him, he welcomes their husbands to his home. When the latter are aristocrats of higher caste, his pride seems the more easily to outweigh any potential hostility toward them.

In orthodox homes today, women's attitudes to their mothers' brothers seem to be variously compounded of fear and admiration. A woman fears her uncle's anger and may resent his harshness toward her brothers and sons. If, however, he manages her household with equity and if his reputation stands high in his neighborhood, he may become a distant hero in her eyes.

MAN-SISTER

Within the kinship circle, a man's concern for his sisters should come second only to that for his mother. He had greater authority over them, but he owed them similar protection and consideration. If he became their kāranavan, he must manage the property on their behalf and educate their children to the best of his ability. A woman owed her brother domestic services, obedience, and devotion. Brother and sister should, when necessary, subordinate their own marital interests to each other's comfort and welfare.

The elder sister shared something of the mother's role; the younger sister, that of the sister's daughter. Indeed, as in all relationships within the taravād, the significance of age surpassed that of generation; for when age and generation were discrepant the attitudes appropriate to age overrode those appropriate to generation.

A much older sister might help to bring up a boy in the same manner as the mother's younger sister. As he grew to maturity her attitude combined sharp criticism with maternal solicitude. When both were adult, however, difference of sex became a greater determinant of authority than did difference of age. Although she might continue to speak informally with him or even to upbraid him mildly, the elder sister stood in her brother's presence and received his commands with respect. If he became kāranavan, the younger brother's ultimate legal authority was unquestioned. His sister might, however, remain his trusted counselor for life.

Until her tāli rite a girl played freely with her elder brothers and was affectionately patronized by them. After this time an outer formality was required between them, identical with that preserved toward the sister's daughter. Inwardly the relationship was expected to be more intense, with less authority and more tenderness on the part of the brother, less fear and more devotion on the part of the sister, and today, in speech with others, young childless women often display a simple hero worship for their elder brothers. As a woman's children grew to maturity, her brother's discipline of them might create tensions in the sibling relationship. She should, however, continue to submit willingly to his wishes. A man who was not her kāranavan had no right to dismiss his sister's husband from their home. Nevertheless, a woman who knew that her brother deeply disliked her husband would feel it her duty to reject him.

The very formal behavior required between a man and his younger sister is consciously related to incest prohibitions. Sibling incest is in fact very rare and was traditionally punished by death. Enough cases are known in modern times however to show that the temptation was real. The reasons for the partial avoidance between men and younger women of the taravād apparently lie in the descent system. Brothers, in common with other men of the taravād, owned the procreative rights in a woman. They shared property and a home with her and were jointly the guardians of her children. With all these shared interests a strong devotion to her was axiomatic and inevitable. Yet brothers must forswear completely the sexual rights in their sister and surrender these to other men. Their formalized, partial avoidance of their younger kinswoman facilitated their continued devotion, side by side with the sexual prohibition. At the same time it completely segregated their interests in her from those of her husbands and thus made tolerable the relationships between brothers-in-law.

Life histories and the behavior of small children suggest that a man's near-conscious attraction toward his sister is a displacement of his earlier and more intense Oedipal attachment to his mother. The latter is apparently repressed at about the age of five, together with similar motives toward other older matrilineal kinswomen. It is uncertain whether Nayar boys developed Oedipal hostility toward their mothers' husbands in early childhood. Perhaps they did, for a child shared his mother's sleeping room until the age of three or four and must have witnessed parental sexual relations. If Oedipal rivalry did develop, much of the hostility seems to have been displaced toward the mother's brothers as they became the significant authorities in the child's world. There is in any case a realistic basis in the mother's brother's hard discipline for aggressive motives toward him. Mythology and religious rites suggest that these two forbidden motives—aggression toward older matrilineal kinsmen and desire for union with matrilineal kinswomen—remained powerful throughout a man's life. It is therefore easy to see why observance of the rules of formal etiquette toward older men and toward younger women of the taravād represented, for a Nayar, the essence of familial piety. The rules counteracted his deepest unsocialized impulses and made possible the harmonious coöperation of the matrilineal group. It is reasonable also to conclude that tensions arising within this natal group must have been eased by the fact that aggression and sexuality, sternly prohibited within the lineage, were encouraged outside it in warfare, organized dueling, and very free sexual relationships.

A man's hidden concern for his sister's sexuality seems to have found an approved outlet in the jealousy with which he was expected to guard her from any taint of contact with low-caste men. Organized duels as well as illegal battles between lineages seem to have been fought chiefly to vindicate a kinwoman from the unproven charge of cohabitation with a man of low caste, or to protect her from any form of obscene slander. Such approved forms of aggression against Nayars of other lineages may have provided outlets for a brother's sexual jealousy, which he might show only covertly toward his sister's socially recognized husbands. If, on the other hand, a woman were finally judged guilty of sexual relations with a man of low caste, the law permitted her brothers to vent their jealous fury by putting her and her lover to death.

BROTHERS

The relationship between brothers had much in common with that between a man and his sister's son. Age rank was of the greatest significance: even twins, or classificatory brothers born on the same day, were mutually ranked in terms of birth order, the elder preceding the younger in succession to the kāranavanship. Brothers near in age played together in early childhood, but toward adolescence their behavior became formalized to the point of partial avoidance. The elder might command the junior to do small tasks for him. A much older brother might inflict corporal punishment within the limits set by the kāranavan's authority. In general, a man's etiquette in the presence of his brother was the same as that shown to the mother's brother. A man whose elder brother was also his kāranavan treated him with even greater respect and when possible avoided his presence.

The social distance required between brothers must have been made possible by the fact that they were often absent from home, and that, when home, they had little need to coöperate in work. In modern times a man who resides with his elder brother or mother's brother usually works independently outside the taravād, spends much time in his wife's house, and restricts his intercourse with his senior to mealtimes and to formal consultations concerning their property. Unfortunately we do not know what, if any, was the structure of authority or the division of functions between brothers who traditionally fought together in war.

Great rivalry was admitted to exist in the relationship between brothers. They were thought of as bound to the taravād through their mother and sisters, rather than directly to each other. At the same time, sons of the same mother could be expected to support each other in conflicts with children of the mother's sister, while both sibling groups might experience a common resentment of their maternal uncles' authority. In broader contexts, the men of a property group supported each other firmly in disputes with other property groups of the lineage, while the men of a lineage were expected to defend each other to the death in outbreaks of violence against other lineages.

Inter-segmental conflicts between classificatory brothers, or between the men of a sibling group and their mother's classificatory brothers, eventually led to division of the taravād. This could not, however, take place until the men of all generations senior to the disputants were dead. As long as the taravād was obliged to cohere, the formalities associated with age rank between men countered incipient tendencies to segmentary fission. Men were ranked by age irrespective of segment and generation, and the same etiquette of formality and partial avoidance was due an elder own brother as to an elder classificatory brother. Thus the etiquette of age rank not only reduced the dangers of open violence between individual "brothers" of any degree of relationship; it also *enforced* estrangement and social distance between full brothers, who in some contexts might otherwise have huddled together in unseemly amity to plot against their classificatory brothers in other segments of the property group.

SISTERS

Sisters shared many experiences and interests. They played together in childhood and often experienced the tāli ceremony together. As adults they cooked, swept, pounded paddy, harvested, and cared for babies together. Women were in some respects ranked on the basis of age in the same manner as men. All who were older had some authority over all who were younger. A younger sister was not permitted to receive a visiting husband until after one had appeared to claim her elder sister's or elder classificatory sister's favors.

However, the age ranking and authority structure between women was less formal than that between men. Women had no legal authority over one another. All women of a household were legal minors, collectively under the authority of the men of their household, represented by their kāranavan. Women had no place in the caste assembly and might not give evidence in trials. Disputes between women of different households or different lineages were not considered serious matters for public consideration. Women could not legally represent their households in relationships with other households, other castes, or political authorities.

For these reasons older women had only moral authority over juniors. They could not enforce their decisions except by appeal

to the kāranavan. Even in relation to small children they tended to
seek the backing of a brother to maintain discipline in the home.
Old women who had passed the menopause had the greatest authority. They could move freely about the village, travel alone on pil-
grimages, and wield influence over their younger brothers and sons.
But even old women in some contexts found themselves united with
their juniors as a group of legal minors under the command of a male
authority.

Under these circumstances the mutual behavior of women was
intimate and informal. Their joint tasks, carried out in the confined
space of the kitchen, encouraged this intimacy. Further, as natal kinswomen they were habituated to each other from birth. Unlike a
woman and her daughters-in-law in a patrilineal household, their
group membership was unitary and they experienced a continuity
in major roles and loyalties from birth to death.

If she were competent, the oldest woman of the household delegated its tasks, allowing flexibility for seasonal variation and unusual
occurrences. Generally, girls who had not reached puberty ran
errands between houses, did small outdoor tasks, and played with
their younger siblings. The younger married women shared the heavy
work of pounding paddy, milking cows, cleaning dishes, and most of
the cooking. Old women had pride of place in the kitchen and living
room. They supervised cookery, occupied the best seats, and controlled their juniors' consumption of betel leaves, areca nuts, and
tobacco from the family box. Elderly mothers took pride in serving
their children and grandchildren with food on birthdays. In a large
house young married women had considerable leisure and privileges.
Through the day they took turns visiting the village bathing pool in
couples, an event which gave opportunity for gossip and allowed them
to be seen by (although not to converse with) the men of neighboring groups. Old women proudly distributed the taravād's jointly
owned jewelry among the young and marriageable women, helped
them to apply cosmetics and to dress their hair, and obtained a
vicarious satisfaction from their marital conquests. For a few years
—until she had several children—a young woman's life was gay and
not overburdened with work. Women of childbearing age also had
periods of respite from the kitchen. They were secluded in an inner
room for three days during menstruation and did no household tasks
for ninety days after a birth. In these conditions the division of labor
was not strict and the segments descended from women were not
segregated in their functions. Women wielded most control over their

own daughters and grandchildren, but sisters "stood in" for one another in caring for their children and contributed their work in a manner conducive to the general welfare.

Between sisters, especially own sisters, there was deep personal affection as well as loyalty to the sibling group and to the taravād. Sisters were also rivals, often squabbling over jewelry, clothing, and favors. Both rivalry and affection were most intense between sisters close in age.

Most women died in their ancestral homes among their siblings and children. Only a woman whose forebears and brothers were all dead might move away from her sisters into a separate property group headed by her son as kāranavan. Even so, sisters often lived to experience covert disputes between their children, who looked forward to the day when they would separate into new branch taravāds. In the last resort sisters would support their own children in quarrels, although they tried not to become involved in such disputes but to preserve their mutual amity.

MARRIAGE

The taravād was obviously of very great strength as an economic and legal corporation. Correspondingly, marriage was the slenderest of ties.

Every ten or twelve years, the immature girls of one generation within a lineage were ritually married on the same day by men drawn from their enangar lineages. Before the ceremony the girls were secluded for three days and caused to observe ritual prohibitions as if they had menstruated. (The actual rite of tying the tāli or gold ornament around the bride's neck is the central rite of "normal" marriage among most of the patrilineal castes of South India.) After the tāli rite, each couple was secluded for three days in a room of the ancestral house. Their seclusion clearly marked a ceremonial if not an actual defloration, and travelers' accounts of the sixteenth to eighteenth centuries indicate that the brides were actually deflowered at this time (Stanley, 1865: 24; Kerr, 1811: chap. 6; Hamilton, ed. Penzer, 1930, I: 174). During the seclusion period, rites were performed to the goddess Bhagavadi to enhance the girls' fertility. On the fourth morning each couple took a purifying bath and ate a meal together. In Calicut and Walluvanad, although apparently not in Cochin, each bridegroom then tore in two the lower cloth worn by the girl in the period of seclusion. He kept one half and handed the other to the girl. Their personal obligations ended, the bridegrooms left the household.

If he wished, a girl's ritual bridegroom might later visit her as one of a series of husbands, but he had no prior claims and was not obliged to do so. The woman in turn owed no obligations to him except that at his death, she and all her children by whatever biological fathers must observe fifteen days of ritual pollution for him. Ritual pollution was otherwise observed only for matrilineal kin. Until modern times it was not observed by a woman and her children for a visiting husband who was not also the woman's ritual husband. In addition, if they knew him, a woman's children called her ritual husband by the Dravidian word *appan,* the term used for the father in the patrilineal castes. Their mother's visiting husbands they called by the Sanskrit term *acchan;* this word means "leader" or "lord" and was also sometimes applied as a title to village headmen and military leaders.

After the tāli rite and shortly before or after puberty, a woman might enter into a number of sexual relationships with men of her local caste group or of an appropriate higher caste. Similarly, a Nayar might visit a number of wives of his own or an appropriate lower Nayar caste. Among retainer Nayars, by far the majority of unions were between persons of the same caste. A very few favored women had husbands from the lineages of temple servants, village headmen, chiefs, or royalty, or from houses of Nambudiri Brahmans of relatively low rank. A smaller number of Nayar retainers had wives in the lower-ranking castes of Nayar temple menials, but not in the servant castes of Nayar washermen and barbers, which were endogamous.

It is not certain how many husbands a woman might have at one time; various writers [8] of the fifteenth to eighteenth centuries mention between three and twelve (Logan, 1951, I: 136–137). Others add that women "never refused themselves" to occasional Brahman or Nayar visitors of appropriate rank. It seems probable that each woman had a small number of husbands from her local caste group who, while their relationship lasted, visited her regularly, but that women also received occasional fleeting visits from itinerant Nayars of appropriate rank, perhaps mainly during military operations.

[8] See, for example, Abdu 'r Razzak (1441), Nicolo di Conti (1444), Hieronimo de Santo Stephano (1563), and Cesar Fredericke (1563), in Hakluyt Society Publications Vol. 22, 1857; Duarte Barbosa (1518) and Joao de Barros (early sixteenth century) in Dames, 1921, II: 124, 241; Ludovico di Varthema (1503–1508), tr. J. W. Jones, 1863; 146; Zein-ud-Deen (1579), tr. Rowlandson, 1833; 63; J. H. van Linschoten (1596) in Hakluyt Society Publications Vol. 71: 279; Pietro della Valle (1624), Hakluyt Society Publications Vol. 85: 579; Hamilton (1727), ed. Penzer, 1930, I: 310; Buchanan, 1807, II: 411.

A husband normally visited his wife after eating supper in his natal home, and left before breakfast. Even today in many orthodox Nayar homes men eat regularly in their taravāds and accept food in their wives' homes only on special invitation from their wives' kāranavans. Traditionally a husband placed his weapons outside his wife's door as a sign to other men that he was within. My informants in a Cochin village reported that, within living memory in the late nineteenth century, if two husbands called on the same night the one who came last might sleep outside on the veranda. Usually a woman's regular husbands knew each other and informally agreed upon their turns.

The relationship with the visiting husband was called *sambandham* (Sanskrit, "joining together"). At the start of a girl's first sambandham her husband came to her house privately at night, sometimes with a few friends of his own age. In the presence of the girl's kin he presented her with a white cloth of the kind worn as a skirt. The occasion was not marked by feasting. Later husbands might or might not present the cloth. A transient visitor is said to have left a gold coin beneath the woman's pillow, and a regular husband might do the same on the first night of his union.

While his relationship lasted, a regular husband was expected to make gifts to his wife at the three main festivals of the year. Vishu, in April, was the Malayalam New Year; Onam, in September, was a harvest festival; Tiruvadira, in December, was a women's festival to Kama Devan, the god of passion. The gifts were of bathing oil, bananas, wafer biscuits, and betel leaves and areca nuts for chewing. In some areas a husband also gave a loin cloth of superior quality at Onam. The gifts were prepared by women of the husband's taravād, and he should present them in person to each of his wives on the festival day. If a husband failed to make these gifts it was a tacit sign that he had ended the relationship. It should be noted that the gifts, trivial in value, were gifts of courtship and were in no sense maintenance. Bathing oil is a feminine toilet requisite; wafer biscuits are delicacies served at feasts; and the giving of chewing materials between a man and a woman is everywhere in South India associated with courtship or with the first night of marriage. A husband had no obligation at all to maintain his wife, for she received her food, shelter, and regular clothing from her taravād.

The only other obligations of a husband came at the birth of a child. When a woman became pregnant it was necessary for one or more men of appropriate caste to acknowledge possible biological

paternity. This they did by making gifts to the woman herself and
to the midwife immediately after the birth. Any man who had visited
the woman in the appropriate time period was required to make
these gifts. If a man refused, he could be called upon by the caste
assembly to fulfill his obligation. The gifts comprised two new
lower cloths for the mother and one cloth and a quantity of paddy
as payment to the Nayar woman barber who attended at the delivery. Again, these gifts were clearly legal and ceremonial tokens
rather than objects of substantial economic value. Legally, however,
their transfer was of the utmost significance. For if no man would
consent to make the delivery payments, the woman was assumed to
have had sex relations with a man of lower caste or with a Muslim
or a Christian. Her caste assembly would temporarily excommunicate
her taravād until she and her child had been driven out by their
kāranavan and the woman's funeral rites had been performed. The
woman, presumably with her child, might be executed by her
matrilineal kinsmen or allowed to become a slave of the district chief
or the king. If the woman and her lover were publicly exposed even
before the birth of the child, both might be put to death.

A woman had no obligations to her husbands other than the
granting of sexual privileges. Nayar husbands of the woman's own
caste occasionally dined in her household but this was a favor and
not a right. Nayar households sometimes provided uncooked food
and a separate building for Brahman or chiefly husbands, but this
again seems to have been a matter of courtesy rather than of obligation. Husbands of higher caste made the same gifts to their wives
as did Nayar husbands.

In the nineteenth century her kāranavan selected a woman's first
husband, and he may have done so at earlier periods. Until the
1930's many kāranavans also retained the right to dismiss a husband
who displeased them. It seems improbable, however, that a woman
or her kāranavan would ever refuse the visits of a Brahman, chief, or
village headman of powerful standing in the community. In some
cases also a husband of higher caste seems to have monopolized the
favors of a Nayar woman, a privilege not accorded to men of her own
caste. K. Kannan Nair reported (1908: 186) that until a century
previously local chiefs sometimes compelled a woman to receive as
husbands those of her enangar who wished to marry her. In general,
however, women seem to have been free to reject particular men, and
both men and women to terminate liaisons without formality.

In all possible respects attempts seem to have been made to reduce the intensity of marital ties for the sake of the unity of taravād, village, and kingdom. Good men were men who devoted themselves first to the service of their feudal lords, and second to the welfare of their taravāds. Weak and immoral men were men who became inveigled by their wives and their children, so that they tried to make unnecessary gifts to their wives and neglected their taravāds. An ideal kāranavan was one who broke off his marital ties in old age and devoted his energies solely to his sisters' children. Institutional recognition of emotional attachments between spouses was reduced to a minimum. If a man by accident died in his wife's house his body was immediately brought home for cremation by his lineage kin. After a man's death his current wives were permitted to come and view his corpse. They were then ceremonially conducted out from the north side of the house—the side opposite to that from which the god of death had come. They must not look back at the house of death and they might never visit it again. They and their children took no part in the funeral or the subsequent anniversary rites nor did they observe death pollution.

In spite of the institutional precautions, undoubtedly some men formed strong emotional attachments to particular wives and their children. The institution of sorcery came into play at this point (Gough, 1958). Among Nayars, sorcery was practiced mainly against affines; it was ineffectual within the lineage. It was believed to be practiced most by junior members of a taravād against the matrilineal kin of their kāranavan's wife. The reason was that if he were particularly attached to a wife, the juniors of a kāranavan might fear that he would transfer to her gifts and cash which belonged legally to his taravād. They could not make their complaint in law, for the kāranavan was their legal representative. Instead, they are said to have secretly engaged low-caste practitioners to recite spells and make offerings to some minor malevolent deity with the object of bringing sickness upon the wife or her kin. If they suspected such evil doing, the members of the wife's taravād might in turn hire a "good" practitioner of their own who would appeal to some other deity to return the misfortune to the senders. It is clear that Nayars did hire "good" practitioners to perform countermagic against affines; whether in fact they hired evil practitioners to perform sorcery in the first place is uncertain. At all events the institution of sorcery provided a covert outlet for interpersonal hostilities between affines which could find no expression in open conflicts between their groups as a whole. The result of the hostilities was often termination of the particular marriage, for the spouses, unable to bear the machinations of their relatives, would often end their relationship.

I have called these Nayar institutions "marriage" because they limited and regulated sexual relationships and because they served to legitimize children. The provisions of both the tāli rite and the sambandham were directed toward these ends. The tāli rite was both a legal and a ritual institution. First, it symbolically conferred sexual and procreative powers upon the girl. The mock menstrual seclusion, the rites to the fertility goddess, and the "defloration" all indicate this. Second, it took the sexual rights in a girl away from her matrilineal kinsmen as soon as they had been conferred. This appears in that the girl and her elder matrilineal kinsmen must observe the rules of etiquette associated with incest prohibitions from the day of the tāli rite. Third, it transferred the sexual (but not the procreative) rights in the girl to a representative of her caste in the person of an enangan. Fourth, however, this man at once renounced his rights in his capacity as an individual, after which they became available to men of the caste, and of appropriate higher castes, as a group. All of this was accomplished in good time *before* the girl actually attained puberty and was capable of entering fruitfully into sexual liaisons. It was strictly forbidden for a man to have relations with a girl before her tāli rite, and if the rite was not performed before puberty she was expelled from caste.

With regard to the sambandham institution, sex relations were not promiscuous. They were forbidden within the lineage, within a certain range of affines (discussed below), and, most categorically, with men of lower caste. It was therefore necessary to have some procedure for legitimizing children, to show that they had been fathered by men standing in the appropriate roles. The legally obligatory payments by husbands at the time of birth accomplished this, and if no one could be found to make the payments, the woman and child were expelled from the caste.

It was appropriate that a woman should wear the tāli throughout her life and that she and her children should observe death pollution for the ritual husband rather than for any particular visiting husbands. For neither the ritual husband nor the visiting husbands had rights in the woman *as individuals*, nor had the woman or her children individual rights in them. After renouncing his individual rights, however, the ritual husband remained for life, in relation to this woman, the representative of his caste, which in law had collectively married her and collectively fathered her children.

As a form of group marriage, the Nayar institutions clearly will not fit the definition of marriage proposed in *Notes and Queries in Anthropology*.[9] It did, however, legitimize children, which seems to me the minimum necessary criterion applicable to all those unions which anthropologists customarily label "marriage." As a new definition of marriage which will cover all the familiar types, the Nayar case, and several other unusual cases which are commonly recognized as marriage, I have suggested the following: "Marriage is a relationship between a woman and one or more other persons which provides that a child born to the woman, under circumstances not prohibited by the rules of the relationship, shall be accorded full birth-status rights in his society or social stratum" (Gough, 1959: 32).

Nayar men seem always to have chosen wives younger than themselves. A man ranked above his wife, who had to show respect to him. In the presence of her kin she remained standing before him and seldom spoke to him; she would not be seen talking to him in public outside her home. A woman never used her husband's name; she addressed and referred to him by plural honorific pronouns. Hypergamous marriage relationships were even more formal than those between Nayars. Caste rules of pollution prevented the husband from receiving food from his wife's kinsfolk. During the daytime, after taking his purifying bath in the morning, he was forbidden to touch her or any member of her family.

THE FATHER AND HIS KIN

The most peculiar characteristic of the Central Nayars is that although a form of marriage existed they did not institutionalize the elementary family of one man, one woman, and their children. This group was in no sense a legal, residential, commensal, productive, or distributive unit. An individual man had no legal rights in a particular wife and her children. He did not reside with them, did not eat regularly with them, did not produce with or for them, and he did not customarily distribute goods to his children. A woman had no legal rights in a particular man—only the right that one *or more* men admit paternity of her children. Similarly, a child correctly begotten was assured of legal paternity, but a group of men might fulfill this role and the child had no subsequent claims on any of them. It might perhaps be claimed that the group composed of the tāli tier, his ritual wife, and her children born subsequently received cere-

[9] "Marriage is a union between a man and a woman such that children born to the woman are the legitimate offspring of both parents" (*Notes and Queries*, 1951: 110).

monial recognition through the performance of death pollution, but that was strictly all.

Nayars did, however, understand and attach significance to the physiological role of the male in procreation. They expected a child to resemble his genitor and to be unusually intelligent if his father were a Brahman or a Nayar aristocrat. A man is said to have been especially fond of a child whom he knew with reasonable certainty to be his own. He would make small gifts to him, play with him on visits, and offer him friendly counsel as he grew older. However, a man had no right to interfere in any way in his child's training, and the child had no customary obligations to him. If he ended his relationship with the mother he had no further contact with the child.

Children addressed all their mothers' husbands as acchan, adding the caste title in the case of a father of higher caste. Both boys and girls stood in the father's presence and accorded him respect, but without the extreme submissiveness due to an older matrilineal kinsman. In spite of the Malayāli adage "No Nayar knows his father," it seems probable that almost every Nayar regarded some particular man as his genitor; but his relationship with this man might be anything from a permanent, warm attachment to almost total lack of recognition. Certainly differences of paternity created no institutionalized divisions within a sibling group.

No rights or obligations existed between an individual and his patrilateral kin. These relationships, when they existed, were a matter of individual friendliness or of polite etiquette. A person might visit his or her father's taravād as long as the father's marriage to the mother endured, especially if the father lived close by. However, although marriage has been monogamous for the past seventy to eighty years, I found in one Cochin village in 1949 that only 48 per cent of sibling groups containing children under fifteen had any contact with their father's matrilineal kin. In the other cases patrilateral relationships were suspended because the father lived at a distance, because he had divorced the mother, or because his kinswomen had quarreled with the mother.

In what follows, the term "father" refers to any husband of the mother in the sambandham relationship, and the term "patrilateral kin," to the matrilineal kin of such a man.

Patrilateral kin of the father's generation or older were accorded friendly respect. Cross cousins of the same sex and caste had a familiar, mildly joking relationship if they maintained contact with one another. If their families remained friendly, cross cousins of opposite sex might talk to each other with rather more freedom than to unrelated persons. In his role of enangan a boy sometimes tied the tāli for his maternal uncle's daughter or stepdaughter of suitable age.

There were no incest prohibitions with patrilateral kin, although a man was unlikely to marry his father's own sister because of age differences. Marriage to the father's or stepfather's brother or brother's son was neither prohibited nor preferred. Modern informants thought that if a girl was known to be one's father's daughter by another wife, marriage with her would be avoided as indelicate, but it was apparently not prohibited. The children of brothers were not considered related, and provided they belonged to different lineages, they might marry or not as they chose.

Bilateral cross-cousin marriage was freely permitted, with some preference for marriage to the mother's brother's daughter or stepdaughter. A kāranavan was particularly likely to encourage his nephew to enter marital relations with a daughter of the kāranavan's favorite wife. In this case it was felt that the marital interests of uncle and nephew would be harmonized and the nephew might be less likely to accuse the uncle of infidelity to the taravād if he favored his wife and her children. Patrilateral cross-cousin marriage is said to have been less favored because it did nothing to smooth the relationships between men of a taravād. It may, also, have been less common because a man had no influence in his son's choice of a wife.

It may seem strange that preferred cross-cousin marriage should have existed side by side with group marriage, for cross-cousin marriage, especially when it is arranged by the senior generation, suggests an interest in prolonging the ties brought about both by paternity and by matrilineal kinship. Group marriage, by contrast, tends to negate the claims and interests of individual fathers. Today, the fact is that cross-cousin marriage is arranged only with the child of an uncle who has had a long and satisfactory marriage relationship. It is never deliberately arranged as a first marriage, with the child of an uncle's previously divorced wife. Further, although young people agree to arranged cross-cousin marriages, they may and fairly often do later dissolve the marriage if things do not go well. One presumes that similar circumstances existed in the days of group marriage. Many men, presumably, entered marriage relations with cross cousins only incidentally—often, presumably, without being fully aware of the blood relationship. It seems quite probable that at other times some men did have an enduring relationship with a particularly favored wife, and that such a man might well arrange for a nephew's first sambandham relationship to be with a daughter of this wife. It seems probable also that such deliberately arranged matrilateral cross-cousin marriages increased in popularity in the nineteenth century, as plural marriages gradually gave place to monogamy. My data suggest also that deliberately arranged patrilateral cross-cousin marriages may have become more popular in the late nineteenth century, as fathers became instrumental in maintaining and educating their sons.[10]

AFFINITY

The members of ego's father's household had less significance to him in their interpersonal relationships than as affines or *bandhukkar* (singular, *bandhu*) of his household as a whole. The bandhus or "joined ones" of a household were acquired through the sambandham relationship. They comprised the current spouses of the property group's members, together with the households from which these people came. *Bandham* (affinity) had no practical significance beyond this range.

Because of the transience of particular marriages, affinal relationships, like those with patrilateral kin, were a matter of etiquette rather than of rights and obligations. Affines of the same caste might visit each other informally and must be received with hospitality. It was also common to invite to the feasts of life-crisis rites the actual spouses of the dwelling group and any close matrilineal kin they might wish to bring with them. Affines, however, had no ceremonial obligations on these occasions and were not under the same categorical obligation to attend as were the representatives of enangar households.

Politeness—masking a greater or lesser degree of covert hostility—characterized affinal relationships in general. A man treated his wife's male elders of senior generations with respect, and stood in their presence unless invited to eat with them. They welcomed him with cordial gravity and with the respect due to his caste status if he were a man of higher caste.

[10] Both types of cross-cousin marriage have however decreased in frequency as a result of the urbanization and mobility of the past thirty years. In one Cochin village in 1949, 7 per cent of living Nayar women had married the father's own or classificatory maternal nephew; less than 2 per cent had married the own or classificatory mother's brother's son. Taking the women of six lineages over five generations, 14 per cent of marriages were to the father's own or classificatory nephew; 9 per cent to the own or classificatory uncle's son. In Walluvanad, of the women of nine lineages over five generations, 11 per cent had married the father's own or classificatory nephew; about 5 per cent, the own or classificatory uncle's son. Patrilateral cross-cousin marriage is of course impossible in hypergamous unions.

A man's relationships with his wife's older matrilineal kinswomen were less formally respectful. He might sit with them and exchange village news. They served food to him when he ate in their house and were the persons who usually greeted him first on an evening visit. Although she welcomed them at first out of pride in her daughter's popularity, a woman was likely in time to become jealous of her sons-in-law. If they were tactful they treated her with courtesy and submitted to her whims.

A man tended to avoid his wife's sisters or classificatory sisters who were younger than himself. They treated him with extreme respect similar to that accorded to an older brother, and avoided him as far as possible after they had reached puberty. Incest prohibitions were relevant here: a man was forbidden to have marital relations with two women of the same household, and a woman, with two men from the same household. These prohibitions of course partly served to prevent father-daughter incest. Marriage to a member of a dead or divorced spouse's household was also forbidden.

These rules in general appear to relate to the need to keep minimal potential rivalries between persons of the same sex within the matrilineal household. They were also consistent with the relationship of extreme respect and social distance between the men of a taravād. Tensions between these men were sufficiently acute in any case; they might have been intolerable if two of them had shared a wife. There was also the attitude that sexual relationships should be kept strictly segregated from ties to matrilineal kin. A boy's matrilineal kinsmen were even forbidden to accompany him to his bride's house at the beginning of his first sambandham. Instead he took with him brothers-in-law, unrelated friends, or sometimes a cross-cousin. For marriage was a gay undertaking, a matter of personal pleasure, and only men who stood to each other in a familiar and non-authoritative relationship might have knowledge of each others' marital affairs.

Similarly, the ban on marriage to two women of the same property group is understandable in that Nayar women were open rivals for the attentions of men. Many writers mention this and it is still discernible at the present day. Apparently the respect and amity required of women of the same household was incompatible with such rivalry.

However, the prohibition of relations with two members of the same property group was less stringent than the rule of lineage exogamy. Nambudiri Brahmans are said to have occasionally pressed their attentions on two sisters in spite of their family's reluctance.

At least during this century, moreover, cases have very occasionally occurred in which a Nayar cohabited both with his wife and with their daughter by the marriage or with his wife and her younger sister. Such affairs are viewed with disgust as evidence of extreme ill-breeding, but they do not merit excommunication or exclusion from public ceremonies, nor are the offenders expected to fall ill through supernatural vengeance. The reason appears to be that traditionally only matrilineal kinsfolk were regarded as kin in the true sense. Incest prohibitions outside this range were apparently a matter of propriety rather than of religious law.

A man's wife's sisters' children, like his own children, had an amicable relationship with him of mingled respect and playfulness. After their tāli rite, however, girls were forbidden to touch their "fathers," own or classificatory, and relationships with these men tended to become more grave.

Brothers-in-law had informal relationships. A man would defer to his wife's much older brother and expect some respect from his wife's much younger brother. Brothers-in-law of similar age had a mild joking relationship. They might chew betel leaves, loll, yarn, and gossip together. A man's sisters' husbands sometimes acted as go-betweens in arranging his first sambandham and accompanied him to the house of his wife. But the surface amicability of brothers-in-law often hid very deep hostility related to conflicting claims upon the woman who linked them. This might break out in quarrels or end in mutual avoidance. The wife's brother was also often instrumental in having a man dismissed from the conjugal house.

A woman's contacts with her husband's kin were obviously less regular than those of a man. A woman never went to her husband's taravād to visit him for personal reasons but only to pay polite social calls on his kinswomen. When a man or girl began their first sambandham the man's mother and sisters customarily went to bring home his wife a few days after the husband's first visit. Often the wife's sisters would accompany her. They were given a small feast in private and the husband's mother might make a gift of jewelry to the girl before she returned home on the third or fourth day. Thereafter the frequency of feminine visits between the two households depended on the stability of the marriage, the proximity of the houses, and the personal feelings between the members. Neither husband nor wife did any tasks at all in each other's homes. Each remained always an outsider to whom polite behavior was due. Because of incest prohibitions a woman paid extreme respect to her husband's elder matrilineal kinsmen and they avoided her except on ceremonial occasions. She had a relationship of mutual courtesy with all of her husband's older kinswomen and was given meticulous respect by her husband's junior kinsfolk of both sexes. The *ammāyi* (mother's brother's wife) and the *chēdatti amma* (elder brother's wife) play a role in Nayar jokes and folk tales somewhat comparable to that of the stepmother in Europe. As was mentioned in connection with witchcraft, junior members of a taravād habitually resented these women's hold over their husbands and represented them as grasping, unscrupulous, and intent on robbing their husbands' juniors. This fear of the mother's brother's wife was however much more pronounced in North Malabar, where marriage was monogamous or polygynous and residence avunculocal.

Co-wives and the wives of brothers, being in different houses, had no institutionalized relationships and apparently very little contact. The husbands of women of a property group also had only slight relationships. There was no structure of authority between them because they performed no activities together. The younger men accorded some deference to the older, but all might sit together informally and exchange news.

Virtually nothing is known of the relationships between co-husbands except the testimony of several writers from the fifteenth to eighteenth centuries that they "agreed very well" with each other. They are said to have distributed the woman's time among them in a convenient manner "according as they can fix a term among themselves" (Hamilton, ed. Penzer, 1930, I: 172).

Among the Nayars of this area, households of the linked lineages or enangar fulfilled the customary obligations and carried out the ceremonial roles which were required of an individual's affinal or matrilateral kin in the patrilineal castes of Kerala. It was enangar who *must* take part in life-crisis rites, make gifts at first menstruation and marriage ceremonies, and come to assist at deaths. Enangar were of course often currently affines of the households in which they officiated, for sambandham relationships took place most intensively between lineages of the local caste group. However, the enangar relationship did not derive from particular sambandham ties nor was it brought about by particular tāli rites. It was rather a hereditary relationship of "perpetual affinity" between lineages as groups, which persisted irrespective of the making and breaking of particular sexual ties. When a man who happened to have sambandham with some woman of a household acted there in his role of enangan, he did so as a representative of his lineage, irrespective of his interpersonal marriage tie. Often, the particular persons who officiated as enangar did not happen to be currently having marital relations with any member of that house. This inter-group relationship of ceremonial obligation fitted the fact that particular marital ties were too transient and slender to carry the normal obligations of affinity.

Prerequisites of the Kinship System of Commoners

It is not definitely known how the institutions of group marriage and linked lineages arose among Central Kerala Nayars. In 1518 Barbosa, writing of the Nayars of Calicut, stated of group marriage: "And it is said that the kings made this law, in order that the Nayars should not be covetous and should not abandon the king's service" (Dames, 1921: 124). Similarly João de Barros wrote at about the same period: "They say that this (polyandry) is a very ancient law among them, and that it springs from the wish of a certain king to relieve the men of the burden of maintaining sons, and leave them ready for warlike service whensoever the king calls upon them" (*ibid.*: 241). Whether or not group marriage was instituted by a particular royal edict, we know that once it had begun it was enforceable by the laws of the Central kingdoms. Thus, according to at least one authority, a chief could compel a woman to receive as marital partners any of her enangar who wished to visit her (K. Kannan Nair, 1908: 186). The rights and duties of enangar in the administration of caste law were also sanctioned by the chief and, ultimately, by the king.

Considerable literary evidence suggests that a form of group marriage similar to that of Central Kerala existed among Nayars in at least some of the chiefdoms of the kingdom of Travancore in Southern Kerala. K. M. Panikkar, it is true, has argued that Travancore Nayar women were never polyandrous (1918: 270–271). Other Malabari writers, however, responding to Panikkar's statement, have argued convincingly that they were (Aiyappan, 1932*a*, 1932*b*, 1934; Iyer, 1932). K. P. Padmanabha Menon, in particular, supports the view that traditionally Nayar women in both Central and Southern Kerala were "held in common, every woman belonging to all the members of the tribe, and resistance to any of them was severely punished." In support he quotes two early statements concerning the chiefdom of Venmani, with its capital of Kartigapally, in North Travancore. Thus the Portuguese Archbishop Menezes in the mid-sixteenth century reported that "the king of Kartigapally enacted that in his kingdom any Nair was at liberty to be free with any woman of the caste high or low, and that he could kill a woman, with impunity, if she refuses a favor"; and the Dutch Captain Nieuhoff observed in 1664 that "It is commonly reported in these parts, that the kings of Venmani made a law, by which a man was empowered to kill any woman that should refuse him a kindness" (quoted in K. P. P. Menon, 1908: vii–viii). These quotations are especially interesting because they suggest that, in Travancore as in Central Kerala, plural unions on the part of women were not merely permissible but, in theory at least, enforceable by law.

Similarly, Nayar informants of a village near Haripad in Central Travancore told me that they understood that "long ago" Nayars of Travancore had the institution of the visiting husband together with polygyny and non-fraternal polyandry, like Central Kerala Nayars. The same informants reported that during the nineteenth century, after the Nayar armies were disbanded, residence became avunculocal among Nayars in this area of Travancore, non-fraternal polyandry died out, and for a few decades some Nayars practised fraternal poly-andry, with a group of brothers assuming collective responsibility for one or more co-resident wives and their young children. Other writ-ers also mention relatively modern cases of fraternal polyandry among Travancore Nayars (Iyer, 1932; Fawcett, 1901: 241). Later in the nineteenth century and during this century, however, Travancore matrilineal property groups began to disintegrate, and fraternal poly-andry gave place to monogamy. The Central Travancore sequence of duolocality with group marriage, to avunculocality with fraternal poly-andry, to partial neolocality with monogamy, is an interesting one in view of the fact that fraternal polyandry has, as far as I am aware, always been strictly forbidden among both duolocal Nayars of Cen-tral Kerala and avunculocal Nayars of North Kerala throughout the historical period. I was able to spend only a fortnight in Travancore and could not pursue the comparison.

The marriage of a woman to more than one man concurrently is not confined to the Nayars in southwest India. The double unilineal Tiyyars and some other higher polluting castes of Central Kerala had fraternal polyandry, and both fraternal and non-fraternal polyandry were customary among the Toda tribe of the Nilgiri hills. The Coorgs to the east of North Kerala are also said to have had fraternal poly-andry associated with patrilineal descent groups. The prevalence of various types of polyandry in southwest India generally suggests that *some* form of plural unions for women may have been very ancient among the Nayars, possibly predating their organization into king-doms.

Leaving aside the problem of origins, however, what I would argue is that the *specific* form of group marriage evolved among Central Kerala Nayars in the period of the native kingdoms was particularly adapted to their military organization, which in turn was made possible by the existence of the lower castes of sub-tenants and serfs. The work of the tenants and serfs absolved Nayar men from the duty of maintaining the women and children of either their natal or their conjugal units by their own productive activities. It set free most of these men for a lifetime of military service; in each matrilineal group only one old man was needed at home to organize the work of the household's retainers. Given matrilineal descent and inheritance, and given the mobility of men and the absence of male economic obligations to kinswomen, there was no reason why either men or women should restrict themselves to particular spouses. There was also, as the early European writers realized, a positive value for the kingdom in their not doing so, for plural marriages discouraged soldiers from forming deep attachments to particular wives and children, and encouraged them to focus their loyalty on military leaders and on the matrilineal groups through which they were recruited. At the same time, plural marriages provided the soldiers with ready comforts and a night's lodging both in their own villages and in other villages of the kingdom through which they might pass. Whether or not chiefs regularly enforced indiscriminate mating among Nayar women of their districts in order to strengthen their soldiers' allegiances, a system of group marriage involving optional multiple alliances certainly fitted the way of life of a landed militia, already (for historical reasons) organized into matrilineal descent groups. A close connection between group marriage and the military organization is further suggested in that, after the British had disbanded the armies in about 1800, although matrilineal descent persisted for over a century, group marriage rapidly died out. Within about thirty years monogamous marriage in Central Kerala, and monogamous or restricted, fraternally polyandrous marriage in Travancore, had become common, and fathers had assumed a definite role in the upbringing of their children.

Kinship in the Aristocratic Matrilineal Castes

THE LINEAGE

Among the retainer Nayars a household whose membership rose above about thirty tended to divide its property between its segments when the senior males who had spanned the segments were dead. Correspondingly, lineages and clans of retainer Nayars went through a gradual process of fission. This state of affairs was in harmony with the small amounts of land controlled by retainer property groups and with the relatively temporary relationship of retainer Nayars to their land. The conditions of kānam tenure not only allowed for changes in the tenures of plots of land within one village, but even permitted segments of an expanding taravād to change their feudal allegiances and if necessary to hive off from their natal village.

The situation was different in the aristocratic lineages of royalty and district chiefs. By jenmam right they owned large domains which could support greater numbers of members. Their members also had a stake in the political office which they were reluctant to surrender. On the whole these lineages tended to cohere for longer periods than did those of retainers. Some of them today number over three hundred members and trace their descent back to the fourteenth and fifteenth centuries. When segments of these lineages did move away from their ancestral lands it was usually because they had been conquered and forced to vacate their territories and offices.

In the beginning, when one of these aristocratic lineages rose to power, it did so as a small property group. It did so either (in the case of royals) through conquest or (in the case of chiefs) through being appointed to office by some royal power. When they acquired office these upstart property groups seem to have severed ties with their former lineages and clans and to have conferred on themselves a higher ritual rank as independent castes.

After a few generations such a property group might expand in numbers and separate out into segments. I lack data on the precise point at which aristocratic property groups segmented; it seems to have been always at a later point with them than with retainer Nayars. (Today, some royal and chiefly property groups have a time depth of eight or more generations and over a hundred members.) When fission did occur the segments moved into separate palaces, each taking a portion of the ancestral domain for its maintenance. The oldest man resident in each segment acted as kāranavan and managed its internal affairs. For a time at least, the political office remained vested in the oldest man of the lineage irrespective of branch. When he was able, he kept a tight hold over all the segments, deflecting part of their income to himself for the upkeep of his palace staff, private army, and the larger forces he mustered through his subordinate vassals in war. The office bearer also retained sole right to the customs dues on trade within his chiefdom or kingdom, and to the tribute from village headmen within his area of rule.

Theoretically, office-bearing lineages were supposed to cohere forever, the officer being the eldest man of the lineage regardless of branch. In fact, if the lineage continued to expand, some other development would occur within a few generations. What its pattern might be depended on the economic and political circumstances of the times. One pattern was for the political office itself to become divided between the segments some time after they had divided their private domain. The head of each segment would then become ruler in his own right over a portion of the original territory, either (in the case of royals) as an independent small king, or (in the case of district chiefs) as a small chief independent of the rest of his lineage but still owing nominal allegiance to the original king of the kingdom as a whole. This type of fission of offices took place in areas and periods in which for some reason trade was declining, customs dues were running low, and neither king nor chiefs could muster enough extra wealth to fight wars which would maintain them in full political control. This process went on apace from the fifteenth century to the end of the seventeenth both in Kolattunad and in Travancore, the northernmost and southernmost kingdoms of Kerala. They had been powerful kingdoms for a period, with the help of Chinese traders, but declined in the fifteenth century after the Chinese trade collapsed and the Arabs built up Calicut. After 1500, different trading powers supported the smaller chiefs of these areas in trade wars against each other, so that these kingdoms remained weak and disunited until the second quarter of the eighteenth century. During this period segments of the royal lineages in both kingdoms carved up much of each kingdom into virtually independent chiefdoms. Within each of these in turn, the lineages of formerly subordinate Nayar chiefs tended also to break into segments, each retaining control over four or five villages. Early in the eighteenth century the British and French each tried to consolidate North Malabar by allying themselves with different local powers, but their struggles were temporarily eclipsed by invasions from Bednur to the north and later, in the 1760's, from Mysore in the east. In Travancore the process of disintegration persisted until the British obtained a trade monopoly and, in the 1730's, helped the king to reconquer his kingdom once and for all and to establish a bureaucratic form of rule (Innes, 1908: 55–75; Pillai, 1940: 266–466; K. M. Panikkar, 1931: chap. V).

The other course of development was for one branch of a ruling lineage to seize the office and most of the private domains and, temporarily or permanently, exclude or banish the others. This process took place in areas and periods where one trading power was in the ascendant and wished to support a strong ruler with taxes, arms, and shipping, and through him to gain a monopoly of the pepper trade. Such maneuvers went on continually in the Cochin lineage during the period of European trade. In the late fourteenth or early fifteenth century the Cochin lineage disintegrated into five property groups. The Zamorins to the north, who were expanding with Arab aid, supported the Mutta ("Elder") branch, installed its head as king, and made him feudatory to Calicut. When the Portuguese arrived in 1500 they took up the cause of the Elaya ("Younger") branch, installed them as kings, and ousted the Elder branch and the Zamorin. By 1656 the Younger branch was dying out, as were the three other branches, and only the Elder branch had members available for adoption. Instead of allowing the king to adopt from the Elder branch as they should by custom have done, the Portuguese forced him to adopt from an unrelated lineage, the Rajas of Bettem, who ruled between Cochin and Calicut and who had just defected to the side of Cochin. The Elder branch then sought the help of the Zamorin and the Dutch, and defeated the Cochin Raja and the Portuguese in the war of 1600. The Dutch ousted the Portuguese from Cochin port and installed the Elder branch as their protégés on the throne. Despite such machinations, the Cochin kingdom never became permanently *divided* between branches of the royal lineage, because the office of kingship, supported by one or another merchant power, retained sufficient funds, equipment, and men to restore control over the whole.

The Zamorin's lineage was unusual in that from at least the thirteenth to the mid-eighteenth centuries it apparently did not greatly expand in numbers or divide into separate property groups. Indeed it several times almost died out and in 1705 had to adopt from the Nileswaram lineage, an offshoot of Kolattiri. There were therefore no dynastic wars in Calicut. Even had there been, however, it is safe to say that they would always have culminated in the supremacy of one branch and not in division of the kingdom. This was because throughout the period the Calicut port remained great. With the help of one trading power after another the kingship remained strong and, except for border losses, was able to maintain central judicial control and a system of differentiated political offices within the heart of the kingdom.

Within the Calicut kingdom, which was the strongest until the mid-eighteenth century, dynastic disputes among the district chiefs were usually settled by the king. Succession to district chiefship and to vil-

lage headships had to be ratified by the king and he could if necessary dispossess disaffected branches and exclude them from office.
This was true in the heart of the kingdom. Between Calicut and
Cochin, the Zamorins' perpetual enemy, lay several small chiefdoms
ruled by formerly independent Kshattriya lineages owing only a tenuous allegiance to one or the other side. In the perennial wars between
Calicut and Cochin disaffected branches of these lineages frequently
changed sides.

Village headmen's lineages, again, had their successions confirmed
by the chief or king to whom they owed immediate allegiance. When
a property group divided into segments, the tendency seems to have
been for the branch having the senior member to retain the ancestral
house, the office, and most of the village domain. The king or chief
sometimes installed a discarded branch of such a lineage in a vacant
office elsewhere, if the office-bearing lineage of that village had died
out. His power to do this rested on the fact that an office-bearing
lineage which was dying out could not adopt without the consent of
the officer of next higher rank. Lopped branches of village headmen's lineages which lost their domains and office seem to have reverted in time to the caste rank of retainer Nayars.

In most of the royal lineages and many of the chiefly lineages there
existed the institution of *sthānams*. These were titles carrying separate estates and sometimes subordinate political offices for the men
next in seniority to the ruler, irrespective of branch. The Zamorin's
lineage had five sthānams. The first was the Zamorin who had palaces
at Calicut and Ponnani. Second came a *sthāni* (title holder) who ruled
as chief of Nedunganad, a large chiefdom near the southern boundary whose former ruler had been conquered and executed. The third
sthāni regularly patrolled the southern frontier with an army. The
fourth and fifth had no political offices but lived on separate estates.
The rest of the lineage occupied one or more palaces in Calicut. When
a sthāni died, those next below him in age rank all moved up one
place. The ruling lineages of Kolattunad, Walluvanad, and Palghat
each had five sthānis and many of the lesser chiefs had two or three.
Cochin had no sthānis other than the king, but originally the eldest
male of the lineage retired into celibacy while the second ruled as
king. When the Portuguese came they abolished this rule and installed
the king themselves.

When a ruling lineage was financially and militarily strong, sthānams
strengthened its rule and helped it to cohere for a longer time than it
might otherwise have done. They lifted the senior men out of their

separate segments, gave them economic independence and a share in the government, and made them representatives of the lineage as a whole. If the lineage separated into two or more branch property groups, their estates were managed by their senior men after the sthānis had been removed. The whole lineage might thus cohere for a number of generations. When, however, taxes ran low and the political offices became financially weak, the sthānis had a tendency to revert to the property groups from which they came and, as heads of them, to seek independent rule over a portion of the chiefdom or kingdom. Sthānams were thus an integrative device which developed when a ruling lineage was already strong. They could not maintain its strength if the economic basis of its power was removed, nor could they ultimately prevent disputes of the branches for the central office if the lineage became very large.

RELATIONS BETWEEN ARISTOCRATIC LINEAGES

Each office-bearing lineage had as its enangar one or two higher-ranking lineages from the range of those within which its women were wont to draw visiting husbands. Thus village headmen often had their district chiefs as enangar. A district chief's lineage might have the royal lineage, a conquered royal lineage, or a Nambudiri Brahman family as enangar. The Calicut royal lineage had two conquered royal feudatory lineages as enangar, and some other royal lineages had Nambudiri Brahman families. The enangar fulfilled the usual ceremonial obligations at life-crisis rites, and tied the tālis of girls. Unlike those among the retainer Nayars, these enangar obligations were not reciprocal. A district chief's lineage might thus receive enangar services from royals, but would give them to village headmen. Appropriately, the enangar relationship among aristocrats, like the marriage relationship, was thus asymmetrical. Unfortunately I lack information about whether aristocratic enangar, like those of retainers, had the right to bring to trial offenders against the religious laws of caste.

It is clear that hypergamous marriages and asymmetrical enangar relations were adapted to the potential political and ritual mobility of office-bearing lineages and to the fact that at any given time such a lineage might not be able or willing to acknowledge others as its equals in political or ritual rank. In most situations therefore an office-bearing lineage could act as though it formed a separate caste. There were some contexts, however, in which this was not possible. One of these was adoption. If a lineage was obliged to adopt, it had to find some other lineage whose members it was willing to acknowledge as peers. This problem was usually surmounted by adopting from a lineage with which one was neither at enmity nor in regular asymmetrical political relationships. Thus the Travancore royal lineage several times adopted from Kolattiri, at the other end of Kerala, and the Calicut lineage from Nileswaram, the northernmost independent chiefdom of the Malabar Coast.

The giving and receiving of food, normally a hallmark of caste ranking, presented other problems. Some royal lineages were vegetarians and employed Nambudiri Brahman cooks who, being ritually higher than themselves, were permitted to serve them with food. Others seem to have drawn to themselves a small group of lineages as cooks and houseservants upon whom they conferred equivalence of caste rank, while maintaining them as their social inferiors and not intermarrying with them.

RESIDENCE AND KINSHIP RELATIONSHIPS

The property groups of village headmen's and chiefly lineages had residential arrangements similar to those of retainer Nayars, except that their houses were larger. The men of these groups visited their lower-ranking wives in the latters' homes. If they lived nearby, visits would occur at night; if at a distance, the husband might visit his wife about once a month and remain for two or three days. Similarly, women of these groups received visits from their higher-ranking husbands at convenient intervals. If he came from a distance the husband brought his own servants and cook, occupied a building near the taravād house, and stayed at his conjugal family's expense.

In the royal lineages each property group occupied a large palace. Within it each princess had her own suite of rooms in company with her children under the age of fifteen. Princes over this age had private rooms in a separate wing. The Nambudiri Brahman husbands of princesses (who were younger sons in their own households and had no managerial duties) lived at the palace for the duration of their marriages and were maintained at its expense. In the daytime they occupied a building within the royal courtyard, with its own bathing pool, kitchen, and servants, and visited their wives' rooms mainly at night. Junior princes visited their wives in nearby retainers' households or in more distant chiefly taravāds. Each royal sthāni had his own palace, estate, and retainers' for the duration of his office. He would normally bequeath a house to a Nayar wife within the palace grounds and visit her and his children there.

Although group marriage appears to have existed in theory among aristocrats, polyandry was in fact perhaps less common than among retainer Nayars. Princesses are said to have been sometimes polyandrous and divorce was freely practiced, but a princess probably did not regularly entertain more than one husband at a time. Older Nambudiri Brahman husbands often introduced their own younger kinsmen into the palace; for this reason both matrilateral cross-cousin marriage and paternal parallel-cousin marriage were common in Brahman-royal unions. Princes, chiefs, and high-ranking Nambudiri Brahmans were sometimes polygynous. Their wives, however, were probably seldom polyandrous; for aristocrats seem often to have exercised the power to monopolize the attentions of their favorite Nayar wives. They were therefore more sure of the paternity of their Nayar sons, upon whom they sometimes conferred military or political offices.

In all hypergamous unions the husband observed the normal all-India caste rules of pollution except with regard to sexual intercourse. He might not receive food from his wife's caste and had little communication with her or her children in the daytime. Affinal relationships were correspondingly more restricted than in the retainer castes, for a woman had very little communication with her husband's natal kin; she and her children used no kinship terms for them. If the wife was of lower social as well as ritual rank than the husband she did not visit his natal home. Conversely, princesses do not seem to have demeaned themselves socially by visiting the homes of their ritually higher-ranking husbands. A Nayar wife who was of similar social rank to her Brahman or temple-servant husband might occasionally visit the womenfolk of his home, but she was received in an outbuilding and might not eat with them. Similarly, husbands in hypergamous unions had highly formalized and restricted relationships with the matrilineal kinsmen of their wives. The wives' elder kinsmen were accorded the respect due their age; the husband, that due his superior ritual rank.

Relationships between matrilineal kin among the aristocrats were a sharpened version of those found among retainer Nayars. Between men, the etiquette associated with age rank was highly stereotyped. Among the senior princes who were likely to compete for political office it reached the point of avoidance, a condition facilitated by their separate residences as sthānis. The etiquette of respect was similarly elaborated between men and women. After the age of fifteen a prince might converse with older women of his palace only by appointment and in some public place. He must scrupulously avoid the presence of younger kinswomen from the time of their tāli rite. In the potentially larger property groups of the aristocrats these rules of etiquette obviously militated against the expression of aggression between men as well as preventing incestuous relations between the sexes.

Kinship Terms

As might be expected, kinship terms were used only between matrilineal kin and between ego and the spouses of members of his lineage. The terms were as follows.

A. MATRILINEAL KIN (extended throughout the lineage)

(1) *Mūttassi* ("Oldest woman"). M. and F. speaking. Woman of the second ascending generation, primarily MoMo. May be prefaced by *valiya* ("big") or *cheriya* ("small") for women respectively older or younger than MoMo.

(2) *Ammāman* ("Male mother"). M. and F. speaking. Men of first and second ascending generations, primarily mother's own brother. May be prefaced by valiya or cheriya for men of first ascending generation respectively older or younger than Mo. May be prefaced by *mūtta* ("oldest") for men of second ascending generation.

(3) *Amma*. M. and F. speaking. Women of first ascending generation, primarily own mother. Prefaced by valiya or cheriya for women respectively older or younger than Mo.

(4) *Jyēshtan*. M. and F. speaking. Men of own generation older than ego, primarily own elder brother. Sometimes corrupted to *ētan*.

(5) *Anujan*. M. and F. speaking. Men of own generation younger than ego, primarily own younger brother. Reference only.

(6) *Jyēshtatti*. M. and F. speaking. Women of own generation older than ego, primarily own elder sister. May be corrupted to *eratti* (South Malabar) or *chēchi* (Cochin).

(7) *Anujatti*. M. and F. speaking. Women of own generation younger than ego, primarily own younger sister. Reference only.

(8) *Āngala*. F. speaking. Own brother by same mother. Reference only.

(9) *Pengal*. M. speaking. Own sister by same mother. Reference only.

(10) *Marumakan*. M. speaking. Male of first or second descending generations, primarily own sister's son. Reference only.

(11) *Marumakal*. M. speaking. Female of first or second descending generation, primarily own sister's daughter. Reference only.

(12) *Makan*. F. speaking. Male of first descending generation, primarily own son. Reference only.

(13) *Makal*. F. speaking. Female of first descending generation, primarily own daughter. Reference only.

(14) *Pērakutti* ("Name child"). F. speaking. Male or female child

of second descending generation, primarily own daughter's child. Reference only.

(15) *Kāranavar* (singular, *kāranavan*). M. and F. speaking. All males of the lineage older than ego, living or dead. Primarily, the eldest living man of ego's property group. Reference only.

(16) *Anandravar* (singular, *anandravan*). M. speaking. All males of the lineage younger than ego. Primarily, junior males of ego's property group. Reference only.

Comment: Older relatives are addressed by terms; younger, by name.

The overriding of generations which appears in terms 2, 10, and 11 is suitable because the men under 2 are not in the direct line of ascent and their authoritative roles are similar. Terms 15 and 16 further emphasize the age rank of lineage males regardless of segment or generation.

The separation of terms 1 and 3 may be related to the fact that women are in a direct line of descent. Moreover, 1's role is more authoritative than that of 3.

The existence of special terms 8 and 9 points up the interdependence of own brother and sister on which the unity of the sibling group and the cohesion of the property group are based.

The merging of lineals and collaterals within each generation points up the lack of institutional segregation of one woman and her children.

B. AFFINES AND NON-MATRILINEAL COGNATES

(1) *Bhārya.* M. speaking. Wi in the sambandham relationship. Reference only.

(2) *Bartāvu.* F. speaking. Hu in the sambandham relationship. Reference only.

(3) *Sambandhakkar.* M. and F. speaking. Collective. Husbands of women of ego's lineage, primarily of ego's property group. Reference only.

(4) *Mūttacchan* ("Oldest father"). M. and F. speaking. Hu of Al.

(5) *Acchan.* M. and F. speaking. Hu of A3, especially of own mother. May be prefaced by valiya or cheriya according to age of the man's wife in relation to ego's mother. Followed by the caste title (e.g., Nambudiri) if he is of higher caste.

(6) *Ammāyi.* M. and F. speaking. Wife of A2.

(7) *Aliyan.* M. speaking. Reciprocal between a man and his wife's lineage kinsmen of her generation, primarily within her property group. Reference only.

(8) *Jyēshtatti Amma.* Wife of A4. M. and F. speaking. Sometimes

corrupted to *chēdatti amma* (Cochin) or *eratti amma* (S. Malabar).

(9) *Chētan.* M. and F. speaking, reference; M. speaking only, address. A particular shortened form of *jyēshtan* (ElBr), reserved for the husband of A6.

(10) *Makan.* M. speaking. Son of ego's wife. Reference only.

(11) *Makal.* M. speaking. Daughter of ego's wife. Reference only.

(12) *Pērakutti.* M. speaking. Child of ego's wife's daughter. Reference only. Not always used.

(13) *Appan.* M. and F. speaking. Ritual husband (*tāli* tier) of ego's mother.

(14) *Manavalan.* F. speaking. Ritual husband. Reference only.

All other affines and cognates were referred to by descriptive compound terms (e.g., *ende acchande marumakan,* "my father's nephew"; *ende anujande bhārya,* "my younger brother's wife"). Persons of 8 and 9 were also often referred to by descriptive compound terms.

A man might *address* his wife's matrilineal kin older than himself by the same terms as she did but he was not obliged to do so. He might also address them by their names and caste titles. They addressed him by his personal name, adding the caste title if he were of higher caste.

A man addressed his wife's younger matrilineal kinsmen by name. Because of the avoidance relationship he and his wife's younger sisters used no terms or names to address each other.

If she knew them and was of the same caste as they were, a woman addressed her husband's older matrilineal relatives by the same terms as he did. She addressed by name those younger than herself. She called her husband's younger sister who was older than herself *jyēshtatti,* (elder sister). Because of the avoidance relationship no terms or names were used between a woman and her husband's brothers who were older than she.

In hypergamous marriages a woman and her husband's natal kin used no terms to address each other.

An individual used no terms, but only names, to address his father's matrilineal kin.

Comment: In general, the restricted use of reference terms for affines and the lack of terms for patrilateral kin other than the father reflect the slenderness of the marriage tie and the lack of obligations to these kin.

Affinal terms were mainly restricted to the spouses of ego's older matrilineal kin, persons with whom he had fairly regular contact. Even these, however, might be *referred* to by descriptive compound terms. When one of these terms applies to more than one relative the equation issues simply from the equation of the matrilineal kin who are their spouses.

There was a lack of terms for affines younger than ego because unless sex difference caused ego to avoid them completely, the principle of age rank made it possible to address them by name. Descriptive compound terms were adequate to refer to them.

However, the existence of the special reciprocal reference term between brothers-in-law points up the uniqueness of the brother-sister tie and the fact that a woman's brothers and her husband were brought into a specially close relationship by virtue of their claims upon the woman who linked them.

The use of B3 as a collective term reflects the fact that, as sex partners and fathers, these men had a common interest in ego's matrilineal group and it in them.

MODERN CHANGES

Since about 1890, as I have described elsewhere (Gough, 1952), Nayar marriage has become monogamous and men have assumed rights in and obligations to their children. The matrilineage is gradually disintegrating and the elementary family is gradually emerging as the key group in a system of bilateral, interpersonal kinship ties.

As a result of these changes, terms formerly restricted to matrilateral kin are today sometimes used to address corresponding patrilateral kin, although this usage is not yet standardized. The most common equations are MoMo = FaMo, MoMoBr = FaMoBr, MoFa = FaFa, MoBr = FaBr, MoSi = FaSi, MoBrWi = FaBrWi, and MoSiHu = FaSiHu. Cross cousins and paternal parallel cousins still have no reference terms but if older are addressed as siblings. No other regular changes are observable for kin of ego's or ascending generations, and no regular changes have occurred in terms for descending generations.

As the system now stands, therefore, ego's matrilineal kin of the same sex are still merged within each generation, but the transferences to patrilateral kin have created a mixture between "lineal" and "generation" systems in the sense of Murdock and earlier writers, as far as the own and ascending generations are concerned (Murdock, 1949: 149). A "generation" classification is used for both sexes of ego's generation, with all cousins equated with siblings. A "generation" classification is also used for women of the first ascending generation, if we discount the age prefixes used to differentiate older and younger sisters of the parents. If we classify the age prefixes as constituting separate terms, we have a "lineal" classification for the women of this generation. Men of the first ascending generation are classified in a "lineal" manner, with FaBr = MoBr, both separated from Fa. Female affines of the first ascending generation are "lineal," with FaBrWi = MoBrWi, both separated from Mo. Male affines of the first ascending generation are "generational," with Fa = MoSiHu = FaSiHu. The terms faithfully reflect an extreme matrilineal system which is in process of breaking down in favor of bilateral kindreds.

Nayar: North Kerala

The Nayars of North Kerala live between the Chandragiri and the Kora rivers. This area lay north of the Calicut kingdom and had been conquered by the Kolattiri kings at some period before the fourteenth century (Logan, 1951, I: 283; Innes, 1908: 57). It then disintegrated into the small kingdoms of Kolattunad, Kottayam, and Kadattunad. North Kerala was invaded from the Bednur kingdom of South Canara in the 1730's. It was later occupied by Muslim armies from Mysore between 1766 and 1792, after which it passed under British rule (Logan, 1951, I: 360, 399–473). This account deals with conditions before 1760, so far as these are known, and with the major changes of the nineteenth century.

Ecology

The mountains approach nearer to the sea in North Kerala than in Central Kerala. There are fewer stretches of lowland suitable for wet-rice cultivation, and gardens of fruits, nuts, vegetables, and spices on hillsides are more extensive. Since rice was the main subsistence crop, population density was lower than in Central Kerala. The houses of a village (*dēsam*) were scattered in gardens on hillsides surrounding a wet-rice flat in a valley. Villages were often separated by three to six miles of uncultivated scrub or jungle. Until the Mysoreans built roads after the 1760's, transport and communication by narrow mountain paths were difficult, especially in the heavy monsoons.

North Kerala had four major ports during the period of European trade—Cannanore, Tellicherry, Mahé, and Badagara (Hamilton, ed. 1727: 369–371). Pepper and other spices were exported from inland villages probably from Roman times, but villages were virtually self-sufficient for food until the mid-eighteenth century. After that time the Mysoreans' roads permitted greater import of goods both from the coast and from Mysore, and greater spatial mobility. In the nineteenth century cash-crop farming for export increased, as did imports of food and other goods. The population expanded and much formerly waste land was brought under cultivation as gardens for the production of coconuts, pepper, cashew nuts, and cinnamon. Higher in the mountains Europeans developed estates of tea, coffee, and spices, which attracted wage labor from villages to the west. The development of the steamship, the opening of the Suez Canal in 1869, and the entry of railways into Kerala in the 1860's were significant events in this process.

Political and Economic Systems

Traditionally, a hierarchy of the major Hindu castes was present as in Central Kerala, except that large areas of North Kerala had no Pulayas or agricultural serfs (*ibid.*, I: 148). Nambudiri Brahmans were fewer than in Central Kerala, but they controlled a small number of temple estates and claimed religious superiority over the Nayar rulers. Muslims were the dominant trading population of the ports and inland trading centers.

The mountainous terrain, heavy rainfall, poor communications, sparse population, and comparatively low productivity made political centralization more difficult than in Central Kerala. The ancient Kolattiri kingdom was divided into chiefdoms and villages in a manner similar to the later kingdom of the Zamorin, but judicial control was perhaps never as well centralized as in the Calicut kingdom. From the fourteenth century, when the Zamorins captured most of the Arab trade, the Kolattiri kingship lost some of its former power. The kingdom disintegrated into three smaller, virtually independent kingdoms—Kolattunad, Kottayam, and Kadattunad—plus a number of small border chiefdoms of uncertain allegiance (*ibid.*, I: 343–344). Each of the three North Kerala kingdoms probably had a population of between 150,000 and 250,000, in contrast to the Calicut kingdom, which seems to have numbered some 600,000 to 720,000 (see note 5, page 473).

After 1500 each of the North Kerala rulers sought the help of one or another of the mutually hostile European and Middle Eastern trading powers, thus maintaining a state of fragmentation until the Mysorean conquest. In the struggles of the seventeenth and eighteenth centuries some new Nayar chiefs also arose with mushroom rapidity on the basis of European support and gained partially autonomous sway over small groups of villages. Political and social mobility among Nayar aristocrats was thus more marked in North Kerala than in the more stable central kingdoms. Indeed, a North Kerala proverb remarks that "When a high-caste Nayar becomes ripe, he turns into a king."

Low productivity and poor communications perhaps made the exaction of tribute more difficult than in Central Kerala, and this fact, plus the uncertain nature of trade, made the local rulers perennially short of funds. This is probably the reason why, although they were trained for warfare in gymnasia in their villages, Nayars were not regularly conscripted into a national army. Instead, they merely fought sporadically on behalf of local chiefs. Further, chiefs and village headmen were insufficiently strong to bring all the land under their control. Their domains were larger than those of Nayar commoners, but most commoner Nayar property groups were independent small landlords in their own right within their villages. Since they were not full-time warriors and since in many areas they had no serfs, Nayar commoners also did part of their own cultivation on their small estates. Part of their land, however, they leased to Tiyyar tenants as in Central Kerala. The polluting castes of village servants had the same rights and spatial distribution as in Central Kerala. In general, the economic processes of reciprocity and redistribution in villages proceeded in a comparable manner.

As independent warrior-cultivators, the Nayar commoners were not divided into separate castes of retainers owing allegiance as vassals and *kānam* tenants to different kinds of lords. Most villages were nominally under Nayar village headmen. In villages of the Kottayam and Kadattunad kingdoms, both the headman's lineage and those of the Nayar commoners belonged to a large caste called Nambiars, who appear to have intermarried throughout the kingdom. Although of the same general caste as commoners, and not forbidden by religious law from intermarrying equally with commoners, Nambiar village headmen's lineages tended, however, to intermarry only with each other or to take wives only from the commoners, occasionally giving their own women in marriage to chiefs or Brahmans. Chiefs claimed a higher caste rank as Samantan Nambiars, and royalty as Kshattriyas. These aristocratic lineages conducted hypergamous marriages with each other and with Nambudiris as in Central Kerela.

Judicial processes were somewhat less centralized than in the Central kingdoms. At least in theory, grave crimes and civil disputes in urban centers seem to have been tried in royal courts, but most civil disputes inland were apparently tried by local chiefs. Under the chiefs, caste assemblies of neighborhoods took care of crimes against religious law as in the Central kingdoms. Murder among Nayars

sometimes led to blood feuds between lineages (*ibid.*, I: 195–196).
Chiefs could usually cut short a feud between commoner lineages, but
even these feuds occasionally ran their course for a generation, although cognatic and affinal ties between lineages helped to bring
them to a close. Greater feuds were sometimes waged between the
lineages of village headmen or chiefs of adjacent districts, in which
the commoner Nayars of each area might participate.

Matrilineal Units

THE CLAN

Among Nambiar commoners the largest matrilineal unit was the clan
(*vamsham* or *illam*). It had the functions of exogamy and mutual
hospitality. Common descent was merely stipulated and not demonstrated and the order of segmentation within the clan was unknown.
The clan might be dispersed throughout a kingdom or even, perhaps,
between kingdoms. Its members might point to a particular village as
their original ancestral site, but each clan seems to have been much
older and its history less clearly documented than among Nayar retainers in Central Kerela. There is no doubt that clans became much
more dispersed in the nineteenth century than they had traditionally
been because of the development of new areas of cultivation and increased mobility between villages. However, even traditionally the
clan seems to have had more members and a wider spread than in the
Central area. Its characteristics may be attributed to several factors.
First, Nambiars were not divided into separate retainer castes. Thus,
although the majority of commoner marriages were within the village,
Nambiars did have greater freedom to marry and move more freely
between villages throughout the realm. Lacking a strong superordinate political structure and internal caste differentiation to give form
to their relationships, they had larger kinship units. Newcomers to a village probably did not need to become affiliated to its assembly by order
of a superior political authority. Instead, they could probably affiliate
themselves with their clan fellows and so at once be provided also with
classificatory affines in other clans. Second, Nambiars practised
avunculocal residence; husband and wife lived in the husband's
matrilineal ancestral house (Buchanan, 1807: 513–514). Sons normally
moved back to their own matrilineal homes at puberty, but daughters
moved to their husbands' homes. However, Nambiar fathers occasionally gave privately acquired land to their wives and children
when they were able. The children might then settle permanently in

the father's village, if this was different from the mother's. In this way, matrilineal kin might become widely scattered between many villages, while remembering the village from which their matrilineal forebears sprang.

THE SUB-CLAN

This group corresponded to the clan in Central Kerala. It was a segment of the clan whose members seem to have been located within one chiefdom. The structure and functions of this group were identical with those of the clan in Central Kerala, the members observing death and birth pollutions as well as exogamy.

THE LINEAGE

As in Central Kerala, the lineage was that portion of a clan located in one neighborhood (tara). Traditionally there seem to have been about six to ten lineages in one neighborhood, as in Central Kerala. A lineage was internally segmented and segmentation was relevant to the reversion of property. Exogamy, the observance of pollution, and the extension of kinship terms inhered in the lineage. Perhaps because village headship was weaker than in Calicut and each commoner lineage stronger as an organized group of kinsfolk, rites connected with the lineage were more prominent in the North than in the Center (Gough, 1958). There were few or no neighborhood temples of Bhagavadi. Instead, each lineage held a grand annual festival to its own patron Bhagavadi and to minor male deities, in which the lower castes took part. We have mentioned blood feuds between lineages, which indicate that a lineage was, in popular thought, if not in law, considered responsible for its members' physical protection.

Little is known today of the enangar relationship in North Kerala. It did exist, and enangar are said to have attended life-crisis rites and to have had some function in neighborhood caste trials of offenders against religious law. However, enangar did not tie the tālis of immature girls and did not participate in any form of group marriage. Among Nambiars and in most of the aristocratic Nayar lineages a girl's tāli was tied before puberty by some local Nambudiri Brahman. He was often an old man, and he appears to have had no right of cohabitation. The woman and her children did not observe pollution at his death. As far as I can judge the tāli rite in this area was merely an initiation rite which, at least in the nineteenth century, removed the ritual danger of cohabiting with a virgin (Gough, 1955). It also instituted the etiquette associated with incest prohibitions between the girl and her matrilineal kinsmen.

THE PROPERTY GROUP

The property group, a segment of the lineage, was among Nambiar commoners of roughly the same size and internal composition as among the Nayar retainers of Central Kerala. Its members jointly owned both movable and immovable property in the same manner. Its kāranavan managed the estate, had legal guardianship over members, and was legally responsible for them to the local caste assembly and to the chief. All Nayar property groups appear to have owned some garden and rice lands as *jenmis*. In addition some leased land on kānam tenure from chiefs, royalty, or Brahmans if any were present in their village. A property group whose membership was expanding might bring under cultivation waste land belonging to the chief on a tenure known as *kurikānam*. The tenant had the right of occupancy for twelve years without paying rent; he then paid an annual share of produce to the landlord. The improvements he made (trees, houses, etc.) were his own and he could not be evicted without compensation for them.

Residence was ideally *avunculocal*. Plural marriages for women were forbidden, and a man normally brought his wife to live with him on his matrilineal estate for the duration of the marriage. This mode of residence was apparently related to population density and to the sexual division of labor. Some duolocal marriages did exist between partners living in nearby houses in the same village. However, houses and villages were so scattered that most men would have had difficulty in maintaining a visiting relationship with a wife. Matrilocal residence was also disadvantageous because men did much of the work of cultivation on their own estates, were required to defend their estates against invaders, and were mobilized by the chiefs in war on the basis of property-group membership. A few junior men lived matrilocally for short periods, but the kāranavan and most of the adult men lived on their own estates.

In the relatively small property groups of commoners, the dwelling group was thus often an avunculocal extended family. It would comprise a group of brothers, their wives and immature children, their adult sisters' sons, and the wives and small children of these men. Divorced or widowed women born into the property group also had the right of permanent residence there, and married women born into it might return to live there for several weeks or months when they wished.

In the larger property groups of some commoners, village headmen, and chiefs, the main ancestral house might be reserved for

divorced or widowed women of the group and their children, together with temporarily divorced men or elderly widowers. The
kāranavan, his wife, and his immature children would occupy a wing
of the ancestral house or a separate building in the same courtyard.
Married men of the group would live with their wives and children
in separate houses, all on the matrilineal estate. The kāranavan would
then allocate separate gardens and rice fields for usufruct to each
married man. A junior would often hold such land on kānam tenure
from the taravād as a whole. The kāranavan would retain a larger
portion of the estate for his own maintenance and that of unmarried
persons living in the ancestral house. In any case he retained ultimate
management of the whole property and might retract portions of it at
will. If, however, a junior man leased new land from the taravād
on kurikānam tenure, the improvements he made on it might, by
custom although not by law, become the separate property of his
mother's matrilineal descendants. If, later, the whole property was
divided between major segments of the property group, each branch
might take as its share the fields and gardens on which improvements
had been made by male members of that branch. In the larger
aristocratic taravāds one or two sthānam estates might be set aside
for the men immediately junior to the kāranavan. Their holders
managed such estates with greater independence than the plots allocated to more junior men. All cultivation was carried on with the
aid of Tiyyar laborers attached by hereditary right to the taravād. In
some cases also plots were given on sub-tenure to Tiyyar cultivating
tenants in the same manner as in Central Kerala.

A man might also—at least in the nineteenth century—with the
consent of his own and his wife's kāranavan, lease land on kānam or
kurikānam tenure from his wife's taravād. A few junior men actually
went to live matrilocally in the wife's ancestral house or in a separate
house which they built on the wife's ancestral estate. Houses and improvements to land provided by a husband in this way customarily
became the separate property of the wife and her matrilineal descendants. Land on which such improvements had been made also
normally passed to the wife's descendants as their share when the
whole property of the wife's taravād was finally divided. Matrilocal
residence by a junior man was rare and could always be objected to
by the man's kāranavan if his services were needed at home. However, a man who was himself a kāranavan had considerable freedom
to build a house and develop new gardens on his wife's taravād
estate, which would later enrich his wife's matrilineal descendants. If

the wife's taravād was near his own he might divide his time between his own ancestral house and the private house he had built for his wife and her descendants on her ancestral estate.

Although this was contrary to customary law, some men also managed to give jenmam land outright to a wife and her matrilineal descendants, thus founding a new branch taravād through the wife. This practice greatly increased in the nineteenth century, when new gardens were continually being developed on former waste land and when land became freely marketable. In 1896, indeed, a law was finally passed enabling a man's wife and children to inherit half of his self-acquired intestate property (Malabar Marriage Act, 1896). Occasional gifts of land to the wife and her descendants were, however, known long before the British period, although they were against the law. At the political level, kings and chiefs occasionally gave large domains, together with the office of chief or village headman, to their wives' matrilineal descendants. The chiefships of both Nileswaram and Kadattunad are said to have been formed in this way by gifts from Kolattiri kings before the fourteenth century; both later became virtually independent kingdoms (Logan, 1951, I: 343; Ayyar, 1938: 4). Many smaller territories and political offices were similarly bequeathed during the period of European trade. On a smaller scale, the kāranavan of a Nambiar taravād sometimes managed to take out a portion of the fallow jenmam land of his own taravād, cultivate it, and give it to his wife and her descendants. Naturally, such gifts, which were in no sense a part of acknowledged lawful custom, led to disputes with the donor's matrilineal kin and sometimes, in the next generation, to feuds between lineages.

Gifts of land or improvements by a man to his wife's descendants led to the existence of branch property groups, called *tāvari-taravāds*, within the main property group. After the donor's death the wife's kāranavan might manage such a small estate on behalf of her branch, retaining the income separately for her and her children. More commonly, the donor's eldest son became the kāranavan of the tāvari property, while the branch also continued to receive its ancestral dues out of the property of the taravād as a whole. When a stirpital division of the whole taravād occurred, this branch might claim both its separate estate and its share of the ancestral property. If the donor had been a chief and the gift was large, the branch to which it was given might, however, choose to leave its taravād without taking a share of the ancestral estate and to found a new taravād home on its new land. Tāvari-taravāds were, however, rare among commoners until the second half of the nineteenth century. Their existence before 1750 seems to have been chiefly associated with conquest of land by chiefs. After the British conquest they became associated rather with the gradual expansion of the population to newly cultivated lands, and with the ability of men to acquire land as personal and freely marketable property.

Recent Developments in North and Central Kerala Contrasted

The modern North Kerala practice, whereby a man acquires newly cultivated garden land and gives it to his wife and children, makes Nayar residence heterogeneous at the present time. My data come from a village of Kottayam division where, in 1948, the great majority of Nambiar men were small owner- or tenant-cultivators. It was found that out of 42 Nambiar houses, 23 (55 per cent) had been built by individual men and given to their wives and children. Only 45 per cent had been built in the traditional manner by a matrilineally related group of men for their taravād.

Regarding the constitution of households, it was found that 29 per cent were "traditional," avunculocal extended family households comprising matrilineally related men, their wives, and small children, with or without divorced or widowed mothers or sisters of these men; 48 per cent contained an elementary family with or without another relative of either husband or wife—a widowed mother, unmarried sibling, etc.; 14 per cent contained a widow or divorcee with her unmarried children; 7 per cent contained a segment of a lineage —a group of matrilineally related men *and* women of the Central Kerala type, with the men visiting their wives in other households; 2 per cent (1 house) contained a man whose wife had just died, and the unmarried children.

Taking the residence of the 53 married couples by household, it was found that 26 per cent lived in the traditional manner in the matrilineal home of the husband. Some of these husbands were kāranavans; others lived avunculocally with a mother's brother. Fifteen per cent lived duolocally as in Central Kerala, with the husband visiting the wife. At least half, however, were couples in which the wife had recently had a child and was only temporarily living in her natal home; she would later return to her husband's matrilineal home, thus bringing the total percentage of couples in the husband's matrilineal home up to about 33 per cent. Six per cent lived patrilocally in the husband's father's private house, while 4 per cent lived matrilocally in a home with the wife's mother and sometimes with others of her older matrilineal kin. Twenty-six couples (49 per cent) lived neolocally in a house provided by the husband and containing no natal kin of either husband or wife. Of these 26 neolocally resident couples, 6 (11 per cent) lived in a house which the husband had inherited from his dead father; 3 (6 per cent of the total) lived in a house which the husband had obtained from his taravād; 14 (26 per cent) lived in a house newly built by the husband for his wife.

These figures may be contrasted with the modern picture in a Central Kerala village, where the marketability of land and labor have also brought about a partial disintegration of matrilineal descent groups and an emergence of the elementary family as a residential and economic unit. Both in Central and in North Kerala, moreover, marriage has been compulsorily monogamous since the 1930's, men have been legally obliged to maintain their wives and children, and the whole of man's private intestate property has passed to his mother, wife, and children at his death (Madras *Marumakkattāyam* Act, 1933; Cochin Nayar Act, 1938; Nair, 1941: 306). In addition, it has now become legally possible for the members of a taravād to divide their matrilineal ancestral property on a per capita basis. Once the ancestral property has been divided into individual shares in this way it becomes private property in law and is heritable in the same manner as are self-acquisitions. Both in Central and North Kerala, therefore, economic change and resultant modern laws have combined to break down traditional matrilineal descent groups.

In Central Kerala, however, population is denser and there has been less waste land available for individual cultivation. Over the past hundred years, therefore, when individual men have acquired private plots, it has more often been through purchase of already cultivated land than through cultivation of virgin land. Further, Nayar men in Central Kerala, having been a professional militia, tended after the disbanding of their armies either to remain noncultivating owners and tenants or where possible to move into new forms of salaried employment. Central Kerala today is more urbanized than is North Kerala, so that a much greater proportion of Nayars have salaried work in factories, as clerks, as government servants, as schoolteachers, or in the armed services. Many are unemployed and merely live from their ancestral lands. Particularly among retainer Nayars, who are relatively poor, men have amassed less self-acquired land than was possible for Nayar cultivators in North Kerala. Moreover, because Nayar men are often not themselves the cultivators of their land, there has been a tendency—under the new law of division of taravād property—for women and immature children to retain the ancestral houses and much of the land and for men to take their individual shares of the property in cash. Thus, having left their taravāds with their shares, some men now find themselves living in a house owned by the wife and her young children. Other men pool their share of property with that of the wife and jointly buy a new garden and house. When the location of their work permits it, most men remain in their ancestral homes until middle age and visit their wives in the traditional manner.

Modern residential patterns in Central Kerala, although moving in the direction of autonomy for the elementary family, thus show a different bias from that seen in North Kerala. Our contrast is made with data from a Cochin village three miles from a large town, where 75 per cent of Nayars of retainer castes worked for wages in the town. Here, out of 65 high-caste Nayar houses, 40 (61 per cent) had been built by kāranavans for their taravāds in the traditional manner; only 22 per cent had been built by a man for his wife and children, and 11 per cent had been built or bought jointly by husband and wife; 3 per cent had been built by a man for his private use, and 3 per cent by a woman for herself and her children.

Taking the constitution of households, we find that 46 per cent contained matrilineage segments more or less of the traditional type, except that one or more husbands of the women might live regularly in the house. Seventeen per cent contained a "broken" matrilineage segment, the adult men of which had left their natal kinswomen, taken a share of the property in cash, and gone to live with their wives. In these houses the husbands of the remaining women might or might not be living with their wives. Twenty-nine per cent of the households were simple elementary families; 3 per cent contained only one man; 3 per cent contained an extended family composed of some modern mixture of matrilineal and patrilateral kin; and one house contained a widow with her small children.

Taking the residence of married couples by household, we find that out of 100 couples, 58 lived duolocally, the husband dividing his time between his natal home and that of his wife in the traditional manner. In some cases the wife might occasionally move for a few weeks to live in the husband's natal home if circumstances made this particularly desirable. Such an arrangement was however very modern in Central Kerala; it was much disliked by women and was seldom resorted to. Eighteen of the couples lived matrilocally; the couple shared a home with the wife's mother and sometimes with others of her matrilineal elders. Twenty-four lived neolocally in a house containing no natal kinsfolk of either partner; of these 24 couples, 7 lived in a private house acquired by the husband; 11 lived in a house jointly acquired by husband and wife; and 6 lived in a house acquired by the wife.

As these figures suggest, duolocality is still the accepted norm of residence for younger married couples in Central Kerala, and avunculocality slightly less so for those in North Kerala. In both areas participation in a market economy has caused a shift toward neolocality, especially for middle-aged couples. In the North Kerala village, however, the modern prevalence of cash-crop farming has carried this tendency further than has small-scale urban wage work in the village in Cochin. At the same time, because of the coöperation of North Kerala men in cultivation, the male sex normally determines the pattern of residence. Couples live avunculocally, neolocally, or even patrilocally because men must live on their land. In the Cochin village, by contrast, the male shift from military to small-scale salaried employment has only partially undermined the position of women as the sex which remains on the ancestral land and for which the land is cultivated by lower-caste servants. It is still women whose claims, in the majority of cases, determine the choice of residence in Central Kerala. Women, whenever possible, remain on their own land and men adapt themselves to this condition by living duolocally, matrilocally, or in some cases neolocally in a house partly provided by the wife.

Kinship Relationships

MATRILINEAL KIN

The etiquette of behavior between matrilineal kin was traditionally the same in North as in Central Kerala, but the emphases in terms of rights and obligations were somewhat different.

The kāranavan's ultimate legal authority was much the same as in the Central kingdoms. However, he lacked domestic authority over women and their small children, who resided elsewhere. Among adults, avunculocal residence caused great emphasis to be placed on the unity of the matrilineally related men, who should coöperate in work and property management for the good of the taravād as a whole. Covertly, their relationships tended to be rivalrous and hostile. Open disputes between them were often avoided through the separate allocation of plots to individual men. The distance thus created between them also permitted the observance of the type of very formal etiquette that existed in the Central kingdoms.

A peculiarity of strict avunculocal residence is that it separates a woman from both her sons and her daughters after they are married. The sons return to their ancestral estates and the daughters leave with their husbands. The relationships of mother and children were therefore less continuous than in Central Kerala. However, various particular arrangements did often permit women to live with some of their children for a great part of their lives. Cross-cousin marriage was one of these. Matrilateral cross-cousin marriage was the most popular, because by this means the daughter of a kāranavan and his wife could be brought into their dwelling group as the wife of the kāranavan's nephew. Patrilateral cross-cousin marriage was also popular but less common.[1] It was less advantageous unless a shift from the normal residential arrangements could be made. This sometimes occurred when a kāranavan succeeded in arranging a marriage between his son and his sister's daughter. The son might then remain on his father's ancestral estate for part of his life in patrilocal residence. Any property which he developed there would pass to his wife's descendants as matrilineal heirs of the estate. In this way a woman might keep one of her sons living with her for a large part of her life.

Women were also commonly reunited with their sons at divorce or widowhood, for they would then return to their taravāds to live. Whatever the circumstances of residence, moreover, a man should place his duties to mother and sisters above those to wife and children. The ideals of devotion and reverence to matrilineal kinswomen were the same as in Central Kerala. Brother and sister were drawn apart by the normal rules of residence but, like mother and son, came together if the sister were divorced or widowed and returned to her taravād. A woman also returned to her taravād for several months at the time of childbirth, for every child had to be born in its own

---

[1] In the Kottayam village already cited, 12 per cent of Nambiar commoner women who had been married had at some time married their father's own or classificatory sister's son; 8 per cent had married their own or classificatory maternal uncle's son. Cross-cousin marriage is, as everywhere in Kerala, more common among the aristocratic lineages of village headmen and chiefs. Of the women of six village headmen's lineages over a period of five generations, 17 per cent had married their father's own or classificatory sister's son, and 13 per cent their own or classificatory maternal uncle's son. Patrilateral cross-cousin marriage is thus more usual in North than in Central Kerala. One reason for this is that fathers in North Kerala more commonly educate and endow their sons. By this means a father acquires the right to a voice in arranging his son's marriage, often to the father's niece.

taravād. A woman might also visit for several weeks each year. Brother and younger sister, like a man and his sister's daughter, observed rules of partial avoidance—associated with incest prohibitions —during their periods of co-residence.

Sisters were always separated upon marriage, for the Nayars of this area, unlike those to the south, forbade the marriage of two brothers to two sisters. They say that such marriages would endanger the unity of the brothers' taravād by introducing into it too strong a contingent from another lineage (Gough, 1952). Sisters were together, however, during childhood in their father's house, and were often reunited in old age when they went back to the taravād. Although they might seldom have stayed there during childhood and early youth, women seem usually to have died in their matrilineal ancestral homes. A woman was often widowed in old age. Alternatively she might elect to leave her husband and return to her taravād and sons when her period of childbearing was ended. In any case a woman's body had to be cremated and her funeral rites performed in the garden of her taravād house.

Women in avunculocal residence were partly maintained by their husbands' taravāds in return for domestic services. Nevertheless, important distributive ties persisted between them and their matrilineal kinsmen. Usually their kāranavan sent quantities of grain and clothing to them and their children twice annually after the harvests as part of their maintenance.

MARRIAGE

Following the tāli rite, a girl entered into a marriage relationship (sambandham) with one man at about the age of eleven. The father's sister's son, if of suitable age, was considered the rightful claimant. If the girl did not marry him her kāranavan must pay a token fine to him at the marriage ceremony. The giving of the cloth by the husband which marked the start of a sambandham was carried out with ceremony in the girl's ancestral house and was the occasion for a large feast to relatives of both parties. After the marriage had been consummated in the girl's house the couple were ceremonially conducted to the bridegroom's taravād and the girl was formally received into it by her husband's mother and his kāranavan's wife.

While a marriage endured the husband had exclusive rights in his wife's sexuality. If he detected her in adultery he might by custom kill her lover, cut off the hair of his wife, and send her home after divorce. A woman was not, however, excommunicated from caste and her children were not illegitimate unless she had relations with a man of low caste.

A woman normally lived with her husband in his ancestral home or in a separate house on his ancestral land. He then owed her physical protection and at least a part of her food and clothing, in return for limited domestic services. Occasionally a man might choose to visit his wife in her ancestral home if she lived nearby. In this case he might work on her ancestral land or bring periodic provisions of grain and clothing to her and her children. He would eat sometimes in his ancestral house and sometimes in the house of his wife. In all marriages a husband was obliged to pay the full expenses of delivery when his wife bore a child in her ancestral home and, additionally, to supply grain and other food to her throughout the six months which she spent in her taravād at this time.

A woman owed respect and obedience to her husband. He had the right to scold or even to beat her if she disregarded his wishes. Polygyny was permitted and was fairly common among village headmen, chiefs, and royalty. The polygynous husband usually provided separate houses for his wives on his ancestral estate.

Theoretically, either party might divorce the other at will, but in fact it was usually the husband who initiated a divorce. We do not know how common divorce was in the traditional period. At present it is rare in wealthy landowning lineages, although it probably takes place rather more frequently than among aristocratic Mappillas of North Kerala. It is more usual among the poorer Nambiar commoners, although probably less frequent than among the poorer Tiyyars of this area.

Widows might remarry freely by traditional law. Today it is somewhat rare for a widow to remarry if she has children under the age of three or four; we do not know whether this was the case traditionally. A widow who does remarry almost invariably leaves her children by the first marriage behind in her taravād, in the care of her mother or some other older natal kinswomen. Such children may visit their mother in their stepfather's house but they have no customary rights of maintenance there, and it is considered that their own taravād is the correct place for them to live.

Thus in North Kerala, by contrast with Central Kerala, differences of paternity may create structural divisions among the children born of one mother. All are of the same taravād and share the same fundamental birth-status rights, but if their fathers were different they

will have had different life experiences. One set of siblings may receive property from their father in which their maternal half-siblings
have no legal rights. Each set of full siblings will have important
relationships with its own paternal kin. In many respects, therefore,
children of the same mother by different fathers have a relationship
more comparable to that of the children of two sisters than to that
which obtains between full siblings. However, the ties between
maternal half-siblings are much stronger than those between paternal
half-siblings, who have only a slight relationship. At best, it may be
comparable to that between paternal parallel cousins; at worst it may
be one of open hostility.

A woman's claims on her husband's taravād ceased absolutely with
his death. As in Central Kerala, a widow was ceremonially conducted
out of her husband's house immediately after the death and could
not enter it thereafter. Husband and wife did not observe death pollution and did not take part in each other's funeral rites.

Hypergamous marriages in aristocratic lineages bore some resemblance to those in Central Kerala, although they were never
polyandrous. Brahman husbands of royal or chiefly women lived
matrilocally at the expense of the palace as in Central Kerala. Royal
and chiefly men, however, brought their lower-ranking wives to live
on their estates in avunculocal residence. The wife and her children
occupied a separate house or else a wing of the palace with separate
cooking arrangements. Husband and wife observed rules of ritual
pollution as in hypergamous marriages in the Central kingdoms.

THE FATHER AND HIS KIN

The kāranavan held ultimate legal control over all his juniors, but
their fathers had limited customary rights in and obligations to them.
A man was expected to care for his children in his home until they
reached puberty or married. Although their own taravād had a legal
obligation to maintain them in food and clothing, the father's taravād
customarily supplied their day-to-day needs as a matter of pride. The
father was expected to train his small children in manners and morals,
to see that they were taught to write, and to give his sons instruction
in cultivation. In return he could ask his children to do small tasks,
could exercise domestic discipline while they stayed with him, and
could expect kindness and occasional help from them when he was
old. His consent had to be sought for his children's marriages and he
often arranged the marriage of his daughter, although he could not
override her kāranavan's wishes. Over and above their customary

obligations, some fathers, especially kāranavans, kept their children residing with them for most of their lives and gave them property. A child owed his father obedience and respect. If a man divorced his wife her children also left him and might see little of him thereafter. However, they had to observe ritual pollution at his death and his eldest son took part in his funeral rites along with the chief matrilineal heir. The eldest son also made annual offerings to his dead father's spirit. In general the relationship with the father was thought of as intimate and loving. Children must respect him and a daughter must not touch him after her puberty. But having no legal authority, the father was not feared. His role was sharply contrasted with that of the mother's brother. Uncles were said to teach by scolding and punishment; fathers, by persuasion and laughter.

The father's kin had privileges and obligations at life-crisis rites—most of which took place in the individual's taravād house—and were feasted and made gifts at the ceremonies of first pregnancy, naming, first rice feeding, tāli tying, marriage, first menstruation, and death. At the naming ceremony, when a baby was one month old, the father's mother chose the name, the father's father conferred it, and the father presented the child with a gold waistband. The kāranavan fulfilled these roles in Central Kerala.

A person was forbidden to marry his father's sibling or paternal parallel cousin of the father's property group. Affectionate respect was the proper attitude toward all the father's older kin. The paternal grandmother played with a child but did not idolize him as she did her daughter's child, for he was not of her taravād. Unless he was also a child's kāranavan, the paternal grandfather was a distant kinsman who had little to do with his grandchild. The mother's father, on the other hand, usually doted on his grandchild and was a cherished companion.

Male cross cousins had a joking relationship and were often close companions. Their relationship might be tinged with hostility concerning the property of their respective father and mother's brother. Sometimes, at least in the nineteenth century, they quarreled openly over the inheritance and became enemies thereafter. Male and female cross cousins had a joking relationship with implicit sexual privileges if the girl was younger than the man. A boy who returned to his taravād at puberty often married his matrilateral cross cousin thereafter. Even if she married someone else he might sleep with her illicitly before or after the marriage. Elders were either ignorant or oblivious of these affairs. If the husband found out he might keep quiet or might divorce his wife, but he would not be likely to take vengeance.

AFFINES

The etiquette of behavior between affines was practically identical in North and Central Kerala, but in the North they had recognized obligations.

During her marriage a woman became partly integrated into her husband's property group. Her husband could request her to cook and do limited domestic work for any of his matrilineal kin. She would do so regularly if she lived in an avunculocal extended family. In such households there was a certain authority structure between the wives of matrilineally related men, based on the relative age of the husbands. The oldest woman directed the group and the younger ones should obey her. Matters went most smoothly when a woman was the mother of her husband's niece-in-law. Older women in avunculocal households did not, however, have the unequivocal authority over junior wives which is found in the patrilocal extended families of the higher patrilineal castes of India. They would never beat a girl and usually courted her affection. If the young wife was dissatisfied she might urge her husband to move to a separate house, go home for long periods, or even seek a divorce.

In strict avunculocal residence the kāranavan's wife had domestic authority, keeping the keys of storerooms and directing the younger wives. However, if any woman born into the taravād returned to live in it she could demand the internal management of the home as a right. The relations between a woman and her husband's sisters and nieces were thus often strained. Soon after such a natal kinswoman returned to her home in this way, the kāranavan would try to move his wife into a separate building to avoid feminine disputes. However, a younger wife often lived for several years in the same house with her husband's widowed mother and was expected to obey her with good grace.

A woman and her husband's older matrilineal kinsmen avoided one another—except on ceremonial occasions—because of incest prohibitions. She was accorded meticulous respect by her husband's younger matrilineal kin, who usually feared and resented her influence over her husband. Gruesome proverbs told of the tortures which men and women would like to inflict on the wives of their elder brothers and uncles, and it was said that "If the uncle's wife and nephews sit down peaceably together, *nux vomica* and bitter gourds will turn to honey."

The wives of her elder matrilineal kinsmen figured prominently in the life-crisis rites of a girl, performing the ritual acts done by enangar women in Central Kerala.

Because of residence patterns men had less contact than did women with the property groups of their spouses. They must be invited to all ceremonies and had ritual duties in those connected with their own children. As sambandhakkar of a property group, the husbands of its female members were usually consulted formally by its kāranavan before he undertook important matters such as building houses or dividing property. He was not, however, obliged to follow their advice.

Kinship Terms

A. MATRILINEAL KIN

The pattern of terms was the same as in Central Kerala. Lexically, the only difference was that MoMo and her sisters (A1) were called *acchamma* (literally, "father's mother"), a term extended to them from FaMo. This usage probably resulted from the fact that a child normally recognized FaMo earlier than MoMo and had more contact with her.

B. AFFINES AND NON-MATRILINEAL COGNATES

In North Kerala, as might be expected, there were customary kinship terms for the patrilateral kin. The terms for affines and non-matrilineal cognates were as follows.

(1) *Bhārya.* M. speaking. Wi. Reference only.

(2) *Bartāvu.* F. speaking. Hu. Reference only.

(3) *Sambandhakkar.* M. and F. speaking. Collective. Husbands of women of ego's lineage, primarily of ego's property group. Reference only.

(4) *Acchappan* ("Father's father"). M. and F. speaking. FaFa and FaFaBr. FaFaSiHu, FaMoBr, FaMoSiHu. MoFa and MoFaBr. MoFaSiHu, MoMoSiHu.

(5) *Acchamma* ("Father's mother"). FaMo and FaMoSi. FaFaBr-Wi, FaFaSi and FaMoBrWi. MoFaSi, MoMo, MoMoSi, MoFaBrWi.

(6) *Amma* ("Mother"). M. and F. speaking. Extended from Mo and MoSi to FaSi and FaBrWi. FaSi is called *valiya* ("big") mother or *elaya* ("younger") mother according to her age in relation to the father. FaBrWi is so designated according to FaBr's age in relation to Fa.

(7) *Acchan.* M. and F. speaking. Fa, mother's current husband,

FaBr, FaSiHu, MoSiHu. The last three are designated "older" or "younger" in the same manner as above.

(8) *Ammāyi.* M. and F. speaking. Wi of any male of first or second ascending generations within ego's lineage, especially within his property group.

(9) *Aliyan.* M. speaking. Reciprocal between a man and Wi's lineage kinsmen of her generation, primarily within her property group. Reference only.

(10) *Jyēshtatti amma.* M. and F. speaking. Wi of older male of ego's generation within his lineage, primarily within his property group.

(11) *Machunian.* M. and F. speaking. Male cross cousin, i.e., male of ego's father's lineage in ego's generation, or So of ego's own, or classificatory MoBr within his lineage. Extended to male cross cousins of either parent.

(12) *Machunichi.* M. and F. speaking. The female equivalent of B11.

(13) *Makan.* M. speaking. WiSo. Reference only.

(14) *Makal.* M. speaking. WiDa. Reference only.

(15) *Pērakutti.* M. and F. speaking. Reciprocal of B4 and B5. Used primarily of own grandchild through either So or Da. Reference only.

A man or woman used the same terms to address the spouse's natal kin as the own natal kin except in case of an avoidance relationship.

An individual *addressed* all cross-cousins in the same manner as siblings, reserving terms B11 and B12 for reference. He addressed and referred to paternal parallel cousins as siblings.

Kinship terms were used in relationships with affines or cognates of higher or lower matrilineal caste but not in relationships with Nambudiri Brahman relatives.

Comment: Males and females of the second ascending generation were equated with grandparents, except for the maternal great-uncle and his wife. This fits the fact that relationships with the maternal great-uncle and his wife were distant and authoritative while those with other kin of this generation were non-authoritative and informal. Similarly, in the first ascending generation the mother's brother and his wife are singled out as distant and authoritative figures. All others of this generation are classed with the parents as non-authoritative figures.

The existence of Iroquois cousin terms for reference fits the special joking relationship and preferential marriage between cross cousins as contrasted with the prohibition of marriage between parallel cousins of both sides.

Tiyyar: North Kerala

Throughout Kerala the Tiyyars (called Iravas in parts of Cochin and Travancore) ranked below the Nayars as a polluting caste and were sharecropping tenants. In the Central kingdoms they had a double unilineal kinship system with localized patrilineages. But in North Kerala, as in parts of Travancore, they had a matrilineal system very similar to that of Nayars.

Little is known of the Tiyyars before the period of British rule. As a "low" caste they tended to be ignored by contemporary writers and, being mostly nonliterate, they left few records. This account deals with Tiyyar kinship in the former Kottayam kingdom over the past hundred years. During this period Tiyyar matrilineal groups have partly disintegrated through extensive cash-crop farming and general absorption in a market economy. We shall indicate what is known of the traditional system as well as outlining modern changes.

Ecology and Economy

The Tiyyars were traditionally sharecropping tenants of gardens and rice fields owned by Nayars and Brahmans. During native rule the tenure of these plots seems to have been hereditary in small matrilineal descent groups. Although this is not definitely established, it seems probable that in North as in Central Kerala a Tiyyar household had to seek the permission of local political authorities before moving to a new village, and that jenmis could not evict their hereditary tenants unless the latter committed some crime. Tiyyar tenants attached to a Nayar taravād also did agricultural work on the Nayars' private domain and could be summoned for various menial tasks such as gathering wood for cremations. These hereditary ties must, however, have been loosened as early as the beginning of the eighteenth century through the opening up of new gardens for export crops and through the employment of some Tiyyars by European traders of the ports. Many hereditary service ties were broken during the Mysorean invasions when a part of the Brahman and Nayar population fled temporarily southward, leaving their estates in the hands of Muslims (Logan, 1951, I: 610–611).

Early in the nineteenth century the British government accorded jenmis absolute ownership of their lands with powers to evict their tenants (*ibid.*, I: 614). Much new land was also brought under cultivation for cash crops. Many Tiyyars therefore became short-term sharecroppers holding gardens as individuals. Others, less fortunate, lost all rights of tenure and became mere wage laborers hired by the day. A few engaged successfully in trade or the professions and became jenmis in their own right. Today very few Tiyyars of this area can trace their ancestry back beyond their own great-grand-parents and most families have lived on their present sites only one or two generations.

Matrilineal Units

The Tiyyars of Kottayam have eight named matrilineal clans dispersed throughout villages of the former kingdom. The clan has no functions other than exogamy. Marriage usually takes place between persons of the same or adjacent villages but it is permitted throughout the former kingdom.

The Tiyyars probably once had localized matrilineages comparable in size and functions to those of Nayar commoners. Like the Nayars they had a neighborhood unit (tara), comprising the Tiyyar community of one or more villages. The neighborhood had a caste assembly of the heads of households; it judged offenders against the religious laws of caste and could fine or expel them from caste with the consent of the Nayar village headman or the chief. As among Nayars, there seem to have been some six to ten lineages in a neighborhood. We do not know what role the lineage may have played in village politics or whether its members performed collective religious ceremonies. We know that the neighborhood assembly had a headman (*Tandān*), whose office was probably hereditary in a matrilineage. He acted as intermediary between the Tiyyar community and the Nayar headman of the village and he witnessed marriages. It is not known whether Tiyyars of this area had an enangar relationship. Their lineage does not appear to have been significant as a vengeance group; crimes and grave civil disputes were tried by the local Nayar chief. The most certain evidence we have of a Tiyyar lineage is that Tiyyars within one neighborhood who knew that they were matrilineally related observed death and birth pollutions for one another.

In the early decades of British rule, even with the possibility of eviction by jenmis, Tiyyars who were able to retain tenure of the same plots for two or more generations tended to form small matrilineal property groups. Wealthier Tiyyars who bought their own land set up more stable matrilineal property groups comparable to those of Nayars. It therefore seems safe to assume that during native rule Tiyyars had had a matrilineal property group whose members jointly owned the hereditary right of tenure of plots of land and were attached to a Nayar landowning family. Ideally Tiyyar residential arrangements in the nineteenth century were the same as the Nayars', with wives coming to live avunculocally in their husbands' property groups and boys returning to their matrilineal kinsmen at puberty or marriage. In at least some cases a group of matrilineally related males occupied one house with their wives and young children. In other cases each man built a small house for his wife and children on the family plot. Divorced or widowed women returned to live in their matrilineal homes under the protection of their brothers and maternal uncles.

In the latter half of the nineteenth century, however, most Tiyyar taravāds lost their hereditary rights to fields. Individual men leased gardens where they could, often developing new ones on kurikānam tenure in former waste areas, far from their ancestral homes. Others became landless agricultural laborers for Nayars. A man took his wife with him to his new home. He built a house in his leased garden or, if he was landless, obtained permission to live rent-free in a hut on some Nayar landlord's land. Men who lived for very long in one place sometimes brought nephews and widowed sisters to live near them. A man who acquired property in the form of land, improvements to land, cash, or movables was in law judged free to give these to his children within his lifetime unless it could be proved that he had earned them through using taravād funds. If he died without having bequeathed his goods they passed jointly to the matrilineal descendants of his mother. Thus some Tiyyar men founded new small matrilineal property groups, while the property of others passed to their children. Even in the latter case, however, Tiyyars in the nineteenth century tended to give their property jointly to the wife and her matrilineal descendants, thus (like Nayars) forming a small branch taravād through the wife. The Tiyyar taravād was however very ephemeral because of its uncertain attachment to land.

In 1896 Tiyyars, like all the matrilineal castes of Malabar District, became subject to a law which stated that if a man registered his marriage half of his self-acquired intestate property should pass to his wife and children at his death, and only half to his matrilineal heirs (Nair, 1941: 233). Since that date more and more houses and fields have descended from fathers to their sons, with married daughters coming back to claim a share only if they were divorced or their husbands failed to provide for their children. Moreover, since 1933 Tiyyars, like Nayars, have come under a further act which permits the per capita division of such matrilineal estates as remain among them. Since 1933 a man is permitted not only to give self-acquired property to his wife and children but also to take one share of any matrilineal joint property and separate it from the shares of his sisters and their children. If a man dies intestate all his separately owned property is now equally divided between his mother, his wife, and each of his (male and female) children (*ibid.*: 308).

The exact provisions of these acts are a somewhat academic matter for the poorer Tiyyar tenants and laborers, who own little property. In general, however, the present tendency, for a man whose marriage is stable, is to give a house and if possible the tenure of a plot of land to his wife and children, while retaining the obligation to give shelter and economic help to any sisters whose husbands have deserted them or failed to provide for them before death.

Residence

These economic and legal developments make residential arrangements heterogeneous in modern villages. Thus, out of 104 Tiyyar houses in one Kottayam village in 1948, approximately 22 per cent were occupied by patrilocal extended families. They comprised a married couple, their sons, unmarried daughters, sons' wives, and sons' children, or else two or more brothers, with or without a widowed mother, together with their unmarried sisters, their wives, and their children. Twenty-eight per cent of the houses contained a simple elementary family; 30 per cent contained a widow or divorced woman and her unmarried children; 20 per cent contained some kind of "mixed" extended family. This last might comprise a married couple, their divorced or widowed daughters, and the daughters' children; a widow, her daughters, and her grandchildren—with or without a temporarily resident son-in-law; a patrilocal extended family with one or more of the men's divorced sisters and their children; one man with his wife, his children, his divorced or widowed sister, and her children; or a group of divorced or widowed sisters with their children.

Taking the residence of married couples by household membership, we find that 50 per cent of married couples lived neolocally, in a house provided by the husband; 33 per cent lived patrilocally, either in a house with the husband's father or in a house which had been provided and inhabited by the husband's father before his death; 7 per cent lived duolocally, with the husband residing with natal kin and visiting his wife in her natal home; 7 per cent lived avunculocally, in a house with the husband's mother's brother; and 3 per cent lived matrilocally, in a house with the wife's mother. In spite of the 7 per cent avuculocal residence it may be noted that no "complete" avunculocal extended family was found in which both an uncle and nephew lived with both of their wives.

Residence was also calculated with regard to the married couples' choice of village. Fifteen per cent of the couples lived neolocally, in a village in which none of their elder kinsfolk had ever lived; another 15 per cent lived avunculocally, in a village where the husband's mother's brothers lived or had previously lived; 53 per cent lived patrilocally, in a village where the husband's father lived or had lived before death; 10 per cent lived matrilocally, in a village of the wife's natal family which was not also that of the husband; 7 per cent lived duolocally, in the same village.

These figures illustrate the fact that today it is rare to find a traditional type of matrilineal group whose members still share joint property or whose male members all live on the same plot or on adjacent plots. Nevertheless, the members of a matrilineal group of three to five generations' depth (counting young children) do often preserve a certain unity. Those who live less than ten miles apart tend to assemble for all life-crisis rites. If at all possible, all members must attend a funeral, make offerings to the departed spirit, and participate in the purification ceremony and feast at the end of their period of death pollution. Impoverished widows or women whose husbands have deserted them normally return to live with or near a brother or, if they have no brother, a maternal parallel cousin. Moreover, in some villages, although not in the village cited, a few wealthier Tiyyars who are landlords still have matrilineal property groups, some of whose members reside together.

Interpersonal Kinship Relationships

The etiquette of behavior, the ritual coöperation, and the ceremonial obligations between all kin were traditionally almost identical with those among Nayars of North Kerala. The kāranavan of a traditional property group was the legal guardian of its members and managed the group's finances. Men born into the group coöperated in cultivating their leased fields, with help from their wives or from sisters who had returned to live with them. Today, maternal uncle and nephew who are both married seldom work together. A group of brothers may however coöperate in cultivation and jointly lease gardens and rice plots from a landlord. Whatever the composition of a household, it is normally a cooking and commensal unit. In elementary family households the man usually either works as a day laborer for wages or else independently cultivates only one or two leased gardens, selling most of his produce to merchants for cash.

Tiyyar women, unlike Nayars, do regular outdoor work. Men tend coconut trees and other cash crops in gardens, plough and sow rice fields, transport and thresh the harvest, build and thatch houses, and tend male cattle. Women grow vegetables, milk cows, weed and transplant in rice fields, and do most of the cutting at harvest. In households which lease land, women—whether wives or sisters of the men —coöperate in outdoor tasks. On the other hand a woman today, like a man, may be employed by a landlord as a day laborer for wages. Thus many women whose husbands have deserted them are able to support their small children independently with only occasional help from brothers. However, such women like to live near a brother so that he may give them physical protection and act as a guardian for their children. A woman who remarries normally leaves all but her youngest children behind in the household of a brother.

Until about thirty years ago Tiyyar girls underwent the tāli rite before puberty. The tāli was usually tied by the girl's mother's brother's wife, her father's sister, or, if she was already betrothed, the mother of her future husband (Aiyappan, 1944: 159; Gough, 1955). Whichever of these women performed the rite did so in the role of potential mother-in-law. In some areas, however, the tāli was tied by a woman of a lower-ranking caste whose members served Tiyyars as barbers and midwives. Tiyyar men might have hypergamous marriages with women of this caste but Tiyyar women might not marry barber men. In all cases the rite seems, as among Nayars, to have been a mere initiation ceremony which rendered the girl marriageable and instituted the etiquette associated with incest prohibitions between her and her matrilineal kinsmen. After the rite, usually before puberty, she entered into a marriage (sambandham) with one man.

Marriage among Tiyyars carried more precise obligations than among Nayars. It was arranged by the kāranavans of the couple, who had to seek the consent of the fathers if they were still married to the couple's mothers. As among Nayars, the girl's father's sister's son was considered her rightful bridegroom and her kāranavan must pay a token fine to him if she married some other boy. In advance of the marriage the boy's kāranavan presented earrings to the bride, which were placed in the tops of her ears; these rings were the mark of a married woman and were removed at divorce or death. The marriage ceremony itself consisted of the bridegroom's presenting one loin cloth to his wife and another to her mother. The marriage feast in the bride's house was jointly supplied by the couple's matrilineal groups. After the feast the bridegroom's kāranavan paid a small bridewealth in *panams* (traditional Malabari coins) to the kāranavan of the bride. The bride's party in turn supplied a dowry of jewelry and cooking vessels. After the marriage had been consummated the couple were blessed by the girl's elders and departed to the bridegroom's house.

Unlike Tiyyars, the Nayars gave neither bridewealth nor dowry. The difference seems to be related to the following facts. First, Nayar women did little outdoor work and were somewhat of an economic liability. It was therefore not necessary to compensate their natal groups in the form of bridewealth for the loss of their services. Second, a Nayar could not demand that his wife live always in his house, although she was expected to do so for a large part of her married life. At all events a Nayar woman did not change her household membership as completely as did a Tiyyar woman. This again is relevant to the payment of bridewealth. Third, a Nayar woman continued to receive part of her maintenance from her natal group in the form of transported food and clothing. A Tiyyar woman must be maintained entirely by her husband's group for the duration of her marriage. Again, a Nayar woman on marriage became attached to a well-equipped conjugal matrilineal group whose members were already well provided with valuable metal vessels as part of their jointly owned property. Conversely, the jewelry which a Nayar woman took with her on marriage remained the joint property of her taravād and could be taken back to it at any time. A Tiyyar woman's dowry of jewelry and cooking vessels, by contrast, was a valuable contribution to her conjugal group, in part compensating them for the burden of her maintenance. In hard times her husband's kāranavan could pawn these goods in order to maintain her. Alternatively, if the woman's husband could be persuaded to build her a separate house she was assured of vessels for her kitchen.

The payment of bridewealth by the husband gave him exclusive rights in his wife's sexuality, rights in her domestic services and out-door work, and the right to have her live with him for the duration of the marriage. He in turn undertook to shelter and maintain her and to maintain her children by him until their puberty or marriage. If a woman divorced her husband without good cause her group must return the bridewealth. A divorced wife took home with her what-ever remained of her dowry. As among Nayars, a Tiyyar woman had no claim on her husband's natal group after his death. Unless he had built her a separate house, she must leave her conjugal home and never return thereafter.

The Tiyyar bridewealth was called kānam, the word used for the sum of money paid by a tenant to his landlord at the start of a period of land tenure. The word indicates that Tiyyar marriage was thought of as a temporary "leasing" of the woman from her natal group (to which she continued to belong) for certain definite and limited forms of "usufruct." Further, this kānam "tenure" of a wife involved certain regular payments in kind to the group to which she belonged, exactly as in the case of a field. After each harvest the wife took home to her matrilineal kin a portion of the paddy she had cut. If a husband withheld this customary gift he could expect his wife to divorce him. It was the wife's contribution to the maintenance of her elders and it gave her the right to visit occasionally and to eat in her natal home. It also renewed her right to return home for the birth of her children and, for the future, to claim help from her matrilineal kin when her marriage was ended.

Today a marriage is usually arranged by the fathers or elder broth-ers of the couple. The male head of the house, whether father, brother, or mother's brother, usually makes the marriage payments. A mar-ried woman carries paddy to her natal home after the harvests, until such time as her husband gives her a house and garden for herself and her descendants.

Bilateral cross-cousin marriage is favored among Tiyyars as among Nayars, some preference being given to matrilateral cross-cousin mar-riage. Incest prohibitions are the same as among Nayars. Polygyny is, and probably was traditionally, more common among Tiyyars than Nayars. A Tiyyar man sometimes brings two wives to live in the same house, although he is today more likely to build separate huts for each. In spite of the more precise obligations of marriage among Tiy-yars, the divorce rate is much higher than among Nayars. Today, the majority of Nayar women in North Kerala do not experience divorce, and those who are divorced or widowed seldom remarry if they are over about the age of thirty. By contrast most Tiyyar women of middle age have married two or three times. The modern economic independence, as wageworkers, of both men and women among Tiyyars may be responsible for this difference. Even traditionally, the fact that women could work independently for landlords may have given them the ability to terminate a marriage at will.

Like Nayars, Tiyyar husband and wife do not observe death pollution or perform funeral rites for ane another. Traditionally a woman left her husband's natal house after his death and before the funeral. Today, if the husband has built a private house for his wife and children, the wife remains in this house. She lives in it throughout the days of the funeral rites but takes no part in them. Traditionally a woman was buried in the garden of her natal house. Today her body may be either buried or cremated in the garden of the house which her husband has given to her. If the husband is living he may finance the funeral, but it is conducted by the woman's children and matrilineal kin, and the husband takes no part in the ceremonies. If the wife's funeral takes place in her natal home the husband usually attends it as a guest.

A Tiyyar's obligations to his children were traditionally much the same as those of a Nayar. His obligations ceased if he was divorced from their mother. While the marriage endured, however, he must maintain his children entirely until they reached puberty or married. He must give consent for their marriages and often arranged the marriage of a daughter. Today a man whose marriage is stable feels that he should provide for his children and give them property, whereas he now feels to have only residual obligations to his sisters' children. If the father has privately leased fields, he and his adult sons may coöperate in cultivation. Children always observed death pollution even for a divorced father, and the eldest son performed the rites of chief mourner along with the eldest matrilineal heir. Today children whose father has given them a house and garden often finance his funeral themselves, inviting the father's matrilineal kin as guests and ceremonial participants.

Among the poorer Tiyyars today both matrilineal and conjugal ties tend to be weak, but they are weak in different ways. Matrilineal ties are still durable; they cannot be entirely renounced unless the individual flees the locality of his birth. However, ties to matrilineal kin may carry very slight obligations unless these kin become destitute and turn to one in emergency. Conversely, the ties of marriage and fatherhood are potentially very brittle. This is because both sexes may now earn a living independently as wage laborers, working in groups not organized on the basis of kinship. A man may also cultivate gardens for cash crops on his own. However, the demands of sexuality, infant care, and housekeeping cause most men and women to be engaged in *a* marriage, however ephemeral, at any time during their youth and middle life. Participation in *an* elementary family, even if it is short-lived, is thus the most regular form of kinship coöperation among Tiyyars today.

Kinship Terms

In spite of some lexical differences of dialect, the pattern of Tiyyar kinship terms was traditionally identical with that of Nayars. A few "peculiar" usages have crept into some modern households but these are not standardized. Thus in a household where brothers jointly share property, junior brothers and their wives may call the eldest brother's wife *ammāyi*, the traditional term for mother's brother's wife. This is presumably because the eldest brother acts as, and is called, the kāranavan of the property-owning group. Again, in families where the mother's brothers have practically lost their traditional authority through modern economic changes, the mother's younger brother may be called *kunnicchan* (a diminutive of acchan, "father") —a word also used for the father's younger brother. This usage of course fits a bilateral system in which neither uncle has authority. Most commonly, however, traditional kinship terms are still used.

Mappilla: North Kerala

The Mappillas are a Sunni Muslim group originated by eighth-century Arab traders and indigenous converts to Islam. They settled mainly in the ports of Central and North Kerala. In this area they numbered over 1,250,000 in 1931, or 26 per cent of the population (Censuses of Madras and Cochin, 1931). Over the centuries the Mappillas have been recruited largely from Mukkuvans, a coastal fishing caste, from Tiyyars, and from other polluting castes. No doubt because of their historical origins, the Mappillas of Central Kerala are patrilineal; those of North Kerala, matrilineal. Although their exploits at sea are well documented, Mappilla social history is sketchy until the mid-eighteenth century. This account deals with the British period and with what is known of kinship in the period of native rule.

Economic and Political Institutions

Arab merchants and their converts dominated Kerala's trade in the fourteenth and fifteenth centuries, exporting spices to the Red Sea and the Persian Gulf and importing metals and luxury goods. In North Kerala the Kolattiri kings gave them land for settlements in ports and on river banks (Ibn Battuta, quoted in Logan, 1951, I: 287). From at least the thirteenth century, a Muslim chief, the Arakkal or Ali Raja, ruled Cannanore, a major port of Kolattunad, with rights comparable to those of a Nayar chief (Hamilton, ed. Pinkerton, 1811: 370). His matrilineage is supposed to have been descended from that of a Nayar minister of Kolattunad who became converted to Islam (Logan, 1951, I: 357). As chiefs of Cannanore, the Arakkal rajas continued to manage the Kolattiri treasury, financed mainly from revenues which they collected in the port (*ibid.:* 358). They rebelled and bid for independence in the late seventeenth century, and in the eighteenth century allied themselves with the Muslim invaders from Mysore against Kolattiri and the British (*ibid.:* 410). They remained a minor merchant power with their own ships until the early nineteenth century and today are still landlords of wealth.

The Portuguese broke the Arab monopoly of overseas trade in the sixteenth century. After this time the Nayar kings and chiefs of North Kerala became entangled in military and trade alliances with Portuguese, Dutch, French, and English trading companies. A few Muslim lineages retained their ships and engaged in sporadic trade with the Middle East, sometimes legally, sometimes as pirates, depending on whichever power dominated at the time (Ayyar, 1938: 210). Most Muslims, however, became inland traders, transporting spices on foot and by water from inland estates to the ports for sale to the European companies. The conditions were not those of a free market during the period of European trade. Each European company made a treaty with the king or chief of the chiefdom containing the port in which it had been allowed to settle (Logan, 1951, I: 306–307). The treaty gave the company a monopoly of the export of spices at a fixed price, usually determined by the year. In each port the ruler accorded to one or two aristocratic Muslim lineages the legal right to supply the spices to the foreign company, and these lineages bought the spices from inland estates at what was nominally the same price. Their profit arose from the fact that the measure they used was, by legal enactment, larger on the inland estates than at the ports. Thus as late as 1800 the *candy* (the standard measure) of pepper which Muslim merchants bought from inland estates near Tellicherry (formerly in the Kolattiri raja's kingdom) weighed 640 pounds. At Tellicherry, where the merchants delivered the pepper to the English East Indian Company, the candy, sold for the same price, weighed 600 pounds (Buchanan, 1807, 533). The Muslim wholesale merchants in turn hired Mappilla middlemen to bring in the pepper for a fee, and the middlemen hired gangs of Mappilla carriers from each local area. Carriers were paid in cash or kind at customary rates. In inland chiefdoms which had no port of their own the price of spices was separately fixed at a lower rate. Aristocratic Mappilla merchant lineages were again given contracts by the ruler to buy the pepper locally and to sell it to Muslim merchants of the nearest port at the price fixed in that chiefdom. Each ruler took a percentage of the profits on exports and imports within his chiefdom. At the ports, spices and other goods which Europeans did not require might be exported by the Muslim merchants in their own ships or sold to merchants from other parts of India. Officially the fixed price still held, but in fact the Muslims were sometimes able to keep back stores of spices and sell them to private Indian merchants at a larger profit. This system seems to have obtained in the seventeenth and early eighteenth centuries at all the major ports of North Kerala.

Outside the small Arakkal domain, Muslim ownership and tenure of land were restricted. The few aristocratic lineages which were granted wholesale trading rights by rulers seem also to have been given estates near the ports and near trading centers on river banks inland, at least by the early eighteenth century. The great bulk of Muslim commoners were middlemen trading agents or carriers of goods, who seem to have held sharecropping tenures of the gardens in which they built their homes, such gardens being owned either by aristocratic Muslims or by Nayars. Muslims did little cultivation, however, relying mainly on cash purchases from trading centers. Some may have leased merely the actual site and not the whole garden on which their house was built.

The Arakkal rajas governed their own small domain and maintained a criminal court of justice for the Muslims and low-caste Hindus who lived within it (Hamilton, ed. Pinkerton, 1811: 369). Elsewhere Muslims came under the judicial authority of the Nayar chief in whose chiefdom they lived. The chief, or a Nayar village headman under him, judged crimes and civil disputes. Muslims had, however, their own neighborhood assemblies comparable to those of Nayars. A neighborhood might comprise the Muslims of one village, a part of a village, or a small group of villages, depending on the density of Muslim habitation. Household heads formed an assembly of elders who managed the neighborhood mosque and tried offenses against Muslim religious law. Their sanctions were fines and expulsion from the community. They elected a *khāzi* or religious leader who conducted trials, witnessed marriages, delivered the Friday sermon in the mosque, and represented the community to higher political authorities. Each neighborhood owned in common its own burial ground, adjacent to the mosque. Aristocratic Muslim lineages which owned estates maintained their private burial grounds and mosques. These lineages may have had some judicial rights—probably equivalent to those of a Nayar village headman—over the Muslim commoners and the Hindu polluting castes who lived on their estates. Only the Arakkal rajas, however, seem to have held rights equivalent to those of a Nayar chief.

The Mysorean Muslim invasion under Hyder Ali in 1766 broke up this social system. Some Mappillas supported the invaders and received land confiscated from Nayars and Brahmans; thousands of the latter fled temporarily south to Travancore. Hundreds of others were forcibly converted to Islam, although almost all reverted to Hinduism when the occupation ended in 1792 (Innes, 1908: 72–73). Some Nayar chiefs were left in charge of their domains but Mappilas were freely employed as soldiers and collectors of the newly instituted land tax. The government set up by the invaders, with the support of the Arakkal rajas, assumed a monopoly of all exports and imports at the North Kerala ports (Buchanan, 1807, 515). Muslim wholesale merchants at the ports, many of whom had opposed the invaders, thus found themselves forced to produce quotas for export in return for moderate fees.

When the English East India Company expelled the Mysoreans and assumed the government of North Kerala in 1792, it reinstated some aristocratic Muslim lineages as suppliers of pepper at fixed prices for export by the company. The company, however, soon found that its interests as merchants and as governors were opposed; it wished to make profits for the English shareholders but also to retain high revenues for public works in Kerala. It therefore gradually relinquished its trade. Free trade in all goods except pepper was instituted in 1792 (Innes, 1908: 77). The company's monopoly of pepper was relinquished in 1813, and in 1833 the company ceased to trade. Most of the aristocratic Muslim wholesalers who had relied on monopolies created by the government also abandoned trade and became wealthy landlords. Many new, independent Muslim merchants arose in the free trade of the nineteenth century and exported independently overseas or became suppliers of spices, timber, coconuts, tea, and coffee to European export firms. Today the Muslim group is extremely heterogeneous in wealth and occupation. It comprises great landlords, wholesale merchants, middlemen traders (and their wage laborers) plying as of old between inland estates and ports, shopkeepers in the bazaars of coastal and small inland towns, and, in a few cases, wage laborers in agriculture along with the poorer Nayars and Tiyyars.

Matrilineal Groups

Mappillas are divided into two, theoretically endogamous castes. The higher-ranking caste is believed to comprise descendants of converts from Brahmans and Nayars. Most of its lineages appear to be those of aristocrats granted land and wholesale trading rights by the native rulers. The Arakkal rajas are the greatest among them but intermarry equally with others of this caste. The members of the caste are divided into six exogamous matrilineal clans called *kiriyams,* dispersed throughout North Kerala. The higher caste is much smaller than the lower caste of Mappilla "commoners," supposed descendants of converts from the polluting Hindu castes. This caste is said to comprise sixty-four dispersed exogamous matrilineal clans called illams (the word used also for the Tiyyar clan). High and low castes may interdine freely and worship together in mosques. With the social mobility which has characterized Mappilla traders in the market economy of the nineteenth and twentieth centuries, the rule of endogamy has been frequently broken and has now practically died out. In both castes the common descent of clan members is merely stipulated and not demonstrated. A clan has no functions other than exogamy and mutual hospitality.

Muslim aristocrats who owned land, wholesale trading rights, or political office in the period of native rule have traditionally had localized matrilineages and property groups almost identical in structure with those of Nayar aristocrats. They had separate sthānam estates for the two or three oldest men of the whole lineage, after the fashion of royalty and Nayar chiefs. If there was a political office it went to the oldest man of the lineage as a whole. Property groups periodically divided in the same way as those of Nayar aristocrats and the legal rights and obligations of a kāranavan were the same. The differences lay in the rules of residence and marriage, discussed below.

A right of wholesale trading granted by a ruling power was comparable to a landed estate. It was granted in the first place to a matrilineal property group under the guardianship of its male head. When the group became large and divided, the trading monopoly was in theory divided too; in fact, as in the case of a political office, one branch might in time manage to dispossess the others. The Mappillas are of interest because they show that it is possible to organize a trading group in a cash economy on the basis of segmentary unilineal descent groups, provided that trade is politically administered, rights to trade are hereditary, and land and labor are not freely marketable. After about 1830 these conditions disappeared: trade became free, land became freely marketable, and in many sectors of the economy labor also went on the market for prices which fluctuated according to supply and demand, rather than being remunerated by customarily fixed amounts of cash or shares of produce. The partial change to a fuel technology involving steamships and railways greatly hastened this process, for it opened up large-scale competitive cash-crop farming and upset the subsistence economy of villages, causing more and more people to rely on marketable commodities for their living. In these conditions the unilineal descent groups of Mappillas, like those of Nayars and Tiyyars, have undergone a slow process of disintegration.

The traditional functions of the lineage and property group among Mappilla commoners who owned no land or trading office are uncertain. The group of matrilineal kin whose members lived in one neighborhood observed exogamy (derived from the clan) and had a distinctive name (derived from the house and garden from which they believed their ancestress to have come). To this extent the group resembled a Nayar lineage. It is not known whether the Mappilla lineage had any joint legal responsibility, whether it acted as a vengeance group, or whether its members ever performed religious rites together. Mappilla commoners did have small matrilineal property groups. The members of such a group jointly owned the tenure of a garden or at least a house and house site. Its oldest male, as kāranavan, was legally responsible for the members and represented them in the assembly of the neighborhood mosque. It is not known whether Mappilla carriers who were employed by traders for customarily fixed wages were traditionally recruited individually or on the basis of property-group membership.

During the nineteenth century, as free trade and cash-crop farming expanded, Mappilla men, like Nayars and Tiyyars, began to acquire by their individual efforts personal property, much of which they gave to their wives and children. Such property might take the form of land, houses, shares in an export and import firm, elephants for use in procuring timber from forests for the timber trade, or retail shops selling cloth, food, or (in this century) a wide range of European machine-made goods. A poor Mappilla engaged in wage work for traders or agriculturalists might, like a Tiyyar, provide a house and the tenure of a garden for his conjugal family.

Tāvari-taravāds, or branch taravāds originated by a father's gift of property to his wife and her descendants, thus became common in the nineteenth century among Mappillas as among Nayars and Tiyyars. Mappilla legislation concerning inheritance has followed similar trends (Nair, 1941: 317). An act passed in 1918 ensured that the self-acquired property of a man who died intestate should pass by Muslim law to his wife and children (The Mappilla Succession Act, 1918). A further Mappilla act of 1939, comparable in its provisions to the Hindu Matriliny Act of 1933, permitted equal per capita division of a matrilineal property-group's estate between its male and female members (The Mappilla *Marumakkattayam* Act, 1939, quoted in Nair, 1941: 318). The general trend among Mappillas, as among Nayars and Tiyyars, has thus been a gradual disintegration of matrilineal groups, coupled with the emergence of the elementary family as a residential and economic unit. Among the wealthy, however, a few large matrilineal property groups of three to five generations' depth still remain, their members owning land, shops, or wholesale businesses in common under the management of a kāranavan.

Residential Patterns and the Constitution of the Dwelling Group

Mappillas, unlike Nayars or Tiyyars, were and are predominantly matrilocal. A young husband customarily moves to his wife's natal house on marriage, where he lives a large part of his time and contributes to the maintenance of his wife and children. In aristocratic taravāds owning land or other property, however, it has traditionally been customary for the oldest man of the taravād, when he succeeded to the headship, to return to live *sororilocally* in or near the ancestral house or houses occupied by his matrilineal kinswomen, their husbands and their unmarried sons. By this means he was able to manage the joint property conveniently. If his wife's natal house was nearby he might leave some of his private effects there and visit her when he could, maintaining an interest in the affairs of her matrilocal extended family and of his children. If his wife's house was at a distance a kāranavan usually brought her and their unmarried children to live for long periods in his own. By contrast, among poorer Mappillas whose property groups owned only a house and garden, even a kāranavan might remain in matrilocal residence in his wife's natal house, returning home to his taravād only for life crises or to settle disputes. This was (and is) especially likely if husband's and wife's natal homes were in the same neighborhood.

With the increasing development of personal property in the past hundred years, it has become fairly common for a midde-aged man to move his wife, daughters, and unmarried sons into a new house which he has provided. The daughters' young husbands are then also likely to live in this house, so that the result is again a matrilocal extended family. In this case however the house and property are managed by the donor husband and father. If such a man later becomes the kāranavan of an undivided matrilineal property group he may divide his time between his natal home and his private conjugal home. Some men manage to provide a house early in life for their wives before their children have married. In this case, at least for a time, the dwelling group is an elementary family.

Even a young man may sometimes divide his time between his own and his wife's natal homes if the two are in the same neighborhood. This is likely to happen if for some reason neither its kāranavan nor the husbands of its women live regularly in the husband's natal house. But such duolocal residence is of a different type from that of Nayars of Central Kerala. The husband visits not only at night, but for several days at a time. He leaves personal belongings in his wife's home; if possible, a private room is reserved for him; and he contributes regularly to the maintenance of wife and children.

In a very few cases a young man who is needed in his natal home but whose wife's house is at a distance may bring her to live for a period in his natal home. Such residence may be patrilocal, avunculocal, or sororilocal, depending on the kinship composition of the husband's home.

Figures for residence were obtained from Mappillas of a Kottayam village two miles from an inland Muslim bazaar town. None of the families were aristocrats; 17 per cent owned one or more gardens of pepper and fruit trees; 33 per cent were sharecropping tenants of gardens owned by Nayars or wealthy Mappillas living elsewhere; and 15 per cent merely rented the patch of land on which their house was built. Slightly over half the men were wage laborers for timber merchants. Their work was to cut trees in the forests of the foothills, move them to a river bank with the aid of elephants, and swim with the logs downriver for some twenty miles to a coast town north of Cannanore specializing in furniture making and timber export. The other men included small shopkeepers in the near-by town, wage workers in the gardens of Nayars or wealthy Mappillas, or small merchants who bought standing crops of spices or nuts from inland gardens and sold them to wholesalers in one of the coastal towns.

In this dominantly lower-class community, 54 per cent of the houses had been provided by a husband or father from his private earnings; 46 per cent by the men of a taravād for their matrilineal kinswomen and the latters' husbands. Seventy-one per cent of the households were matrilocal extended families comprising a woman and her husband with one or more daughters and their husbands and children; 5 per cent comprised a group of widowed or divorced matrilineally related women with their unmarried children; 8 per cent comprised a group of matrilineally related women and their children, with or without husbands, together with a matrilineal kinsman of the women and this man's wife; 15 per cent were elementary families.

Taking the residence of married couples by household we find that

46 per cent lived matrilocally; 25 per cent combined duolocality and matrilocality, the husband dividing his time between his natal home and his wife's; 25 per cent lived neolocally in a house provided by the husband; 4 per cent lived patrilocally in a house provided, and occupied, by the husband's father. Taking the residence of married couples by community, we find that 61 per cent lived matrilocally in the wife's natal village. In some cases this was also the husband's village, but the dwelling was usually nearer the wife's kin than the husband's. Twenty-five per cent combined duolocality and matrilocality: husband's and wife's houses were in the same village and the husband moved between them; 7 per cent lived neolocally: the husband had built a house in a village not previously occupied by his own kin or his wife's; 4 per cent lived patrilocally in the village of the husband's father which was not also that of the wife's kin; 3 per cent lived avunculocally in a village occupied by the husband's matrilineal kin but not by those of the wife.

These figures show a persistent tendency toward matrilocal residence coupled with gifts of houses by middle-aged husbands and fathers and some tendency toward increased autonomy of the elementary family. Like Tiyyars, Mappillas often give houses and gardens to their wives. However, Tiyyars are more likely to locate these near the husband's natal home; Mappillas, near the natal home of the wife.

From general observation, residence arrangements among wealthier Mappilla businessmen of the coast towns and among landowners seemed to be similar to those of the lower class. Two main differences were noted. One was that extended family households among the wealthy might be larger than among the poor, having a depth of four or even five generations and twenty or more members. The other was that kāranavans among the wealthy regularly lived sororilocally so that they could manage the property of their taravāds. The sororilocal residence of elders is much less common among the poor.

At present, dominantly matrilocal dwelling groups may be roughly classified into three main types in terms of their economic constitution. The first is the dwelling group of traditionally aristocratic Mappillas owning large estates. The more traditional type of household contains the matrilineally related women of the property group, their unmarried sons, their kāranavan, and sometimes his wife and unmarried children. Husbands of the women either live permanently in the house or visit for several days at a time. Junior men are absent in their wives' homes and visit occasionally. Both the husbands and the junior men may be engaged in subsidiary business in a nearby town—privately, or occasionally as one of a group of brothers. Downstairs, the large house contains a single communal kitchen, a dining room, several living rooms, and the kāranavan's private suite. Bedrooms may be set aside for junior men of the group on their visits. Taravād members, both male and female, live mainly downstairs in the daytime. Upstairs there will be a second large dining hall and living room. Opening off from these rooms are bed-sitting rooms, which are occupied by the matrilocally resident husbands and their wives. Husbands live mainly on this floor and seldom enter the downstairs kitchen because they may not see or speak to the sisters of their wives who are near to them in age. Taravād members dine downstairs, the men preceding the women. Husbands dine normally upstairs, served by a woman of the older generation, and retire at night to their rooms, where they are joined by their wives. Only children move freely in all parts of the house.

The household is primarily maintained from the produce of the matrilineal estate, managed by the kāranavan. He allocates supplies as in a Nayar property group in Central Kerala. In addition he pays out cash sums once a month to absent junior men. Husbands also pay cash sums to their wives each month, derived either from their own ancestral estates or from their businesses. Each wife retains a portion of her husband's payment for extra clothing and luxuries for herself and her children. The rest she hands to the oldest woman of the house, who uses it to supplement the household's budget for food. Aristocratic husbands admit, however, that while they reside matrilocally their gifts to their wives supply only a small portion of the household's maintenance. If a husband's business has been developed out of funds supplied by his taravād, a large part of his profits will go to his kāranavan to swell the joint property of his matrilineal group. If he started the business privately or with funds from his wife's taravād he will save money to provide a separate house and property for his wife and her descendants in middle age. For this reason, few modern aristocratic matrilocal extended families are "complete"; usually some of the older women live away in the private houses of their husbands.

The second type of dwelling group is that of rising middle-class Mappillas who have gained wealth in business over the past twenty to one hundred years. They include retail shopkeepers and timber merchants or merchants in spices, coconuts, or other garden products. In some cases such property is jointly owned by a taravād, although it was usually originally bequeathed by the husband of the common ancestress. The taravād may also own land, but this, unlike the land of aristocrats, is likely to be forest or newly developed gardens worked only for cash crops, rather than wet-rice land or gardens in long-established villages. (Both aristocrats and middle-class Mappillas have their land cultivated by tenants, either poorer Mappillas or Tiyyars.) Middle-class Mappillas, having no large ancestral estates of grain and subsistence crops, are more exposed to fluctuations of the business cycle than are aristocrats; such land as they own therefore comes and goes with rapidity. At any given time most of the property of this group, whether shops or land, is owned by individual men. At his death the property of such a man may pass jointly to his wife and her matrilineal descendants, thus forming a new small taravād. It is however quite likely to be dissipated in a generation or two. If the man originally used funds from his taravād to start a business, part of his property on his death may revert to the matrilineal descendants of his mother.

When such Mappillas live in matrilocal extended families the woman's kāranavan is less likely to be a permanent resident of their house. If there is taravād land he will come home occasionally to receive the rents and distribute the income, although most of the household's maintenance will be supplied by the resident husbands of the women. Often (as among aristocrats) two or more of these husbands are themselves matrilineally related, for Mappillas favor marriage of matrilateral cross-cousins and of two brothers to two sisters. Husbands who are matrilineal kin may go into business together and jointly supply the household of their wives. In this case—or in any case if the husbands' incomes are similar—the oldest woman manages the household's internal finances and cooking is communal. If, however, as more often happens, the husbands' incomes are disparate, each supplies his wife separately with cash, food, and clothing for themselves and their own children. The wife passes on a portion of her income to the oldest woman for the upkeep of the house, but each wife cooks separately for her husband and children. The houses of middle-class trading Mappillas in small bazaar towns thus often resemble small blocks of apartments. The house is owned jointly by the women's taravād and contains a main kitchen for feasts, a central hall, and rooms for the visiting kāranavan, but each wife occupies a separate wing with rooms and kitchen for her conjugal elementary family. In middle age a woman is likely to move out with her daughters into a new house provided by her husband.

In the matrilocal extended families of the poor, who own no land

and are usually wage laborers, the taravād property, if any, consists only of a small house and the tenure of a garden. Male members come home only for life crises or if they or their natal kinswomen are in urgent need of help. Resident husbands hand almost all of their wages to their wives, who may also work as agricultural laborers if the household is very poor. Divorce occurs more often in this group than in the aristocratic and middle-class groups, where it is very rare. In such poor households the incomes of husbands are usually similar and each may be periodically unemployed. Incomes are usually pooled, so that working members may support the old or the temporarily sick or unemployed. In later life a husband may build a new house for his wife, her daughters, and their husbands. Alternatively, a widow or a destitute divorced woman may occasionally go to occupy a hut near her brother's conjugal household and live from her own earnings and occasional help from her brother. Marriage and fatherhood are less stable than in the upper-income groups.

Given matriliny, the dominantly matrilocal residence of Mappillas, past and present, seems related to their occupations. Mappilla men's work has always tended to take them away from home. Traditionally, merchants of the ports sailed up and down the coast and sometimes to the Middle East. Some had one wife at home and other wives— Arab or North Indian Muslim—in distant ports; for a Mappilla, like all Muslims, may have four wives at one time. Inland traders and carriers also traveled, perhaps thirty or forty miles from home, sleeping often in rest houses and warehouses. Given matriliny, and with the men often away, it was natural that women, as among Central Kerala Nayars, should live in their natal homes protected by the head of their own matrilineal group. If women remain at home, residence must be either matrilocal or duolocal. Duolocal residence was not feasible in much of North Kerala because of distances between homes and between villages. Moreover, there was no special need why most men should live at all in their natal homes unless they were heads of property groups. Mappillas were not, like Central Kerala Nayars, trained for the army or attached to feudal lords on the basis of lineage membership. If there was an estate, the oldest man could manage it, for Mappillas did little cultivation. On the other hand, the demands of sexuality and the desire for domestic comfort would make it likely that, when possible, they would stay in the house of a wife who was conveniently located in relation to their work. The fact that Mappillas even traditionally dealt much in cash made it easy for them to give economic support in both natal and conjugal homes. Among the poor it is probable that even traditionally husbands and fathers provided the bulk of maintenance.

Today, wholesale merchants, middlemen traders, carriers, and wage workers in timber forests have a similar mobility. They may be absent for days or weeks, sleeping in shacks, warehouses, or rest houses, returning to the conjugal house as their home and visiting the natal house when they can. Shopkeepers in modern, crowded bazaar streets may live nearer to their fixed place of work; often, however, they live in gardens outside the town. Near the coast towns men may live ten miles from their work, to which they commute by bus. In these circumstances matrilocal residence is still often the most convenient arrangement, especially if a man's business is private and not a joint concern of his own matrilineal group. Some such men do bring their wives to live in their natal homes if this is especially convenient. Many now build a private house for the wife and children as soon as they can afford it.

Interpersonal Kinship Relationships

MATRILINEAL

The mutual coöperation and authority structure between matrilineal kin are obviously stronger in aristocratic landed taravāds than in those of the landless poor. Traditionally, however, the kāranavan had irreducible legal rights and obligations in all cases. He was legally responsible for his juniors in cases involving religious law and he represented them in the neighborhood assembly. He conducted life-crisis rites and arranged the marriage of a junior, although he sought the individual's father's consent. At a marriage the bride's kāranavan paid over the dowry to the bridegroom's kāranavan and received the bridewealth from him in turn. If the taravād owned property the kāranavan managed it and distributed the income. When at home he held domestic authority over women and children. If he maintained his juniors from a matrilineal estate his authority was great. He might for example compel a sister's son or daughter to divorce a spouse of whom he disapproved, by denying them maintenance until they complied with his wishes. As among Nayars, the Mappilla kāranavan's authority was whittled away by legal and economic changes in the nineteenth century. Since 1918 each man has been the legal guardian over his wife and immature children, although kāranavans who manage estates retain much *de facto* authority.

Matrilineally related men may still occasionally coöperate in business even under modern marketing conditions. If taravād funds are to be used to start a business, however, adult members of both sexes must sign documents accepting responsibility for its losses. It is therefore more common for two or three brothers, or one man and a sister's son, to enter business on the basis of their private earnings, especially if they are married to women of the same household. The profits and property they acquire are then their private concern and, during their lives, may be divided and distributed as they wish— to some few taravād members or to their wives and children. Many men, of course, now do business on their own.

The etiquette of behavior and the emotional ties within a taravād were traditionally very similar to those among Nayars, especially those of Central Kerala, where women lived together. Overt respect, based on age rank and covert hostility, characterized the relations between men: respect and distant behavior, based on the incest prohibitions, those between women and older men. However, Mappilla men, who live apart from their natal kinswomen for much of the time, observe a less formal etiquette of social distance toward their younger sisters and nieces than do Nayars. Mappilla women are not in purdah to their matrilineal kinsmen. They may uncover their faces before them, talk with them in a manner proper to age rank, serve them with food, and move about with them relatively freely in the home.

Great stress was traditionally placed on the unity and coöperation in work of matrilineally related women, as might be expected with matrilocal residence. The oldest woman had most authority in landed taravāds; she managed supplies and organized women's tasks. Women of the oldest generation served younger husbands with food. Feminine relationships in such a house were and are very similar to those among Central Kerala Nayars. In the middle classes today women more often cook separately for their husbands and children. Among wage laborers, the older generation, while receiving respect, in general loses much of its authority. An older couple or a widow who depend on their sons-in-law are apt to withdraw from authoritative roles and seek favor as playmates of their grandchildren.

MARRIAGE

Although Mappillas retained matrilineal descent, they introduced into the marriage institution some of the provisions of orthodox Sunni Muslim law, which they combined with local matrilineal usage. The modern trend is in favor of increased orthodoxy in the observance of Muslim law—a trend which may have begun with the invasions and propaganda of patrilineal Mysorean Muslims in the 1760's.

A Mappilla may have four wives by law, but in modern times few have more than two. Multiple marriages are difficult to combine with matrilocality unless a man travels constantly and visits each wife for brief periods. Whatever the reason, the majority of Muslims today have only one wife. A Mappilla, unlike a Tiyyar, never brings two wives to live in one house. He stays with each in her natal home. Sororal polygyny is forbidden both by local usage in the matrilineal castes and by Muslim law. Polyandry is of course strictly forbidden by Muslim law and in any case has not traditionally existed in any caste of North Kerala.

A Mappilla may divorce his wife by pronouncing the formula of divorce on three separate occasions before the *Khāzi* of his neighborhood, but a wife cannot freely divorce her husband by religious law. By local usage, however, she may ask her matrilineal elders to request a divorce from the husband. He invariably gives it, for his life would otherwise be intolerable in a matrilocal household. Divorce is very rare in the landed and middle classes—rarer than among Nayars. A husband who is dissatisfied usually remarries and visits his first wife less often. He maintains cordial relations with her family for fear of losing contact with his children. The woman's side normally seek divorce only if the husband is impotent or refuses to maintain her. Divorce is more usual among landless wageworkers, as it is among Tiyyars of the same economic level.

Girls traditionally married shortly before or after puberty; men, over the age of twenty. At the marriage, dowry (*strīdhanam*) was and is paid by the girl's taravād and bridewealth (*mahar*) by the man's. Mahar is the Islamic bridewealth, calculated in Arabic coins and then translated to rupees. Dowry is a common institution among the higher patrilineal Hindu castes and among Muslims throughout India. Among North Kerala Mappillas it seems to be adapted to the occupations of men. Both payments are always made but their significance varies by economic class. Among landed aristocrats the girl's kāranavan pays a cash dowry to the husband's kāranavan at the marriage. After the ceremony however the husband's kāranavan hands the dowry sum plus one rupee (a trivial amount) to the husband, who hands it back to the wife and her kāranavan as bridewealth on the night the marriage is consummated. The exchange is therefore a mere formality to mark the marriage contract. However, the dowry sum in theory remains vested in the girl for her husband's use. If the husband later divorces her he must again return the dowry sum to her taravād. Bridewealth is not, however, returnable at divorce. The net effect is that no significant sum changes hands at the marriage, but at divorce the husband must pay what amounts to a cash fine. In this class significant marriage payments are not required by either side because both groups own land and rely chiefly upon it for their maintenance.

Among middle-class Mappillas who own newly acquired land for cash crops and run businesses, the bridewealth is a moderate cash sum. It helps to defray the expenses of the marriage feasts which are provided by the household of the girl. It is not kept for the girl or her husband and is not returnable at divorce. Dowry is a much larger cash sum paid by the girl's kāranavan, sometimes augmented by her father. After the marriage the husband's kāranavan hands it on to the husband himself, who uses it to start a business or to expand a business in which he is already engaged. The husband is expected to maintain his wife and children almost entirely by his business and to leave at least a part of its proceeds to them at his death. If he divorces the wife he must return the dowry sum. In this class the payment of a large dowry is the means by which the girl's taravād relinquishes its obligation to provide the bulk of her maintenance and transfers this obligation to the husband, while giving him the means to undertake it.

Among both aristocrats and middle-class Mappillas the dowry also includes valuable jewelry. This is vested in the girl, but if the husband is in need he may use it as security for loans. At a divorce all her jewelry must be left intact with the girl. Again, the cash value of jewelry is of greater practical significance in the middle class, where ready cash may be urgently needed for business ventures.

In recent years fathers in these two classes have also often given self-acquired immovable property to their daughters as dowry at marriage. Among aristocrats this is often land; among businessmen, a shop. The property is vested in the wife and her matrilineal descendants but the husband controls it and manages the income for the duration of the marriage.

Among wage laborers both dowry and bridewealth are very small cash sums. The bride's family spends the bridewealth on a marriage feast; the dowry reimburses the groom for the wedding clothes he has presented to his wife. In this class, which has little or no capital, dowry and bridewealth thus become a polite mode of sharing the marriage expenses.

At marriage the bridegroom provides his wife with clothing which she wears to visit his family a few days after the marriage. Before this visit, on the night of the consummation, the couple are given a private room in the girl's home in which to enjoy their married companionship. Furnishings in the room, provided by the girl's family, belong to the husband for the duration of the marriage and may not be removed without his consent. He keeps his private belongings in this room and spends most of his time there when home, talking and sleeping with his wife, playing with the children, or, when the wife is absent, entertaining other husbands of the house. This usage contrasts with that among Nayars of Central Kerala: the husband is given no furniture and brings no movables to his conjugal home; he merely visits his wife at night in any vacant bedroom of the house.

A man has exclusive sexual rights in his wife and rights in her domestic services. Even if she cooks the main meals communally with her kinswomen, she must provide tea and snacks privately for her husband in their room when he requests them. All Mappillas have some domestic authority over their wives, but this is greatest in the modern middle class, where the husband provides almost all of his wife's maintenance. Among aristocrats a woman remains primarily under the authority of the matrilineal elders who maintain her. Among the poor the woman may herself go to work and can dismiss her husband if he offends her.

A husband owes his wife maintenance. Among aristocrats he contributes monthly cash sums to the oldest woman of the house and brings occasional clothing for his wife. In the middle and lower classes husbands buy and bring home almost all the household provisions. As has been seen, in all classes a modern husband may elect to move his wife into a private house of his own, of which he then becomes the head. From this time on, he usually assumes the whole responsibility of maintaining his wife and children.

Husbands have special expenses at the birth of a child. The husband or his taravād pay for family feasts at the wife's house during the pregnancy and at the naming ceremony on the fortieth day after the birth. The husband presents his wife with new clothing after the birth and pays the low-caste Hindu midwife in cash and cloths. As among Nayars and Tiyyars, the birth payments indicate the husband's acceptance of his paternity and serve to legitimize the child. Among aristocrats they meet only a portion of the total expense lavished by the girl's taravād in feasts and gifts at a birth. In the middle and lower classes the husband finances the whole affair.

THE FATHER AND HIS KIN

A man normally takes a great interest in his children, caring for them in infancy and attending to their education. He traditionally had domestic authority over them although they were the legal wards of their kāranavan. He must be consulted about their marriages and today may actually read the marriage service for his daughter. Traditionally, a man should at least partially have maintained his children until they married. He was almost certainly not expected to do so if he divorced their mother; today, however, he can be obliged to maintain them by law. Over and above the maintenance he owed them, fathers have for at least a hundred years given self-acquired property to their children when they could, and have augmented the dowries of their daughters. Today a father sometimes introduces a son into his private business, especially if the son has married his father's sister's daughter. Emotionally and in etiquette the relationship with the father closely resembles that among Nayars of this area.

In general Mappillas seem to have tried to strengthen the paternal tie as much as is compatible with matrilineal descent. The wealthy disfavor divorce and regard the separation of father and children as tragic. In order to prolong the paternal tie they encourage a man whose wife has died, leaving young children, to marry her younger sister or her sister's daughter. The bereaved man is usually glad to do so, for this solution minimizes the discontinuity in his own and his children's lives. The children in any case will be brought up by their mother's sisters; if the father marries elsewhere he cannot take them with him, yet he is customarily obliged to contribute to their maintenance. No dowry or bridewealth is required for the second marriage. Such sororatic marriage—common among wealthy Mappillas but forbidden by Nayars and Tiyyars—fits well with matrilocal residence and reflects the Mappilla view of fatherhood as a permanent and stable relationship carrying obligations till death. Leviratic marriage is also occasionally practiced, although it is much less common than among the patrilineal, patrilocal Mappillas of Central Kerala, where it has special utility. It may occur if a man dies leaving property to his young children and there is a brother of suitable age to marry the wife. The brother then manages the property of the dead man's children and is expected to care for them as if they were his own. If no leviratic marriage occurs, a middle- or upper-class widow with children is unlikely to remarry, for it is thought that a strange stepfather might neglect the children and create disharmony in the home. Leviratic marriage, again, is forbidden by Nayars and Tiyyars but is enjoined by Muslim law.

A further marriage favored by Mappillas is that of two or more brothers to two or more sisters. Nayars and Tiyyars of North Kerala forbid such marriages on the grounds that the sisters will ally themselves against other wives of their husbands' residential group and too firmly entrench themselves within it. The children, brought up together as a group of matrilineal kin, might later be unwilling to leave the paternal fold. This view reflects the traditional Nayar attitude that marriage and paternity are personal ties, always potentially breakable if they threaten matrilineal loyalties. The matrilocal Mappillas by contrast already have the children in their mother's home and wish to secure their fathers as permanent financial supports of the mother's taravād. They feel that husbands of the same generation will be more firmly knit to their conjugal home if they enter it as a group of brothers.

Again, funeral rites show that Mappillas do not sever the conjugal and paternal ties at death as sharply as do Nayars. Only aristocrats bury their dead in a private lineage burial ground; other Mappillas inter them in a communal cemetery attached to the neighborhood mosque. The sons of a dead man not only perform the rites of chief mourners but also finance the funeral; they give the money to their sisters' husbands, who pay it out as required. If the deceased leaves no son, his sons-in-law pay for the funeral on behalf of his daughters. A widow formally mourns for her husband for three months after the death; during this time the husband's kin send money to maintain her. A widow is not forbidden to visit her husband's natal home.

Like North Kerala Nayars and Tiyyars, Mappillas forbid marriage to the father's sister, the brother's daughter, and the paternal parallel cousin. Women are not in purdah in relation to their male paternal parallel cousins, for they, like matrilineal cousins, are regarded as brothers. A woman does however observe purdah in the presence of an older male cross cousin unless he is her husband, for he is marriageable and may of course be her actual brother-in-law. Mappillas, like Nayars and Tiyyars, favor both types of cross-cousin marriage, especially matrilateral. Emotionally and in etiquette, male cross cousins have the same type of relationship as among Nayars and Tiyyars.

Paternal kin play a significant role in life-crisis rites. The husband's mother and sisters attend feasts during the wife's pregnancy and on the fortieth day after the birth—the end of the new mother's period of seclusion. The baby's paternal grandmother names him on this day, giving the paternal grandfather's name to the first boy and her own to the first girl. When the child is six months old its parents must present him to his paternal grandmother in her home. He receives a gold waistband from the grandmother and other gifts of jewelry from the father's sisters at this time. The father's mother and sisters are also prominent at a marriage, where they are feasted and where they make gifts of clothing and jewelry.

AFFINES

The husbands who "marry in" to a taravād are obviously its most important affines. The wife's elder kin call them *pudiyāppillais* ("new Mappillas" or "bridegrooms") throughout their lives. In all classes scrupulous politeness is extended to these men, but the relationship is most ceremonious among aristocrats.

In a traditional aristocratic household the taravād under its kāranavan largely maintains the women and children; husbands contribute small sums. Correspondingly, the kāranavan holds ultimate authority in the house. Husbands, as though in compensation, receive lavish hospitality and ceremonial privileges, and ostentatious care is taken to fulfill their limited rights to the letter. The different rights of kāranavan and husbands appear most sharply at life-crisis rites. The kāranavan arranges all of the rites and finances the large feasts from taravād funds. Husbands of the house play a limited—but essential— role by paying the fees of the ritual officiants; they also make gifts to the chief celebrant of the rite. The husbands of the household collectively pay the Hindu goldsmith who pierces the ears of a small girl; they pay the Mappilla barber who circumcises a small boy; and they pay the khāzi who officiates at marriages and deaths in the household. On all these occasions they give clothing and other small perquisites to the chief celebrant. Correspondingly, although it is obvious to all that the kāranavan arranges the ceremonies, he may not do so without first formally consulting all husbands of the house in a solemn conclave. At the feast itself the kāranavan humbly calls on all the husbands to give consent before the company is permitted to sit down and eat.

It is the wife's kāranavan and other matrilineal kinsmen of generations senior to her who must give the greatest overt respect to her husband. The wife's kāranavan urges hospitality on the young husband, addresses him in an honorific way, carefully accords him privacy in his room, and asks consent before sitting in his presence. If the wife's kāranavan is the husband's father, these courtesies are decreased, but still the father must see to it that his son is accorded honor in his house. The young husband's conduct is less formally polite. He lolls and talks freely before the men of his wife's house and may request small favors in a rather cavalier way. Beneath this, however, Mappillas know that the husband is the real subordinate. He may not tamper with the serious management of the house, he avoids the downstairs rooms where the kāranavan wields undisputed authority, and he knows that if he gravely oversteps his limits he can be politely encouraged to leave. The kāranavan is the most scrupulously polite to the husband because it is he who limits the latter's power. Traditionally, her kāranavan remained the legal guardian of the wife; he gave her husband only sexual rights and limited domestic authority. On the other hand he required partial financial support from the husband and wished to keep him as a permanent resident. It was, and in orthodox houses still is, a most delicate relationship, made bearable for the husband by the kāranavan's studied politeness.

The wife's mother and other women of senior generation have a less formal relationship with the husband in aristocratic homes. This is possible because they have no legal authority in the house; at the same time their age makes the difference of sex a comparatively unimportant barrier. It is they who serve food to the husband, chat to him about his home affairs, and plan comforts and delicacies for him. In etiquette the husband may be as free with them as with his own mother. He may for example touch them after they have performed their ceremonial ablutions without endangering the efficacy of their prayers, whereas he is forbidden to touch his wife after her ablutions and before her prayers. The husband, like the Nayar husband in Central Kerala, knows that tact is required if he is to avoid provoking their jealousy over his marital relations with his wife. A thoughtful husband never enters the house without bringing betel leaves, areca nuts, and tobacco for his mother-in-law and her sisters. The senior women evaluate him in terms of these little courtesies.

A man sees his wife's married brothers only occasionally and they have less authority over the wife than has her kāranavan. His behavior to them is informal, and brothers-in-law near in age have a mild joking relationship. Each, however, owes the other favors which must not be neglected. The wife's brothers must at all times urge hospitality on the husband. He in turn must make gifts of clothing to them at his own marriage and at the subsequent marriage of any of them. As among Nayars, a man's sisters' husbands act as groomsmen at his marriage, accompanying him to the house of the bride. Unlike Nayars, Mappillas also invite a man's sisters' husbands on all other important occasions when his taravād is to be represented. Thus at all life-crisis rites in a house, not only the women's husbands' sisters but also *their* husbands—the "bridegrooms" of the husbands' natal houses—must be invited to the feast.

Mappilla women observe a modified form of purdah outside their natal homes. They are not veiled, but they wear a headscarf which they draw across the face when an unrelated man approaches. Purdah is most strictly observed by middle-class women of business communities, who seldom go outdoors. It is less necessary for aristocratic women, whose wealth and rank effectively remove them from contacts with commoners. It is less possible for lower-class women, who sometimes go out to work. In all classes, however, women observe purdah as far as possible in relation to their sisters' husbands. Among aristocrats a woman who has not passed the childbearing age does not sit or loiter in the upstairs hall where the husbands congregate. When summoned, she slips quietly to her husband's room with her scarf drawn across her face. Purdah restrictions thus effectively preclude sexual intrigues between affines and jealousy between resident husbands. At the same time they exclude the husband from participation in the intimate family life of his wife's matrilineal kinsfolk below stairs, and so segregate his field of authority from that of his wife's matrilineal kinsmen. A man may not indeed speak the name of his wife's sister and it is said that he never addresses her "unless the house is burning." He may however play with his wife's younger sister who has not reached puberty or married; he contributes to the expenses of her ear-piercing ceremony, and he presents clothing at her marriage.

A man's children and all his wife's kinsfolk of junior generations treat him with affectionate respect. He is a "father" or "grandfather" to all of them. The children have ready access to his room and the mature women do not observe purdah before him. As he grows older they, and especially his own children, become his allies in the house and stabilize his position. Indeed, in a traditional household a husband literally moves downstairs into intimacy as he attains old age. The men of senior generations in the wife's house die, the women of his own generation avoid him less carefully after the menopause, and the younger women are not in purdah before him. The kāranavan will be his brother-in-law and age mate, toward whom he has learnt to accommodate himself through long association. If he has earned the loyalty of his wife's house he may spend happy hours in the downstairs rooms and the outer veranda, playing with the grandchildren, and his advice will be sought with genuine respect rather than merely ceremonious politeness. Traditionally, of course, it is at this point that a man often becomes the kāranavan of his own natal house and must begin to loosen the ties with his conjugal family. Today many men have by this age built private houses and founded matrilocal extended families of which they are the paternal heads.

The husbands of a traditional aristocratic dwelling group behave informally to one another. They sit, smoke, and joke mildly together, although the husbands of younger women accord some respect to those of older women and do not act boisterously before them. The respect is somewhat more marked toward husbands of a higher generation. Unless they are also matrilineal kin, there is however no authority structure between co-resident husbands, for they perform no tasks in common. Each is separately tied into his wife's house through the payment of money earned elsewhere, and traditionally none had real authority within it. Husbands, especially of the same generation, are thrown together by community of fate. They usually appear friendly; today they often play cards together. But apart from jointly contributing to the expenses of life-crisis rites they practice little serious coöperation.

In a traditional aristocratic household it was her father's personal rights in a woman which the husband took over at marriage. The girl's kāranavan remained her legal guardian exactly as before marriage, but the father's domestic authority passed to her husband. A man therefore had to be careful not to oppose his son-in-law's wishes if he offered advice to his daughter. She in turn must make clear, sometimes in a ceremonial manner, that her husband was her immediate authority in private domestic matters and that her first attachment was to him. Thus, for example, when a woman's father died, she could not by traditional custom view his body or begin to mourn him until she received her husband's formal consent. Her father, by contrast, had nothing to say when a woman mourned for her husband, nor was the husband consulted before she mourned the death of a matrilineal kinsman.

Traditional usages are now being modified through the accumulation of private property and houses by individual aristocrats. Much more drastic departures from ideal traditional custom are however observable in middle-class business and lower-class wage-working communities today; unfortunately I do not know to what extent the ancestors of these commoners observed the "ideal" customs in former days. In newly rich business households today the taravād property is often small and resident husbands provide most of the maintenance of their wives and children. The women's kāranavan is often absent most of the time and the matrilocal extended family may be divided residentially into separate elementary family cells. The wife's older matrilineal kinsmen preserve customary politeness in relation to her husband when they see him, but they surrender to him most of the day-to-day management of his part of the home. The husband today often finances and acts as host at his children's life-crisis rites, merely inviting their kāranavan and matrilineal kinsmen to officiate out of politeness. A young husband often starts his married life as a resident of the private house of his father-in-law, who accords the youth greater overt respect than he would do in a traditional aristocratic household; yet the father-in-law also retains more real authority over the household as a whole. The relationship is not very formal or stereotyped, however, and the young husband may in turn soon move his wife into a home of his own. In the rare cases where the adults of a taravād elect to use their joint capital to start a business venture, the husbands of the women now exercise their modern rights as legal guardians of the women and children. Thus an adult woman may not sign her name to a modern taravād document without her husband's supporting signature, and he may later insist on acting for her in the management of the business. More commonly it is her husband who instigates division of the wife's taravād property on a per capita basis in accordance with modern law. He may even act for her in court cases against her own kāranavan. In general, whereas the traditional etiquette of behavior tends to be preserved in modified form between kinsfolk in modern middle-class families, real financial and legal powers are more often vested in the husbands.

Among lower-class wage workers, houses are perhaps even more often owned by the husband. A woman's kāranavan seldom lives in her home; if he does, he may be there as a dependent and exercise little authority. After marriage the wife's brothers are usually away from her home. The young husband finds himself contributing to the expenses of a household managed by his wife's father or, almost as frequently, by his wife's widowed or divorced mother. He will be accorded customary overt respect, but his real authority will depend on his financial contributions. He may be an actual subordinate of his wife's parents, liable to dismissal if he fails in his obligations. Alternatively he may soon become the chief breadwinner and "carry" the whole household, nominally deferring to his parents-in-law but relatively unhindered by their claims. If this marriage endures he will by middle age, through one means or another, become the head of his conjugal household. In this class wagework is almost always individual and property is reduced to a minimum. Neither matrilineal kinsmen nor affines are therefore likely to be bound for long periods by joint ownership or by coöperation in production.

In all classes a woman's relations with her spouse's kin are slighter than those of a man. She seldom lives with them and her visits are a matter of ceremonial obligation. Mutual politeness characterizes her relations with her husband's kinswomen; avoidance, those with her husband's kinsmen of the same generation; and respect, those with her husband's senior kinsmen. In general a woman is the recipient rather than the donor of gifts and privileges in her husband's home. The husband's kinswomen do not accompany him to his marriage, but they receive the couple in their home a few days later, feast them royally, and give clothing and jewelry to the bride. Later they attend feasts of pregnancy and birth in the wife's home and make gifts to the mother and child. A woman must be invited to almost all life-crisis feasts in her husband's natal home. Only immediate kin of the household, and not guests, however, are present at the nuptials of a bride, which follow in her own home shortly after her marriage. On this day the bridegroom is summoned three times from his home by brothers of the bride. Each time he sends them home with gifts of food and clothing, and only at the third summons does he accept their invitation. He brings with him a large quantity of tobacco which is distributed to women in the house of the bride. They in turn take care to parcel and send portions of it to the wives of their own matrilineal kinsmen in other homes, who must not be forgotten on any important day. Particularly in landed taravāds, relationships with the wife of a matrilineal kinsman are not of the warmest. Especially when she is the kāranavan's wife, Mappillas, like Nayars, may suspect her of seeking undue influence with her husband and thus of endangering the interests of his taravād.

Kinship Terms

Mappillas equate a number of relatives on the mother's and the father's sides. Terms are therefore listed by generation and not by lineage. When a term applies to relatives of more than one generation it is listed under the generation to which it primarily applies.

EGO'S GENERATION:

(1) *Ikkākka, kākka.* EBr. Elder male paternal or maternal parallel cousin. May be extended to MoBr, FaMoBr, WiEBr, HuEBr.

(2) *Ittātta, tātta.* ESi. Elder female paternal or maternal parallel cousin. FaFaSi, HuESi.

(3) *Anujan.* YBr. Younger male paternal or maternal parallel cousin. Reference only.

(4) *Anujatti.* YSi. Younger female paternal or maternal parallel cousin. Reference only.

(5) *Āngala.* F. speaking only. Own brother. Reference only.

(6) *Pengal.* M. speaking only. Own sister. Reference only.

(7) *Machunian.* Male cross cousin. Reference only.

(8) *Machunichi.* Female cross cousin. Reference only.

(9) *Ammāyi.* EBrWi, MoBrWi, MoMoBrWi, WiMo, WiESi, Wi-MoBrWi, HuMoBrWi, HuEBrWi.

(10) *Kunyala.* ESiHu. Sometimes extended to FaSiHu.

(11) *Māppilla.* Hu. Reference only.

(12) *Kettiyōl.* Wi. Reference only.

FIRST ASCENDING GENERATION:

(1) *Uppa.* Fa. Prefaced by *mūtta* (eldest) or *elaya* (younger) for FaEBr or FaYBr, MoESiHu or MoYSiHu, FaESiHu or FaYSiHu. HuFa.

(2) *Umma.* Mo. Prefaced by *mūtta* (eldest) or *elaya* (younger) for MoESi or MoYSi, FaEBrWi or FaYBrWi. HuMo.

(3) *Pettōma, pettāccha.* FaSi. MoFaSi.

(4) *Ammāman.* MoBr, MoMoBr, WiMoBr, HuMoBr. All of these kin may also be called *kākka.*

SECOND ASCENDING GENERATION:

(1) *Ummumma.* MoMo and MoMoSi, Spouse's MoMo and Mo-MoSi, MoFaBrWi.

(2) *Belippa.* MoFa, MoFaBr, MoMoSiHu, Spouse's MoFa, spouse's MoMoSiHu.

(3) *Uppumma.* FaMo and FaMoSi.

(4) *Uppuppa.* FaFa. May be extended to MoMoBr, who is otherwise called *ammāman.*

FIRST DESCENDING GENERATION:

(1) *Makan.* So. SiSo F speaking. Reference only.

(2) *Makal.* Da. SiDa F speaking. Reference only.

(3) *Marumakan.* SiSo, SiDaSo. M. speaking. Reference only.

(4) *Marumakal.* SiDa, SiDaDa. M. speaking. Reference only.

(5) *Pudiyamāppillai, pudiyāppillai* ("new husband"). YSiHu, Da-Hu, SiDaHu, Hu of any younger woman in the household in which one lives or into which one was born.

SECOND DESCENDING GENERATION:

(1) *Pērakutti.* DaCh, SoCh, SiDaCh. F. speaking. Reference only.

Terms are not commonly extended to relatives other than those given. Any distant older male relative may be called *kākka* (EBr); any distant older female relative, *umma* (Mo).

Comment: Leaving aside lexical differences, the Mappilla system is essentially similar to that of North Kerala Nayars and Tiyyars. The main differences are as follows.

Mappillas equate elder brother's wife, mother's brother's wife, wife's elder sister and wife's mother and her sister. The equation of elder brother's and mother's brother's wives, like the occasional equation of elder brother and mother's brother, emphasizes the similar roles of all the older males of ego's lineage. There seems no special reason why Mappillas should emphasize this more than Nayars, unless it be that Mappillas have less need to differentiate between their older matrilineal kinsmen since these kin are usually absent in their wives' homes. The equation of mother's brother's wife with wife's mother fits matrilateral cross-cousin marriage. The equation of elder brother's wife and wife's elder sister fits the common Mappilla practice of the marriage of two brothers to two sisters (forbidden by Nayars).

Second, Mappillas may equate elder brother not only with mother's brother but also with father's mother's brother. The latter equation may reflect the fact that ego acts as his father's equivalent when he visits his father's house, adopting the father's terminology in relation to the latter's kāranavan.

Third, Mappillas distinguish father's sister from mother by a special term, thus making a bifurcate merging system for the parents and their siblings. North Kerala Nayars, by contrast, equate father's sister with mother's sister. The difference probably lies in that Nayar children may be brought up near the father's sister in avunculocal residence and treat her as a permissive motherly figure. Among matrilocal Mappillas she is an affine who officiates and makes gifts at ceremonies and is clearly distinguished from ego's mother's sister who lives in his natal home. The father's sister is also however distinguished from the mother's brother's wife, who has a special affinal role as potential wife of ego's kāranavan. The Mappilla equation of father's sister with mother's father's sister reflects the fact that these women play similar roles as visitors at ceremonies.

Fourth, Mappillas may equate elder sister's husband with father's sister's husband. This, like the second equation, may reflect the fact that ego classes himself with his father for some purposes when he visits his father's natal home.

Fifth, Mappillas sometimes equate mother's mother's brother with father's father. This usage is probably confined to the situation where ego's parents have made a patrilateral cross-cousin marriage.

Sixth, Mappillas equate as "bridegrooms" all the husbands of younger women of the house in which they live or into which they were born. This usage reflects the common role of younger husbands as honored guests and partial outsiders. For the first decade of marriage they are indeed treated as though they were on a perpetual honeymoon in the wife's house.

Variation in
Matrilineal Systems

Introduction to
Parts Two and Three

The Introduction to this book set forth a theoretical statement of the common features of systems of matrilineal descent. It was argued that these features issue from three fundamental premises of matrilineal systems: namely, the rule of matrilineal descent itself, the exogamy of descent groups, and a certain sexual division of functions and of authority. Subsequent chapters analyzed nine matrilineal systems in concrete detail.

In Part Two I attempt to explain some major variations among matrilineal societies.[1] Specifically, I try to state the conditions under which certain special characteristics of descent groups, of residence patterns, of interpersonal kinship relationships, and of marriage preferences are likely to occur.

My method in this part is different from that adopted by Schneider in the general introduction. When, at the close of the seminar, I undertook to explore further the hypotheses which the group had begun to develop about varieties of matriliny, I was impelled by both temperament and training to investigate a small number of societies, in their totality and in detail. I chose this method rather than (like Schneider) attempting a purely theoretical statement of logical possibilities without reference to particular cases, or (like Aberle in the final part of this book) seeking statistical associations of variables

[1] Part Two is based on insights which members of the SSRC seminar reached together in the course of their discussions in 1954, on conversations and correspondence which I have had individually with members of the seminar since our group dispersed, and on my own reading during the past four years. My thinking has been particularly influenced by the work of Marshall D. Sahlins, who participated in the seminar, and by constant discussion with my husband, David F. Aberle. For my training in the analysis of kinship systems I am deeply indebted to Meyer Fortes and to Max Gluckman. Whatever there is of merit in chapters 10 to 16 has grown, directly or indirectly, out of the joint efforts of the seven seminar members. On the other hand, I alone am responsible for this presentation, and other members of the group cannot be held accountable for any particular statements I have made.

445

within a much larger number of systems. All three methods are, I believe, valid types of comparative research for their purposes. All three rely, explicitly or implicitly, both on empirical knowledge and on logical constructs. All three aim to produce exploratory hypotheses which can be checked, modified, amplified, or rejected by future writers working with better materials or larger numbers of societies.

Fifteen societies or part-societies will be considered in Part Two. Nine of them have been described in the ethnographic chapters of this book. In addition, I have included six other societies in my comparative study. They are the Hopi of Arizona, the Minangkabau of Central Sumatra, and four Central African societies: the Mayombe of the lower Congo area of West Central Africa, the Bemba of the northeastern plateau of Northern Rhodesia, the Ndembu or Mwinilunga Lunda of the northwest province of Northern Rhodesia, and the Yao of Southern Nyasaland.

My original plan was to include short summaries of these six systems in the main body of this book. Later this was seen to be impracticable. Only very brief accounts could have been given, and for all six of the societies admirable summaries were already available in recent literature by specialists. Instead, salient characteristics of each society will be brought out in the course of the discussion, and the literary sources indicated.

I make no bones about my reasons for selecting these fifteen systems. Nine of them had been chosen for various personal reasons by members of the seminar, and I had learned much from our discussions of these societies. In addition, Dr. Meyer Fortes' work on the Ashanti had earlier influenced my own research among the Nayars. I added the Bemba, Mayombe, and Yao because of Dr. Audrey Richards' stimulating comparative study (1950) of these and other Central African systems, which provided me with many valuable clues for my own task. The Minangkabau were included because of their obvious and unusual parallels with the Central Kerala Nayars, including that of duolocal residence. I included the Hopi and the Ndembu because I felt "at home" with these systems from the writings and discussions of my friends, Dr. and Mrs. Fred Eggan, Dr. Mischa Titiev, and Dr. Victor Turner. The fifteen societies are thus in no sense a sample, but rather examples of matrilineal systems with which I happened to be familiar. Nevertheless, I began my task with the pleasing awareness that they represented a wide range of possible types of matrilineal society, with regard to subsistence base, political system, descent-group structure, and residence pattern. This variety, as well as the fact that they are drawn from four continents and thus probably issue from at least four independent historical developments of matriliny, has enhanced the breadth and perhaps the validity of my conclusions.

Chapters 10, 11, and 12 attack the problem of variations in the structure and functions of matrilineal descent groups. Three apparent determinants of these variations are considered. They include, first, the qualitative type of the society's ecology or subsistence base and, in particular, the question of whether the society relies for its subsistence primarily on settled or on mobile cultivation. (No noncultivating societies were included in my examples.) The second determinant of descent-group form to be discussed is the quantitative level of productivity of the society. The third determinant is the extent of the society's political centralization.

At this point a few words may be said about definition of terms. By ecology I refer to the interaction between the natural environment and the society's technology. I use White's definition of technology: "The technological system is composed of the material, mechanical, physical and chemical instruments, together with the techniques of their use, by means of which man, as an animal species, is articulated with his natural habitat. Here we find the tools of production, the means of subsistence, the materials of offense and defense" (White, 1949: 365). Technology involves the harnessing and controlling of energy, by means of tools, to serve the needs of man. "Level of productivity" refers to the amount of energy harnessed per capita per year by members of the society. This concept is further explained in chapter 11.

I do not include in "ecology" the system of social relationships through which the society exploits its environment by means of its technology. This system, following common usage, I shall refer to as the economic system. The economic system or system of economic relationships is a dimension of the total social structure, having to do with the allocation of goods and services. The kinship system, or system of genealogical relationships, is a segment of the total social structure which, like all other segments, has its economic dimension. The ecology is the "base" on which the social structure is built up.

By political organization I refer to the allocation of authority and responsibility in the society.[2] By this definition, therefore, all relationships and groups, including descent groups, have political and

---

[2] My definitions of economic and political organizations are influenced by Levy's work on the Chinese family (1949: 22, 28).

economic dimensions. This is true notwithstanding the fact that in general, as technology develops, specialized groups and relationships emerge which have to do primarily with the allocation of goods and services or with the allocation of authority and responsibility in the society as a whole. My concern is to develop a rough classification of types of ecology and types of over-all political organization and economic organization in matrilineal societies. I shall then enquire into the implications of these over-all classifications for the small-scale political and economic organizations of descent groups, and also into their implications for other characteristics of descent groups—for example, genealogical structure and local distribution.

Part of the discussion in chapters 10, 11, and 12 concerns the separate implications for descent-group form of qualitative subsistence type, level of productivity, and degree of political centralization. Because these three determinants do not operate independently of one another, however, considerable space is given to the nature of the connections between them.

Chapter 13 takes up the problem of variation in residence. Here, the major determinants are thought to be economic factors—in particular, the sexual division of labor and its relation to work sites, the constitution of work groups, and the nature of distributive networks. These features of the economic system are in turn thought to stem primarily from the type of ecology and of over-all political and economic system. Both residence patterns and economic variables may, however, *derive* from past historical circumstances and persist, because their subsequent ecological, economic, and political settings have not exerted positive pressures toward change.

The general content of interpersonal kinship relationships, discussed in chapter 14, is in important respects seen to co-vary with the structure and functions of descent groups, and thus to be strongly determined by type of subsistence base, level of productivity, and degree of political centralization. When, however, I turn to specific features of the etiquette of interpersonal kinship relationships, namely, the presence or absence of avoidant and joking patterns, I seek primary determinants in specific types of economic and of residential arrangements. Preferred forms of marriage, discussed in chapter 15, are thought to stem from a rather wide range of factors in the larger social structure, such as the number of descent groups in a given territorial unit, the residence pattern, the economic relationships of production and distribution, and the type of political structure.

Finally, in chapter 16, I explore the several steps in the modern disintegration of matrilineal descent groups and the causes of their decline. The determinants here, in the societies examined, are seen to lie primarily in the area of change to a market system of economic relationships, although direct changes in political structure may also operate concomitantly. It seems appropriate to include these several stages of partial disintegration and dwindling of functions of descent groups as "variations" in matrilineal systems, not least because they are the forms of matrilineal system most frequently encountered at the present time.

In the last chapter (Part Three) David F. Aberle raises the question, "Under what circumstances is matrilineal reckoning likely to arise, to survive, and to disappear?" and attempts to deal with it within the framework of evolutionary theory. He uses many of the major variables discussed in chapters 10 to 16, but does so in terms of correlations and associations provided in Murdock's *World Ethnographic Sample*.

K. G.

Descent Groups of Settled
and Mobile Cultivators

My first classification of descent groups has to do with direct implications of ecology for descent group structure, leaving aside consideration of the over-all economic and political organizations of the societies.
It is a simple dichotomy between societies or part-societies which have
settled subsistence cultivation as the chief means of livelihood, and
societies which lack settled subsistence cultivation.

Groups Which Place Primary Reliance on Settled
Subsistence Cultivation

"Settled" cultivation is of course a relative term. Even under the most
permanent forms of cultivation, some plots may be left fallow, and the
population may periodically expand to newly cultivated land. I use
"settled cultivation" to refer to those forms of cultivation which permit
at least a portion of the population to remain on the same residential
sites for an indefinite period. Of the fifteen groups considered, we may
place in this category Central and North Kerala Nayars, aristocratic
North Kerala Mappillas, North Kerala Tiyyars, Mayombe, Hopi,
Ashanti, Trobriand, Minangkabau, and Truk. Aristocratic Mappillas
are included because—although they were traders—they owned
landed estates from which they derived a large part of their maintenance. Aristocratic Mappillas and Central Kerala Nayars were unusual in that they did not themselves cultivate the land from which
they gained a living. Tiyyars were unusual in that they did not themselves own the land they cultivated. The effects of these conditions
will be considered later. For the present it is enough to note that the
ownership or long-term tenure of fixed plots caused the descent
groups of these castes to have some characteristics in common with
those of other societies of settled cultivators.

    Some of these societies have entered marketing relationships with modern industrial nations and devote a large part of their cultivation to the production of cash crops for export. This chapter will be concerned with what is known of these societies at a time when they cultivated primarily for subsistence, before they became involved in the modern system of marketability of land and labor. Their former primary concern with subsistence cultivation was not incompatible with the fact that many of them had trade relations in a limited range of goods before the advent of the market system.

Reliance on settled subsistence cultivation seems to lead to the following characteristics of matrilineal descent groups.

THE JOINT ESTATE

A landed estate is controlled jointly by the members of one or another order of descent group. This is the case in all my examples, and I suggest that with matrilineal descent and settled subsistence cultivation only land newly brought under cultivation can ever be controlled by individuals. Once it has been inherited, land will be held by some order of matrilineal descent group, although larger territorial units, e.g., the district or the state, may have an overright in land.

The existence of the joint estate seems to be common to patrilineal or bilateral descent groups with settled subsistence cultivation, as well as to matrilineal, at least in the great majority of cases. I am not sure of the precise reasons for this near-universality of the joint estate with settled cultivation. One important characteritic of the joint estate in all our matrilineal examples of settled cultivators is that the estate owned by a descent group is large enough to comprise several different types of crops or of land. In some cases each estate contains all the types of crop found in the society. This would not be possible with individually owned plots. The descent group therefore acts as a simple redistributive unit with regard to its own products, although it will often also exchange some products with other descent groups, especially if resources are widely scattered. Given mixed forms of cultivation (and most types of settled cultivation seem to involve a range of crops and of land types) and given matrilineal descent and inheritance, it is more convenient, stable, and equitable to have a joint estate owned by a descent group than to divide land into individually owned plots.

AUTHORITY

Given the ownership of a fixed estate, its management requires some form of authority structure. There is therefore likely to be a headman of the descent group which owns the estate, or at least a managerial group of elders. If several orders of segments within the descent group have different estates or differential rights in a common estate, as among the Ashanti (chap. 5) or in Minangkabau (DeJong, 1951: 10–12), there will be a hierarchy of elders or of heads of segments within the descent group as a whole.

RESIDENCE AND MEMBERSHIP

In this section I discuss only the broader limits which are imposed on residence by the existence of a joint estate. A more detailed treatment of residence appears in chapter 13.

The joint ownership of a fixed estate ensures, first, that membership of the descent group will be definite and not fluid or optional. Individuals will not be able to move readily from one descent group to another within the same clan merely by changing their residence.

Second, given the joint ownership of a fixed estate, there is a tendency to localize a majority of the members of at least one sex on or near the matrilineal descent group's land. This is obviously necessary because the estate is the chief source of maintenance for at least one sex within the group. Thus, whatever the over-all residence pattern of the community, the choice of residence of married couples in relation to descent groups will be strictly limited, and there will usually be one preferred type to which a majority of the population must conform. Depending on factors to be considered in chapter 13, the residence of married couples may be predominantly matrilocal (i.e., husband and wife live with or near wife's mother, as among the Hopi, Trukese, and North Kerala Mappillas); *or* avunculocal (husband and wife live with or near husband's mother's brother, as among the Trobrianders, Mayombe, some Ashanti, and traditional North Kerala Nayars and Tiyyars); *or* it may be duolocal (husband and wife live apart in their separate lineage homes, as among Central Kerala Nayars, Minangkabau, and some Ashanti). Matrilocality localizes the women of the descent group on or near its estate; avunculocality, the men; and duolocality, both sexes. One or other of these three forms of residence is most likely with settled cultivators, although other forms are possible under certain conditions. They are bilocality (husband and wife live according to convenience with the kin of either partner) and ambilocality (husband and wife live for fixed periods alternately with the kin of each partner). These forms, and the circumstances which encourage their choice, are discussed in chapter 13.

Three forms of residence are unlikely to occur extensively in a matrilineal society with settled subsistence cultivation. One is patrilocality (husband and wife live with husband's father), which permits the localization of neither the men nor the women of the matrilineal descent group. Another is multilocality (free choice of residence with any kin of either spouse), for this requires that the individual's source of livelihood should not be tied to any particular site. The third unlikely form is neolocality, in which husband and wife choose a new place of residence not necessarily located near the kin of either partner. With settled subsistence agriculture, neolocality is impracticable for the same reason as multilocality.

GENEALOGICAL STRUCTURE OF THE DESCENT GROUP In apparently the great majority of matrilineal societies, and in all our examples having settled cultivation, the widest matrilineal unit is a named, dispersed, unorganized, exogamous group of people who stipulate, but cannot demonstrate, matrilineal descent from a common ancestress, and who recognize mutual obligations of hospitality. I shall call this group a clan. In some cases a group of associated clans—which do not necessarily claim to be originally matrilineally related—forms a wider exogamous unit, which I shall call a phratry. Neither clan nor phratry are characterized by organized activities.

All of the fifteen societies studied also have one or more orders of organized matrilineal groups, which I have called descent groups. Where clans are found, the descent group is a segment of the clan. Whatever its form, a descent group is, by definition, characterized by organized activity, through which decisions must be made.

In those societies or part-societies with settled subsistence cultivation, the descent group within the clan tends to be a *lineage*, i.e., a unilineal group within which descent from a common forebear (an ancestress in the case of matriliny) is demonstrated through a determinate number of generations, rather than being merely stipulated. With settled subsistence cultivation, even if exact genealogical relationships are not known within the maximal descent group, it is likely to be divided into segments of varying orders and functions, whose members know the segments' *relative* degrees of relatedness to one another. Within the smaller segments, exact relationships will be known.

Further, in societies with settled subsistence cultivation, when any order of descent group divides to form two or more new descent groups, the division usually takes place between segments of like order whose ancestresses were sisters or putative sisters. With settled subsistence cultivation, I do not normally expect a situation in which members of one generation form a new descent group by seceding from their mothers' own brothers, mother's mother's brothers, or own sisters' sons. Nor do I normally expect a situation in which genealogically distantly related matrilineal kin band together to form a new descent group, excluding from it matrilineal kin who are more closely related to some of them. It follows that division can normally occur only after the death of the ancestress common to the separating segments, and after the deaths of her sons. Under some circumstances division may be delayed much longer.

Related to this cohesion of proximal generations with settled subsistence cultivation is the fact that authority tends to be concentrated with one or more elders of the senior generation. Since this generation has legal authority over all succeeding generations, a marked social equation of alternate generations, at least within the descent group, is not expected to occur with settled subsistence cultivation.

Groups Which Lack Settled Cultivation

Only five societies were studied which lack settled cultivation. Although they vary considerably among themselves, I shall treat them together as a residual category. They are the Navaho and four Central African groups: the Bemba, Yao, Mwinilunga Lunda or Ndembu, and the Plateau Tonga. The Central African societies all rely heavily on some form of slash-and-burn cultivation. The Bemba traditionally combined this with large-scale raiding of subject peoples and with minor hunting and fishing. The Yao combined shifting cultivation with trading and slave raiding on behalf of Arab traders; the Tonga, with cattle herding and minor hunting and fishing; and the Ndembu, with hunting as a dominant male activity. Navaho cultivation is not of the slash-and-burn type; it can be carried out on stable sites, and does not itself require high mobility. It is however combined with sheepherding. The importance of herding, and recent Navaho expansion, seem to militate against stable settlement on landed estates. Hence the Navaho have been classified with groups lacking settled cultivation.

ABSENCE OF JOINT ESTATE

In societies which lack settled cultivation the matrilineal descent group owns no joint estate in land. Land is a free resource or use rights in it are loosely vested in territorial units, not in descent groups.

Among settled cultivators the descent group jointly owns not only land, but also a variety of other types of immovable and movable property—houses, storehouses, water supplies, utensils, livestock, tools, weapons, canoes, or other valuables. In societies without settled cultivation, by contrast, the absence of a fixed estate in land seems to militate against joint holding and management of property of any kind by the descent group. Instead, from the point of view of property, the descent group in these societies is merely a unit which has a lien on the personal property of its members for such purposes as payment of bridewealth or of legal compensation. Within the descent group, also, certain rights over persons, movable property, and sometimes over standing crops, cultivation sites, or houses, are inherited by one or more individuals from another after the latter's death. One probable reason for the absence of a jointly held and managed matrilineal estate in these societies is that the absence of an estate in land encourages some scattering of descent-group members, so that joint ownership of other property would not be feasible. Moreover, productivity on the whole is relatively low in matrilineal societies without settled agriculture, so that there tends to be little valuable durable property either to own jointly or to inherit.

AUTHORITY

In general the authority stucture of matrilineal descent groups without settled cultivation tends to be weaker than that of descent groups with settled cultivation. This is not true of all societies, in all respects. The Bemba or Yao head of a matrilineage, who could traditionally sell junior members into slavery, had in some ways stronger authority than the head of a Hopi local clan element—the most weakly organized of our settled cultivating descent groups. It is however obvious that, lacking a joint estate, the descent group in societies with mobile cultivation will also lack the kind of authority structure necessary to manage an estate.

RESIDENCE AND MEMBERSHIP

In general, membership of a matrilineal descent group in a society which lacks settled cultivation tends to be more fluid and optional than among settled cultivators. Lacking a joint estate, the descent group in such a society is also likely to be less localized than among settled cultivators. Correspondingly, there is less likely to be a single dominant norm of residence for married couples, and husband and wife may move through several communities in the course of their married life.

GENEALOGICAL STRUCTURE OF THE DESCENT GROUP

In societies which lack settled cultivation, the descent group is less likely to be a clearly segmented lineage than in societies with settled cultivation. Among Navaho and Plateau Tonga, whose descent groups may endure through many generations, the descent group is not a lineage at all in the sense of a group within which descent from a common ancestress is demonstrated through a determinate number of generations. It is rather an unsegmented unit in which common descent is merely stipulated (see chaps. 1 and 2). Ndembu, Bemba, and Yao have lineages according to the above definition, but (apart from Bemba royalty) the lineages are small, shallow, and weakly segmented. In all these societies, when a descent group divides to form two or more new descent groups, fission does not necessarily follow the lines of cleavage between major segments of like order. Among Navaho and Tonga, individuals or genealogically haphazard segments may merely float off to other areas and become lost to the descent group. Among Ndembu and Yao, true siblings tend to ally themselves against other sibling groups of the descent unit. Division of the descent group may, however, take place between adjacent generations, between close matrilineal kin each party of whom allies itself with more distantly related matrilineal kin, or even, occasionally, between members of the same sibling group (Turner, 1957: 204–207; Mitchell, 1956: 152–182). The comparative lack of stability of the descent group in relation to land evidently underlies this weak development of segmentation.

Descent-Group Variation Among Settled Cultivators

The distinction between settled and mobile cultivation explains some gross differences of descent-group structure in the fifteen systems. In this chapter an attempt will be made to account for certain other differences through a consideration of levels of productivity.

By level of productivity I refer to a society's ability to obtain need-fulfilling goods and services from its natural environment. Productivity depends on the quality of the natural environment and of the society's tools and techniques for exploiting it. The level of productivity which results from the interaction of these factors can be regarded in White's terms as "the amount of energy harnessed per capita per year," and "the efficiency of the instrumental means of putting the energy to work" (White, 1949: 368–369).

Because all societies must, first and foremost, exploit nature for energy in the form of food, for cross-cultural studies of simpler societies the most useful single measure of productivity is probably one which focuses on the society's production of food (Sahlins, 1958: 107–108). Any precise measure of food productivity is impossible with the ethnographic materials available to us. Two forms of indirect evidence can, however, be used, which afford a very rough rank ordering of most of the fifteen systems. The first is an over-all consideration of those aspects of the society's natural resources and of its exploitative techniques which are relevant to food production. For cultivators, these include such factors as range and types of crops, adaptability of crops to environment, existence and uses of domesticated animals, methods of cultivation, incidence of natural catastrophes such as drought or cyclone, and range and significance of other forms of food getting such as hunting, fishing, and collecting. The second form of indirect evidence of food productivity which I shall use is a rough estimate of the proportion of the population wholly or partly exempt from food production and hence able either to enjoy leisure or to engage in other, specialized types of production or services. The rationale for this criterion is of course that the higher the food productivity of the society, the larger the proportion of people available for activities other than food production (*ibid.*: 109).

I am aware of several pitfalls in this method and in these particular criteria. First, the ethnographic materials do not permit me to use even these criteria with a high degree of precision, for they offer chiefly qualitative statements about resources, technology, and division of labor, whose implications for relative productivity are sometimes hard to assess. Second, formal characteristics of environment and technology, although guides to potential productivity, offer no indication of the extent to which the society actually exploits its productive potential.

In spite of the pitfalls I have used these criteria because differences in the level of productivity *were,* at a glance, obviously relevant to differences between the social structures of some of the societies studied —for example, Plateau Tonga and Kerala. In any event, although my data and criteria of productivity were quite inadequate for a precise, quantitative rating of all the thirteen societies,[1] they did permit me to rank-order, with a high degree of confidence, most of the societies within each of the main categories of settled and mobile cultivators. I am less confident in ranking the more productive mobile cultivators in relation to the less productive settled cultivators, because of wide differences in types of resources and of techniques. For this reason, I shall for the most part limit the discussion to considering implications of level of food productivity for social structure *within* each of these major categories.

Levels of Productivity among Settled Cultivators

The salient characteristics of each of the eight societies of settled cultivators are listed below, with regard, first, to aspects of environment and techniques relevant to food production, and second, to specialization of labor and general exemption from direct food production.

TRUK (ROMONUM ISLAND)
Environment and Technology Romonum (0.288 square miles) is a very small volcanic island on a coral atoll, having a tropical climate

---

[1] The North Kerala and Central Kerala regions are considered as separate types of society because of salient differences of ecology and political structure. North Kerala Nayars, Tiyyars, and Mappillas are thus considered sub-groups of one society, and Central Kerala Nayars a sub-group of a separate society.

with heavy rainfall. Occasional typhoons cause destruction of crops. There is some environmental diversity, including swamp used for taro growing, hill slopes used for breadfruit, and a sandy coastal fringe suitable for coconut. Bone and shell tools and wooden fish spears were traditionally used; iron and steel have been introduced in modern times. The primary crop is breadfruit, stored for off-season consumption. Secondary crops include taro, sweet potatoes, manioc (modern), and (traditionally) arrowroot. Coconut was formerly important as a food crop and is a modern cash crop. There are no yams and bananas are unimportant. Other food sources include fishing (deep-sea and reef), secondary in importance to crops. Pig and other small domesticates were unimportant. There was minor collection of wild fruits and sugar cane.

Specialization and Exemption from Food Production   There is no mention of full-time craftsmen. Part-time specialization in magic, canoe building, and the making of wooden spears, paddles, etc., has been confined to middle-aged and old men. Women were part-time specialists in mat making and basketry. Chiefs and lineage heads were probably only partly exempt from food production, if at all. Men were dominant in production but women also engaged in cultivation and, traditionally, in the more important forms of fishing (Goodenough, 1951: 24; Gladwin and Sarason, 1953: 42, 52–58, 63–64; chap. 3, above).

HOPI

Environment and Technology   The Hopi live in villages on the spurs of a plateau edge, and cultivate in the silt of a basin sloping south to the Little Colorado Valley. They have low and uncertain rainfall, and hence depend on springs and underground seepage for floodwater cultivation. There is some spring irrigation of luxury crops. Fertility is maintained by alluvium and blown soil. The Hopi occupy a greater area and have greater environmental diversity than the Trukese, but suffer the dangers of flood, excess silt, late frost, summer drought, sandstorms, and pests. They are normally able to store one year's food against possible failure of crops. Tools formerly included a wooden digging stick, weed cutter, and rake. The primary crop is maize, and secondary crops include beans, squash, melons, peaches, chiles, onions, and sweet corn. Some land was formerly diverted to cotton growing. Corn was exported to the Navaho in return for skins and meat. Other food sources included wild berries, fruits, nuts, and tubers, all important when crops failed. Deer, antelope, and rabbit were traditionally hunted. Sheepherding has existed since the Spanish period, but was limited before 1860 because of the danger of Navaho raids. A few goats and horses were kept.

Specialization and Exemption from Food Production   The village chief—and sometimes the heads of clans and religious societies—was exempt from most productive labor. Women played only very minor roles in food production as cultivators, and none as herders. There were no full-time craft specialists (Titiev, 1944: 181–201; Eggan, 1950: 17–18; Forde, 1931: 357–406; 1948: 220–246).

THE TROBRIANDS (BOYOWA ISLAND)

Environment and Technology   Boyowa Island is a coral island of about 100 square miles, i.e., over three hundred times larger than Romonum. It has a tropical climate and considerable environmental diversity; the inland plain is fertile and there is intensive coastal fishing. Tools formerly included stone axes and other stone implements; iron and steel are modern. Fields are left fallow about three years in four. The primary crop is yams, of excellent quality, stored in quantities. In modern times the people may grow twice as much food as is needed in one year, but this may be a recent result of the introduction of metal tools. Secondary crops include taro, sweet potatoes, coconut, and bananas. There is local specialization in, and exchange of, taro and yam. Fishing is extremely important, second in significance only to yams. There are quantities of pigs. Yams, taro, coconut, and pigs were exported to other islands in exchange for nonedible goods—stone, clay, rattan, bamboo, and pottery.

Specialization and Exemption from Food Production   Chiefs and the headmen of larger villages were largely exempt from direct food production. In the northern, more fertile half of the island there were specialist villages of woodcarvers, potters, and basket makers—five out of a total of some forty villages—who were probably largely exempt from food production. Other part-time or full-time specialists—in canoe building, carving, and stone-blade and shell-disc manufacture—were supported by chiefs. In general, men were slightly dominant in food production, but women were important in most stages of cultivation, and men spent part of each year in trading expeditions (Malinowski, 1922: 49–70; 81–124; chap. 4, above).

THE MAYOMBE

Environment and Technology   The Mayombe inhabit the coastal region and forested foothills of the Lower Congo area; there are a tropical climate and fertile soils. Metal tools were traditional. Crops included maize, millets, eleusine, manioc, sweet potatoes, sugar cane, bananas, rice, sorghum, mangoes, and other vegetables and fruits. Products of the coconut and other palms have modern importance for export. Domesticated animals include chickens—and goats and sheep in some districts—but few cattle.

Specialization and Exemption from Food Production   Chiefs and their close kin had "great wealth" (De Cleene, 1935: 66), and so may have been exempt from direct food production. There were either full-time or part-time specialists in iron and copperwork, wood and ivory carving, and weaving. Before 1884 some proportion of the free men were engaged in ivory and slave trade with the Arabs; they were perhaps partly freed from food production by the extensive use of slaves. Women seem to have been of equal importance with men in traditional garden cultivation, but in modern times, at least, are subordinate or occasional workers in connection with palm products (Richards, 1950: 212–213; *Encyclopædia Britannica*, 1910, VI: 917–928; De Cleene, 1935: 66; 1937: 4).

THE ASHANTI

Environment and Technology   The Ashanti country shows great environmental diversity, especially between north and south. The north is chiefly savanna and orchard country, having a somewhat uncertain rainfall and with danger of either drought or flood. The south is an extremely fertile, forested plateau with plentiful rain. Metal tools were traditional. There was no use of crop rotation or fertilization, fields being left fallow after a two- to four-year period of tillage. Yams and maize were the important crops in the north; in the south, maize, millets, sorghum, yams, manioc, sweet potatoes, coco yams, pulses, bananas, tomatoes, onions, peanuts, and important palm products. Domesticates included mainly goats and fowl, with occasional sheep, pigs, and a few cattle in some districts.

Specialization and Exemption from Food Production   Royalty and chiefs seem to have been exempt from food production, and perhaps also a body of traders of the chiefs and an administrative and military staff. There were specialists in gold, iron, and copperwork, hand pottery, woodcarving, and, from the seventeenth century, weaving. The northern area appears to have had lower food productivity and less specialization. Men were dominant in cultivation; women, secondary. In the south, with its denser population and urban centers, women appear to have been dominant in cultivation since the men spent a considerable part of their time in organized warfare (chap. 5, above; Service, 1958: 340–342).

MINANGKABAU

Environment and Technology The Minangkabau inhabit the high-lands of west central Sumatra, an area which had access to the east coast by major rivers. The area contains the most fertile soils in Sumatra, with some forest. It has a tropical monsoon climate, but with lower rainfall than Kerala. Cultivation included irrigated wet rice, and some use of the plough with cattle or water buffalo. Water transport was used extensively for trade with the east-coast ports. Crops included wet and dry rice, maize, millets, pulses, sweet potatoes, sugar cane, coconut and other palms, pepper, coffee, oranges, lemons, pome-granates, guavas, pawpaws, and other fruits. Cattle and buffalo were used for meat and draught, and chickens and goats were domesticated. Other food sources included river and pond fish, perhaps imported sea fish, minor hunting, and collection of forest produce.

Specialization and Exemption from Food Production The royal lineage, the king's administrative officials and private small army, district chiefs, lineage heads in villages and their lineage segments, and literate religious officials all appear to have been largely exempt from food production. There were full-time specialists in mining, glasswork, copper, gold, and other metalwork, woodcarving, and building. Some women were specialists (probably part-time) in making pottery and cloth-of-gold. Commoner men appear to have been partly freed from food production by the use of slaves, and to have spent part of their time in trading and warfare. Women were important in cultivation (non-plough) and in minor fishing. Literate persons in general are said to have been unlikely to work in wet-rice fields (Loeb, 1934: 48; Marsden, 1811: 42, 347, 349; Van Leur, 1955: 174; Schrieke, 1955: 55–57; De Jong, 1951: 7–9; Cole, 1936: 19, 25; 1945: 249–250, 260–264, 269–270; Cabaton, 1911: 269).

CENTRAL KERALA

Environment and Technology The area comprises a sandy, coastal plain, the hills and valleys of the midlands, and the forested highlands of the Ghats. Soils were fertile and there was great environmental diversity, with extremely heavy, tropical, monsoon rainfall. The coast was excellent for fishing. Metal tools were traditional, the plough was used extensively, large areas of wet-rice land were irrigated from plentiful streams, tank irrigation was common for garden crops, and animal and leaf fertilizers were employed. Crops included wet and dry rice, millets, sorghum, pulses, legumes, yams, manioc (post-Portuguese), many varieties of bananas, mangoes, tamarinds, jack fruit, pawpaws, guavas, pomegranates, and other fruits. Coconut, areca, and other palms were extremely important, also gingelly, pepper, limes, cashew nuts, and a profusion of minor garden produce. Cattle were used mainly for draught and milk, and were seldom eaten; goats and chickens were eaten by the lower castes. Other food sources included inland and extensive sea fishing, hunting of boar and deer, and minor collection of forest produce. Between 1500 and 1800 rice was increasingly imported to coastal towns from other areas of India, in exchange primarily for spices.

Specialization and Exemption from Food Production Both sexes of the upper, literate castes of royalty, chiefs, administrators, religious specialists, clerks, soldiers, temple officiants, and professional traders were virtually exempt from food production. Middle- and lower-ranking specialists included endogamous castes of goldsmiths, blacksmiths, bell-metal workers, carpenters, leather workers, weavers, builders, basket and mat makers, washermen, barbers, bow makers, wheel potters, middlemen traders, oilmongers, beggars, astrologers, snake charmers, and palmists, all with only very minor, secondary reliance on cultivation. Food producers were divided into the specialist castes of fishermen, palm growers, tenant cultivators of mixed subsistence crops, and serfs, the latter performing the bulk of wet-rice plough agriculture. Women were important food producers only in the serf castes (Forde, 1948: 60–270; chap. 6, above).

NORTH KERALA

Environment and Technology North Kerala was similar to Central Kerala, except that the mountainous area was proportionately greater and inland food productivity was lower because wet-rice farming was less extensive. The more densely populated coast towns relied heavily on imports of rice from overseas, in return for export of spices (chap. 7, above).

Specialization and Exemption from Food Production The general caste structure was similar to Central Kerala, but a smaller proportion of the population was exempt from food production. Administrators, religious specialists, and temple officiants were proportionately fewer. Men of the warrior castes (Nayar) were usually engaged in cultivation, and tenant cultivators of mixed crops were proportionately more numerous than in Central Kerala. Serfs specializing in rice cultivation were much fewer. The craft castes were proportionately smaller, and there was much less intricate caste specialization of such tasks as professional entertainment and ritual services (*idem*).

I tentatively place the foregoing eight societies in the following order of increasing food productivity: Truk, Hopi, Trobriand, Mayombe, Ashanti, Minangkabau, North Kerala, and Central Kerala.

There is doubt as to the rank ordering of Truk and Hopi. Both have very few if any specialists completely exempt from food production. Both have very limited environmental opportunities. I tentatively rank Hopi slightly higher in productivity because of the existence of grain as against only tree and limited root cultivation on Truk, and the generally greater range of food sources among the Hopi. The fact that Hopi women apparently play only minor roles in food production, whereas both men and women are significant producers on Truk, suggests higher productivity for the Hopi.

The Boyowa Island of the Trobriands definitely ranks above Truk and Hopi because of its more diverse environmental opportunities, more fertile soil, great potentialities for fishing, its ability to export considerable food in return for nonedible goods, and the existence of a sizable number of craft and other specialists largely exempt from food production.

Mayombe ranks above the Trobriands by virtue of its greater range of crops, especially grains, its ability to support larger domesticated animals, its high quality of coconut and other palm products, its traditional reliance on metal tools, and the probably larger porportion of the population engaged in specialized crafts or holding privileged political offices.

The materials on Mayombe are too defective for a very definite comparison with Ashanti. However, I rank Ashanti above Mayombe because of the probably larger range of crops in Southern Ashanti, the greater prevalence of domesticated animals, especially cattle, the probably much larger proportion of aristocrats and administrators freed from food production, the partial exemption of Southern Ashanti men from food production, as warriors, and the probably larger number of specialized crafts.

Minangkabau is ranked above Ashanti mainly because of the importance there of wet-rice agriculture coupled with some use of the plough. This ranking is supported by the almost certainly larger number of craftsmen and of aristocrats—including even the senior segments of commoner lineages in villages—exempt from important food production.

North Kerala is ranked above Minangkabau because of the much larger number of specialist groups almost wholly exempt from food production, the probably smaller proportion of women engaged in cultivation, and the fact that most traders were divorced from significant forms of cultivation, rather than being part-time farmers as among the Minangkabau. The probably more extensive use of the plough in North Kerala supports this ranking. It is true that in North Kerala some of the urban specialists on the coast were maintained with imports of rice by sea. Nevertheless, even the relatively self-sufficient inland villages show an apparently greater specialization of labor than in Minangkabau. Moreover, sea fishing was of tremendous importance for the support of dense coastal populations in Kerala.

Central Kerala is ranked above North Kerala for reasons detailed above in the text.

Levels of Productivity and Political Centralization among Settled Cultivators

By degree of political centralization, I shall refer to a cluster of apparently closely related factors concerning the allocation of authority and responsibility. These are, first, the population size of maximal political unit,[2] i.e., the largest territorial unit within which customary mechanisms exist for the ultimate settlement of disputes. Second, the number of hierarchically organized authorities of territorial units above and including the head of the minimal community. Third, the extent and strength of controls exercised by such authorities over resources, goods, and people.

The first two of these factors may be called structural criteria. The last comprises a number of functional criteria. A society is judged politically more centralized, the larger the maximal political unit, the greater the number of hierarchical territorial heads, and the greater the extent and strength of their controls. Where two societies have the same number of territorial heads, exercising similar controls, the one which has more controls vested in the central authority will be considered the more centralized.

Using these criteria I find a strong connection between level of productivity and degree of political centralization among the eight

---

[2] Population *density* was not found to be closely related to either level of productivity or political centralization in this range of societies. Romonum Island on Truk, for example, has a population density of about 800 per square mile. It has much lower productivity and less centralized political structure than Minangkabau, with a density of about 76 per square mile (Foreign Office Handbooks, No. 83, 1920: 10). Evans-Pritchard and Fortes found a similar lack of close connection between density and political centralization in Africa (1940: 7). For the lack of necessary connection between population density and level of productivity, see White, 1959: 291.

societies of settled cultivators. Below are summarized their salient characteristics with regard to political centralization.

TRUK

Size of Maximal Political Unit 64 to 127 (Goodenough, 1951: 130).

Number of Levels of Territorial Authority One: a district chief.

CONTROLS EXERCISED BY TERRITORIAL AUTHORITY

Over resources. The chiefly lineage, as "founder" lineage, may control more land than other lineages and is regarded as a kind of residual titleholder to the district. It apparently has no direct rights over the resources, as distinct from produced goods, of land controlled by other lineages.

Over goods and their redistribution and consumption. The chief collects and redistributes breadfruit, taro, and fish at four annual feasts. He keeps the finest for his own lineage. He receives the first fish at communal fish drives.

Over people. (1) Production: the chief organizes fish drives.

(2) Over organized force: the chief traditionally led the district to war but could not command his subjects to follow him. He had no control of force which could be exercised to maintain law or to enforce decisions.

(3) Settlement of disputes: the chief only "tries to act as mediator" between disputants. He has "little formal authority" and "no legal right to interfere in quarrels and feuds among his subjects" (Goodenough, 1951: 142–143; chap. 3, above).

HOPI

Size of Maximal Political Unit 200 to 300 most common. Oraibi reached about 600 before it divided in 1906.

Number of Levels of Territorial Authority One: a village chief.

CONTROLS EXERCISED BY TERRITORIAL AUTHORITY

Over resources. The village chief and heads of religious societies traditionally had society lands (sometimes of their own clans) set aside for their offices. As head of the "founder" clan, the chief today has the right of allocating spare land. He has very weak control over land once allocated to other clans.

Over goods and their redistribution and consumption. There is village-wide redistribution at feasts connected with numerous religious ceremonies, but this is organized by the heads of religious societies or their members and not dominantly by the village chief.

Over people. (1) Production: commoners, organized by a voluntary leader, join harvesting parties on the chief's and other clan heads' land. Heads do not command this work. Other communal work, e.g., cleaning springs or hunting, is organized by any commoner with the consent of the chief. A clan head other than the village chief fixes the dates of planting, but cannot enforce their observance. Chiefly control of production is thus very weak.

(2) Over organized force: a war chief disciplines the villagers and leads them to war on behalf of the village chief. He could scold, box the ears of or thrash miscreants, or place them in the forefront of battle. He was supported only by popular consent, not by the formal control of force. Force was widely vested in a number of "disciplinary katchinas" representing the village as a whole.

(3) Settlement of disputes: the village chief was the final authority above clan heads in judging disputes over land or destruction of crops; he could award damages. His sanctions were supernatural authority and popular support. Clans were private vengeance groups over which the chief had no formal control in case of murder.

The weakness of Hopi political centralization is seen in the large number of authorities and leaders who act "for" but largely independently of the village chief. Leadership is widely dispersed among clan elders, most of whom are also heads of religious societies of multi-clan membership, and among commoners who volunteer leadership of particular activities. The chief is mainly a ceremonial head in the background of secular affairs (Titiev, 1944: 58–68; Eggan, 1949: 106–109; Forde, 1931: 357–406).

TROBRIAND

Size of Maximal Political Unit About 400 to 800 as a rough estimate.
Number of Levels of Territorial Authority Two: a village of some 30 to 150 people; a chiefdom of up to 12 villages.

CONTROLS EXERCISED BY TERRITORIAL AUTHORITIES

Over resources. The chief has the largest village with the greatest amount of land. Members of chiefly lineage have the right to remain indefinitely in their fathers' villages and take over land there. The chiefly sub-clan and its offshoots thus control the best cultivated land.

Over goods and their redistribution and consumption. The chief maintains the economy in operation by collecting different foodstuffs (yams, coconuts, betel, pigs, fish) from villages with different dominant resources and produce. He collects mainly through urigubu paid by the villages of his many wives, and partly by the help of villages of his own sub-clan (into which he may not marry) in preparing feasts. The chief redistributes food in numerous great feasts, organizes and maintains traders on interisland expeditions, feeds war and work parties, and supports craft specialists. Village headmen organize minor redistribution. Most goods are perishable and are continually redistributed and consumed, but chiefs own the best and most canoes, shell necklaces, armlets, and axe blades. Only the chief and village headmen may own canoes.

Over people. (1) Production: there is chiefly patronage of craftsmen through gifts of food. The chief harbors "vassals" and people of lower clan rank in his village, who work for him. He organizes work parties, especially canoe building, and trading expeditions. The chief may keep his sons with him to work in his own village until his death. He has many wives to garden for him. The chief or village headman can hire out his canoe and so has a lien on fishing. The village headman organizes agricultural work and fishing.

(2) Over organized force: the chief leads war parties against other districts and can command the biggest following among village heads by virtue of the large number of his sons and other personal followers. There is, however, no regular army or formal centralization of force.

(3) Settlement of disputes: commoner sub-clans exact blood revenge privately; the chief cannot interfere. The chief settles some disputes, and controls the most powerful sorcerers to kill those who offend him. His sanctions are mainly supernatural but he occasionally sends henchmen to execute an offender (Malinowski, 1922: 62–70, 464–478; 1932: 18, 89–92; chap. 4, above; Hoebel, 1954: 193–196).

MAYOMBE

Size of Maximal Political Unit The materials are inadequate. About 3,000 to 5,000 as a rough estimate from village size and from the number of chiefdoms in the area.

Number of Levels of Territorial Authority Two: a village of about 100 to 300, under a village headman; a chiefdom under a chief.

Controls Exercised by Territorial Authorities

Over resources. The chief must have controlled extensive land because of the large number of wives, descendants, and slaves who swelled his village population. Other information is lacking.

Over goods and their redistribution and consumption. The chief administered ivory and slave trade with the Arabs; he must therefore have controlled the hunting of elephants. Other information is inadequate. The chief must very probably have drawn tribute from villages, since he is said to have had "great riches." His clothing and movable goods were probably not luxurious, however, as his insignia were a leopard skin, leopard teeth, and body paint.

Over people. (1) Production: the chief had the most slaves and the largest number of wives to work for him. Other information is lacking.

(2) Over organized force: the chief had a monopoly of guns obtained

from the Arabs, and therefore must have held some command over the chiefdom to make war against other chiefdoms. Since there were about 111 chiefdoms in all, some of which might divide into two, or temporarily become subject to a neighboring chiefdom, a chief's monopoly of organized force seems to have been unstable.

(3) Settlement of disputes: the information is inadequate. Oaths were sworn by the chief's fetish, and his sanctions were at least partly supernatural. The chief may have had a court for the settlement of disputes and punishment of crimes, for village headmen are said to have been able to sell or pawn junior lineage members to pay the expenses of a lost lawsuit (De Cleene, 1935: 63–75; Richards, 1950: 214, 219–220).

ASHANTI

Size of Maximum Political Unit About 200,000.

Number of Levels of Territorial Authority Three or four: a village of perhaps 500 to 1,000, under a village headman; in some cases a sub-chiefdom of several thousand under a sub-chief; a chiefdom under a chief; the Ashanti Union under a paramount chief.

CONTROLS EXERCISED BY TERRITORIAL AUTHORITIES

Over resources. A chief controlled extensive lands of his own village and allocated unclaimed land to strangers. New villages could, however, probably be formed fairly freely, subject only to the consent of the chief, although he appointed some village headmen himself and thus maintained indirect control of village lands. The paramount chief had no regular control over the land of chiefdoms other than his own, in contrast to Kerala. He could, however, award villages of his own conquered territories to his own favorites or to other Union chiefs as rewards.

Over goods and their redistribution and consumption. The paramount chief controlled most external trade, especially of slaves, ivory, kola. He obtained the taxes of trade, he had heavier weights than other chiefs, and he had the largest store of gold dust. He had control of the spoils of war, of death duties, and of special imposts for war. Ordinary chiefs, as well as the paramount chief in his own chiefdom, controlled treasure trove, taxes, fines, and tribute from first fruits, hunting, and fishing. Sumptuary regulations reserved certain types of woven cloth, stools, and other luxury items for the chiefs.

Over people. (1) Production: each chief exercised *corvée* for his own farm and for public works; he employed and supported artisans. The paramount chief supported the largest number of craftsmen from his treasury.

(2) Over organized force: each chief had a monopoly of force within

his chiefdom, controlling guns and gunpowder and conscripting able-bodied men for frequent wars. The paramount chief commanded the military support of other chiefs and had the largest army, probably more specialized because (unlike the armies of other chiefdoms) it was not organized on a lineage basis. The paramount chief also used captives and slaves as soldiers, as well as conscripted commoners. Although there were thus no standing armies, the paramount chief had a monopoly of force over subordinate chiefs.

(3) Settlement of disputes and punishment of crime: each chief had his own court for judgment of many private disputes and all crimes against the state. The paramount chief had few or no direct legal rights over "rear vassals"—the subjects of other chiefs—except the right to impose the death sentence on criminals already found guilty by their own chief's court. The paramount chief's judicial and other controls were limited by a council of chiefs, who could try, and destool, an unsatisfactory paramount chief (chap. 5, above; Hoebel, 1954: 211–254).

MINANGKABAU

Size of Maximal Political Unit   Information inadequate. Probably between 500,000 and 1,000,000.[3]

Number of Levels of Territorial Authority   Three: a village of perhaps 1,000 to 2,000 (Foreign Office Handbooks, 1920: 54–56) under a council of lineage heads, usually organized under the one of highest rank; a district of some 20 to 50 villages, under a chief; the kingdom, under the king in the capital town.

CONTROLS EXERCISED BY TERRITORIAL AUTHORITIES

Over resources. The king had large estates near his capital. He bestowed villages on junior royal officials, district chiefs, the prime minister, and the heads of the treasury, of land and sea forces, and of customs dues. The king owned forest and waste land between villages, and monopolized gold mining.

Over goods and their distribution and consumption. The king and chiefs exacted tribute from villages and from some neighboring tribes, especially the Batak. They also drew tribute from Minangkabau settlements at outlying ports. The king tried to monopolize pepper and other trade with the Europeans, and succeeded at some periods. He

---

[3] Loeb states that about one and a half million Malays have remained in Minangkabau in modern times, and through the past six centuries an equal number have settled in the coast towns of Sumatra and in Malaya (Loeb, 1934: 26). Considering the situation in other Asian areas, it seems probable that there has been considerable population increase in the past hundred years.

drew taxes from trade, coined money, and made trade treaties with foreigners, giving them rights to build factories on Minangkabau settlements in the ports. Sumptuary laws probably governed the use of luxury goods, restricting some to royalty, chiefs, or heads of villages. Gold, white horses, yellow umbrellas, etc., were insignia of royalty. The king used his wealth to maintain a private army, to patronize craftsmen in the capital, and perhaps to pay administrative officials.

Over people. (1) Production: the king controlled the work of slaves, having the ownership right of illegitimate persons and runaways from justice from villages of the kingdom. The king, and probably the district chiefs, supported woodcarvers, metalworkers, weavers, brocade makers, and glassworkers. The king and chiefs organized gold mining.

(2) Over organized force: the king had a regular army, the largest in the kingdom. He called together the armies of districts and villages in war, although his controls were uncertain during most of the period of European trade. There was, theoretically, central control of organized force, not always maintained in practice. Chiefs levied smaller armies from villages, whose members foraged for supplies in war.

(3) Settlement of disputes and punishment of crime: there was a hierarchy of courts with appeal from village to district councils, by way of the king's councilor to a junior royal official and thence to the king. Death penalties were imposed. The king had "secret police" to ferret out and assassinate rebels. Murder, however, at least in the nineteenth century, was viewed as a civil offense between lineages and was settled by compensation. The king had a theoretical but imperfect ability to terminate small battles between villages through his emissaries (Marsden, 1811: 41–42, 337–352, 376; Van Leur, 1955: 110, 174; Schrieke, 1955: 17, 55–72, 95–97; Cole, 1936: 25; De Jong, 1951: 7–9, 13–14, 51–52, 74–75, 81, 95–111).

NORTH KERALA (KINGDOMS OF KOLATTUNAD, KOTTAYAM, AND KADATTUNAD)

Size of Maximal Political Unit Appears to have varied between about 120,000 and 250,000 in different localities and at different periods between 1500 and 1760.[4]

Number of Levels of Territorial Authority Theoretically, three or four: a village of about 1,000, under a village headman; sometimes a sub-

[4] These figures are extremely tentative, being derived from traditional lists of the numbers of Nayar soldiers which each chief and king was normally expected to provide in war. I have argued that Nayar soldiers might comprise about one-third of the Nayar population, and the Nayar caste about one-quarter of the total population. By this estimate, for example, the Kottayam kingdom, with 18,000 Nayar soldiers, would have a population of about 216,000 (Ayyar, 1938: 278–279).

district, under a sub-chief; a district, under a chief; the kingdom, under the king. Periodically, an area might in fact have only two levels, during a period of rebellion by a chief against his king.

CONTROLS EXERCISED BY TERRITORIAL AUTHORITIES

Over resources. The kings of the three kingdoms, and the more powerful chiefs on their borders, owned numerous villages and could allocate others to sub-chiefs or to village headmen. A king monopolized gold washing, elephants, and shipwrecks. He could dispossess lesser nobles if they rebelled. If a village headman's or a minor chief's lineage died out, its estates escheated to the king or to a more powerful local chief. The head of each village (village headman, chief, or royal) controlled waste land and allocated it for new gardens.

Over goods and their distribution and consumption. Kings and chiefs called on village headmen for tribute of rice, coconuts, domesticated and hunted animals, forest products, cash levies, a portion of fines extracted from offenders, and succession fees at their own or the subordinate's succession to office. Kings extracted comparable and larger dues from their chiefs when possible. Kings and the greater coastal chiefs made trade treaties with Europeans, monopolizing the export of pepper and the import of guns and gunpowder. They levied house taxes and trade tolls from merchants in towns. In villages, village headmen controlled produce and cash from land allocated to tenants, first fruits, meat of hunting, fish, treasure trove, and fines; in turn they redistributed food to villagers during festivals and life-crisis rites, and supported craftsmen and other village specialists. Kings and chiefs supported numerous craftsmen, and paid soldiers in cash during the continual wars.

Elaborate sumptuary laws regulated differential consumption and enjoyment of goods by priests, royalty, nobles, Nayar commoners, merchants, craftsmen, and menial workers with regard to foods, clothing, house types, use of metals and pottery, personal ornaments, festal regalia, etc.

Over people. (1) Production: village heads controlled much labor by tenants, craftsmen, and menials on their estates; kings and chiefs controlled larger numbers of villagers and more specialized craftsmen. Coastal rulers had an overright of the ships of merchants to carry goods and to prosecute wars.

(2) Over organized force: village headmen had call on Nayar commoner men as soldiers and led them in support of chiefs and kings. Chiefs and kings had direct call on larger numbers from their own villages and, when possible, from their political subordinates. Kings and

larger coastal chiefs maintained small standing armies. A king had theoretical control of organized force throughout his kingdom, but because of intervention by mutually competitive European trading companies in the seventeenth and eighteenth centuries, the greater chiefs often rebelled and broke loose. Even chiefs could not always quell small battles between village headmen.

(3) Settlement of disputes and punishment of crime: there was a hierarchy of courts from the village headman through the chief to the king, with the death penalty theoretically reserved to the king. Chiefs sometimes abrogated his powers. Chiefs tried to control the interlineage feuds of commoner Nayars through the institution of the duel, but village headmen's blood feuds were sometimes prolonged (Buchanan, 1807: 499, 548–551; Innes, 1908: 57–75; Logan, 1887, I: 296–400).

CENTRAL KERALA (KINGDOMS OF CALICUT AND COCHIN)

Size of Maximum Political Unit About 500,000 (Cochin) and 600,000 to 750,000 (Calicut).[5]

Number of Levels of Territorial Authority Three to four: a village, under a village headman; a district, under a chief; in some areas, a feudatory small kingdom, under a feudatory king; the kingdom, under the king.

CONTROLS EXERCISED BY TERRITORIAL AUTHORITIES

Over resources. The situation was similar to North Kerala, except that,

---

[5] These rough estimates are again derived from lists of Nayar soldiers. The Zamorin of Calicut at various times brought between 50,000 and 60,000 Nayars into the field against Cochin and the Portuguese (Ayyar, 1938: 169, 172). By the calculation noted above, this would probably indicate a total population of 600,000 to 720,000 for the Calicut kingdom as a whole. If the lists of soldiers are correct, the estimate of population is probably conservative.

It should be noted, however, that Logan gives an estimate of only 465,594 for the population of Malabar District *as a whole* in 1802, i.e., of the former Calicut kingdom and all the North Malabar kingdoms together (Logan, 1887, I: 81). He does not state the source of the estimate. If it was correct, it might not be incompatible with a much larger population in the first half of the eighteenth century. During the Mysorean invasions of Central and North Kerala, 1766–1792, up to half the population is thought to have fled to Travancore, and of the remainder tens of thousands were slain or died of famine; 15,000 more were deported to Mysore, of whom only 200 are supposed to have survived (Innes, 1908: 67; Logan, 1887, I: 413–414, 437, 449). The population would therefore be greatly depleted in the early decades of British rule. It increased rapidly in the nineteenth century and was 2,365,000 by 1891, the time of the first reliable census. The population of Cochin State was 722,906 in 1891 (Census of India, 1931, Madras and Cochin volumes), but at that date the state comprised only about half the area of the former kingdom.

especially in the Zamorin's kingdom of Calicut, the king had more thorough control of land. He held a larger proportion of it directly as his own royal estates and exercised stronger powers to allocate and dispossess.

Over goods and their distribution and consumption. Identical with North Kerala, except that the king maintained tighter controls over ports, merchants, and foreign traders, deflecting most of the trade to his capital port. The Calicut king reserved the right to coin money and make trade treaties in his kingdom. He was able to extract tribute, succession dues, etc., regularly from his nobles. Until the mid-eighteenth century he maintained the largest number of craftsmen in Kerala. The king's greater power to extract goods from his subjects rested on the greater extractive powers of heads at the village level: village headmen managed almost all land in their villages and extracted large produce from Nayar commoners, who served as perpetual tenants rather than as relatively independent owner-cultivators. Central Kerala's sumptuary laws were correspondingly more elaborate and detailed than in North Kerala.

Over people. (1) Over production: greater controls over production were exercised by all levels of territorial heads and by Nayar commoners, all of whom owned landless serfs to carry out the bulk of cultivation. The king maintained tighter control of the navy by transferring boys of the Hindu fishing caste to the Muslim community to serve as sailors and traders. Persons expelled from caste for religious offenses became slaves of the king.

(2) Over organized force: except in small border districts, the kings, especially in Calicut, maintained tighter control of their chiefs' armies and had the power to assassinate a rebel chief and to dispossess his lineage. Nayar commoner men throughout the kingdom were regularly conscripted as soldiers; the king maintained standing armies in ports and at the frontiers. Battles between chiefs were curtailed, and between village headmen, unknown.

(3) Settlement of disputes and punishment of crime: there was a hierarchy of courts from the village headman through the chief to the king. Only trials of petty civil disputes were permitted to village heads; greater powers were given to chiefs, but the death penalty was reserved to the royal court. Blood feud was strictly curtailed and was replaced by duels supervised by the king or the chief (chap. 6, above; Logan, 1887, I: 197–358, 597; II: clxxvii; Ayyar, 1938: 80–91, 261–296, 325–328).

These data suggest a close connection between productivity and political centralization in the eight societies. In general, so far as can be judged from rough estimates, higher productivity tends to be associated with a larger maximal political unit. It tends to be associated with a larger number of levels of territorial authority. Third, as productivity increases, there is a tendency for the controls of territorial authorities to increase with regard to resources, production, distribution and consumption of goods, organized force, the settlement of disputes, and the punishment of crime. Further, between societies with the same number of territorial heads, higher productivity tends to be associated with stronger controls exercised by the highest authority.

The data cited do not show perfect connections between productivity and political centralization in all respects. Judged by the formal criteria of technology and environment—plus specialization of services other than food production—the levels of productivity of Ashanti, Minangkabau, North Kerala, and Central Kerala were ranked in the order given. The maximal political unit in some areas of North Kerala in the seventeenth and eighteenth centuries, however, appears for all practical purposes to have been considerably smaller than those of Ashanti or Minangkabau. Similarly, the royal control of trade and of organized force in North Kerala and Minangkabau appears to have been weaker than in Ashanti. A more detailed consideration of historical events is needed to explain these apparent anomalies. Thus, the written reports of all these societies apply chiefly to the period shortly before European conquest. Although it may have been preceded in the area by other centralized states, the Ashanti Union itself came into being as late as the early eighteenth century, and reached its height shortly before the British conquest of 1874. Minangkabau and the Central Kerala kingdoms, by contrast, reached their period of maximal centralization in the fifteenth century, and North Kerala, probably in the fourteenth. From the early fifteenth to the late eighteenth centuries these Asiatic kingdoms experienced immense upheaval, and strife between their component chiefdoms, as a result of the competitive struggles of Arab and European trading powers. The three North Kerala kingdoms—originally one kingdom in the fourteenth century—practically disintegrated into autonomous chiefdoms in the early eighteenth century, before their invasion by the Mysoreans in the 1760's and subsequent entry into British rule in 1792. The Minangkabau royal lineage gradually lost power after 1500 with the arrival of competing European traders, and was abolished in 1820 (Cabaton, 1911: 270; Schrieke,

1955: 97; De Jong, 1951: 13–14). After this the area was governed in severalty by the chiefs of districts until the Dutch conquest of 1899.[6] It is arguable that both the Kerala kingdoms and Minangkabau may have had more centralized states in *all* respects in or before the fifteenth century than Ashanti ever attained, but this cannot be proved from the materials presently available.

Two further points are worth noting. One is that during times of internecine strife and temporary abeyance of central controls—such as Kerala and Minangkabau experienced in the period of European trade —actual, as opposed to potential, productivity might fluctuate widely from one year to another. The trade wars of the eighteenth century in Kerala created periodic desperate famines resulting from devastation of crops and stoppage of trade goods. Similarly, between 1820 and 1899, the Dutch severely restricted trade outlets between the Minangkabau highlands and the Sumatran ports, so that productivity of rice greatly declined (Schrieke, 1955: 96–97). Our formal categories of "normal" technology, environment, and specialization do not take account of these fluctuations, and it may be that fluctuation of productivity and of political centralization are in fact more intimately connected than our categories can suggest.

A second point is that in spite of fluctuations in productivity and political centralization, Minangkabau and Kerala, in the periods discussed, were inexorably moving toward greater political centralization as a result of technological innovation and trade expansion from the West. In Kerala, even in the midst of civil wars, some further steps in this direction were taken before the collapse of native rule. The Kolattiri king of North Kerala tried to introduce the first regular land tax in 1731 to meet the increasing cost of wars, and Travancore, the

---

[6] Schrieke's information (1955: 97) indicates that after the royal lineage was extirpated during the Padri rebellion of the 1820's, the Dutch allowed Minangkabau to be governed by the petty chiefs of small districts for the rest of the nineteenth century, and did not take over direct administrative control until 1899. Trade also declined during the nineteenth century, and the *negari* or village seems to have become more self-sufficient than it was traditionally. It may have been this nineteenth-century interim period of political and economic decentralization which led to subsequent anthropological pictures of the self-sufficient and virtually autonomous negari, reigned over by "the poorest pretense at monarchs the world has known" (Loeb, 1934: 28). Marsden's account of 1783 (republished in 1811) indicates, by contrast, that although the Minangkabau kingdom began to decline about 1500, royal control of the tribute, trade, and military power of the several districts and of the outlying ports on the east coast, was still recognized in the late eighteenth century (Marsden, 1811: 334–352). De Jong also opposes the implications of political decentralization contained in the work of Willinck and, later, of Loeb (De Jong, 1951: 16–22).

southernmost Kerala state, replaced its "feudal" system with a bureau-cratic government and mercenary army in the 1730's (Innes, 1908: 56, 308). Eventually (in 1792 in Kerala, and 1899 in Minangkabau), all of these kingdoms were incorporated into much larger, bureau-cratically organized colonial states.

Productivity, Political Centralization, and the Structural Form of Descent Groups among Settled Cultivators

The next step is to examine the implications of the level of productivity and the degree of political centralization for the structure of matrilineal descent groups and the types of relationship which exist between them. The implications which will be examined are the kinship composition of local communities; degrees of stratification and types of marriage re-lations between descent groups; and the size, segmentation, and inter-nal stratification of descent groups.

HOPI AND TRUK

In the two societies of lowest productivity and political centralization, Hopi and Truk, the smallest local community is also the maximal political unit: the village among Hopi and the district on Truk. Each of these communities is a multi-lineage unit. Thus the Hopi village of Oraibi contains some thirty landowning sub-clans [7] grouped into nine exogamous phratries (Titiev, 1944: 53). The Trukese district contains some six to thirteen landowning lineages, usually of different exogamous clans. Occasionally two or more lineages may belong to the same clan and together form a higher order of descent group of limited functions, which Goodenough has called a ramage (chap. 3, above).

Stratification between descent groups is minimal. The chiefly descent group has slightly higher rank as the supposed founder of the com-munity. The chief's own powers are, however, very weak, and his descent group as a whole enjoys no privileges other than a vague pres-tige over other descent groups. Relations between descent groups can thus be classed as near-egalitarian. The chiefly lineage commands no special privileges such as multiple polygyny or enhanced marriage pay-ments. Egalitarian marriages also take place across political boundaries with individuals in other villages or other districts. Named exogamous

---

[7] Because the Hopi clan, as a named exogamous unit, is dispersed throughout different, politically autonomous villages, I shall refer to the members of a clan resident in one village as a sub-clan. This group has normally been referred to as a "clan" in the literature. I do not call it a lineage because its members do not always know their exact genealogical relationships to one another. The sub-clan may contain one or more lineages within which genealogical relationships are known (Eggan, 1950: 77; Titiev, 1944: 46–47).

clans are also dispersed throughout several maximal political units.

The maximal descent group is small—some three to forty members. On Truk the descent group may have a time depth of five to seven generations, including the common ancestress and the youngest children. The time depth of the Hopi sub-clan is unknown.

In both societies the descent group is internally weakly segmented. Among the Hopi, a relatively large sub-clan may contain several genealogically separable descent lines or major lineages (Eggan, 1949: 124; 1950: 77), each having a customary lien on certain fields. Within this lineage each woman's children fall under the special authority of their mother's own brothers, especially the eldest. Segments are not, however, very clearly distinguished from each other in functions, and they have no formal hierarchy of heads with specialized powers. The uncertainties with regard to the number and application of Hopi clan names suggest that, when they divide, Hopi sub-clans may not always divide cleanly along lines of genealogical segmentation (Titiev, 1944: 55–58). If this were the case they would in some respects resemble descent groups in societies without settled cultivation, and differ from most settled cultivators of higher productivity.

On Truk the lineage is sometimes more clearly segmented into descent lines (often sibling groups) having minor heads and each holding some form of title to land or its products bequeathed by a father. The Trukese lineage is, however, a relatively ephemeral unit. It is often *not* composed of functionally discrete segments, and when it is, the life span of the segments is short, for they tend rapidly to separate from each other and to take on the functions of maximal descent groups. Further, when a Trukese descent group divides permanently, fission does not always cleanly follow the lines of genealogical segmentation. Relatively distantly related individuals or sibling groups sometimes combine and separate themselves from others more closely related (Goodenough, 1951: 149). In this respect the Trukese lineage bears some resemblance to those of shifting cultivators and differs from that of most settled cultivators of higher productivity.

Among Hopi and Trukese, inter-segmental stratification within the lineage is either minimal or nonexistent. Trukese lineage segments are of equal rank, and so long as the lineage coheres headship vests in the oldest man regardless of branch. Among the Hopi, it is true, headship of the sub-clan tends to be vested in its senior segment—in a man drawn from the segment descended from eldest daughters, which occupies the main clan dwelling (Titiev, 1944: 47). The head's segment as a whole, however, has no significant privileges apart from its suc-

cession right. Further, descent groups are often so small that the headship may pass into a junior line. If, moreover, the descent group is not
small, other branches tend to develop heads of their own with ceremonial offices comparable in privileges to those of *the* sub-clan head.
At all times, the sub-clan head's authority is shared with all other senior
men of his descent group. While we may perhaps speak of slight inter-
segmental rank in Hopi sub-clans, we can scarcely, therefore, speak
of inter-segmental stratification.[8]

TROBRIAND AND MAYOMBE

The Trobriand and Mayombe systems, the two ranked next higher in
the scale of productivity and political centralization, exhibit certain
other special features in common. Here the smallest local community
tends to be a mono-lineage community, with attached affines and cognates drawn temporarily from other communities. Specifically, it comprises the men of a descent group, together with their wives, immature
children, and sometimes a few mature children and grandchildren of
these men, plus some older women of the lineage who have returned
from their conjugal to their natal villages. This local community is en-
capsulated within a chiefdom as the maximal political unit (chap. 4,
above; Richards, 1950: 218–221).

In the society as a whole, inter-lineage stratification is moderately
developed. Not only the chief but his whole descent group command
respect, superior land rights, material insignia, and authority. Any male
member of the Trobriand chief's lineage may choose to settle for his
lifetime in the village of his commoner father, and even attract matrilineal juniors to him there. If he does not marry his father's sister's
daughter, he may later develop separate land rights for himself and
his matrilineal heirs, who in turn may eventually assume control of the
village. The land rights of Mayombe chiefly lineages are not well described, but they were probably extensive because of the reputedly
greater wealth of chiefs (De Cleene, 1935: 66). In these societies also
there is some stratification between non-chiefly lineages, expressed in
differential control of land and other resources. Landowning descent
groups in these societies also apparently tend to differ in size according to their rank. The smallest contain perhaps some twenty to thirty
individuals, the largest up to 100 or more in the Trobriands, and per-

---

[8] I use Fried's distinction between ranking and stratification. Ranking exists
when there is social limitation of the number of positions of high prestige, when
the principles on which prestige is based involve criteria other than sex, age, and
personal attributes, and when there is consensus within the society concerning
claims to rank. Stratification is a form of ranking in which those of high rank have
privileged rights of access to strategic resources (Fried, 1957: 24–25).

haps 400 among the Mayombe (Richards, 1950: 219). The generation
depth of Trobriand descent groups is unknown. Among the Mayombe
it appears to be anything from five to nine or more generations, including children.

Stratification between descent groups in these societies shows itself
in the form of asymmetrical marriage ties. Marriages take place between lineages at all levels of the society and are in this sense egalitarian, but chiefs engage in multiple polygyny, drawing wives from
many or all of the villages in their chiefdoms. The terms of these marriages also favor the chief. The Trobriand chief draws especially large
and diverse annual affinal gifts (urigubu), amounting to tribute, from
the villages of his brother-in-law headmen. Both Trobriand and Mayombe chiefs commonly exercise a privilege of keeping their adult sons
present in their own villages to swell their following. Among the
Mayombe asymmetrical marriages also take the form of extensive marriages by chiefs and other men of rank to slave women, who come entirely under the control of their husbands. Their children become members of the father's lineage, occupying a rank inferior to that of his
regular matrilineal juniors (De Cleene, 1935: 66).

In both these societies—although no doubt more markedly among
the Mayombe with their greater productivity, trade, and political
centralization—the chief's capital village has a more elaborate kinship composition, with more pronounced stratification between its
component descent groups. In addition to the chiefly lineage, its many
wives, children, and grandchildren, there were traditionally subordinate descent groups of vassals or slaves, who, through capture or political subjection, possessed inferior land rights and swelled the chief's
personal following as his producers and henchmen. It must be emphasized, however, that in these societies with their primarily kinship-based
political structures, such vassals married with chiefs and commoners
and became incorporated into the society as kinsfolk. They might
occupy an inferior status for several generations, but their work and
standard of living were similar to those of commoners.

Intra-lineage segmentation may be slightly more strongly developed
in these societies than among the Hopi or Trukese. The larger localized
lineages of the Mayombe tend to separate into several segments, all
occupying the same village over an extended period but probably
having separate heads. It seems possible, moreover, that among the
Mayombe there may be organized descent groups extending beyond the
village. Richards speaks of a major matrilineage associated with a district, and a clan associated with a "territory." There were apparently

heads of both these units with at least ceremonial functions (De Cleene, 1935: 68; Richards, 1950: 244). Unfortunately we know nothing about the hierarchy of authority, if any, of these heads. "Lateral" succession through brothers and then to sister's sons seems to have been confined to the senior branch of the chiefly lineage, so that there may have been inter-segmental stratification in chiefly lineages (De Cleene, 1937: 69). Within the localized descent group, headship of the village was not vested in the senior line but depended on selection (Richards, 1950: 215). Intra-lineage stratification within the village seems doubtful except as between segments of freeborn and segments descended from slaves. Trobriand descent groups are divided into lineages which regularly lay claim to certain fields and within which inheritance of personal property and of use rights in land tends to take place. Headship of the descent group is vested in the senior segment, which may enjoy special privileges, although the evidence here is unclear. The organized descent group of the Trobriands rarely seems to extend beyond the village. There may be some such extension, however, in the case of a chiefly lineage having branches in other villages, for a chief has call on goods provided by other village headmen of his clan prior to feasts. What evidence there is suggests for both these societies a somewhat more clear-cut and durable intra-lineage segmentation than among the Hopi or Trukese, and possibly, but not definitely, a greater development of inter-segmental stratification within descent groups.

ASHANTI

Among the Ashanti, the society next higher in the scale of productivity and political centralization, the smallest local community was normally a multi-lineage village. It comprised some four to seven lineages of different exogamous clans. The village existed within the framework of at least two larger territorial political units: chiefdom and kingdom or Ashanti Union.

In the society as a whole, inter-lineage stratification had proceeded further than among the Mayombe. Within the village, as its "founders," the village headman's lineage somewhat outranked those of other commoners in terms of political status, often of size, and perhaps also of extent of land rights. Above the village, living in the capitals of chiefdoms and Union, came, in order of rank, the lineages of urban councilors (who were also village overlords), of the chief, and of the paramount chief or king. At each of these levels the whole lineage appears to have enjoyed wealth, authority, and privileges appropriate to the political rank of its head (chap. 5, above). Inter-lineage stratification at the political level found expression, as among the Mayombe, in asymmetrical marriage ties. Whereas most commoners were monogamous, a chief, by virtue of his office, commanded wives from a range of commoner lineages in multiple polygyny (Fortes, 1950: 279). Contrary to normal usage he retained some of his mature sons with him to swell his following, and cemented his political status by appointing some to sub-chiefships within his domain (*ibid.*: 260–261). As among the Mayombe, also, persons of higher political office had more slave wives than did commoners. At the same time, Ashanti marriage ties at the political level seem to exemplify a transitional stage between those of societies with lower and with higher degrees of political centralization and levels of productivity. Apparently the society was not so highly stratified that marriages could not take place between all status levels: there seem to have been no endogamous castes. But in a state of this size and degree of centralization, the relationships between status levels were primarily political and only incidentally affinal or cognatic— the reverse of the Trobriand situation. At most, a chief could probably marry women from only a small proportion of commoner lineages. We do not know how these lineages were selected; possibly they were from the higher ranks of commoners. At all events chiefs also married extensively into each others' lineages within the Union, while even today over 75 per cent of commoners marry into their own rank within the village or within a small group of adjacent villages (*ibid.*: 279). Ashanti society thus perhaps presents the germs of a society with predominantly in-marrying, ranked political classes, each class comprising a number of lineages of roughly equal rank, rather than being a society composed merely of a number of lineages, all of which intermarry, but all of which are mutually stratified.

With regard to intra-lineage stratification, lineage segments composed of freeborn commoners were not mutually stratified. The head was elected from adult, freeborn lineage males regardless of generation or branch. Most lineages apparently had, however, several attached segments of slave origin whose members occupied a somewhat inferior status and could not succeed to the headship (*ibid.*: 255). In the society as a whole, therefore, intra-lineage stratification should perhaps be regarded as more prominent than in those previously discussed. It does not, however, appear to have involved marked hereditary differences in economic rights. The children of captured slaves remained slaves, but more remote descendants of slaves were apparently gradually incorporated as attached segments of their owners' lineages, and the origins of such segments may, even under native rule, have been a source of stigma rather than of practical discrimination (Rattray, 1929: 38–40).

The average size of the localized Ashanti lineage was probably greater than among the Mayombe, but this is not clearly established. Certainly the Ashanti lineage was more elaborately and precisely segmented, at all events at the level of the local descent group. Three functionally differentiated levels of segmentation are distinguishable: the maximal lineage, twelve to fourteen generations deep including children, with its legally appointed head, which acts as a corporate unit in relation to other lineages and to the state; a major lineage five to seven generations deep, which commonly holds land or other resources under the management of an informally chosen head; and a minor lineage which ego reckons as springing from his mother's grandmother, and whose oldest male is his legal guardian. It seems probable that land may traditionally have been vested in the maximal lineage and merely allocated for usufruct to major lineages (chap. 5, above). The major lineage must, however, have had a corporate identity, for it was to this segment that the term "yafunu" ("children of one womb") primarily referred, and witchcraft was effective only within this group (Fortes, 1950: 258).

MINANGKABAU

A similar but more complicated situation presents itself in Minangkabau. Here again the minimal local community was a multi-lineage village or township (*negari*). It commonly comprised some four to nine maximal lineages, called *suku* or *kampueng* in different areas, which may have been traditionally exogamous, and each of which was regarded as the localized element of a dispersed clan. The village existed within the framework of district and kingdom (Loeb, 1934: 28; De Jong, 1951: 11–12, 68).

Social stratification involving lineages and lineage segments had apparently proceeded further in Minangkabau than in Ashanti. The royal lineage was socially and culturally clearly differentiated from the rest of the population. It was patrilineal, not matrilineal, and was endogamous or nearly so, thus forming a royal caste. It comprised three main branches, headed respectively by officials of unequal ranks: the king, the prince of laws, and the prince of religion. Succession to these offices was from father to son by primogeniture. Marriage could take place within or between the three branches (De Jong, 1951: 13–14). The royal lineage was thus internally stratified, in a manner not entirely clear. It is not known how the district chiefs and major administrative officers were organized in terms of kinship, except that they presumably had matrilineal lineages and each had some kind of headship over at least one village. Neither do we know anything about the kinship composition of the royal lineage's personal followers, who appear to have been mostly slaves. The royal lineage does not appear to have been connected affinally with either its personal followers or its (matrilineally organized) subjects in the kingdom at large.

Commoner villages fell into two types of political organization: Koto-Piliang, the more stratified, and Bodi-Tjaniago, the more egalitarian. Bodi-Tjaniago villages seem to have been organized in a manner similar to Ashanti. Four or more localized maximal lineages (kampueng) of roughly equal rank comprised the village population, their heads forming a village council. The council was sometimes led by one of them of slightly higher rank. A maximal lineage comprised several major segments (*parui*), each possessing a head and controlling a section of village lands. The parui counted its common ancestress not fewer than three generations above the oldest living members. A major segment might comprise several households (*rumah*), each normally occupied by a minor segment (*djurai*) under a subordinate head. In some Bodi-Tjaniago villages succession to headship at all levels of lineage stratification was ideally determined in an egalitarian manner. The head might be chosen by popular consent of members, he might be the oldest man of the relevant lineage group, or he might be selected in turn from among the heads of subordinate segments. In other Bodi-Tjaniago villages, however, there was at least some intralineage stratification with regard to succession rules, in that the head of a kampueng was drawn only from the senior segment (parui) of the kampueng as a whole (*ibid.*: 12, 51–52, 59). What is not clear is whether all the lineages of Bodi-Tjaniago villages, like those of Koto-Piliang villages, had—incorporated within them for purposes of administration, exogamy, and residence—landless families or segments occupying a definitely servile status as menial workers, at least sometimes as slaves (Cole, 1936: 22). If they did have, as seems probable, even the lineages of Bodi-Tjaniago villages should perhaps be assessed as internally more stratified than those of the Ashanti.

The lineages of Koto-Piliang villages were internally more elaborately segmented and more stratified. The localized matrilineal unit of highest order was the *nan*, or section, a cluster of genealogically separate maximal lineages grouped together for administrative purposes. The heads of the four or more nans of a village formed the highest village council, headed by one of them as "summit chief" of the village. Each nan comprised several localized lineages (kampueng) whose heads formed a lower-order village council. The lineage was in turn divided into landholding segments (parui) of six or more generations depth including children. The parui was usually divided into smaller segments, each forming a single household. In Koto-Piliang villages, headships of all levels of matrilineal units were vested in supposedly senior lines, a head being succeeded by his full brothers in order of age, and these by their eldest sister's eldest son (De Jong, 1951: 51, 68, 73–75). This mode of intra-lineage stratification appears to have yielded economic classes with differential access to resources in the village, which cross-cut the larger matrilineal groupings. The paruis or landholding segments of the heads of village sections and maximal lineages appear to have formed an aristocracy who were wealthier, owned more land than the "commoner" branches of their own lineages, refrained from most manual work, and intermarried among themselves whenever possible (De Jong, 1951: 60; Loeb, 1934: 48). Below the "commoners" was apparently a still lower category, for each landholding parui commonly had attached to it families or segments of landless persons, sometimes slaves, who lived on its land and worked in a menial capacity (Cole, 1936: 22). It is not clear whether such persons were mainly immigrants from other villages, captives, or members of true matrilineal branches of the lineage who had somehow become dispossessed of their land. These servile persons at all events apparently claimed lineage and clanship ties with their masters, observed exogamy with them, and were legally represented by the heads of segment, lineage, and village section on whose land they lived. It is not clear whether the landed commoners of one lineage could marry the servile attachés of another. Given the tendency toward endogamy of social strata (De Jong, 1951: 60), this would seem to have been unlikely.

It should be noted that at the village level of this society, *maximal* descent groups (kampueng or nan) were not mutually stratified with regard to power or economic rights. They were apparently only vaguely ranked with regard to supposed primacy of settlement. True stratification of power and wealth was rather between the smaller landholding segments (parui), both within the same maximal lineage and across lineage boundaries.

Koto-Piliang villages of Minangkabau thus seem to present a situation in which intra-lineage stratification had proceeded so far with regard to discrepancies in political and economic rights that the higher- and lower-ranking segments of maximal lineages of the village were in process of separating into endogamous castes. We might understand this process better if we knew something about resource control and redistribution of goods in relations between segments of the lineage and section, but unfortunately we do not. We do not even know the economic correlates of the differences between Bodi-Tjaniago and Koto-Piliang villages, except that the latter tended to come under the direct control of royalty, administrative officials, and district chiefs, while the former were less directly related to the central power (*ibid.:* 74–75). Perhaps, therefore, Koto-Piliang villages had higher productivity and were more involved in external, administered trade and in redistribution of goods at the highest political levels. But this is speculation.

The Minangkabau commoner maximal lineage was as large or larger than the Ashanti, numbering in some cases perhaps 200 to 300.[9] The maximal lineage had a time depth of at least twelve to fourteen generations including children; the property-holding segment, at least seven (*ibid.:* 10).

KERALA

In Kerala the movement toward stratum separation and endogamy, apparently incipient in Minangkabau, was much further elaborated and crystallized. The highest stratum of religious specialists, rulers, and military aristocrats (Nambudiri Brahmans, Nayars, and their congeners) were sharply segregated in terms of resource control, authority, general economic privilege, and total severance of kinship and clanship ties, from the many separate endogamous lower castes of traders, craftsmen, menials, and (in Central Kerala) agricultural serfs. This highest stratum itself formed a kind of large endogamous ruling caste, but was also internally minutely stratified into occupational or political status groups between which only asymmetrical, hypergamous marriages were permitted.

In this society, because of the manifold divisions into sharply separated castes, stratification between *lineages,* or between lineage segments, was less prominent than in either Ashanti or Minangkabau. Descent groups *within* each of the castes below Nayars were egalitarian, enjoying equal privileges and intermarrying symmetrically within their small caste communities located in a few neighboring villages. In the highest stratum of religious specialists, rulers, and mili-

---

[9] Loeb states that a household, which may comprise a parui or part of a parui, may contain seventy or eighty members (1934: 30). If, in a given lineage, there were only two parui to each kampueng, and two kampueng in the suku or maximal descent group, this could yield a maximal descent group of up to 300 people.

tary, the same was true within each of the several occupational groups of Nambudiri Brahmans, and also of Nayar commoners who did not hold political offices. *Inter-lineage* stratification was prominent only among the matrilineal royalty, district chiefs, and their village headmen, whose lineages received their rank from the hierarchical political offices vested in them. At this level, inter-lineage stratification was more pronounced than in the societies previously discussed. The ranked office-bearing lineages were sharply separated from each other in terms of resource control, authority, and enjoyment of luxury goods. Concomitantly, instead of two-way marriages with multiple polygyny for those of higher rank, these lineages practiced only asymmetrical, one-way marriage (hypergamy), which emphasized the lower political and economic status of the woman's group. Further, although they probably helped to bolster relationships of political allegiance, these marriages lacked the political content of chiefly marriages in societies of lower productivity. A king or chief might occasionally promote his Nayar son to a subordinate political office—especially, in North Kerala, the area of lower productivity and less developed political centralization. Chiefs did not, however, take large numbers of wives, draw tribute through their wives, or rely on sons and grandsons to swell their following. The relations between office-bearing lineages were overwhelmingly political relations backed by armed force, and marriages between them served for little more than the provision of sexual partnership and the procreation of children.

Among commoner Nayars in villages, the Nayar community, like the village in Ashanti or Minangkabau, was a multi-lineage community of some four to seven maximal descent groups. In accordance with the general increase in social stratification, the village headman's lineage was lifted more sharply above the rest in terms of resource control, prestige, authority, and asymmetrical marriage rules than in Ashanti or Minangkabau. The main difference was, however, that in the Kerala village each Nayar landholding lineage segment had attached to it, by hereditary politico-economic status links and not by ties of kinship status, small descent groups of lower-caste tenants and (in Central Kerala) of serfs. The Nayar community as a whole commanded the services of village specialist workers of still other castes. It was as though the lower-ranking and economically less privileged segments of maximal lineages in a Minangkabau village had been lopped off and segregated as separate, completely endogamous occupational castes, claiming no ties of clanship or lineage membership with their superiors.

The Kerala village was probably roughly the same size or somewhat larger than the village in Minangkabau. Being only one of four or more descent groups within a caste community and not within a total village, however, the Nayar maximal lineage was probably smaller and was internally less segmented than in ·either Minangkabau or Ashanti. The maximal lineages of Nayar royals might number anything from some 5 to 300 members; of chiefs, up to about 100; of village headmen, somewhat fewer; but Nayar commoner lineages probably seldom numbered over 50 members. The maximal lineage among Nayar commoners often had about the same generation depth as the Minangkabau parui or landholding segment—seven to eight generations including children and common ancestress. Below the maximal lineage was only one functionally significant segment, the landholding or property group. This often counted its common ancestress only one to three generations above the oldest living members and normally occupied a single house.[10] Further, the Nayar maximal lineage lacked important political or economic functions. Among office-bearing aristocrats the political office was vested in the maximal lineage. Among Nayar commoners, however, the maximal lineage had no headman, structure of authority, or resource control, and no economic coöperation other than at household feasts. It was not regarded as a legally corporate unit by the state. Nor was it residentially unitary within a ward of the village. It was merely an exogamous group sharing hospitality, death pollution, and·a few other religious observances, and acting as an informal and indeed illegal group in feuds. The legally significant unit among Nayar commoners was the property group, comprising some five to thirty people and normally having a time depth of only four to five generations including children.

Correspondingly, intra-lineage or inter-segmental stratification was absent among Nayars. Headship of a commoner property group passed by strict seniority among males regardless of sub-branch until such time as the group divided between its component segments, each under a separate head. Political offices in theory passed by seniority in perpetuity within maximal lineages regardless of branch, even after the

[10] A significant difference between the Minangkabau and the Nayar property group was that in Minangkabau the property group (parui) was not permitted in law to divide its property between its segments until five generations had passed between the common ancestress and the oldest living members of these segments (De Jong, 1951: 10). Among Nayars, division of the property was permitted after the deaths of the common ancestress and of her sons. I would argue that the shallower generation depth (and normally, smaller size) of the property-holding and legally responsible lineage unit in Kerala was connected with the greater occupational differentiation of the society and its more centralized political structure.

lineage became divided and subdivided into separate property groups. In fact, if an aristocratic lineage became large and segmented into several property groups, in time one of them would seize the political office. But this did not set up intra-lineage stratification. Instead, the other branches appear shortly to have lost unilineal connection with the leading branch and to have sunk to a lower level of caste rank.

THE LIMITS OF MATRILINEAL DESCENT

It is perhaps significant that in Minangkabau and Kerala, the societies of highest productivity and political centralization, not all of the population followed matrilineal descent. In Minangkabau the royal lineage was patrilineal. We do not know about the kinship system of slaves or other landless retainers. In Kerala, Nambudiri Brahmans practiced a peculiar form of patriliny with primogeniture. Most of the other castes of North Kerala had some form of matrilineal descent, but only the descent groups of royals, chiefs, Nayar commoners, and Mappilla aristocrats had strongly corporate characteristics. The descent groups of Tiyyars and other low castes were small, held little property, and had a weak authority structure. These latter groups may also, even traditionally, have practiced a fairly high proportion of patrilocal residence. In Central Kerala, the society of highest productivity and political centralization, only the rulers, chiefs, temple servants, Nayar commoners, and their personal servants had matrilineal descent. Mappilla and immigrant Hindu traders had patrilineal descent groups. Nambudiri Brahmans had their peculiar form of patriliny with primogeniture. Tiyyar tenant farmers, artisans, and some other lower castes in villages had small localized patrilineal descent groups with fraternal polyandry, and dispersed exogamous matrilineal clans—a form of double descent. Serfs appear to have had no descent groups but rather a system of interpersonal bilateral kinship relations spreading outward from the elementary family.

There is some evidence that a larger proportion of Kerala's population may have been matrilineal at an earlier date. Nambudiri Brahmans have a tradition of having been "originally" matrilineally organized into multi-lineage village communities. Indeed, one Nambudiri Brahman village, Payyannur in North Kerala, has this form of descent at the present time. It seems probable that the lower castes of Central Kerala, (Tiyyars, etc.), who in historical times have had double descent, once had only matrilineal descent. I suspect this is so because these same castes, until very recently, followed matrilineal descent in the less productive and centralized kingdoms of North Kerala and also, incidentally, of South Kerala or Travancore. At the same time the widespread tendency toward patrilocality of North Kerala Tiyyars associated with cash-crop farming in the later nineteenth century produced something closely akin to the double descent of their caste in Central Kerala.

I suggest that there is a point on the scale of increasing productivity and political centralization when matrilineal descent is no longer viable, and that the Kerala kingdoms, and possibly Minangkabau, were approaching this point shortly before the European conquest. I do not know precisely what characterizes this stage of development, but it probably has to do with increasing division of labor and the consequent need for very small descent groups or for elementary families as the basic legal units of the kinship system. A division of labor which makes a small household the primary work unit for each single occupation, or a bureaucratic political structure in which individual men are appointed to salaried positions for limited periods, might exemplify such conditions. For reasons given in Schneider's Introduction, matrilineal descent groups do not lend themselves to the extremes of segmentation and fission possible in patrilineal descent groups. In matriliny a group of male and female siblings is the minimal requirement for starting a descent group, and each man has, through his sisters, several sibling sets of potential heirs. In patriliny, by contrast, each man with his wife is the starting point of a potential descent line, and if he is monogamous he has only one sibling set of heirs (his sons). Primogeniture, an institution suitable for stable succession to single occupational or political positions, is also easier to accomplish with patrilineal than with matrilineal descent. These may be some of the reasons why matrilineal descent is not found in very large, bureaucratically organized states. As matrilineal societies go, Ashanti, Minangkabau, and Kerala had large states with a high degree of political centralization, but such states seem to have been rare. As preindustrial states in general go, moreover, they were small and decentralized when compared with such bureaucratically organized patrilineal states as those of the great river valleys of North India and China.[11] In recent times, since they became affected by the fuel revolution and the modern industrial system, the matrilineal descent groups of these societies —like those of many other societies—have begun to disintegrate and to give place to a system of bilateral relationships centered in the ele-

[11] In chapter 6 I emphasized the comparatively decentralized character of the Kerala kingdoms, having in mind the larger patrilineal kingdoms of the great Indian river valleys. In this chapter, having in mind other matrilineal societies, I have been led to emphasize the relatively high degree of political centralization in Kerala.

mentary family. It is suggested here, however, that even if these most modern changes of the market system had not overtaken them, these states could not have expanded greatly or greatly increased their division of labor without shifting to some form of bilaterality, or—probably via an intermediate system of double descent—toward small patrilineal descent groups. In Ashanti, the fact that sons might follow their fathers to war may indicate incipient double descent; this tendency was much more marked among the neighboring Fanti, were the regiments were recruited patrilineally. In Central Kerala, the most advanced of the matrilineal states, shifts to double descent proper or to patriliny were, for large strata of the population, already accomplished.

CONCLUSIONS

Extrapolating from the data presented above, I suggest the following possible general connections between level of productivity and degree of political centralization among matrilineal settled cultivators on the one hand, and descent-group structures and interrelations on the other.

(1) In settled cultivating societies at the lowest levels of productivity, relations between descent groups will be egalitarian or near-egalitarian. This follows from the very low degree of political centralization. With increasing productivity and political centralization, most descent groups in the society will be ranked in relation to one another, with the chiefly descent group of course outranking all and having privileged access to strategic resources. At still higher levels of political centralization and productivity, ranking between individual descent groups will tend to give place to stratification between caste or class groups, each composed of a number of near-egalitarian descent groups. In the most highly centralized and productive matrilineal states, stratification between individual descent groups seems likely to survive longest toward the top of the social hierarchy among descent groups holding hereditary political offices. Egalitarian or near-egalitarian descent groups are expected in societies having only one, if any, level of territorial head; ranked and incipiently stratified descent groups in societies having two levels of territorial head (chiefdoms or protostates); and stratified classes or castes in societies with three or more levels of territorial head (states proper).

(2) In settled cultivating societies at the lowest levels of productivity, with only one level of territorial head, the descent group will tend to be small, of shallow generation depth, weakly segmented, and lacking inter-segmental stratification. In protostates and small states, with higher productivity, it seems likely that localized maximal descent

groups will have greater generation depth, size, and definiteness of division into functionally distinct segments. It is expected that these characteristics will be enhanced by increasing productivity, up to a certain stage of economic and political development, exemplified by Minangkabau. Concomitantly, inter-segmental stratification of some kind within descent groups *may* occur in this stage, although I am uncertain whether this is a necessary feature. Such developments seem likely to continue until productivity, division of labor, and wealth differentiation have reached the point where clearly separate, hereditary or near-hereditary classes of menials, traders, military, literati, and rulers emerge, as in the Kerala kingdoms. When this takes place, descent groups, instead of being the dominant units of social structure within communities, become confined within social classes or castes of differential wealth, resource control, political power, and occupation.

The maximal localized descent group in such societies is likely to be smaller and to have fewer functionally distinct levels of segmentation than in states of relatively high productivity which are not yet divided into occupational classes, such as Ashanti or Minangkabau. The descent group is also likely to be internally less stratified or even completely unstratified by segment. Nevertheless, in these complex states, descent groups in the highest classes, having greatest resource control, will be larger, will have a greater generation depth, and will be more clearly segmented than those of middle-ranking occupational classes. If the lowest classes of the society have no rights or only subsidiary and impermanent rights to hold land or other resources, very small, shallow descent groups may be expected, or descent groups may entirely disappear.

(3) In settled cultivating societies of lower productivity, it seems likely to be the maximal organized descent group which primarily controls land or other resources. As productivity, descent-group size, and degree of segmentation within the descent group increase, direct management of land seems likely to shift to lineage segments intermediate between the maximal lineage and its minimal segments, as in Minangkabau and perhaps in Ashanti. In such societies the maximal lineage seems to be more relevant to judicial administration and its head to be a link with the state, although he may retain an overright in land management. With the highest level of productivity in which occupational classes have emerged, as in Kerala, land seems likely to be vested in very small lineage segments, each normally the nucleus of a household. This segment, through its head, is in law directly responsible to political authorities of the state. The maximal lineage may survive as an

exogamous and ceremonially coöperative group, but it loses its political and economic functions and receives no legal recognition from the state.

(4) There may be some connection between level of productivity and degree of political centralization on the one hand, and the kinship composition of local communities on the other hand, among matrilineal settled cultivators. This is difficult to specify, however, because the kinship composition of communities is no doubt affected by the nature of resources and their distribution, as well as by mere level of productivity. I will simply point out that among the eight examples, four types of community were distinguishable which did not seem to be randomly distributed along the scale of productivity.

These were, first, a small, near-egalitarian multi-lineage community, which was also the maximal political unit, under a weak territorial head. Each descent group also had its head, but he was not thereby the head of a local sub-unit because the descent group was not necessarily residentially unitary (Hopi and Truk). Second, a mono-lineage community with attached affines and cognates, forming a village under a hereditary head responsible to the district chief as head of the maximal territorial unit. The chief's own village might contain more than one descent group with attachments, with his own group outranking the rest (Trobriand and Mayombe). Third, a village composed of several localized lineages, usually four to seven, its hereditary headman being of a higher-ranking lineage, responsible to political officers of chiefdom and kingdom (Ashanti and Minangkabau). Fourth, a village made up of a number of stratified, endogamous occupational castes (Kerala). The lineage composition of the managerial caste (Nayars) was comparable to that of a village of type three, the difference being that Nayar lineage segments, instead of relying on their own production, had attached households of lower castes to serve them.

At the lowest levels of productivity, at least one type of settled cultivating community is known to be possible which is not contained in our examples. This is a small hamlet containing a single descent group with temporarily attached affines and cognates, which has either no head or only informal leaders selected on the basis of personal qualities. The hamlet is set within an acephalous district as the maximal political unit (the peace group). This type is represented by Dobu and the Amphlett Islands. This type is similar to type one, except that a majority of the members of each descent group are localized separately as a small hamlet on their own fields, and neither descent group nor district have hereditary heads. It seems probable that this hamlet type is associated with a region of very low productivity and uniformly distributed resources, such that each descent group can control all available resources on a small, continuous area of land. Type one, by contrast, seems to be associated with a region of relatively low productivity but with scattered resource zones within a limited area, in which each descent group controls more than one resource zone within the small territory of the district or village.

For what it is worth, I suggest that multi-lineage communities *may* be common at the lowest and highest levels of productivity in matrilineal societies, but rare at the middle levels, whereas mono-lineage communities may be common at the lowest and middle levels, but rare at the highest levels. More specifically, one would expect to find multi-lineage communities either as maximal political units in societies with only one or no level of territorial head, or as villages in states with three or more levels of territorial head. Conversely, mono-lineage communities would be expected in societies with none, one, or two levels of territorial head, but rarely in states with three or more levels of territorial head. The reasoning behind this hypothesis is that it seems to be in small chiefdoms or protostates that the descent group is most likely to be utilized as the nucleus of a local unit, whose head is at once a lineage head and a territorial head subordinate to the chief. In more complex states, higher population density and more centralized authority seem likely to force a grouping of several commoner descent groups within each minimal territorial unit under a single political officer who is responsible to the state.

Beyond this, one would of course not expect to find as the minimal local unit of a matrilineal society a village composed of multiple stratified endogamous castes, except at the very highest levels of productivity represented by the Kerala systems. It is impossible to hypothesize about other potential community types at or above this level of productivity, because, so far as I am aware, no matrilineal society is reported to have attained this level outside Kerala.

(5) Increase in productivity and in degree of political centralization is associated with changes in the range and degree of symmetry of marriage ties. In settled cultivating societies of lowest productivity, and only one or no level of territorial head, marriage ties link descent groups in an egalitarian manner. Marriages and ties of clanship are also likely to cross the boundaries of maximal political units unless the latter are isolated by environmental conditions. In chiefdoms having somewhat higher productivity and two levels of territorial head, two-way chains of marriages will still link all or almost all sectors of the society, but

the conditions of marriage will no longer be egalitarian. Chiefs are likely to use privileged forms of marriage as an important basis of their nascent political power, e.g., as a source of labor, tribute, or military followers. Marriage and clanship ties may still cross political boundaries, but a smaller proportion of marriages is to be expected outside the maximal political unit. In matrilineal states having three or more levels of territorial head and the control of force by a central power, chief-subject relations based on affinity and cognation are expected to give place to primarily political relations between ruler and ruled, in which marriage ties are an incidental factor. As resource control and political power become concentrated in a hereditary ruling class, marriage ties are likely to decline or cease between rulers and ruled, and there may be a still further multiplication of endogamous divisions within each category. Ties of marriage and clanship are unlikely to cross the boundaries of these larger states, except possibly between royal lineages of adjacent states. In general, the lower the class, the narrower the range of marriage relations, so that commoners are likely to marry mainly within the minimal local community or a small group of adjacent communities. Between the higher ranks of political officers, where inter-lineage rather than inter-class stratification may still predominate, asymmetrical forms of marriage are likely to persist. Their form will emphasize differences rather than similarities of privilege. They will, however, play a relatively very minor role in upholding the political structure.

Productivity, Political Centralization, and the Functions and Authority Structures of Descent Groups among Settled Cultivators

The kinds of functions fulfilled by descent groups in the eight settled cultivating societies are superficially similar. They include ownership and exploitation of a joint estate; coöperation of at least a proportion of members in production, distribution of goods, and inheritance of individual property; common legal responsibility for at least some of the acts of members; and participation in religious or magical cults associated with the group. The significance of these functions within the framework of the total society varies, however, with level of productivity and degree of political centralization, as well as with other less general factors. So also, of course, do the kinds of controls exercised by descent-group authorities.

It is argued that descent groups are most tightly organized, and the controls exercised by their authorities most comprehensive, at the middle levels of productivity in large chiefdoms or small states. These characteristics appear to be somewhat weaker in descent groups in the largest states with highest productivity. They are weakest of all in the smallest political units with lowest productivity. An attempt will be made to "spell out" this statement by reference to the eight societies.

HOPI

Control and Exploitation of Resources   The sub-clan or maximal descent group jointly owned an estate. Apparently because of low productivity, simple sex division of labor, and relatively uniform distribution of resource types to households and individuals, however, it was largely exploited in severalty and its management required only weak authority. The sub-clan head had residual rights to allocate unused plots and to settle land disputes. Land once allocated tended, however, to remain within subordinate segments, and use rights to be inherited informally by individuals (Eggan, 1950: 58). In general the descent-group head's control of resources must be assessed as very weak.

Production   Low productivity coupled with lack of specialization and fairly uniform distribution of resources permitted the matrilocal extended family, rather than the maximal descent group, to be the major unit of productive coöperation. Within the household, members of the same sex performed the same tasks individually or in small informal groups, so that little authority was needed. Larger communal tasks such as planting and harvesting were formerly carried out by sub-clan members as a group (Titiev, 1944: 184), but this work, too, probably required little division of functions and only weak authority. Other forms of production, relevant not to the joint estate but to the community as a whole, such as hunting, fell to voluntary multi-clan work parties under informal leadership or to groups drawn from multi-clan religious societies (*ibid.:* 188–193).

Distribution of Goods   Distribution of products took the form mainly of simple daily pooling within the household (*ibid.:* 15–24), sporadic informal sharing between households of the sub-clan in time of need, reciprocity between households at marriage and other special occasions, and collective distributions on the part of religious societies to the whole community during festivals. Because households produced the same goods and had little surplus, there was evidently no room for organized redistribution by the heads of either sub-clan or community.

Legal Constitution of the Descent Group   The sub-clan head, the senior woman, or collective elders of the descent group might settle private disputes within it over land or other property (Forde, 1931: 400). They appear to have had no sanctions other than the force of public opinion. In a grave crisis such as the split between Friendlies and Hostiles at Oraibi in 1906, there was no machinery to resolve disputes between sections of the same sub-clan. In this instance a number of sub-clans split permanently between the two factions. One faction remained at Old Oraibi and the other moved out to form a new village (Titiev, 1944: 88–89).

There seem to have been no crimes recognized within the descent group, in the sense of individual offenses to be met by forceful punishment on the part of the group or its authority. It is not clear, for example, what happened in case of incest, but Titiev's material suggests that breaches of exogamy, while considered "illegal" and perhaps sinful, were not forcefully punished by the descent group or by higher authorities (ibid.: 36).

The controls of the sub-clan head or other elders over the personal lives of members were evidently weak. Elders advised in the choice of first marriage partners, for example, but their consent does not seem to have been strictly necessary.

Witchcraft was believed possible between kin of the same as well as of different descent groups. General theory would suggest that witchcraft and sorcery accusations are likely to occur in relationships in which open aggression is not feasible, but which are not regulated by organized authorities to whom effective appeal can be made.[12] Resort to covert forms of self-help is therefore desirable in cases of infringement of norms. If this theory is correct, the prevalence of witchcraft accusations *within* the descent group would reflect the inability of its leaders to take forceful action in case of disputes within it.

The evidence is not clear about the kinds of individual acts for which the sub-clan had collective responsibility in relation to other descent groups. Disputes between people of different descent groups concerning property were settled by the village chief or by a collectivity of sub-clan heads, but there is no evidence that the descent group or any of its segments was collectively responsible for damages. Physical violence was rare within the Hopi community. Titiev suggests that the Hopi themselves were uncertain of the correct procedures in case of assault or murder (ibid.: 162). Eggan states that theoretically the "family" of a slain man should kill the slayer, but that murder was very rare (1950: 108). Although they evidently hastened the offender's downfall through upbraiding and condemnation, Hopi villagers do not

---

[12] This theory was suggested to me by B. B. Whiting's book, *Paiute Sorcery* (1950), and also by an unpublished manuscript on primitive religion by G. E. Swanson, University of Michigan.

seem to have regarded assault or threat of violence as crimes against the community requiring punishment by collective or organized force (Titiev, 1944: 79).

In general the data indicate that the Hopi sub-clan's common legal responsibility in relation to other descent groups and to the community was very weakly developed, and that the controls of its head over members were extremely limited. The fact that the sub-clan head consulted other elders in decision making and that the senior woman was also an important advisory figure reflect the lack of a specialized and differentiated authority structure. Peace among the Hopi evidently depended on the operation of cross-cutting relationships, supernatural sanctions, and diffuse public disapproval, rather than on formal authorities or collective force (Eggan, 1950: 116–120).

TRUK

Control and Exploitation of Resources   Although the Trukese probably had a similar or even lower level of productivity than the Hopi, their descent group was somewhat more tightly organized and its head's authority more extensive. I suggest that this may have been because the slender but diverse resources of the Trukese were less evenly distributed between household and individuals. Given the dense population and small size of plots, there may have been a tendency for some households to produce more breadfruit in a given season, others more fish, etc. This may have been the case even though resource ownership in general was continually evened out through such institutions as adoption and gifts of provisional title by fathers to children. An uneven distribution of resources may have necessitated controls over production and redistribution on the part of authorities of descent group and district. Nevertheless, such controls were weak when compared with those found in societies of higher productivity.

The lineage head allocated land, or the trees and other improvements made on land, at infrequent intervals to subordinate branches and individuals. Once allocated, such resources tended to remain within branches as long as there was a suitable number of persons to inherit their usufruct. The head could not, apparently, supervise the use to which resources were put, nor could he dispossess insubordinate individuals. His control of resources was shared by the sub-heads of component sibling groups within the lineage, especially by those sibling groups which owned branch property inherited from a father (chap. 3, above).

Production   Most day-to-day production by men was carried out individually or in small informal groups. Such groups usually comprised men of different lineages—the husbands of a matrilocal household or a pair of brothers-in-law. There were, however, seasonal forms of work requiring larger teams organized under an authority, such as land clearing, large fishing drives, and breadfruit storage; in this work matrilineally related men coöperated under the head of the lineage or of the larger-order ramage. The women of a lineage also worked regularly as a team under the guidance of their senior in reef fishing (*idem*).

Distribution   The most regular forms of distribution were simple pooling of products for immediate consumption within the matrilocal extended family, or sharing within this unit, in which one husband prepared breadfruit on behalf of the household as a whole. In a larger lineage which provided the female core of more than one household, there was also regular sharing between households. These small-scale forms of distribution normally required no formal authority. The lineage head did, however, act as a formal agent in redistribution in emergencies and on periodic special occasions. He could command products from the plots of one member or household to give to another in time of need. He periodically organized lineage members to produce food for an exchange feast ("feast fight") with another lineage. Four times a year he commanded products from lineage members for surrender to the chief in aid of a district feast (*idem*). The lineage head was thus an occasional agent of redistribution both within his lineage and, as subordinate of the chief, among lineages of the political unit. These roles were, however, of minor significance compared with those of the Trobriand descent-group head. Thus, the Trukese lineage head commanded no regular surplus of food or other goods. As an elder of lesser productive capacity he might, indeed, like other elders, run the danger of hunger in times of shortage. His dependence on the good will of juniors in this respect seems to have tempered the practical exercise of such authority as was theoretically vested in him (Gladwin and Sarason, 1953: 155).

Legal Responsibility   The Trukese lineage was more tightly organized than the Hopi sub-clan, both as a unit of collective responsibility and in terms of its controls over its own members. This may be related to the greater degree of economic coöperation and organization within the Trukese lineage; the much smaller amount of community-wide coöperation in communal tasks in the Trukese district than in the Hopi village; and the less nucleated character of the Trukese community, dispersed in matrilocal extended families on separate plots of land.

The lineage head might settle disputes and intervene in fights between members, although he had no sanctions except the collective support of the group. The greater authority of the group, and of its head, to resolve intra-group disputes is evident perhaps in that sorcery does not seem to have operated within the lineage. Rather, knowledge of sorcery was passed on between lineage members for use against other descent groups (*ibid.:* 149). In theory, the lineage head and the female head approved marriages and had the right to veto an unsuitable choice (chap. 3, above). Their authority might, however, be overridden, and if a couple eloped they had little redress. Incest was a crime within the lineage, and if it took place the group as a whole was expected to kill the offenders. Persistent failure of an individual to meet lineage obligations led to a withdrawal of support which occasionally drove the offender to suicide (Gladwin and Sarason, 1953: 145–146). Other intra-lineage offenses were classifiable as sins. Thus difficulties in childbirth might be interpreted as ghostly punishment for general lack of amity between members (*ibid.:* 150).

The lineage emerged as a vengeance group in support of individual members in disputes with other lineages. Sorcery, assault, or adultery on the part of a spouse were occasions for collective retaliation in the form of counter-sorcery or physical attack. Inter-lineage fights resulting from individual disputes were evidently brief, and compensation in the form of property seems to be modern. More prolonged blood feuds arose in connection with inter-lineage disputes over land and chiefship. These might end in the expulsion of one lineage from the island by another. Collective responsibility was, however, strongest within the sibling group, and descent lines of the same lineage might take opposite sides in district wide disputes. One case of murder and one of attempted murder are recorded between men of different descent lines of the same lineage. No action was possible by the lineage except its fission into separate units. The obligation in this case rested with the classificatory "fathers" and "sons" of the victims (Goodenough, 1951: 149). This situation highlights the relative impermanence of the lineage as an organized group and the tendency for branches owning separate, paternally bequeathed property to split apart at intervals of two or three generations.

This potential striving for autonomy on the part of branch segments appears also in that the major responsibility for discipline in day-to-day events rested with the subordinate heads of adult sibling groups rather than with the lineage head. Elder brothers disciplined their younger brothers, managed their sisters' marital affairs, and, on behalf of the sisters, demanded services of their sisters' husbands. While the lineage cohered, decisions affecting the group as a whole were, moreover, normally made by the head in regular consultation with the senior woman, other male elders of the oldest generations, and the heads of junior segments as a collectivity.

TROBRIAND

Control and Exploitation of Resources   The Trobriand maximal descent unit was in every way more tightly organized and its structure of authority stronger than among Hopi or Trukese. Among Hopi and Trukese, matrilineally related women shared a household. But the households of one maximal descent group might be scattered among those of other descent groups, and they owned plots dispersed among those of the multi-lineage community as a whole. In the Trobriands, by contrast, men of the descent group formed the core of a discrete residential unit, a village, and controlled a continuous stretch of land. The descent-group head, who was also head of the avunculocal village, allocated plots to individual members annually, instead of at irregular intervals. He determined which crops should be grown on each plot and which plots should lie fallow for the year. The descent group as a whole, however, retained ultimate control of its resources, subject to the lien of the chief. Thus it could dispossess and evict temporarily resident sons of male members, even of the headman, if they failed to conform to norms. The head also exercised his authority over many matters in consultation with other elders of the group.

Production   The head of the village directed communal labor on village lands by descent-group men and their wives. Through his monopoly of gardening magic he initiated and supervised major activities on individual plots (chap. 4, above). As owner of the village's canoes he controlled its fishing resources. He organized the teamwork of descent-group men in canoe building and fishing. These tasks, like cultivation, required specialization of functions and thus demanded a clear-cut and differentiated authority structure on the part of the descent-group head and the various experts subordinate to him. As a subordinate in the wider political structure, the village head commanded seasonal labor on behalf of the chief for larger district-wide projects of canoe building, fishing, and overseas trading (Malinowski, 1922: 116–120; 1932: 26–27).

Distribution of Goods   Although the elementary family household was the unit of daily pooling of products and of consumption, three-quarters of the food produced by individual men was distributed elsewhere— to the chief, to sisters' husbands on behalf of sisters in other villages, to the descent-group head for redistribution within the group, or in trade with other islands (Malinowski, 1922: 61). These arrangements were made possible by the relatively high productivity of Boyowa Island, which permitted some village and individual specialization in different forms of food production and crafts, and the export of some food to less productive islands in return for nonedible goods.

These forms of specialization made the head of the descent group and village, under the chief, a regular agent in organized redistribution. He maintained a large store of yams and other foods to dispense to work parties during canoe building and other communal projects. The store came partly from contributions by descent-group members and partly from the garden work of his (several) wives and children. During the dancing season he collected food from members and redistributed it in numerous village feasts. As canoe owner he took charge of and distributed the village's fishing hauls. He could also hire out his canoe to others for a return which helped to swell his stores. He served as agent in the redistributive processes of the chiefdom by collecting tribute of food and other goods from his villagers for surrender to the chief as urigubu (affinal gift). These goods the chief used to support craftsmen, trading expeditions, and communal work parties. Under the aegis of the chief the village head also led his men on overseas trading expeditions for valuables and utilitarian goods. He acted as collector and distributor of trade goods both entering and leaving the village, and retained the major share in his own control (*ibid.:* 64, 192–193, 464–475).

Legal Constitution of the Descent Group   The head's right to settle disputes and control the personal lives of members remained relatively weak in the Trobriands. He seems to have had greater strength to preserve his own inviolacy than on Truk. Through his control of sorcery and gardening magic, for example, he could punish disrespectful people or threaten disaster to the group as a whole (*ibid.:* 64). He seems however to have relied largely on the general support of his kinsmen and to have seldom acted without consulting other male elders of the group. He apparently exercised no force to settle disputes. Disputants over crops or plots harangued each other; no third party intervened to adjudicate between them (Malinowski, 1932: 60). Lineage ghosts were believed to punish with sickness various intra-lineage sins such as incest (Hoebel, 1954: 184). Incest may also, perhaps, be classified as a crime against the descent group, for its public exposure seems to have left the offender no course of action except suicide (*ibid.:* 186).

Feuding between descent groups was more restricted than on Truk. I suggest that this was because of the higher productivity of the society (and thus the greater wealth and power of the chief) and also, probably, because of the greater economic specialization and interdependence of descent groups. Full-scale, prolonged hostilities were prohibited by custom between villages of the same district, although they might fight with spears and throwing sticks and perform isolated killings in cases of grave offense. A sorcerer or an adulterer caught in the act in the village of the offended spouse might be killed by the latter's lineage kin, apparently without much danger of retaliation (Malinowski, 1932: 118). Many offenses were met by sorcery or counter-sorcery. Villagers protected themselves from theft by placing disease magic on trees. Threats of violence between descent groups concerning boundary disputes or insults apparently often gave place to challenges to a "food fight," in which each village in turn tried to outdo the other in presenting gifts of food (Malinowski, 1935: 182–187). Theoretically the descent group should avenge the wanton murder of any member. In fact, however, only the murders of men of "high rank" were normally avenged (Hoebel 1954: 190). It is not clear whether this means only village heads or elders, or (more probably) only members of higher-ranking and consequently wealthier and more powerful descent groups than the murderer's. Such groups would presumably tend to have larger villages and thus would be able to afford retaliation. When they occurred, feuds were short and ended in payment of compensation for every person killed; often compensation was arranged immediately following the murder. If the deceased had deserved his fate, his kin might refrain from vengeance or from demanding compensation. Malinowski's examples suggest that "deserved" may usually have meant that the deceased had offended the chief or another of high rank, so that vengeance would in any case be difficult (Malinowski, 1922: 65). Against more covert offenders the chief could direct the most powerful sorcery in the district, which he alone controlled.

Apparently no offenses were recognized as crimes against the district as a whole. As Hoebel points out, the chief had no publicly recognized authority to settle disputes with organized force or to punish offenders against the common weal (1954: 196–197). Like any other descent group, the village acted to protect its own interests as a private corporation. Because the chief had greater wealth and a larger following, however, because he was indispensable as a redistributive and organizing agent, and because—via the chief's coördination—descent groups were economically dependent on one another, the descent group's access to self-help was curtailed.

MAYOMBE

Resources, Production, and Distribution   Information on the constitution of the Mayombe descent group is inadequate for a thorough comparison, but some salient points are clear.

As a group whose male members, with their wives and children,
formed the core of a village or occasionally a village section, the
Mayombe descent group was tightly organized. The head allocated
unused land, garden sites, and palm trees to its members. He is said
to have wielded "absolute" authority over the labor of its male members, who are spoken of as his "subjects" (Richards, 1950: 219–220).
He commanded their collective services for housebuilding, clearing
fields, harvesting palm wine and nuts, hunting, or carrying trade goods
(De Cleene, 1937: 9), as well as, apparently, supervising individual
tasks. He must formerly have been in charge of all surplus products, if
not all products, of individuals, for redistribution within the group and
perhaps also for surrender as tribute to the chief. Today, with wage
labor and cash-crop farming, he controls a joint purse composed of a
levy on the earnings of men, and of customary contributions from their
earnings made by women of the descent group who live with their
husbands in other villages. Traditionally a married woman received
fields to cultivate in her husband's village and surrendered half of her
produce to the husband and his kin. She carried the other half to her
descent-group head in the village of her natal home. The lineage head
received bridewealth in cloth and cash on behalf of girls marrying out
of the group, met their marriage expenses, and paid out bridewealth on
behalf of male juniors bringing wives into the village. From his store of
surplus wealth he also met the expenses of healers or magicians whom
he was responsible for summoning in case of sickness or other misfortune (Richards, 1950: 219–220). He was similarly responsible for
hiring specialists to treat women and children of the group who fell
sick while living in the villages of their husbands and fathers (De
Cleene, 1937: 7). The head appears to have had charge of the group's
trade with other villages or with foreigners, perhaps under the superior
authority of the chief. As representative of the descent group he was
responsible for its debts. Slaves were also property among the Mayombe, and it seems probable that most of them came primarily
under the authority of descent-group heads (*ibid.:* 8). The head appears also to have controlled the inheritance of individual property of
deceased members by their matrilineal juniors. In sum, it seems clear
that the Mayombe descent-group head controlled a much larger
amount of consumer goods and durable property than did the Tro-

briand head, and that he was a more authoritative agent of redistribution both within and between descent groups.

Legal Constitution of the Descent Group   Information is inadequate on the judicial role of Mayombe chiefs and consequently on the legal constitution of the descent group. It seems probable that some machinery existed above the village for the settlement of inter-lineage disputes, because the descent-group head is reported to have had the right to sell juniors to pay debts or the damages of lawsuits lost by the group (*ibid.:* 11). Since slavery has been abolished in modern times it sounds as though this practice was traditional. There is no mention of inter-lineage blood feuds, which suggests that disputes between lineages may have been settled by higher authorities. Hostilities between descent groups seem mainly to have taken the form of sorcery, from which the head was responsible for protecting his group—if necessary, by hiring expert magicians (De Cleene, 1937: 7; Richards, 1950: 220).

Within the descent group the head had stronger authority over the personal lives of members than did the descent-group head in the Trobriands. He settled disputes between its members, perhaps with the supernatural sanction of ancestral punishment, for the cult of matrilineal forebears was well developed. In addition to his ability to sell junior members into slavery, he arranged marriages, could force an unwelcome marriage on a girl, and could precipitate the divorce of a female member by bringing home her children from her husband's village. A head could beat, kidnap, or imprison a woman who refused to marry the suitor of his choice. In this as in other conflicts with juniors, however, his chief sanction seems to have been the possession of powerful sorcery. In disputes with other groups he was required to use it on behalf of his "subjects," but if they disobeyed him he could direct it against them (De Cleene, 1937: 4, 10–11).

ASHANTI

Resources, Production, and Distribution   The Ashanti descent group had a clearly defined authority structure culminating in the head of the maximal lineage. The extent of coöperation and collective responsibility of lineage kin was impressive, and the headman's authority was at least as extensive (and more strongly sanctioned) as among the Mayombe.

The maximal lineage head appears to have had the ultimate right of allocation of lineage land and other jointly owned property, although land once allocated may have remained more or less permanently with subordinate segments under the management of subordinate heads (Fortes, 1950: 257–258). Privately acquired property and land developed by individuals became lineage property after the death of the owner, to be reallocated by the head. Information on traditional production is inadequate, but there must have been considerable coöperative work on lineage lands, as well as lineage-based work on behalf of the village as a whole (chap. 5, above). The head of the maximal lineage led his male juniors in compulsory military service on behalf of chief and king. Under the chief he summoned them for *corvée* labor in public works of the chiefdom. Only in the most central-ized state, Kumasi, were men organized in the army in groups which cross-cut lineage affiliations, and so must have taken them partially out of the control of lineage elders (*idem*).

Heads of lineages and segments were clearly of great significance for the redistribution of food and of durable movable property. The lineage head gave and received bridewealth on behalf of members, financed funerals and ancestral offerings, was ultimately responsible for the adequate maintenance of members, sanctioned the inheritance of personal movables, and was directly responsible for debts incurred by the lineage as a group (Fortes, 1950: 256). He was ultimately re-sponsible also for the debts of individual members (Hoebel, 1954: 231). There appears to have been no regular system of tribute other than first fruits and certain animals exacted by the chief from villagers. There were, however, special imposts for war and other emergencies. At such times the lineage head must have been responsible for his lineage's quota.

Legal Constitution of the Descent Group   Traditional Ashanti forms an excellent instance of a society in which descent groups (rather than castes, classes, occupational categories, etc.) are still the basic units of organization within local communities, but in which a state with centralized force adapts the lineage to its purposes. Maximal lineage heads, as heads of territories or as councilors of the head in one or another order of territorial unit, thus represent the state to their mem-bers and are endowed with authority by it, while also representing their members' interests to the state. It is perhaps in such states that the lineage achieves its height of collective legal responsibility and its strongest structure of authority.

Within the lineage, small disputes between members could be car-ried for arbitration to any lineage elder. Grave ones were settled by the maximal lineage head. His judgment was sanctioned by the super-natural power of ancestors to punish with sickness, and ultimately by the authority of the state. Reconciliation of intra-lineage disputants was formally marked by the defendant's offering a gift to placate the plaintiff's soul (*ibid.:* 216–218).

After the consolidation of the Ashanti Union, all crimes against the lineage appear also to have become crimes against the state. Incest was a heinous offense against the royal ancestors, punished by death. So also was homicide within, as well as outside, the lineage. At an earlier period persons who killed a lineage mate were expelled by the lineage and might become slaves (*ibid.:* 219, 238). Incest, and probably fraticide, if unintentional, merited only fines and atonement assessments for religious sacrifices; for these the lineage was collectively responsible.

With regard to control over the personal lives of members, the lineage head must give consent and act as representative at marriages and divorces. He could enforce cross-cousin marriage and must give consent for divorce (chap. 5, above). The latter rights seem to have been shared by heads of subordinate segments. A lineage head could pawn or sell into slavery any junior member to meet debts incurred by the lineage or its individual members, or to pay fines which would commute the death sentence passed on a member convicted of capital crime (Hoebel, 1954: 231).

Within the local community many private disputes between people of different lineages, considered "affairs of the household," were brought to a meeting of lineage heads, who passed judgment and exacted fines. The lineages of disputants, under their heads, were collectively responsible for such fines. Under the government of the kings, however, any private delict could be brought to trial as a capital crime by the device of one disputant's swearing a royal or chiefly oath. The chiefs encouraged such procedure to gain revenue from the expenses of trial. Individuals seem to have resorted to it with the hope of achieving a reversal of judgment. The guilty party might merit the death sentence, but it was often commuted for heavy fines for which the lineage was responsible. Capital sentence might also at royal pleasure be commuted for regular crimes against the state. These included homicide, suicide, certain sexual offenses, assault, stealing, cursing the chief, treason, cowardice, sorcery, and violation of local taboos. In the absence of regular tribute, therefore, lineages as units of collective responsibility surrendered heavy dues to the state for a wide range of crimes. Self-help on the part of the lineage as a private vengeance group was forbidden, all punishment of crime or private delict having been taken over by one or another level of public authority within the state (*ibid.:* 219, 231–235, 245).

At least in modern times, Ashanti believe that witchcraft acts only within the lineage (Fortes, 1950: 258). If it is true that witchcraft and sorcery (where they exist) operate in relationships where open aggression is not feasible but where adequate appeal for justice cannot be made to an authority, this belief may reflect an important characteristic of intra-lineage relations. Perhaps witchcraft accusations do not exist between lineages because inter-lineage disputes can (and could) be adequately solved in the courts (Hoebel, 1954: 219). With regard to intra-lineage relations, Fortes notes that the mother and sister are those most commonly accused of witchcraft (1950: 264, 275). I suggest that this may reflect the fact that women are legal minors, under the guardianship of male matrilineal authorities. They cannot therefore readily take to court grievances against each other or against their own matrilineal authorities. Whether or not this is the case today, I would expect that, traditionally, witchcraft accusations would be mainly against those members of the lineage (whether women or junior males) who were legally represented by their lineage heads and could not gain ready access to courts. I would not expect lineage heads to be accused of witchcraft because they held state-backed legal authority (Hoebel, 1954: 243). Witchcraft may therefore have been viewed as a means by which oppressed minors could, illegally but effectively, bring harm to oppressive authorities.

MINANGKABAU

The information on Minangkabau descent groups is inadequate for a thorough comparison with Ashanti or Kerala, but the outline indicates certain likenesses to and differences from both societies.

Resources   As in Ashanti, maximal lineages tended to occupy separate wards of the village and to control separate blocks of land (Cole, 1936: 23). In Minangkabau, however, *de facto* ownership of land and inheritance of movables was vested in a seven- to eight-generation segment (parui). The maximal lineage retained only an overright in land, to the extent that this could not be pawned or sold without the consent of its head—and indeed of the heads of all maximal lineages of the village (Schrieke, 1955: 116; Cole, 1936: 23). It seems probable that in Ashanti the maximal lineage and its head retained greater control over land and other goods than in Minangkabau. I suspect this to be true because, in Ashanti, lineage males are reported to have dined every night in the house of the lineage head (Hoebel, 1954: 214), which suggests tightness of economic coöperation of the lineage. Further, movables could, at least in theory, be inherited by any junior within the maximal lineage (Fortes, 1950: 257); this again suggests that the lineage was the "real" unit of ownership. On the other hand, it is clear that the Minangkabau maximal lineage retained greater control over land than did the lineage in Kerala.

As manager of the estate, the head (*panghulu*) of the landholding segment allocated fields to subordinate household heads (*mama'*) within his segment (De Jong, 1951: 55). The mama' in turn gave plots to each married woman of his household to cultivate, sometimes with the help of her husband (Cole, 1936: 20). It seems clear however that, given the large variety of tree and garden crops in Minangkabau, the landholding segment's head must have retained much land in his direct control. Perhaps it was cultivated by the rather mysterious landless persons who lived on his estate (*ibid.*: 22).

The village council of heads of maximal lineages reserved the right to assign unused land to lineages or lineage segments, and approved the rare sales of land which in emergency might take place between lineages of the town. Individual men had some ability to own privately cleared plots, but they could not give them to their children or other persons without the consent of a full council of segment heads of the maximal lineage (Schrieke, 1955: 115–116; Cole, 1936: 26). At a man's death his segment head took charge of his undisposed private property and reallocated it within the segment (De Jong, 1951: 56).

Production In addition to any control he had over the work of landless servants, the segment head summoned men of his segment to participate in such communal tasks as making roads or building a new mosque on behalf of the village (Loeb, 1934: 31–32). Either he or the subordinate heads of households probably also commanded the work of lineage men in laying fences, building houses, and ploughing on their own estate, and perhaps also in communal hunting and trade. We know that Minangkabau men were "great traders" (De Jong, 1951: 9; Cabaton, 1911: 269), but it is not clear how much if any of their trade was traditionally individual. Since pepper was the main export of Minangkabau, grown largely on lineage-owned land, and since the segment head kept accounts of the contracts and trade of his property-owning unit, it seems probable that most trade was done coöperatively by the lineage segment. Above the level of the lineage, foreign trade appears to have been administered by chiefs and, when he could assert his power, by the king (Marsden, 1811: 337; Schrieke, 1955: 55–60). It is also not clear whether men were summoned to war under the leadership of lineage elders, but this seems probable.

Distribution The segment head was obviously an important agent of redistribution within and outside his group. He kept accounts of the income and expenditures from his segment's estate and from the private property of its members (Loeb, 1934: 31). He had to consent to contracts involving the private property of members, and directed the inheritance of movables within his group. At the marriage of a girl he made a marriage payment to her bridegroom on behalf of her group. If the segment was large he surrendered to the subordinate heads of households the daily management of food supplies which their own segments had produced. He was, however, clearly responsible for collecting and redistributing their surplus. Since the king levied tribute from villages, it seems likely that segment heads were ultimately responsible for supplying it from their estates. They also paid taxes for public works within the village, levied jointly by its council of maximal lineage heads.

Legal Constitution of the Descent Group   Although the maximal lineage—and in Koto-Piliang villages, the larger village section (nan)— had heads engaged in a council as village administrators, the landholding lineage segment (parui) was the chief unit of collective responsibility. This contrasts with Ashanti, where the maximal lineage retained primary collective responsibility for its members' acts. The head of the segment settled disputes between its members (*ibid.:* 35). Supported by the authority of the village council of lineage heads, he could temporarily withhold maintenance from insubordinate junior men. He was also required by the council to expel incorrigible male offenders, thus repudiating his group's responsibility for them (*ibid.:* 36). Such rejects, like illegitimate children, became slaves of the king as in Kerala (De Jong, 1951: 108). Unfortunately we do not know for what offenses they were expelled. In general the segment head was responsible for his juniors' actions to the inferior council of segment heads of the village and to the superior council of heads of maximal lineages or larger village sections. His authority over his juniors' personal lives was extensive, although perhaps less than that of Ashanti lineage heads. He arranged the first marriages of members and was responsible for marriage payments. His consent does not seem to have been needed for divorce or remarriage. Male members had to get his permission to travel outside the village—again a suggestion that trade was very probably lineage-based. It is not known what procedure was followed in case of grave intra-segment offense such as murder or incest; presumably the offenders were expelled and became the property of the king.

The recognition of crime against the state, if it existed, was less developed than in Ashanti. There may have been some capital crimes before the kingdom disintegrated in the 1820's. Marston reports for example that the king had secret police to seek out and assassinate treasonable subjects (1811: 350). Murder was ordinarily, however, a private delict between descent groups. The lineage segment of the deceased took the case to the village council (Loeb, 1934: 36), whence it might proceed through higher authorities to the king himself (De Jong, 1951: 75). Koto-Piliang villages (the most centralized) favored the death penalty for those found guilty of murder. Bodi-Tjaniago villages favored payment of compensation by the murderer's lineage segment to that of the deceased (*ibid.:* 74). This difference suggests the possibility that in Koto-Piliang villages, often ruled directly by royalty or administrative officers of the kingdom, murder was in process of being reckoned a capital crime rather than a private delict. Immediately after a murder the deceased's segment might essay vengeance, but this was normally curtailed in favor of court proceedings. The descent group did, however, retain a limited right of self-help. Thieves or adulterers, if caught in the act, might be killed by lineage mates of the offended person without the possibility of retaliation by their kin. Private delicts concerning property were tried by the highest village council, with possible appeal to the district chief. The offender's descent group was held responsible for fines (Loeb, 1934: 35–36).

KERALA

The constitutions of Nayar commoner descent groups in North and Central Kerala were very similar, with minor differences attributable to the greater political centralization of the Central Kerala kingdoms. I discuss the two groups together with the Mappillas and Tiyyars of North Kerala.

Resources, Production, and Distribution   Unlike those of Ashanti and Minangkabau, maximal lineages in Kerala were not localized in separate wards of the village. Each lineage normally had segments scattered about that ward of the village which was occupied by its caste community. Correspondingly, the small, residentially unitary segment of three to five generations' depth was the unit of landholding, the maximal lineage having no overright other than that of residual inheritance. The property-holding segment among commoners was on the average probably smaller and of shallower generation depth than in Minangkabau, and, especially in Central Kerala, its co-resident members usually occupied a single house. Its component branches could split and divide their property after the deaths of their common ancestress and of her sons, whereas the Minangkabau property group could not divide until five generations had elapsed between the founding ancestress and the oldest living members.

In line with the less centralized political structure of North Kerala, Nayar and aristocratic Mappilla descent groups of this area owned their land subject only to the overright of political authorities. Their heads had large powers of allocation to junior members and to tenants of lower (normally Tiyyar) caste. A property-group head probably could not, however, dispossess his lower-caste tenants except for grave offenses, and had rights only to a stipulated share of their produce. His powers of allocation and usufruct were thus limited by laws of the kingdom.

The role of the North Kerala Nayar head of a property group combined most of the powers held by both household head and property-owning segment head in Minangkabau. He commanded the agricultural labor of his male juniors, as well as services rendered on the unleased fields of the estate by the group's Tiyyar tenants. He might allocate separate gardens and rice fields to junior kinsmen or, especially if the group was small, keep them as a joint work team on the descent group's unleased domain. He was responsible for the military training of boys of his group. In war he might be required to lead juniors to battle on behalf of village headman or district chief.

Normally, the property-group head controlled in person the whole income and expenditure of his group, with its joint avunculocal household. He doled out food from his granary to the communal kitchen and supplied male members with their clothing and personal luxuries. He sent grain, clothing, and other supplies to the married women and their children in other households. He financed life-crisis rites and conducted the descent group's trade. He paid tribute of first fruits to the village headman, and dues to the village council of segment heads for the upkeep of the temple. He acted as redistributive agent outside his descent group in relation to his tenants and to village servants, supplying them with cloth, building materials, and food at ancestral and life-crisis feasts. Within his own small descent group and in relation to low-caste retainers, therefore, the North Kerala Nayar property-group head exercised quite as extensive controls over production and redistribution as did the head of a Minangkabau property group or of an Ashanti lineage. The difference lay in that, in Minangkabau and Ashanti, heads of maximal lineages, jointly or in severalty, exercised important powers over production and redistribution in their village community as a whole. In North Kerala there were no heads of maximal lineages, and the village council of heads of Nayar property groups played only a secondary role in regulating production and distribution in the village at large. These functions of over-all management accrued mainly to the village headman in his role of territorial official in the kingdom.

The aristocratic North Kerala Mappilla head of a property group appears to have had similar rights over resources but less direct control of the labor of junior kinsmen than did the North Kerala Nayar head. Aristocratic Mappillas did little or no agricultural work, which was done by Tiyyar or lower-caste Mappilla tenants. The head of the aristocratic Mappilla descent group might take junior kinsmen with him or send them on trading expeditions, sometimes overseas, and might allocate parts of the estate for their subordinate management. When home from trading, however, junior men lived normally in their wives' houses and appeared at intervals to receive their head's commands rather than working under his daily supervision. The aristocratic Mappilla head seems, however, to have had virtually the same responsibilities of redistribution of goods as did the North Kerala Nayar head within his descent group and in relation to retainers of lower caste.

The low-caste Mappilla head of a descent group probably controlled only the leased garden on which his house was built. He might return to it only for life-crisis rites, and usually lived regularly in his wife's natal home. He probably had little or no control of the labor of his male juniors in the descent group, for like them he worked usually as a carrier for wealthier Mappilla merchants, in groups which may not even have been recruited on the basis of lineage membership. He was, however, responsible for directing life-crisis rites and inheritance, and as one of a council of Mappilla heads he contributed to the village mosque.

The head of a matrilineal property group among North Kerala Tiyyar tenants also appears traditionally to have had only limited control of resources. Members of the group might jointly hold plots of garden and rice land from their Nayar landlord for their own cultivation, but they had limited choice of crops and retained only a small proportion of the produce. A Tiyyar head could direct the work of his nephews in the segment's leased fields, but he and they also owed services on the Nayar landlord's private domain, under his supervision. The Tiyyar descent group's stability on its leased plots seems also to have been relatively weak, and it is possible that even traditionally a proportion of young men remained in the father's house after marriage and worked in partnership with him. Such a situation might be especially likely if both father and mother's brother served the same Nayar landlord. When his household did comprise an avunculocal extended family, a Tiyyar head had the right of distributing their daily maintenance to members. He also controlled produce brought back to the group by its absent married women, directed individual inheritance, financed life-crisis rites, and paid the small bridewealth owed by male members at marriage. He was responsible for surrendering produce to the Nayar landlord and for small dues to the households of the village servant castes. Along with other Tiyyar heads of the village he contributed to the upkeep of the caste's community shrine.

In Central Kerala the Nayar commoner head's rights over resources were more narrowly curtailed than those of the North Kerala Nayar head. He was obliged to lease a larger proportion of his estate to hereditary cultivating tenants. As hereditary landholder rather than landowner, he owed heavy dues in produce and cash to his own village landlord. He retained, however, the direct management of several gardens and rice fields. These were cultivated by Tiyyar tenants who were also his personal servants, and by agricultural serfs.

A Nayar commoner head in Central Kerala apparently had little control over the labor of his male juniors; they did only minor agricultural work under his direction. Boys were trained for war in village gymnasia under village military leaders, and as they grew older many were absent in battle each year. It seems probable that village rather than lineage membership determined young men's military roles. The controls exercised over production by the head of a Nayar commoner descent group in Central Kerala therefore related more to his role as a minor political officer charged with the direction of hereditary low-caste retainers, than to his headship of a matrilineal descent group.

The redistributive functions of the descent-group head were very similar to those in North Kerala. When they returned home junior men seem to have relied entirely on maintenance by their head from descent-group property. In national wars, however, they received personal cash wages from the royal treasury and so participated in the wider redistributive processes of the kingdom.

THE LEGAL CONSTITUTION OF DESCENT GROUPS

The head's rights over persons. The head of a property group among North Kerala Nayars and aristocratic Mappillas held fairly extensive rights over the personal lives of juniors, comparable to those exercised in Minangkabau. Among Central Kerala Nayars the head's authority over males was rather less extensive because of their incorporation in a more centralized state. Among North Kerala Tiyyars the head's rights over both sexes were much less extensive because Tiyyars, as a low caste, came under stronger controls on the part of authorities of higher caste. Too little is known of the legal constitution of low-caste Mappilla descent groups for a comparison to be made.

Among North Kerala Nayars and aristocratic Mappillas, the property-group head arranged all first marriages and gave consent to later ones; he could enforce cross-cousin marriage. Among Central Kerala Nayars the head was instrumental in choosing the ritual bridegroom of a girl. His choice had to be approved, however, by his village caste assembly and the village headman also had to give formal consent to the rite. A head seems to have had very little right over a woman's subsequent choice of husbands, although he might command her to dismiss one against whom he had had special complaints. He probably could not refuse access to a husband of higher caste or to one whose claim was supported by his overlord. North Kerala Tiyyar heads commonly arranged first marriages, but they sought the consent of their Nayar masters. Later marriages tended to be arranged by the couple with their masters' consent.

Heads of descent groups in all the castes settled small disputes between members, especially between women. In both areas grave disputes between adult men of the descent group, especially if they were likely to lead to fission of the group, were taken in arbitration by some popular man of another lineage, in return for a small fee. As a last resort the disputes might be carried to the village headman or to higher authorities. North Kerala Tiyyars referred far more disputes within the descent group upward to Nayar arbitrators or to the village headman than to arbitrators of their own caste. Among Tiyyars even women, especially widows, might refer a dispute in this way, for as servants of the landlord they had a direct relationship with him and were less subordinate to their descent-group head than were women of the higher castes, who remained always legal minors and could not take a dispute to an arbitrator or to court.

In all the groups a descent-group head might in theory inflict corporal punishment on juniors who disobeyed his commands. Central Kerala Nayar heads exercised strongest discipline over women and children, because men were much more under the control of higher authorities. North Kerala Nayar heads exercised stronger discipline over men, because women and children were often absent in the husband's home. Mappilla heads exercised weaker controls over both sexes: men were often absent, and women came partly under the domestic authority of their husbands. A Tiyyar head might more readily inflict punishment on both men and women of his descent group, and also on his wife, but all had recourse to Nayar authorities if his discipline became too irksome. In all the groups, a head had the right to deny maintenance for a time to disobedient juniors. This was least effective among Tiyyars, because adults of both sexes received some individual remuneration in return for services to landlords.

Descent-group heads in Kerala could not sell or pawn juniors to meet debts owed by the descent group. Landed descent groups might sell or pledge gold valuables; Tiyyars, small jewelry; and Central Kerala Nayars, serfs.

In Kerala sorcery was not believed to be effective within the matrilineal descent group. Nayars believed that witches and sorcerers were chiefly low-caste persons who used their powers against high-caste superiors who they believed to have wronged them. Within the Nayar caste, juniors of a descent group were believed occasionally to engage sorcerers to harm the wife and children of their head if they believed that he was unduly favoring his wife and children with gifts. Within the descent group the cult of matrilineal forebears provided juniors with protection against immoral exploitation by their head, for it was believed that ancestral spirits would bring misfortune on a kāranavan who wronged his juniors (Gough, 1959). These institutions in general tend to support the hypothesis that witchcraft and sorcery are likely to operate in relationships where open aggression is not feasible but where disputes cannot be justly settled by recourse to formal authorities.

Private delicts within the community. Private disputes concerning property between persons of different descent groups might be taken to a popular arbitrator. Tiyyars were most likely to take such disputes to Nayar arbitrators. Small disputes not susceptible of arbitration went to the village headman; graver disputes, involving heavy fines, to the chief. The descent group among Nayars, at least, was collectively responsible for fines.

In disputes within the caste community concerning slander or assault, especially of women, hostilities commonly spread to involve maximal lineages and might lead to fights. Such "feuds" were more rapidly curtailed by political authorities in Central than in North Kerala and a formal duel substituted.

Among North Kerala Nayars the descent group reserved a limited right of self-help in case of adultery within the caste. The cuckold's lineage kin might kill an adulterer caught in the act and shave off the hair of the wife before divorcing her. Tiyyars had no right of self-help in case of adultery, but took the case to caste elders or to Nayar masters, who exacted compensation on behalf of the offended party. Adultery within the caste was not recognized among Central Kerala Nayars.

Crime. Crimes against the local caste community, which were also sins against its deity, included incest, murder within or between descent groups, sex relations or interdining with persons of proscribed castes, and many other less grave breaches of caste rules of ritual pollution. In case of a minor offense the caste assembly of descent-group heads ostracized the criminal's descent group until it had paid a fine to the deity's shrine. In case of grave offense, the descent group was ostracized until it had expelled the criminal. The ultimate fate of a male criminal was probably usually decided by the chief or the king: he might be executed or taken as a slave. The fate of Nayar and Muslim women criminals, who were legal minors under the guardianship of male kin, seems to have been left to their descent groups. Her male matrilineal elders might allow a woman who was expelled to become a slave of chief or king, or might themselves put her to death. The fate of Tiyyar criminals is not definitely known: both men and women were probably at the mercy of the chief.

Many offenses, such as slander or assault, which were private delicts within the caste, were crimes if committed against a person of higher caste. So also were sex relations with a woman of higher caste. Conversely, whereas murder was a capital offense within the caste, it was a lesser crime if committed against one of lower caste. The offender's descent group paid a fine to the chief and compensation to the deceased's descent group. Tiyyars were thus subject to a different body of law than aristocratic Mappillas and Nayars, one which emphasized their low-caste rank.

Finally, in Central Kerala at least, a class of crimes seems to have emerged for which the individual alone was responsible. In the city of Calicut, for example, thieves and incorrigible debtors were tried and sentenced to death by a special officer of the king (Ayyar, 1938: 283–288). Their descent groups and local communities do not seem to have been consulted, although their caste rank determined the mode of execution. It seems probable that such forms of individual responsibility for crime were likely to arise in urban centers, to which individual soldiers and traders might travel beyond the sphere of guardianship of their descent groups and natal communities. Within the city, treason seems to have been the only capital crime for which the descent group was held responsible. All members of a Nayar traitor's descent group were liable for execution and their property escheated to the king.

Conclusions

I suggest the following hypotheses concerning relationships between level of productivity and degree of political centralization on the one hand, and descent-group functions and authority structures on the other, in matrilineal societies with settled cultivation.

(1) With the exception of the most highly productive matrilineal states known (Central and North Kerala), the higher the productivity of the society, the more extensive are the controls exercised by descent-group heads over the resources, distribution of goods, and the labor and personal lives of members. In larger chiefdoms and small states, however, the descent-group head comes to exercise his authority by delegation from higher territorial authorities, to whom he is responsible. His controls over members, although extensive, are therefore merely the bottom link in a chain of command not based, or only incidentally based, on kinship. In the largest states (Central and North Kerala) having hereditary occupational castes, the descent-group head loses some of his controls, especially over the labor of members, as they become involved in state or community organizations not based on kinship. In these states, the lower the caste, the greater the area of controls assumed by higher economic and governmental authorities of the state; consequently such controls are lost to the descent-group head.

(2) In settled cultivating societies of lowest productivity and political centralization, there is little division of labor within the descent group except on the basis of sex. In chiefdoms and small states of higher productivity from subsistence cultivation, there is greater division of functions between members of the descent group, requiring stronger coördination by its head. In the most productive states (Kerala), where the commoner population is no longer wholly devoted to subsistence cultivation and where the population is divided into stratified occupational groups, the members of each descent group within one stratum, with the exception of the head, tend to fulfill very similar functions within the occupational and political structure of the community or of the state.

(3) In matrilineal societies of lowest productivity and very weak political centralization, the descent group's collective responsibility seems likely to include some degree of recourse to self-help in cases of grave offense between members of different descent groups. The ex-

tent of this right may vary inversely with the extent of productive coöperation within the society at large. Thus the right of self-help is evidently very weakly developed in a society such as the Hopi, who have a nucleated multi-lineage village community, much community-wide productive coöperation and a council of selected descent-group heads. The descent group's right of self-help is much more pronounced, extending to blood feuds, among the Trukese, where the descent group had comparatively greater productive autonomy and the community was less nucleated and had no council of descent-group heads. In larger chiefdoms of higher productivity (e.g., Trobriand), the descent group's right of self-help is gradually curtailed by the growing power of the chief, and in true states with centralized control of force (e.g., Ashanti) the right of self-help is absent in most or all circumstances. The descent group instead becomes a unit of collective legal responsibility vis-à-vis higher judicial authorities of the state. In the largest states of greatest political centralization (e.g., Kerala), the descent group may lose its collective responsibility for some of the acts of its members—at least of its male members—who in some contexts become individually responsible to the state's judicial authorities. This loss of collective responsibility of the descent group may apply particularly to disputes and offenses of its members in urban centers remote from their natal communities.

(4) In settled cultivating societies of lowest productivity, the descent-group head is likely to be required by custom to consult other adult males of the group, at least of his generation, about major decisions. The higher the productivity, the more likely it is that formal legal authority will be vested in one male head of the group or in a hierarchy of heads having clearly defined powers and responsibilities. This condition is especially likely to occur in states, where the descent-group head is responsible to higher territorial authorities as well as to his group.

Similarly, in societies of lowest productivity (e.g., Hopi and Truk), women, particularly the oldest woman, of the descent group seem likely to participate in the male head's authority, especially in matters pertaining to women. As productivity and political centralization increase, women appear to become more definitely subordinate to their male heads. With the emergence of the state proper they may become legal minors in perpetuity, who can be represented in law only by their male guardians. Senior women of descent groups may retain a formal role in the selection or installation of male heads, but they, too, what-

ever the character of their moral authority, appear to remain legal
minors under the guardianship of male authorities. This situation is
somewhat modified in the case of women in the lower strata of complex states, for example, North Kerala Tiyyars. The economic servitude
of both men and women in this caste makes both directly responsible
in law to male authorities of higher political strata in many contexts,
rather than placing women unequivocally under the male heads of their
own descent groups.

(5) In societies of low productivity and political centralization, incest and murder within the descent group are likely to be considered
sins and/or crimes against the descent group; in states, against the
local community or the state.

(6) The data are insufficient for a precise theory of the incidence
and range of witchcraft or sorcery accusations in matrilineal, settled
cultivating societies. It is clear that these must be explained in terms
of the total framework of economic and authoritative relationships,
and in relation to other modes of aggression and other types of sanctions, whether supernatural or secular. Such data as I have seem to
support the hypothesis that when witchcraft or sorcery accusations are
present in a society, they will occur in relationships where open aggression is not feasible but where satisfactory redress of real or seeming
injuries cannot be obtained through appeal to formal authorities. I may
tentatively suggest that where accusations of witchcraft or sorcery are
widespread at all status levels both within and between descent groups,
as among the Hopi, the society is likely to be one of low productivity
in which the authority structures of both the descent group and the
larger territorial unit are extremely weak. In chiefdoms of higher
productivity but which lack centralized control of force, the more
powerful forms of sorcery or other supernatural power may be monopolized by heads of descent groups and territorial units for use in
the protection of their groups against other groups of like order,
and also, perhaps, against recalcitrant subordinates within their own
groups. This seems to be the case in the Trobriands and among the
Mayombe. A similar situation may have been incipient on Truk, where
elders appear to have had most knowledge of magic and sorcery and
to have gradually taught it to juniors within their descent groups. In
centralized states, by contrast, I would not expect heads of descent
groups or higher territorial units to be the targets of sorcery accusations on the part of their subordinates, for such heads hold judicial
authority sanctioned by force. Accusations of sorcery are more likely
to be leveled against subordinates in the social structure who lack ade-

quate rights of appeal to judicial authorities. Sorcery and witchcraft in such societies are also likely to be viewed as serious crimes against the state. Depending on circumstances which cannot be specified, they may be believed inoperative within the lineage, or, if operative, their use may be ascribed mainly to junior male members or to women.

Descent-Group Variation among Mobile Cultivators

Levels of Productivity among Mobile Cultivators

The five societies of mobile cultivators proved more difficult to rank in terms of productivity than did the settled cultivators. This is no doubt because there was less discrepancy in their levels of productivity, four of them being drawn from Central Africa and having similar technologies. Nevertheless, I have made some attempt to rank them, using the criteria previously employed. But first I will recapitulate the salient characteristics of environment, technology, and specialization of the five societies.

NAVAHO

Environment and Technology   The Navaho country is one of desert and steppe. Cultivation was precarious because of variable rainfall and frost; maize, beans, squash, and potatoes were grown. There was minor hunting and gathering, and sheepherding from the mid-eighteenth century. Navaho life was transhumant, with some families moving annually between a relatively steady farm site and grazing grounds, and others using pasturage and marginal agricultural land for shorter periods. Before 1868 there was some exchange of meat and hides with the Hopi for corn, and some raiding of Pueblos. Since 1868 there has been gradual partial absorption in wage work and the market system, including the sale of meat, wool, and hides, and the purchase of food from traders.

Specialization and Exemption from Food Production   There were traditionally no full-time specialists, but only part-time male silversmiths and female weavers. Heads of matrilineal groups and neighborhoods were not exempt from food production (chap. 2, above).

TONGA

Environment and Technology   The Tonga inhabit a bushy plateau with some flood plain. Rainfall tends to be localized and sporadic, so that cultivation is highly precarious through unpredictable drought. The Tonga have slash-and-burn, hoe cultivation of millet, sorghum, maize (modern), groundnuts, and beans; there are no orchard or root crops. There is minor hunting and fishing. Cattle are herded, and were raided by neighboring tribes in the nineteenth century. Villages traditionally moved every four or five years. In modern times there has been partial absorption in wage work and cash-crop farming.

Specialization There were no full-time specialists, but only part-time specialists in pottery, baskets, wood and stone tools, and metal tools, such specialists also carrying on regular food production. Village heads were not exempt from food production, in spite of the existence of slaves (Colson, 1951: 103–110; chap. 1, above).

NDEMBU

Environment and Technology The Ndembu territory comprises woodland and grassy plain, having higher rainfall and more rivers than the Tonga country. There is shifting hoe cultivation of cassava, millet, maize, and a variety of garden crops; more fertile streamside gardens are also used for millet and maize; there are no orchard crops. Male hunting was traditionally of great importance. The Ndembu have no cattle, but keep some chickens and goats. Villages have traditionally moved every four to five years, perhaps because of hunting rather than agricultural requirements.

Specialization There were probably no full-time specialists. Village heads were not exempt from production, in spite of the existence of slaves (Turner, 1957: 18–33).

YAO

Environment and Technology The Yao of Southern Nyasaland, whom Mitchell studied, lived in an area comprising forested highlands, plain, and swamp. Soil and rainfall were variable, but there were areas of high fertility from plentiful highland streams or from alluvial deposits in the plains. There was shifting hoe cultivation of millet, sorghum, maize, cassava, groundnuts, sweet potatoes, pumpkins, sugar cane, mangoes, pawpaws, bananas, and some rice. The cultivation potential of the soil permitted a thirty-year stay of villages on the same sites, in contrast to the Tonga, Ndembu, and Bemba. Minor hunting and fishing were carried on.

Specialization Traditional specialists were blacksmiths, carpenters, and leeches, perhaps partly freed from food production. Men were partly engaged in raiding and in trading ivory, slaves, beeswax, and tobacco with Arabs on the east coast for guns, gunpowder, cloth, and beads, probably largely in the dry season. Men were perhaps partly supported by the food production of women. Chiefs and higher village headmen were perhaps largely exempt from food production through extensive use of slaves (Mitchell, 1951: 292–304; 1956: 1–21).

BEMBA

Environment and Technology The Bemba inhabit an open, high plateau, with relatively poor soil but ample rainfall. Because of the tsetse fly, there are no cattle other than those obtained by raiding neighboring tribes. There was shifting hoe cultivation of millet, sorghum, maize, pumpkins, beans, peas, and groundnuts; cultivation methods involved rotation of crops. Villages normally moved every four to five years. Hunting and fishing were traditionally fairly important, and done partly by local specialists. In addition to indigenous food production, the majority of men under chiefs performed extensive raiding for cattle and other foods from neighboring and subject peoples. After conquest, regular tribute was exacted from some of these areas. Men are said to have lived "largely" from raiding and tribute (Richards, 1951: 167).

Specialization There were no full-time craftsmen. The royal clan, tribal councilors, perhaps the councilors of the separate chiefdoms, numbers of messengers and courtiers, and the more regular soldiery were probably largely exempt from food production. These men were apparently fed from the proceeds of raiding, foreign tribute, slave labor, and tribute labor supplied by commoners. The Bemba had the largest group of non-food-producers of the five societies (Richards, 1940: 94–95; 1950: 222; 1951: 166–167; 1956: 25–28).

The Plateau Tonga are here tentatively ranked as the least productive of these societies by virtue of their extremely precarious water supply and comparatively narrow range of crops. The Navaho perhaps rival the Tonga for low productivity. The general situation of the Navaho before 1860 was probably better than that of the Tonga, however, since they were in a position to raid the Pueblos. Tonga, by contrast, suffered severe raids from neighboring peoples in the nineteenth century. The Ndembu should probably be ranked slightly above the Navaho and the Tonga by virtue of their more generous water supply and ability to rely on grains and hunting as well as on cassava, the most productive of the root crops. The Yao seem undoubtedly to rank considerably above these three tribes because of their wide range of crops (orchard and root crops as well as grains, including some rice), and high fertility of some areas, and the apparent partial exemption of large numbers of men, as traders, from cultivation.

The Bemba proved the most difficult to classify. Richards has tended to emphasize the poor quality of their natural resources and cultivation techniques, and she seems inclined to rank them below the Yao in general productivity (Richards, 1950: 231). They had ample rainfall and evenly distributed resources, however, which would place them well above the Plateau Tonga in terms of environmental opportunities. They were also apparently able to support numerous aristocrats and administrators, at least partly from tribute labor performed by commoners in addition to their own cultivation. There seems no doubt, however, that the Bemba food supply was enormously augmented by raiding and tribute from neighboring tribes. Their food productivity from their own cultivation was perhaps lower than that of the Yao, but their total food *supply* from all sources, relative to the energy expended in actual food production, was probably considerably greater.

Productivity and Political Centralization among Mobile Cultivators

Below are listed salient characteristics of the political systems of the five societies.

NAVAHO

Size of Maximal Political Unit   The political unit was a loosely organized neighborhood of fluid membership, often referred to as a "band" in the literature, under a popular head. The size of this unit is very uncertain; it may have been as small as 60 to 200 (Hill, 1940), with temporary combinations of two or more units for raiding.

Number of Levels of Territorial Authority   One: A neighborhood leader was chosen by popular consent. There were no hereditary territorial heads.

CONTROLS EXERCISED BY THE NEIGHBORHOOD LEADER

Over resources. Usually none. The leader may possibly have had some right of allocating irrigated lands in a few areas.

Over production. The neighborhood leader set the time for planting and supervised "any communal work" (Hill, *loc. cit.*). He had no coercive authority.

Over distribution of goods. Probably none.

Over people. The leader mediated in individual quarrels and arbitrated inter-group disputes over damages. A separate, popular war leader led men in raiding Mexican and Pueblo settlements (chap. 2, above).

TONGA

Size of Maximal Political Unit   The Tonga political unit was a neighborhood of 400 to 600; it was a peace group, with either an ephemeral popular leader or no leader.

Number of Levels of Territorial Authority   One or two, both very weak: the head of the traditional hamlet of perhaps 5 to 20 people; in some cases, an ephemeral leader of the neighborhood, selected and not hereditary.

CONTROLS EXERCISED BY TERRITORIAL AUTHORITIES

Over resources. None.

Over distribution of goods. The hamlet head collected and distributed beer and food for the harvest-festival and first-fruits ceremonies. He contributed beer on behalf of the hamlet to the feast of the neighborhood's rain ceremony. He may have managed a common cattle kraal. The neighborhood head may have had some power to organize feasts of rain shrines.

Over people. The neighborhood head had no rights over people. The hamlet head performed ritual acts before sowing and harvest, and thus may have somewhat coördinated these activities (Colson, 1951: 110–121, 151–161; chap. 1, above).

NDEMBU

Size of Maximal Political Unit   The largest effective political unit was the sub-chiefship under a "senior headman," apparently a group of about 300 to 900 people. This was the largest unit within which law cases could be settled, although the Ndembu as a whole had a ritual chiefship. The sub-chiefship was divided into villages, each of some 16 to 30 people.

Number of Levels of Territorial Authority   There were two levels of formally recognized, hereditary territorial heads: the senior headman of the sub-chiefship; the village headman. Above the senior headman was the hereditary ritual chief of all Ndembu (Kanongesha). Intermediate between village headman and senior headman, but not acting formally as the senior headman's representative, was the informally selected head of a vicinage or group of some to five to ten villages.

CONTROLS EXERCISED BY TERRITORIAL AUTHORITIES

Over resources. The vicinage head gave permission to incoming villages to build and garden. The senior headman of the sub-chiefship apparently had no rights to allocate resources.

Over distribution of goods. (1) The ritual chief, Kanongesha, occasionally collected tribute from senior headmen for surrender to the chief of the Mwantiyanvwa empire, of which the Ndembu tribe was an offshoot. (2) The senior headman collected tribute and game from village headmen. He traded slaves, which were sometimes raided from his own sub-chiefship, with Ovimbundu traders for guns and cloth. He held feasts at rain and fertility ceremonies. (3) The village headman had rights to first fruits, to the first beer brewed, and to the first share of beer and food at feasts. He distributed meat after the large annual game drive. He was expected to have more food than other men, and to be generous to villagers and guests.

Over people. (1) The senior headman drew tributary wives from certain of his village headmen, whose succession he confirmed. He had no organized control of force but wielded power through access to guns from traders; his poison oracle was the final court of appeal in sorcery cases. He controlled special medicine to protect his own village and special sorcery to punish recalcitrant subordinates. (2) The head of the vicinage settled most disputes at the vicinage level through arbitration, although villages resorted to temporary self-help in cases of homicide. The vicinage head sponsored the boys' circumcision ritual of the vicinage. (3) The village headman arbitrated village disputes, but had no sanction of force; with the villagers' consent he might expel sorcerers or incestuous persons. He organized the annual hunt. He normally had more wives to work his gardens than had other villagers (Turner, 1957: 2–18, 34–44, 129, 318–327).

YAO

Size of Maximal Political Unit The maximal political unit was a loosely organized chiefdom of some 5,000 to 20,000 people.

Number of Levels of Territorial Authority Two: The chief of the chiefdom; the head of a village of some 25 to 100 people. Chiefly villages might contain up to about 300 people.

CONTROLS EXERCISED BY TERRITORIAL HEADS

Over resources. (1) The chief allocated land to his followers to build new villages. The heads of these villages in turn might allocate parts of their shares to subordinate branch villagers. (2) The village headman might allocate scarce streamside gardens within his village area.

Over distribution of goods. (1) The chief monopolized the trade of ivory, skins, and slaves with Arab and Swahili traders in return for cloth, beads, and guns. He distributed the latter to his subordinate village headmen. He organized raids in neighboring areas and distributed the booty, and had rights to meat from hunting. He had more slaves, wives, cloth, and guns than other village headmen and thus commanded more labor and military followers. (2) The village headman had rights to first fruits and to the first beer brewed. He collected food to entertain the chief and visiting village headmen. He had more slaves and wives than other villagers. Higher village headmen had distinctive robes, knives, and other insignia.

Over people. (1) The chief commanded men of the chiefdom in war and raiding. He confirmed the succession of his village headmen and had to be informed if they conducted private "wars" against each other or against outsiders. He controlled the work of slaves in his own village in farming, sewing, and basketry. He settled disputes and charged fines, usually in slaves, from subordinate village headmen when he was powerful enough to coerce them. A powerful chief might kill, enslave, or burn the property of a rebellious village headman who made war or traded without his consent. His judicial powers and control of organized force were much stronger than those of the Ndembu senior headman, but were incomplete and unstable: he did not, for example, interfere in inter-village blood feuds following homicide. (2) The village headman settled disputes within his village. He could fine, enslave, or execute offenders with chiefly support. He led the village in vengeance against other villages after homicide and led men in trading or raiding parties under a higher village headman or under the chief. He controlled the work of slaves in farming and other tasks, and could organize his commoner subjects to dig wells or fish ponds (Mitchell, 1951: 338–350; 1956: 17–20, 31–37, 46–130).

BEMBA

Size of Maximal Political Unit   The Bemba kingdom numbered about 100,000, and had varying controls over outlying tribes which were held for tribute.

Number of Levels of Territorial Authority   Three to four: the king or paramount chief; the chief of a district, himself a member of the royal clan; in some areas, a sub-chief controlling "several" villages; the head of a village of some 100 to 300 people. Chiefly and royal villages might contain 1,000 to 2,000 people.

CONTROLS EXERCISED BY TERRITORIAL HEADS

Over resources. (1) The chief of the district or chiefdom gave permission for the foundation of new villages in his district; cultivation of land was not permitted except within a village recognized by the chief. The chief allocated land for cultivation within his capital village. (2) Village headmen perhaps had no control of resources. They did not allocate land.

Over distribution of goods. (1) The king and the chiefs drew grain, ivory, salt, and ironwork from neighboring subject tribes, which they raided for slaves and cattle and other food, distributed in the chiefdoms. They filled large granaries from royal gardens worked by slaves and by tribute labor from villages, and they exacted some tribute of grain and beer from villages. They monopolized the sale of ivory and slaves to Arab traders in return for guns, cloth, and salt. They kept special elephant hunters, and were responsible for feeding the administrative, religious, military and advisory officials, messengers and courtiers, the soldiers in wartime, and the commoners in famine. (2) The village headman commanded tribute on behalf of the chief. He commanded beer, meat, and grain from villagers, which he redistributed at village feasts and used to entertain guests.

Over people. (1) The king and chiefs in their several districts commanded tribute labor in their own gardens, organized big hunting and fishing drives, and commanded men for raiding and warfare. There was fully organized control of force, men being mustered by their village headmen on behalf of the chief and by chiefs on behalf of the king. Lawsuits went on appeal from the courts of village headmen to those of the chief and of the king. Each chief had the power of enslavement, mutilation, or execution for such offenses against himself or his lineage as wife stealing, laughter, or rebellion. Only the king and a few higher chiefs could conduct the poison ordeal or hear witchcraft cases. The king had the final word over succession to the larger chiefships. The chief confirmed village headmen and could enforce a successor against the people's choice or introduce a stranger headman from outside the village. (2) The village headman organized hunting and fishing parties of the village and initiated agricultural processes. He commanded tribute labor on behalf of the chief and one extra day's work in his own fields for tree cutting and sowing. He settled land disputes, supervised divinations at deaths, disciplined children and young people, and represented his villagers in the higher courts (Richards, 1940*b*: 83–112).

In general these data support the expectation that level of food productivity will be closely associated with degree of political centralization. The Tonga, with probably the lowest productivity, had probably the smallest maximal political unit. Both the Navaho and the Tonga had only popular, nonhereditary leaders of their small neighborhoods, having none but advisory powers. They did not therefore have rank at all in the sense in which this has been defined (see note 8, chap. 11). Within the neighborhood the Tonga hamlet head appears often to have managed a group no larger the Navaho extended family. The Tonga hamlet also had a very short life cycle and its head's powers in all areas were extremely weak. The Ndembu political unit by contrast had at least two levels of hereditary territorial heads. Their authority was weak, but it was stronger than that of the hamlet head and the neighborhood leader among the Tonga. With the Yao we have much larger chiefdoms, with chiefs and village headmen exercising significant controls over resources, goods, and people, and with some approach to political centralization of the chiefdom with regard to organized force and to judicial process. The Bemba present a fully fledged state, less centralized than that of the Ashanti, with greater autonomy for the chiefs of districts, but much more centralized and stable than the chiefdom or protostate of the Yao.

If, however, I am correct in assuming that the Yao had a somewhat higher level of food productivity from cultivation than did the Bemba, the expected connection between food productivity and degree of political centralization is reversed in the case of these two societies. The problem is partly solved if it is assumed, as it probably must be, that the Bemba supported a majority of their non-food-producers from the proceeds of raiding and tribute. This does not explain, however, why the Bemba in the nineteenth century should have formed a centralized state at all out of their previously separate chiefdoms, whereas the Yao, who had if anything higher food productivity and who also had access to trade routes, remained divided into unstable chiefdoms. One may perhaps hazard a guess that the Yao had access to a number of trade routes and to a number of different, mutually competitive trading groups. Such groups may have supported different chiefs against each other, and so (as in the case of North Kerala and Minangkabau) have encouraged political fragmentation, while strengthening each chief's control of his own people through the provision of guns. The Bemba, by contrast, may have had more canalized trading opportunities, which fostered a central monopoly of arms and other trade goods and thus permitted the rise of a kingdom.[1]

The Bemba case shows, at all events, that the connection between level of productivity and degree of political centralization is no simple one-way causal relationship. The Bemba case suggests rather that external trade contacts fostered an internal monopoly of trade goods, especially weapons, and that having acquired these goods the newly centralized authority was able to increase its supplies by external conquest and raiding (Richards, 1951: 165). It was also able to exact maximal productivity from the slender resources of its own subject population through tribute labor on chiefly domains. Although, there-

----

[1] Elizabeth Colson tentatively suggested this explanation to me in conversation.

fore, level of indigenous food productivity probably remains a good average predictor of degree of political centralization for large numbers of primitive societies, other factors—external trade, the resources and political structures of neighboring peoples and the society's relationships with them, natural topography and ease of communications, access to strategic weapons, and unique historical traditions—are likely to be relevant to the presence or absence of states in particular instances. The Bemba, alone of the examples, present an interesting case of a state with relatively low productivity from indigenous shifting cultivation. They thus give an opportunity to disentangle the implications of highly productive settled agriculture for descent-group structure from those of political centralization.

Productivity and Political Centralization among Mobile and Settled Cultivators

The attempt which follows, to rank the total range of the thirteen societies for level of productivity and degree of political centralization, is necessarily very tentative. With regard to indigenous food productivity (other than food getting from raiding or trade) I would place Tonga at the bottom of the scale, followed by Navaho, Hopi, and Truk without definite mutual ranking. They would be followed in order of increasing productivity by Ndembu, Trobriand, Bemba, Yao, Mayombe, Ashanti, Minangkabau, North Kerala, and Central Kerala. With regard to degree of political centralization I would place Tonga and Navaho at the bottom of the scale without attempting to judge between them. They would be followed in order by Hopi, Truk, Ndembu, and the Trobriands. Yao and Mayombe (not mutually ranked because of inadequate material for Mayombe) would rank above the Trobriands, followed by the Bemba. Ashanti, Minangkabau, and North Kerala all rank above Bemba and are each regarded to be—in some respects but not others—more centralized than the other two within this trio. Central Kerala is the most centralized of the states.

If these rankings are at all valid, they indicate, as might be expected, that although mobile cultivating societies no doubt *average* a much lower level of productivity and a weaker degree of political centralization than do settled subsistence cultivators, there is considerable overlapping between the two categories.

In the discussion of descent groups among mobile cultivators which follows, I shall try to disentangle from one another the implications of level of productivity, degree of political centralization, and specific types of mobile cultivation ecologies.

Descent Groups among Mobile Cultivators

The following hypotheses are tentatively suggested with regard to descent-group structure and functions among mobile cultivators.

(1) *Size of descent group.* The size of descent groups may, as among settled cultivators, be related to the level of productivity, although available materials are inadequate to establish this. In all five societies—Navaho, Tonga, Ndembu, Yao, and Bemba—the maximal descent group seems seldom or never to have numbered over 100, and usually considerably fewer; in the Tonga, sometimes as few as ten. The only exception is the Bemba royal lineage, which seems to have numbered several hundreds. I do not expect the maximal descent groups of commoners among mobile cultivators ever to be as large as those of more highly productive settled cultivators such as the Ashanti and Minangkabau, provided that the latter lack elaborate occupational stratification of their commoner populations.

(2) *Extent of residential unity of the descent group.* The extent of residential unity of the descent group among mobile cultivators seems to have some indirect connection with level of productivity, but a closer and more direct connection with certain qualitative ecological factors. Of the five societies, the Tonga descent group was the most dispersed; the Navaho, second; the Bemba, third; the Ndembu, fourth; and the Yao, the most unitary in terms of residence.

Among the Tonga the unit of daily productive coöperation was the single married couple or the polygynous homestead, with a number of unmarried dependents. The Tonga reliance on cattle keeping probably accounts for the fact that the husband, as male head of this unit, normally determined the location of his homestead within a hamlet whose headman was a congenial kinsman. The homestead, however, had to be free to move between hamlets over a wide area because of unpredictable local drought. In the nineteenth century, hamlets seem also often to have broken up in reaction to slave raids, with the component homesteads scattered. Given the need for mobility and the wide choice of residence, it is not surprising that descent-group members were widely scattered. Colson's materials suggest, in fact, that not more than 25 per cent of the members of a hamlet or of the larger village tend ever to be matrilineal kin of its headman (Colson, 1951: 112). There was also, indeed, a positive value in keeping matrilineal kin scattered, i.e., in segregating the field of matrilineal relationships from that of ties of close propinquity; by this means individuals were assured of the mandatory hospitality of unilineal kin elsewhere, if drought struck them in a particular locality (chap. 1, above). This may have something to do with the fact that Tonga marriage prohibitions actually prevent closely related women and their respective children from becoming members of the same conjugal residential unit (chap. 1, above). In this case therefore a particular form of low productivity, associated with sporadic, localized drought, appears to keep the descent group highly dispersed.

The Navaho case is somewhat similar. Here the traditional residential unit of regular productive coöperation is a matrilocal grandfamily: an older couple, their daughters, sons-in-law, and daughters' children. The composition of this unit was suitable to an economy in which women did much cultivation and sheepherding together while men, with horses, might roam afield at intervals on raiding expeditions, leaving the women behind. As a unit in relation to the larger community or neighborhood, the matrilocal grandfamily appears to have been relatively mobile, although probably less so than the Tonga homestead. Here again uncertain rainfall and frosts probably made the scattering of the descent group an asset for purposes of hospitality, rather than a weakness. Thus, although close matrilineal kinswomen did live and work together among the Navaho, the descent group as a whole appears to have been dispersed, perhaps through several neighborhoods.

The Bemba unit of regular productive coöperation was also a matrilocal grandfamily, in this case located within a village as the smallest administrative unit of the kingdom. The residential clustering of a woman, her daughters, and daughters' daughters was again, somewhat as among the Navaho, suitable for an economy in which women coöperated in cultivation while men were periodically absent in raiding and warfare. The location of the grandfamily itself in relation to a village seems to have been chiefly determined by its male head (the husband of the oldest woman), who in middle life might move his wife and her daughters away from their natal village to one headed by a kinsman of the husband. Having no share in a matrilineal joint estate, the husband had a fairly wide choice of residence. He might live in the village of his mother's brother if he hoped to be this man's heir, or might choose that of his father or maternal grandfather—or remain with his father-in-law—if one of them was of higher rank than himself (Richards, 1950: 226; 1951: 172; 1956: 40–41). While the political relations of men determined the location of their homesteads, they did not therefore necessarily bring together groups of matrilineally related men; at the same time, the male choice of residence in middle age prevented the localization of large groups of matrilineally related women. Although a descent group might regard a certain village as its point of origin to which its members might return if they wished (Richards, 1951: 174), each descent group tended at a given time to be dispersed between a number of villages. The Bemba case is thus one in which in spite of relatively high productivity (if we include the products of raiding) and a high degree of political centralization, the descent group remains scattered. The absence of a joint estate, the lack of valuable, heritable personal wealth tied to particular sites, the low population density and amplitude of cultivable land (Richards, 1950: 248), and perhaps the lack of a large, regularly coöperating work group which might bring together one sex of the descent group as a whole, appear to have permitted this dispersal of the descent unit.

The Ndembu appear to have had considerably lower productivity than the Bemba, but their matrilineal descent group was more heavily concentrated within a single village. The core of the village consisted of a majority of adult males of the descent group with their wives and young children. Sons of these men might, however, remain in the paternal village until their fathers' deaths (Turner, 1957: 63–65), and residence seems to have been less strictly determined by matrilineal descent than, for example, in the Trobriands. Older women tended to return to the village of their brothers, where their sons might eventually succeed to headship (ibid.: 52). Two factors seem to have influenced this relative concentration of descent-group members.

First, hunting, the dominant male activity, required the coöperation of a group of men larger than could be provided by the elementary family. The choice of hunting sites seems also to have affected the location and rate of movement of the village, whereas cultivation, managed largely by women, could be carried on wherever the village moved (ibid.: 28–33, 46). Given matrilineal descent and succession to village headship, it was thus likely that matrilineally related men would group themselves together as a residential and productive unit.

Second, the village had a high degree of economic self-sufficiency in a well-watered region of relatively uniform resource distribution. Given the ability to shift site when necessary, villagers did not need dispersed ties of descent-group membership as media for hospitality and aid in times of natural disaster, as did the Tonga and the Navaho. The high degree of economic and political self-sufficiency of villages may indeed account for the fact that exogamous dispersed matrilineal clans died out among the Ndembu as they became established in this region, and that marriage came to be permitted between relatively close matrilineal kin of alternate generations within the village (*ibid.*: 80, 85–86, 109). The Ndembu system is thus one in which, in spite of relatively low productivity, the nature of the productive unit, and the comparative self-sufficiency of small local groups, fostered a rather high degree of residential unity of the descent group.

The economy of the Yao village is not well described, so that my hypotheses here must be tentative. The matrilineal lineage seems, however, to be more strictly localized within a village or village section than in any of the other societies of mobile cultivators. Its residentially unitary core is a group of matrilineally related women of a lineage of five to eight generations' depth, their immature children, most of their husbands, the male head of the lineage and his conjugal family, and some at least of the oldest males of the lineage's component sibling groups. The following factors seem to have fostered this high degree of residential unity of the descent group.

First, population density was higher than among the other mobile cultivators and land was relatively scarce (Mitchell, 1956: 12–13; Richards, 1950: 231–232). Land was allocated to the heads of new villages by the chief or by village headmen of superior rank (Mitchell, 1956: 62–63). Given matrilineal descent, inheritance, and succession to village headship, it was therefore likely that the descent group would focus on a particular village as its home.

Second, Yao village sites were more permanent than those of the other mobile cultivators. A village might remain on its site for thirty years, as against the four or five years of Tonga, Ndembu, and Bemba villages (Richards, 1950: 232; Mitchell, 1951: 301). Further, Yao productivity from cultivation (as distinct from raiding or herding) seems to have been the highest of all the mobile cultivators. Production may have involved trees or other valuable heritable wealth tied to particular sites. Although the Yao apparently have no joint estate in the strict sense of the term, the greater permanence of villages and higher productivity seem to have produced a situation approaching that of settled cultivators owning matrilineal joint estates. These factors would foster residential unity of the descent group.

Third, the literature does not contain information on the composition of the unit of regular productive coöperation or on the precise nature of redistributive relations within the Yao village. Within the village, lineage segments do, however, tend to build in separate clusters (Mitchell, 1956: 164), each, when possible, under its own male head, who is subordinate to the lineage and village head. This situation contrasts with Bemba and Ndembu villages, where proximal generations, cutting across lineage affiliation and segmentation, built in different sections of the village (Richards, 1939: 156–157; Turner, 1955: 130; 1957: 97). Spatial relations in the Yao village, plus the strong authority of segment heads, make one suspect that the lineage segment may be the core of a productive unit for some purposes. The higher productivity of the Yao and the localization and strong authority structure of the descent group and its segments would, at all events, make it probable that lineage and lineage segments are significant units in the redistributive process. I cannot, of course, offer as evidence an argument which starts with lineage localization, from it deduces lineage redistributive processes, and then posits these processes as instrumental in lineage localization. I merely suggest that given relatively high productivity from cultivation plus localized descent groups, productive and redistributive processes involving lineage and lineage segments may be here involved.

The Yao case suggests therefore that high productivity does produce a high degree of residential unity of the descent group, when it is based on cultivation, and when land is scarce and there is valuable heritable property tied to particular sites. High productivity produces descent-group localization, that is to say, when the conditions approach those of settled cultivation. Other types of relatively high energy appropriation coupled with shifting cultivation (e.g., the Bemba type) need not necessarily produce descent-group localization. Correspondingly, relatively low productivity among shifting cultivators *may* be accompanied by descent-group dispersal (e.g., Tonga and Navaho) if productive processes do not foster concentration and if need for aid in emergency positively favors dispersal. Other types of low productivity may be accompanied by a rather high degree of descent-group concentration (e.g., Ndembu) if the productive process requires a tightly organized and nearly self-sufficient local unit.

(3) *Genealogical structure of the descent group.* The genealogical structure of the descent group among mobile cultivators appears to be affected both by the level of productivity and by the degree of residential unity of the group.

Among the Navaho and the Plateau Tonga, where the descent group was dispersed and productivity low, the descent group was a non-segmentary unit having only stipulated as opposed to demonstrated descent, i.e., it was not a lineage (chaps. 1 and 2, above).

Among the Bemba, in spite of relatively high over-all productivity, the commoner descent group tended to be dispersed, and only branches of the royal lineage appear to have had a high degree of residential unity. Correspondingly only the royal lineage appears to have been strongly segmentary in character (Richards, 1940b: 99–103). The internal structure of the commoner descent group is not very clear, but it appears to have been of shallow depth (four to five generations), and, even though descent could be demonstrated, it does not appear to have been strongly segmentary (Richards, 1950: 223–224; 1954: 39; 1940b: 32).

Among the Ndembu with their low productivity but high degree of descent-group concentration, the descent group was a lineage of from three to nine generations' depth including children (Turner, 1957: 82–83). Descent was demonstrated rather than merely stipulated, and there was some tendency toward opposition between segments of like order and toward ultimate fission of the village between its component segments. Neither of these tendencies was very marked. Both were instead overriden by the principle of generation, which, spatially and in other respects, separated proximal generations and allied alternate generations within the village. Segmental and (in the case of the sons of male members) even matrilineal descent-group loyalties were thus submerged in many contexts. Segmentary tendencies were further countered by marriages between matrilineal or other types of kin of alternate generations. When it did divide, therefore, the Ndembu lineage did not necessarily divide cleanly between component segments of like order. Generational or marital allegiances might cause some members to leave more closely related matrilineal kin and to hive off with genealogically more distantly related kin (Turner, 1957: 195–200). Two factors, I suggest, may have been responsible for this weak development of segmentation.

First, there was no valuable, heritable immovable property such as might lead to the spatial segregation of segments and isolate them as units for inheritance. Villages moved often, land was free, and gardens could be made anywhere and had little durable value. Second, productive and redistributive processes, which, given matrilineal descent, were imposed by the ecological setting, emphasized the unity of the individual elementary family; the men of one generation, especially true brothers; and the village as a whole rather than of lineage segments. Women cultivated their gardens separately and cooked separately for themselves and their own children. Each married woman cooked in turn for all the men of the village, who ate in the communal men's shelter. Hunting was done in informal male groups, often of one generation, or in larger game drives by men of the village at large. In larger villages meat *was* distributed to the senior man of each minimal lineage segment, but its distribution does not appear to have fostered permanent lines of cleavage within the lineage as a whole (Turner, 1957: 21–33).

Yao lineages were the most strongly segmented among the mobile cultivators. A dominant lineage provided the core of the village, and in large villages there might be lesser lineages, each tracing its descent from a wife (often a slave wife) of a former village headman of the dominant lineage (Mitchell, 1956: 187–193). Small lineages and segments of larger lineages tended to build their huts in separate clusters within the village (*ibid.*: 164). Each group of true sisters was headed by a brother, usually the eldest, and formed with him a unit which Mitchell calls a sorority group (1949: 316–317; 1956: 145 ff). The sorority-group head was subordinate to the head of the lineage as a whole, and through him to the village headman. The unity of alternate generations was apparent, especially among women, but was much less developed as a principle of social structure than among Ndembu, Bemba, or Tonga (Mitchell, 1956: 175–176). Villages had a stronger tendency than did Ndembu villages to divide between their component segments (*ibid.*: 165). I suggest that the stronger segmentary principle in Yao lineages, like the stricter localization of the descent group, may have resulted from higher productivity through cultivation, more valuable and durable cultivation sites, and higher population density and land scarcity than in the other societies.

It seems probable therefore that among mobile cultivators descent groups will not be segmentary at all unless they have some degree of residential unity. Residential unity, even on very impermanent sites, fosters a tendency toward segmentation, but this becomes strongly developed only with more highly productive cultivation and more valuable, durable immovable property. Given mobile cultivation at all, however, it seems improbable that lineages will ever be as elaborately segmented or have as great a generation depth as among settled subsistence cultivators of high productivity such as the Ashanti or Minangkabau. The Yao have the most developed segmentary lineages of the mobile cultivators, but even among them villages do move and disintegrate, there is free land available for cultivation, and old gardens do in time become exhausted. Correspondingly, the local descent group is less cohesive than among settled cultivators of higher productivity having scarcer and more durable sites, and fission within it is less strictly between segments of like order. The head of a junior sorority group can under some conditions secede from his own mother's brother, and even full brothers may part company, each taking several sisters (Mitchell, 1951: 322). Such procedures are not permitted among settled cultivators of any but the lowest levels of productivity (e.g., Truk).

(4) *The functions and authority structures of descent groups.* I suggest the following generalizations with regard to the functions and authority structures of descent groups among mobile cultivators.

First, with low productivity, a simple division of labor by sex and age, no political centralization, and dispersed descent groups, the descent group's functions are the most limited of the types we have discussed, and it has virtually no specialized structure of authority. These conditions are best illustrated by the Tonga, and almost equally well by the Navaho.

In these societies, the functions of the descent group were restricted to mutual aid in emergencies such as famines or sickness; residual rights on the part of the group in the movable property of individuals, seen for example in the collection and distribution of bridewealth, or in the distribution of the property of a deceased member; and a certain degree of collective legal responsibility for members in their relations with others. Thus the descent group acted as a vengeance unit following homicide, provided or received compensation for members following the compounding of a dispute, provided substitute spouses (if necessary) for the bereaved partners of dead members of the group, and supported members in their relations with spouses or other outsiders to the group. Other descent-group functions lay in certain common ritual observances, but they will not be analysed here (chaps. 1 and 2, above).

Authoritative roles in these groups were unspecialized, and the controls exercised by authoritative figures were very limited. The Tonga descent group had no head: each generation of men exerted authority as a collectivity over the succeeding generation. "Mothers' brothers" arranged the marriages of their "sisters' daughters," held their bridewealth, and represented them in relations with their husbands. Men of the senior generation collectively represented those of junior generation in disputes and could sell a junior member to meet obligations owed by the descent group. Alternate generations of the group were allied as "siblings" in non-authoritative relationships (chap. 1, above).

The Navaho descent group may have had one or more leaders who mobilized the group to collective activities, but it seems clear that their authority was no more extensive and their roles little more specialized than those of seniors in the Tonga unit (chap. 2, above).

Second, provided that the descent group remains dispersed and not focused on valuable, heritable immovable property, a higher level of energy appropriation and incorporation in a state do not greatly extend its functions or strengthen its authority structure. The Bemba case suggests this generalization. It seems obvious that through raiding and exaction of tribute, if not also through indigenous cultivation, the Bemba level of energy appropriation must have been considerably higher than that of the Tonga, Navaho, or Ndembu. There was also a centralized state. Nevertheless, the descent group's functions and the controls of its authorities seem to have been little stronger than among the Tonga or the Navaho. The "commoner" descent group controlled no resources, and only close female matrilineal kin produced together. There were apparently no regular forms of redistribution within the descent group, although personal property (of slight importance) was inherited from a deceased member by his individual heir. The group was apparently primarily a unit of collective legal responsibility in relation to the state and to other descent groups. Succession to political office and to kinship statuses took place within it, and it may have been held collectively responsible for fines and for individual violations of law. There was apparently no single head of a commoner descent group; each individual seems to have been under the authority of a mother's brother, perhaps the eldest. The mother's brother arranged the marriages of his sisters' daughters and protected their interests after marriage. He is said to have been able to command a man's services and to require him to follow in war; he could also sell a junior into slavery under certain circumstances. Since he could apparently compel neither sisters' sons nor sisters' daughters to live in his village, however, his controls would seem to have been weak (Richards, 1940a: 32–33; 1949: 174–175; 1950: 223–224; 1956: 39–40).

The Bemba state did of course create positions of authority involving control of natural resources and, more pronouncedly, of the labor of its subjects and the distribution of goods. As in the other matrilineal states these controls were vested in the heads of territorial units—kingdom, district, and village. But because the descent group was not residentially unitary, it did not—in contrast to the descent group in states of settled cultivators—become involved in this hierarchy of authority as the nucleus of a minor territorial unit.

Third, where the descent group provides the core of a local productive and distributive unit—but where productivity is low, division of labor is based only on sex and age, political centralization is weak, and there is no attachment to valuable heritable sites—the descent group is necessarily more tightly organized as a regular coöperating unit, but its structure of authority remains weak and unspecialized.

The Ndembu seem to exemplify this situation. Here, as we have seen, the maximal lineage provides the core of a village. The men help to clear and hoe each others' gardens and hunt together, usually in informal groups without an authority (Turner, 1957: 22). It has been shown that the village headman's controls over production, distribution, and the settlement of disputes were very weak: he acted mainly as *primus inter pares* within his genealogical generation (*ibid.:* 104). He was, moreover, head of the village as a local group rather than (specifically) of his lineage, although succession to headship was normally confined within the dominant lineage. Resident adult sons of male members coöperated in village affairs as village members, and members of the lineage absent in other villages were "remembered" (*ibid.:* 86) rather than actively engaged in economic or other relationships with it. They had a right to return to the natal village if they wished, but the headman could not command them to live in it.

Within a larger village of some six to eight generations' depth, the effective descent group in many contexts was a minor lineage of five generations' depth including children (Turner, 1957: 195). This unit was normally exogamous, marriage being absolutely prohibited within the own or proximal generations and discouraged between alternate generations (*ibid.:* 86). Collective responsibility was most strongly enjoined within this unit. Its members provided or received most of the cloth, livestock, and guns involved in bridewealth transactions; the property of a dead man was primarily distributed within this group; the group paid or received damages following disputes with people of other descent groups; and the group was responsible for purifying the spouse of a deceased member and for a death payment to the spouse's descent group (*ibid.:* 129, 251). The minor lineage had no formal headman, authority being exercised by each generation collectively over the succeeding one, much as in a Tonga descent group. Alternate generations of both minor and maximal lineages were allied in non-authoritative relationships. Even the minor lineage was a relatively "weak" unit, in that, on the breakup of a village, sub-groups within it might disperse to separate villages.

Fourth, where the descent group provides the core of a local unit or section of such a unit—but where productivity from cultivation is relatively high, and there is attachment to more valuable sites for a longer period—the descent group develops an authority structure somewhat comparable to that found in settled cultivating societies of similar levels of productivity.

As far as can be judged, the Yao exemplify this situation. A dominant lineage provides the core of a village, sometimes with other, cognatically related lineages present which trace descent from wives of former village headmen. The village head's controls over production, distribution, and the settlement of disputes are stronger than among the Ndembu. While the village head has authority over all resident villagers regardless of lineage, moreover, each lineage in the village and each sibling group within the lineage has its own formally recognized head, who is more strictly the head of a descent unit (Mitchell, 1951: 315–320). Heads of lineages and of their component sorority groups often live near their sisters in their natal villages, but if absent in their wives' villages they visit often and are the constant mentors of their junior matrilineal kinswomen. They arrange marriages, act as marriage sureties, and are constantly appealed to in marital disputes. They must give consent to divorce. The head of a sorority group is economically responsible for his sisters if their crops fail, and they in turn must feed him when he requires food in his village. He is responsible for their care and the care of their children during sickness and for consulting diviners on their behalf (Mitchell, 1956: 144–152). In modern times he apparently sends money and brings goods to them when he works as a labor migrant, and he seems to have some control over the earnings of younger men of the group when they work outside the village. Descent-group heads represent both male and female juniors in disputes and are responsible for their fines (*ibid.:* 136). In his youth the head of a sorority group is responsible for his own junior siblings and sisters' children as the subordinate of his lineage head, but as he grows older he assumes increasing authority. Eventually, through "positional inheritance" of the kinship status of a deceased mother's brother, he may come to head a more inclusive lineage unit, or even the village as a whole (*ibid.:* 181–182). Alternatively, if the village grows large, the head of a numerically strong sub-lineage may move out with his followers to found a new settlement.

The traditional economic roles of descent-group heads are insufficiently described for one to see how these articulated with their legal authority. I can only suggest that the relatively high productivity of the Yao from cultivation, their greater land scarcity, their more permanent sites, and perhaps the need for formal redistributive processes within the village, lay behind the more corporate character of their lineage and the stronger controls of its authorities.

(5) *Descent groups and social stratification.* Higher productivity and increase in social stratification, among mobile as among settled cultivators, are necessarily associated with increase in social stratification which in some way involves descent groups. In societies of low pro-

ductivity and no political centralization, like the Navaho and Tonga, relations between descent groups are necessarily egalitarian. In chiefdoms which lack the centralized control of force and which have two main levels of territorial authority, each minimal local unit is ranked in relation to every other. When, in such chiefdoms, the descent group tends to be localized within a minimal territorial unit, as among the Ndembu and Yao, the localization tends to bring about a mutual ranking of all descent groups, much as in the chiefdoms of settled cultivators. Asymmetrical marriage ties such as multiple polygyny on the part of chiefs are also found in these societies, and such ties bolster the nascent political power of chiefs. With shifting cultivation, however, there may be more social mobility of descent groups than among settled cultivators of a comparable level of political centralization. For descent groups move and split more often and, especially at the lower levels, may more readily lose rank through fission or gain rank through augmentation of membership. Nevertheless, the basic principle of ranking is the mutual ranking of individual descent groups.

An interesting situation exists where there is political centralization but the descent group is dispersed, as among the Bemba. Here neither productive processes nor the existence of valuable heritable property foster residential unity of the descent group. Rather, the fact that land is ample, villages move and divide often, and new villages are often formed, gives men a wide choice of residence—with the father, mother's father or some convenient affine, or the mother's brother. For commoners, therefore, descent-group affiliation does not strictly determine either residence or rank. The royal descent group did outrank all others, followed by the descent groups of hereditary councilors. Among commoners, however, there seems to have been a good deal of upward mobility through the paths of cognatic or affinal kinship with chiefs of the royal lineage. Chiefs favored their children, affines, and patrilateral kin with positions at court, with village headships and even sub-chiefships, thus apparently continually drawing some commoners into the ranks of aristocrats (Richards, 1940b: 93). It seems probable that individuals who acquired rank in this way were partly severed from their natal descent groups, although their own subsequent matrilineal heirs would presumably inherit their status. Our reasons for this interpretation are Richards' statements that a Bemba father of high rank could overrule the legal control over his children normally exercised by their mother's brother, and that men with high-ranking fathers tended to join the father's village rather than that of a mother's brother (Richards, 1950: 226–227). Therefore, although the rank of royals and councilors was determined by matrilineal descent-group affiliation, that of commoners was a more individual matter, determined by a variety of cognatic ties.

This discussion is relevant to Richards' hypothesis that the existence of a centralized state strengthens paternal ties and weakens the matrilineal descent group (*ibid.*: 227). We would argue, rather, that in the Bemba case relatively low productivity from shifting cultivation and the absence of valuable heritable sites and other property made for a rather weak matrilineal group in the first place and for correspondingly fairly evenly balanced patrilateral ties. The existence of the state gave special authority to officers of rank, both over their own matrilineal juniors *and* over their children, other cognates, and affines. The state correspondingly gave privileges to all these categories of the officers' kin. Presumably the authority of a mother's brother of low rank was weakened if his juniors could lay claim to rank through paternal ties to officers; similarly, the authority of a father of lower rank would be very weak if his children could claim higher rank through matrilineal affiliation. In states of matrilineal settled cultivators, by contrast, the paternal claims of men of rank do not seem to have been regularly strengthened to the same degree. Chiefs did sometimes promote their sons to office in Ashanti and North Kerala, but for the most part an individual acquired his rank from his matrilineal descent group, with its relatively stable attachment to a joint estate. In Central Kerala, the most centralized state of highest productivity, individual paternal claims were practically eliminated. This problem will be further examined in chapter 14, in connection with interpersonal kinship relationships.

Variation in Residence

Types of Residential Unit

It is possible to classify the residential patterns of the fifteen matrilineal systems in a variety of ways. One may choose to look at the residence of children in relation to older kin, or of married couples at different stages of the life cycle; at the kinship composition of the household, of the group of closely coöperating households, or of the minimal local community, whether it be a village or a less nucleated district. Thus viewed, the fifteen systems offer a bewildering array of residence types—as many types, in fact, as there are systems.

I shall try to cut through this maze by focusing on the kinship composition of a particular residential unit, namely, that localized group of kin whose members regularly coöperate in production and/or the distribution of products. For each society, one such unit does stand out. Sometimes it is a household sharing one roof and one hearth; this is commonly the case among the Hopi, Minangkabau, Mappillas, Tiyyars, and Nayars (Titiev, 1944: 3–10; De Jong, 1951: 10; Cole, 1945: 252–254, 260; chap. 6, above). Sometimes it is a small group of closely coöperating households, as commonly among the Tonga, Navaho, Trukese, Bemba, and Ashanti (chaps. 1, 2, and 3, above; Richards, 1950: 227; chap. 5, above). Sometimes the main coöperating unit is itself a minimal local community or village; this is usually the case in the Trobriands and among the Ndembu, and may be the case in the smaller villages of Yao or Mayombe (chap. 4, above; Turner, 1957: 61; Mitchell, 1956: 140; Richards, 1950: 218–219). Members of the coöperating unit do not coöperate equally closely and frequently in all the societies. My selection of the main coöperating unit is not, however, arbitrary, for it is based on the fact that members do engage in essential economic coöperation either daily or every few days, rather than merely seasonally or annually. I decided to focus upon this unit because comparisons made in terms of it seemed to produce fruitful generalizations. By contrast, comparisons in terms of units sharing a common hearth or occupying a house, a homestead, or a village, proved less fruitful.

Five main types of coöperating units are distinguishable in the fifteen societies.

(1) *The elementary or the compound polygynous unit.* This unit centers about one man with his wife or wives and their unmarried dependents—often, but not necessarily, their own children. Of the fifteen systems, only the Tonga have this group as their main, relatively self-sufficient coöperating unit (the homestead). The homestead may be located in a larger hamlet but its members need not coöperate closely with the rest of the hamlet, and the unit may move freely between hamlets.

(2) *The matrilocal grandfamily.* I use Richards' convenient phrase to refer to the group composed of an older married couple, their daughters, daughters' husbands, and daughters' children (Richards, 1950: 228–229). Unmarried sons or husbands of married granddaughters may also be present in the group. This group is the most common coöperative unit among traditional Navaho, Hopi, Bemba, and landless, lower-caste North Kerala Mappillas (chap. 2, above; Titiev, 1944: 3–10; Richards, 1950: 227; chap. 9, above).

(3) *The matrilocal extended kinship unit with sororilocally resident male head.* This group comprises an older group of sisters, their husbands, unmarried sons, daughters, daughters' husbands, daughters' children, and sometimes granddaughters' husbands and children. A brother or son of the oldest group of sisters—usually the eldest man of the relevant matrilineal unit—either lives permanently with the group or visits frequently to manage its affairs. The male head's wife and children may also be temporarily resident. This group is apparently the dominant coöperating unit among the Trukese, Yao, and aristocratic landowning North Kerala Mappillas. It is sometimes difficult to distinguish from type 2, and there are intermediate states between 2 and 3. Although classed as type 2, the Hopi coöperating unit is closer to 3 than, for example, is that of the Bemba or Navaho, for Hopi men, especially sub-clan heads, regard their natal home as their true home, live very near it even when resident with their wives, and return often to look into its affairs (Eggan, 1950: 34). Some Trukese, again, live in matrilocal grandfamilies or in extended families with the matrilineal male head absent in his wife's house and paying visits to his sisters' home or homes. Indeed, even when a Trukese lineage head comes to live permanently near his sisters' extended family he does not, because of avoidance rules, live *with* them, but in a house near by (chap. 3,

above). In general, however, we have counted the unit as a matrilocal extended family with male head if the matrilineal male head lives near by and is engaged in regular economic coöperation with his unit, and the unit does not normally break up immediately after the death of its female members' common ancestress, but stays together for some time as a unit of sisters and their descendants. Navaho, Hopi (Titiev, personal communication), Bemba, and landless Mappilla units do break up in this way; Trukese and aristocratic Mappilla units traditionally did not. There is some doubt about the Yao unit because the data on economic coöperation are poor. The matrilocal grandfamily may in fact be the most common unit of daily coöperation within the village or village section. On the other hand the fact that heads of lineages and sorority groups commonly return to their natal villages and play such an intimate role in their sisters' lives suggests that the matrilocal extended family with male head may also be a significant unit of regular coöperation.

(4) *The avunculocal extended kinship unit.* This unit comprises the adult men of a matrilineal descent group of varying size, together with their wives and unmarried children. Adult sons sometimes remain in the group during the father's lifetime or even longer, especially if they marry cross cousins within the local group. With varying degrees of strictness, this residence type is found among the Ndembu, Trobriand Islanders, some traditional Ashanti, the Mayombe, at least some traditional North Kerala Tiyyars, and North Kerala Nayars. Among the Ndembu, Trobrianders, and Mayombe, the group may form a discrete small village. There is some doubt whether the main traditional coöperating unit in Ashanti was the local group formed on the basis of a maximal lineage, or of a landholding segment of such a lineage. The fact that "lineage" (presumably maximal lineage) men traditionally ate together in the house of the lineage head each night suggests that in former times the most significant unit of regular economic coöperation was the unit having, as its core, members of the maximal lineage as a whole (Hoebel, 1954: 214). This may have been the case, however, only in some of the northernmost districts (Basehart, personal communication). More recently, at all events, the main coöperating unit seems to have been the local unit formed on the basis of a landholding lineage segment (Fortes, 1950: 257–258).

The North Kerala Tiyyars present a problem because, at least by the second half of the nineteenth century, they had a variety of types of coöperating units. These included patrilocal grandfamilies, larger patrilocal extended families, varying forms of "mixed" or bilateral extended family, and elementary family units, as well as avunculocal extended families. On the basis of information presently available, I am inclined to view this variety as symptomatic of the disintegration of matrilineal descent groups as a result of the growing marketability of land and labor, and to consider the avunculocal extended family as the normal premarket form of Tiyyar residence. The evidence is in-adequate, however, and it is possible that Tiyyars had some amount of patrilocal residence even before the great increase in markets and cash-crop farming of the late nineteenth century. The Tiyyar problem will not be considered further here.

(5) *The lineage segment.* This unit is a matrilineage segment whose members, male and female, engage in regular, daily, or near-daily economic relationships and who co-reside for the greater part of their time. One spouse visits the other rather than living mainly in the other's home, and the economic coöperation of each sex with matrilineal kin is more significant and mandatory than that of spouses with each other. We have called the residence of individual married couples in this system duolocal. This unit is best exemplified by the household or property group of Central Kerala Nayars. I have also included under this classification the main coöperating unit of Minangkabau. It was usually a household whose members shared a common hearth. Often this household was a parui or main property-holding lineage segment; sometimes it was a sub-segment of the parui whose members occupied one house and had a degree of autonomy in managing their share of the joint property (De Jong, 1951: 24). Husbands in Minangkabau did sometimes work in the fields of their wives, in contrast to Central Kerala, but they were not obliged to do so traditionally, their main commitments being to their natal groups (Loeb, 1934: 42). The Minangkabau unit is slightly closer to the matrilocal extended family with male head than is the unit of Central Kerala Nayars, but it is clearly more appropriately classified under type 5.

Some Ashanti apparently also traditionally had type 5 as their main coöperating unit, for many Ashanti women spent all their lives in their natal homes and merely visited the husband's dwelling in a form of duolocal residence (Fortes, 1959: 150). Ashanti women did, however, owe more definite economic duties to their husbands than did Minangkabau men to their wives. The Ashanti as a whole are thus perhaps best classified under type 4.

Levels of Productivity and Residential Units

Table 13-1 gives the fifteen groups of mobile and settled cultivators, listed, so far as I can judge them, in descending order of productivity

TABLE 13-1

	Settled Cultivators	Mobile Cultivators	Main Residential Unit
	Central Kerala Nayar		Lineage segment
	North Kerala Nayar		Avunculocal extended family
	Aristocratic North Kerala Mappilla		Matrilocal extended family with male head
Same society	Low-caste North Kerala Mappilla *		Matrilocal grandfamily
	North Kerala Tiyyar		Avunculocal and variant extended families
	Minangkabau		Lineage segment
	Ashanti		Avunculocal extended kin unit or lineage segment
	Mayombe		Avunculocal extended kin unit
		Yao	Matrilocal extended family with male head
		Bemba	Matrilocal grandfamily
	Trobriand		Avunculocal extended kin unit
		Ndembu	Avunculocal extended kin unit

TABLE 13-1 (continued)

	Settled Cultivators	Mobile Cultivators	Main Residential Unit
Not mutually ranked for productivity	Truk		Matrilocal extended family with male head
	Hopi		Matrilocal grandfamily
		Navaho	Matrilocal grandfamily
		Tonga	Elementary or polygynous family

*The low-caste North Kerala Mappillas are included because they were one of our example systems, but it should be remembered that they are not strictly classifiable as settled cultivators. Although they were a subgroup of a society primarily dependent on settled subsistence cultivation, they were themselves an almost landless group. Only their women did regular cultivation for landlords, their men being carriers in trade. Aristocratic Mappillas also relied partly on trade but they owned landed estates as well.

of indigenous cultivation, together with the main residential units which characterize them.

This list is of course too small to be at all definitive, but it suggests that there may be a general tendency for matrilocal units to predominate in matrilineal cultivating societies of lower productivity, and for avunculocal or lineage-segment residential units to predominate in cultivating societies of higher productivity. Thus, if we divide the list into two sections between the Mayombe and the Yao, we find both lineage-segment systems and four out of six avunculocal systems in the upper section, and (excluding low-caste Mappillas) four out of five matrilocal systems in the lower section. If we consider settled cultivators alone, the results are more impressive: two out of three matrilocal systems fall at the bottom of the list, with five avunculocal and two lineage-segment systems ranking above them in terms of productivity. Only the North Kerala Mappillas are aberrant in this list—and they were not cultivators and not wholly reliant on the produce

of their landed estates, being rather a trading caste *within* a settled
cultivating society. The mobile cultivators are too few to have much
value, but three out of five of them are predominantly matrilocal. In the
other two societies, Tonga and Ndembu, the residence rule seems to
have been fixed by subsistence factors other than cultivation—herding
among the Tonga, hunting among the Ndembu.

Simply on the basis of these general typologies, therefore, I suggest
that in matrilineal societies or part-societies which rely very predominantly on cultivation, dominantly matrilocal residence will be
found among those with lower productivity, and dominantly avunculocal or duolocal among those of higher productivity. Where other
subsistence factors are of major significance, such as hunting, trade,
raiding, or herding, there may be some "aberrant" residence type which
does not fit expectations based on a consideration of level of productivity from cultivation alone. With so few societies to work with, however, these suggestions must obviously be tentative. I have tried to
cast a little more light by considering in greater detail the precise
ecological and economic factors which, given matrilineal descent,
appear to determine the type of residential unit in each particular
case among our examples. These considerations, plus a general knowledge of matrilineal systems, lead to some further hypotheses.

Implications of Ecology and Economic Organization for Types of Residential Unit

Five general considerations, derived partly from the work of other
writers, proved valuable for my analysis of specific residential forms
in the fifteen systems. This section draws in part on theoretical con-
structions developed by David Aberle, and presented more fully by
him in chapter 17.

(1) World distributions suggest that matrilineal descent is most
commonly found in predominantly cultivating societies which lack the
plough, important large domesticates, or extensive irrigation works.
Within the total range of agricultural societies, such horticultural
societies tend to have relatively low productivity.

(2) Matrilocal residence can occur without organized matrilineal
descent groups, as in some hunting, fishing, or cultivating societies of
very low productivity.[1]

---

[1] Murdock lists, in particular, a number of Central and South American tribes
which fit this description. They include the Cuna, Miskito, Cagaba, Callinago,
Motilon (Iroka), Ponare, Warrau, Tapirapi, Cashinawa, Piro, Siriono, Alacaluf,
Caduveo, Chamakoko, Choroti, Lengua, Paressi, Tenetehara, and Tupinamba

(3) It would be very unlikely, if not impossible, for matrilineal descent groups to develop except out of prior matrilocal residence, although matrilocal residence need not necessarily lead to the development of matrilineal descent groups (Murdock, 1949: 209–210). It seems unnecessary to recapitulate Murdock's cogent reasoning here.

(4) Murdock also argues that avunculocal residence can only develop directly as a shift from matrilocal residence, and at a time when organized matrilineal descent groups have already developed. Avunculocal residence can thus never develop directly from patrilocal, bilocal, or neolocal residence (*ibid.:* 207). I agree, except for the small proviso that avunculocality *could* under some circumstances develop from duolocality—if, for example, a previously matrilineal, duolocal group moved into a more sparsely populated area where duolocality was not feasible. But this would be extremely rare because of the rarity of duolocal residence.

(5) I have already tentatively suggested, on the basis of general knowledge and of the fifteen systems, that in matrilineal societies which rely primarily on cultivation, dominantly matrilocal residence tends to be found among those with lower productivity and avunculocal or duolocal residence among those with higher productivity.

These considerations lead to the conclusion that, historically, matrilineal descent groups have probably developed independently in several areas of the world on the basis of prior matrilocality, perhaps usually, although not invariably, under conditions of low productivity cultivation. Further, where they occur, matrilineal avunculocal systems must probably always be a development from previously matrilocal or duolocal matrilineal systems.

The precise conditions under which first matrilocality, and then matrilineal descent groups, have developed *ab initio*, can probably not be firmly established with presently available data. Murdock (1949: 204–205) has tended to relate residence rules to the relative power of the sexes deriving from their relative importance in production. Matrilocal residence would thus, according to him, be likely to develop when, in a previously hunting and gathering society, women become cultivators and begin to produce more food than men, and so are able to dictate the rules of residence.

This argument seems doubtful because, in human society in general, engagement in the most important productive processes seems to bear

---

(Murdock, 1957: 684–686). All have bilateral kinship systems with dominantly matrilocal residence. Their economies comprise various combinations of hunting, fishing, gathering, and low productivity cultivation.

little relation to power. The serfs of Kerala were the most important producers and the least powerful caste. There are, also, at least some patrilocal and avunculocal societies in which women, as far as can be judged, are the more important producers, for example the Shawnee (Murdock, 1957: 684) and the Ndembu (Turner, 1957: 26). In general, finally, female dominance in production apparently never gives women, as a sex, legal authority over men.

A more likely circumstance fostering matrilocal residence might be that in which women gather food, fish, or cultivate in small teams, and in which also their production sites are either stable or, if not stable, dictate the periodic movement of the residential group. If these conditions existed and if, in addition, men were able to hunt in any locality, either individually or in loosely organized groups which did not require long coöperative training, matrilocal residence would seem likely to occur regardless of the relative importance of men's and women's productive activities. A variant condition favoring matrilocality might be one in which couples could reside within a larger in-marrying band or community, with the women cultivating or fishing in small teams and the men hunting in a larger, community-wide group. While living matrilocally with regard to the homestead, both sexes could then remain within their wider natal community. The relatively greater importance of female work sites over those of men, and the existence of small, organized female work groups, are thus suggested as economic prerequisites of a shift to matrilocal residence.

Given matrilocality, organized matrilineal descent groups might then perhaps be expected to develop if women's property, in the form of resources, produce, or equipment, became sufficiently scarce or valuable to require formal inheritance rules, and management and defense on the part of the women's male kin. This suggestion is, however, tentative.

The main point to which I am leading is that, whatever the conditions which originally give rise to matrilocality and, later, to matrilineal descent, there is a sense in which matrilocal residence is the "basic" form with matrilineal descent: most if not all matrilineal societies were once matrilocal at some point in their history. If this view is correct, the problem of residence in matrilineal systems becomes not so much "Why are some matrilineal societies matrilocal?" as "Why are some matrilineal societies not matrilocal?" That is to say, regardless of the circumstances which originally gave rise to matrilocality, we would expect matrilineal societies to *continue* to be matrilocal, or even to revert to matrilocality, under a wide variety of ecological and economic conditions, for negative reasons, because no condition existed which forced them into another residential type. By contrast we would expect other forms of residence to exist with matrilineal descent for positive reasons, because some condition existed which made matrilocality impracticable. An examination of the fifteen systems seems to lend support to this view.

I now consider each of the major types of residential and economic coöperative unit in some detail and, using clues from the concrete examples, try to suggest the conditions under which, given matrilineal descent, each is likely to occur.

(1) *Dominantly matrilocal units in general* (Navaho, Hopi, Bemba, Yao, Truk, Mappilla). It seems unlikely that any of these groups, at the period studied, retained the economic system under which matrilocal residence and matrilineal descent groups had originally developed among them. Certainly none of them combined "pure" female cultivation or settled fishing with male hunting, economic arrangements which, given certain special characteristics of work sites and work groups, have been hypothesized as likely to bring about matrilocal residence.

Nevertheless, the Navaho, Bemba, Yao, and Mappilla systems did, at the period of study, have features of the sexual division of labor, of work sites, and of work groups which I have hypothesized as positively favoring matrilocality. Thus, Navaho women seem traditionally to have gathered food, and later herded sheep, in small teams, and Navaho residential sites were probably, in the latter period, determined mainly by the needs of women's sheep. Men, by contrast, seem traditionally to have hunted, and later to have raided, in larger territorial groups, while much of their supplementary work around the homestead could be done individually within the elementary family unit or in loosely organized local groups. Traditionally Bemba and Yao women appear to have done the bulk of continuous cultivation work in small teams, and village sites were moved mainly in accordance with cultivation requirements (Richards, 1939: 382–384; 1940a: 85–86; 1951: 166; Mitchell, 1951: 328). The less continuous cultivation work of younger men could be done individually in the elementary family or (in the Bemba case) in loosely organized groups of men attached to the wife's residential unit (Richards, 1939: 383–386; 1940a: 85–86; 1951: 166; Mitchell, 1951: 301–302, 328; 1956: 18). Population density permitted many Yao men to work in both the wife's and own natal community, and this was also possible in both societies in the case of intra-village marriage. Men of both societies were also often engaged in larger, mobile territorial units—the Bemba for war and raiding and the Yao for raiding and trade.

Similarly, low-caste Mappilla women cultivated in small teams on the land of high-caste landlords, whose settled location determined their own. Men did very subsidiary cultivation and were primarily engaged, individually or in larger work gangs, as carriers in trade. Aristocratic Mappilla women did no productive work but derived their livelihood largely from landed estates, on which they lived. Theoretically, since high-caste Mappilla women were not producers, it should have been possible for them to live avunculocally on their husbands' lineage estates. The fact that men were often absent in trade, and that women, more than men, were *primarily* dependent for maintenance on the produce of their land, would, however, positively favor keeping the women on their natal estates and so maintain matrilocal residence for the majority of the population. In these four societies, therefore, given matrilineal descent, the nature of work sites and the kinds of work groups of men and women strongly favored, if they did not actually demand, matrilocal residence.

Truk and Hopi present a rather different picture. In both societies, women did work in small teams—Hopi women in minor cultivation and domestic work and Trukese women in reef fishing (Titiev, 1944: 20–21, 24; chap. 3, above). Men worked individually, in pairs, in small, loosely organized groups, in the larger territorial groups of the district or village, or in their own lineage groups (Titiev, 1944: 22, 29, 181–200; chap. 3, above). The lineage groups, in a densely settled multi-lineage community, were readily accessible even with matrilocal residence. Work groups, work sites, and the sexual division of labor were thus quite compatible with matrilocality. On the other hand, they do not seem to have especially *required* it. There seems little reason why both Hopi and Truk should not have lived avunculocally if they had wished. Women's work sites did not, for example, dictate the place of residence, for women's cultivation was relatively unimportant in both societies and houses were in any case not necessarily located on the cultivation sites of their owners (Titiev, 1944: 181; chap. 3, above). In short, Truk and Hopi perhaps offer examples of the retention of matrilocal residence out of the past, under contemporary conditions which no longer especially favor it, because, in the period under discussion, new circumstances had not arisen which made it positively impracticable. Given the development of matrilineal descent groups out of some prior economic conditions, matrilocality could be said to have continuing adaptive significance for the economies of the Navaho, Bemba, Yao, and Mappillas; but matrilocality was perhaps only adaptively indifferent for the economies of the Hopi and Trukese. If this view is correct, it would support my belief that, in general, matrilineal societies are likely to remain matrilocal provided new conditions do not arise which make matrilocality grossly impracticable or impossible.

One specific characteristic of work sites and the division of labor deserves mention which, if other circumstances permit, seems positively to favor retention of, or reversion to, matrilocality. This is the circumstance in which women's work, of whatever kind, is done in or near the home, while men's pursuits periodically take them far from home. If other conditions do not prevent this, it is no doubt congenial for women to stay behind in unilineally related groups, rather than with affines. As already noted, the Navaho, Bemba, Yao, and Mappillas did have these conditions. Similar conditions may be brought about in these societies today by migrant labor.

It should be noted, however, that duolocal residence (both spouses live primarily with lineage kin) can also be a convenient form with frequently absent men, as among Central Kerala Nayars and in Minangkabau. Peripatetic males are not, moreover, a necessary feature of matrilocality, nor are matrilineal societies always matrilocal or duolocal if their men are wanderers. Hopi men stayed mainly in their villages. Trukese men may have sailed considerable distances, but so did the Trobrianders, who were avunculocal. The hunters of an avunculocal Ndembu village might also travel great distances in search of game (Turner, 1957: 31).

Given matrilineal descent, matrilocal residence may therefore exist under economic conditions which demand it, under those which favor it, or under those in relation to which it is adaptively indifferent. Some conditions which fit admirably with matrilocality in one society are found without it in another, where other conditions demand a different residence rule. The main question is, therefore, "Under what conditions is it impossible for matrilineal societies to retain dominantly matrilocal groups?"

(2) *The matrilocal grandfamily* (Navaho, Bemba, and low-caste Mappillas). First, the matrilocal grandfamily (as distinct from the matrilocal extended family with matrilineal male head) can be the main unit of economic coöperation only if the descent group owns no joint estate, or if its joint estate does not require formal redistribution of products on the part of a male head of the descent group. These

conditions are fulfilled among the Bemba, who have no matrilineal joint estate, and among the Navaho, among whom any joint holdings are likely to be transitory. They are fulfilled among low-caste Mappillas, whose "estate" (the lease of a garden) is not their major source of production. They are fulfilled among the Hopi, whose estate can be parceled out for usufruct and does not appear to require redistribution of products by the descent-group head. To the extent, moreover, that Hopi men do come home to manage their sisters' land and redistribute its products, their main unit of economic coöperation approaches a matrilocal extended family with resident male head rather than a matrilocal grandfamily.

Second, similarly it seems that the matrilocal grandfamily can be the major unit of economic coöperation only if the men of the major economic unit (in this case, the husbands) are not committed to continuous, coördinated teamwork or division of labor requiring a strong male authority. Where such a form of male organization is necessary, as often happens for example in societies with joint estates of high productivity, men of the descent group seem always to congregate and work under the authority of their own descent-group head, thus producing avunculocal or duolocal residence. Husbands *can* work together in matrilocal grandfamilies, but their joint work is less continuous, intricate, and authority-ridden than among localized males in avunculocal societies. In all the societies having either matrilocal grandfamilies or matrilocal extended families, the resident husband has opportunities to do some work that does not require coöperation with the group of husbands of his wife's residential unit. Among Navaho, Bemba, and Yao, he can work part of the time with his wife and children (chap. 2, above; Richards, 1939: 131, 162–164, 166, 172). Coöperation in these groups is, moreover, relatively unskilled and unaffected by turnover among young husbands through divorce. It does not require the years of practice needed, for example, to sail a Trobriand trading vessel. Where the residential unit (with or without a joint estate) requires continuous, closely coördinated teamwork by men under a strong authority, matrilocal residence is unlikely.

This argument is supported by observation of certain patterns in societies which do have a joint estate, yet which also have dominantly matrilocal residence and a productive system in which the estate is parceled out for usufruct and does not require continuous, directed, male coöperative work. In such societies, when the estate does demand occasional or seasonal teamwork on the part of a formally organized group of men, it seems likely to be men of the natal unit who will come home to do this work, rather than the co-resident husbands of the women. The Hopi and Trukese illustrate these conditions. Among the Hopi, husbands might work together in small informal groups, cultivating or herding, but men of the sub-clan are said to have formed the larger and more organized seasonal groups for the communal planting and harvesting on sub-clan land (Titiev, 1944: 184). Among the Trukese, husbands coöperated informally in small groups to fish or cook breadfruit, but lineage members coöperated under their head in organized seasonal projects like land clearing or the storage of breadfruit (chap. 3, above).

Third, the matrilocal grandfamily can be the main economic unit only if men do not control domesticated animals whose movements dictate their own.

Dominantly pastoral societies which herd large animals are apparently seldom matrilineal at all, probably because in such societies large animals tend to be managed individually by men, are the most valuable property, and are inherited solely or chiefly by men. Herds of small animals pose a different problem and can under some conditions be handled by matrilineal societies which are also matrilocal. Thus Navaho sheep appear to have been herded mainly by women until modern times. They could be cared for near the home and thus favored matrilocal residence. Men managed horses, but horses were few compared with sheep, could be let loose rather than herded when not in use, and were used for periodic, distant raiding, so that their ownership did not determine the regular residence of men. Hopi sheep, tended only by men, were subordinated to agricultural requirements and remained comparatively few until after the 1860's. Before that date sheepherding on a large scale far from villages was a dangerous occupation because of Navaho raids. Yao and Bemba have few cattle or other large animals; Trukese, traditionally none. Aristocratic Mappillas, like all landowning groups in Kerala, do keep some cattle and water buffalo, chiefly for milk and ploughing, but they are tended and worked by low-caste tenants, usually Tiyyars. Low-caste Mappilla households are unlikely to have more than one cow, grazed and milked by the women. Where matrilineal descent does coexist with male care of large animals as a dominant source of production, we do not expect matrilocal residence.

(3) *The matrilocal extended family with matrilineal male head in sororilocal residence* (Aristocratic Mappillas, Truk, probably Yao). This type may be considered as intermediate between matrilocal and avunculocal residence. The head of the descent group lives with ⌐

near his matrilineal kinswomen and manages their affairs, often bringing his wife and unmarried children with him. Most junior males live in their wives' units, although they may have varying degrees of commitment to their natal units.

First, where this residence type occurs there is likely to be an estate owned jointly by the descent group (aristocratic Mappillas and Truk) or at least a fairly stable site round which the interests of descent group members are focused (Yao). Further, the goods produced by descent-group members are likely to require redistribution on the part of its head.

Second, on the other hand, junior men are not needed for regular, coördinated teamwork on behalf of their descent group on its residential site. Thus most Yao and Trukese men's more regular productive work is done individually or in small informal groups, for immediate consumption, and so can be conveniently carried out on behalf of their wives' units. When a coördinated team of men *is* required for seasonal work on a descent-group's estate, as in the case of land clearing or preparation for lineage feasts (among the Trukese), men of the descent group seem likely to come home and carry out such tasks under their head's management rather than entrusting them to their matrilineal kinswomen's husbands. Among aristocratic Mappillas men did little productive work on their descent group's landed estate. Trading expeditions on behalf of the descent group might carry them far afield and did not necessitate regular residence on its land. It was enough to have one older man living on the estate to manage its laborers and distribute its income to resident and absent members.

It should be noticed, however, that in societies with either matrilocal grandfamilies or matrilocal extended families, the residential habits of men tend to approach something akin to duolocal residence if population density permits this. Where husband's and wife's natal units are far apart, as sometimes among Bemba and Navaho, the matrilocally resident husband necessarily has to make his major commitment to his wife's unit. When, however, husband's and wife's units are within easy walking distance—as is usual among the Hopi, many Trukese, some Mappillas, and many Yao—husbands are likely to drift home often on visits to their matrilineal kin. Thus, although he works mainly for his wife's household, a Hopi considers his natal house his chief home. Mappilla husbands visit the natal home often, sometimes for several days each month. Trukese husbands clearly maintain constant concern with their sisters' affairs, and Mitchell "found that [Yao] husbands were often away on a visit to their matrilineal relatives' village" (1951: 328).

The fact that men have authoritative roles in their own descent groups, although descent is matrilineal, explains this less complete commitment of matrilocally resident men to their wives' units, as compared with the commitment of a patrilocally resident woman to her husband's unit in patrilineal descent (Introduction, above).

(4) *The avunculocal extended kin unit* (Ndembu, Trobriand, Mayombe, Ashanti, North Kerala Nayar, some North Kerala Tiyyar). First, avunculocal residence seems most likely to occur where the descent group jointly owns an estate of relatively high productivity, in relation to which the products of the men require redistribution, and their labor, regular coördination, on the part of an authority. These conditions exist in the Trobriands, among the Mayombe, in traditional Ashanti, among North Kerala Nayars, and to a less marked extent among traditional North Kerala Tiyyars.

Second, the Ndembu differ from the other avunculocal groups in having relatively low productivity and no joint estate. Here again, however, as Turner points out, "the majority of productive activities involving collective work are carried on by men—clearing the bush, hunting, and also hut-building" (1957: 31, 33). Men's production from hunting also traditionally required redistribution of meat by a village head, and long-distance hunting parties presumably required habituation of men to each other and some direction by an authority. Women's cultivation, by contrast, was almost entirely individual or part of the combined effort of the elementary family and could be carried on in any place. The relative economic autonomy of the Ndembu village and its need for common defense in feud or against marauders are also significant. Given matrilineal descent, these conditions would seem to explain dominantly avunculocal residence. It should be noted, however, that Ndembu residence was less strictly avunculocal than in the Trobriands or among the Mayombe. There was no rule that sons must normally move to their mothers' brothers at puberty; many men moved only after the father's death (Turner, 1955: 126; 1957: 64–67). Amplitude of land and the lack of a joint estate made possible this more flexible choice of residence.

Third, given the conditions outlined, avunculocality is still likelier to occur if, in addition, women work mainly individually or with their conjugal elementary families, rather than in teams, and/or the natal homes of husband and wife are too far apart to permit duolocal residence. Both these conditions tend to be fulfilled among the Ndembu, Mayombe, North Kerala Nayars, and Trobriand Islanders. North Kerala Tiyyar women worked in teams, often organized on the basis of households, but they were directed by a landlord rather than by a senior woman, and their natal homes were often far from those of their husbands. Where, however, women as well as men can profitably engage in teamwork and where the natal homes of husband and wife are close together, duolocal residence may be preferred to avunculocal, each spouse remaining primarily with the natal unit. This was the case among many Ashanti and some North Kerala Nayars, and was of course the dominant residence pattern of Minangkabau and Central Kerala Nayars.

(5) *The lineage segment residential unit* (Central Kerala Nayar and Minangkabau). First, it has been already noted that duolocality or residence in lineage-segment units requires dense settlement, preferably in multi-lineage communities. Given a joint estate, duolocality is common in many matrilineal societies as a temporary alternative for a minority of couples whose natal homes happen to be near by. As the dominant residential pattern, however, duolocality is very rare. With only two cases as examples, we can do little more than state the conditions which appear to have made duolocality especially congenial in both societies.

Second, both societies had (for matrilineal systems) unusually high productivity from valuable joint estates in densely settled communities where land was scarce. These estates required strong male management and redistribution of many types of products among members of the descent group. Such conditions required, at the least, residence on the estate by its male head, and made congenial a system in which as many members of the descent group as possible were localized in its home.

Third, in both societies, men other than the descent-group head were often absent—among Nayars, during warfare, and among Minangkabau, in trade. This favored women's remaining on their own estates, in their own homes, under their own matrilineal guardian's control.

Fourth, when men were at home they were engaged in work associated with estates owned jointly by descent groups and directed by the heads of these groups. Nayar men did minor garden work, helped to direct their descent-group's servants, and acted as bailiffs on the village landlord's estate, recruited through their descent groups. Minangkabau men were cultivators. The latter, unlike Nayar men, sometimes did minor agricultural work for their wives in fields allotted to the women by the heads of their own descent groups for their private usufruct. Such work on the part of husbands could be done individually.

In Minangkabau as in Kerala, however, the bulk of the agricultural work and products of both men and women must have been coördinated by descent-group heads. For in both areas crops were extremely varied and each estate had many different kinds of fields and gardens, at least some of which could not be allocated for usufruct to members or to servants but were kept under the management of the head (Cole, 1945: 263–264). In both societies it was also necessary for heads to train male juniors for their own eventual headship of this complicated enterprise. As in the case of the avunculocal societies, such conditions fostered the residence of men in their own natal units during their periods at home.

Fifth, in Minangkabau, women's work in cultivation was also extremely important. Since much of it required coördination to the collective ends of the descent group, and subsequent redistribution of women's products, women's work, too, was more likely to be done on behalf of the own rather than the husband's natal unit. Nayar women's cultivation was minor, being confined to the harvest season; it involved teams under the authority of older women and of male heads. Nayar women were, however, recruited through their descent groups to work in the houses of village landlords. These conditions probably further fostered female residence in the natal unit.

Sixth, in spite of occasional work, junior Nayar men were of minor significance in actual production, as distinct from management, the land being worked chiefly by lower-caste tenants and serfs. Except for their senior male guardian, Nayar women had little need, strictly speaking, of either husbands or brothers to maintain them and their children. Matrilocally resident husbands would therefore have been superfluous from an economic point of view. Since, however, both sexes depended on their matrilineal estates for maintenance, it followed that both lived in the natal home.

Junior men may have been similarly unproductive in the senior and wealthier descent groups of Minangkabau lineages (Loeb, 1934: 48). If my argument here is correct, we should perhaps expect stricter duolocality in these descent groups and a greater tendency toward matrilocality in poorer descent groups where men were more productive, provided that in the latter groups men had some ability to produce on their own or to work individually for aristocrats. The Minangkabau data are not adequate to test this hypothesis.

Seventh, both societies had much durable heritable property, both movable and immovable, and a considerable range of trade goods in which both sexes were interested. Colson has argued convincingly that the conflict between natal and conjugal loyalties becomes most acute in matrilineal societies where there is durable heritable wealth and a productive surplus above immediate subsistence needs (chap. 1, above). In both these societies there is evidence not only that the residence of both sexes in their lineage units was seen as the most convenient means of handling the lineage's productive and redistributive processes, but also that conjugal and paternal ties were seen as actively endangering the integrity of the descent group and the safety of its joint estate. There was thus a host of stipulations designed to reduce the shared interests of spouses and of father and children—for example, strict rules limiting gifts of personal property to wives and children. A Nayar woman was not even permitted to enter a husband's natal house after his death lest she should try to continue meddling in its affairs. Duolocal residence should therefore perhaps be seen as part of a general attempt to limit conjugal and paternal ties, which in these societies were both irrelevant to the economic processes of the joint estate and actively dangerous to these processes.

(6) *The elementary and the compound polygynous unit.* Of the fifteen systems, only the Tonga had one or the other of these groups as their main unit of regular economic coöperation. Strictly speaking, the simple elementary family was probably rather rarely found as an autonomous homestead; it seems often to have had attached to it other children or oldsters related to one of the married partners. Young couples also attached themselves for a few years to the homestead of some older married couple before their marriage could become established. Such initial residence appears traditionally to have been matrilocal, probably because the girl's parents, in the period of slave raiding, feared to allow her to leave them until they were convinced of the husband's ability to protect her. At any given time, therefore, some of the traditional Tonga residential units were matrilocal grandfamilies. At the present time young couples may attach themselves to any older kin (chap. 1, above).

The composition of the Tonga homestead seems explicable in that it was the smallest group which could exist as a viable, relatively autonomous reproductive and productive unit in this economic system, which combined male cattle keeping with female cultivation; and it could not incorporate itself with any predictable degree of permanence in any larger residential unit because of the need for frequent dispersal of homesteads as a result of sporadic local drought, and perhaps, also, of slave raiding.

The Tonga homestead thus moved often and freely between hamlets,

attaching itself temporarily to such a wide possible range of kinsfolk
that, in relation to the larger community, the residence of Tonga married couples can justly be termed multilocal. At the same time it should
be noticed that choice of residence, although wide, rested with the
male head of the homestead after the initial period of his first marriage. Although multilocal, the residence of married couples was thus
also dominantly virilocal (Colson, 1951: 112).

There seem to be several reasons why the Tonga choice of residence
should rest chiefly with men. First, although the homestead could be
a near-autonomous unit for much of the year, men did form larger
seasonal work parties to clear land, build huts, sometimes to weed
and harvest, and to organize fish and game drives (*ibid.*: 105–106).
Large work parties seem almost always to have concerned men, while
women worked primarily within the homestead unit. Second, the needs
of cattle caused annual movement to dry-season cattle camps. Women
had no part in the care of cattle after puberty, so that men would be
likely to reserve the choice of suitable sites for pasturage. Again, there
seems to have been some male coöperation in herding, since the head
of a hamlet was considered the owner of the kraal which housed the
cattle of its male members (*ibid.*: 105, 108–109, 117). Such forms of
male coöperation, which in a less chancy environment might have
produced regular avunculocal (or possibly patrilocal) residence, seem
among the Tonga to have given rise to the strong virilocal bias within
their multilocal residential pattern.

Bridewealth and Residence

In her pioneering comparative study of Central Bantu matrilineal systems, Richards has argued that where a substantial bridewealth is
paid the residence of married couples is invariably virilocal, but that
where the bridegroom gives only service or token payments it is not.
As examples of virilocal matrilineal societies she cites the Mayombe,
who paid a heavy bridewealth in cloth and cash and were avunculocal, and the Ila (a society closely related to the Tonga), who paid
cattle, hoes, shells, and blankets, and appear to have been mainly patrilocal with some avunculocality (Richards, 1950: 249).

In the context of a much broader theory, Murdock has advanced a
similar argument. He argues that in a matrilineal society where men
acquire durable movable property such as herds, slaves, money, or
other valuables, they are likely to use this as bridewealth in order to
induce parents to part with their daughters, and so to bring about a
shift to either avunculocal or patrilocal residence. He leaves open the

question of which choice will be made, except to note that "the adoption of a pastoral economy has almost universally resulted in patrilocal residence" (Murdock, 1949: 206–207). He further argues that where patrilocal residence becomes established there may be an eventual shift to double-unilineal or to patrilineal descent (*ibid.*: 208–212).

It does seem to be true that in the great majority of societies where the dominant mode of production involves male-managed herds of large animals, patrilineal descent is the rule, and that where matrilineal descent is found, as among the Tonga and the Ila, residence is dominantly virilocal. It may well be that when a matrilineal society comes to rely predominantly on herds managed by individual men, and when cultivation, or any form of attachment by the matrilineal group to specific sites and collective economic activities, becomes insignificant, a shift to patrilocal residence and eventually to patrilineal descent is likely to occur. The data are insufficient to handle this problem fully here.

If we restrict ourselves to the problem of bridewealth within matrilineal societies, it seems preferable to place it within the context of a more general theory of relations between residence and the system of allocation of goods and services. Thus I would argue, along the lines laid down above, that avunculocal residence is likely to occur in any matrilineal society where men work regularly in teams or through a coördinated division of labor requiring authority, where the products of men require coördination and redistribution by such an authority, and, in particular, where the work and products of men are connected with a matrilineally owned joint estate. I am less sure of the general economic conditions likely to foster dominantly patrilocal residence with matrilineal descent, but they may be, as suggested above, those in which men, as individuals, come to control the dominant forms of movable property in the society, where such property determines residential sites, and where the matrilineal descent group lacks, or has lost, any basis in regular collective economic activities.

Certainly the range of matrilineal societies in which the over-all economic system favors or demands virilocal residence is likely to include many in which men do control durable movable property. Given the economic need for virilocal residence, the transfer of such property as bridewealth may then in many cases be an institutionalized mode of establishing the marriage and, incidentally, of according to the husband the right of bride removal. Thus, six out of seven of the sample societies with virilocal residence do pay some form of bridewealth. The Mayombe paid a substantial sum in cloth and cash

(Richards, 1950: 216); the Tonga, in cattle (Colson, 1951: 145–149). The Trobrianders paid shell valuables (chap. 4, above); the Ndembu, guns, cloth, and livestock (Turner, 1957: 265); the Tiyyars, a small sum of money; and the Ashanti, among whom residence was sometimes avunculocal, a basic payment consisting usually of two bottles of gin, which might be followed later by a more substantial gift (Fortes, 1950: 280–281).

It should be noted, however, that there is great variation in the value of these gifts relative to the total male wealth of the society in question —and also relative to any return gifts which may be made by the bride's kin. The Mayombe, Tonga, and Ndembu payments seem to have been substantial in terms of the economies of these societies. The Trobriand gift was substantial, but was equally compensated by gifts of food from the wife's kin during the first year of marriage, and more than compensated by later annual gifts of foodstuffs. The Tiyyar sum can probably be considered only as a minor payment, for which the bride's dowry of jewels and cooking vessels more than compensated. The basic Ashanti payment must surely be considered trivial considering that Ashanti movable wealth included shell money, cloth, slaves, guns, livestock, etc. It is true that many Ashanti women did not live avunculocally with their husbands, that larger sums might be given for wives of rank, and that a later substantial payment might be made, but there seems to be no evidence that such larger payments were associated with a definite right of bride removal. It is also perhaps relevant to notice that in all these societies the one crucial claim which payment of bridewealth is invariably said to confer is exclusive rights in the woman's sexuality, to which the right of removal of the wife may be viewed as secondary. In some cases, indeed, rights in sexuality may be separated from the right of removal and specifically attached to the main marriage payment. Thus among both the Ndembu and the Tonga, after the initial period of uxorilocality, a smaller preliminary payment grants the husband the right to remove the wife to his village, but only the full payment gives him exclusive, permanent sexual rights and the right to claim damages for adultery (Turner, 1957: 265; Colson, 1951: 145–146).

In general, in societies which pay bridewealth the amount and quality of the goods paid are probably understandable only in terms of a range of economic factors such as the economic significance of the various movable goods available to men and the relative value of women's productive activities, as well as the type of residence and the degree of severance of the woman from her natal unit imposed by modes of production and distribution and by demographic factors. In short we would see both residence rules and bridewealth payments as functions of the total system of allocation of goods and services, rather than seeing residence rules as determined by the type of payments made at marriage.

One advantage of this approach over Richards' theory is that it can attempt to take care of societies in which residence is avunculocal although no bridewealth is paid, and also of cases (no doubt rare) in which bridewealth may be paid although residence is matrilocal. The North Kerala Nayars are an example of the former; and the Navaho, of the latter. Among North Kerala Nayars men certainly controlled ample movable goods with which bridewealth could have been paid—far more, for example, than the Tiyyars, who actually paid a small bridewealth. Such goods included money, gold and silver, jewelry, weapons, tools, cattle, and elephants, but the marriage contract involved only the gift of a single cloth by the bridegroom to the bride. The absence of bridewealth seems to be related to the fact that although residence was virilocal, a wife's obligations to her husband and his group were very limited. Commoner Nayar women did no productive work other than occasional harvesting; aristocratic women, none. Further, the fact that the sources of wealth were landed estates and movable goods owned jointly by descent groups required boys normally to return to their taravāds during adolescence. These conditions made a woman's ties to her conjugal group temporary and limited; many women in fact probably spent most of their declining years in their own taravāds with their sons. A Nayar woman was thus loaned temporarily to her husband as a sexual and domestic companion, rather than, like a Tiyyar woman, being "leased" to provide well-defined and valuable economic services.

The circumstances surrounding Navaho payment of horses as bridewealth are not well described. One possible explanation may be that this was related to a growing heterogeneity of wealth during the nineteenth century (Aberle, personal communication). Before 1860, men appear to have owned horses individually for raiding and as a prestigious mode of investing accumulated wealth, while sheep were probably managed largely by women in the matrilocal extended family. Payment of bridewealth in horses by some, but not all, men, may thus have reflected a process of economic selection in marriage, with the men of wealthier families thereby acquiring the privilege of attaching themselves to women of other similarly wealthy families. Although residence was matrilocal, the husband who married into a wealthy family would obtain definite economic advantages such as sharing in the benefits of large herds of sheep. In return the woman's kin would need some assurance that the husband's kin were people of substance who could assist him in time of need. Bridewealth payment perhaps provided such assurance, rather than (as in some avunculocal societies) compensating the woman's kin for any specific loss of services on the part of the wife.

In sum we may suggest that bridewealth is likely to be paid in matrilineal societies where men control durable movable property, and where the property or services which a woman brings to the marriage have high economic value to the husband and/or his descent group. Payment of bridewealth probably has a high statistical correlation with virilocal residence, but the two are not *always* found together. Whatever its economic significance, payment of bridewealth in matrilineal societies seems always to be regarded by the people as primarily payment for exclusive sexual rights in the wife. It appears normally also to accord the husband some kind of legal paternity of his wife's children, although this is vested with widely varying rights and obligations in different matrilineal societies. Payment of bridewealth cannot, of course, normally accord the father or his descent group complete rights in the woman's children, for this would be a negation of matrilineal descent. It is true that in some matrilineal societies, for example the Mayombe, payment of an unusually large bridewealth may in some circumstances give the husband and his descent group complete control of the wife and her children, thus severing their matrilineal ties (Richards, 1950: 250; De Cleene, 1937: 5). It seems probable, however, that such societies will always be ones in which slavery is institutionalized, and that in these unusual cases the wife and children become, strictly speaking, slaves of the husband and his descent group. Normally, payment of bridewealth confers only secondary claims on the woman's children which do not conflict with the claims of their matrilineal descent group, and the crucial emphasis is placed rather on the acquisition of exclusive sexual rights in the wife.

Types of Residential Mobility and Variability

Our classification of societies in terms of their dominant economic-residential units has not taken account of either the extent of spatial mobility in the society or the range of possible alternate forms of residence. Four possible types of spatial mobility can be distinguished in these societies.

(1) Movement of the minimal local community as a whole, as ex-

emplified by the movement of a village to new lands every few years among many slash-and-burn cultivators.

(2) Movement of the main economic-coöperative unit from one minimal local community to another—in societies such as the Bemba, where the main economic-coöperative unit is smaller than the village.

(3) Movement of individual married couples and their unmarried dependents from one main economic-coöperative unit to another, as well as from one local community to another. Often such movement is part of the fission of one economic-coöperative unit into two, as when a Bemba couple in middle age move out of the wife's parents' grandfamily to found one of their own in another village.

(4) Movement of an adult individual, with or without dependents, on the breakup of a marriage. We shall not deal with such movement here.

On the whole, the first three types of mobility occur more frequently among mobile than among settled cultivators. Movement of types 2 and 3 means that there is greater residential variability among married couples in relation to wider local units, on the average, among mobile than among settled cultivators. Movement of type 3 also means, in particular, that although there is one dominant structural type of economic-residential unit in each society, on the average the dominant type tends to be statistically less dominant and variant types tend to occur more frequently in mobile than in settled cultivating societies. We illustrate this with reference to the two main types of ecology.

MOBILE CULTIVATORS

Among the Tonga, as we have seen, the group composed of the individual married couple and their unmarried dependents, or of the polygynous family, is also normally the main unit of economic coöperation. Occasionally this unit is in addition coextensive with the hamlet or minimal local community, but more often it is temporarily located within a larger hamlet. I have already argued that the high mobility of the homestead and its wide choice of residence in relation to hamlets were made possible by low productivity and lack of attachment to particular sites, and were actively encouraged by fluctuating water supplies. I have also argued that the tendency for virilocal residence of the homestead head and his wives in relation to the hamlet head was fostered by cattle herding and male coöperation in larger work parties. In this society also, the main economic-coöperating unit (the homestead) was not only mobile in relation to larger units but was itself very impermanent because it was based on marital rather than lineal ties and so disintegrated after death or divorce. This fact is again attribut-

able to the ecological need for small, highly mobile economic-coöperating units. The uncertain natural resources and the continual need to
strike a balance between a homestead too small to provide adequate
labor and one too large for available resources, may also in part explain the fact that even children could move between the homesteads
and hamlets of a range of older kinsfolk rather than staying permanently with their parents.

Among the Navaho the matrilocal grandfamily as the main economic-
coöperating unit seems to have moved freely both within and between
larger communities or neighborhoods. Choice of the location of the
grandfamily in relation to other grandfamilies of the neighborhood
seems to have had no perceptible bias to either virilocality or uxorilocality (chap. 2, above); the grandfamily could settle near any of a
wide range of affines or cognates of either the senior man or his wife.
The residence of individual married couples should therefore be classified as matrilocal during youth, in relation to the main economic-
coöperating unit, and multilocal in later life (after the death of the
wife's parents), in relation to the wider neighborhood. There was also,
however, possible variation in the composition of the main coöperating
unit itself, patrilocal or bilateral grandfamilies being found in a minority
of cases. The near-absence of heritable immovable property made possible these alternatives, the patrilocal one being especially desirable for
a family which had no daughters. Today there is also a high proportion
of independent, neolocal elementary family units (chap. 2, above).
I suspect that at least some of them may result from the entry of individual men into the modern labor market, but the evidence is inconclusive.

Among the Ndembu an avunculocal extended kinship unit of varying
size formed the core of both the main coöperating unit and the
minimal local community. It moved freely within or between vicinages or between the larger areas headed by senior village headmen.
Such movement was made possible by low productivity, lack of heritable immovable property, abundance of land and evenly distributed
resources (Turner, 1957: 6). Within the main coöperating unit the
residence of married couples was more flexible than is usual among
avunculocal settled cultivators. Traditionally it normally began with a
short period of matrilocality, followed by the husband's taking his wife
to a village of his choosing—sometimes to his father's village for a
time, but eventually to that of his own matrilineal lineage. A man might
also have a choice of residence with one or another set of matrilineal
kinsmen, if his village divided during his lifetime to form two or more

villages. Again, this relative flexibility of residence choice is attributable to available land and absence of a matrilineal joint estate.

Among the Bemba the matrilocal grandfamily as the main coöperating unit was incorporated within a larger village. The grandfamily's choice of village was largely determined by its senior man, who, when he founded the unit in middle life, might choose to move his wife and their daughters out of the wife's natal village to one headed by his own mother's brother, father, brother, maternal grandfather, or other relative. Alternatively, the middle-aged husband might himself succeed to headship of a deceased matrilineal elder's village or might found a new village with the consent of his chief (Richards, 1950: 226). The residence of married couples was thus at first matrilocal for varying periods, followed often, but not always, by virilocality of varying forms. Here the political relations of men—their ties through one or another form of kinship to heads of larger or smaller territorial units of the kingdom—primarily determined the location of the main coöperating unit. As we have seen, the absence of matrilineal joint estates, combined with enough land, allowed men to choose among a range of such relationships.

Yao residence appears to have been less flexible because of greater land scarcity and more stable village sites. Villages moved less frequently than among the Tonga, Ndembu, and Bemba, and the main economic-coöperating unit (presumably a matrilocal grandfamily or a matrilocal extended family) was more stably embedded within the natal village of its female members. The majority of married couples thus appear to have lived matrilocally throughout their married life, although some men who became heads of lineages or sorority groups might persuade their wives and children to move temporarily to the husband's village (Mitchell, 1951: 332–333). When a village did divide, its sections often did not sever their ties but remained within the same neighborhood, linked, within the political structure of the chiefdom, through ranked relationships of perpetual kinship between their heads (Mitchell, 1956: 122, 206–207). As has been noted, therefore, Yao residence seems to have approximated more closely to that of settled cultivators, probably as a result of their higher productivity from cultivation, higher population density, and more stable village sites.

SETTLED CULTIVATORS

Among settled cultivators the local community as a whole is obviously more stable than among mobile cultivators, and the main economic-coöperating unit moves less frequently between communities. There are, however, various forms of mobility and residential variability among settled cultivators which can be linked with particular ecological, economic, or political conditions. Here I merely draw attention to some of the more outstanding forms.

Some forms of residential variability are, as might be expected, characteristic of certain types of low productivity in settled cultivation. Truk offers an example of one such type. Here are very small islands with small populations divided into small descent groups. It is necessary to maintain some kind of balance between the size of descent groups and of economic-residential units and the amount of land to which they have access (Goodenough, 1951: 166). The Trukese seem to use three main methods of adjustment: paternal bequests of various types of land right, which run counter to matrilineal descent; adoption of children; and a fairly flexible allocation of married couples to economic-coöperating units. In this last connection, matrilocal residence is preferred, but a given couple may for economic or demographic reasons live instead with the extended family associated with the lineage of the husband—or even occasionally of the husband's father—of the wife's father, or of some other less close relative (chap. 3, above). This type of variability, which approaches bilocality, may be characteristic of small island populations divided into small descent groups.

Ambilocality is another but rare form of residential mobility which seems to be possible only with certain types of low productivity settled cultivation. It is not found among my examples, but the Dobuans exemplify it. Here a core of matrilineal descent-group members form the nucleus of a small village located on the descent group's land. Each married couple normally moves annually between wife's and husband's village for the duration of the marriage (Fortune, 1932: 4–5). Such a residential type probably requires: low productivity with lack of need for a strong descent-group authority to coördinate labor or to redistribute products; close proximity of villages so that frequent movement between them is feasible; and the elementary family as the main economic-coöperative unit, so that it does not matter much in whose village it lives.

Some forms of residential *variability*, which may or may not be associated with *mobility* of the couple or of the economic unit, are connected with varying degrees of political centralization, in that office bearers or their near kin are able to practice privileged forms of residence. Thus among the Trobrianders a chief might with the consent of his own lineage keep a married son living with him patrilocally until the chiefly father's death. If the son married his patrilateral cross cousin he might even stay in the village throughout his own lifetime, in what amounted to combined patrilocal and matrilocal residence. After the son's death the abnormal residence pattern came to an end, for his children would be matrilineal heirs of the village in which he had lived. Conversely, however, the son of a *woman* of chiefly rank had an unchallenged right to live patrilocally in the village of his lower-ranking father and to receive land there. If he married a patrilateral cross cousin this aberrant residence form, too, might end with his death. Alternatively, such a son sometimes brought his own matrilineal heirs to the village. They later inherited from him and might eventually even take over the village from its former owners (chap. 4, above).

Among the Mayombe a chief or village headman of high rank might keep with him numerous sons and sons' children throughout his life (De Cleene, 1935: 66). Unless they were slaves actually owned by the father and inherited by his descent group, however, such sons seem normally to have returned to their own villages after the father's death. Ashanti chiefs had similar privileged controls over their sons, some of whom were given positions of rank in the army and perhaps kept in temporary residence with their fathers. Additionally, some subordinate chiefships were regularly given to the sons and sons' sons of the chiefs in whose domains they were located (Fortes, 1950: 260–261).

We do not know what privileged forms of residence, if any, were associated with chiefships in Minangkabau. In both North and Central Kerala, however, the women of royal and chiefly lineages normally kept their Nambudiri Brahman husbands with them in a form of matrilocal residence. The husbands in the daytime occupied buildings of the palace, with separate cooking arrangements appropriate to their higher caste rank, and visited the wives in the latters' private rooms. Such an aberrant residence form was a political privilege for the princess, who could monopolize her husband by keeping him within her lineage's precincts. It was an economic privilege for the husband, who was maintained in style at the palace's expense. Men of royal and chiefly lineages, however, usually followed the normal residential patterns in relation to their wives. In Central Kerala princes visited their wives like other Nayars, sometimes in commoner, vassal Nayar lineages located in the royal village, and sometimes in village headmen's lineages in various parts of the chiefdom. In North Kerala princes usually brought their Nayar wives to live temporarily in avunculocal residence in buildings within or near the palace grounds. Occasionally a king or chief carved out a new estate or political office for a favorite son, which then became the hereditary property of the son's descent group. This happened more frequently in North than in Central Kerala, the political structure being less centralized and rigid in the north. It was, however, always an aberrant and strictly speaking illegal procedure, for the estate first had to be expropriated from some other office-bearing lineage or from the royal lineage itself.

Privileged forms of residence were of course also practiced by office bearers and their kin among mobile cultivators like the Bemba and Yao. Yao chiefs and village headmen might move their wives to their own villages on marriage and later keep adult married sons living patrilocally with them. Such sons sometimes stayed in the village by virtue of patrilateral cross-cousin marriage, as among the Trobrianders. Sometimes, however, daughters of the headman might also settle with him, whose descendants in time formed new, patrilaterally linked lineages. Some if not most of these lineages seem traditionally to have been those descended from slave wives, but some were apparently descended from free women who left their natal villages (Mitchell, 1956: 188–189). In time, if the village grew large, such linked lineages might hive off to found new villages.

Bemba chiefs of districts, who were all of the royal clan, had the privilege of removing their wives to their own villages on marriage and founding one or more grandfamilies there (Richards, 1950: 228–229). In his capital village a chief also had a numerous following of various types of affines and cognates: not only sons, sons' sons, and daughters' sons, but also often his father, paternal half-brothers, and other patrilateral kin and various affines. Some of these kin had political positions as advisors of the chief. Some received subordinate chiefships or village headships within the chiefdom. Moreover, when such royally related persons died, their political positions and statuses in the kinship structure were filled by their individual matrilineal heirs through the institution of positional inheritance. Thus, in theory at least, any person who could claim matrilineal descent via positional inheritance from a son or grandson of a former chief could consider himself of royal rank (Richards, 1940b: 93–94).

The extent to which interpersonal affinal or cognatic relationship to office bearers can influence residence and political rank in these matrilineal states and protostates seems to depend on the degree of stability of the population on its cultivable land, and the level of productivity and thus the heritable value of land. The two extremes in this respect are the Bemba and Nayar, both with relatively centralized states, but at opposite poles with regard to stability of cultivation sites and the heritable value of land. Among the Bemba, villages moved every four or five years; they fragmented often, some died out, and new ones were constantly being formed. The descent group was not focused at all on heritable immovable property. It was thus possible for the chief in each generation to bring in a range of people from his own personal kindred—sons and grandsons especially, and sometimes patrilateral kin and affines—and to settle them in his capital, give them minor political positions, place them as heads of new villages, or even put them in charge of older villages whose former heads had been ousted. Once granted, these positions were, in theory at least, inherited by their holders' matrilineal heirs, and some heirs probably renewed their right through cross-cousin marriage back into the royal clan. Nevertheless, it seems likely that within a few generations the claims of many of the heirs would wear thin, their rank would lapse, or they would be replaced by members of the interpersonal kindreds of incoming chiefs. In this society, therefore, only the highest offices in the royal lineage itself and in some of the higher councilors' lineages seem to have been stably inherited by matrilineal descent, while many minor positions at court and many village headships were constantly replenished by personal kin—especially filial descendants—of those of higher rank.

In Kerala, by contrast, cultivation sites were stably occupied and highly productive, land was scarce, and the population of most areas (especially in Central Kerala) was densely settled. Among Nayars and the higher aristocrats estates were held for many generations by the same matrilineal descent groups. The various ranked upper castes of commoner Nayars, village headmen, chiefs, royalty, and Brahmans also held their estates with graded rights to share produce and stewardship, which corresponded with their ritual and political rank. Economic rights and political status were inherited almost solely by unilineal descent. The non-unilineal, interpersonal kindreds of chiefs and royals received minimal concessions on the basis of these personal ties. True, the sisters' husbands and fathers of chiefs and royals were wealthy Brahmans and their sons were themselves chiefs, village headmen, or honored vassals of the realm. They held these roles, however, by virtue of unilineal inheritance of statuses politically established in perpetuity, and only incidentally through interpersonal kinship with rulers. The royal lineage might modify the residence rules for its Brahman husbands and Nayar wives, but it did so without normally tampering with established political offices or major hereditary estates. Brahman husbands living in the palace had no part in its management and were given no political office; they were, rather, "like breeding bulls," as one Calicut prince remarked, the pensioned guests of their royal affines. It is true that personal kinship with royals did occasionally bring political advancement. Over several generations of favorable alliances with aristocrats, a commoner Nayar descent group might rise to village headship or even to chiefship. This was more usual in North than in Central Kerala, for in North Kerala the political system was less centralized, there was more internal strife, and there was also more land for new settlement. But such upward mobility was everywhere rare— it was against the rules and was stiffly resisted by lineages of established rank. Further, once a descent group had attained high office in this way, the office was inherited in virtual perpetuity by matrilineal descent.

In protostates of settled cultivators of lower productivity, such as the Trobriand Islands, there seems to be a situation somewhere intermediate between those of the Nayar and the Bemba. Here the aberrant residential patterns of the children of chiefs do sometimes give rise to the formation of new descent groups within villages, so that there is a constant reshuffling of descent groups within and between villages and also a constant rearrangement of their rank in relation to one another. But the process is a gradual one, and, once established, descent groups tend to inherit their rank and sites over a number of generations. A rather similar type of gradual mobility goes on among the Yao, the least mobile of the mobile cultivators we examined. Here again the sons and daughters of village headmen, by residing aberrantly, sometimes give rise to new patrilaterally linked lineages within established villages, and occasionally even eventually take over the village (Mitchell, 1956: 162–163). In neither society was there the degree of permanence of territorial group membership and succession to office seen in Kerala, nor was there the constant turnover through interpersonal cognatic and affinal ties apparent in Bemba villages. In general we may suggest that in matrilineal states and protostates, filial and other interpersonal, non-unilineal relationships to office bearers modify residence patterns and the political process less, the more stable the cultivation sites of the society and the higher its productivity from cultivation.

Variation in Interpersonal
Kinship Relationships

It has been argued that in general, excluding the most highly productive states with stratified occupational classes, the higher the productivity of a matrilineal society from cultivation, the more tightly organized the descent group and the stronger its authority structure. The particular factors most relevant to descent group strength appear to be: first, localization of the descent group on a relatively permanent site, especially if this is a jointly owned estate; second, land scarcity and the existence of valuable heritable immovable property such as buildings, trees, and other improvements to land; third, teamwork or division of functions within the descent group, requiring strong coordination of production; fourth, the need for redistributive processes by the head within the descent group and by higher authorities through the instrumentality of descent-group heads; and fifth, to some extent, incorporation of the descent group in a centralized state, since this gives its authority structure the sanction of organized force wielded by higher political authorities on behalf of the descent-group head. It was seen, however, that in the most centralized states with highest productivity, the descent group loses some functions and its head's authority narrows because of the development of a stratified occupational structure.

Correspondingly, I would argue that as the descent group becomes stronger as a result of increased productivity associated with these various factors, the ties of marriage, paternity, and affinity become proportionately weaker by comparison with matrilineal ties. Thus, in societies with lowest productivity from cultivation, an individual's shared interests in relation to his father, paternal kin, children, spouse, and spouse's kin are most evenly balanced against those with his matrilineal kin. In societies with higher productivity from cultivation, the marital, paternal, and affinal ties are proportionately weaker. There then appears the classic matrilineal contrast between the mother's brother as stern and disciplinary and the father as intimate and non-authoritative. Further, when we come to the most centralized states with highest productivity, even though the descent group surrenders some of its functions to the state and its head's authority is narrowed in the landowning, upper strata of the population, the shared interests of marriage, paternity, and affinity are not thereby strengthened but seem to reach their weakest point. In lower strata of the population with no rights or only slender rights in land produce, however, marital, paternal, and affinal ties are relatively strong by comparison with matrilineal ties, although all types of kinship relationships are subordinated to the obligations owed to higher economic and political authorities. I shall try to illustrate these statements by reference to the fifteen matrilineal systems.

Mobile Cultivators

TONGA AND NAVAHO

The Tonga and the Navaho were judged to have the lowest productivity of the mobile cultivators. In both these societies, in addition to his own matrilineal group, an individual has a kind of honorary life membership in his father's matrilineal group. This is legal and not merely affective. The group helps to provide and also receives bride-wealth; it becomes operative in vengeance; and it can be called on to pay compensation on ego's behalf. Among the Tonga the father's group supports a person in disputes with his own matrilineal kin and it can demand compensation from them if they wrongfully accuse him of sorcery. A man and his father's group also have obligations of mutual aid similar to those shared by matrilineal kin. The father's group must help an individual, ritually or practically, in illness, and among the Tonga it must propitiate the spirits of the father's matrilineal forebears on his behalf (Colson, 1951: 143–151).

The regularly shared interests of spouses are very strong in these societies. For many purposes they and their unmarried dependents form a separate coöperating unit, pooling products which are for immediate consumption. Divorce can certainly occur, and the individual may be involved with several different spouses at different periods. Nevertheless, economic coöperation with *a* spouse is most intensive during the greater part of most people's adult lives (chaps. 1 and 2, above).

The paternal tie is correspondingly important, legally and economically as well as affectively. The father is normally his young son's authority in matters of work, and he shares discipline of the children with the wife's male kin and may physically chastize them. Even after the parents' divorce, sons customarily help to support their fathers in later life, and may receive gifts of stock or other property from them. The father has recognized legal claims in relation to his children at their marriages, and an interest in their property if they predecease him.

In each society, also, a particular range of affinal ties has great significance for one or the other sex. Among the Tonga a youth was traditionally closely involved with his wife's parents or other elders in the initial period of uxorilocal residence. Later the wife might have close involvement with her husband's co-wives and their children. Among the Navaho, a man's relations with his wife's parents and other kin of the matrilocal grandfamily were the affinal ties of crucial significance.

NDEMBU

Among the Ndembu, ego is not separately attached as an honorary member of his father's matrilineal group, but other circumstances give a strongly bilateral character to the kinship system. Cross-cousin or alternate-generation marriage within the same village on the part of the parents causes many children to have their most significant paternal and maternal kin concentrated within the same relatively autonomous economic-coöperative unit. In the case of marriage to the matrilineal classificatory daughter's daughter, indeed—a preferred marriage among Ndembu—children of the marriage have their paternal and maternal kin within the same maximal matrilineage (Turner, 1957: 86, 244–247).

With regard to the father himself, Turner has described in some detail how the father's and mother's brother's roles are equivalent in many respects, rather than being sharply contrasted as in most matrilineal societies with settled cultivation (ibid.: 237). A son often stays in his father's village until the latter's death, rather than returning to his mother's brothers before or shortly after puberty, as is commonly the case among Trobriand Islanders, Mayombe, and North Kerala Nayars. Fathers commonly train their sons in hunting, house building, blacksmithing, and in the laws of the tribe. Most fathers assist their sons with bridewealth, and today represent them when necessary in court cases. When a youth's father and mother's brothers occupy the same village, both have predominantly authoritative roles in relation to him, the mother's brother's authority being only slightly stronger. The mother is similarly equated with the father's sister in many situations (ibid.: 237).

All of these kin are contrasted with affines of the preceding generation, relationships with whom are tense, avoidant, and non-authoritative
(*ibid.:* 240). Both the consanguine-affinal and the matrilineal-cognatic
distinctions tend to be obliterated in the non-authoritative relationships between kin of alternate generations (*ibid.:* 247). In general,
the marked spatial and social dichotomy between proximal generations
in the village and the alignment of alternate generations override distinctions between the roles of matrilineal and patrilateral kin.

In spite of a high divorce rate, again, the marriage tie is spoken of
by Ndembu as "the strongest and deepest they know" (*ibid.:* 78). The
elementary family coöperates in cultivation, pooling many products for
immediate consumption. Husband and wife are initiated into curative
and fertility cults together. Wives are said to outrank sisters in importance, a strong contrast to the situation found in settled cultivating
societies of higher productivity. High tension and partial avoidance
characterize both sexes' relations with affines of proximal generations,
but affines living in the same village are necessarily forced into common interest in its economic enterprises.

BEMBA

Kinship among the Bemba, with their relatively low productivity from
highly mobile cultivation, again has a markedly bilateral character.
The category of ego's personal bilateral kindred through both father
and mother has a collective name, *lupwa*. They figure collectively in
his life-crisis rites, they offer generalized support, and among them
they determine his status in society (Richards, 1951: 176). Fathers discipline and train their children. They later build up a following through
their daughters, daughters' children, and sometimes through their
sons. As in the tribes previously discussed, a father retains certain legal
rights in his children even if he divorces their mother. He must, for
example, be consulted about his daughter's marriage, and must receive
a part of her small marriage payment. Children take their father's name
as a kind of surname. They honor both father's and mother's ancestral
spirits, and they may have the spirit of a patrilateral ancestor reincarnated in them (*ibid.:* 174–175, 180). Through the father's authority
a special relationship obtains between a girl and her father's sister.
The latter plays an important part in a girl's initiation rites, and has the
right to request her brother's daughter as a co-wife. Frequently an older
woman may choose to leave her husband's village and go to live with
her brother; she may then bring in her brother's daughter as a substitute wife for her husband (Richards, 1940a: 45; 1951: 181). This
institution, in particular, points up the almost evenly balanced claims

of a woman's husband and her brother. In old age the latter may receive back his sister and her descendants to swell his village following,
provided that he surrenders a daughter in exchange.

The whole process of Bemba marriage seems in fact to be something
in the nature of a cycle. During initial uxorilocal residence the young
husband gradually weans his wife from her family, gaining more and
more rights in and control over her (Richards, 1940a: 50–72). In
middle life he may remove her completely to his own village, later to
surrender her to her family again in return for a younger spouse
(Richards, 1939: 115). Correspondingly, a man's main economic involvements in the early part of his marriage are with senior affines,
especially the wife's parents in the matrilocal grandfamily. His later
involvements are with his own descendants, daughters' husbands, and
sometimes sisters' children.

YAO

Among the Yao, with their probably higher productivity from cultivation and more stable cultivation sites, marital, patrilateral, and affinal
ties are much weaker by comparison with matrilineal ties than in the
tribes so far discussed. A matrilocally resident husband helps his wife
in her gardens and helps to support her children. His duties to her
parents are, however, more restricted than among the Bemba and he
is often absent in his natal village (Mitchell, 1951: 328–329; 1956:
118–119; 183–184). He is always an outsider in his wife's village—a
"billy goat," a "chicken rooster," or a "beggar," who merely followed
his wife (Richards, 1950: 233; Mitchell, 1956: 184). The importance
of the brother-sister tie is stressed at the expense of the marital one: a
woman summons the older brother who is her guardian to intervene in
every marital dispute, and he may command her to divorce her husband (Mitchell, 1951: 326, 335; 1956: 145–152). Correspondingly, only
the children of slave wives seem traditionally to have retained permanent obligations to the father and his lineage. The free children of a
headman might live for a time in his village, but before or after his
death they normally returned to their own. If they did stay to found a
new lineage in the village, this lineage shortly assumed considerable
autonomy and segregated itself spatially from the patrilateral kin.

A man who divorced his wife had no rights in nor legal obligations
to his children. While they were young they came under the paternal
care of the woman's subsequent husbands, and differences of paternity
did not create significant divisions within the sibling group. A divorced
father might choose to help his children from kindness, but his was a
highly personal, nonlegal relationship. It was contrasted for its in-

timacy but relative slightness with the harsher, more disciplinary, and legally significant relationship with the mother's brother (Mitchell, 1956: 163, 177–179; 186–197). In these respects the matrilineal-patrilateral contrast was comparable to that commonly found in settled cultivating societies. The difference was that among the Yao, new villages *could* be founded, and sisters' children could, therefore, sometimes secede in later life from their mothers' brothers. Probably for this reason, the guardianship of a woman and her children gradually passed from her mother's brother to her brother until the latter took over complete command of her minimal lineage.

Settled Cultivators

Among the settled cultivators, again, it is in the societies with lowest productivity that marital, patrilateral, and affinal ties are strongest by comparison with matrilineal ties. The former types of ties are probably never as evenly balanced against the matrilineal as in mobile cultivating societies of lowest productivity, but there are nevertheless significant differences of emphasis within the range of settled cultivating societies.

TRUK

Among the settled cultivators studied, marital and paternal interests are probably strongest on Truk. Divorce is "not uncommon," but while a marriage lasts a man works chiefly to support his wife, children, and wife's matrilocal extended family. He has authority over his wife and may beat her, but he must also respond to requests made on her behalf by her brother. A man spends most of his adult life working on the lineage land of one or another wife, coöperating in work with her brothers or sisters' husbands, and building up improvements to the land which will be inherited by her children.

As has been seen, a slow process of continual reallocation of land and/or its improvements goes on between lineages through the mechanism of paternal bequests to children, and this gives fathers early authority over—and later, claims on—their children (chap. 3, above). A man is his children's chief disciplinarian before puberty; the affective relationship seems to be harder and less sentimental than is common in settled cultivating societies of higher productivity (Gladwin and Sarason, 1953: 86–88). Even if he divorces their mother, a man owes maintenance and shelter to his young children and they owe him services both in youth and in later life. Children also have legal obligations to their father in that they must act as a vengeance group on his behalf if he is murdered by a lineage kinsman, or if he or his lineage kinsmen are driven by enemies from their land (Goodenough, 1951: 149). Children inherit full title to the land of a father whose lineage is dying out for lack of women. They are bound to their father through the gift of provisional title to improvements which he makes on their own lineage land and bequeaths to them, for they must pay him a share of the produce as long as he is alive. While his children are young, therefore, a father appears to exert authority over them comparable to that exercised by their mother's brother.

Probably because the Trukese lineage has a short life cycle due to fluctuations in land tenure, and also because the younger generation are chiefly responsible for the food supply, both father and mother's brother lose much of their disciplinary authority after a child reaches puberty, and authority passes instead to the eldest brother of the sibling group (Gladwin and Sarason, 1953: 95–97; Goodenough, 1951: 76–77). The segmentary character of the lineage structure—with its active younger heads of sibling groups and its weaker older head, and the eldest brother's legal guardianship of his juniors and power to coerce his sisters' husbands—thus in many ways resembles the Yao situation. The chief difference is that Yao sibling groups segregate themselves through acquisition of new lands which they develop, whereas Trukese sibling groups segregate themselves from the rest of the lineage through paternal bequests of land and its improvements. This difference accounts for the greater strength of marital and paternal interests on Truk.

HOPI

Although their descent group has a longer life cycle than the Trukese lineage and greater permanence in relation to land, the Hopi have relatively strong marital, patrilateral, and affinal ties by comparison with settled cultivators of higher productivity. Divorce is common and Eggan states that both men's and women's primary loyalties are to their own clans; nevertheless, while a marriage endures the husband must devote most of his energies to working his wife's fields and contributing generally to the support of his wife, her children, and her matrilocal grandfamily (Eggan, 1950: 31, 34). Indeed, at a marriage the mother's brother of the bridegroom adjures him to coöperate diligently with his father-in-law and to work harder on his wife's clan's land than on his own (ibid.: 55–56). The shared interests of Hopi spouses are, certainly, weaker than among the Navaho with their mobile cultivation and herding, for a Hopi man keeps his most important ceremonial objects and other movables in his natal house and returns to it as his home. Marriage, or a series of marriages, does however involve a man in extensive economic coöperation with his father-in-law and his wife's sisters' husbands on behalf of their common conjugal household.

Correspondingly, the father has well-defined obligations to and rights in his children, whether or not he subsequently divorces their mother. He instructs his sons in farming and herding, chooses their ceremonial fathers for the initiation rite, and gives them sheep and other movable property at their marriages. Often a father gives his son a piece of his own clan land to cultivate after the latter's marriage. Sons must officiate at their father's funeral, the one who plays the most important role inheriting the bulk of his movable property. A father contributes to the expenses of his daughter's marriage, makes her marriage clothing, and later maintains a close and indulgent interest in her children (*ibid.:* 31–33). Similarly, the father's matrilineal kin have strong interests in his children, even if he should divorce their mother. The father's sister makes gifts at all the life-crisis rites in which a girl is involved, and should in return receive help from her in various household tasks such as house plastering or water carrying. The father's sister names a boy by the name of one of her own clansmen. When he grows up the boy makes gifts to her and has an intimate joking relationship with her. This is also extended in the form of rough joking with her husband concerning mutual jealousy over the woman who unites them (*ibid.:* 39–41; Titiev, 1944: 27–28).

The Hopi do make what has usually been regarded as the typical "matrilineal" contrast between the mother's brother's role as distant and disciplinary, and the father's role as intimate and relatively unauthoritative. The contrast does not, however, appear to be as sharp as in settled cultivating societies of higher productivity. Male authority in the descent group is, as we have seen, rather diffuse and unspecific, for land is allocated in severalty to sub-clan members, and the group coöperates only seasonally in collective economic activities. The etiquette of behavior in relation to the mother's brother is relatively informal. Indeed, a woman may joke mildly with her mother's brother about her jealousy of his affection for his father's sister. Such a form of behavior would be unthinkable in the more "classic" matrilineal societies with strongly organized descent groups. Correspondingly, the father's role is gently authoritative and disciplinary, as becomes an elder who is largely responsible for his children's training and welfare (Titiev, 1944: 17–19, 25–26).

TROBRIAND

With the Trobriand Islanders we have a somewhat more "classic" matrilineal pattern than appears among either the Trukese or the Hopi.

Within the avunculocal village, husband and wife coöperate as a gardening team and manage their separate household. The husband has considerable authority, and can claim damages and may beat his wife if she commits adultery; in this respect his rights in her are stronger than those of a Hopi husband. Nevertheless, husband and wife retain their strongest economic and emotional ties with their own descent groups, in particular with their respective linked siblings of opposite sex. Throughout her married life the wife is maintained almost entirely by gifts of food brought by her brother to her husband on her behalf, while the husband is busy amassing yams to give to his sister elsewhere. The men of a descent group are, moreover, involved together in many important economic undertakings from which their wives are excluded. Neither sex is involved in extensive productive coöperation with affines.

The father's role, correspondingly, is polarized with respect to that of the mother's brother. The father is nurse and early protector of his children, exercising only the mildest discipline. By the dogma of descent he is not really a kinsman at all, his obligations to his children being phrased as payment for sexual rights in their mother. He is expected to show a personal interest in his children if they experience distress, illness, or danger from enemies, and he has certain customary obligations: he performs ceremonies and averts black magic from his daughter during her pregnancy and at the birth of her child. As representative of her mother he may arrange his daughter's marriage, but he cannot gainsay the girl's mother's brother if the latter requests her as a wife for his son. A father receives valuables as part of the bridewealth paid by his daughter's husband. After their marriages, however, a father normally loses control over his children of both sexes, for they disperse, the sons to their natal villages and the daughters to their husbands'. The mother's brother, by contrast, has permanent legal rights in a man's services and a woman's procreative powers by virtue of descent-group membership. His juniors owe him formal respect and his relationship with them, especially with the sister's sons, is disciplinary and emotionally tense.

The father's descent group appears to retain only a weak interest in his children in the Trobriands with no mandatory legal rights or obligations, although the son has a privileged relationship of sexual joking with women of his father's generation and may marry one of their daughters (chap. 4, above).

MAYOMBE

The information available on the Mayombe points to strongly organized descent groups based on valuable immovable property and a corresponding weakness of normal marital, affinal, and patrilateral ties. The situation was evidently complicated, however, by male management of trade and by the existence of numerous slaves, circumstances which may have been responsible for the apparently subordinate position of women in the society as a whole. De Cleene describes the wife as no more than a servant in her husband's avunculocal village; he could have her killed, for example, if she committed adultery (De Cleene, 1937: 4). Marriage was often polygynous, and some men, especially chiefs and perhaps village headmen, had numerous slave wives who, with their children, belonged entirely to the husband and were inherited by his descent group.

On the other hand, a free wife owed strictly limited obligations to her husband and his descent group and maintained her strongest ties with her natal unit. "Marriage dies," say the Mayombe, "but relationship (i.e., matrilineal kinship) does not die." A woman had her own fields within her husband's village and owed the husband only half of her crop; the rest she sent to her matrilineal kin to pave the way for her sons' future residence in their village. She owed only limited and well-defined services to her husband's descent groups, and for extra work such as processing palm products she had to be paid a fee which went back to her natal group. Conversely, a wife had no rights in her husband's personal fields, cloth, money, or other movable wealth. His matrilineal kin kept a strict eye on her and became jealous if the husband gave her more than was necessary for subsistence—a situation exactly duplicated among avunculocal North Kerala Nayars. Marriage was thus a restricted contract in which the woman's descent group, on reception of bridewealth, "hired" her to provide limited services for the period of her married life. In return, the woman's group demanded children as its heirs, judged the husband by his worth as a genitor, and if the marriage was childless might divorce him, return the bridewealth, and give the woman in marriage elsewhere.

The father's rights in his freeborn children were correspondingly restricted. While they lived in his village he could command his sons' labor and earnings and was responsible for their debts and maintenance. On her marriage day the father of a girl had rights to a small portion of her bridewealth as compensation for her early care. Free children were, however, unequivocally under the authority of their own descent-group head. The father had no right to discipline them, but sent a recalcitrant son to his mother's brother for correction. Conversely, a son whose father ill-treated him ran away to his mother's brothers, who returned him only if the father pleaded for pardon. Their descent-group head could if he wished command children to come and live with him, and boys usually left the father's village as early as the age of ten. If their mother died or was divorced, children were removed by their guardian. If a child fell ill, his father had to summon the head of the child's descent group so that the latter might consult a diviner; if the father failed in this obligation and the child died, the father owed damages to his wife's descent group. Similarly, if the diviner judged the father guilty of witchcraft, he had to pay damages to the child's guardian, but if a matrilineal kinsman of the child was accused, the father received no compensation. The father's normal relationship with his children is described as affectionate and unauthoritative, their mother being the disciplinarian in their early childhood, and the mother's brothers, in later life. If a son's descent group became involved in feud with that of his father, however, the son was obliged to oppose him on behalf of his own matrilineal group. A father could demand no services of his adult children, and is reported therefore to have often shown preference for his slaves. In general the elementary family is described as very weakly structured, with the wife constantly reminding her husband that he had no rights in her children, and with the children normally leaving their father's care at an early age (*ibid.*: 3–14; Richards, 1950: 215–221).

ASHANTI

The Ashanti in most respects typify what have often been regarded as the "classic" characteristics of matrilineal descent. Among them the married couple need not even necessarily co-reside, and apparently seldom did so traditionally (Fortes, 1959, *passim*). Marriage, established by the bridewealth payment, gave the husband exclusive sexual rights in his wife and the "right to essential domestic and economic services" (Fortes, 1950: 280). These services must have been quite limited, for the wife did not have to reside in her husband's home; traditionally, a woman appears to have been obliged to cook for her husband, at least the evening meal, which she carried to the house of his lineage head (Busia, 1951: 6–7). The husband in turn owed his wife sexual satisfaction, care in sickness, payment of any debts she contracted, clothing, and housing if she had none. He had to obtain her consent before he remarried. A husband also owed his wife food, but presumably women grew a large proportion of their food in their own lineage fields, at least traditionally. Since only 26 per cent of married women lived with their husbands at Agogo, the more traditional of the two modern villages studied by Fortes, it seems probable that both sexes have traditionally maintained by far the strongest shared interests with their own matrilineal kin (Fortes, 1949: 77). Typically, a man is said to have entrusted weighty matters to his sister, never to his wife (Fortes, 1950: 274–275).

The marriage payment gives the father legal paternity of his children, but this again involves very restricted rights and obligations. It is true that the patrilineal descent line is emphasized in the concept of ntoro; as Fortes points out, however, this does not involve any corporate organization based on the father's line, but only common ritual observances and an emphasis on the personal nature of the tie between father and son (*ibid.*: 266–267). The father has "no legal authority over his children" (*ibid.*: 268) and his only strictly legal obligation appears to have been to pay damages if his son committed adultery. A father cannot require a child to live with him. It is his "duty and pride" to feed, clothe, and educate them, but if he divorces the mother, only a "conscientious" father continues to care for them, from choice rather than necessity. A father has customary rights to help in the arranging of his children's marriages, he may make gifts of property to them, and they play a role in his funeral rites. In general, as Fortes notes, it is to social relationships in which voluntary choice can play a part that the paternal tie gives a man access, but these relationships affect only his personal life and not his public character and roles. Correspondingly, the affective tie with the father is typically represented as one of "warmth, trust, and affection" and is sharply contrasted with the stern, legally authoritative and often unaffectionate relationship of mother's brother and sister's son. The father's sister and other kin are respected because of the personal tie with the father, but a man evidently has no definite customary obligations to or rights in them. Correspondingly, neither sex becomes regularly involved with affines, even the parents-in-law, in mandatory forms of economic or other coöperation (*ibid.*: 270, 277–278, 283).

MINANGKABAU

In Minangkabau, one of the societies with highest productivity from cultivation, the shared interests of marital, affinal, and paternal ties are considerably weaker even than in Ashanti. Traditionally, husband and wife did not normally co-reside: a husband visited his wife, chiefly for sexual purposes. He was a "borrowed man" and a "rooster"; he had no rights in his wife's lineage's property, nor she in his (Cole, 1936: 20). The only definite legal claims which marriage seems to have involved were exclusive sexual rights on the part of the husband and rights to very limited domestic services from the wife, and on the wife's side, claims on the husband's sexuality and perhaps rights to certain small personal gifts. Wealthy men might have as many as four wives, whom they visited in turn. Divorce was freely available for both partners, so that a girl of twenty might have already married five or six times.

In contrast to Central Kerala Nayars, the Minangkabau did permit limited, optional economic coöperation on the part of husband and wife and of the elementary family. This seems to have resulted from the fact that (in contrast to Nayars) Minangkabau women did some agricultural work in severalty. Thus, when she married, a woman was given a plot of her own to work. If he wished, her husband might help her with her plot; in this case the couple jointly controlled the produce, although they also had to contribute to the upkeep of the woman's matrilineal household (*ibid.:* 20). Any earnings from a couple's joint work were divided equally at divorce or death—the husband's share in the latter case going to his lineage (De Jong, 1951: 56–57).

Correspondingly—again in contrast to Central Kerala Nayars—the elementary family had some spatial segregation within the wife's lineage household: each married woman had a room set aside for herself, her husband, and children. Her brothers might not enter it, but instead occupied the common room at the front of the house. When they were not with their wives they slept with bachelors in the communal religious house (Cole, 1936: 20). In spite of this potential exclusiveness of the elementary family, however, cooking was communal in the wife's joint household. Moreover, marital economic coöperation was strictly voluntary. A man in any case owed by far his most onerous economic obligations in his own lineage home. Traditionally, in fact, most husbands gave their wives only "small presents and a little cash," each woman being maintained very largely by her brothers and her lineage as a whole (Schrieke, 1955: 117). A man could not give self-acquired property to his wife or children except with the consent of his lineage and of a village council. If he did not work for his wife, a man paid her family separately for any food they served to him. If he wished, he might live always in his natal home, eat there, be nursed there when sick, and visit his wife only at night (Cole, 1936: 20). De Jong seems justified in regarding the Minangkabau as a society in which the elementary family was not, therefore, legally organized as a co-residential and economic unit, although it might in fact be so optionally in a minority of cases (De Jong, 1951: 11).

Father and children, correspondingly, appear to have had no mutual legal rights, and hardly any customarily recognized moral rights. A man might if he wished give movables to his children, but he need not do so (*ibid.:* 89–90). He evidently owed them no maintenance in law,

and they owed him no support in old age. He had no right whatsoever
to discipline them, shape their careers, or even arrange their marriages.
The affective content of the relationship is not described, except that
Loeb says the father displays "not the least concern" with his children
(1934: 47). The relationship with the mother's brothers, by contrast,
has all the classic components of authority, respect, sternness, and
social distance. The father's kin are said to have sent small presents to
the mother's house on the occasion of his child's first haircutting and at
other life-crisis rites. The obligations of affinal and patrilateral kin seem
in general to have been confined to such limited gift giving and ceremonial duties (De Jong, 1951: 64).

MAPPILLA, TIYYAR, AND NAYAR
(NORTH AND CENTRAL KERALA)

In North Kerala, a society with probably higher productivity from
cultivation than Minangkabau, the less nucleated settlement pattern
necessitated at least partial co-residence of spouses. This led, of course,
to more regular association between them, between father and child,
and between certain categories of affines. In the landowning castes of
North Kerala Nayars and aristocratic Mappillas, however, the legal
obligations of these relationships were no stronger than in Minangkabau, and the customary ones only slightly more so. Among Nayars
marriage gave the husband exclusive rights in his wife's sexuality and
the right to have her live in his natal home if her own was too distant
for him to visit her conveniently. If her home was near by, however, he
could not complain if she lived there for long periods. In any case she
spent the greater part of a year at home each time a child was born.

While she lived in his house the wife owed her husband very limited
domestic services, chiefly cookery. If the husband's mother or widowed
sisters lived at home, they would in fact shoulder most of the burden,
giving the wife the less arduous tasks and leaving her largely free to
care for her children. Women did little agricultural work for either
their husbands or their natal groups. A wife and her children were at
least partly maintained by grain sent from their natal household, a fact
which further weakened the economic coöperation of the elementary
family. Given matrilineal descent, therefore, high productivity from
settled agriculture—plus the Nayars' role as a landowning aristocracy
only partly responsible for the agricultural work on their property—
reduced marital coöperation to very limited proportions. A wife left
her husband's lineage home immediately on his death, was forbidden to
reënter it thereafter, and had no rights in any of his property after his
death. Theoretically, at least, a husband could give his wife self-ac-

quired property during life only with the consent of his property group, which meant, in fact, that only heads of property groups, and seldom those, could do so. Neither spouse mourned formally for the other or had any part in the other's funeral rites.

Among North Kerala Nayars the father owed his children shelter and, if necessary, food, while they lived with him as children. Their taravād was expected to supply most of their food and clothing. The father had limited *de facto* authority over his young children, but he exercised it with great restraint and commonly with tenderness. He could not override their matrilineal guardian in any important matter. He was customarily consulted about their marriages, especially that of his daughter, over whom he had a kind of moral claim as a wife for his own nephew. The father had no redress, however, if a child's kāranavan arranged a marriage against his will. For all practical purposes the father's claims lapsed when his children left his house—the son, normally, about the time of puberty, and the daughter, on marriage. A man who divorced or was divorced by his wife lost all customary claims on his children's attention, although they were expected to observe ritual pollution at his death and might return out of respect to take part in his funeral rites. Until 1896, children had no right of inheritance of the father's personal property. Patrilateral kin and affines had only ceremonial obligations, such as the giving of small gifts and a minor role in the life-crisis rites of birth, girls' initiations, and marriage. Thus, in spite of the co-residence of married couples, the obligations of both sexes were overwhelmingly to their own matrilineal kin.

With minor differences traceable to the different norms of residence, and perhaps, also, to differences of religious ideology, the aristocratic Mappilla system was very similar to the Nayar. The husband was normally involved in no productive coöperation with his wife or her natal unit, even though he lived with them. He owed his wife's household gifts of food or cash which would cover his own expenses while he lived with them and, if anything, leave only a small margin as contribution to the upkeep of the household as a whole. He was not strictly required to make personal gifts to wife or children other than those needed to establish his legal paternity at the birth of a child, although he often did give them at least part of their regular clothing, and might provide other movable wealth. The husband had exclusive sexual rights in his wife and rights in her domestic services as long as he lived with her, and, as among the Minangkabau, he and she enjoyed the use of a room set aside for themselves and their children. Mappilla marriage seems even traditionally to have been endowed with a kind of religious sanctity not found among the matrilineal Hindus—as seen, for example, in the practice of ceremonial mourning by a bereaved spouse. But until the second half of the nineteenth century, when men became able to endow their wives with property acquired personally through transactions of the market, the legal and customary obligations of marriage were extremely restricted.

Correspondingly, aristocratic Mappillas had very few categorical rights in their children. A child owed his father respect, affection, and a measure of obedience in return for care and partial maintenance, but the father had no legal guardianship and always deferred to the resident head of the child's matrilineal property group. Fathers were consulted about their children's marriages but probably could not enforce their choice. We have seen also that a man's slender personal rights in his daughter were in large measure transferred to her husband at her marriage, and that he lost all practical claims on his son when the latter married and moved to the house of his wife. As among Nayars, adult children's customary and mandatory obligations to their father consisted of little more than ceremonial obligations at his funeral. Patrilateral kin and affines, especially the co-resident husbands of a matrilocal household, owed gifts and ceremonial participation in life-crisis rites. They were not, however, traditionally involved in productive or other regular forms of coöperation.

The North Kerala Tiyyars and low-caste Mappillas are interesting examples of what can happen to matrilineal systems in the lower strata of a highly productive, centralized, and heterogeneous society. The ideal residence form among Tiyyars as among Nayars was the avunculocal extended family, but the matrilineal, joint property-owning unit was not securely based on the control of a highly productive landed estate. The "estate" of the Tiyyar matrilineal group consisted rather of the hereditary right to a house site and garden, and to serve and lease fields from a Nayar landowning lineage segment. Such matrilineally inherited ties to landlords may also not have been very stable, so that it may even traditionally have been possible for some sons to acquire attachment to their fathers' landlords, but the evidence here is uncertain. In any case, women's agricultural work was important, so that a woman became an integral productive member of her husband's residential unit. While her marriage endured a woman owed her husband exclusive sexual privileges, full domestic services, agricultural work such as weeding and harvesting in his family's leased fields, and also, as a member of his family, seasonal work on the private domain of his

Nayar landlord. The husband owed shelter, food, and clothing to his wife and their immature children.

Polygyny was fairly common, so that a wife often coöperated in production with co-wives as well as with other wives of the husband's residential group. On the other hand, a woman received separate remuneration in grain and other perquisites from her husband's landlord for her services, and these gave her a measure of independence. After a few years of marriage a Tiyyar wife commonly insisted on a separate hut and hearth for herself and her husband and children. The woman's personal productive work thus permitted the elementary family an exclusiveness not found among Nayars. At the same time, however, it allowed a woman to reinforce her ties with her own natal unit, for she customarily took back a part of her earnings to her mother's household to pay for her own visits home and to keep the way open for her sons' later return there. The husband's group also owed the wife an annual portion of the paddy she cut in their own leased fields, for surrender to her natal family.

Although spouses coöperated continuously in daily life, therefore, the woman's personal services to landlords gave her a measure of economic independence. Further, any surplus wealth earned by either sex was, as probably in all matrilineal cultivating societies, regarded as rightfully belonging to their own matrilineal groups. Finally, the economic independence of women appears to have facilitated a high divorce rate, so that marital economic coöperation, although the most important form, was often of short duration in particular instances.

The father among Tiyyars was wholly responsible for his immature children's care and maintenance, and could wholly command their labor as long as they lived with him. If his marriage endured, he had the right to arrange his daughter's marriage. Marriage to the father's nephew was regarded as a prescribed form and not merely a preferential one as among Nayars or Mappillas. A man whose daughter made such a marriage would retain a measure of legal authority over her, as head of her husband's residential unit. Alternatively, if a son married his father's niece the father might also keep the couple living with him for a time, and might later retain their sons as members of his residential unit, as occasionally happened among Nayars. Patrilocal residence seems traditionally, however, to have been a privileged rather than a customary form. A father whose children married elsewhere lost all claims on them, although they were expected to mourn his death. A man who divorced his wife also lost his rights in the children, who were cared for by their mother's brother or else moved temporarily with the mother to a subsequent husband. Apart from the economic coöperation engendered by co-residence and joint production in the avunculocal extended family, patrilateral and affinal ties among Tiyyars, as among Nayars, involved only small gift giving and ceremonial obligations at life-crisis rites.

Information on the traditional low-caste Mappilla system is inadequate for full comparison, but a general picture emerges which is somewhat similar to that of the Tiyyars. The husband, here matrilocally resident, was largely responsible for maintaining his wife and children as long as he stayed with them, and so he wielded a measure of domestic authority. On the other hand women's personal work in agriculture for landlords seems here, as among Tiyyars, to have permitted a high divorce rate, and the divorced husband lost his claims on the children. In general, in both of these lower castes, it may be said that absence of a valuable joint estate weakened the economic coöperation and authority structure of the descent group. Matrilineal ties remained the only durable ones, focused on a hereditary house site and the hereditary right to work for and receive produce from higher-caste masters. These ties also provided the nucleus of the main economic-coöperative unit, as an avunculocal or a matrilocal extended family, but members absent in their spouses' units had much less intensive ties with their natal units than in the landowning castes. Correspondingly, the elementary family had much more intensive ties of daily economic coöperation. At the same time, women's productive work for landlords gave them a comparative independence which permitted a high divorce rate, so that elementary family ties, though strong, were also brittle. In emergency, also, the individual could turn as of right only to matrilineal kin; he had no durable legal ties to his father's matrilineal group, as he had in the societies of lowest productivity from mobile cultivation. Finally, the authority of higher-caste landlords overrode that of kinsfolk both in the operations of production and, ultimately, in the legal sphere.

Central Kerala Nayars belong to the society of highest productivity from cultivation and greatest degree of political centralization. Among them the shared interests of marital, paternal, and affinal ties reach their absolute minimum. Marriage was a group sharing of sexual rights. It was in law limited only by incest prohibitions extending to the clan and to a narrow range of affines, by the prohibition of sexual relations between a Nayar woman and a man of lower Nayar caste, and by the prohibition of relations between Nayars as a caste category and all members of lower, non-Nayar castes. The individual marital tie (sam-bandham) involved as economic obligations only the husband's small seasonal gifts signifying continuance of the relationship, and other token gifts to establish legitimacy at the birth of a child. It did not involve co-residence, sexual exclusiveness, maintenance, or domestic services. Except for the establishment of legal paternity, father and child had no legal or customary rights in each other. Individual patri-lateral and affinal kin lacked even the customary ceremonial obliga-tions at life-crisis rites required of them in North Kerala. These roles were fulfilled instead by the linked lineages in their hereditary relation-ship of "perpetual affinity."

I have argued already that the absence of any significant economic content in the marital and paternal relationships was made possible by the Nayars' reliance on highly productive, matrilineally owned joint estates, by the nucleated settlement pattern which facilitated duolocal residence, and perhaps by the fact that Nayar men did very little productive work in any case, so that they could hardly have been called on to produce on behalf of their wives and children. The institu-tion of group marriage itself, which dispersed the slender roles of hus-band and father between a number of men, I have tentatively traced to the military organization, suggesting as a probability that political officers may have encouraged or even enforced group marriage as a means of minimizing the individual familistic ties of their vassals.

General Comments

(1) I have argued that in matrilineal societies, the higher the produc-tivity of the society from subsistence cultivation, the weaker the shared interests of spouses, father and child, patrilateral kin, and affines, rela-tive to those of matrilineal kin. This may seem strange in view of my earlier argument that there is a point on the scale of increasing pro-ductivity and political centralization where matrilineal descent be-comes no longer feasible and a shift must be made to some form of bilateral or patrilineal system. One might therefore have expected that the matrilineal societies at the top of the scale of productivity and political centralization would have been the least strongly rather than the most strongly matrilineal. The crux seems to be that increasing productivity does strengthen the matrilineal descent group and weaken both marriage and ties of complementary filiation, so long as the matri-lineage or lineage segment can remain as the unit of joint ownership of property and coöperative economic enterprise. The latter situation ceases to exist, however, when economic changes occur which permit

men to enter individual positions of access to livelihood or to accumulate personal property as a source of livelihood. The conditions which brought this about in Kerala—as in many other matrilineal societies in modern times—were those of entry into a market system in the second half of the nineteenth century, in which both land and the labor of individuals became treated as commodities. Then, even though the Nayars had probably had the "strongest" matrilineal system in the world, the disintegration of matrilineal groups, and the emergence of the elementary family as the key unit in a bilateral system, proceeded apace.

(2) It should be noted that although my hypothesis relates to the strength of shared interests of various kinship relationships, it tells us nothing about divorce rates. All the societies of our examples—and, I would hypothesize, all matrilineal societies—permit divorce, but the information is inadequate for a ranking of divorce rates. What information there is suggests that this is not very closely related to mere levels of productivity, but to more specific economic factors. Thus the Ndembu, Hopi, Minangkabau, and Central Kerala Nayars appear to have had very high rates of divorce or marital separation, whereas those of the Tonga, Bemba, and North Kerala Nayars were probably lower, and that of North Kerala aristocratic Mappillas very low. The amount of bridewealth paid and the productive importance and potential economic independence of women may be among the significant influential factors, as well as the extent of reliance of each spouse on the natal matrilineal group. I have no hypothesis to offer for divorce rates, other than the negative comment that these rates do not seem to be closely related to the extent of economic or other coöperation between husband and wife, as opposed to that between matrilineal kin.

(3) It may be worth pointing out that if my hypothesis concerning levels of productivity from cultivation and strength or weakness of marital and paternal ties in matrilineal societies is correct, the converse may be true of patrilineal systems. Thus in patrilineal societies one would expect that the higher the productivity from subsistence cultivation, the tighter the organization of the patrilineal descent group and the stronger its authority structure. This would mean, however—contrary to the situation in matrilineal descent—that in societies of higher productivity women would be *more* closely incorporated into their husbands' descent groups and their ties with their natal units more severely weakened, because women, in patriliny as in matriliny, give birth to the descent group's heirs. Correspondingly, one would expect matrilateral and affinal ties to be weakest in patrilineal societies

of highest productivity from subsistence cultivation, and strongest in those of lowest productivity. This suggestion is very tentative, but it may merit further exploration. I cannot even guess whether this hypothesis would also apply to patrilineal societies primarily reliant on some subsistence base other than cultivation.

(4) I must emphasize that the hypothesis concerning levels of productivity and descent-group strength in matrilineal systems refers only to those groups primarily reliant on subsistence cultivation. The examples are too few to judge what happens when a matrilineal society shifts from cultivation to some other dominant subsistence base. I suspect that if it comes to rely very predominantly on male hunting, herding, or trade, a move toward patrilineal descent is likely, regardless of the level of productivity. The Tonga, Ndembu, and low-caste North Kerala Mappillas may all be examples of societies in which a partial shift from cultivation to some other subsistence base had in one way or another weakened matrilineal descent groups, but in which cultivation was still important enough for weak matrilineal units to endure. Historical evidence is lacking, however, with which to support or refute such a suggestion.

Factors Influencing the Etiquette of Behavior in Interpersonal Kinship Relationships

Although my study led to interesting insights into connections, in each particular society, between descent-group structure, economic relations, and residence patterns on the one hand, and the etiquette of behavior between various categories of kin on the other, it did not prove possible to develop comprehensive theories covering all relationships in all the societies. Thus, for example, the study led to no general theory of avoidance and joking relationships in matrilineal systems. Some limited hypotheses for particular relationships did, however, emerge, which will now be presented.

MATRILINEAL KIN

Brother and Sister As Schneider has pointed out in the introduction, a particular type of tension is likely to exist in the brother-sister relationship with matrilineal descent. On the one hand brother and sister are bound by common descent-group membership, which requires special coöperation and amity and may well engender deep affection. The brother is, further, specifically interested in his sister's sexual and reproductive capacities as a source of potential heirs. On the other hand the incest taboo precludes sexual intimacy between them.

This source of tension often appears to receive recognition in the form of prohibitions of behavior between brother and sister which might be construed, in the society concerned, as having a directly or indirectly sexual content. The picture *is* complicated by the fact that in societies where, in addition to common descent-group membership, the brother has legal authority over his sister (e.g., Yao and Truk), restrictions of behavior associated with dominance and submission are added to those associated with the incest taboo (chap. 3, above; Mitchell, 1956: 145–152). Further, the "sexual" prohibitions themselves range from prohibition of a limited number of behavioral acts, such as touching the bridewealth cattle of the sister or sitting on her bed, as among the Tonga, to the much more extensive avoidance found, for example, among Central Kerala Nayars (chaps. 1 and 6, above).

In general, however, it seems probable that the majority of matrilineal societies will have *some* forms of restriction—other than the incest taboo itself—relating to sexually relevant behavior between brother and sister, and that certainly such restrictions will, on average, appear more prominently in matrilineal than in patrilineal societies. Thus, of the fifteen groups studied, twelve are known to have had some such forms of prohibition in the brother-sister relationship: Tonga, Navaho, Ndembu, Bemba, Yao, Truk, Trobriand, Minangkabau, and the four Kerala castes. Information is lacking for the Mayombe; the Hopi and Ashanti do not appear to have had any special prohibitions (Eggan, 1950: 36; Fortes, 1950: 273–274).

No very satisfactory theory was developed to account for these differences. A possible explanation may, however, lie in residence patterns. Thus, the kinds of taboos discussed *may* be most likely to develop in societies where the woman's brother and her husband are in close residential proximity, either sharing the same homestead or small settlement or frequently visiting it. The taboos are relatively limited among the Tonga, Navaho, Bemba, and Ndembu, among whom the husband and brother of a woman may sometimes occupy the same settlement but often do not do so (chaps. 1 and 2, above; Richards, 1940a: 41–42, 47; Turner, 1957: 251–252). The taboos appear to be more strongly developed among Yao, Trukese, and Trobriand Islanders (Mitchell, 1956: 146; chaps. 3 and 4, above). Among the Yao and Trukese the woman's husband and her brother are in frequent close contact since the brother is his sister's immediate legal guardian in many respects and either lives near her or visits frequently. Trobriand brother and sister are more frequently separated in different villages, but brothers-in-law may occupy the same village in cases of cross-cousin marriage, and a brother must visit his married sister often in connection with urigubu payments.

The prohibitions seem to be most pronounced among Minangkabau and Central Kerala Nayars (Loeb, 1934: 42; Cole, 1936: 20). Here brothers share a joint homestead with their sisters and come into frequent contact with the sisters' visiting husbands. In both cases the brother is allowed to enter only the communal portions of the homestead and may not penetrate the rooms occupied by his sisters and their husbands. Brother-sister avoidance reaches its highest point among Nayar royalty, where both husbands and brothers of the women live permanently in the palace. A prince born into the palace may not enter the private suites of his kinswomen after the age of fifteen. He may request an audience with a kinswoman of his mother's generation in a public room of the palace, but should not see "sisters" of his own generation except at a distance. Brahman husbands of the princesses, by contrast, have free access to the private rooms of their wives. Compared with Central Kerala Nayars, brother-sister taboos are slightly less emphasized among North Kerala Mappillas, where brothers are more often absent. Nevertheless they are similarly restricted from visiting their sisters' rooms when on visits to the natal home. Although definite prohibitions exist, they are still less emphasized among North Kerala Nayars and Tiyyars, where husband and brother-in-law only infrequently co-reside.

It may be, therefore, that Hopi and Ashanti do not require special taboos in the brother-sister relationship because brothers-in-law seldom co-reside. Hopi brothers-in-law normally occupy the same village, but a man and his wife's married brother would seem less likely to converge often on the same homestead than, for example, among Central Kerala Nayars or in Minangkabau. Among the Ashanti, brothers-in-law apparently never co-resided (Fortes, 1949: 76). They occupied different wards of the village and a woman either lived with her husband or else lived with her brothers and visited the husband in his home.

It must be admitted, however, that although residential patterns do seem to have some relevance to the strength of brother-sister taboos, they probably do not wholly explain either the incidence or the strength of these prohibitions. As Murdock (1949: 273) and others have pointed out, some societies simply do not use "external," formal prohibitions to enforce sexual restrictions, but seem to rely instead on internalization of prohibitions during socialization. This may well be the reason for the absence of brother-sister behavioral taboos among Ashanti and

Hopi, for neither society had well elaborated patterns of avoidance toward any categories of kin.

Matrilineally Related Men A different kind of social distance, sometimes amounting to partial avoidance, may exist between matrilineally related men. In this case the degree of social distance seems to be directly related to the degree of authority in the relationship, and its function seems to be to prevent overt aggression or rebellious action on the part of the junior man.

In all matrilineal descent groups there is some social distance between men of proximate generations, associated with authority on the part of seniors and respect on the part of juniors. The etiquette of behavior is least formal, however, in societies of lower productivity such as the Tonga, Navaho, Ndembu, and Hopi (chaps. 1 and 2, above; Turner, 1957: 240–242; Titiev, 1944: 25). It is also rather informal among Trukese, where the descent group has a relatively short life cycle and *de facto* authority early tends to pass from the mother's brother to the eldest brother in ego's own generation (Goodenough, 1951: 113; Gladwin and Sarason, 1953: 95). Formal respect toward the mother's brother is more strongly emphasized in the societies of higher productivity, and reaches its peak of social distance among Central Kerala Nayars. Here the relationship is almost one of avoidance: the junior must not approach within several feet of his senior, must not address him first, speaks softly behind his hand when required to speak, and when possible avoids the senior's presence. In this group such very formal behavior is made possible by the fact that senior and junior men seldom engage in joint productive activities. Rather, both depend for their livelihood on land cultivated mainly by caste subordinates; they are therefore able to avoid frequent contacts and even to live in separate parts of the homestead. His lack of significance as a producer also traditionally made the junior male's role more dependent and submissive, since he owned his livelihood almost entirely to the descent-group head. The formality of this relationship was somewhat relaxed among Nayars of North Kerala, who cultivated together. It was still more relaxed among North Kerala Tiyyars and low-caste Mappillas, where descent-group men came collectively under the authority of high-caste superiors and employers, and the descent-group head's authority over his matrilineal juniors was correspondingly weaker. Young men's importance in production was also relevant here.

Differences in the social distance between older and younger brothers are apparently similarly related to levels of productivity and descent-group strength. The relationship is least formal among Navaho, Tonga,

Ndembu, and Hopi, is more formal among Yao and Trukese, where the eldest brother is normally the immediate legal guardian of the sibling group, and is most markedly formal in the societies of highest productivity, especially the Kerala aristocratic castes (Titiev, 1944: 21–22; chaps. 1 and 2, above; Turner, 1957: 249–250; Gladwin and Sarason, 1953: 96; Mitchell, 1951: 321–323). It is again somewhat less formal in the lower strata of this society, among low-caste Mappillas and Tiyyars.

Relationships between alternate generations of the descent group seem to follow a similar trend of association with types and levels of productivity. In all the societies there is some tendency for authority and social distance to be relaxed between alternate generations, *de facto* authority being wielded most strongly by men of the first ascending generation, who are in the prime of life while ego is a child. A marked equation of, and a high degree of equality between, alternate generations occurs, however, only in some of the lower productivity societies, for example the Tonga, Ndembu, and to a lesser degree the Bemba (chap. 1, above; Turner, 1957: 245; Richards, 1951: 181; Turner, 1955: 130). Among the Yao, with their more stable cultivation sites and stronger descent groups, there was a much slighter tendency toward equation of great-uncle and great-nephew, with a stronger authoritative component (Mitchell, 1956: 176–177). Information on the mother's mother's brother is inadequate for the Navaho, Trukese, Trobrianders, Mayombe, and Minangkabau. The relationship was a somewhat formal one among the Hopi, where the mother's uncle was ritual head of ego's natal household and might act as teacher (Titiev, 1944: 26; Eggan, 1950: 38). On the other hand he was often called "elder brother" and usually left actual disciplining of a child to the latter's mother's brother (Eggan, 1949: 135).

Among the Ashanti the mother's mother's brother is looked up to with reverence, often as head of the lineage segment, and may punish for minor acts of impropriety, although he calls on the mother's generation for major disciplinary action (Fortes, 1950: 276). Among Kerala aristocrats there was probably the highest degree of social distance in this relationship. The mother's mother's brother was primarily an authoritative and revered figure, often head of the descent group, although his behavior was more genial and he was less feared and avoided than the mother's brothers. In the low-caste Kerala groups, as might be expected, the authoritative element was weaker and there was slightly more playful relaxation in this relationship. On the whole, therefore, a marked social equation of alternate generations of the descent group can only be expected in mobile cultivating societies of low productivity. This generalization can also probably be extended to cover both sexes and other kinsfolk of the grandparental generation: thus, out of the examples, it was only among the Tonga, Ndembu, and Bemba that preferential marriages occurred between kin of alternate generations.

Other Matrilineal Kin   Allowing for differences of etiquette associated with difference of sex, the component of social distance associated with authority in the relations of brother and sister, mother's brother and sister's daughter, and great-uncle and great-niece, appears to vary with levels of productivity in a similar manner to that described for matrilineally related men.

Social distance is probably never as marked in relations between matrilineally related women as in those between men, or between men and women, of a descent group. Relations between matrilineally related women are apparently always informal, no doubt because women as a collectivity come under the legal authority of the descent group's men. The mother's mother does, however, achieve a position of authority and reverence in many matrilineal societies. This appears to be most marked in matrilocal and duolocal systems. In these societies no significant differences in this relationship were detectably associated with levels of productivity.

AFFINES

Information was inadequate for a complete comparison of affinal relationships. The following comments are restricted mainly to relations of men with their wives' kin in matrilocal residence.

Schneider has pointed out that in matrilineal systems neither spouse is ever as fully incorporated into either the conjugal descent unit or the conjugal residential group as in the case of the wife in most patrilineal systems. The matrilocal husband is not fully integrated with his wife's unit because his primary authority relates to his matrilineal heirs, who live elsewhere. The wife is not fully integrated with her husband's local or descent unit in avunculocal or patrilocal residence because her children do not belong to this group by matrilineal descent and will soon go to live elsewhere. Of the two, the position of matrilocally resident husbands is probably the more onerous, however, for men as a sex do hold authoritative positions in society at large. It is therefore perhaps more difficult for them to live in a group where their authority is at best equivocal and subject to question. Because of differences of descent-group membership, a very strong, unquestioned structure of authority apparently never exists among the husbands of a matrilocal

unit, nor between the husbands and men born into the descent group
of their wives. Since these men normally engage in some forms of economic and other coöperation, relations between them are likely to be
of a particularly delicate nature.

Husband-Wife's Elders In all the fifteen systems, men show some respect toward affines of the wife's parental generation. Formal avoidance, either total or partial, of the wife's parents or other kin of this
generation seems, however, to occur exclusively, or almost exclusively,
in matrilocal systems or in duolocal systems of the "visiting husband"
type, although not in all of those systems. Such forms of avoidance
seem, therefore, to be related to particular tensions in the role of the
resident or visiting husband in certain particular forms of matrilocal
or duolocal residence. The question is, "What are these forms?"

Avoidance or partial avoidance of the wife's parents and any other
resident kin of the wife's parental generation is found among the
Navaho, Bemba, Yao, and in Minangkabau (chap. 2, above; Richards,
1940a: 72; Mitchell, 1951: 328). Avoidance is most marked in relation
to the wife's mother, but there are strong taboos also in the father-in-
law–son-in-law relationship. These restrictions are gradually relaxed
among the Bemba as the son-in-law's position becomes established, and
cease finally at the point when he is accorded full control of his elementary family and receives permission, if he wishes, to move his wife
to another village. Similar avoidant relations exist among the Tonga
and Ndembu in the early, uxorilocal period of marriage, before the
husband and wife have been given full control of their household and
hearth, but are relaxed among the Tonga at the time of bride removal.
Among Ndembu both sexes maintain relations of partial avoidance with
all affines of the parental generation in whichever village they later
choose to occupy (Turner, 1957: 240). Normally, however, the couple
do not live matrilocally after the early period of marriage.

By contrast, avoidance patterns in relation to the wife's parents are
not found among the matrilocal Hopi, Trukese, or Mappillas, nor
among the duolocal Central Kerala Nayar. In these societies the husband treats his wife's parental generation with informal respect. Among
Mappillas the wife's elders in turn accord the young husband marked
politeness and a kind of ceremonious deference.

Following the hypothesis outlined by Aberle for the Navaho (chap.
2), I suggest that avoidant patterns with the wife's parental generation
may be most likely to occur in matrilocal societies or in duolocal societies of the "visiting husband" type, when husband and wife have
some exclusive forms of productive coöperation or sharing of goods

which threaten to shut out the rest of the wife's residential unit, yet the wife, or both husband and wife, also have productive and/or distributive coöperation with the wife's residential group as a whole, organized by the wife's older kin. The husband is then an interloper who threatens to segregate his wife from her parental generation, but is also linked to the latter through his wife's continuing ties to them, and sometimes also through his own coöperative efforts on their behalf. Tensions between conjunctive and disjunctive elements in the affinal relationship are thus particularly acute, and avoidant patterns may be a mode of handling them. The societies studied seem to fit this hypothesis fairly well, although it is freely admitted that other factors may also be involved. An additional sexual element may, for example, be present in the particularly strong mother-in-law taboo. Nevertheless, the conjunctive-disjunctive factors referred to above may also heighten sexual ambivalence toward the mother-in-law in those societies where avoidance occurs.

Taking first the societies where husbands practice avoidance patterns, we find the Navaho husband occupying a separate hogan with his wife and cultivating or building up sheep herds with her, yet both husband and wife also coöperate in the wider economic activities of the matrilocal residential unit. Among both Bemba and Yao, again, the young husband may cultivate some plots separately with his wife, yet he also does varying amounts of work for her parents and is largely dependent on them for his food (Mitchell, 1951: 328; Richards, 1950: 225–226, 228). The young husband's dependence is here greater than among the Navaho, but at the same time, if the marriage succeeds, he is gradually working toward a more exclusive relationship with his wife. The avoidant patterns cease only when the young couple are judged capable of managing their own household with its granary, hearth, etc., without constant intervention on the part of the wife's elders. A similiar situation occurs in the initial uxorilocal period of Tonga and Ndembu marriage. It ends when the Tonga husband leaves the matrilocal homestead to become the head of his own, usually in some other hamlet of his choosing. Among the Ndembu, avoidant patterns continue in relation to all affines of the parental generation of the village in which the couple later reside. This situation fits my hypothesis well, because wherever they live the Ndembu couple are involved in perpetuity in conjunctive-disjunctive relations with affines of proximate generations of the type we have described. On the one hand, husband and wife cultivate their own fields alone; on the other, the husband hunts, clears fields, and builds huts with men of the village as a whole; and both spouses are concerned in economic redistributive relations and in cooking arrangements which encompass the village (Turner, 1957: 23–33).

According to my hypothesis, avoidant patterns with the wife's elders should have less relevance to the Minangkabau situation, where the husband is overwhelmingly involved in economic activities with his natal kin in another household. In fact, the avoidances are less stringent than in the other societies; they involve only taboos on physical contact, commensality, and joking (Loeb, 1934: 42). There is, however, some basis for the hypothesis among the Minangkabau. The young husband may, if he wishes, work separately in his wife's private fields and accumulate minor forms of property jointly with her, while the wife remains largely concerned with economic coöperation with her natal household as a whole (De Jong, 1951: 56).

Turning to the matrilocal or duolocal systems which lack avoidance of the wife's parental generation, we find a variety of situations all of which conform fairly well to our hypothesis. Among the Hopi, husband and wife seldom work as an exclusive team, for women play a minor role in cultivation. Women of the matrilineal household work mainly together; husbands work alone, with other husbands of the household, or with brothers or other kin (Titiev, 1944: 22, 29; Eggan, 1950: 33). The husband contributes produce and support to the wife's household as a whole, as a resident member, and household budgeting is (traditionally) unitary (Eggan, 1950: 56; Titiev, 1944: 24). Unless he remained to old age, the husband was never very fully integrated into his wife's household, but, on the other hand, neither did he work exclusively on her behalf in ways likely to separate her from her kin. Instead he worked directly with and for her elders and, if the marriage was successful, came to occupy a role somewhat comparable to that of a son.

Among Trukese, again, male and female productive roles were largely segregated. Women did domestic work and fished, under the authority of their senior in the matrilocal household; men fished, cultivated, or cooked in groups, chiefly with other husbands of the dwelling unit. Except for small snacks, daily food supplies were pooled within this unit and cooked jointly or in turn by the husbands (chap. 3, above). A husband might, it is true, plant trees or develop other forms of property on behalf of his own children. Such activity was probably less important in the early years of marriage, however, and in any case it seems likely that the produce would be pooled with the wife's parents as long as they lived.

Among aristocratic Mappillas the young husband normally did not coöperate in production at all with either his wife or her kin. He drew funds from his taravād or was engaged in its behalf in trade elsewhere. Except for small personal gifts, his slender contributions to the wife's household went directly to her resident elders, usually her mother, and were lost in the common budget. In this system the characteristic feature of affinal relationships was the marked deference owed by the wife's elders *to* her husband. This had no avoidant features, but seems to have been related to the fact that the husband did *not* produce on their behalf and so had no significant authority in the household. He was rather a paying guest, necessary for his procreative capacities, and was accorded punctilious respect as though to compensate for his exclusion from any significant managerial role. Among low-caste Mappillas the husband contributed to his conjugal household's funds and had real authority. He did not work coöperatively with his wife, however, and while the household cohered its goods were pooled. Accumulation of separate property by the Mappilla husband on behalf of his wife and children has in modern times occurred chiefly in middle-class groups engaged in market trade. In these households the elementary family may occupy a separate apartment and kitchen in a portion of what was formerly the wife's ancestral home. In such situations, however, the elementary family's finances are managed with virtual autonomy. The husband merely pays rent to his wife's parents and contributes to life-crisis rites. Affinal relations in such households are often extremely tense, and at the earliest opportunity the husband moves his wife to a separate house.

Among Central Kerala Nayars, finally, the husband traditionally played no significant role at all in the economy of his conjugal household, nor had he any authority. He came always as a guest and an outsider, and his relations with his wife's elders were respectful, as became a junior village neighbor, but informal and slight. An underlying hostility often characterized the mother-in-law relationship, but patterned avoidances were scarcely likely to develop in so slender a relationship. Instead, the husband who did not meet with familial approval would speedily be dismissed.

Brothers-in-Law I suggest the following hypotheses concerning the etiquette of behavior between brothers-in-law in matrilineal societies.

(1) A relationship of respect, which may involve partial avoidance, is expected when the husband is partly engaged in separate economic coöperation with his wife, but where husband and/or wife also coöp-

erate economically with the wife's family unit, of which her brother is a member, thus bringing the husband into a close yet disjunctive relationship with his wife's brother. Navaho, Bemba, Yao, Minangkabau, Trukese, Trobriand, and to a much milder degree, Ashanti brother-in-law patterns would exemplify this situation (chap. 2, above; Richards, 1939: 122; Mitchell, 1956: 329; Loeb, 1934: 42; chaps. 3 and 4, above; Fortes, 1950: 283).

(2) Given the conditions described above, if neither husband nor wife's brother has superior authority in the relationship of economic coöperation, a symmetrical relationship of mutual respect or partial avoidance is expected. The Navaho, Bemba, and Minangkabau situations would exemplify this. In the Navaho case the wife's brother, especially if unmarried, may be a member of the matrilocal homestead. If so, the husband will work with him on behalf of the homestead as well as working separately with his wife. Neither party has particular authority in respect of the coöperative work, which will probably be organized by the wife's father. A similar situation may arise among the Bemba if the wife's brother is unmarried or has married in his natal village. It may also arise among Minangkabau if the husband is helping his wife with her separate fields as long as she remains within the more significant economic unit of her lineage segment, which includes her brother. A somewhat similar but much weaker brother-in-law relationship appears to exist among the Ashanti. Husband and wife coöperate economically, but the wife retains economic ties with her natal lineage of which her brother is a member, and the husband may help his wife's natal family with occasional tasks (Fortes, 1950: 283). The husband is, however, residentially and economically much more segregated from his wife's brother and her family generally than in the other societies just mentioned. Correspondingly, brothers-in-law appear to have a slighter relationship of less formal respect.

(3) If the conditions of category 1 are fulfilled, and the wife's brother is the chief legal authority with regard to the economic coöperation in which the wife and her husband are involved, an asymmetrical relationship of respect or partial avoidance is expected in which the wife's brother has some power to command the husband, and the husband employs an etiquette of submission. The Yao and Trukese cases exemplify this situation. In the Yao case the husband lives matrilocally and works for his wife in her fields, but he also works for her parents and extended family as a whole. The wife's brother, as head of her sorority group, is her immediate legal guardian and mar-

riage surety. The brother-in-law relationship is tense and formally respectful, with the husband playing the more submissive role (Mitchell, 1956: 329).

In the Trukese system the husband works along with other husbands of the matrilocal household toward the daily subsistence of his wife and her matrilocal dwelling group as a whole. The relationship between the husbands is relatively informal—because, I have argued, they coöperate on behalf of the household and not separately with their own wives. The wife's brother is, however, in a more disjunctive relationship with the husband, although a very close one. He does not live *in* the matrilocal household and may not even live very near it, being largely concerned with his own wife's matrilocal dwelling group. He is, however, his sister's immediate legal guardian, works on her behalf on large projects connected with their lineage, and represents her to the lineage and the society at large. Because of his legal tie with the sister he can demand special forms of work and gifts from her husband. He is also, however, potentially segregated from the sister and her husband in that the husband may be gradually making improvements on the lineage land allocated to his wife, or supplying new land to his children. The wife's brother will be excluded from control of this property, which may eventually allow the wife's children to secede from their mother's brother. The brother-in-law relationship here is extremely tense and avoidant, with marked submission in etiquette on the part of the husband (Goodenough, 1951: 113; chap. 3, above).

(4) Given the conditions of category 1, if residential and economic patterns are such that the husband has primary, immediate control of his wife, while the wife's brother is in a position where *he* works for the sister and her husband, an asymmetrical relationship of respect is expected, in which the husband has authority over the brother. This is apparently the Trobriand situation. The wife lives in her husband's village under her husband's temporary guardianship and works in her husband's gardens. On the other hand, the wife's specially chosen brother brings from his own village the food supplies which largely maintain his absent sister and her elementary family. The relationship appears to be respectful, with the brother in the subordinate role (chap. 4, above).

(5) A more informal etiquette is expected between brothers-in-law in societies where they neither coöperate regularly in economic matters nor simultaneously coöperate economically with the woman who links them, as well as in societies where brothers-in-law *do* coöperate on be-

half of the wife's natal extended family or larger unit as a whole, but the husband is not engaged in separate coöperation with his wife. These conditions seem to be fulfilled by the Hopi, Ndembu, Tonga, and the four Kerala groups. The information is inadequate for the Mayombe.

In the Hopi system the woman's married brother seems to work chiefly for his own wife's household, coming home only for seasonal work on clan land or to help out his sister if she is divorced (when the brother-in-law relationship has already lapsed). If the woman's marriage is successful, her husband and brother may choose to cultivate or herd together (Titiev, 1944: 29). It is not clear, however, whether such voluntary coöperation is focused on the woman herself or whether it is simply a matter of congenial brothers-in-law deciding to work together, each on behalf of his own wife. If, however, this coöperation *is* on behalf of the woman who is sister to one man and wife to the other, it is also on behalf of the matrilocal dwelling group as a whole. The husband does not, moreover, also work separately with his wife. The brother-in-law relationship in this society is informal.

Among Ndembu and Tonga the woman's brother and her husband seldom seem to be economically associated with her at the same time, or to coöperate in production together. The woman goes to the husband's village and is chiefly supported by his and her joint efforts. She seems normally to return to her brother only if her marriage fails. Further, even if husband and brother do temporarily occupy the same village, they work together not specifically on behalf of the sister, but as village work partners, each engaged primarily with his own elementary family. In the four Kerala systems, again, there is little specific economic coöperation between husband and wife's brother. In Central Kerala the Nayar husband traditionally did no work for his wife and made only small personal gifts. Among North Kerala Nayars the wife was partly maintained by her husband in his home and partly by food sent by her own taravād; but the latter responsibility lay with the wife's kāranavan, not specifically with her brother, and her brother was likely to become kāranavan only late in life. Among North Kerala Mappillas the husband contributed modestly to his wife's matrilocal family as a whole; he was not engaged in separate economic coöperation with his wife and did not work with his brother-in-law. Among Tiyyars, finally, the husband was responsible for his wife's maintenance as long as the marriage lasted. The wife did take home annual quantities of grain, earned by herself, but these did not involve her husband in close coöperation with her brother.

In all these societies the etiquette of behavior between brothers-in-law was informal. It was actually a joking relationship among the Tonga, and may have had an element of joking among Ndembu, since it seems to have been partly assimilated to the cross-cousin relationship (chap. 1, above; Turner, 1957: 253). It was, however, a very hostile relationship too among the Ndembu, since both brother and husband wished to have the woman and her children living in his village (Turner, 1957: 260). In the Kerala groups the relationship was informal, with mild joking between brothers-in-law near in age, especially while they were young. In a relationship between brothers-in-law of very disparate age, the junior showed mild respect to the senior. This was not, however, at all comparable to the formal and avoidant respect-relationship which obtained between matrilineally related men.

Within category 5, I suggest that an element of joking may be particularly likely to exist if the brother of the woman has no legal authority over her. This is the case among the Tonga, where only the mother's brothers, and not the brothers of a woman, have authority over her and represent her at law. It is probably also the case among Ndembu. In the Kerala groups, again, a young woman's legal guardian was normally her mother's brother or great-uncle, and her brother had no particular legal responsibility for her. He was likely to become her kāranavan only late in life, if at all. She might by that time have left her husband, and if she had not, the brother-in-law relationship tended to be less jovial than among youths. It might become a relationship of mutual trust and companionship, or, occasionally, one of hostility with voluntary (though not customary) avoidance.

In general, therefore, I would argue that the relationship between male affines tends to be extremely formal or partly avoidant when they coöperate most closely, yet the husband also has separate forms of economic coöperation with the wife. It is less formal if the two coöperate jointly without other, divided interests, and is least formal when their spheres of interest in the linking woman are most segregated. A positive element of joking seems to be possible only when the linking woman's natal kinsman has no immediate legal authority over her.

Husband-Wife's Sister No single variable was found to be very closely associated with forms of etiquette in relation to the wife's sister in matrilineal systems. The data were inadequate for the Mayombe and the Ndembu, so there were only thirteen systems to work with. It seems probable that any or all of the following factors may be relevant in a given culture: whether the society permits sororal polygyny and/or sororatic marriage, or regards sex relations with the wife's sister as incestuous; residence type; economic and other relations between a man and his wife's sister; economic and other relations between a man and his wife's sister's husband.

Of the thirteen societies, the Tonga, Trukese, and Bemba had various types of joking relationship with the wife's sister (chap. 1, above; Richards, 1940a: 46; Gladwin and Sarason, 1953: 116). The Navaho, Northern Mappillas, Minangkabau, Central Kerala Nayars, and Yao had avoidant, partially avoidant, or very respectful relations (chap. 2, above; Loeb, 1934: 42; Mitchell, 1951: 329). Relative age may be a differentiating factor in these cases. Central Kerala Nayars, for example, have a friendly and informal relationship with the wife's prepubertal unmarried sister, an informally respectful one with the wife's older sister who is older than ego, and an extremely respectful, partially avoidant relationship with the wife's sister who is younger than ego but has attained puberty. In general in these societies, however, very respectful and/or avoidant patterns are predominant. Milder, less formal respectful behavior seems to be required among the Trobriand Islanders, Ashanti, and Hopi, as well as among North Kerala Nayars and Tiyyars (chap. 4, above; Fortes, 1950: 283; Titiev, 1944: 28–29).

(1) More or less respectful attitudes seem to prevail where there is no sororal polygyny or sororatic marriage and where sex relations with the wife's sister are regarded as incestuous. In such societies the relationship may be avoidant (Mappillas and Central Kerala Nayars), extremely respectful (Yao), or more mildly respectful (Northern Nayars and Tiyyars, Trobriand, Ashanti, and Hopi). It does not seem likely, however, to contain any element of customary joking.

(2) Joking may occur when the society permits sororal polygyny and/or sororatic marriage, but it need not necessarily do so. Joking is found among the Tonga, who permit classificatory sororatic marriage, and among the Bemba and Trukese, who have both sororal polygyny and sororatic marriage. It does not occur, however, among the Navaho, who have both sororal polygyny and sororatic marriage. Here the relationship with the wife's married sister is respectful and partly avoidant.

(3) When residence is matrilocal or duolocal (husband visits wife), so that husband and wife's sister are likely to be in frequent proximity, there tends to be a more extreme etiquette of behavior between them than when some other residence type keeps them normally apart. Thus, Trukese and Bemba have matrilocality with joking; Navaho,

Northern Mappillas, Central Kerala Nayars, Minangkabau, and Yao have matrilocal or duolocal residence with complete or partial avoidance or extreme respect. Among the "mildly respectful" societies, only the Hopi are matrilocal; the rest—Northern Nayars and Tiyyars, Trobriand, and Ashanti—are dominantly avunculocal. The Tonga are the only society of the sample which has joking without matrilocality.

(4) Given matrilocal or duolocal residence, it may be that the wife's sister relationship will be avoidant or extremely respectful if *either* there is no sororal polygyny or sororate in the society, so that all sex relations with the wife's sister would be incestuous, *or* the husbands of the two sisters have special cause to be jealous of one another because of divided economic or other interests. Central Kerala Nayars and Yao are societies which prohibit any form of marriage to the wife's sister, are matrilocal or duolocal, and have relations of extreme respect with the wife's sister. Navaho, Mappillas, Minangkabau, and Yao have relations between the husbands of sisters of a kind which might create tension between them, which if extended into the sexual sphere would result in avoidance of each others' wives. Thus Navaho, Minangkabau, and Yao have situations in which husband and wife work together and exclusively, yet the wife and her sister also coöperate in work and share products; their husbands may also occasionally work together. Along the lines of my earlier arguments about affinal relations, this situation may create tensions which could reflect into the wife's sister relationship. The reason for Navaho avoidance of the wife's sister, at all events, is given as the jealousy and hostility of her husband (chap. 2, above). Mappillas have a different situation: here husbands do no work for or with the wife's sister or her husband. Unless they are previously related, the husbands of sisters remain more or less strangers enjoying an overtly friendly but slight relationship. The prohibition against seeing each others' wives may be related to this tenuous tie between the husbands. Among low-caste Mappillas, where husbands do sometimes work jointly on behalf of the matrilocal household, the etiquette of behavior to the wife's sister is less strict. This may, however, have to do only with the fact that women in this caste go out to work and observe all religious avoidances less strictly. Among Central Kerala Nayars, finally, it is no doubt the "incestuous" ban rather than the jealousies of husbands which lies behind partial avoidance of the wife's younger sister. Her husband's jealousy could scarcely be invoked in this case, for this is the society in which traditionally even co-husbands of the same woman are said to have "agreed very well together."

Of the matrilocal societies, only Bemba and Trukese have joking. Both also have sororal polygyny and sororatic marriage, and the joking is explicitly related to the fact that under other conditions the husband might have married the wife's sister—or may even do so in the future (Richards, 1940a: 46; Gladwin and Sarason, 1953: 116). The Trukese situation with regard to economic coöperation between the husbands also seems to favor their close intimacy: they work together on behalf of the wives' joint household, and not separately with their wives. They may also be brothers, another relationship in which men have privileged sexual joking with each others' wives. We do not argue that these factors wholly explain the Trukese form of joking, which is particularly obscene, but they may be relevant. It is not clear how "rough" the Bemba joking with the wife's sister may be, or whether it operates equally in the presence or absence of her husband. On the face of it I would have expected the Bemba relationship to have been very respectful or avoidant, as in the Navaho case, because the husbands both work together and also separately with their wives, so that one might have expected certain tensions in their relationship. The precise conditions of these relationships are, however, not known to me.

In general, therefore, there appears to be no one-to-one correlation between etiquette of behavior between husband and wife's sister on the one hand and residence, preferential and prohibited marriages, or economic patterns on the other, yet it seems probable that any or all may be relevant in given cases. Joking tends not to occur where sororal polygyny and sororatic marriage are prohibited. A more extreme form of etiquette—joking *or* avoidant—seems likely when the husband and his wife's sister are in close proximity through matrilocal or duolocal residence. Informal or joking behavior *may* be more likely, in addition, if the husbands work closely together on behalf of their matrilocal household, and not separately with their wives. Very respectful or avoidant patterns *may* be more likely if the co-resident husbands have both conjunctive and disjunctive economic relations, or none at all.

Variation in Preferential Marriage Forms

The fifteen groups offer a rather wide variety of preferred marriages. I shall comment on only five types: cross-cousin marriage, general polygyny, sororal polygyny, sororatic marriage, and widow inheritance (including leviratic marriage). It has already been mentioned that marriage between kin of alternate generations is probably only to be expected in mobile cultivating societies of low productivity.

Cross-Cousin Marriage

Within the range of matrilineal systems, cross-cousin marriage appears to have no relation to levels of productivity. It is true that the three societies which prohibited cross-cousin marriage all had low productivity: Truk, Navaho, and Hopi. So also, however, had several societies with preferred cross-cousin marriage, for example, Tonga and Ndembu.

The most fruitful line of enquiry seems to be to ask first, not specifically about cross-cousin marriage, but about whether or not marriage is permitted into the father's descent group. Among the fifteen examples such marriage is not permitted among Trukese, Hopi, and Navaho; it is permitted for both sexes among Tonga, Ndembu, Bemba, Yao, Ashanti, Minangkabau, and the four Kerala groups; and it is permitted for men but not women in the Trobriands. Data are lacking for Mayombe.

A possible explanation of these differences may lie in the number of organized descent groups existing within the largest territorial unit of the society whose internal organization is based on kinship. If the number of descent groups is small (about eight or less), marriage into the father's descent group seems very likely to be permitted. If the number is large (about twenty or more), marriage into the father's descent group seems almost certain to be prohibited. If the number is intermediate (between about eight and twenty), a variety of compromises may be possible. Marriage may, for example, be permitted in more distantly related sections of the father's descent group or of his wider exogamous clan, but seems likely to be prohibited with his immediate matrilineal kin.

This argument refers, of course, to the necessity, in territorial political units structured predominantly or entirely through kinship, for a large proportion of the unit's population to be linked by kinship ties for which customary rights and obligations are prescribed. If there are few descent groups in the unit, some members of ego's descent group will be married into each of them and will thus provide him with classificatory kinship ties without the need for further extension of incest prohibitions to his father's descent group. If there is a large number of descent groups in the relevant territorial unit, permission to marry back into the father's group would mean permission to form small knots of closely in-marrying groups within the larger political unit, thus leaving the larger unit without a firm basis for structuring its relations as a whole.

It should be emphasized that this hypothesis refers to the number of organized, maximal descent groups in that territorial unit whose structure is based on kinship, and not to the number of larger, exogamous clans or phratries represented in this unit or in the society as a whole. The reason for this is that because the exogamous clan is not an organized group, its members as a whole are not drawn into active participation in the affinal or patrilateral ties set up by any one of them. In most societies, for example, kinship terms are not even extended to members of the spouse's or of the father's whole clan, but only to kin of these relatives' maximal descent groups. Although it sets the extent of unilineal marriage prohibitions, therefore, the clan or phratry is not normally relevant to the extension of affinal or patrilateral kinship obligations. Again, the hypothesis refers specifically to the largest territorial unit of the society *whose structure is kinship-based*, and not necessarily to the society as a whole. This is because kinship in states is only incidental to the political organization of the state as a whole, although marriage may well be permitted throughout or even beyond it. It is therefore not necessary for kinship ties effectively to link members of the state as a whole.

The fourteen documented cases lend support to this theory. In Ashanti and Minangkabau the political unit whose internal relations were mainly structured through kinship was the village or township. This seems in each case to have contained some three to seven maximal descent groups (chap. 5, above; De Jong, 1951: 68). Some marriages seem to have taken place outside the village, but the majority in any generation were within it (Fortes, 1950: 279; Cole, 1936: 24). The most important relationships between villages and between larger political units were not kinship ties, but political relationships. Given a high proportion of marriages within the village, and given the number of descent groups within it, it would scarcely have been possible to forbid marriage into the father's descent group.

The Kerala case was similar. In the Kerala kingdoms, the kinship-based territorial unit was the tara or caste neighborhood. It normally contained some four to eight maximal descent groups of the relevant castes. Marriage into the father's descent group was freely permitted by the Nayar group-marriage regulations of Central Kerala, and was a preferred type in the North Kerala matrilineal castes.

Among the Ndembu the main political unit within which relationships were predominantly structured through kinship was evidently the vicinage, which traditionally appears to have contained some four to seven villages, each dominated by one maximal lineage (Turner, 1957: 48, 281). In this society the maximal lineage was not exogamous, marriage being permitted between a man and his classificatory matrilineal great-niece. Marriage was, however, prohibited between adjacent generations, and also within any one generation, of the localized maximal lineage, or of any larger matrilineal group within which relationships were remembered. Although villages did not remain permanently within the same vicinage, and although each village had far-flung affinal ties in villages all over the Ndembu territory, the most concentrated network of reciprocal marriage ties was between villages of the same vicinage. Further, vicinage organization depended on these ties (ibid.: 261, 274–287). Marriage into the father's descent group was common.

Among the Tonga the neighborhood was the main political unit whose internal relations were structured entirely through kinship. A majority of marriages also took place within it, and marriage into the father's descent group was permitted. It is not quite clear how many organized matrilineal groups were represented in each neighborhood. There was a rather large number of clans in the society as a whole. Twelve predominated throughout most of the Tonga area, and were apparently widely though unevenly dispersed throughout the several neighborhoods. Colson states that most modern villages (smaller than neighborhoods) include representatives of from eight to ten clans. Clans are, however, very uneven in size: six or eight of them numbered between about 4,000 and 8,000 in the whole area studied; one, only about 94; and two others, no more than 10 (Colson, 1951: 131). Thus in any given neighborhood there would likely be no more than about six organized matrilineal groups represented by any significant number of members. With uneven clan representation, a total neighborhood population of about 500, and a high proportion of marriages within the neighborhood, therefore, it would be possible to permit marriage into the father's matrilineal group and still have the whole neighborhood population linked by ties of (classificatory) kinship.

Among the Yao and Bemba the largest political unit whose internal relations were mainly structured through kinship was the village. In each society a village seems to have seldom contained representatives of more than five or six descent groups, one of which was likely to be numerically and politically dominant (Mitchell, 1956: 188; Richards, 1939: 112–119; 413–415; 424). In these societies a higher proportion of marriages took place outside the village than was the case in the larger states. Inter-village relations were, however, primarily political relations, even though (in the Yao case) they might be phrased in terms of "perpetual kinship" between village heads. Given a need for some proportion of marriage within the village, prohibition of marriage into the father's descent group was not feasible.

It might be argued that intra-village marriage was not a necessary feature of these systems, and that they could have provided for intra-village cohesion equally well by forbidding marriage into the father's group and making the village, in effect, into a single exogamous unit. The answer to this argument seems to have to do with the optimal size of kinship-based economic-coöperative units, as opposed to the optimal size of villages. Among both Bemba and Yao the main unit of regular economic coöperation between kin was usually a sub-section of the village—a matrilocal grandfamily among Bemba, and probably a matrilocal extended family, based on a small lineage or lineage segment, among Yao. Nevertheless there seems to have been some reason—perhaps political, or connected with wider, seasonal economic coöperation—for maintaining villages large enough to contain several economic-coöperative units. If the village as a whole were exogamous, there would be less cohesion between its component economic-coöperative units than if there were intermarriage between them, for a rule of exogamy sets up parallel rather than reciprocal relations between the sections of the maximal descent group. Thus, unless the sections have a basis of cohesion in joint ownership of resources and regular productive and distributive relations, there is little to counter fission between them. Intra-village marriage *between* the main economic-coöperative units, by contrast, keeps on affirming reciprocal relations between them with each new marriage. Intra-village marriage does not, of course, prevent village fission when the village has become too large to continue as a viable political unit. By providing cross-links, however, it does prevent the formation of permanent cleavages of interest between the component village sections for as long as the village, for political or wider economic reasons, is obliged to cohere.

In the Trobriand Islands marriages could take place across the boundaries of districts, but the district, headed by a chief, was the main political unit whose internal relations were structured primarily through kinship. A district seems to have contained about ten to twelve descent groups, each having as its home base one village or a local section of a village (Malinowski, 1922: 66–67). From the point of view of number of descent groups in the relevant territorial unit, therefore, the Trobriands are a borderline case. Their rules concerning marriage into the father's descent group are also of a "borderline" character. Matrilateral cross-cousin marriage is strongly disapproved, and very rarely occurs. When it does occur, it is apparently classificatory and perhaps usually takes place only between chiefly descent groups of different districts (Leach, 1958: 139). Examples cited are those of the Kwoynama and Tabalu sub-clans, which apparently intermarry reciprocally as part of a special arrangement. The marriage of a commoner woman into her father's descent group is, however, evidently prohibited. Limited patrilateral cross-cousin marriage is, by contrast, permitted. It usually takes place between the son and the own sister's daughter of a chief or village headman. It is associated with aberrant patrilocal residence on the part of the marrying couple. It apparently permits a chief or village headman to keep his son as a permanent member of his village, while also, perhaps, relieving the chief's heir of the obligation of paying urigubu to a sister's husband outside the village (*idem*). At all events, the marriage of either man or woman into the father's descent group is unusual in the Trobriands, and is connected with the special political privileges of village headmen or of chiefs.

On Truk the most significant territorial unit whose structure is based on kinship is apparently a "community" containing anything from one to four political districts (Goodenough, 1951: 145). Romonum Island, which forms one community and was until recently one political district, contained some thirteen matrilineal descent groups (*ibid.*: 71). Not surprisingly, marriage was prohibited within the father's descent group, although not within his wider clan (*ibid.*: 120).

The village is the significant territorial unit among the Hopi. Oraibi village had twenty-one descent groups (local elements of clans), divided between nine exogamous phratries (Titiev, 1944: 49). Marriage was strongly disapproved with members of the father's own descent group or clan element, but permitted within his wider phratry. These patrilateral prohibitions, together with the exogamic rules of the phratry system and the institution of ritual fatherhood, caused most members of the village to stand in some kind of real or fictive kinship relations with one another.

The Navaho case is somewhat unclear but suggests similarity to the Hopi with regard to number of descent groups within the relevant territorial unit. The largest organized political unit seems to have been the local community. Navaho married widely, however, throughout their territory, and seem to have relied on far-flung kinship ties as a basis for extensive spatial mobility, and perhaps, also, for settlement of some disputes between communities. There were about fifty matrilineal clans in the society as a whole, grouped into nine main phratries, probably with a number of clans not associated with any phratry (chap. 2, above). The number of organized matrilineal groups must have been very large. Marriage was prohibited within the father's whole clan, and disapproved within his phratry. These prohibitions seem to have extended effective kinship ties throughout the population at large.

I suggest therefore that marriage into the father's descent group will tend to be either restricted or prohibited when the largest territorial unit whose relations are structured primarily through kinship contains more than eight descent groups. The larger the number of descent groups, the more rigorous in character and the more comprehensive in range will be the patrilateral marriage prohibitions.

This hypothesis serves to explain the simple presence or absence of bilateral cross-cousin marriage in a matrilineal society. For cross-cousin marriage (own or classificatory) is merely marriage, by a man or by a woman, into the own generation of the father's descent group.

Needless to say, however, there is much concerning cross-cousin marriage which this hypothesis does not explain. First, in societies where marriage into the father's descent group is permitted at all, it usually takes the form of (classificatory) cross-cousin marriage, rather than marriage to the father's "sister," to the father's "daughter's daughter," or to the father's "brother." Indeed, many matrilineal societies actually prohibit these marriages, while favoring cross-cousin marriage. Why should marriage into the father's descent group usually take the form of cross-cousin marriage? I have little to say on this problem except the obvious point that ego's own generation is usually the most likely to contain spouses of suitable age. In most societies, moreover, relationships of authority may be likely to militate against inter-generational marriage.

It may seem surprising that I have not advanced any of the common arguments about the domestic advantages of cross-cousin marriage. Richards and many other writers, myself among them, have for example argued that cross-cousin marriage helps to solve the "matrilineal puzzle" of the male's divided loyalties. Matrilateral cross-cousin marriage ensures that mother's brother and sister's son have harmonious instead of conflicting marital interests. In particular it gives the wife's father assurance that his daughter and her children will continue to be linked to his own matrilineal group, and so to himself. Patrilateral cross-cousin marriage provides the husband's father with a similar assurance with regard to his son, and in addition ensures that the former's grand-children will be members of his own matrilineal group. Matrilineal peoples themselves often advance these and similar arguments in favor of cross-cousin marriage, while patrilineal peoples have corresponding arguments concerning the advantages of cross-cousin marriage under patrilineal descent.

There are two reasons why I do not offer these arguments as objective reasons for the *existence* of cross-cousin marriage. One is that the "matrilineal puzzle" presumably occurs equally among all matrilineal peoples, yet only *some* of them "solve" it through cross-cousin marriage. The existence of a variable cannot be convincingly explained in terms of a constant. The other reason is that plausible arguments can also be brought *against* the domestic value of cross-cousin marriage. Indeed, such arguments often are brought today by young people in societies where cross-cousin marriage is dying out. It can be argued, for example, that in a matrilineal system a young man is already under the authority of his mother's brother with respect to his property. He does not, in addition, want to marry the uncle's daughter and pass under his authority with regard to conjugal affairs as well. In short, I suggest that arguments in favor of the domestic advantages of cross-cousin marriage are rationalizations of a state of affairs which exists for economic and political reasons, and "explain" nothing in themselves.

The hypothesis presented earlier does not explain the conditions under which cross-cousin marriage will be prescribed or preferred, rather than merely permitted. It seems possible that cross-cousin marriage will be the more strongly preferred, the smaller the number of descent groups found in that territorial unit whose internal structure is based on kinship. I would expect it to be more strongly preferred, for example, if there were four such groups than if there were eight. Universally *prescribed* cross-cousin marriage can presumably occur only with a moiety system. I have no hypothesis to account for the situation in which one or two children in each sibling group are obliged to marry cross cousins, while other siblings may marry according to choice. No examples occurred in the societies studied.

Again, no hypothesis was developed to account for the existence of either form of unilateral, as opposed to bilateral, cross-cousin marriage, i.e., for the societies in which only one type of cross-cousin marriage is permitted, while the other is prohibited. The Trobrianders were the only example studied having unilateral (patrilateral) cross-cousin marriage, and even there the rule was apparently imperfectly observed.

Given bilateral cross-cousin marriage, it seems probable that the type of marriage which is the *more* preferred will depend on the kinship composition and on the economic and political structures of local groups. Given bilateral cross-cousin marriage, the matrilateral type seems to be the more preferred type with both avunculocal and matrilocal residence. This is the case among the Bemba, Ashanti, Minangkabau, and the three North Kerala groups. The Tonga, with multilocal residence, also have a very slight matrilateral preference. The Ndembu preference is not known. The Yao prefer patrilateral cross-cousin marriage to matrilateral, but the former seems to occur only in conjunction with patrilocal residence on the part of a village headman's son. It is interesting that patrilateral cross-cousin marriage occurs primarily or solely in conjunction with patrilocal residence among both Trobrianders and Yao. This may be part of a more widespread tendency among matrilineal societies having some patrilocal residence as an alternative form.

The preference for own or classificatory cross-cousin marriage seems also to depend on local group composition and on the structure of economic and political relations within and between local groups. Thus among Yao, Bemba, Ashanti, Minangkabau, and the Kerala groups, cross-cousin marriage serves mainly to weld together lineal groups of the minimal local community. From the point of view of community cohesion, therefore, own and classificatory cross-cousin marriages have the same significance provided they are within the same village, and the people themselves seem to merge them in ordinary parlance. Among Ndembu, by contrast, the chief function of cross-cousin marriage is to weld together different villages of the larger vicinage. Cross-cousin and alternate-generation marriages do take place within the village, but the former are perhaps less essential for its cohesion than among Bemba and Yao, because the village is built up on a single main lineage and forms a single economic-coöperative unit. Inter-village marriages within the vicinage are, however, very desirable for the promotion of cohesion within this unit. This is because the vicinage lacks strong headship or regular economic coöperation as a basis for cohesion, yet peace must be maintained and disputes settled within it because the gardens of its several villages are interspersed with one another. Ndembu thus prefer cross-cousin marriage into other, near-by villages above that within the village, which in practice tends to mean a preference for classificatory rather than "direct" cross-cousin marriage (Turner, 1957: 20–21, 254–255, 279–287).

General Polygyny

General, or non-sororal, polygyny was permitted in all the groups studied except the matrilocal Hopi, who were monogamous. However, in the other predominantly matrilocal societies (Navaho, Yao, Trukese, Bemba, and Northern Mappillas), matrilocally resident husbands also seem very seldom to have engaged in general polygyny, no doubt because of the difficulty of combining it conveniently with matrilocal residence. Even discounting the plural marriages of political officers, non-sororal polygyny seems to have been slightly more common for the population at large among the avunculocal Ndembu, Mayombe, Ashanti, Trobrianders, and Northern Tiyyars than in the matrilocal societies. It was slightly more common among avunculocal Northern Nayars than among matrilocal Northern Mappillas, but much less common than among avunculocal and patrilocal Tiyyars. The reason for the latter situation seems to have been that wives were an economic liability among Nayars rather than a productive asset, as among Tiyyars. For the population at large a much higher proportion of non-sororal polygyny seems to have occurred among the Tonga, with virilocal residence in independent nuclear or polygynous households, than in any of the groups so far mentioned. The highest proportion for the population at large was of course that of Central Kerala Nayars, where it was universally combined with polyandry in the institution of group marriage. Apart from the Central Nayars, the highest proportion for particular individuals was found among political officers of those chiefdoms and kingdoms where women's productive work was valuable and their children had value as followers and political supporters—Trobriand, Yao, Bemba, Mayombe, and Ashanti. The existence of slavery further encouraged general polygyny among political officers in the last four of these societies. General polygyny was, however, much less common among political officers of North Kerala, where women's productive value was low and the political and economic structure permitted only slender ties between men of rank and their children.

In general, therefore, if we leave aside the unique Central Nayar case of group marriage, the following factors seem to favor general polygyny in matrilineal societies: virilocal as opposed to matrilocal residence; given virilocal residence, a high productive value of women; the existence of stratified political offices, in societies where there is free land or other resources which officers can give to their children to entice them to live with them; and slavery. Factors specifically working against general polygyny seem to be: matrilocality; and, in the case of stratified societies, a dearth of free land or other resources which political officers could give to their children.

Sororal Polygyny

By contrast, sororal polygyny was permitted in only three of the fifteen societies, all of them matrilocal: Navaho, Bemba, and Truk (chap. 2, above; Richards, 1940a: 46; chap 3, above). On logical grounds it seems probable that the great majority of matrilineal societies which permit sororal polygyny will be matrilocal, since matrilocality in any case normally demands co-residence of a man and the sisters of his wife. On the other hand many matrilocal societies—e.g., Yao, Hopi, and Mappillas—do not permit sororal polygyny; neither do the duolocal Minangkabau or the Central Kerala Nayars. I suggest that the factors which foster sororal polygyny in matrilineal systems are matrilocal residence combined with a weak descent group not permanently attached to stable and scarce cultivation sites. Under these conditions a father contributes heavily to his wife and children's maintenance and possesses strong rights in them. He may also endow them with movable goods or, as in the Trukese case, with land or improvements to land. On the other hand both mother and child have close ties with their co-resident matrilineal kin, even though they are not permanently and overwhelmingly committed to a large, strongly structured, and stably located descent group. In these conditions, from the point of view of the wife's group, sororal polygyny increases the husband's commitment to this conjugal unit and to his children, simplifies the conjugal unit's problem of harmonizing the interests of co-resident husbands, and perpetuates the ties between sisters and their children. From the husband's point of view, sororal polygyny gives him the pleasures and productive labor of further spouses and children, and allows him to increase his personal following in spite of matrilocal residence. Where, by contrast, the descent group is more strongly structured and more stably located on scarce, valuable, and highly productive land, the matrilocally resident husband has lower stakes in his conjugal unit and in his children. The descent group then keeps the husband more at arm's length as an outsider and does not permit him to monopolize two women and two sets of children, lest his interest in the group and influence over its property become too great and threaten the cohesion of the descent group as a whole.

Sororatic Marriage

Sororatic marriage, or marriage to the dead wife's sister, seems also to occur mainly in matrilocal societies. It exists as a preferential form of secondary marriage among the Bemba, Navaho, Trukese, and Northern Mappillas, and also among the Minangkabau, who have the institution of the visiting husband (Richards, 1940a: 46; chaps. 2 and 3, above; Loeb, 1934: 42). Among Mappillas in modern times it is most common in upper- and middle-class trading families where descent groups own land, men earn cash and other personal property in trade, and a cash bridegroom wealth is paid by the wife's group at marriage. Sororatic marriage is much less common among low-caste Mappillas, who own no land and little movable wealth.

A mild preference for remarriage to a classificatory sister of the dead wife also occurs among Tonga, who are virilocal, but is prohibited with the dead wife's own sister (chap. 1, above).

"Direct" sororatic marriage seems likely to occur wherever sororal polygyny is permitted, and also in some matrilocal systems where sororal polygyny is prohibited. One would expect it to be permitted or preferred in those societies where it is to the husband's or the wife's group's special advantage (or both) to have the husband remain bound to his wife's group even after the first wife's death. It also seems likely to occur where it is to the children's special advantage to remain bound to both matrilineal kin and father after the mother's death. These conditions seem likely to arise in all matrilineal systems which permit sororal polygyny, and also in some others where sororal polygyny might be considered too great a danger to the husband's conjugal descent group.

Among Bemba and Navaho sororatic marriage can have obvious

advantages for husband, wife's group, and children. Starting as a junior worker in his wife's homestead, the husband gradually builds up an independent homestead through his wife and daughters. If the marriage is successful but the wife then dies young, the husband is compensated for the loss of his labor by acquiring the dead wife's sister, and the wife's group retains a satisfactory worker. This arrangement could be particularly advantageous for Navaho, among whom the husband may have accumulated sheep in joint ownership with his dead wife. If, alternatively, the wife dies after several years; leaving children, the husband, by marrying her sister, keeps control of his children, who would otherwise be likely to leave him and stay with their own matrilineal kin. The situation is similar among the Trukese, where the husband is likely to have grown trees and made other improvements for his children's benefit on land owned by the lineage of his wife. Sororatic marriage has particular advantages for the first wife's children. Marriage of the father to the mother's sister allows the children to remain in his custody and receive benefits from him without being removed from their lineage home.

Among Mappillas sororatic marriage has especial advantages in modern landowning families whose men are individually engaged in trade. We do not know whether it has increased in frequency in modern times, but it is certainly most common today in families which combine landowning with trade. Here the wife's group is likely to have paid at the marriage a cash bridegroom price with which the husband entered business, at least partly on behalf of his wife and children. If the wife dies young, the husband wishes to retain his capital and the wife's group wants to obtain him as husband for their second daughter without paying a second bridegroom wealth. If the wife dies later and there are children of the first marriage, there may be added advantages to a sororatic union. The husband may in modern times have already given a house and property to his wife and children; he will wish to remain with them and they will wish to retain his care without losing the benefits of close connection with their lineage. In this situation, if the dead wife left no younger unmarried sister, the husband may marry his wife's sister's daughter by an extension of sororatic marriage.

The frequency and circumstances of sororatic marriage in Minangkabau are not described. I suspect that they may be similar to those among Mappillas, since the Minangkabau also combine landownership with trade and with some ability on the part of men to accumulate personal property. In modern times they also pay a bridegroom price similar to that of middle-class Mappillas. Cash payments to bridegrooms, and gifts of personal wealth by fathers to children, have greatly increased in both societies in modern times. Nevertheless it may be significant that both Minangkabau and Mappillas were even traditionally trading groups in which individual men seem to have had some limited opportunities to acquire personal movable goods which they could give to wives and children, even though descent groups were based on highly productive, stable cultivation sites and a child's legally sanctioned claims on his father were correspondingly very weak. By contrast, in matrilocal or duolocal societies which had strong descent groups and high productivity from cultivation but in which men had little or nothing of personal wealth available for private disposal (e.g., Yao and Central Kerala Nayar), the husband had little basis, either voluntarily or legally, for forming an enduring economic relationship with his conjugal descent group and his children. In such societies neither sororal polygyny nor sororatic marriage is to be expected.

The Tonga "sororate" has a somewhat different form from that of the matrilocal societies discussed above. Here marriage to the dead wife's own sister is forbidden, apparently as part of a series of incest prohibitions which segregate conjugal and local ties from close matrilineal and consanguineal ones. There is, however, some preference for remarriage to a classificatory sister of the dead wife. A relevant factor here may be that the husband has paid bridewealth for his wife and, if she dies young, expects to receive value for the cattle he gave. There are also, however, advantages for the first wife's children. They have a life attachment to their father's matrilineal group, can claim definite support from their father even after the termination of his marriage, owe him services as they grow older, and have a right to live in his homestead. It is to their advantage to remain with him, provided that their stepmother will be a woman of their own matrilineal group and not a stranger whose matrilineal affiliations are opposed to their own. Similar considerations for the children also exist among Navaho and Trukese, both societies which, like the Tonga, accord children lifelong legal claims in and obligations to their fathers' matrilineal groups.

Widow Inheritance

Widow inheritance, the reverse of sororatic marriage, occurs when a widow marries a man of her dead husband's descent group. The second mate becomes the woman's legal husband and the legal father of her subsequent children. Widow inheritance is distinguished from the levirate, in which an heir of the dead man cohabits with the widow in order to raise children who will be the legal children of the deceased. The widow also remains the legal wife of the dead man, for whom his heir is merely a surrogate. No cases of levirate occurred among my examples.

Widow inheritance is usually phrased both as an obligation on the part of the widow to continue rendering services to her dead husband's descent group, and also as an obligation on the part of the husband's descent group to continue to provide for her and (usually) her children. The former obligation is probably stressed when the widow is young; the latter when she is old. In none of the example societies, however, was widow inheritance legally absolutely obligatory for either party; there was merely a stronger or weaker preference for it as opposed to remarriage to a stranger. It was a preferred marriage among Tonga, Bemba, Mayombe, Ashanti, Navaho, and Trukese; it occasionally occurred among Yao and was permitted among Mappillas and in Manangkabau (chap. 1, above; Richards, 1940a: 46–47; Fortes, 1950: 271; chaps. 2 and 3, above; Mitchell, 1956: 121; Loeb, 1934: 42). In the Trobriand Islands it was approved only for the widows of chiefs (chap. 4, above). It was not found among Ndembu except in the case of slave widows, inherited by the heir as slaves (Turner, 1957: 190), and was forbidden among Hopi (who were monogamous), Central Nayars, and Northern Nayars and Tiyyars.

Widow inheritance thus occurred in all the societies which had sororatic marriage. At least in some cases, however, the strength of the preference was different for the two marriages. Thus Northern Mappillas definitely preferred sororatic marriage, which, as has been seen, fitted well with matrilocal residence combined with voluntary gifts of personal property by the husband to his wife and children. Widow inheritance by the dead man's younger brother, although permitted by Muslim law, was, by contrast, very rare among Northern Mappillas. This seems to have been because the wife and children's relationship to their husband and father, whether economically significant or not, was a strictly personal relationship involving no significant relationship to his descent group. The reverse was the case among patrilineal Mappillas of Central Kerala: here widow inheritance was very common, and sororatic marriage, although permitted, extremely rare. It would be interesting to know the strength of both preferences among Minangkabau, but this is not indicated in the literature; both widow inheritance and sororatic marriage are merely said to have been approved.

The form of widow inheritance varies with the modes of succession and inheritance of the society. Among Tonga the widows of the deceased were distributed among different classificatory brothers, but not own brothers, of the dead man. Among Mayombe, Navaho, Trukese, Minangkabau, and Mappillas, the deceased's own brother was usually selected, although a classificatory brother might also fill the role of second husband. Yao and Ashanti inheritance patterns involved inheritance of the widow by that sister's son of the deceased who was chosen as his heir in "positional inheritance"; among Bemba the "positional heir" might be the deceased's sister's son or sister's daughter's son.

Since it occurs where sororatic marriage occurs, widow inheritance is obviously found in some predominantly matrilocal societies (Bemba, Navaho, Truk, and Mappillas, and also the matrilocally visiting Minangkabau). It is also, however, important in some avunculocal societies which do not permit sororatic marriage (e.g., Ashanti), and in some virilocal societies which do not greatly stress the sororatic preference (Tonga and Mayombe). In general, taking the societies where one or both customs exist, one would expect a stronger emphasis on widow inheritance with virilocality, and a stronger emphasis on sororatic marriage with matrilocality. This is because one would expect to find widow inheritance in matrilineal societies where either the widow and children, or the husband's descent group, or both, have some special interest in perpetuating the bond between them which was set up by the first marriage. Such a bond between wife and husband's descent group seems more likely to arise in virilocal than in matrilocal societies, although this is not necessarily the case. Certainly there are avunculocal societies where such a durable bond is not set up and widow inheritance is prohibited. Ndembu, Northern Nayars and Tiyyars, and Trobriand commoners are examples.

The following seem to be the chief circumstances under which special interests can be set up between the wife and children and the husband's matrilineal descent group, leading to widow inheritance. First, the children have a life attachment to the father's matrilineal group which persists after the father's death. This is the case among Navaho, Tonga, and, in a somewhat different manner, Trukese. Here legal obligations between the child and his father's group persist throughout the child's life. Remarriage of the mother to a man of her husband's group gives the children a stepfather in the group to which they already have legal attachment. Second, payment of bridewealth gives the husband's group specific, if limited and temporary, claims on the wife's sexuality and on her own and her immature children's labor. This appears to be the view of Tonga and Mayombe, the two societies where valuable bridewealth is paid. A similar but much more complete relationship exists when the wife and her children are slaves subject to inheritance by the husband's heir, as might occur among Ashanti, Yao, Bemba, Tonga, Ndembu, and Mayombe. Third, the society is a stratified one in which, through their wives and children, men can acquire laborers and a following, and thus attain to political office or bolster an office already held. The heir to the deceased's political office thus needs to take over the deceased's followers as his own supporters. Correspondingly, the wives and children of the deceased have acquired a privileged political status and perhaps a desirable place of residence through the former marriage, which they wish to retain. These conditions apply to the widows and children of Trobriand chiefs, of Bemba village headmen and chiefs, and perhaps of political officers among the Mayombe and Ashanti. It is noteworthy also that Yao widows are seldom inherited unless they have already come to settle in the village of the first husband, who was a village headman or a chief.

The societies which lack widow inheritance have none of these special conditions. Among Ndembu a child's personal legal relationship with his father is relatively strong, and it may happen in addition that his father's close kin are also his own matrilineal kin or that they live in the village of his matrilineal kin. If this is not the case, however, the child has no continuing claims on them; ultimately his status and residence are determined by matrilineal affiliations. The bridewealth paid for his mother is also of no great value and does not set up permanent obligations on her part. Among Hopi, again, the child's personal attachment to his father and father's descent group, although of great significance, do not depend on his mother's continuing association with this group. The father's group will continue to live in the village and be available to the child; in any case, moreover, his chief public statuses are acquired through matrilineal descent or non-kinship associations and not through paternal ties. The same is true in the Trobriands except in the case of the wives and children of chiefs. Similarly, among North Kerala Tiyyars, although the relationship of the wife and children with her husband is one of close economic coöperation, it is completely personal, gives them no significant public status, and ceases with the husband's divorce or death. Among Nayars of both areas, finally, we have seen that marriage involves no marriage payments of value, sets up no new public statuses, and initiates only the most slender personal obligations. Every effort is made, indeed, to keep the obligations personal and to sever them at the death of either spouse. It is for this reason that, on the husband's death, a Nayar widow is conducted ceremonially from his natal home even before the funeral takes place, and is never permitted to return.

I have tried to suggest connections between preferential marriages and the general content, especially the economic content, of relationships between kin. It is possible, however, that some forms of marriage may become prohibited or preferred through the spread of a major religion, whether or not the society's economic system is changed. Thus the prohibition of sororal polygyny and the permission of sororatic marriage and of widow inheritance, found among Mappillas and in Minangkabau, are in accordance with Muslim law. The data do not permit estimation of the relative strength of religious and economic determinants in these cases.

The Modern Disintegration of Matrilineal Descent Groups

Part Two has focused on the comparison of matrilineal systems in their "traditional" forms. It would be incomplete, however, without some reference to the radical changes going on during this century in matrilineal societies throughout the world. Recent literature has accumulated evidence to show that under economic changes brought about by contact with Western industrial nations, matrilineal descent groups gradually disintegrate. In their place, the elementary family eventually emerges as the key kinship group with respect to residence, economic coöperation, legal responsibility, and socialization, with a narrow range of interpersonal kinship relationships spreading outward from it bilaterally and linking it with other elementary families. The interim steps in this process of change vary in different societies and in different strata of the same society. There is also great variation in the degree of change at present experienced both within and between matrilineal societies. Nevertheless, given continued exposure to the same kinds of economic processes, the directions and end products of the change seem to be essentially the same.

Evidence tending toward this view is available for fourteen of the fifteen systems studied; it was considered inadequate for the Trobriands. Changes noted in each of the fourteen systems are summarized in this chapter.

Among the Tonga, Colson notes that modern cash-crop farming and the accumulation of wealth above subsistence needs intensify traditional tensions between matrilineal relationships on the one hand and conjugal and paternal relationships on the other. With the growth of new forms of production and of wealth, there is a tendency for matrilineal groups to break down, especially for purposes of inheritance, into small groups composed of uterine siblings and their immediate descendants through females. Many who are most deeply involved in the new economic processes desire a further change to elementary familial inheritance (chap. 1, above).

Among the Ndembu, Turner notes that cash-crop farming and migration to wagework have produced similar tendencies. In villages where subsistence farming has given place to cash-crop farming, men no longer eat together in a common village shelter, served in rotation by their several wives. Instead, each elementary family eats separately from the rest (Turner, 1957: 24). Eventually, men who specialize as petty traders or cash-crop farmers tend to build modern "farms" separate from the villages. They use their earnings primarily for their elementary families and neglect their traditional obligations to matrilineal kin. In the early stages of breakdown the matrilineage tends to split into groups of uterine siblings and their immediate descendants, often through *both* males and females—a small-scale replica of the traditional Ndembu village. A single elementary family, however, normally forms the social core of the modern "farm." Older men who have acquired wages or money from farming may for a time expend these in efforts to seize headship of more traditional villages. Younger men, however, tend to invest savings in capital goods—a bicycle for trading, a storehouse, or a sewing machine—rather than spend the money to gain followers, and these young men remain heads of separate elementary family units (*ibid.*: 133–136, 218–221).

De Cleene notes that among the Mayombe the lineage head's authority has been weakened by the modern individual wagework of men. Women, too, are sometimes able to earn wages and thus to free themselves both from the authority of their lineage head and also, in consequence, from the obligation to enter a traditional form of marriage. De Cleene reports a general move toward the development of personal wealth and toward inheritance from the father of both movable and immovable property (1937: 9–15).

Mitchell's data for the Yao are less conclusive but suggest the beginning of a similar trend. There is some cash-crop farming and wagework (Mitchell, 1956: 20–21). Such "paying" jobs tend to create, in some villages, new forms of wealth-heterogeneity which run counter to the traditional hierarchy of political status (*ibid.*: 213). Newcomers have settled in some villages among strangers, especially in villages near larger towns. In some cases at least, such newcomers arrive in elementary families and settle near the husband's place of work (*ibid.*: 192, 204–205).

Richards has written at length on the effects of labor migration on Bemba kinship. In this society, indeed, wagework on the part of temporarily absent men seems to be the chief source of kinship change, few new forms of internal production having as yet been introduced. With labor migration, matrilocal residence was rare among young couples in the 1930's. In place of several years of service in the wife's matrilocal unit, the husband gave money and a range of new goods to her family. By this means he gained a large measure of control over her early in the marriage. At the same time, the fact that marriage gifts were provided by the husband personally from his earnings rather than by his relatives gave him independence of both his own family and his wife's, so that he was free to divorce the wife at will or to move her to a place of his choosing (Richards, 1940a: 78–80). Instead of settling in the wife's family, the wageworking husband either left her behind temporarily with her parents or else took her to live nearer his place of work (ibid.: 36–38). While it seems to have increased the divorce rate, therefore, the major effect of wagework was evidently to break down descent groups and traditional matrilocal grandfamilies and to increase the autonomy of the elementary family, however temporary its association in particular cases (ibid.: 76–77). Richards notes, moreover, that nowadays the power of the father has "immeasurably" increased, since as a wage earner he "naturally" acquires new rights over his children in modern economic conditions (Richards, 1951: 175). In general she concludes that European influence and paid work for European employers have cut across the traditional kin groupings with their "system of relationships based on the exchange of services and the links of ritual" (Richards, 1940a: 14–15).

Economic change had apparently made deeper inroads in rural Ashanti at the time of Fortes' study in the mid-1940's than it had in the societies so far discussed. Cash-crop farming of cocoa was particularly important; it began about forty years previously in the villages studied intensively by Fortes (1949: 61–62). The maximal lineage, a majority of whose male and female members had "until recently" occupied a ward of the village, was no longer residentially unitary, and there appeared to be "no fixed norm of domestic grouping" (idem). Towns and industrial centers had different dwelling-group patterns than villages. Fortes notes that, in general, "the solidarity of the maximal lineage has declined in matters of a personal or domestic nature" (Fortes, 1950: 261). As in the case of the more "modern" Ndembu and Tonga, moreover, the matrilineal group having significance for the inheritance of property was often no longer either the maximal lineage or a major segment, but the immediate descendants of the deceased's own mother (idem). In spite of this

crumbling of the larger lineage groups, Fortes argues that "the strength
of matrilineal kinship within the constellation of kinship ties crystallized in the domestic group remains unimpaired" (*idem*).

Fortes' own data lead me, however, to doubt this assertion. He reports, for example, that the conflict between conjugal and paternal
ties on the one hand and matrilineal ties on the other had been much
aggravated by "missionary and modern economic influence," and
notes specifically that "modern opportunities for accumulating private means and holding fixed property such as cocoa farms and buildings, work in favor of the ties between parents and children" (*idem*).
About one out of four cocoa farms, in fact, seems to have passed from
father to children (*ibid.:* 272). There were widespread complaints
against the "frustrations" of matrilineal descent, although the rule was
still followed because "its force derived from the political and legal
system" (*ibid.:* 262). Matrilineal inheritance was "denounced on all
sides" and attempts had been made by the Confederacy Council to
introduce a rule which would cause a dead man's estate to be divided
into three shares—for the wife, the children, and the matrilineal heir.
It is true that the rule had had little effect outside the Christian community, for there was no means of enforcing it, but Fortes notes that
public opinion appeared to support it. There was particular complaint
against those matrilineal heirs who ejected their predecessors' wives
and children "from the enjoyment of properties in the building up of
which they have often assisted" (*ibid.:* 271–272).

It is not clear from the literature consulted whether houses were
traditionally owned by maximal lineages, lineage segments, or individuals. Even if they were built by individuals, however, the lineage
clearly had some lien on them, since they were built in the lineage
ward and presumably inherited by matrilineal heirs. Today individuals often build or buy houses with the aid of privately earned money,
so that headship of a house in "very many cases" results from personal economic achievement (Fortes, 1949: 65).

Fortes' detailed statistical analysis of the composition of dwelling
groups in two villages nicely illustrates variations in the relative
strength of matrilineal and conjugal ties in different localities. A part
of the differences in domestic unit composition seems to result, as
Fortes notes, from differences in the length of settlement. While both
communities had existed for a long time, Agogo (population about
4,000) had escaped severe disturbance from outside for several generations. By contrast, Asokore (population about 900) was broken
up after a rebellion in 1870 and only a fraction of the survivors later

returned to the town. Fortes states that the effects of "missions and schools, modern commerce, British rule, and all the other agencies of Western influence" had been about equal in the two places and that the range of occupations was similar. Nevertheless, Asokore was only twenty-five miles from Kumasi on a modern motor road in a thickly populated area, whereas Agogo, more isolated, was at the end of a second-class road eighteen miles from a mining center. "Urban contacts and influences," Fortes states, "were therefore much stronger at Asokore than at Agogo" (*ibid.*: 62–63). It was probably these "contacts and influences" which mainly accounted for differences of emphasis in the composition of domestic groups. This view finds support in Fortes' statement that at Asokore, "owing to the instability of the lineage organization and the opportunities for individual enterprise offered by the nearby city," the children of a dead woman tended to separate into independent domestic units (*ibid.*: 73).

The strength of lineage ties was thus much greater at Agogo than at Asokore. At Asokore, significantly more non-matrilineal kin lived with both male and female household heads than at Agogo, and further, Agogo households tended to contain matrilineal kin more distantly related to the household head than was the case at Asokore (*ibid.*: 79). Of the married women, 52 per cent lived with their husbands at Asokore, and only 18 per cent at Agogo (*ibid.*: 77). Correspondingly, only 20 per cent of children under the age of fifteen lived with matrilineal male guardians at Asokore, while 52 per cent did so at Agogo (*ibid.*: 79). Fortes concludes that a house headed by a man at Asokore was much more likely to be based on the man's own children than on his sisters' children, whereas the chances were about even at Agogo (*ibid.*: 82).

Whether or not these differences were related to differences in degrees of participation in the modern economy, there seems no doubt that in Ashanti, as elsewhere, modern conditions, in which cash-crop farming and wagework have great importance, are tending, first, to narrow the generation depth and span of the effective matrilineage, and second, to strengthen the elementary family as a more-than-traditionally significant economic, residential, and socializing unit.

The well-known studies of the Hopi by Titiev, Eggan, and Forde, which were the ones I consulted, give only hints of changes of the kind so far described. Nevertheless there is evidence of the beginnings of such change. At the time of Titiev's major field study in the early 1930's, land was still largely controlled by matrilineal descent groups at Oraibi and was never bartered or sold, and only rarely exchanged (Titiev, 1944: 181). The Hopi had, however, entered into important economic relationships with Americans; they imported tea and coffee and bought wagons on time payments from the United States government (*ibid.*: 195, 199). Sheep were privately owned, mostly by men, and a few men raised sheep to obtain cash through sales, although this practice was still despised by the majority (*ibid.*: 194). Two facts suggest that descent-group solidarity was declining and the elementary family growing stronger in the new conditions: first, clan coöperation in planting and harvesting had died out, and second, married couples no longer lived within the matrilocal grandfamily (*ibid.*: 16, 184). A young married woman might continue to work and cook with her mother, but she normally acquired a house of her own shortly after the marriage.

Eggan's and Forde's data suggest similar trends. Eggan notes that a man's personally acquired property, especially sheep, is divided between his children, particularly his sons (1950: 58). Forde noted in 1931 that some men were passing on land of their own clan to either their sons or daughters, and thought that this practice might have increased with a recent population decline coupled with the departure of some men and women to work in the towns (1931: 400).

Eggan also gives information on deeper-lying changes in the modern village of New Oraibi, founded in 1906 (1950: 134–138). Houses are usually occupied by elementary families, although the houses of close matrilineal kinswomen may be clustered together. "Occasionally," however, "a son or brother will build near by as well, adding a bilateral note to the extended family grouping" (*ibid.*: 135). Modern houses tend to be owned by individual men, who have either learned stonemasonry themselves or accumulated sufficient wealth to hire builders. "With this shift comes still further emphasis on patrilineal inheritance and patrilocal residence" (*idem*). There is a decline in observance of exogamy of the phratry and the clan, and of traditional sub-clan activities. Within the sub-clan the small lineage tracing descent from a known common ancestress still "frequently cooperates in various enterprises. But where these enterprises are modern rather than traditional, the problem of sharing the profits becomes a crucial one and causes much conflict" (*ibid.*: 136). "Younger Hopi at New Oraibi use a narrower range of kinship terms than was traditional, and their usage shows a shift toward a bilateral treatment of relatives" (*ibid.*: 137).

This information suggests a transitional picture, familiar from other societies, of initial decay of the larger unilineal groupings and narrowing of the span of the effective descent group, followed by conflicts within the latter unit as the elementary family asserts increasing autonomy. The economic system of New Oraibi is not explored, and Eggan tends to emphasize the effects of education and missionary teachings on kinship relationships. If, however, personal accumulation of wealth and new profit-making enterprises are involved, it seems probable that modern changes in the structure of production and hence in economic relations have been at least partly instrumental in the process of kinship change.

Connections between economic and kinship changes among the Navaho have not been adequately explored. From the data available on both types of change there seems little doubt that such connections exist, but I can only note the changes and hypothesize the connections. Thus, it is known that many Navahos have in recent decades been engaged in wagework or otherwise involved with the American economy, and we know that about 36 per cent of individuals probably lived in elementary family units in the 1930's (chap. 2, above). The extent of connection between these facts is not known; clearly, however, in some instances wagework caused a man to move his wife and children away from the matrilineal kin of both partners into or near a town.

The precise effects of modern economic change on Trukese kinship are likewise somewhat unclear, but there is again evidence of the expected trends. After 1918 the Japanese made major capital developments on the Trukese islands, which included refrigeration and drying plants for fish, beds for shellfish required for the making of buttons, and the large-scale expansion of manioc as a cash crop. "Many jobs" became available for manual wageworkers. The subsistence economy was undermined, and the Trukese began to buy quantities of foreign tools, clothing, canned fish, and, especially, rice (Gladwin and Sarason, 1953: 43). During World War II Truk became a base for Japanese military operations, and after the blockade of 1944 the need to feed 35,000 trapped Japanese, as well as 10,000 Trukese, greatly depleted the islands' resources. After World War II an economic decline set in: the Americans had no use for the Trukese exports and could do little more than assist them to export to other areas. No new important capital investments have been made, many sources of cash have dried up, and the Trukese are consequently unable to buy many goods to which they had become accustomed (ibid.: 45). The Trukese are, however, still involved in foreign markets: United States whaleboats and motor launches have replaced Japanese power boats and sailboats, coconuts are an important cash crop, and there is much importation of flour and rice, canned meat, fish, and cloth (*ibid.:* 55–56, 61).

The Trukese descent group seems to have been surprisingly resilient in the face of all these changes. One reason for this may be that the production of coconuts and the processing of copra for export can still be carried out on a lineage basis under the direction of the lineage head, who in turn is responsible for paying the government head-taxes for adult male members (*ibid.:* 138–139). Another reason for the partial survival of the matrilineal principle may be that young wageworkers, who often travel abroad, can seldom take their wives with them, so that the latter tend to remain with older matrilineal kin. The wageworker's earnings, however, belong to him as an individual and tend to be given over chiefly to his wife, her father, and her brothers (*ibid.:* 139). There is some evidence of the strengthening of the elementary family in the fact that small houses for married couples and their dependents have largely replaced the old dwellings designed for matrilocal extended families. Further, although the small houses still tend to cluster in matrilocal extended family aggregates, they are often built on separate plots owned by different individuals and acquired from different lineages—which scarcely sounds like a primitive economic situation. Only 6 per cent of the population, however, live in economically independent elementary family units; they are church officials and "those seeking to break with traditional ways" (chap. 3, above). Finally, the historical evidence concerning bequests of trees and other improvements to land by fathers to their children is unclear; Fischer's view is that the custom is of pre-German occupation status but that it may have increased in frequency during recent decades (chap. 3, above). In general the Trukese lineage seems to have stood up to modern economic change better than one would have expected, but there is evidence that the seeds of decay have been sown.

De Jong has summarized the modern changes in Minangkabau kinship without linking them to wider economic change. He notes that during the present century the sale of ancestral, lineage-owned property has become common, and privately owned property has correspondingly increased. The lineage segment which used to own property jointly (the parui) is now no longer universally exogamous, and cross-cousin marriage is declining in frequency. The members of many lineages have become territorially scattered, and in those which retain some unity there is an increasing tendency for headships to be filled by appointment after general discussion, rather than by succession laws. The authority of matrilineal guardians has declined. Individuals now tend to arrange their own marriages, and married couples increasingly occupy elementary family households or else live together in the extended family house of the partner of higher rank. Correspondingly, the father now often pays his children's school fees, may act as their legal guardian, and makes large bequests to his sons, sometimes to the extent of his whole personal property (De Jong, 1951: 115–119).

Schrieke provides valuable historical and economic information as a context to these changes. He points out that after the Dutch opened up the Padang Highlands at the end of the nineteenth century, they at first enforced the compulsory cultivation of coffee for export by the government, prohibited the export of rice, and in general restricted private trade. Government export of coffee ceased in 1908, and the prohibition of rice exportation was lifted in 1912. After this time both coffee and rice began to be exported privately as cash crops and money circulated more freely (Schrieke, 1955: 97–98). The traditional law forbidding the sale of matrilineally owned property ceased to be observed in practice as early as 1907, and such sales are now very common. In some areas (Solon and Air Dingin), all land has now become privately owned, freely marketable property. Schrieke sees these changes as fundamental to the decline of matrilineal ties, to the change to neolocal residence in elementary family households, to the great increase of paternal gifts and bequests by will, and in some cases, to the intestate inheritance by children of their father's personal property. He notes that these changes were already apparent in 1895 among those most involved in the cash economy—traders, *hadjis,* and chiefs —but that they have now spread to the population at large (*ibid.:* 107–123).

What precise characteristics of modern conditions bring about the disintegration of matrilineal descent groups? They have not always been adequately pinpointed in the literature on social change. Fortes, for example, writing of the fact that "there appears to be no fixed norm of domestic grouping" in modern Ashanti, sees this as one sign of "a diversified and in parts unstable social system." The unstable social system he sees as in turn produced by "occupational differentiation, stratification by income, education, and rank, geographical and social mobility, as well as disparate values in religious belief, morality, law, and personal ideal" (Fortes, 1949: 60–61). All of these characteristics, are, no doubt, present in modern Ashanti, but such a global description does not focus on the root cause of kinship change. Some of the characteristics which Fortes notes—for example, some degree of stratification by education and rank, and of social and geographic mobility—must also have been present in pre-British Ashanti when the cohesion of descent groups was unimpaired. If, moreover, we are seeking a general theory of the disintegration of matrilineal systems, we must recognize that every one of the characteristics which Fortes lists was present in Kerala for at least three centuries before the British conquest.

I suggest that certain specific characteristics of modern economic organization, found in varying degrees in all the societies we have discussed, bring about the disintegration of matrilineal descent groups. These are not, however, "trade" per se, or the use of money, or even the existence of markets. These factors were present in Kerala in the fifteenth century. The root cause of modern kinship change in these societies appears rather to be the gradual incorporation of the society in a unitary market *system,* in which markets cease to be isolated and are linked in a common standard of value, and in which all produced goods, but more particularly land and other natural resources, and human labor itself, become privately owned and potentially marketable commodities (Polanyi, 1957: 68–69). The capitalist market system is of course based on the fuel technology of industrial nations, and it is the economic relationships with these nations which primarily bring about the modern kinship change.

Obviously, to assess the character of these relationships, it is necessary also to take account of the political context in which they have developed, namely, the circumstance that all the societies studied were obliged to enter the market system through restricted channels, as a result of political conquest or other forceful pressures on the part of expanding industrial nations. Thus the industrial nations have normally exported only very limited parts of their fuel technology, such as transport facilities, to the societies we have discussed. In the case of Truk, the various African societies, Minangkabau, and Kerala, members of the conquered societies seem in varying degrees to have entered the market system as a result of three main pressures: the industrial nations' search for raw materials or semiprocessed materials such as cash crops and minerals; their search for markets for their own manufactured goods; and, as a corollary of political conquest, their need to gather cash taxes to support new administrative institutions. It seems to have been mainly these pressures which directed the conquered peoples into wage labor, cash-crop farming, and, in some instances, into professions and salaried occupations made necessary by the new political structures.

The Hopi and Navaho cases are somewhat different. Having conquered the surrounding, more valuable territory, the industrial nation here had no special need either to draw raw materials from these tribes or to use them as markets. Its need was rather to keep the tribes pacified, to make them self-sufficient on the slender resources of their reservations, or, to the extent that this last proved impossible, to educate them so that they could support themselves within the economy of the larger society. The Hopi and Navaho were thus subjected to less forceful pressures from the market system than most truly colonial societies tend to be. This may account for the greater durability of their traditional institutions and the fact that their descent groups seem only recently to have shown signs of disintegration. Pressure of population on the poor resources of their reservations seems to be the chief factor which has directed them into participation in the market system.

As a final example, I examine the major changes in Kerala which have been responsible, directly or indirectly, for the disintegration of matrilineal descent groups during and since British rule. This case is presented in rather greater detail because historical materials allow me to trace steps more clearly than in the other examples I discussed.

After the British conquest of 1792, the structure of Kerala's production was radically changed under British influence. For many centuries Kerala had had foreign trade, administered by royalty with treaty-fixed prices, but this trade had mainly involved the export of surplus raw materials, chiefly pepper, and the import of metals, weapons, and limited luxury goods (Logan, 1951, I: 300–399). There had also been isolated local markets, but villages had produced mainly for their own subsistence, supplying most of their own basic necessities. During British rule, but particularly after the development of the railways from 1860 on, and the opening of the Suez Canal in 1869, the subsistence economy of most villages was undermined. Kerala began to produce vast quantities of cash crops for export and to import both essential raw materials and manufactured goods (Innes, 1908: 259–261). Cash crops, especially coffee, rubber, and tea, were drawn partly from newly developed plantations in the hilly regions, owned chiefly by Europeans. Other crops such as coconuts, pepper, cashew nuts, areca nuts, and cardamoms were, however, grown in quantities in villages. Correspondingly, in many areas villages ceased to produce enough rice and other subsistence crops for their own necessities. Thus by 1940 roughly half of the cultivated land of Kerala was devoted to cash crops. In Travancore State, in 1937, 65 per cent of exports were cash crops or their semiprocessed products such as copra and coir, while 59 per cent of imports were essential consumer goods, mainly rice, cloth, and kerosene (Namboodiripad, 1952: 74–76). Certain hand industries expanded to employ large numbers in wagework, largely in the manufacture of coconut products. Machine industry, by contrast, was introduced very slowly, so that by 1947 there were only a few machine factories in the larger coast towns, producing mainly textiles, oil, and soap. Moreover, while the largest sector of the population remained engaged in production of primary products through agriculture or fishing, there was great expansion in the sectors concerned in trade, transport, the professions, and public administration. Adequate figures are not available to me for Central and Northern Kerala, but the 1931 figures for Travancore illustrate the rough proportions of the population engaged in primary, secondary, and tertiary occupations:

Primary occupations (agriculture, unskilled labor, mining, fishing): 428, 321.

Secondary occupations (hand and machine industries): 201, 659.

Tertiary occupations (transport, trade, public administration, professions, religious work, arts): 241, 935.

(*ibid.:* 76; quoted from the 1931 Economic Census of Travencore).

These changes in the structure of production and of occupations brought about the private ownership and marketability not only of produced goods but also of land and labor. Before British rule, no one had "owned" land in Kerala in the Western capitalist's sense (Logan, 1951, I: 110–112, 269, 270, 596–608; Baden-Powell, 1892, III: 151–184; Innes, 1908: 288–304). Land was managed, as has been seen, by descent groups of the dominant caste or castes in each village—usually Nayars and Brahmans. The managers owned not the land, but hereditary rights in a portion of its produce, and judicial rights over those of lower caste who lived and worked on it. Descent groups or families of each of the lower castes also owned hereditary rights in the produce of land in return for their services. The various types of "managerial" descent groups—jenmis and kanakkar—could sell their combined managerial, judicial, and economic rights to other descent groups. They did so, in fact, with increasing frequency in the period of European trade before the British conquest. These sales did not, however, take place in the conditions of a free market. They were restricted to descent groups of the same or of similar caste to the sellers, and they had to be sanctioned by district chiefs or royalty, who probably also fixed the price of the rights which were sold (Logan, 1951, I: 603; II: cxxxi–clv).

By 1805 the system of land tenure was changed and jenmis became recognized in law as landowners in the capitalist sense (Innes, 1908: 305–306; Logan, 1951, I: 613–614; II: ccl–ccli). Correspondingly, tenants, sub-tenants, and serfs ceased to own hereditary, inalienable rights in the produce of the land they lived on. Tenants became renters of land who paid cash or produce for their leases and held varying rights in the land for varying periods of time. Serfs became daily wage laborers—either for produce or cash—and could be evicted by the landlord. These changes came about first through misinterpretation of the traditional law on the part of British administrators, who wished to isolate a class of "owners" and make them responsible for payment of land revenue, and who translated the native situation into capitalist concepts with which they were familiar at home. Given the changes in the structure of production which were taking place, however, some such legal changes in landownership would have been inevitable in any case before the mid-nineteenth century. Indeed, it was only after changes in the types of production occurred that the new legal concepts were extensively acted upon in villages. Thus, eviction of tenants by landlords scarcely occurred until after 1831, when the market began to expand and prices of agricultural produce, to rise (Logan, 1951, I: 614–615). In areas where cultivation remained primarily for subsistence, moreover, the old modes of land usufruct by hereditary caste right were clung to as far as possible—even, in a few villages, into the 1940's. Where, however, land became extensively converted to cash-crop farming, it was no longer possible to give castes hereditary rights in the produce. Since no governmental authority took over these forms of production, jenmis and kanakkar became capitalist entrepreneurs. They produced only partly for subsistence, rented out some land to sub-tenants by the year, sold a large part of their produce in the market, hired and dismissed laborers as they needed them, and paid them wages at market rates, increasingly in cash. Wage labor, beginning in the European cash-crop plantations, thus spread to the traditional villages as the latter relied increasingly on exports and imports for their maintenance. Meanwhile, of course, vast new sources of wagework and salary work were opening up in connection with government service, transport, "coolie" labor on behalf of traders, mills for hand industries, and the processing of cash crops for export.

Having passed into private ownership by descent groups, land could be sold freely in the market, and was sold increasingly frequently from about 1830. In some areas the larger aristocratic landowners, taking advantage of their profits from cash crops and also from the new forms of professional or salary work, were able to buy up the land of smaller owners in their vicinity. Thus, for example, in the Kottayam district of North Kerala, one Nayar descent group, formerly district chiefs, profited so much from sales of cashew nuts and coconuts that it was able to buy thirty square miles of rice, garden, and forest land. It dispossessed the village headmen and independent Nayar cultivators of this area and reduced them to the status of tenants. In other cases, families of the new middle class of independent traders—chiefly Mappillas—were able to seize the land of impoverished Nayars as payment for urban purchases of manufactured or consumer goods (*ibid.:* 617). The lack of development of machine industries which was a feature of British colonial policy made land sales ever more frequent, for land purchase was almost the only form of secure investment for successful salary workers, traders, or the more prosperous farmers. The rapidity of land sales was of course also affected by business cycles of the Western nations to whose economy Kerala had become linked. Thus, for example, many of the larger owners greatly increased their estates in the inflationary period after World War I, but some were obliged to sell again during the depression of the early 'thirties (Namboodiripad, 1952: 88). In general, however, the period up to 1955 was one of increasing concentration of land and other capital goods in the hands of a small number of large landowners and traders. Estimates from sample villages in Cochin and Travancore indicated that in each village between 60 and 80 per cent of the rural population owned no land or less than one acre per family, while in most villages only from 3 to 10 per cent of the families owned more than five acres (*ibid.:* 92).

While to a large extent all became engaged in new, caste-free occupations, Nayars, Tiyyars, and Mappillas tended to move into different niches of the new economic structure. In the nineteenth century large numbers of the wealthier Nayars entered salaried occupations in government service or became lawyers, doctors, or other professional workers. This was especially true in Central Kerala, where Nayars had traditionally done little cultivation, and where the collapse of the military organization left men without occupations. Over the decades many commoner Nayars in both Central and North Kerala were obliged to sell their small holdings to larger capitalists. The impoverished Nayars then leased land from others or became wage or salary earners as agricultural laborers, bailiffs, schoolteachers, cooks in restaurants, petty clerks or messengers in government offices, or (in recent decades) bus drivers or factory hands. The great majority of North Kerala Tiyyars became agricultural "coolies" for daily wages on the cash-crop farms of large Nayar owners, petty traders of cash crops, or else small tenants of plots devoted to mixed subsistence and cash-crop farming. A few became rich through trade or the processing of coconut products and bought cash-crop estates of their own. Aristocratic Mappillas in North Kerala, like the wealthier Nayars, devoted a large part of their estates to pepper, timber, coconuts, and other cash crops. From both high-caste and low-caste Mappillas there arose a new middle class of private merchants engaged in export and import trade or owning retail businesses in the towns. The poorer low-caste Mappillas of North Kerala became chiefly agricultural laborers, petty traders, or "timber coolies," who transported logs downriver from the forests of the Western Ghats for export from coastal towns.

In each of these castes, few of the new economic undertakings proved practicable for long-term joint enterprise on the part of matrilineal descent groups. The collapse of the descent group has been most rapid and thorough in the case of the poorest, landless wageworkers and small tenants. Among them the descent group has lost its basis in the hereditary, matrilineal tenure of fields and ownership of rights in produce. Agricultural labor on the new cash-crop farms is not recruited on the basis of descent groups: it requires large gangs of coolies who participate as individuals, regardless of kinship affiliations. Where, in the nineteenth century, a Tiyyar family was able to hold on to a few plots of rice and garden land for two or three generations, a small descent group with avunculocal residence might grow up and engage jointly in production. In the past hundred years, however, with the growing frequency of evictions and with the vast increase in population, men have wandered much between villages in search of wagework or of plots to rent. In such conditions the only viable mobile kinship unit is a married couple or an elementary family; men cannot often take sisters with them on their enterprises because sisters normally have husbands who are seeking work elsewhere. Neolocal residence in elementary families, or small patrilocal grandfamilies, occasionally with divorced or widowed sisters, have thus become the dominant forms of domestic grouping among Tiyyars. Ancestral or once-inherited property is in law still subject to joint matrilineal ownership among Tiyyars as among Nayars, although such property may now be divided into individual shares among members of the matrilineal descent group. Few Tiyyars possess such ancestral property, however, and most fathers bequeath their private property and earnings to their wives and children before their deaths. The Tiyyar and also the low-caste Mappilla descent group has thus in most cases become no more than a scattered exogamous unit, whose members may or may not congregate for life-crisis rites.

The descent group cohered more strongly and for a longer period among Nayars and aristocratic Mappillas, who were able to retain their estates. Some very large descent groups of former royalty, chiefs, and wealthy commoners still jointly owned estates in 1950. The great majority, however, divided their property between individuals or between groups of uterine siblings soon after the acts were passed in the 1930's which permitted such division. In most taravāds which had not divided their property, moreover, "partition suits" were pending in the courts. Nevertheless, some descent groups did retain a measure of unity for a hundred years after the capitalist market system began to get underway. In these landowning property groups the kāranavan normally managed the whole estate. In the largest ones he might give portions of it into the management of one or two other seniors, who lived separately with their wives and children and had partial autonomy over their finances. Junior members were paid in cash from the proceeds of cash-crop farming, and provided with subsistence goods if they lived in or near the ancestral home. Many younger men, however, moved elsewhere in search of careers, as professional men or government servants in the case of Nayars, or into private trade or small retail businesses in the case of Mappillas. Some Mappilla businesses were started with descent-group funds and held for short periods as joint property, but often such a plan was not feasible. Many forms of small business thrived best on individual initiative and daring. Larger enterprises such as export firms, mills for hand industries, and banks, required more capital than most descent groups could muster and tended to be run by joint-stock companies composed of individuals who invested independently of their descent groups (Namboodiripad, 1952: 78–79). In general, given the fluctuations of the market system, investment in business was too risky for a kāranavan charged with the management of jointly owned funds, which tended therefore to be invested in land whenever possible. In most cases where junior Nayars or Mappillas left the taravād to seek employment elsewhere, their earnings were personal property and they lived with, and maintained, their wives and children. Often, too, they invested their savings in land and houses, and, having lived for many years in private elementary family homes, it was natural that they should bequeath such property to the wife as a joint holding for herself and her matrilineal descendants. In the later nineteenth century, therefore, new, small branch-property groups were perpetually being founded through the wives of individuals who had amassed personal property. These circumstances greatly exacerbated the traditional tensions between conjugal and paternal ties on the one hand and matrilineal ties on the other. Litigation over property between men of the same taravād and bitter quarrels between the children and matrilineal heirs of men who died intestate thus became regular features of family life in the higher matrilineal castes. The Malabar Marriage Act of 1896 was an attempt to regulate this situation and to give legal support to the increasing demands for recognition of the status of the elementary family. It provided that if a man registered his marriage with the authorities he should be responsible for maintaining his wife and children, and that if he died intestate half of his personal property should go to them and half to his matrilineal heirs (Nair, 1941: 300). For about a decade afterward, these provisions were seen as premature by the majority of Nayars, but by the 1930's they had come to be regarded as wholly inadequate. Popular pressure had arisen for the enforcement of marriage registration, the voluntary per capita division of such matrilineal ancestral properties as remained, and the inheritance of all personal property by the wife and children. Various acts were passed in the 1930's which fulfilled these conditions, thus providing for the final dissolution of matrilineal descent groups.[1] By 1947 very few descent groups remained which had not divided their property according to the provisions of these acts, or whose property was not in process of partition by the courts. Although the extent of its decline was by no means uniform, the matrilineal principle was universally regarded as obsolescent. In its place the elementary family was rapidly becoming the effective unit of residence, economic coöperation, legal responsibility, and socialization.

[1] The Madras *Marumakkattayam* Act (XXII of 1933) and the Cochin Nayar Act (XXIX of 1938). The corresponding enactments in Travancore were the Travancore Nayar Act of 1922 and the Irava and Nanjinad Vellala Acts of 1923.

It is not suggested that economic change, brought about by internal changes in the structure of production and by changed relationships with other societies, is always and everywhere solely responsible for kinship change. I have already noted that the economic changes mentioned were themselves carried out in the context of political conquest, and could not have been carried out without corresponding changes in political institutions, laws, and education. Moreover, changes of political structure resulting from conquest by a market-organized nation may in some cases directly weaken descent groups by eliminating some or all of their traditional legal functions. One can also imagine other types of conquest, for example by a Communist society, in which enforced political change might involve the immediate abolition of descent groups, and perhaps even of elementary families, and their replacement by quite other institutions for production, distribution, reproduction, and socialization. In other contexts it is conceivable that without any profound economic change the spread of a major religion such as Christianity or Islam may change the character of some kinship relationships, particularly of marriage. What is suggested, however, is that in the particular circumstances of domination by market-organized industrial nations, whatever the character of the preceding or accompanying legal or religious changes, entry into the market system is in fact causing the disintegration of matrilineal descent groups in the societies I have discussed, and the emergence of the elementary family as the core unit in a bilaterally extended system of interpersonal kinship relationships.

There seems little doubt that entry into the capitalist market system also tends to break down descent groups in patrilineal societies, at least for large sectors of the contacted population. Patrilineal descent groups in agrarian societies, like matrilineal ones, lose their economic basis when land is constantly being bought and sold, individuals work chiefly for wages, production becomes vested in such groups as the factory or the plantation, and ownership is by individuals or by joint-stock companies. There seem, however, to be characteristic differences in the processes through which matrilineal and patrilineal descent groups disintegrate in these modern conditions.

In the early phases of entry into the market system, descent groups often seem able to persist in an attenuated form in those sections of an agrarian society which still rely partly on traditional subsistence production, having wagework or sale of products as supplementary sources of wealth. This seems to be the case where the degree of dependence on the market does not allow its fluctuations to cause frequent buying and selling of land or other subsistence resources. It is in this stage that differences seem most marked in the processes of change in matrilineal and patrilineal systems. Matrilineal groups seem to be badly hit as soon as their members enter the market system. Although they may not disintegrate altogether for many decades, they are likely to break down into their minimal segments. Further, as soon as individuals begin to acquire private earnings, violent tensions occur between conjugal and paternal ties on the one hand and matrilineal ties on the other. Patrilineal groups seem better able to weather the early changes and may even give a temporary appearance of increased durability. The reason for this is that, because of the different reproductive and authoritative roles of men and women, wives are more fully incorporated into their conjugal descent groups in patriliny than is either spouse into the conjugal descent group in matriliny. Because wives, as the mothers of heirs, are partly incorporated into the patrilineal descent group, the elementary family operates as a minimal segment of this unit. In matriliny, by contrast, the elementary family is torn between two descent groups—that of the husband and that of the wife and children.

We may illustrate differences in the process of change by contrasting the Nayars with the patrilineal Tamil Brahmans of Tanjore District, both castes who have combined landowning with salary work in the past hundred years.[2]

The joint property-owning unit of the Brahmans was formerly either a patrilocal grandfamily or a patrilocal extended family, incorporated within a larger localized lineage comparable in size and functions to the Nayar maximal lineage. In both castes conditions associated with the market system and with the new political structure have, in the past hundred years, caused almost total disintegration of the maximal lineage. In both castes, however, until recent years, the head and some junior members of the smaller, property-owning descent group have, in many instances, tended to remain on an ancestral estate and to organize the cultivation of both subsistence and cash crops by hired servants. Other male members have typically gone to live in towns with their wives and children and to earn salaries or fees. In the Nayar case the absent male member would usually devote most of his earnings to his wife and children, with whom he lived and who

[2] Richards mentions similar forms of adaptation of the patrilocal extended family to new economic conditions among the Ngoni and other African patrilineal tribes, contrasting them with the breakdown of Bemba descent and residential units (Richards, 1940a, 10, 38).

rendered him services and comforts. At the same time the wife and children would typically draw maintenance allowances from their own descent group. After a few years the husband might invest his earnings in a new house and land for his wife and her immediate matrilineal descendants. He would be reluctant to contribute to his taravād's investments because this would detract from the welfare of his children, for whom, through close association, he had come to regard himself as responsible. By the time he became kāranavan of his descent group he would probably have built up a small estate for his children, and might thenceforth be tempted to add to it from the profits of his own descent group. In such conditions acute tensions arose at the outset between the matrilineal kin and the elementary families of male members. At worst, these families could ruin the taravād financially, through litigation; at best, they often caused the members of the taravād to live apart in bitterness.

In the Brahman case, by contrast, an absent salary-earning man tended to maintain close ties with his natal patrilineal kin. While using part of his salary for the current needs of his wife and children, he would invest part in the joint estate, knowing that this would one day benefit his children as heirs. He and his elementary family returned to the ancestral house as of right. His wife might give birth there to their children. The husband might leave small children behind there, or take away the older children of his brothers to be educated in the town. In at least some cases, brothers whose parents had died found it profitable to keep their property undivided for one or two decades longer than they traditionally would have done. They would pool part of their earnings and leave the land in the care of a brother who consented to remain at home.[3] There were, of course, as in all patrilineal systems, tensions between the component elementary families, of which the several wives were the focal points. These tensions deepened as elementary families gained residential and partial economic autonomy—especially if their earnings were uneven. Nevertheless, the fact that the elementary family was already part of the patrilineal descent group, instead of cutting across two descent groups, allowed the descent group to function as a single corporation so long as fluctuations of the market did not force it to sell its joint

[3] In other cases a group of brothers might jointly buy a restaurant or other small business in a town, and later invest their profits in new, jointly owned land in the natal village. In patrilineal India generally, larger businesses and industrial concerns are often owned jointly by wealthy patrilineal descent groups. In Kerala, by contrast, joint ownership of shops or factories by matrilineal descent groups has usually proved unsuccessful and has been rare.

estate. Such descent groups seem to have been common among Tanjore Brahmans until the depression of the 1930's, and some persist today (Gough, 1956).

Even in the most recent, postwar phase of absorption into the market system, in which both Brahman and Nayar descent groups are tending to disintegrate completely, the process is less striking and less immediately apparent among Brahmans than among Nayars. Differences in the generation depth and lines of fission of the two types of traditional property group are relevant here. The traditional Nayar commoner property group, as has been seen, could not divide into segments until after the deaths of the common ancestress and of her sons. This was because, given dependence on a joint estate, brothers could not be severed from the uterine sisters whose children were their closest heirs. The property group therefore had a minimal depth of three to four generations. At the least, it comprised a group of true brothers and sisters with their uterine descendants. Among Brahmans, by contrast, daughters left the property group on marriage and wives became legal members of it, with rights to maintenance till death. The group could divide into its minimal segments after the death of the common ancestor and ancestress. That is to say, true brothers could, if they wished, divide their property after the deaths of their parents, provided all were adult and married. A new property group might therefore occasionally start out as a simple elementary family, although it would quickly grow to become a patrilocal grandfamily and for a time, probably, a patrilineal extended family, before it redivided.

In the Brahman system an elementary family was thus, even traditionally, the core of each seceding unit at the time of division of the descent group, whereas among Nayars the seceding unit was a matrilineage segment. Eventually, the end result of modern change seems likely to be the same in both castes, at least for large sections of the population. With the further decline of subsistence production and with fuller incorporation into the market system, involving frequent sales of land, ancestral joint properties are sold. Land and other goods become personally acquired property subject to the disposal of the individual owners. Individuals rely for a livelihood on their own enterprise or employment, and each elementary family, as in the West, tends to attain independence early in its career, even before the deaths of the parents. Recent and pending legislation in India, which provides for equal inheritance of intestate property by both daughters and sons, is evidence of the advanced stage of decline of patrilineal descent groups. Its parallel in Kerala was the legislation of the 1930's, which provided for per capita division of matrilineal ancestral property between both male and female members, and for the equal inheritance by sons and daughters of the intestate personal property of their parents.

In the Brahman case, however, disintegration of the minimal descent group merely involves earlier fission into elementary families of the small patrilineal unit. If the ancestral estate is completely lost, young men today may leave their parents to earn money in the towns even before marriage, and the old couple may eventually be left alone, to live on their savings or a government pension. Nevertheless there is less sharp discontinuity in the content of patrilineal relationships, because the patrilineal unit is itself an outgrowth of an elementary family. Children still visit their parents, older parents may live with a married son, brothers make loans to one another, and the destitute go to live with close patrilineal kin. Among Nayars, disintegration of the descent group involves sharper discontinuities in some key relationships. In particular, men now divide their property and fortunes from those of their uterine sisters, and correspondingly completely lose their authority over the sisters' children.

Although, therefore, absorption into the capitalist market system eventually appears to bring about the disintegration of both patrilineal and matrilineal descent groups as organized units, one may perhaps expect decay to become earlier apparent in the matrilineal system. There are also more intermediate steps in the process of change, and the end results shows greater discontinuity with traditional forms than appears to be the case in a patrilineal society.

PART THREE————————————————————

Cross-cultural
Comparisons

Matrilineal Descent in Cross-cultural Perspective

This chapter was originally intended to test a number of the generalizations made by Schneider and Gough on a larger sample than the ethnographic cases familiar to the authors of this book.[1] Murdock's *World Ethnographic Sample* (1957) provided a selected sample of 565 societies classified with reference to 30 variables, and included 84 matrilineal cases.[2] It seemed likely that the sample could be used to test these generalizations, but as work progressed it became clear

[1] A non-statistician who embarks on this kind of effort is helplessly dependent on advice and assistance. H. M. Blalock spent many hours in patient and illuminating discussion of choice of statistical techniques, as well as in substantive and theoretical discussions on the topic of this chapter. I am deeply indebted to him. David Goldberg was most helpful with statistical advice. Allan G. Feldt did most of the tabulating, preparation of tables, and computing, as well as providing statistical advice and critical reading of the manuscript at various stages. His efficiency, accuracy, and unfailing good cheer were important assets in a task which extended over more than a year, and which involved discarding or compressing and redoing many of the tables we ran. Marshall D. Sahlins was a major source of theoretical stimulation. I have greatly benefited from extensive discussions of this chapter with my wife, Kathleen Gough, and from her editorial comments. I hold none of these persons accountable for the use I made of their advice.

The work was supported in part by a Ford Foundation Behavioral Studies Grant, and time for analysis and writing came partly from a University of Michigan fund for released time, subsidized by the Ford Foundation.

[2] This chapter makes passing comments on some twenty-five or thirty cultures. In some instances the remarks are based on a single source, but in others they rest on many sources and several years' reading. Since the entire chapter is quantitative in emphasis, an ethnographic bibliography of upward of twenty-five items seemed out of proportion to the attention given to specific instances. North American references were drawn from Murdock (1953). Materials on South America were almost exclusively based on Steward (1946–1959). The bibliography on African and Circum-Mediterranean cases was culled from Murdock (1959). In the case of groups from other areas, sources are as follows: Belu: Vroklage (1952); Garo: Playfair (1909); Karen: Marshall (1922); Khasi: Gurdon (1914); Minangkabau: Part Two of this volume and references cited there; Tiwi: Hart and Pilling (1960); Vedda: Seligman and Seligman (1911).

that most of the variables used by Schneider and Gough were not coded in the sample, so that only a few of their propositions could be tested in this way. I was not prepared to develop a new "world sample" and code it for the relevant variables, nor to return to Murdock's sources in order to add the relevant data to the 565 cases in his sample.

In the meantime, however, as I worked with the sample I became involved with the issue of the place of matrilineal systems in the world's cultures, and in the problems of method raised by working with a large body of coded materials—and coded by someone who did not have my immediate problems in mind. Hence this chapter will deal primarily with a general view of matrilineal cultures, secondarily with problems of method associated with the use of coded data on large samples of cultures, and only briefly with tests of Schneider's and Gough's propositions.

The Problem

For the most part, the authors of this book have chosen to take matrilineal systems as given. They have asked what resemblances we find among all of them, or what systematic variation we find among them, but seldom do they raise the question of the circumstances which give rise to or perpetuate matrilineality—or any other form of descent system. (Gough's chapter on residence does discuss this issue.) Yet the question of the locus of matrilineal, patrilineal, non-unilineal, and double-unilineal systems has long been of concern to anthropologists, and did concern our group when it met in the SSRC Summer Seminar of 1954.

The usual question is, "Where *do* we find matrilineal kinship?" One major problem about answering the question has to do with the comparability of various systems commonly regarded as matrilineal. Matriliny consists simply in assigning individuals to kinship categories by reference to descent traced through females. Such categories may be dispersed or localized, organized or unorganized. There may be a dispersed unorganized category, such as a clan, and a localized, organized one, such as a lineage or sub-clan, in the same system. The primary function of the category may be the extension of hospitality and protection, the inheritance of property, mutual defense, redistribution of goods, or authoritative regulation. Or all of these functions may be so important that no one of them can be called primary. When we ask under what conditions matriliny is found, we seem to be attempting to account simultaneously for the conditions which create and those which perpetuate a wide variety of types of units lumped together solely by the pattern of descent reckoning. Gough's comparative chapters indicate that only when the precise structure and functioning of matrilineal groups are defined, and the various types of groups categorized, does it become possible to show that certain features of these groups co-vary with such factors as productivity, political centralization, and economic processes. It is highly probable that if patrilineal systems were similarly categorized, equivalent co-variations could be demonstrated. Hence it might be far more meaningful to try to explain the circumstances under which kinship units at various levels of organization occur, without respect to lineality, than to try to explain the distribution of matriliny. Nevertheless, systems which employ matrilineal reckoning are by no means randomly distributed on the face of the globe, so that there is a question to be answered: "Under what circumstances is matrilineal reckoning likely to arise, to survive, and to disappear?"

I should like to put the question in the context of evolutionary theory. As Sahlins has recently pointed out, there are two perspectives necessary for the understanding of either biological or cultural evolution: that of specific evolution and that of general evolution (1960). The perspective of specific evolution is familiar in biology. It deals with adaptive differentiation: with the radiation of forms to fit various niches. In this perspective, other things being equal, complex and simple forms may be seen as equal in degree of adaptation. An earthworm, because of its simpler structure, is no less perfectly adapted than a polar bear. A South Malabar kingdom is, by virtue of its greater complexity, no more perfectly adapted than a Hopi village. The study of specific evolution is concerned with phylogeny in biology, with cultural heritage in anthropology, and with ecology in both sciences: with sequences of genetically related forms and their adaptation to new niches.

The perspective of general evolution is concerned with advance, with increases of complexity, with levels of integration of biological or cultural systems. "An organism is at a higher level of integration than another when it has more parts and subparts (a higher order of segmentation); when its parts are more specialized; and when the whole is more effectively integrated. . . . Higher organisms . . . adapt to a greater variety of particular environments . . . [and are] less bound to any limited niche. . . . [They] have greater dominance ranges than less developed types" (Sahlins, 1960: 22). "The difference between higher and lower life forms . . . is not how efficiently energy is harnessed, but how much. Thermodynamic achievement is the ability to concentrate energy in the organism, to put energy to work building and maintaining structure" (*ibid.:* 20–21). An advanced system is more organized and uses more energy than a simple system. In terms of this perspective, we can see that advances in organization have occurred in a variety of genera, and in a variety of cultures, whose historical sources may be quite different. (Summarized from Sahlins, 1960.) Complex eyes have developed in several phyla; in each case they represent a general evolutionary advance, increasing the organization of the organism and extending its range of dominance. There seem to have been agriculturally based, general evolutionary advances in several areas. A single case of increase in energy appropriation or organization is a general evolutionary advance; a set of parallel developments of this sort is also an instance of evolutionary advance. Finally, the advance may rest on borrowed cultural items or on items developed locally. There is no issue of diffusion versus evolution.

From this point of view, the development and survival of matrilineal forms is an issue of specific evolution. Matriliny is not a feature of cultural systems which represents a particular *level of social organization*, as we may speak of band, chiefdom, or state as levels of organization. It is only a *type of membership criterion*. Matrilineal groups or categories may be found in cultures organized at various levels, and at many of these levels patrilineal, double-descent, and non-unilineal membership criteria may also be found.

Matriliny is not a stage in general evolution, just as red-skinned as opposed to black-skinned reptiles are not a stage. Red coloring may be adaptive for reptiles in particular environments—and for other animals as well. Matriliny may be adaptive in certain niches, in the same way. Even if we could assert confidently that matriliny first arose in conjunction with horticulture, or that it is an invariant feature of first adoption of horticulture everywhere, it still would not be a stage in general evolution. For some hunters and gatherers, some fishers, and some pure pastoralists would belong to the same stage as some horticulturalists, in terms of utilization of energy and level of organization.

Hence the study of the place of matrilineal systems in the world's cultures is at least partly a study of convergent adaptations. Of course many instances of matriliny occur under conditions where we must assume a common cultural heritage which included matriliny. Such is the case with the Central Bantu cluster. But we find clusters of matrilineal peoples, and isolated instances, in Africa, Eurasia, the Insular Pacific, and the Americas. It would require an heroic myth to supply all of them with a single historical tradition distinct from other traditions; their historical unity is found only in the human cultural tradition. Hence convergence must be assumed as a significant force.

Therefore I abjure efforts to decide whether matriliny preceded patriliny, or vice versa, since these efforts assume that the question is one of general evolution. I also refuse to divorce the question of the level of organization achieved by different matrilineal systems from the issue of general evolution. But fundamentally I am attempting to find convergent adaptations, and making the attempt fairly crudely. The matrilineal systems in question cannot be classified by type of organization with sufficient accuracy from Murdock's data. Some have descent categories and no organized descent groups, some have organized descent groups, and some have organized descent groups themselves arranged in hierarchical order. The level of political organization can only be approximated using the *World Ethnographic Sample*. There are few data permitting inferences about level of productivity, and many other types of relevant data are lacking.

An attempt to find correlates of matriliny is impeded by the fact that we are obliged to assume that it survives under conditions other than those which gave rise to it, that we cannot outlaw the possibility that it can spread to groups where it would not originate, and that we cannot deduce theoretically the conditions likely to terminate it. My discussion of these problems is based partly on Gough's chapters, but echoes at points the views of Lowie, Mead, Murdock, Schmidt, White, and doubtless many others. Gough has suggested that matrilocality is a necessary but not sufficient condition for the development of matrilineal descent groups, which perhaps cohere about the control of resources worked by women, women's production, or their equipment. She points out that matrilocal, matrilineal descent groups can survive with changes in division of labor, or the introduction or loss of economic activities, where there is no positive selective pressure for residential change. In addition, she abundantly illustrates ways in which changes in productivity, division of labor, or political centralization may result in the retention of matrilineal descent groups with shifts to avunculocality or duolocality and a corresponding "tightening" of the descent unit, or to patrilocality, bilocality, neolocality, or multilocality, with a corresponding decrement in the functions carried on by the descent group. All these considerations press me to conclude that matrilineal descent groups survive under conditions quite dif-

ferent from those under which they presumably originated. The large
number of non-matrilocal matrilineal systems in the world make it
necessary to assume that major changes have occurred in a very
large number of matrilineal systems (see table 17-3). This follows
from the initial assumption that matrilocality is a necessary precondi-
tion for matriliny.

Let us briefly consider the problem of the origin of dispersed unorganized matrilineal clans, since there are some of these in the
World Ethnographic Sample. (I am *not* discussing the question of
the *coexistence* of organized descent groups and dispersed categories.) These categories would appear to arise *ab initio,* in the absence of prior matrilineal descent groups, only under somewhat unusual circumstances. The most probable one is the recognition of a
"submerged line" through preferential inter-group marriage, as in the
case of some Australian moiety systems. Such systems are normally
accompanied by patrilocal, exogamous groups as well, and are commonly described as double-descent systems. It appears to me unlikely
that they can give rise to matrilocal residence, and it must be rare
for the matrilineal category to survive when the patrilocal, exogamous
group breaks down. In sum, the creation from scratch of a distributed,
unorganized, matrilineal clan except through double descent seems
to me an improbable course of events. Most cases of dispersed matrilineal clans in the absence of matrilineal descent groups probably
represent the erosion of the matrilineal descent groups and the survival of the dispersed clan for its value in interlocale relations. Other
possibilities are discussed below.

I have thus far considered the cases where matrilineal reckoning
arises in a previously non-matrilineal society or cluster of societies,
without impact from neighboring matrilineal systems. This has been
called the origin of matriliny *ab initio.* Matriliny, however, may spread
from one society to another. If a cluster of societies of similar organization exists under virtually identical technico-environmental
conditions, and if matrilineal descent groups originate in one society
and spread across such a unitary area, the situation conforms fundamentally to the model of origin *ab initio* and requires no further discussion. We cannot, however, refuse to recognize the possibility that
kinship forms diffuse. It is one thing to assert that peoples do not say,
"Go to, now, let us borrow that pretty kinship system," and quite
another to eliminate any theoretical possibility of inter-societal transmission. Kinship organization, like many other forms of social organization, represents an adaptation to the cultural as well as to the natural

environment of a society. Two kinship-based societies have as one major method of articulation the development of connections between their kinship systems. Where one of these societies is dominant, or where the kinship forms of one society are highly suitable to its natural ecology, and the other society exists in a setting which permits several possible forms of kinship organization, then there may be at least a partial adoption of the forms of the first society by the second. At a minimum, those forms which tie together groups, rather than those which organize the local community, may spread—so that the second group may accept clans but not descent groups from the first. To the degree that such events can occur, matriliny can disperse beyond the range of the conditions under which it originates.

Matrilineal descent groups arise, then, in connection with women's work groups and the resource bases which these groups control. They survive as organizations under a variety of conditions which would not suffice to create them. The avunculocal and duolocal systems, which exhibit the most tightly organized of matrilineal descent groups, must exist under conditions quite unlike those which promote the origin of matrilineality. This is also true of groups which exhibit other residence rules, and of most instances where there are no descent groups but only dispersed clans.

Although matrilineal descent can survive with residence changed or unchanged, with descent groups unimpaired, strengthened, weakened, or vanished, it clearly does disappear under a variety of conditions. Gough has suggested that when the small household becomes the primary work unit for each occupation, when bureaucratic political structures arise, or when a matrilineal system enters a market economy, matriliny disappears. She has also suggested that it disappears when the subsistence base shifts to one primarily dependent on movable property, e.g., domesticates, which can be controlled by individual men. There are probably still other considerations that effect the breakdown of matriliny in societies less complex than those with which she has dealt.

To summarize, matrilocality is a necessary but not sufficient condition for the development of matrilineal descent groups. Matrilineal descent groups, once developed, can survive under conditions other than those which created them. Matrilineal descent categories, in the absence of descent groups, probably arise *ab initio* very rarely. In most instances the descent groups have probably disappeared, leaving the dispersed clan. Clans at least, and perhaps descent groups, can, in theory, spread to new groups as modes of articulation of two kinship-based societies. It is impossible to specify all the conditions under which matriliny is likely to disappear.

All these factors make it exceedingly difficult to state the precise circumstances under which matriliny will be found. Several conditions permit it; only a few require it; some terminate it. For these reasons the present chapter will be content with relatively weak statistical associations between factors regarded as influencing lineality, and the forms of lineality found in the *World Ethnographic Sample*.

The Ecological Distribution of Matrilineal Systems

I now proceed to an examination of the place of matrilineal systems in the world's cultures, using Murdock's *World Ethnographic Sample* as the main basis for the discussion. The sample contains 565 cultures and aims to be representative rather than random. It divides the world into six major areas: Africa, Circum-Mediterranean, East Eurasia, Insular Pacific, North America, and South America. Each major area is divided into ten minor areas. In some cases this division required the lumping of several small areas normally recognized by specialists, and in others the subdivision of large, heterogeneous areas often considered as units in the literature. Within each minor area at least five and no more than fifteen cultures were selected. Criteria for selection of cultures within a minor division were as follows:

1. The most populous society in the area, or, in default of reliable population data, the society occupying the greatest expanse of territory. 2. The best described culture in each of the other recognizable cultural subareas [of the minor division]. 3. An example of each basic type of economy (agricultural, pastoral, fishing, or hunting and gathering) and of each major rule of descent (matrilineal, patrilineal, double, or bilateral) represented in the area, even though there might be only a single and otherwise unimportant case. 4. One example from each linguistic stock or major linguistic subfamily found in the area. 5. Additional cultures which appeared for any reason to be relatively distinctive within the context of the entire area (Murdock, 1957: 667). [In addition,] we have wherever possible avoided the selection of two cultures from the same [minor] area that are either (a) geographically contiguous or (b) characterized by mutually intelligible languages unless they reveal such major differences in either their basic economy, their social organization, or in the former instance their languages, as to assure that they have achieved independent integration. . . . We set for all areas an absolute maximum of ten societies belonging to the same linguistic subfamily" (*idem*).

The sample includes from Africa, 116 cases; Circum-Mediterranean, 78; East Eurasia, 85; Insular Pacific, 99; North America, 110; and South America, 77.

This sample clearly minimizes associations of traits based simply on the accident of common historical antecedents. By the same token, it maximizes "odd ball" systems, tending to produce a large list of "exceptions" to one or another trend. We do not yet know how to draw a random sample of world cultures; this sample would appear to be as satisfactory for the statistical testing of theoretical generalizations as any yet devised. It certainly makes it difficult to overlook embarrassing exceptions.

TABLE 17-1

Frequency of Types of Descent

Descent Type	Number of Cultures	Percentage
Patrilineal	248	44
Bilateral	204	36
Matrilineal	84	15
Duolineal	28	5
Unclassifiable	1	*
Total	565	100

* Less than 0.5%.

Each culture is classified with respect to thirty variables, including subsistence bases, sexual division of labor in various subsistence activities, certain features of community composition, various characteristics of kinship units, forms of marriage, residence, certain features of kinship terminology, scope of political organization, certain signs of stratification, and so on. Not all these variables have been used in this chapter.

To begin with, matriliny is a relatively rare phenomenon in this sample. Only 15 per cent of the cultures in it are matrilineal (table 17-1). Matrilineal systems are distributed most unevenly on the face of the globe (table 17-2). They are conspicuously underrepresented in the major areas of plough cultivation (Circum-Mediterranean and East Eurasia) and overrepresented in the horticultural areas. There is no major area where matrilineal systems predominate. They represent only 22 per cent of the cultures of the Pacific and of North America, where they are most common. They are concentrated in Africa, the Insular Pacific, and North and South America. Although the cultures of this area make up 71 per cent of the total sample, they include 91 per cent of the matrilineal systems.

Furthermore, among the matrilineal systems of the world, less than 50 per cent are matrilocal or predominantly matrilocal (table 17-3). There is considerable variation among major areas. Matrilocality is common in North and South America, and avunculocality in Africa. The Insular Pacific is diversified, with matrilocal trends the modal type but making up less than 50 per cent of the total. The number of cases elsewhere in the world is too small for discussion. Although argument does not permit me to infer that matrilocal areas preserve matrilineal systems unchanged since their beginning, I am forced to consider that Africa in particular and the Insular Pacific to a considerable degree are areas where we are examining the conditions under which matriliny can survive, rather than the conditions under which it develops.

Of Murdock's 60 minor areas, only 33 have one or more matrilineal systems. Thirty-seven of the total of 84 matrilineal cases are found in 5 of the 60 areas: Central Bantu, 7; Micronesia, 7; Western Melanesia, 8; Eastern Woodlands of North America, 8; and Southwestern United States, 7. These five areas are all horticultural.

Although I had intended using the coded *World Ethnographic Sample* statistically with a minimum of reference to other sources, I was unable completely to overcome habits of some years' standing. I was driven to a rather uneven coverage of the literature on some of the matrilineal groups where I had little prior information. The compromise between rigidity and usual habits of scholarship may not be a happy one, but it led ultimately to a non-statistical effort to examine the distribution of matrilineal systems on the face of the globe, with due attention to vegetation maps for Africa and North and South America, linguistic affiliation, and history and historical reconstruction where these were available. Some of the results of this exploration are now presented, before I proceed to statistical treatments.

Since matrilineal systems are relatively rare in association with pure or dominant pastoralism, hunting, gathering, and fishing, it is most

TABLE 17-2

Distribution of Types of Descent

World Area	Descent System									
	Patrilineal		Bilateral		Matrilineal		Duolineal		Total	
	No.	%	No.	%	No.	%	No.	%	No.	%
Africa	77	31	10	5	17	20	12	43	116	21
Circum-Mediterranean	43	17	31	15	4	5	1	4	79	14
East Eurasia	64	26	14	7	5	6	1	4	84	15
Insular Pacific	28	11	34	17	22	26	14	50	98	17
North America	19	8	67	33	24	29	0	0	110	19
South America	17	7	48	23	12	14	0	0	77	14
Total	248	100	204	100	84	100	28	101	564	100

Test: Matrilineals versus others, tested for non-random
distribution in the six major areas.

$x^2 = 19.94; p < .01$

TABLE 17-3

Distribution of Types of Residence in Matrilineal Systems

World Area	Type of Residence															
	Matrilocal		Dominantly Matrilocal		Avunculocal		Dominantly Avunculocal		Dominantly Duolocal		Dominantly Patrilocal		Dominantly Neolocal and Bilocal		Total	
	No.	%	No.	%	No.	%	No.	%	No.	%	No.	%	No.	%	No.	%
Africa	1	6	1	6	4	24	7	41	0	0	4	24	0	0	17	101
Circum-Mediterranean	1	25	0	0	0	0	0	0	0	0	3	75	0	0	4	100
East Eurasia	3	60	1	20	0	0	0	0	1	20	0	0	0	0	5	100
Insular Pacific	4	18	5	23	1	5	5	23	2	9	4	18	1	5	22	101
North America	10	42	6	25	3	13	0	0	0	0	3	13	2	8	24	101
South America	9	75	0	0	0	0	2	17	0	0	1	8	0	0	12	100
Total	28	33	13	16	8	10	14	17	3	4	15	18	3	4	84	102

convenient to begin with the agricultural world. I shall use the term "agriculture" to refer to all cultivation of plant domesticates by whatever techniques. "Plough agriculture" or "plough cultivation" will be used for all cases where the plough is used, and "horticulture" for the remainder. Matrilineal systems are strikingly infrequent in those areas of the world where plough cultivation dominates, where there is intensive wet-rice agriculture, or where there are extensive irrigation works coördinated and maintained by supra-community organizations. Of matrilineal systems based on plough agriculture in the sample I can name only the Nayar, the Minangkabau, the Kunama (in Africa), and the lowland Karen (if indeed they are matrilineal). Even among these three cases, the Nayar are not farmers but managers of farm land, and the plough is used by tenant and serf cultivators whose patterns of descent are for the most part not matrilineal. Matriliny is lacking in the highlands of South America, with its extensive irrigation systems, and in China, Japan, and those areas of India where irrigation works are most extensive. Where matrilineal systems survive in plough areas or wet-rice irrigated areas, they tend to appear in highland refuges, based on dry rice or wet rice without extensive irrigation, and lacking the plough. Such, for example, is the case for the Garo and Khasi of the Assam Hills, the hill Karen of Burma, and the Belu of Timor. The Guanche of the Canary Islands represent a pre-plough neolithic survival through geographic isolation, in the Circum-Mediterranean plough area.

I turn now to the question of vegetation cover and the distribution of matrilineal peoples in Africa and the Americas. Africa contains a large, more or less continuous stretch of tropical forest, including a considerable part of the Congo basin, the area between the Congo and the Sanaga, and the coastal area from Duala to Monrovia. There are few matrilineal peoples in this tropical forest region. Most such groups, like the Kongo and Mayombe, occupy mixed tropical forest and high-grass savanna areas. North of the tropical forest are east-west bands of savanna, semidesert, and desert, which contain many tribes with cattle, a good many patrilineal systems, and few matrilineal ones. Abyssinia and the Horn fall into Murdock's Circum-Mediterranean area, and are not discussed at this point. The region surrounding Lake Victoria and east of Lake Tanganyika has few matrilineal peoples, in contrast to the area east of Lake Victoria. These areas are complex from the point of view of vegetation and cannot be discussed in detail here. South of the tropical forest is a high-grass savanna zone with few cattle and a fair number of matrilineal peoples. South of this is a scrub or dry forest area mostly occupied by matrilineal peoples. South of this is tall- and short-grass savanna and some temperate rain forest. This area is mainly patrilineal. Maps of cattle and tsetse-fly distribution in the area south of the tropical forest give rise to the strong impression that most matrilineal peoples live in areas where the tsetse-fly makes it impossible to raise cattle. This point cannot be firmly established, however, since sources conflict as to cattle distribution, and the tsetse-fly distribution itself is not static. The association is not perfect.

There are conspicuous exceptions to the general statement that matrilineal peoples are rare in the African tropical forest, but if tribal distributions are compared with vegetation maps the closeness of fit in some areas near the Congo is surprising. Where there are lobes of savanna extending into the tropical forest regions, matrilineal groups are found; in adjoining tropical forest, patrilineal groups. All in all, matrilineal peoples seem to be weakly represented in the tropical forest and in those areas where mixed stock raising and agriculture are possible. The largest single concentration of matrilineal peoples, among the Central Bantu, is found in the high-grass savanna south of the tropical forest, and in the dry forest zone just south of that.

In North America there are two major clusters of matrilineal peoples. In the temperate forests of the Southeastern United States are found the politically centralized and elaborated matrilineal systems of the Southeast, living on some of the better horticultural land (from the point of view of the aboriginal economy) north of Mexico. In the Southwest are found matrilineal groups in the semidesert, occupying there a series of small, relatively productive, nucleated, permanently reusable resource zones. The high civilizations of Mexico and Central America lack matrilineality.

In South America, Steward and Faron (1959) comment on the relative lack of matrilineal peoples in the tropical forest zones. Horticultural matrilineal groups fill zones in northern South America bordering on, rather than in the midst of the tropical forest. The politically and technically most elaborated areas of South America—though by no means those with most agricultural potential—are the highlands, where matrilineal systems are lacking.

Within the world's horticultural zones, then, matrilineal peoples seem to be found, in the main, outside of or bordering on the tropical forest, and outside those zones where cattle can be raised in numbers. Numerous possible reasons for this pattern of distribution suggest themselves, but at present I regard them all as too speculative to merit discussion here.

We turn now to hunting, fishing, and gathering societies. The sample provides thirteen matrilineal instances. The largest single group of these is to be found in northwestern North America, which includes seven. This cluster is worth discussing, since in some respects it fits our general ideas—with only a little squeezing. A notable feature of a number of these cultures—Upper Carrier, Tanaina, Eyak, Haida, and Tlingit—is their heavy dependency on stream salmon fishing and their unusually sedentary settlements. Although the women do not play a predominant role in this fishing, I am indebted to Mr. Daniel A. Grossman for some historical data suggesting a more prominent role, at least among the Carrier, in the past. Be that as it may, this cluster is not featured by a roving hunting and gathering existence, which seems less compatible with matriliny. Adjoining them and groups like them are other groups, such as the Kaska and Kutchin, which lack this sedentary quality and the localized monopolizeable resources that go with it. These cultures have dispersed clans but lack descent groups, so far as I can determine. I believe that the clans have either been retained in the eastward movements of these cultures, or less probably borrowed, as devices for articulating with more coastal tribes—a proposition whose support would require more space than is available here. In any event, the organized matrilineal descent groups of the area are associated with stable, localized resources, and the dispersed unorganized clans with tribes adjoining the richer area but whose ecological base is fluctuating.

Of the six remaining groups, four are South American. In most of these cases there is a suspicion of prior horticultural bases. Thus the Yaruro were formerly more agricultural. The Bororo possibly had agriculture at one time. Although Murdock regards Timbira agriculture as unimportant, they moved their communities to find more gallery forest land to clear for agriculture. In the case of the Guahibo there is doubt as to whether they are matrilineal. One of these systems, then, has a significant amount of agriculture; two others seem to have a recent horticultural past. South America is an area in which numerous peoples have suffered ecological downgrading in the post-Columbian period, many agriculturalists having been pushed into marginal or non-agricultural territory. Under these circumstances, the hunting and gathering base does not seem to be the logical starting point for determining why they are matrilineal; at most it permits them to retain matriliny.

The Vedda of Ceylon are a matrilineal hunting and gathering group for whose lineality I have no plausible explanation. The Tiwi of Australia are a special case, where patrilocal groups of kin have been broken up under the impact of recent acculturation, and the matrilineal totemic categories have survived.

All these associations suggest that matriliny is most likely to develop on a horticultural base, with women doing the agricultural labor. It is most likely to disappear in the face of increased importance of large-scale coördination of male labor; increased importance of property such as domesticates in the hands of males—property, that is, which is divisible and which can multiply; male control of the major tools of production; and the regulation of economic and political life through non-kinship devices. Most, if not all, of these features are likely to be associated with increased productivity. For this reason, matrilineal systems tend to cluster in a relatively narrow range of levels of productivity. They are not found among the largest political units based on high agricultural productivity, and are not found at all at the highest level of productivity.

Subsistence Base, Size of Political Unit, and Descent

The substantive findings of this inquiry center on the relationship between the major bases of subsistence and descent reckoning, the size of the political unit and descent reckoning, and the combined relationship between subsistence base and size of political unit on the one hand, and descent reckoning on the other. Various other lines of endeavor were pursued and abandoned, sooner or later, but these two variables were subjects of repeated investigation.

It must be remembered that it is no small task to deal with subsistence base as classified in the *World Ethnographic Sample*. The sample categorizes four types of activities—agriculture, animal husbandry, fishing, and hunting and gathering—as dominant; co-dominant; important; present but unimportant; or absent, insignificant, or sporadic. In each society one of these four activities is coded as dominant, or two are coded as co-dominant. Other activities may be classified in any of the three remaining categories. In addition, the plant base is classified as to whether the primary dependency is root, tree, or grain crops. In cases where agriculture is absent, trivial, or recent, the importance of gathering is indicated. The domesticated-animal base is classified as: large domesticated animals kept and milked; large domesticated animals kept and not milked; small domesticated animals kept; domesticated animals an important post-European contact phenomenon; and domesticated animals absent or unimportant.

With no less than six variables of potential importance for a classification of subsistence bases, the number of combinations is enormous.

After much trial and error, I adopted a classification system for subsistence base which seemed reasonably satisfactory, if a bit rough. It must be kept in mind that although the data are Murdock's, the classification is my own, dictated in part by the exigencies of his coding system.

In attempting to utilize the coded data, I made certain decisions. Although there are obvious errors in the classification of various cultures, it was decided not to recode any item in Murdock's tables. If I were to correct only cases which I knew to be in error and were to fail to recheck the remainder, an element of distortion would be introduced into the data. Considerations of time, however, made impossible the recoding of *all* cultures on *all* variables used. As Driver (1956) has pointed out, random error in large bodies of data reduces the chances of finding statistically significant associations; it does not tend to provide numerous erroneously based positive findings. Hence, given random error in the data, we can place considerable reliance on those relationships that do emerge. Systematic coding errors, however, do artificially raise statistical associations. Thus if a coder were to use cousin terms to infer the rule of descent, the result would be an artificial association between rule of descent and cousin terms. To date, there is no evidence of this type of contamination. Finally, it was decided not to add new items to the variables coded by Murdock, even if these were important to the investigation, but rather to use certain rough guides to approximate what was needed—a point discussed below in connection with plough agriculture. This decision was made because of the difficulty of securing new information on each of the 565 cultures, for even one new variable. Throughout the analysis that follows, Murdock's sample is assumed to represent the range of the cultures of the world.

My study of the distribution of matrilineal systems around the world indicated that it was important to separate plough agriculture from horticulture in the sample, even though Murdock does not provide information on this score. This was done, and in the process a general classification of subsistence bases for the cultures in the sample was developed. This classification entailed either gathering further information on many of the cultures, or using certain rough rules of thumb which, it was recognized, would result in some erroneous classification. Error which did not bias the results in favor of the theory could be tolerated, and the decision was to use the rough measures. The subsistence typology follows.

Predominantly plough agriculture. Two steps were used to classify cultures in this group. First, all areas where the plough was entirely lacking before the recent expansion of Western European culture were eliminated from this group: Africa, the Americas, Melanesia, Polynesia, Micronesia, Australia, and New Guinea. It should be noted that Murdock includes the Moslem Sudan, the Horn, Ethiopia, and the Sahara in the Circum-Mediterranean area but not in Africa. Second, the remainder of the world—Circum-Mediterranean, Eastern Eurasia, and a portion of the Insular Pacific (Indonesia, Philippines, and Formosa)— was now considered. Cultures in which agriculture was listed as the dominant subsistence base, and in which large domesticated animals (cattle, buffalo, horses, etc.) were listed as important, were assumed to constitute a category the majority of whose members had plough agriculture. This is certainly not a "pure" group, since it includes some groups where cattle are kept but the plough is not used, and some where water buffaloes are used to tramp out rice fields but the plough is lacking. Furthermore, it may omit some groups where large domesticated animals are listed as unimportant, but where in fact the plough is used, and some plough agriculturalists whose agricultural subsistence is not coded as dominant (thus they may be equally dependent on a pastoral complex). In spite of this imprecision, this category will be used because the difference between plough agriculture and horticulture seems critical, and because of unwillingness to recode Murdock's data completely for this variable. These cultures appear on tables as "plough agriculture," but, it must be remembered, are actually "predominantly plough agriculture." [3]

African horticulture with important use of large domesticated animals (cattle in almost all cases, horses in a few). This category emerges as residual to the preceding category. It rests on the assumption that a combination of dominant horticulture with important large stock to manage makes different demands in terms of division of labor and has

---

[3] An intensive check on the nine matrilineal "plough" systems indicates that, as pointed out earlier, only the Nayar, Minangkabau, Kunama, and lowland Karen (whose lineality is in doubt) have the plough. The Fur, Gaunche, Garo, Khasi, and Belu do not. If the tables were rectified by recoding these systems, which would reduce matrilineal "plough" cases by more than 50 per cent, the negative relationship between plough agriculture and matriliny would be strengthened. But this rectification would not be legitimate without a similar recoding of all bilateral and patrilineal cases. Such a recoding would certainly not reduce the number of "plough" cases in patrilineal and bilateral systems by more than 50 per cent. The known error in the tables, then, is permitted, first, because of the labor involved in completely rechecking all instances; and second, because it does not bias the results to favor my own views, but rather to reduce my chances of finding significant associations. Hence such results as do emerge are exceedingly likely to be based on actual trends.

different property implications than dominant horticulture in the absence of such stock. It is homogeneous in that it contains no cases of plough agriculture. Its regional nature, in a list of categories most of which are general, is unfortunate, and emerges from certain difficulties in coding and from one somewhat unwise decision. In the first place, the "plough" and "African horticulture" categories exhaust virtually all cases in which native large domesticates play an important role. Second, as will be seen, it was decided to treat post-Columbian domesticates as a special case in the New World (see "New World Pastoralists," below). Third, the "small" domesticates are a far more variable group in the sample, including sheep and goats in Africa, Asia, and Europe, pigs in Oceania, and the llama and vicuña in South America. These various animals make different demands on labor, localization, etc. Fourth, an initial inspection seemed to indicate that lineality did not tend to vary with the use of small animals. Hence, by disregarding small animals, treating post-Columbian cases separately, and coding "plough agriculture" as we did, Africa was the only area in which horticulture and important large domesticates emerged as a configuration. In any event, it would have been wiser to include in one category all cases where horticulture is dominant and where domesticates, small or large, are important and do not stem from Western contact. The present category, then, includes only Africa horticulturalists with important large domesticates.

Dominant horticulture. This category includes all systems not already classified where agriculture is the dominant mode of subsistence. Some of the cultures in this group have large domesticates as an unimportant, or unimportant and recent (post-Columbian) concomitant, and several have small domesticates as an important subsistence element. It is possible that in a few instances the systems with agriculture dominant and unimportant large domesticates are in fact plough agriculture systems, but the vast majority of these systems are horticultural.

Other horticulture. This category includes all cases where horticulture is either a co-dominant or an important subsistence activity, but not a dominant one, except for the next two categories discussed below, where the rationale for them and the present category is discussed.

Old World pastoralists. This category includes all Old World groups where the care of large domesticated animals is a dominant or co-dominant activity. The subsidiary or co-dominant base may be agriculture, hunting and gathering, or fishing. Old World immigrants to other continents are included here. It is assumed that systems in which the care of large livestock plays so important a part will be different from dominantly agricultural and from largely extractive cultures (see "Extractive Cultures," below). This grouping includes a few cases where plough agriculture is of equal importance with care of large domesticates for the sake of animal products, or where plough agriculture is less important than the care of such large domesticates. There is one case in which domesticates and agriculture are important and fishing is dominant. In the tables these cases are labeled "pastoralists."

New World pastoralists. This category includes all groups native to North and South America where the care of domesticates introduced as a result of post-Columbian contacts is dominant or co-dominant. Most of these cultures are horse-herding hunters, rather than peoples who derive sustenance from the animals they keep. They are, however, different enough from ordinary hunters and gatherers to require separate treatment. There is one case where domesticates are important, agriculture and hunting being co-dominant.

The category "other horticulture" includes all cultures other than those grouped under the present category and the preceding one, where horticulture is co-dominant (with fishing or hunting and gathering) or important (with fishing and/or hunting and gathering more important than horticulture). The decision to use this category rests on the assumption that a culture with a co-dominant or important horticultural base should be separated from a primarily extractive culture which lacks important agriculture, but that systems in which care of domesticated animals plays a dominant or co-dominant role are more importantly influenced by that activity than by horticultural activities.

Extractive cultures. This category includes all cases where agriculture and animal husbandry are unimportant or absent. Hunting and gathering and/or fishing are major activities. The term is used to avoid repetition of the phrase "hunting and/or gathering and/or fishing."

Before discussing results, it is necessary to comment on statistical procedures. Ideally, the sample should have been used to test theories developed before the sample itself had been inspected. Instead, theory construction went hand in hand with tabulation. Under these circumstances, it might have been appropriate simply to present percentage distributions in various categories, since it is not entirely legitimate to utilize tests of significance *post hoc*.

Nevertheless, it seemed advisable to have some device to decide whether it was reasonable to assume that the data showed a trend, or to assume that the results could have arisen by chance. For this purpose, in most instances, chi-square (χ^2) was used to calculate probabilities. Where expected frequencies fell below 5 for any cell, Fisher's exact test was used. The 0.05 level of significance (using two-tailed tests) is used throughout as providing a level at which the trends manifested in the tables are worth further investigation with other samples. In most cases, significance levels are rather better than 0.05.

In addition, it seemed important to use some measure of the strength of the trends found. Significance levels are not a guide for this, since a relationship can be highly significant (be most unlikely to be found by chance) and yet be weak. For the same reason, chi-square values are not an adequate guide, since they depend in part on the number of cases being tested. If the number of cases is doubled, and the distribution remains the same, chi-square is also doubled. Phi-square (ϕ^2) values are used as measures of the strength of relationship, since they are independent of the number of cases, though unduly affected by the relative size of the smallest row or column ($\phi^2 = \chi^2/N$). In a two-by-two table, phi-square is a measure of the amount of variation accounted for by the independent variable in question, with respect to the dependent variable. In such tables, the phi value (square root of phi-square) is a special case of a coefficient of correlation (r). Thus if the association between lineality and subsistence type in a two-by-two table has a phi-square value of 0.09, then 9 per cent of the variance is accounted for by subsistence, and the correlation between the two variables is 0.3, the square root of 0.09.

Where expected cell frequencies fall below 5, chi-square (and hence phi-square) values are corrected for continuity. This reduces both values. Probabilities, however, in such cases, are based on Fisher's exact test.

In the case of tests of Gough's and Schneider's hypotheses, the tests are not done *post hoc*, since the theories were recorded before the tests were carried out. In these cases, the 0.05 level of significance is used, but one-tailed tests are employed, since the theory specifies the direction of the results. Use of chi-square and phi-square is the same as in the remainder of the chapter. Again, since the sample is not random, the use of these tests is open to some criticism.

In the bulk of this chapter, then, "significant" results (at better than the 0.05 level) are results worth taking seriously. They probably did not arise by chance. In the case of tests of Schneider's and Gough's hypotheses, "significant" results may be understood as supporting the hypotheses in the usual sense. In all instances, phi-square values are a guide to the importance—the strength—of the relationship between two variables.

The relationship between the rule of descent and the type of sub-

sistence base is shown in table 17-4.[4] The most striking feature of the
distribution of matrilineal systems in this table is the fact that 56 per
cent of them are found in the category of "dominant horticulture," uncomplicated by the plough or by important quantities of large domesticates. If we compare "dominant horticulture" with all others, we find
that matrilineal systems tend to be found significantly more often in this
category than either patrilineal or bilateral systems. Patrilineal and
bilateral systems are not significantly different from each other in this
comparison.

Although it would be unsafe to assume that horticulturally based
societies lacking large domesticates or the plough are likely to be
matrilineal, it would be reasonable to assume that matrilineal systems
are likely to be "dominantly horticultural" as this term has been defined.

Within the group of cultures based to any important degree on agriculture, the relationships of lineality and subsistence type are straightforward. This set includes "plough agriculture," "African horticulture,"
"dominant horticulture," and "other horticulture." In the comparison
of patrilineal and matrilineal systems, the matrilineal are relatively
prominent in the "dominant horticulture" category. This is so whether
"dominant horticulture" is compared with "plough agriculture," "African horticulture," both of these, or the combination of "plough agriculture," "African horticulture," and "other horticulture." Matrilineal
systems show virtually the same pattern by comparison with bilateral
systems, but the differences are less marked. The only exception is that
both bilateral and matrilineal systems are rare in "African horticulture"
as compared with "dominant horticulture," and in this respect do not
differ significantly from each other. This effect carries over in the comparison of "dominant horticulture" with "plough agriculture" and "African horticulture" combined. Bilateral systems show the same pattern

---

[4] Although the main interest is in matrilineal systems, it is necessary for some
purposes not only to compare matrilineal cases with patrilineal and bilateral instances, but also to compare patrilineal and bilateral distributions. Duolineal systems have been virtually ignored in all comparisons. They are few in number, so
that statistical analysis becomes impossible in any but the largest tables, and in addition they are particularly heterogeneous, including, as they do, seven quite special Australian cases, 25 per cent of the total. Although it would be valuable to
examine at least some of the remainder as representing a transition between matrilineal and patrilineal principles, this would require a detailed inspection more particular than that attempted for other categories. Nevertheless, many of the tables
present distributions for all types of descent, since the tabulations involved a considerable amount of work and presumably have interest for readers over and
above the immediate purposes of this chapter.

TABLE 17-4

Descent and Types of Subsistence

Subsistence Type	Descent System									
	Patrilineal		Bilateral		Matrilineal		Duolineal		Total	
	No.	%	No.	%	No.	%	No.	%	No.	%
Plough agriculture	69	28	38	19	9	11	1	4	117	21
African horticulture	32	13	3	2	5	6	6	21	46	8
Dominant horticulture	66	27	68	33	47	56	7	25	188	33
Other horticulture	11	4	15	7	5	6	2	7	33	6
Pastoralists	51	21	8	4	3	4	4	14	66	12
New World pastoralists	0	0	11	5	2	2	0	0	13	2
Extractive	19	8	61	30	13	16	8	29	101	18
Total	248	101	204	100	84	101	28	100	564	100

TABLE 17-4 (Continued)

	Lineality								
	Matrilineal vs. Patrilineal			Matrilineal vs. Bilateral			Patrilineal vs. Bilateral		
Subsistence	x^2	p	ϕ^2	x^2	p	ϕ^2	x^2	p	ϕ^2
H vs. all other	24.029	<.001	.072	12.578	<.001	.044		NS	.023
H vs. PA	20.199	<.001	.106	6.875	<.01	.042	5.649	<.02	.120
H vs. AH	9.643	<.01	.064		NS		20.248	<.001	.120
H vs. PA, AH	25.271	<.001	.111		NS		13.839	<.001	.050
H vs. PA, AH, OH	22.465	<.001	.092	4.896	<.05	.025	9.368	<.01	.031
PA vs. AH		NS		4.867*	<.05	.088	9.308	<.01	.066
H vs. P	22.721	<.001	.136		NS		23.634	<.001	.122
H vs. AH, P, NP	24.146	<.001	.117		NS		22.161	<.001	.093
E vs. all other	4.392	<.05	.013	6.508	<.02	.023	38.029	<.001	.084
E vs. H		NS		11.299	<.001	.060	13.659	<.001	.064

Key:

PA = plough agriculture
AH = African horticulture
H = dominant horticulture
OH = other horticulture
P = pastoralists
NP = New World pastoralists
E = extractives
NS = not significant (at .05 level)
* = x^2 corrected for continuity

Where results are significant, matrilineal systems are relatively commoner in "dominant horticulture" than in any other category, by comparison with patrilineals or bilaterals. Bilaterals show the same pattern by comparison with patrilineals. Exceptions: bilaterals more common in "extractive" than in "dominant horticulture" by comparison with matrilineals or patrilineals. Other results: bilaterals commoner in "plough" than in "African horticulture" by comparison with matrilineals or patrilineals. Bilaterals more common in "extractive" than in "other" by comparison with matrilineals or patrilineals. Matrilineals more common in "extractive" than in "other" by comparison with patrilineals.

of relationships in comparison with patrilineal systems as do matrilineal ones, but in most instances the relationships are weaker. Thus matrilineal and bilateral systems show an affinity for uncomplicated horticulture, and patrilineal systems for "plough agriculture," "African horticulture," or horticulture subsidiary to, or equal in importance to, extractive activities.

On the other hand, in the comparison of "plough agriculture" and "African horticulture," bilateral systems are relatively more common in the "plough agriculture" category than either patrilineal or matrilineal ones; there is no significant difference in the preferences of patrilineal and matrilineal systems. These results repeatedly demonstrate that within the agricultural groups matrilineal systems continue to display a tendency to be horticultural without such supplements as important large domesticates, the plough, or dominant or co-dominant extractive activities. Bilateral systems are, in general, intermediate between patrilineal and matrilineal systems in these respects. But in spite of a bias toward "dominant horticulture," they also have a greater tendency to appear in the "plough agriculture" category than in "African horticulture," by comparison with other patterns of descent. This pattern would probably be much simplified if bilateral systems were categorized as to the scope and nature of their descent groups, if any. Presumably many of the bilateral systems based on horticulture would prove to have non-unilineal descent groups, whereas those based on plough agriculture would prove either to have none or very small ones. Analysis along these lines would clarify these trends.

If we compare "dominant horticulture" with the various categories involving large domesticates not used for plough agriculture, a somewhat different, but equally straightforward pattern appears. The categories are "African horticulture," "pastoralism," and "New World pastoralism." The "New World pastoralist" category is small and is not treated separately. Both matrilineal and bilateral systems are less likely to have a pastoral as compared with a dominant horticultural base, in contrast with patrilineal systems. They are not significantly different from each other. The same is true with respect to the comparison of "dominant horticulture" and "African horticulture," as has been said. If the three categories are combined, the same trend is found. Matrilineal systems are more likely than patrilineal systems to be "dominantly horticultural" than to make important, co-dominant, or dominant use of large domesticates. They share this characteristic with bilateral systems. The intermediate position of bilateral systems disappears here.

Finally, bilateral systems are more likely than either matrilineal or patrilineal systems to be based on extraction, by comparison with all other subsistence bases. There is, however, a trivial tendency for matrilineal systems to be more common than patrilineal systems among extractives, by comparison with all other subsistence bases. This surprising but very weak trend is accounted for almost entirely by seven cases in North America and four in South America, discussed in a previous section. When dominant horticulture and extraction are compared, bilateral systems are more likely to be extractive than either matrilineal or patrilineal systems, and matrilineal and patrilineal systems do not differ significantly from each other.

These statistical results generally confirm the somewhat subjective description of the ecological niche of matrilineal peoples provided in Part Two. More refined analysis must wait upon a more careful coding of types of kinship organization found in all three patterns of descent reckoning. They indicate that the cow is the enemy of matriliny, and the friend of patriliny. When cattle are hitched to the plough, however, bilaterality tends to emerge, although patriliny is well represented. The findings would be sharpened if we could distinguish in the code those instances in which the plough is power-driven. The familiar tendency for extractive systems to be bilateral is also attested.

These conclusions will surprise few people, but it is worth while to have statistical support for one's impressions as to the impact of subsistence type on lineality. The phi-square values for significant relationships range from 0.013 to 0.136, with corresponding phi values (equivalent to correlations) of 0.11 to 0.37. Five of these are correlations of less than 0.20, nine of 0.20 to 0.29, and nine of 0.30 or above. They express relatively weak but in most cases not unimportant trends.

Before we turn to the associations between size of political unit and lineality, it is necessary to examine the associations between size of political unit and subsistence base. This, however, requires some explanation of Murdock's classification of "political integration" (hereafter "size of political unit" or "size of unit"). There are seven categories. First, societies where there is no authoritative regulation above the family level. Second, societies where authoritative regulation occurs at the community level. Third, "peace groups," where "the basis of unity is other than political, e.g., derived from reciprocal trade relations, defensive military agreements, or a common cult or age-grade organization" (Murdock, 1957: 674). Few systems, and only one matrilineal case, are thus classified. (Note that thus far the classification is based on levels of authority and, in the third category, on relations between units.) Fourth, "minimal states," independent political units of between 1,500 and 10,000. Fifth, "little states" of between 10,000 and 100,000. Sixth, "states" of 100,000 and above. (Here a size classification is substituted for levels of authority, with some anomalous results. In political theory the concept of "state" normally implies centralized control of the legitimate use of force. Yet this classification includes among "minimal states" the Trobriands, Nootka, Shasta, and Crow, none of which would normally be considered states of any sort, and among "states" such units as the Kazak. Nevertheless, probably many of the "minimal states" are chiefdoms, most of the "states" are states, and the "little states" are a mixed bag including a number of states. Hence the classification does have utility.) Seventh, "dependent societies," those which form "an integral part of some larger political system and those governed exclusively and directly by agents of another and politically dominant society. Colonial governments operating through indirect rule are ignored" (idem). Since my theoretical concerns are not related to this last category, it is omitted in most of the tables and in all of the interpretations that follow.

Murdock's first three levels—family, community, peace group—can be combined for statistical analysis into cases of authority at or below the community level (table 17-5). For most purposes "little states" and "states" are combined, since there are relatively few of either. When this is done, it is possible to see a regular progression among the systems with any agricultural base. As we go from "plough" agriculture to "African horticulture," and thence to "dominant horticulture" and "other horticulture," the percentage of cases at or below the community level rises regularly, and by the same token the percentage above this level falls. The percentage of "states" falls regularly, and the intermediate categories—"little" and "minimal states"—show mild curvilinear trends. "Extractive" systems bring up the bottom of the list. The "pastoral" systems are intermediate between "African horticulture" and "dominant horticulture" in respect to the percentage of systems at or below the community level, but between "plough" and "African horticulture" regarding the percentage of "states." This is undoubtedly a reflection not of their tendency toward greater political complexity, but of the capacity of pastoralists to achieve loose political unity involving quite large numbers. The "New World pastoralists" are also anomalous, because of the very large percentage of cases organized above the "community" (in this case band) level as "minimal" states— the familiar Plains political structures which coördinate tribal activities when the bands congregate.

No tests of significance have been employed for table 17-5, but cer-

TABLE 17-5

Subsistence Type and Size of Political Unit

Size of Unit*	Subsistence Type															
	Plough Agriculture		African Horticulture		Dominant Horticulture		Other Horticulture		Pastoralists		New World Pastoralists		Extractive		Total	
	No.	%	No.	%	No.	%	No.	%	No.	%	No.	%	No.	%	No.	%
Family level	3	3	1	2	14	8	1	3	1	2	0	0	15	15	35	7
Local communities	12	12	15	33	78	44	24	75	17	27	5	39	74	76	225	43
Peace groups	1	1	1	2	3	2	0	0	7	11	2	15	4	4	18	3
Minimal states	20	20	15	33	53	30	6	19	13	21	6	46	5	5	118	22
Little states	9	9	9	20	17	10	1	3	15	24	0	0	0	0	51	10
States	53	54	5	11	11	6	0	0	10	16	0	0	0	0	79	15
Total	98	99	46	101	176	100	32	100	63	101	13	100	98	100	526	100

* 35 cases of dependent communities omitted; 3 cases of data not available are omitted.

TABLE 17-5 (continued)

Subsistence Type and Size of Political Unit, Reduced

Subsistence Type	Plough Agriculture %	African Horticulture %	Dominant Horticulture %	Other Horticulture %	Pastoralists %	New World Pastoralists %	Extractive %	Total %
Family, community, pact	16	37	54	78	40	54	95	53
Minimal states	20	33	30	19	21	46	5	22
Little states, States	63	31	16	3	40	0	0	25
Total	99	101	100	100	101	100	100	100

tain patterns emerge fairly readily from inspection of this table. Matrilineal systems are underrepresented in the three subsistence types in which the largest percentage of "little states" and "states" are found— "plough agriculture," "African horticulture," and "pastoralism." By the same token, matrilineal systems are overrepresented in "dominant horticulture," where there is a rather large number of systems integrated at the "peace group," community, and family levels.

These distributions would suggest that there should be a tendency for matrilineal systems to occur in the smallest three categories of size. The actual trends, however, are somewhat different (table 17-6).

Both matrilineal and patrilineal systems tend to cluster at the "minimal state" level by comparison with bilateral systems, which tend to appear at the extremes of political scope. The phi-square value is larger for the matrilineal-bilateral comparison than for the patrilineal-bilateral one. Nevertheless, matrilineal systems do not differ significantly from patrilineal ones in their tendency to cluster in the middle of the range. If we examine only "little states" and "states," the same pattern appears. Bilateral systems are more likely to occur at the "state" level than either patrilineal or matrilineal ones, which do not differ significantly from each other. The phi-square value is larger for the bilateral-matrilineal comparison, and both phi-square values are larger than for the previous comparisons.

Our observation that the over-all relationships between size of unit and lineality were weak compared with many of the findings in table 17-4, in spite of what seemed to be a strong relationship between subsistence base and size of unit, led to a good deal of reflection and experimenting with the data. Finally, the device was hit upon of controlling for size of political unit and examining the associations between subsistence base and lineality which were found in each of three major size groups. These three groups were those previously used for comparing lineality and scope of political system. Family, community, and peace group are lumped as "at or below the community level"; "minimal states" are kept separate; "little states" and "states" are combined. The three groups are labeled "large," "intermediate," and "small." The results are presented in table 17-7.

Subsistence type distinguishes patterns of descent reckoning far more strongly, in terms of phi-square values, and far more often, in terms of number of significant results, among large units than among intermediate or small ones. Phi-square values are slightly stronger, and there are more significant results among intermediate units than among small ones. The absolute size of the largest phi-square values must be

TABLE 17-6

Descent and Size of Political Unit

Size of Unit	Descent Systems									
	Patrilineal		Bilateral		Matrilineal		Duolineal		Total	
	No.	%	No.	%	No.	%	No.	%	No.	%
Family level	13	5	16	8	5	6	1	4	35	6
Community level	75	30	93	46	38	45	19	68	225	40
Peace groups	12	5	6	3	0	0	0	0	18	3
Minimal states	58	24	28	14	27	32	5	18	118	21
Little states	33	13	8	4	9	10	1	4	51	9
States	37	15	36	18	4	5	2	7	79	14
Dependent societies	18	7	16	8	1	1	0	0	35	6
Not ascertained	2	1	1	*	0	0	0	0	3	0
Total	248	100	204	101	84	99	28	101	564	99

* Less than 0.5%.

TABLE 17-6 (continued)

Descent and Size of Political Unit

	Patrilineal and Bilateral			Matrilineal and Bilateral			Patrilineal and Matrilineal
	x^2	p	ϕ^2	x^2	p	ϕ^2	p
Middle vs. Extremes	6.909	<.01	.017	10.941	<.001	.041	NS
States vs. Little states	9.780	<.01	.086	10.051*	.002**	.176	NS

"Middle" equals minimal states, "Extremes" equals all others, cases of dependent societies and no data omitted.

* x^2 corrected for continuity.

** p–based on Fisher's Exact Test.

Bilaterals at extremes in first test; bilaterals at "state" level in second test.

TABLE 17-7

Size of Political Unit, Subsistence Type, and Descent

Subsistence Type	Large Little State and State				Intermediate Minimal State				Small Family, Community, Pact				
	Pat.	Bilat.	Mat.	Duo.	Pat.	Bilat.	Mat.	Duo.	Pat.	Bilat.	Mat.	Duo.	Total
Plough agriculture	30	29	2	1	15	1	4	0	9	4	3	0	98
African horticulture	11	1	1	1	9	1	3	2	12	1	1	3	46
Dominant horticulture	9	9	9	1	19	14	17	3	36	35	21	3	176
Other horticulture	0	1	0	0	2	3	1	0	9	11	3	2	32
Pastoralists	20	4	1	0	12	0	1	0	17	3	1	4	63
New World Pastoralists	0	0	0	0	0	5	1	0	0	6	1	0	13
Extractive	0	0	0	0	1	4	0	0	17	55	13	8	98
Total	70	44	13	3	58	28	27	5	100	115	43	20	526

Dependent societies and those not ascertained are omitted.

TABLE 17-7 (continued)

Size of Unit	Subsistence	Pat. vs. Mat.			Mat. vs. Bilat.			Pat. vs. Bilat.		
		χ^2	p	ϕ^2	χ^2	p	ϕ^2	χ^2	p	ϕ^2
Large	H vs. PA	10.212*	.0013**	.204	10.246*	.0011**	.209		NS	
	H vs. AH	3.907*	.0417**	.130		NS		3.907*	.0417**	.130
	H vs. PA, AH	12.512*	.0006**	.202	8.847*	.0036**	.174		NS	
	H vs. PA, AH, OH	12.512*	.0006**	.202	8.818*	.0031**	.170		NS	
	H vs. AH, P, NP	10.724*	.0011**	.210		NS		6.252*	<.02	.116
	H vs. all others	17.520*	.00013**	.211	8.932*	.0036**	.157		NS	
Intermediate	H vs. PA		NS			NS		6.644	<.01	.136
	H vs. AH		NS			NS			NS	
	H vs. PA, AH	4.390	<.05	.066		NS		9.040	<.01	.153
	H vs. PA, AH, OH	4.188	<.05	.060		NS		5.286	<.05	.083
	H vs. AH, P, NP	5.105	<.05	.082		NS			NS	
	H vs. all others	6.975	<.01	.082		NS			NS	

TABLE 17-7 (continued)

Size of Unit	Subsistence	Pat. vs. Mat.			Mat. vs. Bilat.			Pat. vs. Bilat.		
		χ^2	p	ϕ^2	χ^2	p	ϕ^2	χ^2	p	ϕ^2
	H vs. PA		NS			NS			NS	
	H vs. AH		NS			NS		7.855	$<.01$	.094
	H vs. PA, AH		NS			NS		7.048	$<.01$	.073
	H vs. PA, AH, P, NP		NS			NS				
Small	OH		NS			NS			NS	
	H vs. AH, P, NP	7.777	$<.01$	.087		NS		5.913	$<.02$	.054
	H vs. all others		NS		4.701	$<.05$	.030		NS	

Key:

PA = Plough; AH = African Horticulture; H = Horticulture Dominant; OH = Other Horticulture; P = Pastoralists; NP = New World Pastoralists; Other = PA, AH, OH, P, NP, and Extractives.

* = χ^2 corrected for continuity.

** = p based on Fisher's exact test.

NS = non-significant ($p > .05$).

Where results are significant, matrilineal systems are relatively more common in "dominant horticulture", than in other categories, by comparison with patrilineals or bilaterals. The same is true of bilaterals as compared with patrilineals.

used with caution, however, since these values are unduly dependent on the smallest row or column. Within the large group, the small number of matrilineal cases provides a small column, in comparison with either patriliny or bilaterality, and this raises the phi-square values.

The over-all pattern of results is similar to that found in table 17-4. Matrilineal systems tend toward "dominant horticulture," and other descent systems depend relatively more on other bases, wherever significant results appear. Not all the comparisons supplied in table 17-4 can be presented here, because of the small number of cases in some cells. In general, among large units, matrilineal systems are more inclined to have "dominant horticulture" than patrilineal ones, regardless of the particular subsistence type or combination selected. "Plough agriculture," "African horticulture," "other horticulture," and "pastoralism," singly or in combination, are more likely to involve patriliny. Where the "plough" category enters, matrilineal systems can be distinguished from bilateral systems as more inclined toward "dominant horticulture." Where other use of domesticates, as in "pastoralism" or "African horticulture," appears, matrilineal and bilateral systems cannot be distinguished. The comparison of bilateral and patrilineal systems is complementary to this. Bilateral systems resemble matrilineal ones in their lack of affinity for "pastoralism" and "African horticulture," in various combinations, and can be distinguished from patrilineal ones in these respects. They cannot be distinguished from the patrilineal where "plough agriculture" enters the comparisons.

Among intermediate groups the pattern is partly the same but fewer results are significant and phi-square values drop. Only the massed effect of various patterns other than "dominant horticulture" distinguishes between matrilineal and patrilineal systems. No differences between matrilineal and bilateral systems emerge. There is some shift in the pattern for the patrilineal-bilateral contrast, since patrilineal systems at this level incline more toward "plough agriculture" and bilateral ones more toward "dominant horticulture." Animal husbandry and pastoralism in various combinations fail to distinguish patrilineal from bilateral systems.

At the lowest level, few relationships appear. Matrilineal systems are no longer distinguished importantly from either patrilineal or bilateral systems. Bilateral systems favor "dominant horticulture" by comparison with patrilineal ones, the difference apparently depending on "African horticulture" rather than "plough agriculture." (Luckily I do not have to explain the patrilineal-bilateral comparisons in detail for present purposes.)

The phi-square values for the entire table range from 0.030 to 0.211, with corresponding phi values of 0.17 to 0.46. There are twelve significant results in the group of large units—seven among intermediate units and five among small units. All but three phi-square values in the "large" group are stronger than the highest value in table 17-4. All but three phi-square values in the "large" group are higher than any in the "intermediate" group.

This general pattern requires explanation. Let us return to the raw distribution scores for table 17-7. Here it becomes apparent that as size of political unit increases, the percentage of dominantly horticultural matrilineal systems (ignoring extraction) remains relatively constant, at about 66 to 75 per cent, with insignificant rise in the "large" category. The percentage of bilateral and patrilineal systems based on dominant horticulture (again ignoring extraction) drops sharply. In the case of bilaterals, it goes from 58 and 63 per cent to a little better than 20 per cent. In the case of patrilineals, it moves from 39 and 33 per cent to 13 per cent. In the case of bilaterals, the shift is into the "plough" category in the "large" category. In the case of patrilineals, it is into "plough agriculture," "African horticulture," and pastoralism. Thus the marked statistical differences in the largest political units do not result so much from the decreased subsistence variability of matrilineal systems, as from the increased tendency of patrilineal and bilateral systems to have other than "dominant horticulture" bases. But why should this shift be associated with size of political unit?

I believe that the explanation is to be found in the differing ecological range of matrilineal systems, as contrasted with the patrilineal and the bilateral. Matrilineal systems tend to have a horticultural base, and tend not to be found with the plough, animal husbandry, or dominant pastoralism. On the other hand, patrilineal and bilateral systems are quite commonly found with horticultural bases, as well as with these other bases. Thus far the explanation describes the state of affairs manifested in table 17-4.

The explanation of table 17-7 requires an additional assumption: that size of political unit has some rough association with level of productivity. The reasons for assuming this involve theoretical excursions not entirely germane to the present essay. Let me deal somewhat summarily with the issue. Murdock's size of political unit is roughly associated with actual degree of political centralization. Degree of political centralization (e.g., autonomous band or acephalous tribe, as contrasted with chiefdom or state) is associated with actual level of productivity. Without inquiring into the cause for this, it is necessary only to observe that an elaborated political organization has as a requirement the production of surplus to support it, so that higher productivity is a necessary condition for higher political centralization. Various subsistence bases have different surplus potentials. Extraction pure and simple apparently produces only sufficient surplus for chiefdoms, and rarely accomplishes that. The same is largely true for cultures where extraction is dominant and horticulture secondary, or where horticulture and extraction are co-dominant activities. Agriculture, however, can support a state under appropriate conditions. Murdock's classification would require us to assume that pastoralism can do likewise, but this is one of the points at which the size of the largest political unit is most at variance with the elaboration of political hierarchy. Pure pastoral systems do not ordinarily rise above chiefdoms, even when very large.

By and large, the combination of animal husbandry and horticulture, the use of the plough, and irrigation agriculture (not coded in Murdock's system) *on the average* probably supply higher levels of productivity than does pure horticulture. This means that as size of political unit (now used as an index of productivity) rises, we tend to get proportionately more "plough," "African horticulture," and "pastoral" systems (the last because of coding peculiarities). Hence as productivity rises, horticulture, which is the only base which is peculiarly suitable for matriliny, declines in frequency, whereas all bases suitable for patriliny and bilaterality that select against matriliny rise in frequency. Therefore, subsistence type becomes a better index for lineality with large than with small political units. This explains the table, but it also has some relevance for the real world.

Politically centralized matrilineal systems tend to occur, it seems, only under special ecological conditions. ("Only" here refers to a trend, not to an absolute.) They tend to occupy a niche where horticulture can be quite productive; the plough has not yet reached or cannot reach; important animal husbandry is impossible; large-scale, supra-community irrigation is impossible or unnecessary. In all probability, they must also have developed at a lower level in a similar niche, except that the initial niche need not have a high horticultural potential. Patrilineal systems, and bilateral ones, can occupy not only niches with these characteristics, but also, they can occupy niches where—to different degrees for each descent type—animal husbandry, plough agriculture, or large-scale irrigation are possible. Hence the ecological range of matrilineal systems is relatively narrow compared with patrilineal systems or bilateral ones. This does *not* mean that matriliny keeps a cul-

ture from occupying a more abundant niche or from adding a new
technical device to its productive apparatus. It means only that the
matrilineal system that does so is likely to become patrilineal or
bilateral.

In small political units we tend to find less "plough agriculture" and
"African horticulture," simply because of the general tendency of these
technical forms to be associated with high productivity. Hence matrilineal, patrilineal, and bilateral systems at low levels tend to be based
on horticulture (omitting extraction), and cannot be distinguished. To
distinguish between the horticultural conditions that promote matriliny
and those that promote other descent forms requires data of a sort not
available in the sample—both historical and relative to resources and
work organization. Hence the statistical differentiation largely disappears in small units.

There are three corollaries of the theory just presented. First, we
should find that within any given subsistence type, the relationship between size of unit and lineality disappears. We have claimed that the
societies with the largest political units are the most productive, and
hence the most likely to depend on agriculture supplemented by the
plough and by animal husbandry (or pastoralism, with qualifications
noted). For this reason the patrilineal and bilateral systems are likely
to depend on these productive bases, and not on horticulture, whereas
the matrilineal systems will depend on dominant horticulture, since
other bases are to a degree incompatible with matriliny. Thus size of
political unit is not a factor "causing" lineality in these tables, but one
which selects a group of cultures in which the maximum effect of certain subsistence bases in selecting against matriliny is manifest.[5] The
findings conform approximately to these expectations. The only significant differences within subsistence types occur in connection with
plough agriculture. Here bilateral systems are significantly more likely
to be found at the "little state" and "state" level than are patrilineal or
matrilineal ones. Unilineal systems are not significantly differentiated.
This result is partly a product of the fact that the bilateral systems
include a number of modern, industrialized Western groups. There is
a non-significant tendency for matrilineal systems to have more groups
above the community level among horticulturalists than is the case for

[5] To the degree that size is associated with bureaucratization, Gough's theory
suggests that there would be a connection between size of unit and lineality—via
the nature of political unit. Bureaucratization leads to the disappearance of matriliny, and ultimately of patriliny, in favor of bilaterality. The sample cannot be used
to test this line of inquiry without further codes.

either patrilineal or bilateral groups, and various other small non-
significant trends appear with different classifications of political integration—"minimal states" versus others, "community" versus "minimal states" verses "little states" and "states," etc. In general, then, these
results fit the theory. (Tests and tables are not presented, because of
space considerations. Data can be found in table 17-7.)

Second, if our assumption that size of political unit is an index of
productivity is correct, we should find that other indices of productivity are associated with it, and with subsistence type as well—since
we have assumed an over-all connection between subsistence type and
productivity. In general the facts are consonant with this corollary.
The major available alternative index for productivity in the *World
Ethnographic Sample* is Murdock's "social stratification of freemen." It
includes five categories: none; age groups only; wealth without definite
crystallization into hereditary social classes; hereditary aristocracy or
nobility; and complex stratification into three or more social classes or
castes, exclusive of slavery (Murdock, 1957: 673). For present purposes, Murdock's first two categories are lumped as "no stratification."

As in the case of size of political unit, the argument connecting
stratification and productivity is that stratification is impossible at the
lowest levels of productivity, being permitted at higher levels by surplus. Further elaboration of the ramifications of this proposition is unnecessary for present purposes.

Stratification shows a significant, strong over-all association with
size of political unit, with a strong tendency for complex stratification to
be associated with "states," and hereditary aristocracy with "little
states" (table 17-8). These relationships are conceptually almost
tautologous, but for present purposes the tautology does not matter.
What is important is that similar results are produced by two measures
of the tendency for productivity, political centralization, and stratification to develop *pari passu*. By the same token, high stratification of
freemen is associated with hereditary slavery, and low stratification
with the absence of slavery (table 17-9). I have not further pursued
the associations of slavery with political integration and subsistence.
Furthermore, percentage distributions make it clear that stratification
is closely connected with subsistence type (table 17-10). Here percentages have been allowed to stand without significance tests. "Plough
agriculture" shows the highest stratification, "African horticulture"
next, "dominant horticulture" next, and "other horticulture" next, in
the agricultural series. "Pastoralism" shows a level intermediate between "plough agriculture" and "African horticulture," somewhat

TABLE 17-8

Stratification and Size of Political Unit

Size of Unit	Level of Stratification											
	None and Age Grades		Wealth		Hereditary Aristocracy		Complex		Not Ascertained		Total	
	No.	%	No.	%	No.	%	No.	%	No.	%	No.	%
Family	30	13	6	7	0	0	0	0	0	0	36	7
Community	147	63	45	56	28	26	1	1	4	44	225	43
Peace group	9	4	5	6	3	3	1	1	0	0	13	3
Minimal state	44	19	17	21	40	36	14	15	3	33	118	22
Little state	5	2	7	9	27	24	10	11	2	22	51	10
State	0	0	1	1	12	11	66	72	0	0	79	15
Total	235	101	81	100	110	100	92	100	9	99	527	100

Dependent societies are omitted.

Tests: 1) Little state and state versus other, hereditary aristocracy and complex stratification versus other.
$x^2 = 182.35$; $p < .001$; $\phi^2 = .346$

2) Little state versus state, hereditary versus complex.
$x^2 = 37.41$; $p < .001$; $\phi^2 = .325$

TABLE 17-9

Stratification and Slavery

Level of Stratification	Slavery									
	Hereditary		Non-hereditary		Type Unspecified		Absent		Total	
	No.	%	No.	%	No.	%	No.	%	No.	%
None and age grades	10	10	30	45	16	25	172	62	228	45
Wealth	12	13	16	24	10	15	41	15	79	16
Hereditary	36	38	13	19	28	43	26	9	103	20
Complex	36	38	8	12	7	11	37	13	88	17
Not ascertained	1	1	0	0	4	6	2	1	7	1
Total	95	100	67	100	65	100	278	100	505	99

Dependent societies and those not ascertained are omitted. Test constructed for extremes.

Test: No stratification and age grades versus hereditary and complex stratification; hereditary slavery versus slavery absent.

$x^2 = 92.613; p < .001; \phi^2 = .292$

TABLE 17-10

Stratification and Subsistence

Level of Stratification*	Subsistence Type															
	Plough Agriculture		African Horticulture		Dominant Horticulture		Other Horticulture		Pastoralists		New World Pastoralists		Extractives		Total	
	No.	%	No.	%	No.	%	No.	%	No.	%	No.	%	No.	%	No.	%
None and age grades	10	9	20	46	96	54	24	75	13	21	7	54	70	69	240	44
Wealth	20	17	3	7	22	12	2	6	21	33	2	15	20	20	90	16
Hereditary aristocracy	17	15	12	27	45	25	5	16	20	32	4	31	11	11	114	21
Complex	68	59	9	20	15	8	1	3	9	14	0	0	1	1	103	19
Total	115	100	44	100	178	99	32	100	63	100	13	100	102	101	547	100

*18 cases of data not available omitted.

similar to its position in table 17-5. "New World pastoralism" and "extraction" bring up the bottom of the list. These associations are consistent with the theory provided earlier.

Parenthetically, descent shows a relationship with stratification somewhat similar to that with size of political unit (table 17-11). There is not quite the curvilinear pattern which emerges in table 6, but matrilineal systems tend to have hereditary, rather than complex stratification to a greater degree than is the case for patrilineal and bilateral systems. Patrilineal systems also tend more toward hereditary stratification than do bilateral ones.

The third corollary of the interpretation of table 17-7 is that an analysis of the relationship between subsistence and lineality, controlling for stratification or for slavery, should show a pattern like that of table 17-7. A detailed analysis of the scope attempted in table 17-7 is out of the question. I have, however, presented one compressed test, using only stratification and only those subsistence types which tend toward larger political units: "plough agriculture," "African horticulture," and "pastoralism," by comparison with "dominant horticulture" (table 17-12). The first three subsistence types have been lumped, and stratification has been dichotomized: "high" stratification includes complex and hereditary; "low" includes none, age grades, and wealth only. Matrilineal systems are relatively more frequent in the "dominant horticulture" category than either bilateral or patrilineal systems, at high levels of stratification. They are more commonly in the "dominant horticulture" category than patrilineal systems at low levels; there is no significant difference between matrilineal and bilateral systems at this level. Phi-square values rise in the matrilineal-patrilineal comparison from the low to the high stratification category; in the matrilineal-bilateral comparison there is a shift from non-significant to significant. The patrilineal-bilateral comparison does not concern us here. Thus, in broad outline, the relationship between subsistence and lineality, controlling for stratification, resembles that between subsistence and lineality, controlling for size of political unit.

One would also expect that if subsistence type is controlled and the effect of stratification on lineality is then examined, the relationship between stratification and lineality should disappear. I have not carried out statistical tests on this, nor on a variety of sub-tables dealing with subsistence and lineality, controlling for stratification, because of limitations of time, space, and effort. But inspection of table 17-12 indicates that within the "dominant horticulture" category there is little percentage difference in the distribution of levels of stratification

TABLE 17-11

Descent and Stratification

Level of Stratification	Descent System									
	Patrilineal		Bilateral		Matrilineal		Duolineal		Total	
	No.	%	No.	%	No.	%	No.	%	No.	%
None and age grades	91	40	89	47	40	49	14	50	234	45
Wealth	34	15	29	15	11	13	7	25	81	15
Hereditary	57	25	27	14	23	28	3	11	110	21
Complex	42	18	41	22	6	7	3	11	92	18
Not ascertained	4	2	2	1	2	2	1	4	9	2
Total	228	100	188	99	82	99	28	101	526	101

Dependent societies are omitted.

Tests:

1) Patrilineal versus matrilineal, hereditary versus complex.
   $x^2 = 4.565; p < .05; \phi^2 = .036$
   Patrilineals more complex.

2) Bilateral versus matrilineal, hereditary versus complex.
   $x^2 = 12.919; p < .001; \phi^2 = .133$
   Bilaterals more complex.

3) Patrilineal versus bilateral, hereditary versus complex.
   $x^2 = 5.145; p < .05; \phi^2 = .031$
   Bilaterals more complex.

TABLE 17-12

Descent, Subsistence Type, and Stratification

Stratification	Subsistence Type	Descent				
		Patrilineal	Bilateral	Matrilineal	Total	
High (Hereditary and complex)	PA, AH, P	80	34	7	121	
	H	17	21	16	54	
Low (None, age grade, wealth)	PA, AH, P	56	10	8	74	
	H	45	36	30	111	
Total		198	101	61	360	

TABLE 17-12 (continued)

	Descent								
	Mat. vs. Pat.			Mat. vs. Bilat.			Pat. vs. Bilat.		
Stratification	χ^2	p	ϕ^2	χ^2	p	ϕ^2	χ^2	p	ϕ^2
High	25.433	<.001	.212	6.433	<.02	.082	7.896	<.01	.053
Low	13.156	<.001	.095		NS		14.638	<.001	.098

Key: PA = plough agriculture; AH = African horticulture; P = pastoralists; H = dominant horticulture.

Matrilineal systems more common in horticulture relative to patrilineal and bilateral systems, where relationships are significant. Bilateral systems more common in horticulture than patrilineal ones.

Duolineal systems, dependent societies, and other subsistence types are omitted.

among the three descent categories. Within the combined "plough," "African," and "pastoral" group, the difference is slight between patrilineal and matrilineal systems as to level of stratification, but bilateral systems show a tendency toward higher stratification than either the matrilineal or patrilineal. These same tendencies are to be found in the analysis of table 17-7, and again can probably be attributed to modern, industrialized, bureaucratized bilateral systems found in the "plough" category, all of which show complex stratification.

Thus a second index of productivity shows the same tendencies as size of political unit. I have explained table 17-7 by reference to the limited ecological niche of matrilineal systems. The corollaries that follow from this explanation are supported by an analysis of the tables dealing with stratification.

In sum, all non-extractive subsistence types except "dominant horticulture" tend to select against matriliny. Horticulture itself does not select *against* patriliny and bilaterality, but all other non-extractive types select *for* one or the other. For this reason the ecological range of matrilineal systems is relatively narrow, and among highly productive systems is particularly narrow because ecological niches which permit high productivity on a horticultural base are relatively less common than those which permit it on other bases. Finally, however, I have been unable to define empirically the precise conditions within the horticultural type most likely to differentiate matrilineal from other descent systems.

At this point I must return to the focus on general and specific evolution. Matriliny, it must be stressed, is a special adaptation to certain productive conditions, capable of surviving under other—but by no means all other—conditions. Matriliny itself is not a level of organization, but on the contrary, various levels of organization occur among matrilineal, patrilineal, and bilateral systems. Its association with certain productive systems, its incompatibility with others, and its incompatibility with extensive bureaucratization imply that matriliny is largely limited to a certain range of productivity and a certain range of centralization—ranges narrower than those of either patrilineal or bilateral systems. Matriliny, however, is only one of the principles of descent reckoning which can occur within this range, and cannot be viewed as a "stage" or "level" of general evolutionary development.

Difficulties, Complexities, and Hunches

This chapter describes only a small amount of the work done in the analysis of the *World Ethnographic Sample*. In this section I shall deal briefly with various sorts of attempts to analyze the data which are not represented by tables here, and with the problems that arose in these connections. The first set of problems is connected with the categorization of subsistence activities. The code as finally developed disregards the difference between root, tree, and cereal crops, the importance of small animal domesticates, and subsidiary subsistence activities in agricultural and pastoral societies. The distinction among crops was omitted because no convincing association with lineality could be shown. In fact, of course, the "plough" systems are based on cereal agriculture, but the remainder are mixed.

The case of ancillary subsistence activities was given a good deal of attention. It developed that among cultures where agricultural or pastoral activities were dominant, or where agriculture was important, there was some tendency for fishing to be associated with matrilineality. This was true in the entire sample, and true in Africa, where the phi-square values for the association between fishing and matrilineality in non-extractive cultures ran particularly high. Indeed, the association for the entire sample is probably largely the product of the data for Africa. Consequently, the logical possibility exists that the connection between matrilineality and horticulture is accidental, and that the crucial issue is the amount of fishing or the kind of fishing done. It is also possible, however, that environments conducive to horticulture without important animal domesticates are also conducive to fishing, so that the association between fishing and matrilineality is accidental. Various other causal chains can be imagined. A brief examination of African ethnographic materials did not seem to support the notion that the processes of fishing, the division of labor in fishing, the work groups for fishing, or the control of fishing territories showed any clear correspondence with matrilineality. Efforts failed to demonstrate statistically that the impact of fishing on matrilineality was or was not a statistical artifact. Hence, the only thing that can be done at this point is to mention the tantalizing fact that there is *some* tendency for fishing to be connected with matrilineality in non-extractive cultures, to say that there is no obvious reason why this should be so, and to leave the issue for future investigation. Hunting and gathering, in non-extractive cultures, showed no association with lineality.

A second type of investigation which took a good deal of effort was an attempt to prove that the relationships I have discussed for the entire sample were to be found in each major area of the world. This attempt was only partly successful, but the partial lack of success does not seem to undermine the entire approach. In Africa the "plough agriculture" and "New World pastoralist" categories are lacking. There are very few bilateral peoples among non-extractive groups. The tendency for "African horticulture" to be associated with patrilineality and dominant horticulture to be associated with matrilineality was present, but not to a statistically significant degree. This prompted me to recategorize the African cultures, so as to classify together all those in which horticulture is dominant and animal domesticates, small or large, are important, and to compare them with all those in which horticulture is dominant and no animal domesticates are important. The tendency for patrilineal systems to be associated with the first of these and matrilineal with the second was now significant. This result led to a reëxamination of the case of small domesticates. It was discovered that the strength of a number of the associations would have been improved if all predominantly horticultural systems where large or small domesticates are important had been classed together, omitting only cases where the pig is important. The remainder of the "dominant horticulture" group would then include only cases with large or small domesticates unimportant, or with the pig as an important domesticate. But it was by then too late to undertake this step for the entire sample.

In the Circum-Mediterranean and in East Eurasia there were too few matrilineal systems for any statistical analysis.

In the Insular Pacific, no significant associations of subsistence type and lineality appeared. A further attempt was made by analyzing as a group Melanesia, Micronesia, Polynesia, New Guinea, and Austrialia, omitting Indonesia, the Philippines, and Formosa. Again, nothing emerged, although no trends contrary to theoretical expectation appeared. There is a slight tendency for cases with horticulture and with important fishing to be more often matrilineal than those with horticulture which lack important fishing, but it is not statistically significant. In the Oceanian tables, the range of subsistence types is very limited, including only dominant horticulture, other horticulture, and extractive. Almost all extractive systems are duolineal, which involves problems not discussed in this chapter. Hence, the comparison is between "dominant horticulture" and "other horticulture" types not statistically distinguished in the total sample. In the total Insular Pacific table there are only fourteen cases of "plough agriculture," and these show no statistically significant distribution with reference to lineality. Limited range of subsistence types therefore seems to be of some importance in the lack of significant results.

In North America, matrilineal systems are proportionately more fre-

quent among "dominant horticulturalists" than among "other horticulturalists," "New World pastoralists," and extractive systems, by
comparison with bilateral systems but not by comparison with patrilineal ones, although the trend there is the same. The importance of
fishing does not distinguish types of descent within the groups with
horticulture, but there is a significant tendency for matriliny to be
associated with fishing in extractive cultures—a function of the North-
western matrilineal fishing group.

In South America there are virtually no findings, but one disrupts
the general trend. There are proportionately more matrilineal than
patrilineal extractive cultures, but no differences between bilateral and
matrilineal ones. Fishing seems to show no relationship with lineality.
I have elsewhere suggested that these results may reflect relatively
recent changes in subsistence type, and have demonstrated that most
of the matrilineal groups have some amount of horticulture. The question must be left there.

Thus, in Africa and North America certain of the associations found
in the total sample reappear, but only when the African cases are
slightly reclassified. Reduction of the frequency of matrilineal systems
in the Circum-Mediterranean and in Eurasia makes statistical analysis
impossible, but points again to the relative incompatibility of matriliny
and plough agriculture or pastoralism. Reduction of the range of subsistence types in Oceania is an important source of the inability to find
associations there. In South America certain special considerations have
been invoked.

A third problem was that of the division of labor. Since theories of
matriliny center heavily on the contribution of each sex to important
subsistence activities, it was attempted, particularly in the early
phases of the investigation, to find connections between lineality and
division of labor. The various activities were tried singly and in combination, using residence as a control, using political integration as a
control, and so on and on. Literally no results emerged.

I will not say that no results connecting lineality and the division
of labor can emerge from the sample, but only that I tried every trick
I could think of until I gave up. In terms of the theories advanced both
in Gough's chapters and here, the lack of results is not entirely surprising; nor is it unexpected in the light of our general impressions
from various areas of the world. In the first place, Gough's theory, and
a number of cases, indicate that at low levels of productivity with
sedentary agriculture and descent group control of reusable land,
horticultural activities may be in men's hands (presumably having

shifted from women's) and matriliny may survive. Second, avunculocal residence may accompany either a shift in the division of labor or the concentration of more power in men's hands—as in a redistributive system—or both. Third, we know as an empirical fact that in a number of African systems where most subsistence is derived from women's hoe cultivation but where men care for cattle, descent is likely to be patrilineal. Fourth, the classifications of division of labor tell which sex does what, but tell us nothing about work groups or work sites, which is probably a critical variable. For these, or for other reasons, nothing developed from efforts to use the division of labor as an independent variable.

Finally, I have been unable to make sufficient progress with two critical problems. First, although it can be shown that matrilineal systems tend to be horticultural, I have been unable to provide any theoretical or empirical basis for predicting the conditions under which horticultural systems will be matrilineal, patrilineal, bilateral, or duolineal. Division of labor has thus far not proved helpful. It is possible that ecological niche may prove to be a good predictor, but the reasons for this, if it is so, are unclear. I have claimed that matrilineal systems are rare in the tropical forest, but I have not attempted to prove that they are disproportionately rare. On a purely random basis, they would represent about 15 per cent of the cultures in the tropical forest, since they represent about 15 per cent of the total sample. Since, however, matrilineal systems are only slightly less common than bilateral or patrilineal systems among "dominant horticulturalists," they should be almost as generously represented among tropical forest horticulturalists as patrilineal or bilateral systems. The survey provided earlier in this chapter strongly suggests that this is not the case, but a strict demonstration of this proposition has not been attempted.

Thus, in the very niche (horticulture) in which matrilineal systems flourish, the conditions which produce or permit them remain least clear.

Second, although there are theories as to why plough agriculture, horticulture with important cattle, horses, sheep, goats, etc., and pastorialism tend to eliminate matrilineal systems, these theories have not been tested. That this sort of selection operates seems unquestionable, but it has not yet been demonstrated how it happens. More comparative work, using detailed case analysis of smaller samples and more sharply specified variables on a large sample, is required to answer this problem.

Some Constants and Variables of Matrilineal Systems

This section will be devoted to the use of the *World Ethnographic Sample* to test some of Schneider's and Gough's propositions. At times the test must be somewhat approximate, and at times other, closely related issues will be discussed. The data in the sample cannot be used at all to test most of the propositions advanced earlier in this volume, since the sample does not include codes for the relevant variables. I have abandoned a number of efforts at indirect support for various propositions, because the links connecting the sample data and the propositions seemed too tenuous.

SCHNEIDER'S HYPOTHESES

Lateral Succession   Schneider has argued that lateral succession is more likely for matrilineal than for patrilineal descent groups. Direct evidence on this score is not available. The sample, however, affords a classification of the rules of succession to the headman's position in the local community (table 17-13). If we assume that these rules are likely to conform to the general rules of succession in the society, an indirect test of Schneider's argument can be made. For this purpose we must ignore bilateral and double-descent systems. In addition, we must exclude cases where there is patrilineal succession to the headman's position in matrilineal systems, since by definition the headship of a matrilineal unit cannot follow the patriline. In addition, we must ignore all cases where headship is not hereditary. Finally, there is an unfortunately large number of cases where succession is hereditary but cannot be classified as lineal or lateral. For this, as for succeeding tables, one-tailed tests of significance are used, since the predictions are directional and *a priori*. Table 17-13 shows a highly significant association between lateral succession to the headman's position and matriliny, and lineal succession and patriliny. The phi-square value is also fairly high. These data support, though they do not confirm Schneider's theory.

Segmentation   Schneider has pointed out the difficulties in "neat" segmentation for matrilineal systems. But again, a simple, direct test of this hypothesis is impossible. It should be noted, however, that there is a very strong tendency for segmentary units (in Murdock's classification) to be associated with patriliny, and that indeed only one matrilineal system is classified as having segmentary units (table 17-14).

Merging Terminology   Schneider argues that matrilineal systems are more likely than patrilineal ones to have merging, rather than col-

TABLE 17-13

Descent and Succession to the Headman's Position

Mode of Succession	Descent System									
	Patrilineal		Bilateral		Matrilineal		Duolineal		Total	
	No.	%	No.	%	No.	%	No.	%	No.	%
Patrilineal, lineal	49	23	46	27	7	9	4	17	106	22
Patrilineal, lateral	12	6	2	1	0	0	2	8	16	3
Patrilineal, not ascertained	75	35	22	13	0	0	10	42	107	22
Matrilineal, lineal	0	0	2	1	12	16	0	0	14	3
Matrilineal, lateral	0	0	0	0	14	19	0	0	14	3
Matrilineal, not ascertained	0	0	1	1	18	24	2	8	21	4
Appointment	11	5	7	4	1	1	0	0	19	4

TABLE 17-13 (continued)

Descent System

Mode of Succession	Patrilineal		Bilateral		Matrilineal		Duolineal		Total	
	No.	%	No.	%	No.	%	No.	%	No.	%
Election	15	7	28	16	3	4	1	4	47	10
Consensus	18	8	40	23	9	12	0	0	67	14
No headman, councils	19	9	6	3	5	7	4	17	34	7
No headman	18	8	18	10	6	8	1	4	43	9
No data*	31		32		9		4		76	
Total	248		204		84		28		564	
Total minus no data	217	101	172	99	75	100	24	100	488	101

*Excluded in computation of significance.

TABLE 17-13 (continued)

Tests: 1) Test for non-random distribution, among patrilineal and matrilineal systems, using all patrilineal systems with patrilineal succession, all matrilineal systems with matrilineal succession. Test undertaken because in over 50 per cent of cases there is no information regarding lineal versus lateral succession.

$x^2 = 16.72; p < .001$ (two-tailed test).

2) Test for matrilineal versus patrilineal, matrilineal-lineal and patrilineal-lineal succession versus patrilineal-lateral and matrilineal-lateral succession.

$x^2 = 10.050; p < .005$ (one-tailed test); $\phi^2 = .116$

TABLE 17-14

Descent Units in Patrilineal
and Matrilineal Systems

| Descent Units | Descent System | | | | | |
| | Patrilineal | | Matrilineal | | Total | |
	No.	%	No.	%	No.	%
Segmentary lineages	35	14	1	1	36	11.
Lineages	42	17	9	11	51	15
Sibs	144	58	45	54	189	57
Phratries	10	4	7	8	17	5
Exogamous moieties	10	4	16	19	26	8
Agamous moieties	3	1	3	4	6	2
Not ascertained	4	2	3	4	7	2
Total	248	100	84	101	332	100

Each system is classified by reference to the *largest* unit found. If there are lineages and sibs, the system is classified "sibs."

Test: Segmentary lineages versus all other categories (omitting those not ascertained).

$\chi^2 = 10.62$; $p < .005$ (one-tailed test); $\phi^2 = .032$

lateralizing terminology. The sample can be used to test this proposition directly for avuncular terminology in the first ascending generation. There are, however, two complications in making the test.

In the *World Ethnographic Sample* Murdock has modified Lowie's familiar fourfold classification of first ascending generation terms, supplying six categories. To the usual set of bifurcate merging, bifurcate collateral, lineal, and generational, he adds "descriptive" and "derivative bifurcate merging" terminology. Terminology is "descriptive" when the terms for father's brother and mother's brother can be analyzed into component elements which mean "father's brother," and "mother's brother." These systems are not too common, and in any case conform to the definition of a bifurcate collateral system, since father's brother is not equated with father or with mother's brother. "Derivative bifurcate merging" terminology involves the use of such terms as "little father" for father's brother. Hence, in one sense, he is equated with father, because he *is* called by the term for father, and in another, he is separated, because that term is qualified. Therefore these systems could logically be classified with bifurcate merging, or with bifurcate collateral, or omitted as intermediate.

A second problem arises because Schneider speaks of "merging," not "bifurcate merging" terminology. Hence, generational terminology, which merges father and father's brother, could appropriately be considered merging, and lineal terminology, which does not, could be considered collateralizing. These considerations mean that the tests must be done in a variety of ways if the results are to be convincing.

By comparison with bifurcate collateral terminology, bifurcate merging terminology tends to be associated with matriliny, although the association is not very strong (table 17-15). By comparison with derivative bifurcate merging terminology, it is also associated with matriliny, but less strongly. Derivative bifurcate merging terminology does not differ significantly from bifurcate collateral in its affinity for matriliny, so that it is, in fact, more like bifurcate collateral than like bifurcate merging. Too few descriptive, lineal, or generational systems are found among matrilineal and patrilineal groups for satisfactory analysis of each category. When derivative bifurcate merging, bifurcate collateral, and descriptive systems are grouped, the results remain significant and in the expected direction. When bifurcate merging and generational systems are lumped together and compared with derivative, descriptive, bifurcate collateral, and lineal systems, the results remain significant. If the same test is done with derivative bifurcate merging systems combined with bifurcate merging and generational, the results remain significant. Phi-squares change only within a fairly narrow range, 0.03 to 0.06, remaining fairly low throughout.

These findings support Schneider's hypothesis. Nevertheless, it must be said that it would take a far more exhaustive analysis to have real confidence in the theory that lineality and associated segmentation processes are the causal factors in producing these differences. Murdock's work indicates the large number of factors affecting first ascending generation terminology. Probing for causes of kinship terminology becomes complicated because of the possibility that factor A (say lineality) tends to be associated with factor B (say marriage form),

TABLE 17-15

Descent and Avuncular Terminology

Terminology	Descent System									
	Patrilineal		Bilateral		Matrilineal		Duolineal		Total	
	No.	%	No.	%	No.	%	No.	%	No.	%
Bifurcate merging	65	33	27	15	41	53	20	74	153	32
Derivative bifurcate merging	51	26	14	8	14	18	4	15	83	17
Bifurcate collateral	60	30	52	29	11	14	2	7	125	26
Descriptive	8	4	4	2	1	1	0	0	13	3
Generational	5	3	17	9	6	8	1	4	29	6
Lineal	10	5	66	37	4	5	0	0	80	17
Not ascertained	49		24		7		1		81	
Total	248	101	204	100	84	99	28	100	564	
Total minus Not ascertained	199	101	180	100	77	99	27	100	483	101

TABLE 17-15 (continued)

Tests: Relative frequencies in patrilineal and matrilineal systems of:

1) Bifurcate merging versus bifurcate collateral.

$x^2 = 11.11$; $p < .0005$ (one-tailed test); $\phi^2 = .06$

2) Bifurcate merging versus derivative bifurcate merging.

$x^2 = 5.42$; $p < .02$ (two-tailed test); $\phi^2 = .03$

3) Derivative bifurcate merging versus bifurcate collateral. Not significant.

4) Bifurcate merging versus derivative bifurcate merging, bifurcate collateral and descriptive, together.

$x^2 = 13.46$; $p < .0005$ (one-tailed test); $\phi^2 = .05$

5) All "merging" systems (bifurcate merging and generational) versus all "collateral" systems (derivative bifurcate merging, bifurcate collateral, descriptive, and lineal).

$x^2 = 15.30$; $p < .0005$ (one-tailed test); $\phi^2 = .05$

6) Same as above, with derivative bifurcate merging lumped with "merging" systems.

$x^2 = 8.35$; $p < .005$ (one-tailed test); $\phi^2 = .03$

In all cases, "merging" is associated with matrilineality.

thus making quite difficult a decision as to which one is in fact efficacious. A start was made in this problem by controlling for marriage form. The result was the finding that the association of merging with matriliny and collateralizing with patriliny holds up in systems with monogamy and limited polygyny, but not with sororal and limited sororal polygyny, non-sororal polygyny, or general polygyny. For the most part, demonstrating these relationships requires that derivative bifurcate merging terminology be ignored or treated as a case of collateralizing terminology. Phi-squares rise to a range of 0.07 to 0.134 (no tables supplied). The further complexities of controlling for residence, type of descent group, community composition, etc., seemed too extensive to warrant an exhaustive analysis of the problem. Finally, then, the data fit Schneider's hypothesis, but the analysis has not been carried to the point of definitive support.

Mono-Lineage Communities Schneider argues that mono-lineage communities are likely to be rarer in matrilineal than in patrilineal systems. This hypothesis can be tested approximately by the use of Murdock's classification of community composition in the *World Ethnographic Sample* (table 17-16). The following categories used by Murdock define what seem *not* to be mono-lineage communities.

(1) Demes: communities with a marked tendency toward local endogamy, but not divided into localized exogamic units.

(2) Agamous communities: no report of localized clans within the community, no report of marked local endogamy or exogamy.

(3) Exogamous barrios, wards, hamlets, or localized lineages, where the community normally includes several such units but is not itself an exogamic unit.

The following categories reflect local exogamous units, although one of these is perhaps not a mono-lineage community.

(4) Exogamous communities: marked local exogamy but the local community does not constitute a clan.

(5) Clan communities: those which are essentially localized exogamous lineages or sibs. (This is presumably in contrast to category 4, where a clear-cut rule of descent is lacking.)

(6) Absence of localized clans but no specific evidence on local endogamy or exogamy. (This category provides insufficient information and must be disregarded for this problem.)

We would expect matrilineal systems to be more frequent among the non-exogamous communities (categories 1, 2, and 3), and rarer among exogamous local units (categories 4 and 5). This is the case. A more explicit test, which uses less of the cases, is a comparison of exogamous

TABLE 17-16

Descent and Community Composition

	Descent Systems									
	Patrilineal		Bilateral		Matrilineal		Duolineal		Total	
Community	No.	%	No.	%	No.	%	No.	%	No.	%
Demes	27	13	42	21	13	17	1	4	83	16
Agamous communities	35	16	80	40	15	20	4	15	134	26
Exogamous barrios	52	24	0	0	20	27	7	26	79	15
Exogamous communities	20	9	37	18	5	7	0	0	62	12
Clan communities	75	35	0	0	12	16	14	52	101	19
No local clans	6	3	42	21	10	13	1	4	59	11
Not ascertained	33		3		9		1		46	
Total	248		204		84		28		564	
Total minus										
Not ascertained	215	100	201	100	75	100	27	101	518	99

Tests: 1) Non-exogamous communities (demes, agamous communities, and exogamous barrios) versus exogamous communities (exogamous communities and clan communities), against patrilineal versus matrilineal descent.

$\chi^2 = 7.69$; $p < .005$ (one-tailed test); $\phi^2 = .03$ Matrilineality favors non-exogamous communities.

2) Exogamous barrios versus clan communities, against patrilineal versus matrilineal descent.

$\chi^2 = 4.79$; $p < .025$ (one-tailed test); $\phi^2 = .03$

barrios with clan communities, with the expectation that matrilineal systems will be more common in the former category. This is also true. Thus the data here provide significant support for Schneider's hypothesis.

Four of Schneider's propositions have been examined. Those respecting terminology and community composition are supported by the data. Those relating to succession and segmentation have been tested somewhat indirectly, with results supportive of the hypotheses, so far as the tests themselves are appropriate. In no case are the hypotheses challenged, and in none is found simple random distribution of the relevant data.

Cousin Terms Before passing from the subject of terminology, one point might be mentioned which is not a focus of attention in either Schneider's or Gough's materials. Over 70 per cent of all matrilineal systems for which there is information have either Crow or Iroquois cousin terms (table 17-17). The bulk of the remainder have Hawaiian cousin terms. Nearly 80 per cent of all Crow cousin terminology is found in matrilineal or double-descent systems.

GOUGH'S HYPOTHESES

A large-scale test of Gough's theoretical propositions is a feasible enterprise, but it is impossible to test most of them by using the *World Ethnographic Sample*. In most cases, either her independent or her dependent variable is so specified that the appropriate cases cannot be sifted from the sample. Thus, for example, many of her propositions apply specifically to sedentary or to shifting cultivators, but the sample does not provide information for making this distinction. Appropriate tests of most of her theories are impossible without recoding a large number of cases with respect to a large number of variables. This leaves but few propositions to be tested.

Distribution of Matrilineal Systems Gough points out that matrilineal systems are likely to be rare in association with conditions of the highest productivity and political complexity. This point has been supported by the earlier discussion of the distribution of matrilineal systems. They are rarely based on plough agriculture or wet-rice agriculture and are totally lacking in modern industrial systems.

Polygyny Gough argues that general and non-sororal polygyny are favored by virilocal residence, and that matrilocality militates against them. Given matrilineal descent, she also expects sororal polygyny to be more common in matrilocal systems. Her predictions regarding monogamy involve factors of descent-group structure on which the sample provides no data. Hence, the appropriate test of the hypothesis

TABLE 17-17
Descent and Cousin Terminology

Cousin Terminology	Patrilineal No.	Patrilineal %	Bilateral No.	Bilateral %	Matrilineal No.	Matrilineal %	Duolineal No.	Duolineal %	Total No.	Total %
Omaha	42	22	2	1	0	0	1	4	45	10
Descriptive or derivative	30	16	5	3	0	0	1	4	36	8
Murngin	7	2	1	1	2	3	1	4	11	2
Buryat	1	1	0	0	0	0	0	0	1	*
Iroquois	49	26	23	13	27	37	13	50	112	24
Eskimo	9	5	51	29	3	4	1	4	64	14
Equivocal Eskimo	5	3	5	3	0	0	0	0	10	2
Hawaiian	39	21	85	48	15	21	3	12	142	30
Crow	3	2	3	2	25	34	5	19	36	8
Unusual	5	3	3	2	1	1	1	4	10	2
Not ascertained	58		26		11		2		97	
Total	248		204		84		28		564	
Total minus Not ascertained	190	101	178	102	73	100	26	101	467	100

*Less than 0.5%.

would seem to be a comparison of general and non-sororal polygyny with sororal and limited sororal polygyny on the one hand, and matri-local versus other forms of residence on the other (table 17-18). (No prediction is made regarding limited polygyny; so it is omitted.) The relationship of sororal and limited sororal polygyny with matrilocality, and of general and non-sororal polygyny with virilocality is strong and significant. It is worth mentioning also that the association of general and non-sororal polygyny with avunculocality and sororal and limited sororal polygyny with matrilocality is even stronger. What is surprising is the additional strong association of monogamy with matrilocality, as compared with other forms of marriage and other forms of residence. In all these calculations the few bilocal, neolocal, and duolocal cases are removed, since they are not involved in Gough's predictions. They would not sizably affect the results.

Bridewealth Gough's predictions regarding bridewealth and resi-dence in matrilineal systems are not subject to check with the sam-ple. Murdock and Richards argue that bridewealth is connected with bride removal, a contention strongly supported by the data (table 17-19). Support for their views, however, does not contradict Gough's arguments, which represent a refinement of, rather than a reversal of their interpretations.

Two of Gough's propositions have been subjected to direct test, although in one case the test was not statistical. Both were strongly supported. No others can be strictly tested with the sample.

Residence and Stratification One other point connected with varia-tion in matrilineal systems emerged in the course of the analysis of the sample: a relationship between residence and stratification in matrilineal systems. I have tested for the relationship between matri-local residence on the one hand and avunculocal and duolocal resi-dence on the other, and extremes of stratification. For these purposes "no stratification" and "age grades only" are lumped, and are compared with "hereditary aristocracy" or with "hereditary aristocracy" and "complex stratification." In both cases, matrilocality is associated with minimal stratification, and avunculocality with maximal stratification (table 17-20). This finding is consistent with the trend of Gough's argu-ment on residence, but not a direct test of it.

Retrospect and Prospect

THE USE OF LARGE CROSS-CULTURAL SAMPLES

It must be borne in mind that this chapter grew out of an effort to use the *World Ethnographic Sample* without supplementing its data, and

TABLE 17-18

Residence and Forms of Marriage in Matrilineal Systems

Form of Marriage	A Patrilocal, Avunculocal Secondary		B Other primarily Patrilocal		C Bilocal or Neolocal Primary		D Matrilocal Primary		E Avunculocal Primary		F Duolocal Primary		Total	
	No.	%	No.	%	No.	%	No.	%	No.	%	No.	%	No.	%
General polygyny	2	13	3	20	1	7	2	13	7	47	0	0	15	100
Non-Sororal polygyny	2	40	0	0	0	0	0	0	3	60	0	0	5	100
Limited polygyny	0	0	4	16	0	0	11	44	9	36	1	4	25	100
Sororal polygyny	0	0	1	9	1	9	6	55	2	18	1	9	11	100
Limited sororal polygyny	0	0	0	0	0	0	4	100	0	0	0	0	4	100
Monogamy	1	5	1	5	1	5	17	81	1	5	0	0	21	101

TABLE 17-18 (continued)

Form of Marriage	A Patrilocal, Avunculocal Secondary		B Other Primarily Patri-Local		C Bilocal or Neolocal Primary		D Matri-local Primary		E Avunculocal Primary		F Duo-local Primary		Total	
	No.	%	No.	%	No.	%	No.	%	No.	%	No.	%	No.	%
Polyandry	0	0	0	0	0	0	0	0	0	0	1	100	1	100
Not ascertained	0	0	1	50	0	0	1	50	0	0	0	0	2	100
Total	5	6	10	12	3	4	41	49	22	26	3	4	84	101

Tests: 1) General and non-sororal polygyny versus sororal and limited sororal polygyny, against matrilocal versus other forms of residence (D versus A, B, and E).

$\chi^2 = 14.37$; $p < .0005$ (one-tailed); $\phi^2 = .45$

Virilocal residence is associated with general and non-sororal polygyny.

2) General and non-sororal polygyny versus sororal and limited sororal polygyny, against avunculocality versus matrilocality.

$\chi^2 = 10.68$; $p < .005$ (one-tailed); $\phi^2 = .45$

Avunculocal residence is associated with general and non-sororal polygyny.

3) Monogamy versus other forms of marriage, against matrilocality versus other forms of residence, duo-locals omitted.

$\chi^2 = 10.63$; $p < .01$ (two-tailed); $\phi^2 = .13$

Matrilocal residence is associated with monogamy.

TABLE 17-19

Residence and Considerations at Marriage in Matrilineal Systems

Considerations at Marriage	Residence													
	Patrilocal, Avunculocal Secondary		Other primarily Patrilocal		Bilocal or Neolocal Primary		Matrilocal Primary		Avunculocal Primary		Duolocal Primary		Total	
	No.	%	No.	%	No.	%	No.	%	No.	%	No.	%	No.	%
Brideprice	4	15	6	23	1	4	4	15	11	42	0	0	26	99
Bride service	1	6	0	0	0	0	9	56	6	38	0	0	16	100
Token bride service	0	0	0	0	0	0	1	50	1	50	0	0	2	100
Gift exchange	0	0	0	0	0	0	0	0	1	100	0	0	1	100
Exchange	0	0	1	100	0	0	0	0	0	0	0	0	1	100
No consideration	0	0	3	8	2	5	27	71	3	8	3	8	38	100
Total	5	6	10	12	3	4	41	49	22	26	3	4	84	101

Test: Matrilocal and duolocal versus other forms of residence, brideprice versus other arrangements at marriage. $x^2 = 20.58$; $p < .001$; $\phi^2 = .24$

Other forms of residence favor brideprice.

using machine tabulation techniques wherever possible. (The entire sample was transferred to IBM cards.) I did not adhere strictly to this program, since I examined ethnographic materials on some baffling cases and plotted the distribution of the South American and African samples on vegetation maps. It is notable that, by and large, associa-

TABLE 17-20

Stratification and Residence in
Matrilineal Systems

| Stratification | Residence | | | |
	Primarily Matrilocal	Primarily Avunculocal and Duolocal	Other	Total
None or age grades only	28	6	7	41
Wealth	3	5	3	11
Hereditary aristocracy	8	12	5	25
Complex stratification	4	1	2	7
Total	43	24	17	84

Tests: 1) No stratification versus hereditary aristocracy against matrilocal versus avunculocal and duolocal.

$x^2 = 10.096; p < .01; \phi^2 = .186$

2) No stratification versus hereditary aristocracy and complex stratification, against residence as above.

$x^2 = 7.627; p < .01; \phi^2 = .129$

Higher stratification favors avunculocality and duolocality.

tion between features of kinship systems were stronger than associations between some feature of a kinship system and something external to that system, such as subsistence base or size of political unit.

Where the categories of the sample are germane to one's interests, it affords an unusually satisfactory basis for the testing of—or discovery of—generalizations. The basis on which it was selected puts these generalizations to a fairly severe test, by virtue of the effort to include exceptional cases in each minor area. Effects of accidental historical co-variation are also minimized. It is hence satisfying to me, at least, to find in the sample substantiation of the common claim that matrilineal systems tend to have a horticultural base. I no longer feel ringed about with the dozens of exceptions that can so easily be cited. (Perhaps it should be mentioned here that the citing of exceptions to my general-izations is not a valid argument against them. Disproof would require the assembling of an equally adequate sample in which the generaliza-tion was not statistically substantiated.) Where the sample does not code cultures along lines of specific interest to me, of course, I am frustrated, but this is not a defect of the method of large-scale compara-tive work.

Certain reflections on the use of large-scale samples have occurred to me in the course of my intensive concern with this one, as well as cer-tain specific comments on the *World Ethnographic Sample*. Murdock's presenting the anthropological world with these data is an act of great generosity; I trust that negative comments will not be understood as ungrateful in intent.

There is no question that reliability checks should become a routine feature of large-scale coding operations. They are not mentioned in Murdock's article, although they are routine in the work of Whiting and Child. Often 100 per cent reliability checks are called for. Various other quibbles sometimes raised with reference to work of this sort, like the reliability problem, are not irremediable defects, but technical problems only. Thus it is possible to eliminate sources because of their inadequacy, to develop complex codes for complex problems, and so on.

Murdock has developed a particularly ingenious sample, but sooner or later we must face the question of whether a random sample of cul-tures can be drawn. This is difficult on at least two counts: we do not have, and will presumably never have full coverage of the world's cultures; and, even if we did, we still do not always have a rule for deciding when we have one culture and when we have two or more. In the absence of random sampling, samples for purposes other than those Murdock has in mind are imaginable—samples, for example, which maximize historical contact rather than minimizing it.

There are at least three common-sense variables which, it would seem, should be coded for any large sample where subsistence activi-ties are of any concern, but which do not appear in Murdock's sample. These are the distinction between plough agriculture and other, be-tween shifting and sedentary cultivation, and between relatively industrialized and relatively non-industrialized or un-industrialized cultures.

Some of Murdock's codes are multidimensional in ways that affect their utility. This is conspicuous in the case of size of political unit, outlined in detail above, where the code begins with levels of authority and finishes with size of unit. A similar problem arises in connection with the classification of stratification systems.

The codes of types of descent groups do not reflect close attention to organization, but rather to the largest inclusive unilineal system found. There is no satisfactory classification of bilateral systems.

Nevertheless, the ingenuity of the sample, the precision of much of the classification, and the scope of the approach are admirable. I have only tried to mention certain minimum improvements which might result in more useful work in the future.

THE RESULTS OF THIS INQUIRY

Matriliny, as a category for analysis, suffers from being only a membership criterion, rather than a type of organization. The study of the place of matrilineal systems in the world is a problem in convergent specific evolution, rather than general evolution. The origins of matrilineal systems are probably to be sought in technology, division of labor, organization of work groups, control of resources, types of subsistence activities, and the ecological niches in which these activities occur. In general, matriliny is associated with horticulture, in the absence of major activities carried on and coördinated by males, of the type of cattle raising or extensive public works. It tends to disappear with plough cultivation and vanishes with industrialization. In plough cultivation areas it is often found in "refuge areas," where a horticultural group exists in an environment marginal for plough cultivation or in geographical isolation from plough cultivation. Where it is found in hunting and gathering groups, it is often associated with stable fishing resources.

The increased effectiveness of subsistence base in distinguishing matrilineal from patrilineal and bilateral systems among large political units is a function of productivity and its correlative dependency on agriculture either supplemented by animal husbandry or based on the plough. Gough's work strongly suggests that bureaucratization is inimical to matriliny, so that the largest (and hence often most bureaucratized) units are unlikely to be matrilineal, whatever the subsistence base. This theory is not testable with the sample.

Matrilineal systems tend not to be found in dense tropical forest nor where cattle can be raised, but in other areas of agricultural potential.

They also tend not to be found where pre-industrial irrigation works are highly developed and regulated above the community level.

Many of the matrilineal systems of the world, and particularly those of Africa and Oceania, are transformed: they have undergone a shift from matrilocal to other forms of residence, presumably in the process of accommodating matriliny to changed conditions. There is some tendency for avunculocality to be associated with higher stratification, and matrilocality with little stratification.

SOME PROBLEMS FOR THE FUTURE

The Distribution of Matrilineal Systems   More work must be done before we understand where to lay the weight of emphasis in explaining the origins, maintenance, and disappearance of matrilineal systems: in what connections to stress the organization of labor, the forms of property, the types of subsistence base, the contributions of the two sexes (almost certainly best viewed in the context of work organization, and not by itself), the level of productivity, the level of political complexity, the nature of the authority system, the size and proximity of communities in their relationship to the technical and environmental base, and the relationship of the culture in question to other cultures. Unless some of these variables can be rejected out of hand, large-scale work will be required for a final solution. Research is needed on the causes of the ecological distribution described here.

Historical and historical reconstructive work will also be required for the solution of some of these problems. The Crow Indians are matrilineal, in spite of a dependency on large-game hunting and horse herding. A theory which would attempt to account for the origin of matriliny from this base would have heavy going. In this case, we know that the Crow are an offshoot of a semisedentary agricultural and hunting group represented in historic times by the Hidatsa. We would be greatly aided in other cases if we knew the degree to which we could assume matrilineal survival under greatly altered circumstances. Thus, for example, the Kaska Indians have dispersed matrilineal clans, base their economy on fishing and hunting, do not have lineage or clan control of resources, and do not, indeed, have organized descent groups. Are they to be regarded as a watered-down version of more sedentary systems like the Tahltan and Upper Carrier? Are the clans adaptive in their relations with such groups? Or did Athapaskan clans develop under just such exiguous conditions? I believe that I have a solution for this problem, but the more difficult it is to choose between conditions favoring survival for purposes of internal organization or external relationships, and conditions favorable to the

development of clans *ab initio*, the worse off will our tests of theory be.
Broader Comparative Work   This book has progressed from theoretical explanation of the constant features of matrilineal systems to a
description of factors external to the kinship system which create
variability in matrilineal units. These factors are themselves clearly not
specific to matrilineal systems: for example, levels of productivity,
levels and types of authority, organization of production, and organization of distribution. The next major comparative step to be taken is the
effort to generalize these findings—to state the relationship between
external factors and kinship organization in such a way that the propositions apply to patrilineal and non-unilineal systems as well. Should
they prove valid in this context, we would clearly have a general theory
relative to the organization of kinship systems.

Bibliography

Bibliography

Preface

Adam, L.
1947. Virilocal and uxorilocal. American Anthropologist, 49: 678.

Colson, E.
1958. *Marriage and the Family among the Plateau Tonga*. Manchester: Manchester University Press.

Fortes, M.
1953. Structure of unilineal descent groups. American Anthropologist, 55: 17–41.

Goodenough, W. H.
1956. Residence rules. Southwestern Journal of Anthropology, 12: 22–37.

Hogbin, H. I., and C. H. Wedgwood
1953. Local grouping in Melanesia. Oceania, 23: 241–276; 24: 58–76.

Kroeber, A. L.
1938. Basic and secondary patterns of social structure. Journal of the Royal Anthropological Institute, 68: 299–309.

McLennan, L. H.
1886. *Studies in Ancient History*. New York: The Macmillan Company.

Morgan, L. H.
1870. Systems of consanguinity and affinity of the human family. Smithsonian Contributions to Knowledge, 17: Art. 2.

1877. *Ancient Society*. New York: Holt and Company.

Murdock, G. P.
1949. *Social Structure*. New York: The Macmillan Company.

Radcliffe-Brown, A. R.
1924. The mother's brother in South Africa. South African Journal of Science, 21: 542–555.

1935. Patrilineal and matrilineal succession. Iowa Law Journal, 20: 286–303.

Richards, A. I.
  1934. Mother-right among the Central Bantu. In: *Essays Presented to C. G. Seligman,* ed. by E. E. Evans-Pritchard *et al.* London: K. Paul, Trench, Trubner and Company, Ltd. Pp. 267–280.

  1939. *Land, Labour and Diet in Northern Rhodesia.* London: Oxford University Press.

  1950. Some types of family structure amongst the Central Bantu. In: *African Systems of Kinship and Marriage,* ed. by A. R. Radcliffe-Brown and C. D. Forde. London: Oxford University Press. Pp. 207–251.

Rivers, W. H. R.
  1914*a*. *Kinship and Social Organization.* London: Constable and Company, Ltd.

  1914*b*. Mother-right. In: *Encyclopaedia of Religion and Ethics,* ed. by James Hastings. Edinburgh: Clark; New York: Scribner.

Thomas, N. W.
  1906. *Kinship Organisations and Group Marriage in Australia.* Cambridge, Eng.: Cambridge University Press.

Tylor, E. B.
  1889. On a method of investigating the development of institutions. Journal of the Royal Anthropological Institute, 18: 245–272.

Introduction

Fallers, L. A.
  1957. Some determinants of marriage stability in Busoga. Africa, 27: 106–121.

Firth, R.
  1957. A note on descent groups in Polynesia. Man, no. 2, January, pp. 4–8.

Gluckman, M.
  1950. Kinship and marriage among the Lozi of Northern Rhodesia and the Zulu of Natal. In: *African Systems of Kinship and Marriage,* ed. by A. R. Radcliffe-Brown and C. D. Forde. London: Oxford University Press. Pp. 166–206.

Goodenough, W. H.
  1955. A problem in Malayo-Polynesian social organization. American Anthropologist, 57: 71–83.

Homans, G. C., and D. M. Schneider
  1955. *Marriage, Authority and Final Causes.* Glencoe, Ill.: The Free Press.

Murdock, G. P.
  1949. *Social Structure*. New York: The Macmillan Company.
Radcliffe-Brown, A. R.
  1924. The mother's brother in South Africa. South African Journal of Science, 21: 542–555.
Richards, A. I.
  1934. Mother-right among the Central Bantu. In: *Essays Presented to C. G. Seligman*, ed. by E. E. Evans-Pritchard *et al.* London: K. Paul, Trench, Trubner and Company, Ltd. Pp. 267–280.

  1950. Some types of family structure amongst the Central Bantu. In: *African Systems of Kinship and Marriage*, ed. by A. R. Radcliffe-Brown and C. D. Forde. London: Oxford Unisity Press. Pp. 207–251.
Schneider, D. M.
  1953. A note on bridewealth and the stability of marriage. Man, no. 75, pp. 55–57.

Plateau Tonga

Allan, W., M. Gluckman, D. U. Peters, and C. G. Trapnell
  1948. Land holding and land usage among the Plateau Tonga of Mazabuka District. A reconnaissance survey, 1945. Rhodes-Livingstone Paper 14.
Colson, E.
  1948a. Rain shrines of the Plateau Tonga of Northern Rhodesia. Africa, 18: 272–283.

  1948b. Modern political organization of the Plateau Tonga. African Studies, 10: 85–98.

  1950. A note on Tonga and Ndebele. Northern Rhodesia Journal, 2: 35–41.

  1951a. The Plateau Tonga of Northern Rhodesia. In: *Seven Tribes of British Central Africa*, ed. by E. Colson and M. Gluckman. London: Oxford University Press. Pp. 94–162.

  1951b. The role of cattle among the Plateau Tonga. Rhodes-Livingstone Journal, 11:10–46.

  1951c. Residence and village stability among the Plateau Tonga. Rhodes-Livingstone Journal, 12: 41–67.

  1953a. Social control and vengeance in Plateau Tonga society. Africa, 23: 199–212.

  1953b. Clans and the joking-relationship among the Plateau Tonga of Northern Rhodesia. Kroeber Anthropological Society Papers, 8–9: 45–60.

1954. Ancestral spirits and social structure among the Plateau
       Tonga. International Archives of Ethnography, 47: 21–68.

1958. *Marriage and the Family among the Plateau Tonga.* Man-
       chester: Manchester University Press.

Doke, G.
1945. *Bantu, Modern Grammatical, Phonetical and Lexicographi-
       cal Studies since 1869.* London: Percy Lund, Humphries
       & Co.

Jaspan, M.
1953. *The Ila-Tonga Peoples of North-Western Rhodesia.* Ethno-
       graphic Survey of Africa.

Navaho

Aberle, David F., and Omer C. Stewart
1957. Navaho and Ute peyotism: a chronological and distribu-
       tional study. University of Colorado Studies, Series in
       Anthropology no. 6. Boulder: University of Colorado Press.

Adair, John
1944. *The Navajo and Pueblo Silversmiths.* Norman: University
       of Oklahoma Press.

Bailey, Flora L.
1950. Some sex beliefs and practices in a Navaho community,
       with comparative material from other Navaho areas. Re-
       ports of the Ramah Project, no. 2. Papers of the Peabody
       Museum of American Archaeology and Ethnology, Har-
       vard University, vol. 40, no. 2. Cambridge, Mass.: Peabody
       Museum.

Bellah, Robert N.
1952. *Apache Kinship Systems.* Cambridge, Mass.: Harvard Uni-
       versity Press.

Bourke, John G.
1890. Notes upon the gentile organization of the Apaches of
       Arizona. Journal of American Folklore, 3: 111–126.

Carr, Malcolm, Katherine Spencer, and Doriane Woolley
1939. Navaho clans and marriage at Pueblo Alto. American An-
       thropologist, 41: 245–257.

Collier, Malcolm Carr
1946. Leadership at Navaho Mountain and Klagetoh. American
       Anthropologist, 48: 137–138.

1951. Local organization among the Navaho. (Unpublished MS.)

Curtis, Edward S.
1907. *The North American Indian.* Vol. 1. The Apaches. The

Jicarilla. The Navaho. Cambridge, Mass.: Harvard University Press.

Dapah, Jimmie
1954. DFA's unpublished notes of discussions with this Navaho, formerly of Coolidge and Pinedale.

Dyen, Isidore
1956. Language distribution and migration theory. Language, Journal of the Linguistic Society of America, 32: 611–626.

Dyk, Walter
1938. *Son of Old Man Hat, a Navajo Autobiography.* Recorded by Walter Dyk. New York: Harcourt, Brace and Co.

1947. A Navaho autobiography. Viking Fund Publications in Anthropology, no. 8.

Forbes, Jack D.
1959. The appearance of the mounted Indian in Northern Mexico and the Southwest, to 1680. Southwestern Journal of Anthropology, 15: 189–212.

Franciscan Fathers
1910. *An Ethnologic Dictionary of the Navaho Language.* St. Michaels, Ariz.: The Franciscan Fathers.

Goldfrank, Esther S.
1945. Irrigation agriculture and Navaho community leadership: case material on environment and culture. American Anthropologist, 47: 262–277.

1946. More on irrigation agriculture and Navaho community leadership. American Anthropologist, 48: 473–476.

Goodwin, Grenville
1942. *The Social Organization of the Western Apache.* Chicago: University of Chicago Press.

Government Survey
n.d. Various manuscript items consulted at Window Rock, Arizona. Presumably overlaps with Kluckhohn and Spencer, 1940, pp. 44–45, items listed under United States, Department of Agriculture, Soil Conservation Service.

Haile, Berard (Fr. Berard)
1941. *Learning Navaho.* Vol. 1. St. Michaels, Ariz.: St. Michaels Press.

1950–1951. *A Stem Vocabulary of the Navaho Language.* Vol. 1, Navaho-English. Vol. 2, English-Navaho. St. Michaels, Ariz.: St. Michaels Press.

1954. Property concepts of the Navaho Indians. The Catholic University of America Anthropological Series, no. 17. Washington, D.C.: The Catholic University of America Press.

Henry, William E.
  1947. The Thematic Apperception Technique in the study of cul-
          ture-personality relations. Genetic Psychology Monographs,
          35: 3–135.
Hill, W. W.
  1936. Navaho warfare. Yale University Publications in Anthro-
          pology, 5.
  1938. The agricultural and hunting methods of the Navaho In-
          dians. Yale University Publications in Anthropology, 18.
  1940a. Some Navaho culture changes during two centuries (with
          a translation of the early eighteenth-century Rabal manu-
          script). Essays in historical anthropology of North America
          published in honor of John R. Swanton. Smithsonian Mis-
          cellaneous Collections, 100: 395–416.
  1940b. Some aspects of Navaho political structure. Plateau, 13:
          23–28.
  1943. Navaho humor. General Series in Anthropology, no. 9.
          Menasha: George Banta Publishing Co., Agent.
  1944. The Navaho Indians and the Ghost Dance of 1890. Amer-
          ican Anthropologist, 46: 523–527.
  n.d.   Various notes on Navaho clans, clan groups, kinship, con-
          sulted in the files of Clyde Kluckhohn. Includes kinship
          terminology charts, part of which are published in Bellah,
          1952. Also notes on Navaho law, supplied to DFA.
Hoijer, Harry
  1938. The Southern Athapaskan languages. American Anthro-
          pologist, 40: 75–87.
  1956. The chronology of the Athapaskan languages. International
          Journal of American Linguistics, 22: 219–232.
Jones, Paul
  1950. DFA's notes of various discussions with this Navaho, for-
          merly of Naschitti, long resident at Piñon, former inter-
          preter, District Superintendent, and now (1958) Chairman
          of the Navajo Tribal Council.
Kaut, Charles R.
  1957. The Western Apache clan system: its origins and develop-
          ment. University of New Mexico Publications in Anthro-
          pology, no. 9. Albuquerque: University of New Mexico
          Press.
Kimball, Solon T.
  1950. Future problems in Navajo administration. Human Organ-
          ization, 9: 21–24.

Kimball, Solon T., and John H. Provinse
  1942. Navajo social organization in land use planning. Applied Anthropology, 1: 18–30.

Kluckhohn, Clyde
  1939. Some personal and social aspects of Navaho ceremonial practice. The Harvard Theological Review, 32: 57–81.
  1944. Navaho witchcraft. Papers of the Peabody Museum of American Archaeology and Ethnology, Harvard University, vol. 22, no. 2. Cambridge, Mass.: Peabody Museum.
  1945. A Navaho personal document with a brief Paretian analysis. Southwestern Journal of Anthropology, 1: 260–281.
  1956. Aspects of the demographic history of a small population. In: *Estudios Antropológicos, Publicados en Homenaje al Doctor Manuel Gamio.* Mexico, D.F.: Dirección General de Publicaciones.

Kluckhohn, Clyde, and Dorothea Leighton
  1946. *The Navaho.* Cambridge, Mass.: Harvard University Press.

Kluckhohn, Clyde, and Katherine Spencer
  1940. *A Bibliography of the Navaho Indians.* New York: J. J. Augustin.

Leighton, Dorothea, and Clyde Kluckhohn
  1947. *Children of the People.* Cambridge, Mass.: Harvard University Press.

Leighton, Alexander, and Dorothea Leighton
  1949. Gregorio, the hand-trembler: a psychobiological personality study of a Navaho Indian. Reports of the Ramah Project. Report No. 1. Papers of the Peabody Museum of American Archaeology and Ethnology, Harvard University, vol. 40, no. 1. Cambridge, Mass.: Peabody Museum.

McAllester, David P.
  1954. Enemy Way music: a study of social and esthetic values as seen in Navaho music. Reports of the Rimrock Project Values Series no. 3. Papers of the Peabody Museum of American Archaeology and Ethnology, Harvard University, vol. 41, no. 3. Cambridge, Mass.: Peabody Museum.

Mandelbaum, David G.
  1949. *Selected Writings of Edward Sapir in Language, Culture, and Personality.* Berkeley and Los Angeles: University of California Press.

Matthews, Washington
  1890. The gentile system of the Navaho Indians. Journal of American Folk-Lore, 3: 89–110.

1897.   Navaho legends. Memoirs of the American Folk-Lore So-
        ciety, vol. 5. Boston and New York: Houghton, Mifflin and
        Company.

Mooney, James
1896.   The ghost-dance religion and the Sioux outbreak of 1890.
        Fourteenth Annual Report of the Bureau of American
        Ethnology, part 2. Washington, D.C.: Government Print-
        ing Office.

Murdock, George Peter
1957.   World ethnographic sample. American Anthropologist, 59:
        664–687.

Navajo Yearbook, The
1954.   The Navajo yearbook of planning in action, no. 4. Comp.
        by Robert W. Young. Window Rock, Ariz.: Navajo Agency.

1957.   Report No. 6. Comp. and ed., with articles by Robert W.
        Young. Window Rock, Ariz.: Navajo Agency.

Packard, Robert L.
1882.   List of Navaho clans. 4-p. MS in Bureau of American
        Ethnology Navaho 183. Transcript of copy prepared by the
        BAE for W. W. Hill consulted in the files of Clyde Kluck-
        hohn. Letter from M. W. Stirling of the BAE (attached to
        transcript) dates MS as 1882. Presumably same item listed
        by Kluckhohn and Spencer, 1940, p. 44 (dated 1881 or
        1889), and by Pilling 1892, p. 76.

Pilling, James C.
1892.   Bibliography of the Athapascan languages. Bureau of Amer-
        ican Ethnology Bulletin 14. Washington, D.C.: Govern-
        ment Printing Office.

Radcliffe-Brown, A. R.
1952.   *Structure and Function in Primitive Society*. Glencoe, Ill.:
        The Free Press.

Ramah Files
n.d.   Files on the Ramah Navaho by various field workers. Main-
        tained at Harvard University by Clyde Kluckhohn.

Rapoport, Robert N.
1954.   Changing Navaho religious values: a study of Christian
        missions to the Rimrock Navahos. Reports of the Rimrock
        Project Values Series, no. 2. Papers of the Peabody Museum
        of American Archaeology and Ethnology, Harvard Uni-
        versity, vol. 41, no. 2. Cambridge, Mass.: Peabody Museum.

Reichard, Gladys
1928.   Social life of the Navaho Indians, with some attention to

minor ceremonies. Columbia University Contributions to Anthropology 7.

1939. *Dezba: Woman of the Desert.* New York: J. J. Augustin.

Roessel, Robert A., Jr.
1951. Sheep in Navaho culture. M.A. thesis, Washington University, Department of Sociology and Anthropology. (Mimeo.)

Sapir, Edward
n.d. MS on Navaho clans and clan groups, consulted in the files of Clyde Kluckhohn. See also Mandelbaum, David G.

Sapir, Edward and Harry Hoijer
1942. Navaho texts. William Dwight Whitney linguistic Series. Iowa City: Linguistic Society of America.

Spuhler, James N., and Clyde Kluckhohn
1953. Inbreeding coefficients of the Ramah Navaho population. Human Biology, 25: 295–317.

Stephen, Alexander M.
1890a. Marriage among the Navajoes. Our Forest Children, 3: 222.

1890b. Notes about the Navajoes. Canadian Indian, 1: 15–16.

Strodtbeck, Fred L.
1951. Husband-wife interaction over revealed differences. American Sociological Review, 16: 468–473.

Swanson, G. E.
1958. The birth of the gods. (Unpublished MS.)

Underhill, Ruth
1956. *The Navajos.* Norman, Okla.: University of Oklahoma Press.

[1953]. Here come the Navaho! A history of the largest Indian tribe in the United States. Indian Life and Customs 8. United States Indian Service.

Van Valkenburgh, Richard
1936. Navaho common law. Museum Notes, Museum of Northern Arizona, 9: 18–22.

Vogt, Evon Z.
1949. Navaho Veterans: a study of changing values. Reports of the Rimrock Project Values Series, no. 1. Papers of the Peabody Museum of American Archaeology and Ethnology, Harvard University, vol. 41, no. 1. Cambridge Mass.: Peabody Museum.

Young, Robert W.
1957. *See* Navajo Yearbook, The.

Young, Robert W. and William Morgan
    1951. A vocabulary of colloquial Navaho. United States Indian
           Service.
    1954. Navajo historical selections. Navajo Historical Series, 3.
           Bureau of Indian Affairs.
    n.d.   The Navaho language: the elements of Navaho grammar
           with a dictionary in two parts containing basic vocabularies
           of Navaho and English. A Publication of the Education
           Division, United States Indian Service.

Zelditch, Morris, Jr.
    1959. Statistical marriage preferences of the Ramah Navaho.
           American Anthropologist, 61: 470–491.

Truk

Fischer, Ann
    1950. The role of the Trukese mother and its effect on child
           training. National Research Council, Pacific Science Board,
           Washington, D.C. (Mimeo.)

Fischer, J. L.
    1950. Native land tenure in the Truk District. Civil Administra-
           tion of Truk. June 6, 1950. (Mimeo.)

Gladwin, T.
    1953. The role of man and woman on Truk. Transactions of the
           New York Academy of Sciences, Series II, Vol. 15.

Gladwin, T., and S. B. Sarason
    1953. Truk: Man in paradise. Viking Fund Publications in An-
           thropology, no. 20.

Goodenough, W. H.
    1949. Premarital freedom on Truk. American Anthropologist,
           51: 615–620.
    1951. Property, kin and community on Truk. Yale University
           Publications in Anthropology, no. 46.
    1956. Residence rules. Southwestern Journal of Anthropology,
           12: 22–37.

Murdock, G. P., and W. H. Goodenough
    1947. Social organization of Truk. Southwestern Journal of An-
           thropology, 3: 33–43.

Swartz, M. J.
    1958. Sexuality and aggression on Romonum, Truk. American
           Anthropologist, 60: 467–486.

Trobriand

Fortune, R. F.
    1933. A note on some forms of kinship structure. Oceania, 4: 1–8.

Leach, E. R.
    1951. The structural implications of matrilateral cross-cousin marriage. Journal of the Royal Anthropological Institute, 81: 21–55.

    1958. Concerning Trobriand clans and the kinship category "tabu." In: The Developmental Cycle in Domestic Groups, ed. by Jack Goody, Cambridge Papers in Social Anthropology. Vol. 1.

Malinowski, B.
    1926. *Crime and Custom in Savage Society*. London: Kegan Paul and Co.; New York: Harcourt, Brace and Company.

    1927. *Sex and Repression in Savage Society*. London: Kegan Paul and Co.; New York: Harcourt, Brace and Company.

    1929. *The Sexual Life of Savages in North-Western Melanesia*. New York: Halcyon House.

    1932. *Argonauts of the Western Pacific*. London: George Routledge & Sons, Ltd.; New York: E. P. Dutton & Company.

    1935. *Coral Gardens and Their Magic*. Vol. 1. New York: American Book Company.

    1948. *Magic, Science and Religion and Other Essays*. Glencoe, Ill.: The Free Press.

Murdock, G. P.
    1949. *Social Structure*. New York: The Macmillan Company.

Ashanti

Beckett, W. H.
    1944. *Akokòaso: A Survey of a Gold Coast Village*. London: Percy Lund, Humphries & Co.

Busia, K. A.
    1952. *The Position of the Chief in the Modern Political System of Ashanti*. London: Oxford University Press.

Fortes, M.
    1948. The Ashanti social survey: A preliminary report. Human Problems in British Central Africa, VI.

    1949. Time and social structure: An Ashanti case study. In: *Social Structure, Essays Presented to A. R. Radcliffe-Brown*, ed. by Fred Eggan and Meyer Fortes. London: Oxford University Press. Pp. 54–84.

1950. Kinship and marriage among the Ashanti. In: *African Systems of Kinship and Marriage,* ed. by A. R. Radcliffe-Brown and C. D. Forde. London: Oxford University Press. Pp. 252–284.

Fortes, M., R. W. Steel, and P. Ady
1948. Ashanti survey, 1945–46: An experiment in social research. Geographical Journal, 110: 4–6.

Manoukian, Madeline
1950. *The Akan and Ga-Adangme Peoples of the Gold Coast.* Ethnographic Survey of Africa. Western Africa, part I.

Matson, J. N.
1953. Testate succession in Ashanti. Africa, 23: 224–232.

Meyerowitz, Eva L. R.
1952. *Akan Traditions of Origin.* London: Faber & Faber.

Rattray, R. S.
1923. *Ashanti.* London: Oxford University Press.

1927. *Religion and Art in Ashanti.* London: Oxford University Press.

1929. *Ashanti Law and Constitution.* London: Oxford University Press.

Richards, A. I.
1950. Some types of family structure amongst the central Bantu. In: *African Systems of Kinship and Marriage,* ed. by A. R. Radcliffe-Brown and C. D. Forde. London: Oxford University Press. Pp. 207–251.

Steel, R. W.
1948. The population of Ashanti: A geographical analysis. Geographical Journal, 112: 1–3.

Nayar: Central Kerala

Aiya, V. Nagam
1906. *The Travancore State Manual.* Vol. 1. Trivandrum: The Travancore Government Press.

Aiyappan, A.
1932*a*. Nayar polyandry. Man, 32, no. 99.

1932*b*. Nayar polyandry. Man, 32, no. 337.

1934. Nayar polyandry. Man, 34, no. 55.

1935. Fraternal polyandry in Malabar. Man in India, 15: 108–118.

Aiyar, P. R. Sundara
1922. *A Treatise on Malabar and Aliyansantana Law.* Rev. by B. Sita Rama Rao. Madras: Madras Law Journal Office.

Ayyar, K. V. Krishna
    1938.   *The Zamorins of Calicut*. Calicut: Norman Printing Bureau.
Baden-Powell, B. H.
    1892.   *The Land Systems of British India*. Vol. 3. Oxford: Claren-
            don Press.
Buchanan, Francis (Hamilton)
    1807.   *A Journey from Madras through Mysore, Canara and
            Malabar*. Vol. 2. London: Black, Perry and Kingsbury.
Burnell, Arthur Coke (ed.)
    1885.   *The Voyage of John Huyghen Van Linschoten to the East
            Indies*. From the Old English translation of 1598, of the
            1596 original of Linschoten's *Itinerario*. London: Hakluyt
            Society Publications, no. 70.
Cochin Government Press
    1938.   The Cochin Nayar Act of 1938. Ernakulam: Cochin Gov-
            ernment Press.
Dames, Mansel Longworth (ed.)
    1921.   *The Book of Duarte Barbosa*. An account of the countries
            bordering the Indian Ocean and their inhabitants, written
            by Duarte Barbosa and completed about the year 1518 A.D.
            Translated by the Royal Academy of Sciences, Lisbon.
            London: The Hakluyt Society.
Fawcett, F.
    1915.   The Nayars of Malabar. Madras Government Museum
            Bulletin, 3: 3.
Gibb, H. A. R.
    1929.   *The Travels of Ibn Battuta in Asia and Africa, 1325–1354*.
            London: Routledge and Sons.
Gough, E. K.
    1952a. Changing kinship usages in the setting of political and
            economic change among the Nayars of Malabar. Journal of
            the Royal Anthropological Institute, 82: 71–88.
    1952b. Incest prohibitions and rules of exogamy in three matri-
            lineal groups of the Malabar Coast. International Archives
            of Ethnography, vol. 46, no. 1.
    1955.   Female initiation rites on the Malabar Coast. Journal of
            the Royal Anthropological Institute, 85, pt. 2: 45–80.
    1958.   Cults of the dead among the Nayars. Journal of American
            Folklore, vol. 71, no. 281.
    1959.   The Nayars and the definition of marriage. Journal of the
            Royal Anthropological Institute, 89: 23–34.

Gray, Albert (ed.)
1887. *The Voyage of Francois Pyrard de Laval to the East Indes, the Maldives, the Moluccas and Brazil.* Translated from the 3d French edition of 1619. London: The Hakluyt Society.

Gray, Edward (ed.)
1884. *The Travels of Pietro della Valle in India.* Vol. 2. First issued in Rome in 1662. London: The Hakluyt Society.

Hamilton, Alexander
1727. *A New Account of the East Indes.* 2 vols. Edinburgh: J. Mosman.

Innes, C. A.
1908. *Malabar and Anjengo.* Madras: Madras District Gazetteers.

Iyer, L. K. Anantha Krishna
1909–1912. *The Cochin Tribes and Castes.* 2 vols. Madras.
1932. Nayar polyandry. Man, 32, no. 320.

Jones, J. W. (ed.)
1863. *Travels of Ludovico di Varthema, A. D. 1503–8.* London: Hakluyt Society Publications, no. 32.

Kerr, Robert (ed.)
1811. History of the discovery and conquest of India by the Portuguese, between the years 1479 and 1525, from the original Portuguese by Herman Lopez de Castaneda. In: *A General Collection of Voyages and Travels.* Vol. 2, pp. 292–505. Edinburgh.

Logan, William
1887. *Malabar.* 2 vols. Madras: Government Press. (Reprinted, with additional papers, in 3 vols., Madras, 1951.)

McCrindle, J. W.
1897. *The Christian Topography of Cosmas, an Egyptian Monk of the Sixth Century A.D.* London: The Hakluyt Society.

Major, R. H. (ed.)
1857. *India in the Fifteenth Century.* A collection of narratives of voyages to India. London: The Hakluyt Society.

Menon, C. Achyuta
1911. *The Cochin State Manual.* Ernakulam: Cochin Government Press.

Menon, K. P. Padmanabha
1908. Report of the Marumakkathayam Committee (Enclosure B). Trivandrum: Government Press.
1933. *History of Kerala.* 3 vols. Ernakulam: Cochin Government Press.

Menon, K. R. Krishna
    1894. *Report of the Malabar Marriage Commission.* Madras: Government Press.

Moore, Lewis
    1905. *Malabar Law and Custom.* Madras: Government Press.

Murdock, G. P.
    1949. *Social Structure.* New York: The Macmillan Company.

Nair, K. Kannan
    1908. The matrimonial customs of the Nayars. Malabar Quarterly Review, vol. 7, no. 3.

Nair, K. Madhavan
    1941. *The Malabar Law Digest and Acts, 1861–1941.* Calicut: The Vidya Vilasam Press.

Nambudiripad, E. M. Sankaran
    1952. *The National Question in Kerala.* Bombay: People's Publishing House.

Neale, W. C.
    1957. Reciprocity and redistribution in the Indian village. In; *Trade and Market in the Early Empires,* ed. by K. Polanyi. Glencoe, Ill.: The Free Press.

Panikkar, K. M.
    1918. Some aspects of Nayar life. Journal of the Royal Anthropological Institute, 48: 254–293.

    1929. *Malabar and the Portuguese.* Bombay: D. B. Taraporevala Sons and Company.

    1931. *Malabar and the Dutch.* Bombay: D. B. Taraporevala Sons and Company.

    1945. *India and the Indian Ocean.* Birkenhead, Eng.: Willmer Bros. and Co., Ltd.

Panikkar, T. K. Gopal
    1901. *Malabar and Its Folk.* Madras: G. A. Nateson.

Pillai, T. K. Velu
    1940. *The Travancore State Manual.* Vol. 2. Trivandrum: The Travancore Government Press.

Rao, M. S. A.
    1957. *Social Change in Malabar.* Bombay: The Popular Book Depot.

Report of a Joint Commission from Bengal and Bombay
    1862. Commission appointed to inspect into the state and condition of the Province of Malabar in the years 1792 and 1793. Madras: Government Press. (Reprint.)

Report of the Census of India for 1931
    1931.   Cochin State. Ernakulam: Cochin Government Press.
Ricci, Aldo
    1931.   *The Travels of Marco Polo in the Thirteenth Century.*
            Translated into English from the text of L. F. Benedetto,
            with an introduction and index by Sir E. Denison Ross.
            London: George Routledge and Sons, Ltd.
Richards, A. I.
    1950.   Some types of family structure amongst the Central Bantu.
            In: *African Systems of Kinship and Marriage,* ed. by A. R.
            Radcliffe-Brown and C. D. Forde. London: Oxford Uni-
            versity Press. Pp. 207–251.
Sastri, K. A. Nilankanta
    1955.   *A History of South India.* London: Oxford University Press.
Stanley, E. J. (ed.)
    1865.   *A Description of the Coasts of East Africa and Malabar in
            the Beginning of the Sixteenth Century, by Duarte Barbosa,
            a Portuguese.* Translated from an early Spanish manuscript
            in the Barcelona Library. London: Hakluyt Society Pub-
            lications, no. 35.
    1869.   *The Three Voyages of Vasco da Gama to India.* London:
            The Hakluyt Society.
Stephenson, Carl
    1942.   *Medieval Feudalism.* Ithaca, N. Y.: Cornell University
            Press.
Thurston, Edgar
    1909.   *Castes and Tribes of Southern India.* Vol. 5. Madras: Gov-
            ernment Press.
Zein-ud-Deen
    1833.   *Tohfut-ul-Mujahideen. An Offering to Warriors Who Shall
            Fight in Defence of Religion Against Infidels.* Written in
            1579, translated by Rowlandson. London: The Hakluyt
            Society.

Nayar: North Kerala

Aiyar, P. R. Sundara
    1922.   *A Treatise on Malabar and Aliyasantana Law.* Rev. by
            Sita Rama Rao. Madras: Madras Law Journal Office.
Ayyar, K. V. Krishna
    1938.   *The Zamorins of Calicut.* Calicut: Norman Printing Bureau.
Buchanan, Francis (Hamilton)
    1807.   *A Journey from Madras through Mysore, Canara and Mal-
            abar.* Vol. 2. London: Black, Perry and Kingsbury.

Gibb, H. A. R.
1929. *The Travels of Ibn Battuta in Asia and Africa, 1325–1354.* London: Routledge and Sons.
Gough, E. K.
1952. Incest prohibitions and rules of exogamy in three matrilineal groups of the Malabar Coast. International Archives of Ethnography, vol. 46, no. 1.
1955. Female initiation rites on the Malabar Coast. Journal of the Royal Anthropological Institute, 85, pt 2: 45–80.
1958. Cults of the dead among the Nayars. Journal of American Folklore, vol. 71, no. 281.
Hamilton, Alexander
1727. *A New Account of the East Indies.* 2 vols. Edinburgh: J. Mosman.
Innes, C. A.
1908. *Malabar and Anjengo.* Madras: Madras District Gazetteers.
Logan, William
1887. *Malabar.* 2 vols. Madras: Government Press.
Major, R. H. (ed.)
1857. *India in the Fifteenth Century.* A collection of narratives of voyages to India. London: The Hakluyt Society.
Menon, K. P. Padmanabha
1933. *History of Kerala.* 3 vols. Ernakulam: Cochin Government Press.
Menon, K. R. Krishna
1894. *Report of the Malabar Marriage Commission.* Madras: Government Press.
Moore, Lewis
1905. *Malabar Law and Custom.* Madras: Government Press.
Nair, K. Machavan
1941. *The Malabar Law Digest and Acts, 1861–1941.* Calicut: The Vidya Vilasam Press.
Rao, M. S. A.
1957. *Social Changes in Malabar.* Bombay: The Popular Book Depot.
Report of a Joint Commission from Bengal and Bombay
1862. Commission appointed to inspect into the state and condition of the Province of Malabar in the years 1792 and 1793. Madras: Government Press. (Reprint.)
Ricci, Aldo
1931. *The Travels of Marco Polo in the Thirteenth Century.* London: George Routledge and Sons, Ltd.

Tiyyar: North Kerala

Aiyappan, A.
    1944. Iravas and culture change. Madras Government Museum
           Bulletin, n.s., gen. sec., 5 (4).
Gough, E. K.
    1955. Female initiation rites on the Malabar Coast. Journal of the
           Royal Anthropological Institute, 85, pt. 2: 45–80.
Logan, William
    1887. *Malabar*. 2 vols. Madras: Government Press. (Reprinted,
           with additional papers, in 3 vols., Madras, 1951.)
Nair, K. Madhavan
    1941. *The Malabar Law Digest and Acts, 1861–1941*. Calicut:
           The Vidya Vilasam Press.

Mappilla: North Kerala

Ayyar, K. V. Krishna
    1938. *The Zamorins of Calicut*. Calicut: Norman Printing Bureau.
Buchanan, Francis (Hamilton)
    1807. *A Journey from Madras through Mysore, Canara and Mal-
           abar*. Vol. 2. London: Black, Perry and Kingsbury.
Gibb, H. A. R.
    1929. *The Travels of Ibn Battuta in Asia and Africa, 1325–1354*.
           London: Routledge and Sons.
Gough, E. K.
    1952. Incest prohibitions and rules of exogamy in three matri-
           lineal groups of the Malabar Coast. International Archives
           of Ethnography, vol. 46, no. 1.
Hamilton, Alexander
    1727. *A New Account of the East Indies*. 2 vols. Edinburgh:
           J. Mosman.
Innes, C. A.
    1908. *Malabar and Anjengo*. Madras: Madras District Gazatteers.
Logan, William
    1887. *Malabar*. 2 vols. Madras: Government Press. (Reprinted,
           with additional papers, in 3 vols., Madras, 1951.)
Nair, K. Madhavan
    1941. *The Malabar Law Digest and Acts, 1861–1941*. Calicut:
           The Vidya Vilasam Press.

Variation in Matrilineal Systems (Introduction and chaps. 10–16)

Ayyar, K. V. Krishna
    1938. *The Zamorins of Calicut*. Calicut: Norman Printing Bureau.

Baden-Powell, B. H.
  1892. *The Land Systems of British India.* Vol. 3. Oxford: Clarendon Press.

Buchanan, Francis (Hamilton)
  1807. *A Journey from Madras through Mysore, Canara and Malabar.* Vol. 2. London: Black, Perry and Kingsbury.

Busia, K. A.
  1951. *The Position of the Chief in the Modern Political System of Ashanti.* London: Oxford University Press.

Cabaton, A.
  1911. *Java, Sumatra and Other Islands of the Dutch East Indies.* Translated and with a preface by Bernard Miall. London: T. F. Unwin.

Cole, Fay-Cooper
  1936. Family, clan and phratry in Central Sumatra. In: *Essays in Anthropology Presented to A. L. Kroeber,* ed. by R. H. Lowie. Berkeley: University of California Press. Pp. 19–27.

  1945. *The Peoples of Malaysia.* New York: D. Van Nostrand.

Colson, E.
  1951. The Plateau Tonga of Northern Rhodesia. In: *Seven Tribes of British Central Africa,* ed. by E. Colson and M. Gluckman. London: Oxford University Press. Pp. 94–162.

De Cleene, N.
  1935. Les chefs indigènes au Mayombe. Africa, 8: 63–75.

  1937. La famille dans L'organisation sociale du Mayombe. Africa, 10: 1–15.

De Jong, J. P. B. De Josselin
  1951. *Minangkabau and Negri Sembilan.* Socio-political structure in Indonesia. Leiden: E. Ijdo.

Eggan, Fred
  1949. The Hopi and the lineage principle. In: *Social Structure, Essays Presented to A. R. Radcliffe-Brown,* ed. by Fred Eggan and Meyer Fortes. London: Oxford University Press. Pp. 121–144.

  1950. *The Social Organization of the Western Pueblos.* Chicago: University of Chicago Press.

Evans-Pritchard, E. E., and Meyer Fortes (eds.)
  1940. *African Political Systems.* London: Oxford University Press.

Forde, C. D.
  1931. Hopi agriculture and land ownership. Journal of the Royal Anthropological Institute, 61: 357–406.

1948. *Habitat, Economy and Society.* 6th ed. London: Methuen.

Fortes, Meyer
1949. Time and social structure: An Ashanti case study. In: *Social Structure, Essays Presented to A. R. Radcliffe-Brown,* ed. by Fred Eggan and Meyer Fortes. London: Oxford University Press. Pp. 54–84.

1950. Kinship and marriage among the Ashanti. In: *African Systems of Kinship and Marriage,* ed. by A. R. Radcliffe-Brown and C. D. Forde. London: Oxford University Press. Pp. 252–284.

1959. Primitive kinship. Scientific American (June), pp. 147–158.

Fortune, R. F.
1932. *Sorcerers of Dobu.* London: Routledge and Co.

Fried, M. H.
1957. The classification of corporate unilineal descent groups. Journal of the Royal Anthropological Institute, 87: 1–29.

Gladwin, T., and S. B. Sarason
1953. Truk: Man in paradise. Viking Fund Publications in Anthropology, no. 20.

Goodenough, W. H.
1951. Property, kin and community on Truk. Yale University Publications in Anthropology, no. 46.

Gough, E. K.
1956. Brahman kinship in a Tamil village. American Anthropologist, 58: 826–853.

1959. The Nayars and the definition of marriage. Journal of the Royal Anthropological Institute, 89: 23–34.

Hill, W. W.
1940. Some aspects of Navaho political structure. Plateau, 13: 23–28.

Hoebel, E. Adamson
1954. *The Law of Primitive Man.* Cambridge, Mass.: Harvard University Press.

Innes, C. A.
1908. *Malabar and Anjengo.* Madras: Madras District Gazetteers.

Leach, E. R.
1958. Concerning Trobriand clans and the kinship category "tabu." In: The Developmental Cycle in Domestic Groups, ed. by Jack Goody. Cambridge Papers in Social Anthropology. Vol. 1.

Levy, M. J., Jr.
  1949. *The Family Revolution in Modern China.* Cambridge,
         Mass.: Harvard University Press.
Loeb, Edwin
  1934. Patrilineal and matrilineal organization in Sumatra. Pt.
         2: The Minangkabau. American Anthropologist, 36: 25–56.
Logan, William
  1887. *Malabar.* 2 vols. Madras: Government Press. (Reprinted,
         with additional papers, in 3 vols., Madras, 1951.)
Malinowski, Bronislaw
  1922. *Argonauts of the Western Pacific.* London: Routledge and
         Sons.
  1926. *Crime and Punishment in Savage Society.* London: K. Paul,
         Trench, Trubner and Company, Ltd.
  1935. *Coral Gardens and Their Magic.* Vol. 1. New York: Amer-
         ican Book Company.
Marsden, William
  1811. *The History of Sumatra.* London: Longman, Hurst, Reese,
         Orne and Brown.
Mitchell, J. Clyde
  1951. The Yao of Southern Nyasaland. In: *Seven Tribes of British
         Central Africa,* ed. by E. Colson and M. Gluckman. London:
         Oxford University Press. Pp. 292–353.
  1956. *The Yao Village.* Manchester: Manchester University Press.
Murdock, G. P.
  1949. *Social Structure.* New York: The Macmillan Company.
  1957. World ethnographic sample. American Anthropologist, 59:
         664–687.
Nair, K. Madhavan
  1941. *The Malabar Law Digest and Acts, 1861–1941.* Calicut:
         The Vidya Vilasam Press.
Nambudiripad, E. M. Sankaran
  1952. *The National Question in Kerala.* Bombay: People's Pub-
         lishing House.
Polanyi, Karl
  1944. *The Great Transformation.* New York: Rinehart & Company,
         Inc.
Rattray, R. S.
  1929. *Ashanti Law and Constitution.* London: Oxford University
         Press.

Richards, A. I.
    1939.   *Land, Labour and Diet in Northern Rhodesia.* London:
            Oxford University Press. (Reprinted 1951.)
    1940a. *Bemba Marriage and Present Economic Conditions.* Liv-
            ingstone: Rhodes-Livingstone Institute.
    1940b. The political system of the Bemba tribe. In: *African Polit-
            ical Systems,* ed. by E. E. Evans-Pritchard and Meyer Fortes.
            London: Oxford University Press. Pp. 83–120.
    1950.   Some types of family structure amongst the Central Bantu.
            In: *African Systems of Kinship and Marriage,* ed. by A. R.
            Radcliffe-Brown and C. D. Forde. London: Oxford Uni-
            versity Press. Pp. 207–251.
    1951.   The Bemba of North-Eastern Rhodesia. In: *Seven Tribes of
            British Central Africa,* ed. by E. Colson and M. Gluckman.
            London: Oxford University Press. Pp. 164-193.
    1956.   *Chisungu: A Girl's Initiation Ceremony among the Bemba
            of Northern Rhodesia.* London: Faber & Faber.
Sahlins, Marshall D.
    1958.   *Social Stratification in Polynesia.* Seattle: University of
            Washington Press.
Schrieke, Bertram
    1955.   *Indonesian Sociological Studies.* 2 vols. The Hague: W. van
            Hoeve.
Service, Elman R.
    1958.   *A Profile of Primitive Culture.* New York: Harper & Broth-
            ers.
Sumatra Handbook
    1920.   Handbooks prepared under the direction of the Historical
            Section of the Foreign Office, no. 83. London: H. M. Sta-
            tionery Office.
Titiev, Mischa
    1944.   Old Oraibi: A study of the Hopi Indians of Third Mesa. Pa-
            pers of the Peabody Museum of American Archaeology and
            Ethnology, Harvard University, vol. 22, no. 1. Cambridge,
            Mass.: Peabody Museum.
Turner, V. W.
    1955.   The spatial separation of generations in Ndembu village
            structure. Africa, 25:
    1957.   *Schism and Continuity in an African Society.* Manchester:
            Manchester University Press.
Van Leur, J. C.
    1955.   *Indonesian Trade and Society.* The Hague: W. van Hoeve.

White, Leslie A.
   1949.   *The Science of Culture*. New York: Farrar, Straus.
   1959.   *The Evolution of Culture*. New York: McGraw-Hill.

Cross-cultural Comparisons

Driver, H. E.
   1956.   An integration of functional, evolutionary, and historical theory by means of correlations. Indiana University Publications in Anthropology and Linguistics, Mem. 12.

Gurdon, P. R. T.
   1914.   *The Khasis*. London: Macmillan and Company.

Hart, C. W. M., and Arnold R. Pilling
   1960.   *The Tiwi of North Australia*. New York: Henry Holt, Inc.

Marshall, Harry I.
   1922.   The Karen people of Burma: A study in anthropology and ethnology. The Ohio State University Bulletin, vol. 26, no. 13. Contributions in History and Political Science, no. 8.

Murdock, G. P.
   1949.   *Social Structure*. New York: The Macmillan Company.
   1953.   *Ethnographic Bibliography of North America*. 2d ed. New Haven: Human Relations Area Files.
   1957.   World ethnographic sample. American Anthropologist, 59: 664–687.
   1959.   *Africa, Its Peoples and Their Culture History*. New York: McGraw-Hill.

Playfair, A.
   1909.   *The Garos*. London: David Nutt.

Sahlins, Marshall D.
   1960.   Evolution: specific and general. In: *Evolution and Culture*, ed. by Marshall D. Sahlins and Elman R. Service. Ann Arbor: University of Michigan Press.

Seligman, Charles G., and Brenda Z. Seligman
   1911.   *The Veddas*. Cambridge, Eng.: Cambridge University Press.

Steward, Julian H. (ed.)
   1946–1959.   Handbook of South American Indians. 7 vols. Bureau of American Ethnology Bulletin 143.

Steward, Julian H., and Louis C. Faron
   1959.   *Native Peoples of South America*. New York: McGraw-Hill.

Vroklage, Bernardus A. G.
   1952.   *Ethnographie der Belu in Zentral-Timor*. 3 vols. Leiden: E. J. Brill.

Index

Index